Essentials of
Learning and Cognition

Essentials of
Learning and Cognition

David L. Morgan
Spalding University

Boston   Burr Ridge, IL   Dubuque, IA   Madison, WI   New York
San Francisco   St. Louis   Bangkok   Bogotá   Caracas   Kuala Lumpur
Lisbon   London   Madrid   Mexico City   Milan   Montreal   New Delhi
Santiago   Seoul   Singapore   Sydney   Taipei   Toronto

McGraw-Hill Higher Education

*A Division of The **McGraw-Hill** Companies*

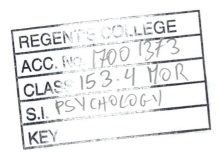
1 2 3 4 5 6 7 8 9 0 DOC/DOC 0 9 8 7 6 5 4 3 2

Library of Congress Cataloging-in-Publication Data
Morgan, David L. (David Lloyd)
    Essentials of learning and cognition / David L. Morgan
        p. cm.
    Includes bibliographical references and index.
    ISBN 1-55934-572-1
        1. Learning, Psychology of. 2. Learning in animals. 3. Cognition. 4. Cognition
in animals. 5. Psychology, Comparative. I. Title.

BF318 .M67 2001
153.1'S–dc21

2001057915

Sponsoring editor, Ken King; production editor, Holly Paulsen; manuscript
editor, Judith Brown; design manager and cover designer, Violeta Diaz; art editor,
Emma Ghiselli; text designer, Linda Robertson; illustrator, Judith Ogus; photo
researcher, Brian J. Pecko; production supervisor, Richard DeVitto. The text was
set in 9.5/12 Sabon by Thompson Type and printed on acid-free 45# Scholarly
Matte by R. R. Donnelley & Sons Company.

Cover images: Tiger: © Jake Schoellkopf / AP/WideWorld Photos; Scuba diver:
© Corbis; Infant: © Elizabeth Crews.

Text credits appear on a continuation of the copyright page, page 361.

www.mhhe.com

To Robin, for reminding me of the reinforcing properties of smiles and chocolate.

Contents

CHAPTER 4   Operant Conditioning and Reinforcement 93

Preface

Alanis Morissette, in her song "Ironic," reminded us a few years back that life is full of ironies, events that seem to contradict themselves. In the world of academic psychology, the learning textbook has become the living embodiment of irony for generations of college students. A book about learning and cognition is, among other things, the autobiography of every student who ever cracked open a book or sat through a lecture. As a college student, you are the consummate *learner*, largely because your life is virtually defined by efforts and opportunities centered around learning new concepts and facts and acquiring new skills. *How might this concept apply to me? How am I going to pass this upcoming test? What point am I trying to make in this term paper? How can I convince my professor I understand this concept? When will I be able to utilize this skill to make a difference in my life or that of others?* Such questions emerge naturally in the course of a formal education, and they should be anything but rhetorical. A textbook purporting to deal with learning and cognition should offer some insight, even a few tentative answers to such questions.

And here's precisely where the irony comes into play. Traditionally, textbooks in the psychology of learning have been notoriously unreadable and inaccessible to all but a few students with graduate-school aspirations. To be sure, the study of learning is among the oldest research endeavors in psychology, and much of this enterprise has consisted of well-controlled laboratory studies involving nonhuman animal subjects. For the scholar in search of specialized, technical language and complex, experimental design, the study of learning and cognition can be a fine repast. There's enough sophistry and laboratory lore here to whet any scientist's appetite. But there is a larger, perhaps more important story to be told about learning and cognition, and this story, more often than not, gets lost amidst the esoteric pages of many learning and cognition textbooks. *Learning and cognition are the primary vehicles by which all organisms, humans included, adapt to the circumstances of their existence.* Perhaps more than any other course that you will take as a college student, the study of learning and cognition is all about what you do and why you do it. Naturally, the story doesn't end with you. Children learning language, animals finding hidden food, assembly-line workers operating new machinery, and prospective pilots flying on simulators are all undergoing behavioral adaptations similar to those encountered by college students. A textbook about learning and cognition should reveal what we have learned about these adaptive feats and many others. But it should do so in a compelling way and, whenever possible, with language that doesn't disenfranchise the reader.

My goal in writing *Essentials of Learning and Cognition* was to offer undergraduate students an introductory text that describes the work being done by learning and cognitive psychologists, but in a more user-friendly way than is characteristic of most texts in the field. This is by no means an easy task, particularly given the enormity and historical precedence of the subject matter. As mentioned previously, the study of learning is one of psychology's oldest preoccupations, and the current discipline of cognitive science boasts thousands of scientists and dozens of research journals. From the outset, it was clear that some big decisions had to be made about both presentation style and coverage. The result is a book that, I believe, differs substantially from others in the field both in content and in writing style. As much as possible, I have tried to use the very facts contained in this book as a guide for writing the text. After all, if the scientific study of learning and cognition is at all justified, then a teaching tool, such as a textbook, ought to embody the wisdom that such a science entails. In several ways, I have tried to remain true to this observation in the writing of *Essentials of Learning and Cognition.*

One of the first lessons you learn as a college professor, and a fact that will become apparent as you read this book, is that people (and other animals, too) are limited in their ability to handle and digest information. Given its prolific history, a book on learning and cognition could easily exceed 1,000 pages of text. Such a book would perhaps be a rich repository of information for the dedicated scholar, but it would most likely be a poor teaching tool for the new student. The sheer amount of information would easily overwhelm the student for whom the concepts and findings would be entirely novel. Consequently, early on in the project I decided to write a book that had no pretense of being comprehensive. In my opinion, that's the job of professional journals, not textbooks. The inclusion of the word *essentials* in the title is significant. I like to think that in the process of reading this book you will be exposed not only to a representative sample of what learning and cognition researchers do, but also to the fundamental empirical findings that most professors would view as essential material, those things that a student having taken a course in learning and cognition simply "must know." As the reader, you will be the ultimate judge of whether or not I have succeeded in meeting this objective.

In addition to forgoing an exhaustive presentation of the field, I have attempted to make the everyday relevance of learning and cognition come alive for you as a student. This has been done both through the use of chapter opening vignettes, some of which deal specifically with student-related issues, and with ample examples throughout the book of the real-world significance of basic learning and cognition principles. As you will learn in this book, material presented in this way is more effectively processed and therefore more easily remembered than simple lists of concepts and research findings. The role of research in the psychology of learning and cognition can hardly be overstated, but the story can and should be told in a manner that does not obscure the big picture. I believe that minimizing the number of experimental studies described while increasing the discussion of significance and application of research is a more effective pedagogy. You are also encouraged to make use of the book's other learning tools, including marginal glosses and interim summaries and thought questions. These tools are intended to foster more active processing of the material, enhancing the quality of your learning and cognition.

Conceptual understanding often requires the integration of ideas and facts as well as the acknowledgment that two things can be different in some ways and alike in others. Historically, the psychologies of learning and cognitive science developed as relatively separate disciplines, and researchers in each area adopted their own philosophy of science, subject populations (nonhuman animals vs. humans), and research methods. Consequently, integration has been hard to come by in the study of learning and cognition. But the similarities that characterize these fields are, arguably, much more important than their differences. A major theme of this text is that both learning and cognition are methods of adaptation. That is, the ability to process information and to be affected by experience are functionally similar aspects of the behavior of organisms. This similarity, often overlooked, does much to bring the sciences of learning and cognition together, and this is important not only for psychology but also for the student trying to pull sometimes difficult material together. I hope you find this integrative theme useful.

Perhaps it will be of some comfort to know that the process of writing this book was a considerable learning experience for me, just as reading it should be for you. An author faces numerous challenges in deciding how best to present any scientific discipline to the uninitiated reader. Questions about writing level, presentation of technical language and experimental findings, depth of coverage, use of illustrations and artwork, and pedagogy (interim summaries, thought questions, and so on) emerged frequently throughout the project. I have tried to tackle these issues by relying on what the science of learning and cognition tells us about these matters—and by imagining what I would have found useful as a student (all those years ago). I hope you will assist me in this learning endeavor by letting me know what you think of the book. What worked for you and what didn't? How might it have been a more useful learning tool as you negotiated the diverse terrain of learning and cognition? Your feedback would be much appreciated. Send your comments to me at dmorgan@spalding.edu.

ACKNOWLEDGMENTS

The challenge of writing this text was significantly mitigated by the talent and professionalism of many folks at Mayfield/McGraw-Hill. As a first-time textbook author, I was guided through the sometimes mazelike world of book publishing by many capable individuals. I would like to thank Ken King, Holly Paulsen, and Georgia Gero-Chen for their guidance and patience during the production process. Judith Brown's masterful copyediting resulted in a more consistent and, I think, readable manuscript. Finally, I am especially indebted to Frank Graham, who was there at the beginning, now so long ago, with enthusiasm and collegiality. I am thankful to all who made this a rewarding experience, and I look forward to further collaboration. Special thanks also goes to the reviewers, for their many helpful suggestions. These included Joel Alexander, Western Oregon University; Mary M. Brazier, Loyola University New Orleans; Robert T. Herdegen III, Hampden-Sydney College; Michael Kane, Georgia State University; Michael J. Renner, West Chester University; Barbara S. Turpin, Southwest Missouri State University; and Sheree Watson, Jackson State University.

CHAPTER ONE

Introduction

Showing up late for the movie, you stumble down the darkened aisle of the theater, groping for an empty seat and hoping not to fall into another movie-goer's lap. Less than halfway through the film, the audience materializes around you in vivid detail. Magically, it seems, the veil of darkness has lifted.

Six months ago, Ted moved into a neighborhood next to the regional airport. For the first few weeks he wondered whether the move might have been a mistake, as the constant roar of aircraft overhead turned everyday conversations into comical shouting matches. Now, however, Ted hardly notices the jet engine reveilles that send his unsuspecting houseguests diving for cover.

Brandon thought he was ready for this anatomy and physiology exam, but he was a bit surprised to learn that he was expected to know all 12 cranial nerves! Now, let's see, there's the oculomotor, the trigeminal, the hypoglossal, um.... It took him a while, but Brandon was eventually able to come up with all 12. Fortunately, he had listened carefully in study group when Lisa had described the acronym strategy that students had used for years to memorize the nerves.

When Chelsea started college, her study habits left much to be desired. She took poor notes, seldom read her textbook, and studied for exams in one long cramming session the night before. Now, as a senior, Chelsea takes the best notes in class, reads and highlights important sections of her book, and studies a little each day for exams. Consequently, she now makes As and Bs in all of her classes, rather than the Cs and Ds she made as a freshman.

On the surface, there doesn't seem to be any common theme running through the above vignettes, as each seems to depict a person encountering a very different kind of circumstance. In one important way, though, these encounters or experiences are similar. Each case describes how, over time, a person comes to respond more effectively to a situation that initially proved problematic. In other words, each person exhibits an ability to *adapt*, or adjust, to his or her environment over time. Adaptation manifests itself in behavior in a variety of ways—many more, in fact, than the above vignettes could possibly depict. To a large extent, the study of learning and cognition *is* the study of behavioral adaptation. This book focuses on learning and cognition as adaptive mechanisms, whether applied to rats negotiating mazes, Seeing Eye dogs pushing elevator buttons, or humans learning the names of the 12 cranial nerves.

LEARNING AND COGNITION AS ADAPTATION

Adaptation takes many forms and can occur over very brief or enormously long periods of time. For example, entire species adapt over very long time periods, usually measured in geological epochs. The fur of the polar bear, the shell of the turtle, and the tongue of the anteater are all adaptations caused by a gradual evolutionary process taking more years than you or I care to think about. Individuals adapt, too, and in ways that are quite different from the long-term adaptation of a species. Only some forms of individual adaptation, though, are relevant to the study of learning and cognition. To put the psychology of learning and cognition into its proper context as a type of adaptation, let's first consider some basic concepts of evolutionary biology and the different levels at which adaptation may take place.

Levels of Adaptation I: Phylogeny

One of the most fascinating, yet difficult, topics in all of science concerns the question of when, where, and how different species originated on this planet. When did life begin? What was the earth's climate and geography like when the first life-forms emerged? How do the physical features of species change over time and why? Why do some species enjoy extended longevity while others seem to disappear in a blink of geological time? All of these and a host of other related questions lie at the heart of the science of evolutionary biology. Biological evolution is understood to be a process by which species change or adapt to the physical environment over extremely long periods of time. Thus, evolutionary biologists focus their scientific energies on the

phylogeny evolution and development of a species over time

process of **phylogeny,** the evolution and development of a species over many generations. Change at the phylogenetic level occurs over time spans that most people find inconceivable, such as hundreds of thousands, even millions of years. Consequently, you can't readily observe the evolution of a species the way you can, in a sense, watch a child grow up in front of your eyes. Instead, biological evolution is an event that must be inferred from the fossil record and research in genetics, biology, geology, and other related fields.

Although the precise details of biological evolution are not completely understood, scientists generally agree that the process entails two important and complementary components: genetic variation and natural selection. **Genetic variation** refers to the fact that individual genotypes, or genetic characteristics, differ within any group of organisms. The number of possible combinations of genes is staggering when you consider that human beings possess between 50,000 and 100,000 genes (Plomin, DeFries, McClearn, &

genetic variation the fact that individual genotypes, or genetic characteristics, differ within any group of organisms

Rutter 1997). This means that no two individuals, even of the same species, are the same genetically, with the exception of identical twins.

In fact, the study of twins has contributed much to understanding how genes affect behavior. The logic of twin studies relies on the fact that identical twins share 100% of their genetic endowment because they develop from the same fertilized egg. Fraternal twins, on the other hand, develop from separate fertilized eggs and, consequently, share 50% of genetic material on average, as do any two siblings. If genetic endowment plays a significant role in the development of personality and behavior, it is logical to expect identical twins to be more alike on these dimensions than either fraternal twins or any other pair of siblings. Research in behavior genetics substantiates this expectation. Identical twins tend to demonstrate greater similarity on such matters as temperament and personality, intelligence, and personal preferences than do fraternal twins or other sibling pairs (Bouchard, 1994; Jeste, 1990).

But are the sometimes striking similarities observed in identical twins due solely to their shared genetic endowment, or is there another explanation? Could it also be the case that identical twins share environments that tend to be more alike than the respective environments of other siblings? Are identical twins more likely to be dressed alike, exposed to the same kinds of activities, and, in general, treated more similarly than any other siblings? If so, as scientists, we cannot unequivocally interpret behavioral similarities in identical twins as being due entirely to genetic similarity. The issue is a difficult one to resolve to the satisfaction of scientists, because the influence of genes cannot effectively be separated from the influence of environment when looking at behavior. To conduct a proper experiment to disentangle the effects of genes and environmental variables would require separating identical twins immediately after conception (do you see why they could not experience the same intrauterine environment?) and raising each twin in a separate, qualitatively different environment. Should the twins nevertheless demonstrate substantial similarities in personality and behavior, we'd be inclined to view their identical genetic makeup as largely responsible. Clearly, ethical considerations prohibit conducting such an experiment, thus making empirical resolution of this issue improbable.

Sources of Genetic Variation   Genetic variability is believed to be due to two processes: sexual reproduction and mutation. **Sexual reproduction** occurs when the gametes, or sex cells, of two separate individuals combine to produce offspring. Sex is not the only way to reproduce, however. Certain animals reproduce asexually, simply making copies, or clones, of themselves. The desert whiptail lizard, for instance, goes by the very apt scientific name of *C. uniparens*, which means, of course, one parent. There are no males in desert whiptail society. The unfertilized eggs of whiptail mothers simply develop into genetically identical daughters (Daly & Wilson, 1983).

Method of reproduction has important consequences for the evolutionary process, particularly with respect to genetic variability. Asexual organisms exhibit little genetic variability from one generation to the next. If all members of the species are genetically alike, they will also share physical and behavioral similarities. Because these physical and behavioral features have

sexual reproduction when the gametes, or sex cells, of two separate individuals combine to form offspring

evolved within a specific environmental or ecological niche, they will continue to serve the organisms in their struggle to survive. Thus, the species will continue to thrive so long as environmental features remain constant. Major environmental change, however, as in climate shifts, altered food availability, or change in predator populations, may spell disaster for asexual species. Because of nearly identical genetic makeup, there may be no individual members of the species who can survive significant changes in the environment; thus no individuals live long enough to reproduce. If no members of the species, by virtue of different genetic makeup, are able to adapt to the changed environment, the entire species is destined for extinction.

Fortunately, much of nature has discovered the overriding benefits of a diverse and ever-changing gene pool. As it turns out, sexual reproduction is a marvelous way of stirring up genetic material, because each parent in a sexual union provides different genetic characteristics to the offspring. A species characterized by genetically different organisms is more likely to survive should major environmental changes occur. Consider, for example, an automobile mechanic faced with repairing a vehicle. You would not predict much success for the mechanic if he or she was in the possession of only a hammer to conduct repairs. On the other hand, if the mechanic had a diverse collection of wrenches, screwdrivers, hammers, and other relevant tools, each designed to handle a specific task, you would be much more confident in his or her ability to repair the vehicle, no matter what the problem might be. Similarly, sexual reproduction increases the chances that at least some members of a species will possess characteristics better adapted to environmental change. Jacob (1982) suggested that ". . . sex provides a margin of safety against environmental uncertainty. It makes extinction less likely. It is an adaptation to the unforeseeable" (pp. 8–9). Is it any wonder, then, that sex remains the predominant mode of reproduction in the animal world?

Sexual recombination is not the only source of genetic variation, though. **Mutations** are spontaneous, often unpredictable changes in genetic material. Although the cause of any specific mutation may be hard to identify, mutations are known to occur in response to exposure to certain environmental agents, such as radiation, chemicals, and extreme temperatures. Mutations are rare, but when they do occur, their effects are usually harmful (Plomin et al., 1997). Why? Imagine what might happen if you were to choose some food or seasoning at random and pour it into a cake mix. Would the cake be edible? Possibly, but the odds are against it, since you've unsystematically introduced an ingredient not called for by the recipe. Of course, there is some outside chance that your new ingredient will revolutionize the baking industry and become a culinary standard, but you wouldn't bet your next paycheck on it. The same is believed to be true of mutations. Though occasionally a mutated gene may bestow some advantage on its host, most would be expected to be of little benefit.

mutations spontaneous, generally unpredictable changes in genetic material

Natural Selection   So, why all this talk about genetic variation? Here is where the concept of natural selection comes into play. **Natural selection** entails differential reproduction: Some organisms will reproduce more offspring than will others, thus sending more copies of their own genes into

natural selection differential reproduction of organisms within a population

future generations. As a result, those specific genes and gene combinations will, over very long periods, become more frequent in the population. Those organisms that do not reproduce do not send their genes on to future gene pools. What determines who reproduces and who doesn't? That is the tricky question in evolutionary theory, because the answer is conditional: It comes down to which organisms have the physical and behavioral attributes that best match the conditions of their local environment at any given time.

In order to survive to an age of reproductive maturity, an organism must avoid predators and succeed at finding the food and shelter it needs. And, of course, it must find a mate with whom to reproduce. So how, precisely, does the organism do all of this? Here is where the organism's genetic endowment becomes important. Perhaps the organism's success is related to certain physical attributes, such as size, strength, speed, coloration, or other features inherited from its parents. The giraffe's long neck, for example, affords it the opportunity to reach leaves at considerable heights. The beaver's strong teeth assist it in the downing of trees it uses to construct a home. The box turtle's shell is a nearly impenetrable shield into which the animal tucks its more vulnerable body parts when threatened by another animal.

All of the above physical features are represented in the respective animal's genetic blueprint. More important, they are features that aid the animal in adapting to the characteristics of its environment, thereby solving the problem of finding food, shelter, a mate, and so on. By adapting to the peculiar conditions of their world, these animals ensure for themselves a long life and the possibility of reproducing. The new generation of giraffes, beavers, and turtles will inherit many of the same genes that allowed their parents to survive. This is why biologists say that the environment has "selected for" those genes that produce long necks, strong teeth, hard shells, and other features that aid organisms in adapting to their environments. Features that prove less adaptive are, in a sense, weeded out, because organisms that possess them do not live long enough to mate, thus failing to pass such characteristics on to future generations.

What all of this means is that some genetic variations seem better suited than others to a particular habitat. These are the variations that are selected for over time, while others are selected out, no longer to be represented in future populations. A frequently cited illustration of differential reproduction is the case of peppered moth coloration in pre- and postindustrial England. Prior to industrialization, large numbers of peppered moths populated downtown London. As with any other species, individual moths differed from one another along many characteristics, including size, shape, and coloration. However, most of the moths were fairly light in coloration, exhibiting primarily off-white to tan hues. This coloration proved to be adaptive, because it allowed moths to blend into the structures in their environment to which they clung, including buildings and trees. In the natural world, many creatures avoid predation through natural camouflage provided by coloration or markings. Because they were able to avoid the many bird species that would otherwise prey upon them, these lightly colored moths were more likely to reproduce, thus sending their genes for light coloration on to further generations of moths (Figure 1.1).

FIGURE 1.1 Moth
Coloration.

With the growth of industry, the environment in and around London changed. The buildings, trees, and other structures began to take on darker coloration, due to increased emissions produced by local industry. To their considerable misfortune, lightly colored moths now stood out against the darker background of trees and buildings and were easily preyed upon. Darker moths, however, were now at a distinct advantage, as they blended in well in this changed environment. Consequently, darker colored moths outreproduced their lightly colored counterparts. Over time, the darker moths outnumbered lightly colored moths.

This example elegantly demonstrates the mechanisms of evolution at work. Because moths reproduce sexually, genetic variation is inevitable and results in individual differences within the moth population. Due to characteristics of the local environment, however, certain physical features proved more adaptive than others. As a result, individual moths possessing this feature (darker coloration) reproduced more successfully, eventually becoming more numerous in the population. The evolutionary process, then, represents an ongoing interplay between genetic variation and environmental conditions, thus resulting in differential reproduction.

At this point, it might be useful to note that biologists disagree about the actual mechanics of the evolutionary process. That is, different theories have emerged to explain biological evolution. In science, theories are collections of formal hypotheses or postulates that attempt to explain documented natural phenomena. As scientists, we might, for example, propose a theory of human aggression. Such a theory does not begin with the proposition that human aggression exists. No one would question this fact; we observe enough instances of aggression to be more than convinced of its reality as a natural occurrence. The purpose of a theory of aggression would be to identify possible causes of aggression, such as frustration, personality disorders, alcohol abuse, poverty, and so on.

It is important to keep in mind that the phrase "theory of evolution" refers to attempts by scientists to explain the biological facts that all scientists take as evidence of the evolutionary process. In other words, the work of evolutionary biologists is not centered on *proving* that evolution occurs; there is simply no debate among biologists that evolution is responsible for the diverse life-forms that inhabit this planet. Theories of evolution are not claims or arguments that evolution is real. They are, instead, attempts at explaining how and by what specific mechanisms evolution works. And on this topic, there is considerable room for debate and disagreement. Traditionally, evolutionary thinking suggested that changes in species occur in small steps and over enormously long time periods or epochs. An example of a rival way of thinking, however, is the theory of punctuated equilibrium, which suggests that evolutionary change is not evenly gradual. This theory argues that abrupt and dramatic physical change may be the rule, rather than the exception, in the evolutionary development of a species (Eldredge & Gould, 1972; Gould, 1995). Thus, while evolutionary biologists all accept evolution as the process that shapes life on this planet, they disagree, sometimes adamantly, about the details of this process.

Demystifying Evolution   "The theory of evolution is quite rightly called the greatest unifying theory in biology. The diversity of organisms, similarities and differences among kinds of organisms, patterns of distribution and behavior, adaptation and interpretation, all of this was merely a bewildering chaos of facts until given meaning by the evolutionary theory" (Mayr, 1970). Despite its status within the biological sciences, the concept of evolution has been mired in nearly continuous controversy since the publication of Charles Darwin's *On the Origin of Species* (1859). Great ideas, particularly those that challenge conventional belief systems, incite not only enthusiasm but also zealous opposition, and evolutionary theory is no exception to this rule. The evolutionary process has not always surrendered itself readily to human understanding, perhaps partly due to its complexity and the controversial nature of its view of human origins.

Critics of evolutionary theory often attack the idea that it operates without any apparent purpose or guiding design. In one famous critique, theologian William Paley (1802) argued that if, while wandering in the woods, one were to come upon a watch lying on the ground, there would be little mystery as to the watch's origin. Unlike the rocks, trees, and other natural objects characterizing the woods, the watch, with its exquisite details and workmanship, clearly implies a creator, a watchmaker. Similarly, Paley suggested, the various life-forms on this planet, especially humans, represent marvels of design and deliberate creation, and could therefore hardly be considered the result of such an unsystematic process as evolution.

However unsystematic the evolutionary process might appear, it is certainly anything but simple. Understanding how such diverse life-forms might have evolved requires an appreciation for the subtle interplay between genetic variation and natural selection. Consider, for instance, the complexity of inheritance. It is simply not possible to know ahead of time which genes will be handed down by each parent in a sexual union because the possible combinations are numerically overwhelming. Nor is it possible to predict when mutations will occur, because not enough is known about either their natural or human-produced causes. Nor can anyone be sure which genes will be affected by mutation. Consequently, predicting the specific genotype of any single organism remains, at least for the time being, the stuff of science fiction.

Remember that the ultimate test of an organism's genetic endowment is whether it will adapt to its local environment and pass its genetic material along to offspring. Predicting that an organism will successfully adapt requires detailed knowledge, not only about its genetic makeup, but also about the specific features of its local environment and whether they remain stable or change over time. Scientists are still grappling with the question of how to classify natural ecosystems, which include not only all plant and animal species occupying a particular region but also geological and climatic features of the habitat. These features of the environment represent the *selective pressures* that any organism must negotiate in order to pass its genes on to further generations.

Sometimes very subtle changes in ecology can render entire populations of animals unfit for a particular habitat. The eastern brook trout, for instance, is the only member of the trout family native to streams in the southern Appalachian mountains. In recent years, increased acidification of these streams has reduced the population of this native species, whose members require cold and well-oxygenated water to survive. This change in the brook trout's ecosystem, introduced by various sources of industrial pollution, threatens to eradicate this species from its natural habitat (Camuto, 1990). The plight of the brook trout is but one example of how the environmental pressures that bear upon a species can be significantly altered by other species, in this case human beings.

All of this uncertainty paints a rather messy picture of biological evolution. As a result, many critics of evolutionary theory have argued that such a haphazard process could not possibly have created something as intricate in structure and function as, for example, the human eye. What must be remembered, however, is that for every physical feature that proves advantageous, many others prove less so and consequently are selected out of the gene pool. Indeed, many more species have become extinct over geological time than presently inhabit the earth. As you read this book, remember that the finished product is only the most recent version of an evolving manuscript. Throughout its development, the text has undergone immense change, with entire paragraphs, or even sections, having been culled, and others added or refined. The final product you now hold in your hands is the result of a rather convoluted process of which *you remain completely unaware.* Evolution, according to Jacob (1977), is a grand tinkerer, but the process itself is not easily observed. Humans must be content to gaze upon the product and make educated guesses about the tinkering itself.

Unlike the text you now hold in your hands, the process of biological evolution unfolds over thousands and even millions of years and over countless generations of organisms. This means that the selective pressures of the environment have ample opportunity to whittle away at genetic features and produce organisms well suited to local conditions. Events that seem inconceivable if observed over a short time span become much more likely if considered over longer periods. Consider a tragic event, such as the crash of a major commercial airplane. Suppose you had to predict the probability that such an event would occur within a specific time period, say the first week of January 2010. How likely would you estimate such an event to be? Now, consider the same prediction, but for a period of 100 years. Would you be more confident in predicting a crash sometime between the year 2010 and the year 2110? Notice how altering the temporal window for such an event makes a big difference in estimating its likelihood. The same event that may seem unlikely over a short interval becomes almost inevitable if considered over a much longer interval. Similarly, evolutionary theorists point out that the human eye, like the rest of our anatomy, is the result of genetic variation and selective pressures operating over countless eons.

The fact that happenstance and randomness play such a vital role in evolution is rather fitting when you consider the series of events that led up to the publication of *On the Origin of Species.* Shortly after graduating in theology from Christ's College, Charles Darwin served as naturalist aboard the HMS *Beagle* in its 5-year voyage to circumnavigate South America (Figure 1.2). During the voyage, Darwin observed and collected an unprecedented array of plant and animal specimens. The tremendous diversity characterizing the life-forms he collected would make a lasting impression on him. Darwin would devote much of the rest of his life to grappling with ultimate questions concerning the origins of life. What would eventually emerge was the theory of evolution by means of natural selection, among the most powerful and controversial ideas in the history of human thought.

The voyage of the *Beagle* ended in 1836, yet *On the Origin of Species* was not published until 1859. Why the delay? Darwin, it seems, was very much aware of the furor that the publication of his ideas would occasion. Both his personal and educational background made him especially sensitive to how people, particularly those possessing strong religious beliefs, would receive the claim that all earthly creatures, humans included, evolved from

FIGURE 1.2
Charles Darwin.

simpler forms of life. Yet Darwin was hardly the first to suggest such a possibility. His was a unique dilemma, though, for unlike many others whose ideas and theories had to stand on their own, Darwin possessed an unparalleled collection of biological specimens. He had painstakingly acquired the kind of evidence that he knew such a volatile theory would require. Despite this, Darwin agonized over the prospects of going public with his ideas.

But such a confession would be necessary sooner than he had expected, for reasons that Darwin could not have foreseen. In June 1858, Darwin received a manuscript from a young naturalist, Alfred Russel Wallace, who had made similar observations of the flora and fauna of South America. To Darwin's astonishment, Wallace had independently created a theory of evolution nearly identical to his own. Rather than be scooped by the younger scientist, Darwin agreed to write a paper to be presented, along with Wallace's paper, at the esteemed Linnean Society of London. As it turned out, neither Darwin nor Wallace attended the meeting, and both papers were read in their absence. A year later, one of history's most important and anticipated books, *On the Origin of Species,* received much fanfare and sold out on its first day of publication.

It is important also to remember that contemporary biologists do not view evolution as a process leading toward some ideal form of life. Rather than conceptualizing biological life-forms as inhabiting different rungs on an evolutionary ladder, recent depictions have relied on a tree or bush analogy, with separate limbs representing diverging lines of descent (Gould,

1995). A logical by-product of this perspective is that biologists aren't tempted to view species as less or more evolved than one another. The tree sloth is as well adapted to its unique habitat as is the dolphin to its watery domain, and the physical diversity between these two animals is well accounted for by the differences characterizing their respective local environments and evolutionary histories.

In summary, biological evolution is uniformly accepted within the sciences as that process responsible for the origination of biological life-forms and their adaptation to the planet's varied ecosystems. On the phylogenetic level, adaptation reflects a continuous interplay between genetic variation and natural selection. The crucial thing to remember is that evolution, as a phylogenetic form of adaptation, occurs at the level of a species, not individual organisms. Individuals don't *evolve*; they change over time and adapt to specialized environments, but they must do so through other than evolutionary means, since biological evolution occurs across time spans that would be of no use to individuals.

Levels of Adaptation II: Ontogeny

Because humans are an evolved species, biological evolution is relevant to an understanding of human behavior. Each one of us possesses characteristics that have been selected for in our species over many thousands of years. These features, such as an opposable thumb, an upright stance, relatively little body hair, and many others, are a part of our species' genetic endowment. We possess these traits simply by virtue of being a member of the human family. This does not mean that adaptation during our life is impossible; quite the contrary is true. Our perceptions, thoughts, and behaviors are constantly undergoing change, and it is to this type of adaptation that I will now turn.

All of the vignettes presented at the beginning of this chapter deal with adaptation. The adaptation described in each case occurs at the level of the individual, not the species. In this book, the primary emphasis will be on this type of adaptation, known as **ontogeny**, or development of the individual organism throughout its life span. Ontogenetic adaptation exhibits itself in many ways. For example, in the moviegoing scenario, adaptation occurs through a physiological process known as *dark adaptation*. When you enter the dark theater, special receptors in your eye, called rods, must adjust before you can see anything but the brightly lit screen. This adjustment takes almost half an hour.

ontogeny development of the individual organism throughout its lifetime

The airport example represents another kind of adaptation, known as **habituation**, which occurs when the response to a stimulus becomes less intense with repeated presentations of the stimulus. Imagine how frustrating it would be to live next to an airport if every window-rattling takeoff sent you running for cover. You have surely noticed that you usually adjust to repeated occurrences of most distracting, but nondangerous, sounds, sights, and smells, and go about the business of attending to more important events in your environment. Eventually, you may even become unaware of their occurrence. Habituation, while perhaps not always appreciated, is a form of adaptation that serves humans well in our busy and stimulating environments.

habituation decrease in intensity of response to a repeatedly presented stimulus

The other two vignettes describe the kind of adaptation that is the primary focus of this book. This adaptation manifests itself in an ability to process relevant information about one's environment and to benefit from experience. In the absence of learning and cognition, human adaptation would be nearly unthinkable. Even such mundane daily tasks as brushing your teeth, getting dressed, fixing breakfast, driving a car, balancing a checkbook, or talking on a cell phone would prove impossible in the absence of such adaptive mechanisms. And it would be difficult to overstate the role that learning and cognition played in some of humanity's more revolutionary achievements, including splitting the atom, going to the moon, and curing polio and other historically devastating diseases.

✖ INTERIM SUMMARY

Adaptation to the environment is a central feature of all biological life and occurs at different levels. Through biological evolution, entire species adapt to changes in habitat. This process unfolds over very long geological time periods. Individual organisms also adapt to their local environments, but over much shorter time spans. Much of this adaptation is behavioral in nature and is particularly evident in the phenomena of learning and cognition.

✖ THOUGHT QUESTIONS

1. Research has shown that the world's entire population of cheetahs may be nearly identical in genetic makeup. Given our current understanding of the evolutionary process, how might this genetic similarity among cheetahs prove harmful to the species' long-term survival?
2. What is the difference between phylogeny and ontogeny? Why does it make sense to say that only species, not individuals, evolve over time?

LEARNING AND COGNITION DEFINED

Learning

Learning is one of those words that ordinarily conjures up all kinds of images, and this is no less true for psychologists than for nonspecialists. Nevertheless, a scientific approach to learning requires that the subject matter be defined in a way that meets with general approval, especially among researchers who study learning in all of its many guises. A definition that has become fairly standard, and which seems to embrace what psychologists mean when they use the term, goes something like this: **Learning** is a relatively permanent change in behavior potential brought about by practice or experience. Notice that the term *adaptation* could be substituted for *change* without altering the definition's essential meaning. Whatever else learning entails, it involves adaptation in behavior potential over time. There are, however, some aspects of this definition that require discussion.

First, change due to learning is considered to be permanent, not temporary. Many changes in human behavior are the result of transient causes,

learning a relatively permanent change in behavior potential brought about by experience

such as mood states, muscle fatigue, or altered states of consciousness. For instance, a person who is known to be an excellent driver may exhibit very slow reaction times and be unable to control a vehicle after consuming significant amounts of alcohol. Although the driver's ability may be impaired for several hours after alcohol consumption, this deficit would not necessarily last. In short, the dramatic change in driving ability is brought on by temporary chemical changes in the nervous system, not by learning.

Nor is it always possible to observe learning directly. You might have learned how to drive a car, but until I observe you driving, I have no *objective* evidence that you have learned this skill. Until such observation can be made, I can only assume that you have the potential to drive. College students have been known to haggle over grades with their professors, arguing that they really knew the answer to this question or understood a particular concept. The problem is that the student may very well have learned the material, but he or she must be capable of demonstrating this knowledge to the professor. This distinction between learning and performance brings up an important historical controversy about the significance of measurement in the behavioral sciences.

Finally, notice that learning occurs as the result of some kind of experience. This is an important element of the definition because many changes in behavior occur for other reasons. For example, simple physical maturation results in changes in body posture, coordination, and muscular ability. Most 9-month-old infants cannot walk on their own, whereas most 15-month-olds can readily do so. This maturational development primarily reflects one's genetic endowment and nutritional and medical history, not learning.

Cognition

The term *cognition* is similarly nontechnical in that it wasn't invented by scientists for the purpose of identifying a particular subject matter. If you consult a dictionary, you will likely come upon some reference to *knowledge* or *thought,* and this comes pretty close for nonspecific purposes. Even these words, however, call for more clarity. A bit more specificity was provided when Ulric Neisser (1967), in a landmark book in the field, defined cognition as ". . . all processes by which the sensory input is transformed, reduced, elaborated, stored, recovered, and used" (p. 4). This is a rather extensive landscape, as will be revealed by even a brief glance at a contemporary textbook in cognitive psychology or cognitive science.

Cognitive psychologists study such varied phenomena as perception, memory, problem solving, concept formation, and language. In fact, cognitive psychology's research agenda is one you'll likely recognize. Why do people have such vivid recall of certain personal events, sometimes years after their occurrence, but find remembering somebody's phone number for 5 minutes nearly impossible? What intellectual prowess allows a chessmaster to "see" his or her opponent's moves ahead of time and then adapt to each of these with a strategic response? How does the 2-year-old figure out which animals belong to the category *dog* and which belong to the category *cat,* particularly since adults provide minimal feedback about such concepts? And how does this same 2-year-old manage to put words together into coherent, meaningful sentences, despite receiving no formal instruction on how to talk? These kinds of questions have defined the discipline of cognitive psychology for decades, and today contribute to the larger enterprise of *cognitive science,* which represents a corroboration between psychologists, physiologists, and computer scientists.

An important assumption guiding research in cognitive psychology is the idea that information processing is a complex activity, driven more by the nature of the system (human vs. computer) than by the material being processed. In other words, cognitive scientists believe that environmental information only makes sense because of the way humans, as biological organisms, are designed. For example, there are no visually sensitive cells located on that part of the retina at the back of the eye where the fibers of the optic nerve exit the eye. Nevertheless, you and I don't perceive a literal hole in our visual field. We are, instead, blissfully unaware of the blind spot, in part because higher centers of our nervous system do a masterful job of filling in, or compensating, for this physical deficit. The idea that the human mind was designed to process certain kinds of information, and that certain biases in processing characterize human cognition, is a significant contribution of recent writings in evolutionary psychology (Crawford & Krebs, 1998; Newell, 1990; Wells, 1998). This exciting and somewhat controversial approach to understanding human cognition is explored in later chapters of this book.

The Importance of Learning and Cognition

The purpose of most psychological research is to understand behavior. This goal requires that researchers consider the many possible determinants of behavior, be they historical or contemporary, biological or social, and so on. Unlike biologists, psychologists are more likely to focus on behavioral adaptation in a single organism than on the adaptation of a species. And, as is apparent in this chapter's opening vignettes, individual adaptation occurs in a variety of settings and as the result of different processes. Learning and cognition represent the most influential mechanisms for adaptation to environmental change, at least during the lifetime of an organism. Let's take a look at why this is so.

Variability of the Environment   The world in which some animal species live is characterized by tremendous stability over time. Climatic conditions, food availability, shelter from the elements or predators, and other physical features change little. For example, the bacteria that inhabit the geothermal pools in Yellowstone National Park have been exposed to relatively constant water temperature and chemical composition for many thousands of years. To survive in such environments, animals simply must possess certain physical and behavioral features that are fit for that environment; there is little need to be able to change or adapt new characteristics or behavioral strategies because the demands of the environment remain so constant. Bacteria have apparently adapted quite well to their stable environment, as they are considered among the oldest and most plentiful of all biological organisms (Gould, 1995).

An organism that is well adapted to a stable environment has little need of a nervous system that is sensitive to large changes in the environment. As a result, many species have evolved such that their nervous systems are relatively closed to or unaffected by experience. Such organisms are said to possess a **closed genetic program** (Mayr, 1976). For instance, in many bird species, chicks automatically begin gaping, or opening their mouths, at the return of their food-bearing mother to the nest. This behavior is elicited, or provoked, by a very limited stimulus complex, including the shape, color, and movement of the mother's beak (Gould, 1982). Because these stimuli are constant, predictable aspects of their environment, it is not necessary for the chicks to learn new colors or shapes or to alter their reaction in general to these stimuli.

Stimuli that elicit such simple reflexes are called **releasing stimuli,** and the response of the chicks to the maternal stimuli is adaptive. Only under unusual circumstances that would ordinarily never occur in nature does such behavior prove problematic. For instance, researchers have demonstrated that the same gaping behavior can be elicited by sticks, wood models, and other artificial stimuli, so long as these stimuli contain certain features resembling the natural mother's beak (Gould, 1982). What this reveals is that the chicks' behavior is highly dependent on an unchanging feature of the mother; it is not likely to be affected by experience. It is important to understand that this is not a sign of poor adaptation, incomplete evolutionary development, or anything of the sort. Since such reflexive behavior patterns are crucial to survival, they make adaptation through learning unnecessary.

Humans, on the other hand, inhabit remarkably varying environments. In any given week, in fact, most of us find ourselves in such diverse places as classrooms, offices, grocery stores, video stores, churches, museums, and friends' houses. And, as if this isn't enough variety, many of these specific environments change dramatically over time. If you have ever updated a computer word processing program or changed Internet providers, you know that either change can be frustrating. It may take you considerable time to learn the new program or Internet menu; often this translates into an initial drop in productivity until you have mastered the new environment. This adaptation is challenging, but not impossible. In fact, the speed with which the contemporary computerized environment changes is ample testimony to the general ease with which the human nervous system can handle such rapid change.

It is a hallmark of the human species that we find ourselves adapting to environments that often undergo rapid and sometimes dramatic change. Learning and cognition are the processes by which this adaptation takes place. We may not have the strength of the gorilla, or the speed of the gazelle, but our ability to adapt quickly to new surroundings is unmatched by other members of the animal kingdom. We respond rapidly to the changing lights at intersections and the sometimes bewildering and surprising actions of other drivers. As a student, you are required to master various kinds of information, often across several disciplines, within a given semester. And, although

closed genetic program characteristic of organisms possessing a nervous system that benefits little from experience (learning)

releasing stimuli environmental stimuli that provoke a simple reflex

you may not appreciate it, you possess a keen ability to size up other people in social settings. Humans are a tremendously social species, and as such we must constantly interpret the behavior of others in our environment. Who can I trust? Will this person be a faithful marriage partner? Will I get my money back from this individual? Can I trust this person with my children? In fact, as you will learn in Chapter 6, a good deal of the cognitive effort expended by humans is devoted to figuring out the nuances of social interaction. The mechanism for doing so must be flexible, because the kind of information we receive differs over time and across individuals and physical environments.

Learning and cognition, then, are powerful modes of adaptation for animals that live in an ever-changing world. But it's important to understand that these adaptive mechanisms are themselves the result of a long evolutionary process. That is, the ability of humans to process environmental stimulation and to benefit from experience is as attributable to the forces of natural selection as our upright stance and our opposable thumb. Evolution has provided us with an **open genetic program**—a nervous system capable of being modified by experience. An open genetic program is just the ticket for animals who encounter rapidly changing environments, and humans certainly meet that requirement. In a sense, an open genetic program is itself an evolved adaptation that makes additional, special kinds of adaptation possible within the life of the organism.

open genetic program characteristic of organisms possessing a nervous system capable of being modified by experience (learning)

Humans' Limited Instinctive Repertoire The genetic program is viewed as a continuum because behavioral adaptation results from a complex combination of both highly stereotyped, rigid behavior patterns and more flexible, environmentally sensitive actions. Most animals possess such combined behavioral repertoires, and humans are no exception. We even possess a limited collection of behaviors that come close to paralleling the gaping of the baby birds in the nest. All healthy human babies enter the world possessing a small, but very practical, collection of behaviors called **neonatal reflexes.** For example, when the cheek of a newborn is gently stroked, the infant will turn his or her head toward the source of stimulation. What's more, if the stimulating object is within reach, the baby will latch onto and begin sucking it.

neonatal reflexes collection of inborn responses to specific stimuli and common to all humans at birth

This behavior is actually a sequence of two reflexes, the *rooting,* or *orienting, reflex* and the *sucking reflex* (Figure 1.3). You can probably see that this behavior is adaptive to the newborn human, one of nature's most helpless creatures. In addition, babies show strong startle responses to loud noises or to the sensation of falling or losing bodily support. All of these reflexes are, in important ways, very much like the gaping of baby birds at the return of their mothers to the nest. Neonatal reflexes are simple, innate behaviors, usually involving few muscle systems, that occur automatically in response to specific environmental events or stimuli. An interesting fact is that many neonatal reflexes disappear before the end of the first year of life. It's almost as if these behaviors serve the sole function of helping the newborn adjust initially to its environment during a time when mobility and muscular con-

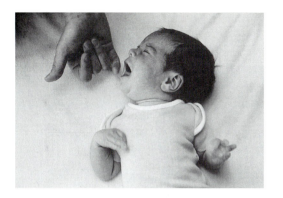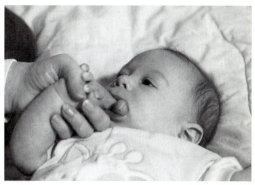

FIGURE 1.3 Rooting Reflex (left) and Sucking Reflex (right).

trol are otherwise severely restricted. Later, as behavior patterns become more sophisticated, the reflexes play less significant adaptive roles (Touwen, 1984).

There is another way that nature might provide a shortcut for developing adaptive behavior. In many species, survival is largely dependent on **fixed-action patterns,** which are highly stereotyped behaviors involving more than one muscle system, but which are nevertheless inborn and affected minimally by experience. Unlike the rooting and sucking reflexes, fixed-action patterns (Figure 1.4) unfold over longer time spans and involve more general activity on the part of the organism.

fixed-action patterns
highly stereotyped, inborn behavior patterns involving multiple muscle systems

Web spinning in spiders illustrates the typical features of fixed-action patterns. First, the behavior itself is not composed of a singular action, like reflexes, but a sequence of many movements. Second, the behavior is stereotypic within a species. Members of the same species of spider all make precisely the same movements when spinning their webs. Finally, once initiated, web spinning seems to run its course, as if by autopilot, until completion. It is remarkably difficult to interrupt.

A spider's web is not only a marvel of geometry, it also serves some vital biological functions. The female spider captures her food with the web and deposits her eggs on it during mating season. The web building itself is no small endeavor. A typical spider web is the result of slightly more than 6,000 spinning, or *dabbing,* movements (Eibl-Eibesfeldt, 1970). Perhaps most interesting about the actual building process is the fact that the movements of the spider do not appear to be sensitive to their consequences. For example, the lights that scientists use to study this behavior often have the effect of drying up the glands that the spider uses to secrete the webbing material. Nevertheless, the spider continues to make dabbing movements until the required number of movements have been made. Because many of these dabbings produce no webbing material, a large hole is present in the finished web, and when the spider deposits her eggs on the web, they will fall through it. None of this seems to influence the behavior of the web-spinning mother. It is this apparent lack of responsiveness of web-spinning behaviors to their consequences that makes this behavior a fixed-action pattern.

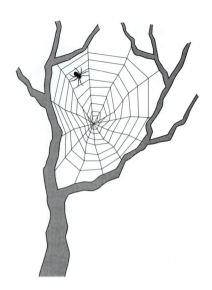

FIGURE 1.4 Web Spinning as Fixed-Action Pattern in Spiders.

Fixed-action patterns are viewed as phylogenetically shaped behaviors that are, for the most part, inborn; that is, they are the genetic endowment of organisms whose ancestors survived, in part because of the adaptiveness of these behaviors. But even fixed-action patterns must be interpreted with caution, for it turns out that they aren't always so fixed after all, but rather evidence surprising variability (Dewsbury, 1978; Siemann & Delius, 1992; Wishaw & Gorny, 1994). In fact, some contemporary biologists have recommended that the term *modal-action pattern* be substituted for fixed-action pattern, recognizing the somewhat plastic nature of some of these behaviors (Archer, 1992; Barlow, 1977). This point may bear special significance when applied to humans. Although psychologists have not always viewed human behavior through a phylogenetic lens, there are advantages to doing so. The last chapter of this book covers the contemporary writings of evolutionary psychologists, including some compelling arguments for the application of concepts such as instinct and fixed-action pattern to various human behaviors, particularly those within the social domain.

Learning and Cognition as Evolved Adaptations

Throughout this book, I will be stressing the theme of adaptation. In particular, the book looks at how scientists study learning and cognition as modes of adaptation across an enormous array of species—from rats, pigeons, cats, and dogs to chimpanzees and human beings—and in various settings, including high-tech laboratories and natural wildlife reserves. In the process, you will find that the terms *learning* and *cognition* encompass an inconceivably large category of behavior, from simple reflexes to problem solving, from tying shoes to hitting a golf ball, from using a word processor to playing roulette in a casino. Regardless of the many surface differences that distinguish these behaviors, all entail adjustment or adaptation in the behavior of an individual. Keep in mind that the focus is primarily on changes in behavior that take place over relatively short time periods, like hours, days, or weeks, because learning and cognition are sources of ontogenetic change—that is, change that occurs during the lifetime of an individual. Yet the very fact that this kind of change is possible, and that people can study it, is due to changes that have occurred on a much larger time scale and for entire species, not just individuals.

Animals go about solving the challenges of their environment in a host of ways. Some animals are bigger or stronger or fiercer than the other inhabitants of their niche. Others evade predation by running fast or by blending in with elements of their surrounding environment. Some of these attributes are specific, in that they represent adaptations that serve a particular group of animals in a fairly restrictive environment, and others prove useful across a broad spectrum of ecosystems. Camouflage, for instance, is an adaptation that aids many animals in avoiding predators, including such forest-dwelling animals as rabbits, raccoons, and deer, all of which fade imperceptibly into the browns and tans of the forest floor. In the ocean, many species of fish have taken on the basic shape and coloration of the coral and polyps that adorn the seafloor. The ability to blend into one's environment is a fairly common or general strategy for avoiding being eaten by one's enemy.

Yet, learning and cognition may be the most generic and useful methods devised by nature to assist organisms in what Darwin called the "struggle for existence." The ability to distinguish food-rich environments from depleted ones, or remember areas where food has been stored, or identify the silhouette or scent of a predator would have had enormous adaptive benefits to animals, especially those, like humans, who eventually found themselves inhabiting very different kinds of environments. Thus, the capacity for sizing up one's environment and benefiting from experience would be expected to become a dominating feature of most organisms, and in fact it has. Scientists say that learning and cognition have been selected for because these basic abilities must be "hard wired" into the nervous system, and natural selection is the only mechanism that could account for these abilities being so common throughout the animal kingdom. Learning and cognition are properly identified, therefore, as evolved adaptations, but cognitive and learning processes are only observable and measurable ontogenetically. And it is to these processes, in all of their complexity, that this book is devoted.

✖ INTERIM SUMMARY
Many species, possessing closed genetic programs, adapt to their surroundings through largely inherited behaviors, such as reflexes and fixed-action patterns. Humans, however, seem to possess a more limited repertoire of reflexive behaviors. Fortunately, we possess instead an open genetic program, which means that we can benefit substantially from experience.

This is an especially important aspect of our evolution as a species, because we tend to inhabit very dynamic, ever-changing environments. Thus, much of our adaptation occurs not as a result of phylogenetic behavior patterns, but from our ability to process environmental information and modify our behavior accordingly.

✖ THOUGHT QUESTIONS

1. Try to recall an example from your own life when some important part of your environment underwent a significant change. How much of a challenge did this change pose for you, and what did you do to adjust? In what way does this example illustrate the difference between closed and open genetic programs?

2. Why is the concept of motivation important to the learning versus performance distinction? Can you see the relevance of this distinction in your own experience as a student?

LEARNING AND COGNITION AS SCIENTIFIC SUBJECT MATTERS

Humans are a particularly curious species. We possess an insatiable desire to understand the world around us, from the smallest microbes to the origin of the universe. To this end, we have developed various methods for acquiring and transmitting knowledge. Frequently we rely on casual observation, intuition, or the voice of authority to help us make sense of things. This commonsense approach to acquiring knowledge seems to work well enough, so we seldom question its effectiveness. And in case such tactics fail, there is no shortage of self-proclaimed soothsayers, psychics, astrologers, clairvoyants, and others boasting privileged access to the workings of the universe, not to mention the human mind. You might be tempted to view such practitioners as part of an isolated fringe movement, unconnected to mainstream society. Such is not the case, however. Those who have enlisted the aid of psychics, both in the past and currently, include American presidents, other heads of state, and contemporary police departments. Moreover, as noted by the late astronomer Carl Sagan (1995), belief in various pseudoscientific practices appears to be increasing among the American populace.

At the same time, the establishment of the scientific method stands as one of the crowning achievements in human evolution. As a way of knowing, science represents a major departure from common sense and pseudoscientific pursuits. The hallmarks of science include the practice of asking specific and well-reasoned questions about natural phenomena and undertaking systematic experiments to answer such questions. On balance, science has been awfully good to us over the years. Modern humans, especially those living in highly technological societies, benefit from science and its application in innumerable ways every day. It may be no exaggeration, in fact, to suggest that we have been spoiled by technology and take for granted the marvelous enterprise that is science. Imagine, for instance, life without automobiles, telephones, air conditioning, VCRs, computers, microwave ovens, antibiotics, birth control, food preservatives, immunizations, heart bypass surgery, and a host of other technological offspring that have become commonplace. How many of us would genuinely wish to return to a world in which there was no science?

Science as Systematic Inquiry

As much as it affects our lives, the scientific method remains something of a mystery to most of us. We continue to hold to the stereotype of the scientist as a mysterious recluse, clad in a white lab coat and surrounded by intimidating electronic gadgetry and chemicals festering in test tubes. We think, also, of the disciplines so indelibly associated with science—such as physics, chemistry, math, and biology. There is nothing in the scientific method, though, that requires lab coats, electronic instruments, and test tubes. Nor are physics, chemistry, and biology, themselves, sciences. They are, instead, subject matters or fields of knowledge. We call them scientific disciplines simply because our understanding of the natural world has largely developed through practices that all scientists find useful, regardless of subject matter. Indeed, what makes science such a powerful way of knowing is that its practices are not specific to any subject matter, but are universally applicable to all aspects of nature, including ourselves. Let's take a look at why this is so.

Science is a means of systematically asking questions about some natural phenomenon. Scientists develop specific questions concerning their subject matter that can be answered through experimentation. Scientific questions may come from several sources. Personal experience, for example, often serves to stimulate interest in a research subject. A case in point is social psychologist Robert Cialdini (1988) who, recognizing his own vulnerability to sales pitches, fund-raising requests, and other attempts at persuasion, developed a program of empirical studies aimed at uncovering the interpersonal dynamics that facilitate or impede such efforts. Cialdini actually worked alongside such *compliance experts* to learn the tricks of the trade. The result has been an enhanced understanding of the special strategies invoked by salespeople, politicians, and other compliance experts to get others to do their bidding.

Research questions also emerge from the ongoing research of one's colleagues. Every study, no matter how well designed, tends to generate as many questions as answers, and this makes the accumulation of knowledge in any field a continuous, albeit gradual, process. In this regard, publication of research results in professional journals serves a critical scientific function. After reading the results of a published study, a researcher may devise a question that, although not addressed in the original account, may be addressed through additional research. As more such research is conducted in the area, additional specific questions are answered, and a fuller understanding of the phenomenon of interest emerges.

Finally, research is frequently conducted for the purpose of testing theories. In general, a **theory** is a series of statements about relationships between variables that, taken together, attempts to explain some natural phenomenon. Each individual statement, or **hypothesis**, is something like an educated

theory a series of statements about relationships between variables that, taken together, attempt to explain some natural phenomenon

hypothesis an educated guess about relationships between variables that can be tested through experimentation

guess that can be directly evaluated through experimentation. For instance, a researcher may have a theory of aggression that includes many such hypotheses, one of which might be that high levels of the hormone testosterone will be associated with high levels of aggression. It would be possible to arrange an experiment in which testosterone is injected into laboratory animals in order to assess whether aggression and testosterone are indeed related. The results of such an experiment could then be used as confirmation or rejection of this particular hypothesis. Note, however, that this experiment is relevant only to this specific hypothesis. The status of the theory would not likely be determined by this one experiment, because most theories involve complicated networks of related hypotheses. A theory would suffer major damage, of course, if none of its hypotheses survived experimental scrutiny.

Science Up Close and Personal:
Exploring Spatial Memory

spatial memory
ability of an organism
to recall specific loca-
tions in its environment
over time

To get a better feel for how science is actually done, let's take a look at research on rats' **spatial memory,** which refers to how well organisms can remember specific locations in their environment. This ability is especially important to animals who forage, or move about their environment in search of food. Finding food in this way imposes two important restrictions on an animal. First, energy and stamina levels will place limits on the size of an area in which the animal can forage. Second, when food availability in a particular area becomes scarce, it is clearly to an animal's advantage not to visit that area again, at least until that food source has been replenished. This means that an ability to remember those areas from which food has been gathered becomes an essential component in this animal's adaptation to its world.

Consider for a moment how as researchers we might go about studying spatial memory in animals. There exist a number of possible strategies. For instance, we could carry out such a study by observing rats, or other foraging animals, in their natural habitat, but this is extremely difficult for practical reasons. Such habitats are often not very accommodating to humans. In addition, our very presence in such a habitat is likely to disrupt the animals' natural behavior patterns. An additional drawback to the natural setting is that we would not have control over the availability of food in the environment or the comings and goings of the animals themselves. Consequently, several factors that may be influencing the animals' behavior may go completely overlooked. As a result, we would be hard pressed to explain how the animals were able to forage so successfully. Without the ability to control the conditions under which the animals forage, discovering the causes or role of spatial memory in foraging is unlikely.

To get useful results, many researchers conduct studies in laboratory settings. Consider, for example, the research on foraging conducted by David Olton over the course of several years (Olton, 1978, 1992; Olton, Collison, & Werz, 1977; Olton & Samuelson, 1978). The apparatus Olton uses to study spatial memory is called a *radial arm maze.* This device contains a central

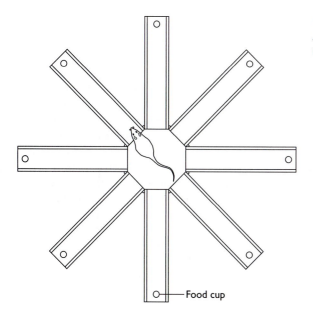

FIGURE 1.5 Radial Arm Maze for Studying Spatial Memory.

platform from which eight runway arms radiate (Figure 1.5). At the end of each arm is a container into which food is placed. In a typical experiment, rats are placed in the middle platform and are observed as they venture out to the radiating arms to collect food. The central question in such research is whether the animals will revisit arms from which they have previously taken the food. This kind of behavior represents poor foraging strategy because it wastes precious time and energy and would hardly prove adaptive in the animal's natural setting. As it turns out, rats perform quite successfully on this task, seldom revisiting arms from which food has already been taken. In fact, their performance remains high even when the maze contains as many as 17 arms.

Testing Hypotheses   How do the rats perform this impressive feat? Does their nearly flawless foraging represent an ability to remember locations, or is there another explanation? Is it possible, for instance, that as the animals visit each arm, they urinate in the arm in order to mark locations? Thus, on subsequent trips into the maze, the rats, known to be very sensitive to odors, simply refuse to enter arms that were previously marked in this way? This possibility represents a specific hypothesis that could account for the animal's impressive performance in the maze, and it is the business of good research to test the validity of such hypotheses.

Remember, though, scientific logic dictates that you rule out all possible explanations, or hypotheses, for a phenomenon before settling on any one definitive account. In order to rule out the possibility that rats were marking maze arms, Olton conducted an experiment in which the rats were allowed to visit several arms before they were removed from the maze. After the animals were removed, the maze itself was rotated 45 degrees, so that arms that had been marked by urine were now lined up with food cups. If the rats were to use the scent marker as an indication of visitation, the researchers would expect them not to enter arms that had been so marked. However, when placed back in the maze, rats continued to visit arms that held food, even if these arms had been scent marked. Thus, the animals' foraging success appeared to be due to something other than olfactory cues. In fact, the role of odor cues was even more convincingly ruled out by Hyde, Hoplight, and Denenberg (1998), who conducted a series of experiments using a water version of the radial arm maze.

The radial arm maze represents a controlled, yet fairly complex, environment in which to observe foraging behavior. Because of the scientist's easy access to the maze, such things as the number of maze arms, food availability, maze orientation, and visual cues external to the maze can be precisely manipulated. These factors, or *variables*, can then be altered in programmatic ways in order to see how they affect the animals' spatial memory.

Manipulating Independent Variables   In learning and cognition experiments, **independent variables** are manipulated in order to bring about some effect on behavior. In the case of spatial memory in rats, there are several such variables that we, as scientists, may want to study. On the one hand, we may want to know whether the ability to remember locations is impaired by increasing the number of available food sites. If, as the number of arms in the maze increases, revisitations (returning to arms from which food has already been collected) increase, we would know that foraging does in fact decline as a function of number of arms. On the other hand, we may be interested in whether memory is disrupted when animals are removed from the maze after being allowed to visit several, but not all, maze arms. When placed back in the maze later, do the animals revisit arms or simply pick up where they left off? Moreover, how long of a delay would it take to disrupt the animals' ability to forage efficiently? Answering these questions helps us to understand how animals solve similar problems in their struggle to survive in the wild. Perhaps most important, these are all questions that could be put to experimental test because the researcher can control and manipulate such variables within a laboratory setting. Each manipulation adds a small piece of information to the understanding of this species' ability to acquire food efficiently.

Scientific Skepticism

Another valuable principle in scientific investigations is **skepticism,** the tendency to suspend judgment until there is reasonable certainty that all possible explanations for a phenomenon have been considered. Scientists make an effort to refrain from uncritically accepting an explanation for behavior until adequate experiments have been conducted to rule out other possibilities. In the case of Olton's research, it is tempting to conclude that rats have wonderful spatial memories, but other possible explanations must be eliminated first. One such explanation was the possibility that the rats were simply marking the maze arms with urine. Only when this possible explanation

independent variable factor manipulated by an experimenter to evaluate its effect on other variables

skepticism the tendency to suspend judgment until you are reasonably certain all explanations have been considered

could be ruled out did it make sense to attribute efficient foraging to spatial memory. Over time, and as the result of many such experiments carried out perhaps by many scientists in different laboratories, knowledge of spatial memory accumulates. This cumulative aspect of knowledge is a defining feature of scientific understanding but is seldom a feature knowledge acquired through casual observation or authority.

Many other details go into any scientific research program, and the strategies and instruments used will depend on the field of study. The beakers and test tubes used in chemistry are the mazes, operant chambers, computerized games and puzzles, and so on used in the psychology of learning and cognition. What remains constant from one field to another is the critical thinking, logic of experimentation, and the unrelenting desire to rule out all but the most compelling explanations for a given phenomenon. These remain the enduring features of the scientific method, and they distinguish science from other ways of knowing, such as appeals to authority or common sense.

The Intuitive Psychologist

The skepticism and rigorous control that represent the scientific method are particularly invaluable when the subject matter is behavior. This is true because, to a considerable extent, most people consider themselves to be knowledgeable about behavior, particularly that of their fellow humans. We naturally spend large amounts of time trying to figure one another out, be it our children, our spouses, our employers, or strangers in line at a grocery store. To some degree, this is possible because behavior does in fact exhibit a certain amount of predictability. When you meet someone for the first time and extend your hand, don't you fully expect the person to reciprocate by reaching for and shaking your hand? Wouldn't you be surprised, or even offended, if he or she refused to do so? If you are at a stoplight behind another vehicle, don't you expect the driver to accelerate when the light turns green? If he or she fails to do so, would you offer some polite encouragement to move? In short, much of what we and others do is commonplace and consequently taken for granted.

But it is just this predictability or ordinariness in behavior that gets us into trouble. Because we can so often anticipate what people will do, we are misled into thinking that we understand the causes of their behavior. The faulty nature of this logic is well illustrated by a thoroughly documented instance of human bias. Social psychological research has shown that we are all strongly inclined toward the **fundamental attribution error,** or the tendency to view other persons' behavior as reflective of their personal dispositions, rather than as responses to social or situational factors in the environment (Jones & Harris, 1967; Ross, 1977; Storms, 1973).

fundamental attribution error the tendency to view others' behavior as resulting from personal dispositions rather than from situational factors

If you were shown a picture of homeless people congregating on an urban street and were asked to speculate on the possible causes of homelessness, what explanation would you offer? Would you suggest that homeless people are just lazy and can't hold down a job? Perhaps they're afflicted by mental illness, drug addiction, or even an inherent lack of character and internal strength. Notice how all of these possible causes of homelessness focus on the *personal* attributes of the homeless themselves.

Now, what do you suppose would happen if you were to ask the homeless person to explain his or her own predicament? Would you expect his or her attributions to be the same as yours? Of course not—you would, in fact, hear a very different explanation. He or she would tend to attribute the current situation to such factors as losing his or her job, perhaps being discriminated against by employers or society in general, or having suffered a devastating personal loss such as a death of a spouse or divorce. In other words, homeless individuals will tend to attribute their predicament to conditions outside themselves, conditions in the local environment. This is quite the opposite of the outside observer's attribution, which places emphasis on the homeless individual's personal weaknesses or shortcomings.

Simply put, the actor and the observer in any particular behavioral episode are looking at different things: The actor looks out at the world surrounding him or her, whereas the observer focuses on the actor and his or her behavior. The differential attributions that are made by actor and observer can probably be readily accounted for by this distinction in perceptual salience; each person attends to a separate aspect of the situation (Storms, 1973).

The fundamental attribution error is a pervasive reminder that personal *biases* can distort the ability to understand behavior. It is precisely for this reason that the scientific method holds such promise as a way of knowing. Without its built-in skepticism and self-corrective nature, people are at risk of allowing personal opinion to cloud their understanding of the subject matter. Without the objectivity of science, we are left more vulnerable to the alluring promises of the pseudoscientific practices that, as Sagan (1995) reminds us, continue to grow in popularity.

✖ INTERIM SUMMARY

Science is among the many ways that humans have developed for trying to understand more about their world. Unlike intuition, appeals to authority, and pseudoscientific practices, however, science boasts many advantages as a method of inquiry. Objectivity, skepticism, and experimentation aimed at answering specific questions make science an especially powerful tool for investigating nature. Science is a particularly important method for studying behavior because everyone harbors various misconceptions about this very personal subject matter.

✖ THOUGHT QUESTIONS

1. Why is skepticism such an important practice when trying to understand behavior? Can you think of an instance in which you may have misinterpreted the behavior of a friend or family member? What advantages would a more skeptical approach have afforded you in this case?
2. Can you identify the fundamental attribution error at work in your own behavior? How would it operate in the context of an argument with a friend or spouse?

HISTORICAL INFLUENCES ON THE PSYCHOLOGY OF LEARNING AND COGNITION

By now you should appreciate the nearly exhaustive influence of learning and cognition in our lives. Few of our behaviors, from simple to complex, or routine to novel, would be conceivable in the absence of these rather encompassing processes. In fact, this realization is hardly the brainchild of modern scientists and scholars. The question of how and why we process information about our environment and adjust our behavior to the changing world has probably taken center stage ever since humans first developed an interest in understanding behavior. It is difficult to put a date on such an occurrence, but attention to such matters can be traced to ancient times. Early Greek orators, not yet blessed by the wizardry of word processing programs, faced the daunting task of memorizing long, complicated speeches. This challenge led them to devise various rehearsal techniques, called *mnemonics,* some of which entailed dramatic and interactive visual images. Using these vivid tools, these scholars committed to memory amounts of verbal information that would probably astound most of us today.

In short, humans have a long history of contemplating the cognitive operations and learning phenomena that define so much of what we do. This section surveys some of the more significant features of this history, including the thoughts of important figures in the history of philosophy. You will see how the study of learning and cognition was affected by early schools of thought and movements within the fledgling discipline of psychology and how the disparate worldviews that emerged from these movements created an unfortunate partisanship that continues to artificially separate the important work being done by contemporary learning and cognition researchers.

Philosophical Contributions

Much of the intellectual fabric of psychology, particularly the study of learning and cognition, originated in the influential writings of scientists, scholars, and philosophers during the 17th and 18th centuries. These great thinkers were motivated, as are today's scientists and philosophers, by a deep passion to understand the complexities and paradoxes of the human mind. What are its central features, abilities, and functions? Is the mind a separate entity acting on the body, and, if so, how does it do so? Is the mind equipped at birth with the capacity to understand the world, or does it require lengthy and comprehensive input from the senses? As shown throughout this book, these are hardly the trivial preoccupations of a bygone generation of thinkers. They are instead timeless speculations about the human condition, many of which continue to inform the work of contemporary scientists.

Descartes and the Doctrine of Innate Ideas   Frenchman René Descartes (1596–1650) was a gifted thinker whose contributions to human knowledge knew few boundaries. Like many of his intellectual contemporaries, Descartes's influence ranged across a diverse collection of disciplines, from philosophy to science and mathematics. In addition to his enormous contributions to the methods of philosophical argument, Descartes conducted important experiments in optics and founded the discipline of analytic geometry. Descartes's legacy to psychology is probably unparalleled among early philosophers. In addition to his speculations on the mind, he may well have been the first to suggest the reflex as a fundamental unit of behavior. Descartes's speculations about reflexive behavior preceded Pavlov's groundbreaking experimental work and the grand era of learning theory by nearly 300 years. In addition, Descartes's philosophical work led him inevitably to a consideration of the mind-body problem. The question of whether mind and body represented qualitatively separate entities, and how one could influence the operation of the other, would entertain generations of philosophers and scientists. Descartes's position, known as *dualism,* was that mind, nonphysical and unextended, could nevertheless affect the physically extended body. It would not be an exaggeration to claim that this fundamental issue has preoccupied philosophers and scientists, including psychologists, ever since.

rationalism the idea that knowledge and truth are to be sought through logical reasoning

Descartes was a representative of a philosophical position commonly referred to as **rationalism,** the major tenet of which is that knowledge and truth are to be sought primarily through the process of logical reasoning. Such reasoning is a natural faculty of the human mind. Closely aligned with this notion is Descartes's doctrine of innate ideas, which claimed that human beings come into the world equipped with certain fundamental ideas or knowledge. Descartes argued, for instance, that such concepts as self, God, and infinity do not depend on experience and must therefore be a basic, irreducible property of the human mind. In many ways, this doctrine, though perhaps in more modern guise, informs the work of many contemporary researchers. For instance, evolutionary psychologists argue quite forcefully that the human mind must consist of numerous specialized modules for processing information, problem solving, and acquiring language and that successful adaptation would simply be unthinkable in the absence of such innate structures (Buss, 1999; Cosmides & Tooby, 1994; Pinker, 1997).

empiricism the idea that knowledge is acquired through the senses

Empiricism   Keep in mind that during the 17th century Europe was a hotbed of science and philosophy; it was a time of intellectual excitement perhaps unequaled during any other period of human civilization. Challenging Descartes's doctrine of innate ideas was a group of British philosophers who believed that all human knowledge was derived from experience—an idea known as **empiricism.** Foremost among these empiricists was John Locke (1632–1704). In his influential "Essay Concerning Human Understanding," Locke (1690/1959) claimed that humans can have no knowledge without prior sensory input. Indeed, the word *emperia,* from which the empiricists derived their name, means "of the senses." Locke revived Aristotle's concept of the *tabula rasa,* suggesting that at birth the mind is a blank slate waiting to be written on by experience. It might occur to you that those scientists who today endorse an empiricist orientation are likely to investigate ways in which personal experience influences behavior and, from this book's perspective, adaptation over time. In some sense, modern research in learning and cognition is an important part of the legacy of the empiricist tradition.

Locke's empiricism laid the foundation for learning and cognition by suggesting that the mind benefits from two separate processes: *sensation* and *reflection*. Sensation refers to the process by which sensory receptors in the body are stimulated by light, sound, and other kinds of physical energy in the environment. To be of any use, though, these basic sensations must be processed, or meaningfully integrated, and this was the primary purpose of reflection. But what is being reflected upon are the basic facts of the world provided by the senses, and this means that Locke's philosophy remained unapologetically empirical. From the data of the senses, simple ideas emerged, and these ideas could be combined with others to produce complex ideas. In addition, Locke recognized that ideas could be associated— that is, certain concepts could be viewed as related to one another. For instance, the concepts *red* and *green* are both names of colors and are, as such, meaningfully related. Locke also claimed that, through various experiences, ideas or events could become connected and that this connection could be established and retained, through memory, in the mind indefinitely. In other words, Locke appreciated the mind's ability both to process complex ideas and to retain this knowledge over long intervals of time. Nevertheless, as an empiricist, Locke maintained that the essential *content* of mind comes, via the senses, from the world at large.

Behaviorism and the Psychology of Learning

By the early 1900s, psychology was not only a separate discipline, but also had become a distinct experimental science. Early experimental psychology had significant ancestral ties to the science of physiology, and this connection was especially notable in the work of Nobel Prize–winning physiologist Ivan Pavlov. In the process of studying the activity of the salivary glands, Pavlov had stumbled upon a learning phenomenon that would have relevance considerably beyond the physiology laboratory. (Pavlov's important work is the topic of the next chapter.) Pavlov's research would become a model for psychologists interested in pursuing a scientific study of learning, in large part because of his commitment to experimental rigor and objective measurement. Still in its infancy as an empirical discipline, psychology during the early 20th century was distancing itself from its early philosophical moorings, and many of its practitioners were quick to identify with established experimental sciences, like physiology. Learning psychologists, in particular, were convinced that the study of learning could be an objective and sophisticated laboratory-based enterprise worthy of the prestige accorded the natural sciences.

The psychology of learning, then, developed within an environment infused by Pavlov's important discoveries and by a general enthusiasm for experimentation. By the 1930s and 1940s, experimental and theoretical work in learning dominated the psychological landscape, particularly in American colleges and universities. But the study of learning was characterized by more than its experiments. Many of those who ushered in this discipline harbored strong opinions about how this young science of psychology was to be conducted. How was the subject matter to be defined? What were its essential properties, and how were they to be measured? What terminological conventions would serve the discipline best? There were, in short, differing ideas on matters of **epistemology,** the collection of rules or criteria to be used in establishing truth or knowledge. One particular epistemology, behaviorism, would eventually win the day, largely through the efforts of two influential American scientists.

epistemology collection of rules or criteria for establishing truth or knowledge

John B. Watson and Methodological Behaviorism   The drive to make psychology an experimental science and to emancipate the discipline from philosophy could not have had a more forceful spokesperson than American psychologist John B. Watson (1878–1958). Somewhat ironically, Watson had originally studied under the noted educational philosopher John Dewey at Chicago University. Finding little of value in philosophy, Watson later studied biology and physiology, the latter under renowned physiologist Jacques Loeb. Having conducted his dissertation research on rats, Watson would become an ardent supporter of animal research, believing that well-controlled studies of nonhuman species could shed light on human behavior as well. Watson had little patience for armchair musings about human behavior and the frequent allusions to *consciousness* and *mind* that seemed to flavor many psychologists' conversations about people. Such accounts were often idiosyncratic and lacked the dimension of public verifiability so central to science. Watson was convinced that a purely experimental approach to studying behavior, one free from personal opinion and subjectivity, was not only possible but was the only defensible way to construct a science of behavior. Watson provided an outline for this new science of psychology in an influential, though controversial, article:

> Psychology as the behaviorist views it is a purely objective experimental branch of natural science. Its theoretical goal is the prediction and control of behavior. Introspection forms no essential part of its methods, nor is the scientific value of its data dependent upon the readiness with which they lend themselves to interpretation in terms of consciousness. (Watson, 1913, p. 158)

Watson argued that there were many aspects of private experience, such as thoughts, emotions, and visual images, that defied objective observation. In claiming such phenomena to be inappropriate subject matter for a science, Watson wasn't denying their existence. After all, how could one deny that people think? The difficulty for the scientist lies in identifying what, precisely, one means by the word *think*. If thinking entails some metaphysical, ghostly process in an unextended mind, as suggested by Descartes, then such an event would be inaccessible to a natural science. On the other hand, if thinking is merely subvocal speech, as Watson claimed, then such a phenomenon might be amenable to scientific investigation. But such research would require extraordinarily sensitive instruments capable of recording miniscule laryngeal movements not detectable by the naked eye. Psychology possessed no such equipment at the turn of the 20th century, and the discipline was consequently restricted in its ability to investigate such elusive inner processes. On the other hand, the overt behavior of an organism, be it human or nonhuman, was directly observable and measurable, as were sources of stimulation in the environment. Psychology should be, Watson claimed, a science concerned with studying systematic connections between the stimulating environment and the behavior of the organism. Watson's position eventually became known as **methodological behaviorism,** both because of its emphasis on experimentation and its claims about the scientific inaccessibility of private experience (Baum, 1994; Day, 1980; Skinner, 1974).

B. F. Skinner and Radical Behaviorism

B. F. Skinner (1904–1990) was born in Susquehanna, Pennsylvania, as the son of a lawyer. His ambition in life, after graduating in English from Hamilton College in New York, was to become a writer. Skinner spent the year following graduation in Greenwich Village, discovering that his future as a writer was not promising, for by his own admission he had nothing to say (Skinner, 1979). Instead, he enrolled in graduate school in psychology at Harvard, where he read widely in physiology and psychology. He was particularly impressed by Pavlov's meticulous and rigorous research and by Watson's iconoclastic and revolutionary writings. It was in fact the behaviorist banner that Skinner would eventually take up from Watson, becoming over the course of more than five decades the single most influential spokesman for behavioral psychology.

Though he assumed the throne as America's preeminent behaviorist, Skinner advocated a philosophy of science that departed considerably from Watson's. Promoting what he referred to as **radical behaviorism,** Skinner claimed that a natural science of behavior must eventually come to terms with the "private events" that Watson had excluded from consideration. According to Skinner (1953, 1974), thoughts, feelings, and other subjective or private experiences are not different from overt behavior simply because they cannot be verified by others. A complete account of behavior would eventually require a description of such private events, including how people become aware of them and how they learn to describe and talk about them with others. Indeed, as you will learn in Chapters 4 and 5, this and other aspects of Skinner's philosophy have been widely misunderstood both within and outside of psychology (Catania, 1991; Todd & Morris, 1992).

Skinner made numerous methodological and empirical contributions to psychology, particularly with respect to the study of learning and conditioning, and he was widely known for his controversial views regarding the role of theory in science. In a classic paper titled "Are Theories of Learning Necessary?" Skinner (1950) argued that theories that refer to events going on inside the organism, rather than simply to behavior-environment interactions, are actually harmful to progress in the study of learning. In his view, science first needs to accumulate a substantial amount of basic empirical facts to serve as a foundation for meaningful theory building, and, as of the late 1940s, psychology had not yet acquired a sufficient database. Unfortunately, Skinner's critics interpreted the article as evidence that he discounted entirely the usefulness of theory of any sort. For this reason, Skinner is often referred to as the grand antitheoretician in psychology. But as explained in subsequent chapters, Skinner's formulation is in all practical senses a theory of behavior, though it contained few of the formal postulates that characterized other learning theories in psychology.

The Cognitive Revolution

The philosophy of behaviorism, especially as promulgated by Watson and Skinner, was the dominant interpretive force that informed research on learning during the first five decades of the 20th century. But by the 1960s, factions within psychology and from related disciplines such as computer science and information theory converged to bring about a major shift in the way psychologists viewed their subject matter. Because such a shift represents a fundamental change in the kinds of questions researchers ask and the nature of the theories they develop to explain their subject matter, some writers have referred to the events taking place during the 1960s and 1970s as the beginnings of the *cognitive revolution* in psychology (Baars, 1986; Gardner, 1985). Whether the term *revolution* is justifiable or not, there is no denying the extent to which cognitive theory has affected virtually every area of research within the discipline of psychology, including the study of learning. To better understand how this came to be, let's examine some of the historical developments leading to the cognitive revolution in psychology.

Information Theory and the Computer Metaphor   Two significant events outside of psychology made enormous contributions to the acceptance of a cognitive approach to studying learning. One of these, **information theory**, suggested that how an organism (or machine, for that matter) responds to the environment depends on the capacities of the organism to handle input or information from the environment. In many ways, information theory views the human being as a general information processor much like a computer or calculating machine. And, of course, computers are limited by how much information they can retain, the speed at which such information can be handled, and so on. In addition, the computer cannot accept certain kinds of input as information, so the nature of the information itself is critical. For example, while the command "RUN TAX PROGRAM" may be accepted by the computer, the command "RIN TAC PROGRAM" will not because the information in the latter is not within acceptable parameters. Similarly, although I can understand the claim that "Liberals often vote against capital punishment," the statement "Often against capital vote punishment liberals" is not interpretable. The gist of information theory is that human beings have limitations as information processors just as do machines, and these limitations must be taken into account in any theory of human learning and behavior.

As is probably already clear, the way theorists have come to think about humans as information processors has been influenced dramatically by the computer, a machine whose popularity and practical importance began to grow during the 1960s. Just as we talk about the input, processing, and output functions of computers, cognitive psychologists believe it can be helpful to describe much of human cognition in similar terms. Of course, cognitive psychologists fully understand that this is only an analogy; we are biological

information theory
the ability to process information from the environment is dependent on properties of the system (human or machine)

as opposed to electronic information processors. However, we share certain functional similarities with computers, despite our other obvious differences. It is instructive, for example, to observe how much the terminology of computer science has become standard within the cognitive lexicon. Chapter 7, on memory and forgetting, describes what psychologists have learned about the encoding, storage, and retrieval of information by humans. These are all familiar concepts to those who work with computers.

The RAND Conference   In 1958 a conference at the RAND Corporation brought together a number of scholars from diverse scientific backgrounds. Included at the conference were not only psychologists but also researchers interested in *artificial intelligence,* which involves the design of machinery capable of complex humanlike behavior, such as thinking and problem solving. Among the objectives of the conference was to demonstrate to behavioral scientists how programs used to run computers and other machines might serve as models for talking about human behavior. The overall theme of the conference was that complex behavior might be generated by particular rules or plans, in much the same way that a computer exercises a particular function written into a program. Impressed by the topics discussed at the RAND conference, psychologists George Miller, Eugene Galanter, and Karl Pribram (1960) began exploring the possibilities of describing the rule-governed nature of human cognition and behavior. Their influential book, *Plans and the Structure of Behavior,* contained a provocative alternative to behavioristic accounts of complex human behaviors like logical reasoning and problem solving. In a sense, the conference served as a catalyst for change in psychology, in that it brought together for the first time those scientists whose names would ultimately become associated with the cognitive revolution.

Among the many events giving rise to the cognitive revolution, the publication of Ulric Neisser's *Cognitive Psychology* in 1967 deserves special mention. Neisser not only offered the first explicit definition of cognitive psychology, but also tied together many issues coming out of artificial intelligence, computer science, and psychology. While aware of the conceptual offerings of information theory, Neisser warned against a simplistic adoption of these ideas to understanding human beings as information processors. He contended, for example, that it is dangerous to assume that the information that goes into a system is identical to what comes out of the system, especially when the system is a thinking, active, problem-solving human being. Finally, Neisser described the research programs currently being conducted under the banner of cognitive psychology and possible future directions for the new discipline.

Explanation in Behavioral and Cognitive Psychology

The cognitive revolution within psychology is indicative of the kinds of change that scientific disciplines often encounter at different times in their history. Thomas Kuhn (1970), a historian of science, has argued that most sciences evolve through varying periods of discord, characterized by disagreement about the discipline's essential *paradigm,* which refers to such varied aspects as the definition of the subject matter, how best to submit the subject matter to investigation, and the actual facts thus discovered. Eventually, this discord leads to a paradigm shift in which empirical progress is made and a general consensus emerges concerning basic conceptual and methodological practices. This latter condition Kuhn has called "normal science," and it is representative of those disciplines whose relative maturity can be seen in a progressive and cumulative knowledge base and empirically related technological achievements. Kuhn considers the natural sciences, such as biology, chemistry, and physics to be in a state of normal science.

The question of whether the behavioral and social sciences can be said to be in a period of normal science is certainly contestable. To some, the cognitive revolution represented a clear paradigm shift within the discipline of psychology. But it is not particularly evident whether a unified paradigm has emerged in psychology or, for that matter, whether the discipline more closely resembles normal science today than it did before the cognitive revolution. Paradigm consensus has proven terribly elusive for psychologists, particularly those representing different experimental or theoretical traditions. It would be misleading to ignore this divisiveness, particularly in a text on learning and cognition.

The absence of a unifying paradigm in psychology is visible throughout the discipline, but the chasm that separates the work of behavioral and cognitive psychologists has always been particularly conspicuous. This state of affairs is truly unfortunate, because psychologists from both of these camps have made substantial contributions to the understanding of how organisms process information and benefit from experience. As this section explores some of the historical and conceptual reasons for this separation, you will discover that despite the often dramatically disparate explanatory styles that emerge from these separate orientations, considerable similarities can be identified as well. In a general sense, both fields of research make use of the experimental method and pursue functional relationships between environmental variables and the behavior of the experimental subject. In addition, both cognitive and behavioral psychologists have increasingly relied on the theme of adaptation to make sense of their subject matter.

The major difference between behavioral and cognitive explanations is the causal status given to private events, that is, processes occurring inside the organism. Consistent with the definition offered by Neisser (1967), it is precisely the agenda of cognitive psychology to describe and explain these processes and how they contribute to behavior. For the cognitive psychologist, research on memory, decision making, and concept formation is important to the extent that it helps explain how humans process information and how this information then allows us to emit adaptive responses to our environment. Cognitive psychologists observe and measure overt behavior, but their reason for doing so is to be able to make statements about the inner processes that produced the behavior. In this sense, cognitive psychologists consider behavior to be important, not so much in and of itself, but for what it can reveal about the private machinery of the mind. In its early days, cognitive psychology was limited to somewhat speculative descriptions of these internal processes, because direct observation of the intact human brain was very limited. In more recent years, however, imaging devices, such as PET and CAT scans and MRIs, have made it possible to peer in on the nervous system and observe the neurological events that correspond to the memory and decision-making tasks manipulated by cognitive psychologists. In fact, the study of the relationship between brain function and cognition, known as **cognitive neuroscience**, is among the fastest growing subfields of contemporary psychology (Gazzaniga, 2000; Nilsson & Markowitsch, 1999).

cognitive neuroscience scientific discipline concerned with the relationship between brain function and cognition or information processing

The behavioral psychologist, on the other hand, views behavior as *the* principal subject matter of psychology, not merely as an index of internal processes. By manipulating environmental variables and observing their direct effects on behavior, it has proven possible for psychologists to establish predictable, orderly relationships, many of which approach the kind of quantitative precision seen in other sciences. For the behavioral psychologist, establishing such orderly relationships between behavior and its controlling variables (environmental stimuli) serves both a descriptive and explanatory purpose within a science of behavior. Behavior is never viewed outside its relevant context, and the context itself takes on substantial causal status. This does not mean, nor has any behavioral psychologist ever claimed, that the organism is a black box or that things happening inside the organism are irrelevant. It might be useful to let B. F. Skinner, a major proponent of the behaviorist position, speak on this matter:

> But we cannot say that what goes on inside is an adequate explanation until we know what the black box does. A behavioral analysis is essentially a statement of the facts to be explained by studying the nervous system. It tells the physiologist what to look for. The converse does not hold. We can predict and control behavior without knowing how our dependent and independent variables are connected. Physiological discoveries cannot disprove an experimental analysis or invalidate its technological advances. (1969, p. 283)

Skinner's point is central to radical behaviorism, the epistemology that he endorsed throughout his career. An independent science of behavior, in which orderly behavior-environment relations are uncovered, is not rendered obsolete by separate observations of neurological functioning. Knowing precisely what is happening in the nervous system when an organism is engaged in a particular behavior certainly adds to the understanding of the entire behavioral episode, but it does not alter in any way the fundamental behavior-environment interaction. Moreover, Skinner frequently claimed that it is the specific environmental contingencies that bring about physiological changes in the first place and that for this reason there is little need, at least for the behavioral scientist, to go beyond this level of analysis. In a sense, Skinner was suggesting that behavioral research was necessary in order for the neuroscientist to know what to look for in the nervous system. Modern research on the brain has for the most part vindicated Skinner on this matter. Researchers are learning some pretty amazing things about how even basic sensory and learning experiences affect the development of neural pathways in the brain, especially during childhood (Rosenzweig & Bennett, 1996; Shatz, 1992). On the other hand, it is understandable that neuroscientists would focus on the details of these neural processes, both because their primary subject matter is the nervous system and because they possess the appropriate technological equipment for its examination.

An additional source of division between behavioral and cognitive psychologists has been their respective choices of experimental participants. Behavioral psychology, particularly as manifested in the era of grand learning theory, was dominated by the experimental study of nonhuman participants. In fact, Watson rather forcefully defended the use of nonhumans in this research:

> I never wanted to use human subjects . . . With animals I was at home. I felt that, in studying them, I was keeping close to biology with my feet on the ground. More and more the thought presented itself: Can't I find out by watching their behavior everything that the other students are finding out by using O's [human subjects]? (1961, p. 276)

The use of nonhuman animal subjects in psychological research has long been a bone of contention among researchers. The justification for doing so includes both practical and theoretical dimensions. For instance, animals bred and raised in the controlled environment of a laboratory remain "uncontaminated" by experiences and personal histories outside the laboratory. Consequently, their behavior in learning experiments can more readily be attributed to the variables manipulated by the researcher. Interpreting the behavior of a human subject in such an experiment is more challenging because extra-experimental influences are assumed to be substantial, since human subjects spend little time in the experiment, but lead full, busy, social lives outside the lab.

continuity Darwinian notion that natural selection should have led to certain universal features in all biological organisms

In addition, many psychologists who study behavior in nonhuman animals operate according to the principle of **continuity**, Charles Darwin's notion that natural selection should have led to certain universal features in all biological creatures. That is, the evolutionary process might be expected to have produced similarities in how organisms make contact with and respond to their physical environment. This claim is consistent with the view held by most behavioral psychologists that details of the learning process (though not the content) should be similar both within and across species. If this is the case, then studying learning in virtually any organism should help shed light on the essentials of the learning process in all organisms, humans included. The principle of continuity has been an enduring facet of behavioral epistemology for many years, but as shown in later chapters, its validity has been increasingly questioned in recent years.

Psychologists who view cognition as their subject matter, however, have historically considered nonhuman animal research to be of very limited utility, at least in understanding humans as information processors. For much of its history as a discipline, cognitive psychology has focused on such phenomena as concept formation, problem solving, and language—capacities long thought peculiar only to humans. This has, of course, changed in recent years. Many scientists now believe that the information-processing ability of nonhuman animals may very well rival that of humans, and it has simply taken science a long time to develop methods that are up to the task of identifying these skills. Contemporary research in *animal cognition* has produced an impressive inventory of memory, conceptual, and, possibly, linguistic feats among nonhuman animals (Roberts, 1998; Wasserman, 1997; Zentall, 1993), some of which will be examined later.

The fact that behavioral and cognitive psychology boast historically divergent intellectual roots and scientific epistemologies would seem to preclude much integration. These differences, however, all too often mask some of the inherent similarities that characterize work in these fields. Most important, and as will become apparent throughout this book, the two disciplines share much in the way of subject matter; that is, the phenomena studied in learning and cognition laboratories often show remarkable overlap. In addition, both cognitive and behavioral psychologists carry on a long legacy within experimental psychology, in which the rigors of controlled experimentation and precise measurement take center stage. Indeed, the data generated by cognitive and behavioral psychologists are among the best replicated and most firmly established that the discipline of psychology has to offer. In recent years behavioral and cognitive psychologists have increasingly appealed to adaptationist interpretations of their subject matter. This growing tendency to view learning and cognition as adaptive processes by which organisms negotiate complex environments goes a considerable distance toward bringing these otherwise disparate worldviews under a common conceptual umbrella. In keeping with this observation, a chief goal of this book is to encourage the reader to appreciate both the variability defining the historical and contemporary landscape of learning and cognition, and the growing potential for meaningful integration.

✖ INTERIM SUMMARY

The psychology of learning and cognition derived much of its early subject matter from 18th-century philosophers who disagreed about the mind's essential makeup and its curious relationship with the physical body. As a separate scientific discipline, the psychology of learning was initially dominated by the behaviorist school of thought, particularly as elaborated in the works of John B. Watson and B. F. Skinner. During the 1960s, a change in the general orientation of psychological theory occurred in the form of the cognitive revolution. Fueled by information theory and the computer metaphor, cognitive psychology adopted a different explanatory style from that of behavioral psychology, and the two schools of thought developed independently of one another. Nevertheless, cognitive and behavioral psychology share a common subject matter, and contemporary efforts at reconciliation, encouraged by the common theme of adaptation, appear promising.

✖ THOUGHT QUESTIONS

1. Do you consider yourself to be more of a rationalist or an empiricist when it comes to understanding human behavior? In other words, do you accept the doctrine of innate ideas, or do you think all that we know comes from direct experience? Explain your answer.

2. Behavioral psychologists argued, from the continuity principle, that studies of learning in nonhuman animals could shed a good deal of light on learning in humans as well. Do you agree or disagree with this position, and why?

CHAPTER TWO

Pavlovian Conditioning
Basic Principles

Nathan is a bright, energetic, and intelligent 18-year-old high school senior with a big problem: He is also a heroin addict. As the result of an adolescent dare, Nathan joined a group of friends for a night of "innocent" experimentation. For Nathan, though, the one-night experiment became much more, and, six months later, he now meets regularly with his user friends on weekend nights filled with music, companionship, and ritualistic heroin use. On one lonely night, unable to get together with his friends, Nathan decides to partake of the drug by himself in his bedroom at home. Early the next morning, Nathan's sister knocks on his door to awaken him. When there's no answer, she enters his room to find Nathan unresponsive, slouched over his desk. Despite taking a dose of heroin he had long since developed a tolerance for, Nathan is dead, at 18, of a drug overdose.

If you have taken an introductory psychology course in college or high school, you have no doubt been exposed to the pioneering conditioning research of Russian scientist Ivan Pavlov. Pavlov's name has become so strongly associated with psychology and the study of learning, that comic strips and jokes about bells and salivating dogs have become a common part of American culture. Unfortunately, students often come away from the study of Pavlovian conditioning (also referred to as *classical conditioning* and *respondent conditioning*) with little understanding or appreciation of its importance or of Pavlov's contribution to the study of learning. Indeed, many a professor has heard a refrain from students that goes something like this: "Big deal! So dogs learn to salivate to a ringing bell. What on earth does that have to do with me, or with how people acquire new knowledge or behavior?"

In actuality, Pavlov's salivating dogs have considerable relevance to the tapestry of human learning and behavior, even in its more complicated manifestations. As this and subsequent chapters will explain, the basic conditioning process explored by Pavlov may shed substantial light on how and why humans sometimes develop violent aversions to novel or unusual foods, or why our immune systems may become suppressed simply as a function of walking into a hospital or medical center. This relatively simple process may

FIGURE 2.1 Ivan Petrovich Pavlov.

also help explain why certain words, written or spoken, may move us to anger or sadness, or why an old song may evoke distant memories, along with the powerful emotions that accompany them. And yes, Pavlov's work may go a long way toward helping us to understand Nathan's untimely death, even though the amount of heroin he consumed *should not* have killed him.

IVAN PETROVICH PAVLOV: THE MAN AND HIS SCIENCE

Ivan Pavlov (1849–1936; Figure 2.1) was born in Ryazan, southeast of Moscow. The eldest of 11 children, he was the son of a priest who also taught Greek and Latin. Having originally attended a theological seminary, Pavlov later studied physiology at St. Petersburg University, from which he graduated in 1875. It is no exaggeration to say that Pavlov was the quintessential experimenter, and he was, by all accounts, a meticulous and rigorous scientist. In fact, his devotion to research and to his laboratory was so complete that he was often given to ignoring some of the more annoying details of daily life, such as which clothes to wear or when and what to eat. Indeed, Pavlov's wife, Sara, apparently had to remind the famous scientist on more than one occasion to collect his paycheck (Schultz & Schultz, 2000).

Pavlov's scientific curiosity first led him to study the nerve fibers that innervate, or connect, to the heart, but it was his later work on the physiology of digestion that would lead to worldwide recognition. The process of digestion is a complicated one, and, contrary to what you may think, it doesn't all happen in the stomach. In fact, the process begins in the mouth, as food, broken down by chewing and mixed with saliva, is made more suitable for swallowing and further digestion. Pavlov knew that saliva was secreted by salivary glands in the throat, and he was interested in how and under what conditions the salivary glands operated. To subject this process to scientific scrutiny, Pavlov placed dogs into leather harnesses to restrict movement and then put them through a surgical procedure, exposing the salivary ducts so that the saliva could be collected outside the body. Then, by presenting a stimulus that naturally provokes salivation, such as dried meat powder, Pavlov could reliably produce the physiological process in which he was interested. This pioneering work earned Pavlov a Nobel Prize in 1904, catapulted him to the ranks of the world's most respected scientists, and established Pavlov as one of the most revered citizens in the history of Russian culture. Perhaps most relevant is the fact that Pavlov's research would take a somewhat unexpected turn, and the result would forever change the young science of psychology.

Historians of science are fond of pointing out that great scientific advances often emerge not from brilliant theories or steadily accumulating work, but rather from unfortunate mistakes and, for lack of a better phrase, "happy accidents." In his search for the physiological mechanisms of digestion, Pavlov would hit upon just such an accident, and his work would take on significance far beyond the scope of the biological sciences. Recall that Pavlov was a strict and rigorous scientist who took pains to ensure that experimental procedures and protocol were adhered to religiously. Such attention to detail is an admirable trait in a scientist, but it can lead to considerable frustration when things don't unfold quite as expected, and this is inevitable at some point in the course of an experimenter's work. In Pavlov's case, the problem emerged in the unexpected salivation of his subjects in the *absence of any direct stimulation to the mouth*. Remember that Pavlov presented food powder directly to the mouths of his canine subjects, eliciting the natural salivary reflex. What eventually proved problematic for Pavlov was that increasingly his subjects began to salivate *before* any food had been placed in their mouths. Because no direct contact with food had yet occurred, Pavlov called these unexpected occurrences "psychic secretions." Fortunately for the future of science, Pavlov interpreted this phenomenon not so much as a procedural annoyance, but as a fascinating event in need of explanation. On the basis of this serendipitous occurrence, he redirected the nature of his research and in so doing made a landmark contribution to the science of behavior.

When experiments go wrong and things don't turn out as planned, researchers go in search of possible reasons, just as you might lift the hood to inspect the engine when your car has failed to start. Pavlov wasted little time in troubleshooting his experiments, and he soon realized that the psychic secretions occurred regularly and predictably as a result of various activities in the laboratory. For instance, he observed that salivation frequently occurred when a laboratory assistant, carrying food powder, approached the harnessed animal. In fact, sometimes the very sight of Pavlov or his assistants resulted in salivation. This led Pavlov to the conclusion that many sources of stimulation, including various sights and sounds common to the laboratory, though unplanned and uncontrolled, could reliably elicit salivation. Always the experimenter, Pavlov devised a formal procedure for evaluating this "accidental" relationship. Why not present a stimulus (such as a buzzer or tone) to the animal in a controlled way, and, after doing so, present food to the animal's mouth. If this procedure were followed, would the buzzer or tone eventually come to substitute for the food, thus provoking the same salivary response as the food? This simple logic, originally fueled by an accidental occurrence, led to hundreds of experiments, most carried out by Pavlov's very able assistants, and to an important recognition of the role played by environmental events in the development of behavior.

The Pavlovian Conditioning Paradigm

The essence of a Pavlovian conditioning experiment is actually quite simple, but students often become confused, perhaps in large part because of the terminology used to describe the experiment. All sciences use technical terms to describe their subject matter, and although learning such terminology may be challenging, there is no way to understand the phenomenon being described without the proper language. One of the most important functions of language, especially in scientific context, is to make distinctions between relevant elements or procedures. In Pavlovian conditioning, as in other forms of learning, language serves primarily to distinguish between environmental events, technically referred to as *stimuli*, and behavioral events, referred to as *responses*.

In Pavlov's research, food powder placed in the mouth of the dog serves a particular stimulus function: It produces salivation. In fact, for all mammals the salivary response is natural; that is, it occurs involuntarily in response to food being placed in the mouth. Because food provokes salivation naturally, or automatically, Pavlov called food an **unconditional stimulus (US)**. Unconditional stimuli, then, are events in the environment that produce reflexive, involuntary reactions. Food in the mouth provokes salivation, unexpected loud noises produce natural startle reactions, and severe heat applied to skin elicits an automatic withdrawal response. Notice that the reactions to unconditional stimuli resemble the simple reflexes discussed in the first chapter. Such an involuntary or automatic response is referred to as an **unconditional response (UR)**. Thus, quite intuitively, unconditional stimuli result in unconditional responses, just as when Pavlov's dogs salivated in response to food powder being placed in their mouths.

There isn't anything earth-shattering about the observation that dogs salivate when food is placed in their mouths. Pavlov would hardly have achieved exalted status in the scientific world on the basis of this discovery. The significance of Pavlov's experiments is that other stimuli in the environment that would not ordinarily produce salivation could, through a conditioning process, come to do so. In a typical experiment, Pavlov presented a stimulus, such as an auditory tone, just before presenting the food powder.

unconditional stimulus (US) event in the environment producing reflexive, involuntary reaction

unconditional response (UR) involuntary or automatic response to a US

Initially, the tone was considered a neutral stimulus, because its presentation did not result in salivation. This is not to say that the animal would not react at all to the tone, for most assuredly it would, primarily by propping up its ears and looking in (orienting to) its direction. But if the tone was sounded and then shortly followed by the presentation of food (US), and this pairing occurred several times in succession, at some point the dog would begin to salivate when the tone was sounded, *and before the presentation of food.* Salivation to the tone alone, since no contact with food had occurred, is what Pavlov originally called a psychic secretion, but later referred to as a **conditional response (CR)**, also known as *conditioned reflex*. Finally, the tone itself, initially a neutral stimulus without the ability to provoke salivation, is referred to as a **conditional stimulus (CS)** once its presentation produces salivation. Thus, a conditioned reflex has been *acquired* when the CS, by itself, first produces a CR. The entire process of bringing about a conditioned reflex is referred to as *Pavlovian conditioning,* though it also goes by the name classical conditioning. The terms refer to the same process, the former quite obviously giving homage to the man who brought this learning process to the attention of the scientific community.

> **conditional response (CR)** learned or conditioned reaction to conditional stimulus (also referred to as conditioned reflex)

> **conditional stimulus (CS)** stimulus which when paired with US comes to elicit conditional response

So far, you may find it difficult to appreciate the power of Pavlov's findings. After all, isn't it obvious that dogs, and people too, learn to respond to stimuli in the environment that signal, or stand for, other stimuli? Yes, it is, but it's important to remember that advances in science don't necessarily come in the form of surprising discoveries, but rather in more sophisticated and comprehensive understanding of a phenomenon that may be generally familiar to everyone. After all, most people appreciate and understand intuitively the principle of gravity, but this doesn't mean that they can describe or explain Newton's laws of gravitational force. Most historians in psychology don't credit Pavlov with the *discovery* of the conditional reflex. Bower and Hilgard (1981) point out that the essential elements of conditioning were known before Pavlov's time, but that the Russian scientist was the first to ". . . study exactly what happened and to vary the parameters that controlled the events" (p. 50). In addition, an American psychology student, Edwin Twitmyer, may have actually scooped Pavlov. At the 1904 convention of the American Psychological Association, Twitmyer reported the results of a study in which human subjects developed a conditional knee-jerk response. For reasons that are unclear, Twitmyer's results aroused little interest, and he apparently decided not to pursue them further. Pavlov's contribution came in the form of exhaustive and intensive research, over many years, in which the details of the conditioning process were eventually revealed.

Conditioning Methods

Creating a conditional reflex, such as salivation to a tone or buzzer, requires the establishment of particular experimental conditions or procedures. In a typical Pavlovian experiment, an animal is exposed to a series of trials in which the conditional stimulus (CS—tone or buzzer) is paired with the unconditional stimulus (US—food). As can be seen in Figure 2.2, there are various ways to pair these two stimuli, and one of the first questions the researcher

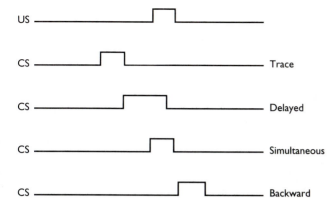

FIGURE 2.2
Pavlovian
Conditioning
Procedures.

might ask is whether these procedures result in differing rates or amounts of conditioning. The two stimuli (CS and US) can be presented simultaneously, one before the other (both trace and backward conditioning), or with some overlap between the two (delayed conditioning). In general, most research seems to suggest that optimal conditioning tends to occur under delayed conditions and in the trace condition when the US follows the CS closely in time, approximately .5 second (Schneiderman & Gormezano, 1964). Neither simultaneous conditioning nor backward conditioning seem to be very effective ways to produce a conditioned reflex, although there are some reported exceptions to this rule (Ayres, Haddad, & Albert, 1987; Cole & Miller, 1999).

One important matter in Pavlovian conditioning is the nature of the conditioned reflex, or CR. In Pavlov's original experiments, the CR was salivation; thus, the conditional response was the *same* response as the unconditional response (UR). So, how do experimenters know when a response is a CR or a UR? Remember that acquisition of a CR occurs when the response is first observed following the CS and before the US. Testing for the presence of a conditional response is not difficult; it simply requires presenting the CS by itself on a particular trial, without following it with the US. Any response to the CS, in the absence of the US, can be interpreted as a conditioned reflex, or CR. Researchers have long known, however, that CRs are not always identical to URs. Frequently, the CR is not as strong, or of as large a magnitude, as the UR. In Pavlov's research, this often meant that the amount of saliva produced in response to the CS (tone, buzzer, etc.) was usually less than that produced in response to the US (food). As explained later, some contemporary researchers believe that certain kinds of conditional responses are actually complete opposites of their respective unconditional responses.

Variables Influencing Pavlovian Conditioning

Although most people are content to grasp the general idea behind a specific phenomenon, it is the business of science to expose all the nuts and bolts, and the study of Pavlovian conditioning during the 20th century has led scientists to a deeper appreciation of what appeared at first to be a relatively simple process. Let's consider in turn how each element in the process contributes to the establishment of a conditioned reflex.

The Nature of the US   Clearly, the unconditional stimulus (US) is at the heart of the conditioning process, and it follows that it would receive a good deal of research attention. There are, of course, innumerable stimuli that provoke involuntary, natural responses in various animal species, and any one of these could, in principle, be employed in an experiment. Among those that have been utilized by researchers, in addition to food, are electric shock (Kamin, 1965), puffs of air presented to the eye (Durkin, Prescott, Furchtgott, Cantor, & Powell, 1993; Gormezano, Kehoe, & Marshall, 1983), and even social approval in the case of humans (Cramer, Weiss, Steigleder, & Balling, 1985). One dimension of the US that may influence conditioning is its intensity, or magnitude. For instance, a strong electric shock might be expected to produce more rapid conditioning than a milder shock. (In such studies, the UR and CR are usually some kind of withdrawal response.) For the most part, this expectation is upheld by research, probably for reasons that make sense phylogenetically. For most animals, including humans, very intense stimuli are not to be ignored. Loud noises may often portend danger, such as when distant thunder signals a violent storm or when a large boulder comes crashing down a hillside. Painful stimulation of the skin, in the form of intense heat or pressure, is disregarded only at our peril. Indeed, all major theories of conditioning formally recognize the role played by US intensity in the Pavlovian paradigm.

The Role of the CS   Perhaps more than any other element, the CS is the celebrity of Pavlovian conditioning. It is in fact the ability to transform the CS from a neutral, meaningless stimulus into a functionally useful signal of the US that designates Pavlovian conditioning as a type of learning. For this reason, numerous experiments have been conducted for the purpose of identifying the various stimuli that can function as CSs and the conditions that affect their suitability. In his original work, Pavlov used such varied stimuli as buzzers, tones, car horns, and a clicking metronome as conditioned stimuli (CSs), and most of these proved to be effective when paired with such USs as food and electric shock. It probably goes without saying, but to be an effective CS, a stimulus must be capable of being detected; that is, the subject must possess sensory receptors that are responsive to the form of energy represented by the CS. Not all organisms rely equally on all senses, so certain stimuli will function more effectively than others as CSs. For instance, because of their superior auditory sense, dogs were easily conditioned to buzzers and tones in Pavlov's experiments. Researchers who utilize avian species (such as pigeons), on the other hand, often cater to the tremendous visual acuity of these animals by utilizing visual CSs (lights and various geometric patterns) projected on response keys.

Intensity also matters with respect to the CS for reasons that seem to mimic the importance of US magnitude. In general, intense stimuli are readily noticeable, and they are consequently more effective as signals for the US. In addition, CS novelty appears to play a substantial role in conditioning. In studies of the **CS preexposure effect**, the CS is presented by itself on several trials before being paired with the US. Numerous experiments of this sort demonstrate that prior experience with the CS alone tends to impair or inhibit conditioning. (This phenomenon also goes by the name *latent inhibition*.) In other words, the conditioned reflex during CS-US pairings is slower to develop, if it develops at all, when the animal has had previous exposure to the CS by itself. The preexposure effect may be due to the phenomenon of habituation, which was discussed in Chapter 1. Recall that habituation refers to a decreased response to a repeatedly presented stimulus. Preexposure to the CS may reduce the novelty of the stimulus (habituation), making it a less effective candidate for later conditioning (Lubow, 1989; Lubow & Gewirtz, 1995). Another possibility, discussed in the next section, is that the CS is simply not as good a predictor or signal of the US because it failed to predict the US during the preexposure phase of the experiment.

CS preexposure effect impairment of conditioned reflex by repeated presentations of CS by itself

Compound Stimuli

To understand the role that Pavlovian conditioning might play in behavior in the world at large, certain matters of complexity must be considered. One of these has to do with the fact that in natural settings organisms are seldom responding to single, isolated stimuli. Rather, the context within which most behavior occurs is characterized by a mosaic of stimulation, and relevant stimuli may be impinging on various sensory modalities (auditory, olfactory, tactile, visual) simultaneously. Given this complexity, an especially important question to be answered is Which of these various stimuli enter into the conditioning process, and why? Why, for instance, do students attend (usually) to the voice of a lecturing teacher, when other sounds and sights could just as easily command interest? No organism can pay equal attention to all sources of energy falling upon it at a given time, and certain stimuli must take precedence over others in the business of adaptation. Indeed, Pavlov was well aware of the importance of this question, and both he and subsequent researchers have pursued answers to the question by investigating the role of *compound stimuli* in the conditioning process.

Overshadowing The phenomenon of **overshadowing** occurs when a compound CS is presented in a standard Pavlovian procedure, and one element of the compound stimulus elicits a CR while the other does not. Suppose both a tone and a light (compound CS) are presented simultaneously to a pigeon prior to delivery of grain (US). Following several pairings of the compound stimulus and the US, each component is presented by itself to evaluate whether that component has become a CS. The presence of a CR is taken as evidence of conditioning having taken place. In this example, overshadowing would be demonstrated if the bird developed a CR to the light, but not to the tone. Of course, responding only to the tone, and not the light, would also be evidence of overshadowing. In this particular case, a response to light is more likely (and thus overshadows of the auditory stimulus) because pigeons are primarily visual creatures likely to give some attentional precedence to the light.

overshadowing differential conditioning to one element of a compound stimulus when stimuli are presented simultaneously

The overshadowing phenomenon has been demonstrated in humans as well. A particularly interesting case is the verbal overshadowing effect (VOE), which occurs when subjects' verbal descriptions of visual stimuli actually impair their ability to recognize these same stimuli later. In such a study, subjects might initially be exposed to a target stimulus, such as a human face, and asked to describe it verbally. During a later recognition test phase, subjects would be presented with the same target stimulus, among other distractors and would be asked to identify the original target stimulus. A number of studies have shown that recognition during the test phase is poorer for subjects who previously described the face than for subjects who were presented with a separate, unrelated task. As with other overshadowing phenomena, VOE is believed to occur as the result of competition between one source of information (visual) and another (verbal description) (Dodson, Johnson, & Schooler, 1997; Ryan & Schooler, 1998).

Overshadowing is probably a pervasive aspect of adapting to the world, and its relevance is easily appreciated in numerous everyday contexts. Perhaps the last time you visited the dentist, you had the misfortune of having to undergo some drilling for a cavity. A dentist's drill makes an ominously distinct sound, and it isn't difficult to imagine why you might begin to squirm with anxiety when first hearing the drill. To whatever extent the drill's humming has been followed by the discomfort of the drilling itself, the sound could have become an effective CS for an anxiety reaction on your part. What is curious about this example, though, is that many other stimuli, in addition to the drill, are present when the drilling begins, yet most of these stimuli *do not* become CSs for anxiety. Why don't such things as the dentist's voice, upward or downward movement of your chair, the various odors that permeate any medical office, or the sight of the dentist's masked face hovering overhead produce the anxiety response?

Clearly, overshadowing represents a kind of selective conditioning in which certain stimuli seem more salient, or command more attention, than do others. Why one component of a compound stimulus is more salient than the other is a complicated question that has occupied researchers for some time. It may simply be that greater salience is attached to the more physically intense stimulus. As discussed earlier, intense CSs do tend to support more conditioning, and this appears to be just as true of compound stimuli (Kasprow, Cacheiro, Balaz, & Miller, 1982). On the other hand, one component in a compound stimulus may be more "biologically meaningful" to the organism involved. That pigeons, for example, will more readily condition to a light than to a tone makes sense given their keen and highly evolved visual acuity.

Blocking   In overshadowing, both elements of a compound stimulus are presented simultaneously from the outset of the experiment. In **blocking**, an initial stimulus previously associated with the US impairs, or blocks, conditioning to a new CS when the two elements are presented as a compound. In the classic experiment on blocking, Kamin (1968, 1969) exposed different groups of rats to a conditioning sequence in which either noise (CS_1) or light (CS_2) were paired with shock, with an anxiety response serving as the CR. In the next phase of the experiment, noise and light were presented together

blocking   initial conditioning to a CS_1 impairs later conditioning to a separate CS_2

as a compound stimulus prior to presentation of shock. In the experiment's final phase, the light and tone were presented by themselves to determine whether they had acquired CS properties. Animals who received preexposure to noise and shock did not develop a fear CR to light during training to the compound stimulus. Similarly, animals who were preexposed to light and shock failed to develop a CR to noise during compound training. In both cases, pretraining to a particular stimulus element (light or noise) blocked conditioning to the other stimulus element. It is almost as if the novel element of the compound stimulus proves redundant in signaling the US, as the initial element has already acquired properties of a CS. Blocking has since been shown to be a reliably produced phenomenon in nonhumans and humans alike (Arcediano, Matute, & Miller, 1997; Pellon, Garcia, & Sanchez, 1995).

The phenomena of overshadowing and blocking illustrate that not all stimuli that impinge on animals' sensory receptors are created equal. Pavlov had shown, as have many other scientists since, that some events in the environment are simply more meaningful or relevant. William James (1890/1981), America's preeminent psychologist at the turn of the 20th century, alluded to the selective nature of attention in his classic work *Principles of Psychology:*

> A distinction in which we have a practical stake is one which we concentrate our minds upon and which we are on the look-out for. . . . Where, on the other hand, a distinction has no practical interest, where we gain nothing by analyzing a feature from out of the compound total of which it forms a part, we contract a habit of leaving it unnoticed, and at last grow callous to its presence. (p. 487)

CS-US Contiguity and Contingency

By now you may have come to appreciate the fact that Pavlovian conditioning is not as simple a process as usually portrayed in the popular media. The plot, however, has only begun to thicken. Although the unique features of both the CS and the US are important, it is obviously some kind of association between them that brings about the phenomenon of interest, the conditioned reflex. The previous discussion has shown how the CS and US can be paired in a variety of ways, both in terms of their sequential order and the temporal interval separating them. There is, in fact, an even more fundamental dimension of the CS-US relationship that bears significance for the conditioning process. In short, the issue revolves around the question of whether simply pairing the two will produce conditioning (*contiguity*) or if some kind of if-then predictability must be evident before conditioning can take place (*contingency*).

The issue is fundamental because it draws attention to notions about the learning process that have been of concern to philosophers and scientists for hundreds of years. Much of the psychology of learning is founded on the idea of *associationism,* a position often attributed to the empiricist philosophers of the 17th century, whose ideas about learning were touched on in Chapter 1. The basic assumptions guiding the associationist movement revolved around the idea that events that are contiguous—meaning they occur together in place or time—and become associated in the mind, and this crucial fact is largely responsible for both simple and complex forms of learning and memory. Thus, the associationist position might expect conditioning to occur in a Pavlovian experiment because the CS and US have been associated through pairing. As long as the two occur together on the same trial, an association should be formed and exhibit itself in the conditioned response.

For many years, this associationist explanation satisfied researchers studying Pavlovian conditioning. It seemed as if mere contiguity was sufficient for conditioning to occur. But in the 1960s, Robert Rescorla conducted a series of influential studies that not only shed new light on the CS-US relationship, but also established the fundamental control procedures that have become standard practice in contemporary Pavlovian conditioning studies. In a classic article, Rescorla (1967) reasoned that it might not be simple pairing of the CS and US that leads to conditioning, but a predictable, *contingent* relationship between the two. The idea of contingency will prove of paramount importance elsewhere in this book, so let's take a look at this concept and what it means for the phenomenon of Pavlovian conditioning.

In somewhat ordinary parlance, a contingency is an *if-then* relationship, meaning that if one event (A) occurs, another event (B) will follow. In some respects, all scientific experiments pursue contingent relationships, and in a general sense the language of causality is all about contingencies. In Pavlovian conditioning, a contingency is in effect only if the CS becomes a reliable predictor of the US; and this contingency does not automatically eventuate just because the CS and US are paired occasionally. To test the necessity of CS-US contingency, Rescorla conducted a study in which different groups of subjects experienced varying degrees of CS-US arrangements. Figure 2.3 shows a sample of 10 trials experienced by three different groups of subjects. Notice that although each group differed in terms of the pattern of CS-US arrangements received, all three groups experienced some trials in which CS and US appeared together (CS-US were contiguous). If mere contiguity is the key to conditioning, then all three groups should exhibit the same degree of conditioning. This is not what happened though. The only group to develop a CR in Rescorla's study was group A. This group never experienced the CS by itself, nor did it experience the US by itself. Thus, the CS was a perfect predictor of the US. In the other groups, although the CS and US were paired on three trials, either the CS or US could occur by itself on other trials. Because either stimulus could occur by itself, the CS does not become a reliable predictor of the US; that is, there is no CS-US contingency, although there is some CS-US contiguity. Thus, what Rescorla had shown is that for conditioning to occur, the CS must be a reliable predictor of the US. It is not sufficient for the two to be paired occasionally.

Nothing is ever as simple as it seems, and in the years since Rescorla's article, the question of what specific circumstances are necessary for conditioning to occur has remained contentious. Researchers have shown that some degree of conditioning may in fact occur even in subjects for whom the CS does not reliably predict the US. Depending upon the nature of the two stimuli, including their importance and intensity, a few pairings of CS

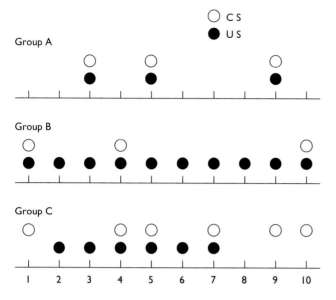

FIGURE 2.3
Importance of CS-US Contingency in Pavlovian Conditioning.

and US, even in the absence of a true contingency, may lead to conditioning (Papini & Bitterman, 1990). It may very well be that many organisms, humans included, react to stimulus pairings as if there is a contingency, even when there isn't. This tendency to see things as being connected may be responsible for some interesting, though unsupported, belief systems and various types of superstitious human behavior.

✖ INTERIM SUMMARY

Pavlovian conditioning represents a process by which initially neutral stimuli acquire conditioned properties through association with unconditioned stimuli. The pairing of these stimulus events can vary with respect to sequence and timing, with particular kinds of arrangements resulting in more rapid and stronger conditioning. In addition, both the intensity and biological meaningfulness of the conditioned stimulus (CS) and the unconditioned stimulus (US) make significant contributions to the learning process. The phenomena of overshadowing and blocking demonstrate that certain components of a compound CS can take precedence over others, leading to differential responding. Finally, the ability of a neutral stimulus to acquire conditioned properties depends upon its ability to reliably predict the US (contingency), not merely on its occasional pairing with the US (contiguity).

✖ THOUGHT QUESTIONS

1. All sciences employ technical terms in their language. What are some of the technical terms in Pavlovian conditioning? Do these terms help you to better understand the processes involved? Why or why not?

2. Food and loud noises are salient USs for most animals, including humans. Can you think of three additional stimuli that provoke URs in humans?

3. Describe a real-world example of your own behavior undergoing Pavlovian conditioning. Be sure to identify the CS, US, CR, and UR. Why do you think the stimulus you identified as the CS acquired its conditional properties, rather than other stimuli in your environment?

EXTINCTION AND INHIBITORY CONDITIONING

Learning is an adaptive process because behavior can change in response to momentary fluctuations in environmental events. Pavlovian conditioning occurs when a previously neutral stimulus, as a result of being paired with a biologically relevant stimulus (US), eventually comes to elicit the same response (or so Pavlov thought) as the US. But to say that the behavior is truly adaptive, wouldn't it have to remain sensitive to future contingencies or lack of contingencies between the CS and US? What would happen, for instance, if a previously conditioned CS no longer predicted the occurrence of the US? The question is easily answered by arranging a series of **extinction** trials in which the CS is presented repeatedly, but never followed by the US. Under such conditions, Pavlov found that the conditional response eventually disappeared. Thus, a conditioned reflex built up by frequent CS-US contingencies could be abolished by removing the contingency. Dogs that had learned to salivate upon presentation of such stimuli as buzzers, tones, and metronomes quit doing so when these CSs no longer signaled the presentation of food.

> **extinction** elimination of a conditional reflex by repeated presentations of the CS by itself

You might naturally question, though, what exactly is being learned by the animal during extinction. Is the CS-US association simply being forgotten in the same way that you might forget a phone number after using it? Or is it instead the case that the animal is learning a new association, one between the presence of the CS and the *absence of the US*? Testing the former hypothesis, that extinction involves forgetting the CS-US relationship, isn't difficult. Suppose that following extinction of the conditional response, the experimenter takes the animal out of the experimental apparatus and returns it to its home cage in the laboratory. Several days later, the animal is put back into the apparatus and presented with the original CS *by itself*. What do you think might happen? If the animal had forgotten the CS-US association as a result of extinction, you wouldn't expect any reaction at all in this follow-up condition. Nevertheless, there is a response, and it resembles very strongly the conditional response that was initially established in the experiment. This tendency for previously conditioned reflexes to occur subsequent to an extinction phase is referred to as **spontaneous recovery**, and it is a well-documented aspect of many types of learning phenomena, not just Pavlovian conditioning.

> **spontaneous recovery** the tendency of a previously conditioned reflex to occur subsequent to having been extinguished

Further evidence that the CS-US association isn't "forgotten" by the animal comes from reconditioning trials. If the animal is reexposed to CS-US pairings, a CR will result much more rapidly than during the original conditioning, indicating that the learning that occurred initially hasn't simply faded away. The fact that relearning occurs more rapidly than original learning is sometimes referred to as *savings,* and it, too, represents a very general behavior principle having implications for many kinds of learning. If you took an algebra course in high school, and are currently enrolled in a college algebra course, it is valid to expect that you will master the material more effectively the second time around. Although you may not fully appreciate it, as a student you probably benefit from the phenomenon of savings all the time.

Inhibition

The acquisition of a conditional salivary response, or the eye-blink response frequently studied with rabbits, is often referred to as *excitatory conditioning,* because the conditioning process ultimately involves the occurrence of some measurable aspect of behavior. Moreover, it is generally easy to observe and measure the results of this kind of conditioning, because an overt response readily lends itself to objective measurement. But would it not be equally adaptive for animals to learn *when not to behave* as well? If so, it would be worthwhile to consider conditions that would serve to suppress a response or make responding less likely. This is precisely the focus of research on conditioned inhibition, and this phenomenon comes in several forms and has been studied through various kinds of experimental arrangements.

Latent Inhibition   One instance of inhibition has already been described. Recall that if the CS is presented by itself on several trials before pairing it explicitly with the US, conditioning occurs, if at all, more slowly than if no such CS-alone trials were presented. This impairment of conditioning, the CS preexposure effect mentioned earlier, is also referred to as **latent inhibition (LI).** Perhaps because the organism learns at first that the CS signals nothing (that is, it remains a neutral stimulus), in the subsequent phase of the experiment, the CS comes to signal the US only with great difficulty. Some researchers have also suggested that the CS-alone trials result in habituation to the CS, and this habituation must be overcome during conditioning before a CR can be acquired. After all, a stimulus that has been habituated to receives little or no attention and is therefore a poor candidate for conditioning.

latent inhibition (LI) impaired conditioning due to previous presentation of the CS by itself (also referred to as CS preexposure effect)

Researchers often use the *summation test* to evaluate the inhibitory properties of a stimulus. Suppose a subject has been exposed to various experimental trials, each trial begun with one of two conditioned stimuli (CS_1 and CS_2). Whenever CS_1 is presented, a US follows. Thus, excitatory conditioning to CS_1 would be expected to occur. However, whenever CS_2 is presented, the US does not follow. It is valid to expect, therefore, that CS_2 will acquire inhibitory properties. One way to assess whether this is the case is to present both CS_1 and CS_2 together, as a compound stimulus, and measure whether and to what extent a CR occurs. If a CR fails to occur, or if it occurs at less strength than would ordinarily be observed in response to CS_1, inhibitory conditioning has occurred to CS_2.

The learning that exhibits itself in latent inhibition may be just as adaptive as that associated with excitatory conditioning. In fact, recent research on LI has led to the fascinating suggestion that the phenomenon may help to distinguish between normal information processing and the disturbed processing that characterizes severe psychological disorders like schizophrenia (Cassaday, 1997). Some experiments have demonstrated a reduced LI effect in both schizophrenic patients and in nondiagnosed subjects who nevertheless may be predisposed to developing psychoses (Vaitl & Lipp, 1997). In essence, this finding suggests that this population finds it difficult to distinguish between relevant and irrelevant stimuli in their environment. This reduction in LI in schizophrenic patients is also consistent with major theories of the disorder that claim ineffective filtering of environmental stimuli leads to much of the characteristic disturbed behavior (Baruch, Hemsley, & Gray, 1988; Brebion, Smith, Gorman, & Amador, 1996; Jones, Gray, & Hemsley, 1992; Williams, 1996). In addition, some researchers have argued that the LI research paradigm holds considerable promise, not only as a potential marker for schizophrenia, but also as a preventive measure against acquisition of phobias and some of the more debilitating side effects of chemotherapy (Braunstein-Bercovitz & Lubow, 1998; Lubow, 1998; Rachman, 1990).

Conditioned Emotional Responses   The effects of inhibitory conditioning can be seen beyond the confines of the typical Pavlovian procedure. In an intriguing combination of learning procedures, a CS associated with an aversive US, such as shock, is superimposed on an operant task (see Chapter 4), such as lever pressing for food, resulting in inhibition of the operant behavior. The suppression of the operant behavior as a function of the presentation of the inhibitory CS is referred to as a **conditioned emotional response (CER),** and was first demonstrated by Estes and Skinner (1941). Rats were first trained to press a lever in an operant chamber in order to obtain food pellets. Once this operant behavior had been established and lever pressing was observed to occur at a steady rate of response, the Pavlovian procedure was introduced. After pairings of the CS with shock, the CS was presented during the operant task. Response rates on the lever during the CS were suppressed relative to response rates in the absence of the CS, thus this phenomenon has also been referred to as *conditioned suppression.*

Conditioned suppression is not difficult to spot in everyday behavior. Imagine a group of juveniles, hanging out on a street corner at night, conducting themselves in a less than admirable way, perhaps drinking beer, maybe spouting loud obscenities, and occasionally defacing street signs, benches, and other public property. How would this behavior change as a police patrol car turns the corner, heading straight for the group? At the very least, much of the activity, particularly the drinking and vandalism, would come to a halt, or at least diminish, in the presence of the officer (CS), though this effect may be short lived. As the patrol car disappears down the street, much of the suppressed activity may reemerge to its pre-CS levels.

Of course, this kind of suppression is not unique to juvenile delinquents. Something of the same sort probably accounts for similar shifts in behavior among more law-abiding citizens. Consider how common it is for most drivers to let up suddenly on the gas (speeding or not) at the appearance of a state highway patrol car. Spontaneous student conversations often termi-

conditioned emotional response (CER) suppression of an operant response due to presentation of a classically conditioned inhibitory stimulus

nate (or should) when the instructor is ready to lecture, and sibling spats may transform into relatively amicable conversations when parents enter the room. A lesson to be learned from such real-world occurrences is that the same phenomena that researchers dissect and analyze in the laboratory, such as conditioned suppression, can be readily seen within the context of a larger, naturally occurring behavioral episode. These real-world examples also demonstrate that learning represents a fundamental process by which animals adapt to the changing conditions of their environment.

✖ INTERIM SUMMARY

Extinction of a conditioned response involves elimination of the response as a result of repeated presentations of the CS by itself. Responses placed on extinction will often reemerge later under similar conditions, a phenomenon known as spontaneous recovery. Inhibitory conditioning is demonstrated when conditioning to a CS is impaired or when suppression of a separate response occurs in the presence of a CS. In latent inhibition, preexposure to a CS by itself produces impaired conditioning in a subsequent condition when the CS is paired with a US. In conditioned suppression, a CS previously associated with an aversive US is superimposed on an operant task, resulting in a suppression of the level of responding on the operant task.

✖ THOUGHT QUESTIONS

1. What evidence is there to suggest that extinction in Pavlovian conditioning is not due merely to forgetting?
2. Think of an original example of conditioned suppression in your own behavior. What is the CS, and how might it have acquired aversive properties for you?

GENERALIZATION, DISCRIMINATION, AND HIGHER ORDER CONDITIONING

Take a moment to read the words in Figure 2.4. Of course, it won't take but a moment, for this is a simple task, almost ridiculously so. The figure merely depicts the name Pavlov in several different sizes and styles of typefaces. Remember, though, that psychologists find even the most mundane behaviors rather compelling, and the present example is no exception. Chances are you have seldom, if ever, encountered the type of lettering depicted in Figure 2.4, because *Pavlov* has been rendered in some of the more obscure fonts in my word processing program. Despite the novelty of the fonts, your ability to read the letters is probably not impaired. Due to having long ago learned to read and write in the English alphabet, you have no difficulty recognizing either the individual letters or the word itself, although you may not have encountered them printed in quite this way. This simple example is meant to illustrate our vital ability as humans to respond effectively to stimulus conditions that we've never experienced, particularly since our moment-to-moment encounters with the world frequently bring novelty. In fact, the philosopher Heraclitus (500 B.C.) suggested that we never step in the same

FIGURE 2.4 Generalization and the Written Word.

Pavlov   Pavlov

PAVLOV   *Pavlov*

Pavlov   **PAVLOV**

Pavlov   PAVLOV

river twice. If this is so, it becomes especially important that specific learning experiences prepare us not only for precisely the same conditions but for similar conditions as well. Fortunately, such a process is pervasive in all learning, and this section considers its role in Pavlovian conditioning.

Generalization

Suppose we are researchers, and we use a tone presented at 1000 Hz as a CS and food as the US in Pavlov's standard conditioning procedure. Once salivation (CR) to the tone is well established, we conduct a second phase of the experiment, during which tones of varying frequencies (250 Hz, 500 Hz, 750 Hz, 1250 Hz, 1500 Hz, and 1750 Hz) are presented by themselves in random order and *without any presentation of the US*. The question we're trying to answer is whether salivation will occur to these novel stimuli, even though they've never been paired with food. The results? Salivation does in fact occur to these various tones, and this tendency to respond to stimuli resembling the conditioned stimulus is called **generalization**. Although salivation does occur in the presence of these other tones, the CR is not equal in intensity to that occurring to the CS, but actually diminishes increasingly as a function of distance away from the CS. This systematic response pattern during the generalization test produces the standard *generalization gradient* depicted by the dotted line in Figure 2.5. As you can see, the maximum amount of salivation, as measured by drops of saliva, occurs to the original CS (1000 Hz tone), and this amount drops off as we move away from the CS in both directions. In other words, those tones that are most similar in frequency to the CS elicit the most salivation, and those that are less similar produce a less intense CR.

generalization tendency to respond to stimuli similar to the CS, despite no explicit training to these stimuli

It's certainly not hard to see why generalization is both readily produced and of such adaptive significance to biological creatures. If it was necessary to learn, through intensive conditioning, the meaning or significance of every stimulus in the environment, there wouldn't be much time left to actually *respond* effectively to these events! The point was powerfully made by Pavlov (1927/1960):

> . . . natural stimuli are in most cases not rigidly constant but range around a particular strength and quality of stimulus in a common group. For example, the hostile sound of any beast of prey serves as a conditioned stimulus to a defence reflex in the animals which

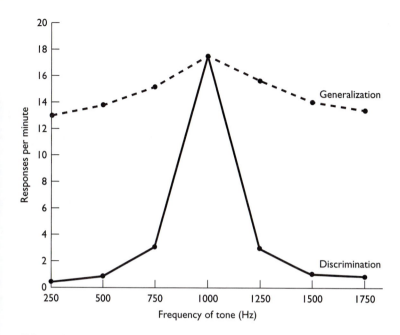

FIGURE 2.5 Generalization/Discrimination Gradient for Pavlovian Conditioning.

it hunts. The defence reflex is brought about independently of variations in pitch, strength and timbre of the sound produced by the animal
according to its distance, the tension of its vocal cords and similar factors. (p. 113)

Generalization, then, is a flexible mechanism by which singular learning
experiences can be usefully extended to conditions not present during the
original learning (Epstein & Burstein, 1966; Hovland, 1937). In the absence
of such a capacity, venturing out into a world of potentially surprising and
unpredictable events could be dangerous. Most animals, humans included,
are pretty well attuned to visual, auditory, and olfactory cues in their environment that signal important biological events, such as food or danger, and
it makes sense that a wide array of such stimuli can serve this purpose. Of
course, generalization has its limits, and adapting to one's environment entails
more than responding identically to all stimuli. Generalization's behavioral
counterpart, discrimination, refines the adaptation process further.

Discrimination

Just as it is important for animals to respond in similar ways to stimuli
resembling one another, adaptation at times also requires differential
responding. When responding occurs in the presence of one stimulus, but
not in the presence of another, **discrimination** has occurred. Take another
glance at the dotted line in Figure 2.5. This figure shows that following
training solely to the 1000 Hz tone, the dog salivates in response to tones
of varying pitch, even though these tones were not paired with food. In fact,

discrimination ten-
dency to respond only
to the CS and not to
other similar stimuli

the animal does not even encounter them until the generalization phase of the experiment. Nevertheless, some responding does occur when they are presented.

Returning to our experiment, suppose we wanted to discover whether the animal could maintain its response to the original CS (1000 Hz tone), but stop responding to the other stimuli. How could we go about producing this discrimination? What Pavlov discovered, and others since him have similarly observed, is that discriminated responding can be strengthened by occasional presentations of the CS accompanied by food (US). In such a procedure, the original CS is designated CS+ because it is always paired with food. The other stimuli are designated CS– because they are always presented by themselves, never with food. Notice that this procedure differs from the one utilized in generalization training. During generalization, all of the stimuli (CS and novel tones) are presented in random order, and the US is never presented. If, however, we always pair the US with our original CS (CS+, 1000 Hz tone), and mix our presentations of the CS-US with presentations of the CS– stimuli by themselves, we will produce the sharp gradient depicted by the solid line in Figure 2.5. Notice that this gradient is similar to the generalization gradient, except responding drops off rapidly when moving away from the CS+. A sharp gradient like this represents maximal discrimination responding, for the animal continues salivating to the CS+, but salivation has nearly disappeared altogether in the presence of the other tones.

It has probably become apparent to you that generalization and discrimination are simply opposite sides of the same behavioral process. Strong generalization clearly means very little discrimination, and vice versa. There is a constant interplay between the two, and the relative degrees of generalization and discrimination that describe any particular behavior would be expected to change largely as a function of the specific environmental pressures to which the organism is responding. For instance, a lone deer in the forest might be expected to respond to any unusual sound coming from behind a rock or tree by fleeing or preparing to defend itself. It isn't essential that the deer identify the specific source of the sound. Any defensive response to a range of such stimuli (generalization) is likely to have survival value for the animal. On the other hand, it is also important that the deer be able to distinguish between other deer, including perhaps its mate, and animals with whom it would rather not socialize, such as mountain lions or bears (discrimination).

Virtually any behavioral episode, no matter how simple, can be conceptualized as an exercise in generalized and discriminated responding. How well this balance is struck at any given moment can have serious ramifications, not just for deer, as in the preceding example, but for humans as well. Being able to read road signs, instructions on medicine labels, computerized instructions, and questions on a class exam, regardless of their size or font, is an essential skill for most modern humans. Similarly, appropriate responses to traffic lights, verbal commands, and odors that may portend danger (smoke) contribute to the daily adaptations we all too often take for granted. In fact, humans living in industrialized nations may be required to generalize and discriminate across more stimulus dimensions than any other species, largely because we have created an environment populated by inanimate features, including electronic technology, that do not even exist in natural habitats. Fortunately, the processes of generalization and discrimination serve a vital purpose in helping us to bring some of this confusion under control.

Higher Order Conditioning

At this point it should be clear that the significance of Pavlovian conditioning lies in what it reveals about how initially neutral environmental events come to play a role in behavior. If Pavlov had done nothing else but demonstrate the basic CS-US relationship and elucidate some of the factors that facilitated or impaired conditioning, his contribution to psychology would have been substantial. But Pavlov had bigger aspirations, and like many great scientists before and after him, he would eventually push the boundaries of his "psychic secretion" to their logical limit. In the process, he would try to explain much more sophisticated behavioral phenomena than were evident in his salivating canines.

When a principle is first uncovered, researchers tend to explore the parameters, or boundary conditions, of the phenomenon. They often do this simply by extending the logic of their experimental manipulations until the phenomenon disappears or manifests itself in some substantially different way. In the case of Pavlovian conditioning, the discovery of the conditioned reflex set the stage for asking questions about which properties of the CS, US, and the relationship between the two contribute to the conditioning process. If you begin with the observation that a completely neutral stimulus can, through conditioning, come to elicit a response that would not ordinarily occur, then you might reasonably entertain the possibility that this CS can support further conditioning in a completely novel CS. Pavlov did indeed entertain this possibility and in the process determined that a previously established CS could lead to conditioning of a novel stimulus, a procedure he called **higher order conditioning**.

To see how higher order conditioning is brought about, let's return to our experiment. Assume that we have already conditioned a salivary response to a neutral stimulus, such as a light, using food powder as our US. Once conditioned, the light becomes CS_1. In the next phase of the experiment, trials begin with the presentation of a novel stimulus (tone), followed by the light (CS_1). Note that during these trials, no food powder (US) is presented. In a sense, higher order conditioning unfolds like any other Pavlovian procedure, but we are using the CS_1, which already reliably produces salivation, as a substitute for the US. By presenting our novel stimulus, followed by the CS_1, we are closely following the same procedure we initially used to transform the light into a conditional stimulus. Now, however, the salivation occurring is in response to the CS_1, not in response to the US. Pavlov showed that with repeated pairings of the novel stimulus (tone) and the CS_1, salivation would eventually occur in response to the novel stimulus (tone) alone. At this point the stimulus has become a *second-order* conditional stimulus (CS_2). What is remarkable about this phenomenon is that the novel stimulus has acquired CS properties despite never having been

higher order conditioning conditioning to a neutral stimulus as the result of pairing with a previously established CS

paired directly with the US. Remember, the tone has been paired with the original CS (light), but never on trials accompanied by the US.

If you have followed the procedural logic of higher order conditioning to this point, then perhaps you have already identified the next question to confront Pavlov. Using our experiment as an example, once we have established a second-order CS (CS_2), such that salivation occurs reliably with its presentation, can we then use this CS_2 to establish an additional conditioned reflex in the presence of a novel stimulus? That is, can we establish a third-order CS? As it turns out, Pavlov found third-order conditioning in dogs to be nearly impossible, at least as long as food was the US. He did have some success in producing a third-order conditioned reflex when electric shock served as the US. Neither Pavlov nor his colleagues were able to produce a fourth-order CR, regardless of which stimulus served as the US.

The phenomenon of higher order conditioning underscores the tremendous flexibility and power of the conditioning process, as it suggests that nearly any stimulus to which an organism can respond may come to serve as a CS, even through distant and indirect connection to other stimuli. Thus, the whole world becomes, in principle, a smorgasbord of signals, helping animals to identify things in the environment that can hurt or help them. In fact, Pavlov was convinced that higher order conditioning would eventually become an indispensable component in any theory of human behavior dealing with complex thought, language, problem solving, and other advanced cognitive capabilities. The possible role that higher order conditioning might play in human behavior would eventually become a major theme in the research programs of several psychologists who study semantic conditioning.

Semantic Conditioning   The power of language in human behavior can hardly be overstated. Words can entertain, instruct, confuse, lead to hurt feelings and even to war. Any complete account of language must eventually explain not only how humans acquire language as young children (see Chapter 9) but also how words come to acquire meaning and an ability to evoke the full spectrum of human emotion. Arthur Staats and colleagues (Staats, 1975; Staats, Staats, & Crawford, 1962) were among the first researchers to consider the possibility that words may acquire certain meanings or emotional effects through a Pavlovian conditioning process. Moreover, these researchers questioned whether it was possible that words might become second-order CSs as a function of their relationship to other words.

In higher order verbal conditioning experiments, words chosen to function as USs are typically words that already possess emotional meaning for subjects. For instance, such words as *joy, fun,* and *candy* might be expected to elicit positive reactions in most English-speaking people. By pairing such words with relatively neutral words, such as *rock* or *carpet,* researchers have demonstrated that the emotional value attached to the US words (*joy, fun,* and *candy*) can be transferred to the neutral words (Early, 1968; Eifert, 1984; Page, 1969; Razran, 1961). This finding is consistent with a higher order conditioning interpretation because the original words that served as USs must be assumed to have acquired their emotional properties prior to the experiment.

It is important to point out that the researchers in such studies do not explicitly condition emotional responses to the spoken (US) words by way of paired unconditional stimuli. Many emotionally charged words only become so because of their association with other positive and negative events. It's unlikely, for instance, that any human infant has an aversion to the word *no* until such time that this word has been paired with unpleasant stimulation. Indeed, according to Staats (1975), "When the parent says 'No, bad!' to his child as he applies some aversive stimulus, the parent is conditioning his child to respond with a negative emotional response to the words" (p. 126). Raskin (1969) also demonstrated conditioning of emotional responses, using galvanic skin response and finger vasomotor responses as CRs. White noise was used as the US, and vocally presented words served as the CSs. Emotional responding developed to the CS words over the course of conditioning, and generalization to novel words was also demonstrated.

✖ INTERIM SUMMARY

Generalization refers to responding that occurs in the presence of stimuli resembling the CS, even though these stimuli have not been directly paired with the US. The behavioral complement to generalization is discrimination, in which responding occurs in the presence of the CS, but not in the presence of other stimuli resembling the CS. Higher order conditioning can be brought about by pairing a previously conditioned CS with a novel stimulus, though never presenting the US on such trials. If the novel stimulus comes to evoke a CR, it has acquired second-order conditioning properties. Several research programs using human subjects have demonstrated the possibility that meanings and emotional properties of words may be acquired through higher order conditioning.

✖ THOUGHT QUESTIONS

1. Using the concept of generalization, describe why you might experience a strong positive feeling when hearing a song on the radio, even though you have never heard the song before.
2. Why did Pavlov consider higher order conditioning to be important in explaining complex cognition and language in humans? What is the difference between the CS_1 and the CS_2 in higher order conditioning?
3. How might Pavlovian conditioning, particularly higher order conditioning, help explain the sometimes strong attitudes and stereotypes directed toward the following groups: police officers, politicians, psychiatric patients, car salespersons, and lawyers?

EXPLANATIONS OF PAVLOVIAN CONDITIONING

It might interest you to know that Pavlov's primary concern wasn't in studying the salivary reflex itself. Recall that he was a physiologist, not a psychologist, and he was fascinated, quite naturally, with the underlying activity of the nervous system that was responsible for the conditioned reflex. Indeed, the subtitle of his classic work *Conditioned Reflexes* (Pavlov, 1927/1960) is *An Investigation of the Physiological Activity of the Cerebral Cortex*. Unfortunately, Pavlov lived at a time when the activity of the nervous system remained aloof and hidden, unavailable for direct observation. No technology existed that allowed scientists to peer into an organism's intact nervous system to see the anatomical events giving rise to observable changes in behavior. Imagine how Pavlov would have greeted the advent of high-tech imaging instruments, such as PET scans, CAT scans, and MRI systems, that let contemporary scientists literally watch the activity of the human brain as it puzzles over a math problem or solves a riddle. No doubt he would have been like the proverbial child in a candy store.

Despite lack of access to the nervous system, Pavlov was devoted to understanding how this marvelous machinery could organize the various sensory experiences of the organism while simultaneously coordinating the necessary motor responses. In short, Pavlov believed, as modern-day researchers still do, that the higher centers of the nervous system (particularly the cerebral cortex) play a critical role in synthesizing the various information coming into the organism and mapping this information onto a response system in such a way as to make ongoing adaptive behavior possible. Pavlov was not, therefore, an idle spectator of the conditioned reflex. His training in physiology led him necessarily to speculate about the details of nervous system activity that accompanied conditioning, and he was convinced that this level of analysis would prove useful to any scientific investigation of behavior:

> It is my conviction that a purely physiological interpretation of much of what was previously called psychical activity has gained sure ground, and that in the analysis of the behaviour of higher animals, man included, every effort should be legitimately made to interpret phenomena in a purely physiological way, on the basis of established physiological processes. (1957, p. 442)

Consequently, Pavlov offered explanations of the behavioral phenomena he observed (the conditioned reflex, inhibition, higher order conditioning, etc.) couched in the appropriate language of physiology. As it turns out, he had a pretty good handle on the underlying events, even though modern research, aided by instrumentation Pavlov could not even dream of, has served to clarify parts of his account and, in some cases, correct some of his errors. Let's take a look at the effort Pavlov made at explaining the acquisition of a conditioned reflex.

Stimulus Substitution Theory

Pavlov's explanation for the conditioned reflex relied heavily on the knowledge that cells in the nervous system communicate with one another by way of electrical and chemical signals. Moreover, the specific pattern of communication between different groups or collections of cells can be altered as a result of particular kinds of environmental experience. Pavlov theorized that certain regions of the nervous system experienced an increase in neural excitation when the US (say, food) was presented. In addition, a separate collection of cells becomes activated when the CS (light) is presented. Although these two separate collections of cells might not ordinarily be connected, or communicate with one another, the conditioning process serves to connect them. In essence, Pavlov argued that repeated pairings of the CS and US caused a pattern of neural transmission in which activation in one part of the cortex spread to other areas, thus linking these otherwise separate circuits. Eventually, whenever the CS was presented, the same brain center that ordinarily responded to the US would respond in a similar way to the CS. This means that Pavlov considered the CS to be a neural substitute for the US; thus his explanation has been referred to as **stimulus substitution theory.**

Although stimulus substitution theory has not gone completely unchallenged, it remains a viable account of some instances of Pavlovian conditioning, particularly those cases in which the conditioned response (CR) appears nearly identical to the unconditioned response (UR). For example, experiments with pigeons in which lighted keys in a cubicle serve as the CS and either food or water serves as the US provide evidence that the CS comes to substitute for the US. When the light signals the onset of water, pigeons will approach the key and begin pecking with their mouths closed and their eyes open (Jenkins & Moore, 1973), as seen in Figure 2.6. On the other hand, when food serves as the US, pigeons will approach the key and peck with their mouths open and their eyes closed. These different key-pecking *topographies,* or forms, are consistent with the pigeon's natural way of consuming water and food, respectively (Jenkins & Moore, 1973). This kind of behavior seems to support the notion that the CS simply becomes a substitute for the US.

In addition, contemporary research in the neurosciences has done much to shed light on the physical underpinnings of the Pavlovian conditioning procedure. Several neural structures, including the *thalamus* (a central way station for sensory information coming into the brain) and the *amygdala* (one of several structures that make up the limbic system), seem to play an important role in conditioned emotional responding. When an auditory CS is paired with shock as the US, activity in both of these structures increases. Once a conditioned reflex has been acquired, presentation of the CS by itself leads to increases in neural activity in both of these structures (Iwata, LeDoux, Meeley, Arneric, & Reis, 1986; Sananes & Davis, 1992), indicating that CS-US pairings have created a circuit, or excitatory pathway, that was not present before conditioning.

Despite the previously described behavioral and physiological evidence, stimulus substitution does not seem capable of explaining all cases of Pavlovian conditioning. In particular, sometimes the conditional response (CR) barely resembles the unconditional response (UR) (Guha, Dutta, & Pradhan, 1974; Zener, 1937). Indeed, the strongest case against stimulus substitution is provided by those instances in which the CR is actually the *opposite* of the UR, and modern research on conditioning has uncovered many such cases, as discussed next.

stimulus substitution theory Pavlov's idea that the CS becomes a neural substitute, or representation, for the US

FIGURE 2.6 Differential Response Form to Water (left column) and Food (right column).

Compensatory Response Theory

The essence of **compensatory response theory** is that the CR represents an attempt by the body to prepare itself for the onset of the US. To illustrate this type of explanation, consider the case of Nathan, the unfortunate high school senior described in this chapter's opening vignette. Remember that Nathan died of an overdose of heroin, despite the fact that the dosage he took was one to which he had already developed a tolerance. The way the body develops a tolerance for a chemical is a fascinating process that scientists once thought was a purely physiological occurrence. Contemporary research, however, has shown that learning, particularly in the form of Pavlovian conditioning, may play an especially important role in tolerance development. Heroin, an opiate-based narcotic, produces a number of physiological effects, among them a reduced heart rate and a reduced sensitivity to pain. Curiously, though, individuals who are about to ingest the drug often experience physical reactions that are the precise opposite of those produced by the drug itself, that is, an increased heart rate and heightened sensitivity to pain. This opposing reaction is believed to be the way the body prepares itself for the introduction of the drug. In essence, by altering some of its basic physical parameters, the body compensates for the potential effects of the drug.

Learning is germane to this process because these compensatory changes aren't happening in response to the drug itself, *for the drug hasn't even been ingested yet.* They are, instead, reactions that must be explained in some other way. Some scientists believe that the compensatory physical reactions constitute a conditioned reflex (CR) in response to environmental stimulation that has reliably accompanied ingestion of the drug. Shepard Siegel (1983, 1989) has been a particularly vocal proponent of this view and has amassed some impressive evidence indicating that drug tolerance may often result from just such a conditioning process. According to Siegel, because Nathan's ritualistic drug use ordinarily occurred in a predictable setting, this ensured that certain stimuli, including the furniture and physical ambience of the environment, the type of music played, and the presence of friends, were also reliable predictors of heroin use. These various stimuli consequently became conditioned stimuli (CSs) for the compensatory response (CR) of the body just before ingestion of the drug. As long as these stimuli remained constant from one instance of drug use to the next, Nathan's body would have reliably prepared itself for the administration of heroin. Under such conditions, repeated over several months, Nathan would be able to ingest a fairly large dose of heroin with little ill effect.

But remember that Nathan's fatal drug episode occurred at home and by himself. Because his drug use never before occurred in this environment, the ambient stimulation available in his room had no history of association with drug use. Thus, unlike the sights and sounds that ordinarily accompanied his heroin use, the stimuli impinging on Nathan that night did not serve as CSs for the compensatory response that had become common just before ingestion of the drug. As a result, Nathan's body was not prepared to handle the heroin, even though the dose was no more than he had taken many times before. In a sense, the drug "surprised" his body, overwhelming its normal capacity to deal with a foreign agent, and Nathan succumbed. That Nathan's overdose occurred under physical conditions that differed substantially from those in which he ordinarily took heroin is consistent with a considerable amount of recent research literature. Siegel (1984) has reported, for instance, that overdoses leading to hospitalization are more likely to follow from administering the drug in unfamiliar surroundings than in familiar surroundings. In addition, in a laboratory study, rats were given repeated injections of heroin (Siegel, Hinson, Krank, & McCully, 1982). Some animals received all injections, including a final large dose, in the same environment, whereas other animals received their final dose in a novel environment. Twice as many rats injected in the novel environment died following the large dose, supporting the idea that these animals' bodies did not sufficiently compensate for introduction of the drug. The novel environment did not contain stimuli that had acquired conditional stimulus properties, thus morbidity rates were higher in this group of animals.

The Rescorla-Wagner Model

Rescorla-Wagner model a mathematical model describing the accelerating course of learning in studies of Pavlovian conditioning and other forms of learning

Like all scientists, psychologists make considerable use of theories and models to explain the behavior in which they are interested. Of course, not all models are created equal, and the test of a good model or theory is its ability to account for a wide variety of research findings. In the psychology of learning, there is probably no better example of such a theory than the **Rescorla-Wagner model,** first proposed in 1972. The model represents a relatively simple mathematical account of how associative strength, and therefore conditioning, builds up over the course of a learning experiment. Although originally proposed as an explanation of Pavlovian conditioning, the Rescorla-Wagner model has proven itself applicable to a broader body of learning procedures, and remains one of the more influential theories of learning some three decades after its original publication (Kop & DeKlerk, 1994; Miller, Barnet, & Grahame, 1995; Siegel & Allen, 1996).

As with many scientific models, the Rescorla-Wagner model is expressed in mathematical terms in the form of the following equation:

$$\Delta V_A = \alpha_A \beta (\lambda - V_A)$$

Students are often intimidated by mathematical equations such as this, but there's really no reason to be. The Rescorla-Wagner model is actually pretty simple as mathematical models go, especially considering the wide range of learning phenomena that this simple equation explains. Let's take a look at the elements of the model and at what it tells us about the process of classical conditioning.

ΔV_A This part of the equation refers to the associative strength that has built up between the CS and the US on a particular trial of the experiment. The rest of the equation actually explains how the CS-US association, or response strength (ΔV_A), changes (increases or decreases) from trial to trial.

$\alpha_A \beta$ These variables represent constants, or parameters, in the equation. Ordinarily, they would reflect certain features of the CS or US, such as intensity or salience, that would be expected to affect the learning process. Both the speed and degree of learning that occurs would be expected to vary from experiment to experiment, in part because these

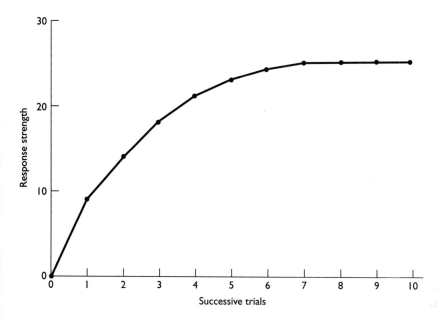

FIGURE 2.7 The Negatively Accelerated Learning Function as Predicted by the Rescorla-Wagner Model.

parameters would be expected to be differentially influential across experiments as well.

$(\lambda - V_A)$ This part of the equation represents, at any given point in the experiment, the difference between the theoretical maximum amount of learning or response strength that would be associated with a particular US (λ), and the degree of response strength or conditioning present on that particular trial (V_A). In other words, although any US would be predicted to produce some ultimate degree of conditioning, on any particular trial, especially early in the experiment, the amount of learning would be something less than this maximum. In general, the quantity $\lambda - V_A$ is usually quite large during the experiment's early trials, and it decreases systematically as a function of continued learning.

The essence of the Rescorla-Wagner model is that conditioning occurs because the presence of the US is surprising to the organism. Before the first trial, the difference between λ and V_A is very large, because the US has not yet been encountered. This means that the US is maximally surprising on the first trial, and this leads to a substantial reduction in the difference between λ and V_A. The model therefore suggests that substantial learning or conditioning occurs as a result of the first CS-US pairing. However, with additional pairings, the amount of learning that occurs in each successive trial decreases; that is, the amount of change in the difference score ($\lambda - V_A$) becomes smaller and smaller. Thus, the model predicts that learning will follow a fairly standard pattern characterized by a negatively accelerated curve, as depicted in Figure 2.7.

As you can see in Figure 2.7, the amount of learning, or response strength (depicted on the vertical axis), increases substantially on the first trial (depicted on the horizontal axis), but the amount of learning actually diminishes with each successive trial. One of the reasons that the Rescorla-Wagner model has been so influential in accounting for various learning phenomena is that this classic negatively accelerated function is an extremely common feature of learning, and it is an essential prediction of the model. This does not mean that the rate and amount of learning remains the same across experiments, or learning tasks, or subjects, for it certainly doesn't. That's where the parameters $\alpha\beta$ become important in the model. Remember, these are parameters associated with the CS and US that influence the learning process. These are, indeed, among the variables that researchers intentionally manipulate in order to evaluate the role they play in the conditioning process. For instance, a very intense CS, such as a bright light, might lead to more rapid learning than would a less intense CS. Factoring this consideration into the equation, the Rescorla-Wagner model would produce a learning curve in which the maximum associative strength, as represented by the leveling off of the curve (also known as its *asymptote*) would occur more rapidly with the intense CS than with the weaker CS. The general shape of the curve won't differ, but the rapidity with which the maximum strength is achieved would.

Because the Rescorla-Wagner model was first proposed in 1972, and has inspired research ever since, it has undergone considerable scrutiny and been exposed to various efforts to prove it false. Not many theories in any discipline would survive this kind of scientific attention completely unscathed, and the Rescorla-Wagner model is no exception. As it turns out, the model has been found deficient in handling some of the facts of classical conditioning (Miller, Barnet, & Grahame, 1995). The model, for instance, does not account for the fact that some CSs may have both excitatory and inhibitory effects (Tait & Saladin, 1986). In addition, the model suggests that extinction simply involves a reduction of response strength to zero, a claim that doesn't correspond well to contemporary research and theory arguing that extinction involves the learning of a new association between the CS and the absence of the US. Finally, although the model does a fairly good job of accounting for results in which singular or two-stimuli CS compounds are used, it falls short in circumstances in which the CS-US associations occur within a larger stimulus context (Kimmel & Lachnit, 1988).

Limitations notwithstanding, the Rescorla-Wagner model remains an extremely influential theory within the psychology of learning because of its ability to account for many of the fundamental phenomena of classical conditioning, including acquisition, blocking, overshadowing, and others. In addition, the theory has been used to predict some rather counterintuitive empirical findings that were not anticipated by researchers. Thus, the model is something of a rarity in psychology, in that it not only accounts for a large amount of experimental data, but accurately predicts some novel results as well. This is an impressive achievement in any science. Good theories should be able to accommodate a diverse collection of facts in their respective fields, and they should also help to generate additional questions that lead to further research. As discussed in Chapter 1, that is precisely what makes evolutionary theory so important within biology. After all, the fundamental mechanism for evolution resides in but two complementary factors—genetic variation and natural selection. Out of this dynamic interaction has come the remarkable diversity characterizing life on this planet. That is an undeniably powerful explanatory device. Such strong claims are rare in psychology, but the Rescorla-Wagner model has earned its status as one of the discipline's more prestigious theoretical achievements.

✖ INTERIM SUMMARY

Efforts to explain the various phenomena of classical conditioning have run the gamut from speculations about the creation of neural connections in the brain to mathematical models describing the decreasing "suprisingness" of the US across experimental trials. As a trained physiologist, Pavlov's explanation for his "psychic secretion" was couched in the acceptable language of physiology. Pavlov suggested that pairing the CS and US led to a neurological connection between two previously separate brain centers and that, over time, the CS comes to act as a substitute for the US, provoking neural activity in the brain region associated with the US. Stimulus substitution theory is consistent with certain aspects of classical conditioning phenomena, but not others. Compensatory response theory argues that conditioned responses represent an effort on the part of the body to prepare for US onset, and that these responses are often the precise opposite of the unconditioned response. Compensatory response theory has been especially influential in attempts to explain the phenomena of drug tolerance and drug overdoses. Finally, the Rescorla-Wagner model has for nearly three decades been the seminal mathematical theory of classical conditioning, and its ability to predict and account for various conditioning phenomena has ensured its continued popularity and preeminence within the psychology of learning.

✖ THOUGHT QUESTIONS

1. What kind of evidence argues against Pavlov's idea that the CS represents a substitute of the US?
2. Why is it perplexing that Nathan died from a heroin overdose, and how would an understanding of Pavlovian conditioning explain his death?
3. What role does surprise play in Pavlovian conditioning, according to the Rescorla-Wagner model? Also, why is the theory held in such high regard by psychologists?

THE ADAPTIVENESS OF PAVLOVIAN CONDITIONING

The scientific study of Pavlovian conditioning remains a vibrant area of research within psychology, and as Robert Rescorla (1988) reminded psychologists in a thought-provoking article, there is a good deal more to the phenomenon than meets the eye. No doubt continued research will uncover aspects of the conditioning process that are currently sources of contention and debate. But it's hardly necessary to answer all of these questions to appreciate the relevance or adaptive nature of Pavlovian conditioning. Whatever else may be said about this learning phenomenon, Pavlovian conditioning represents a process by which organisms learn about the relationships between potentially important events in their environment. If hearing the growl of a predator precedes actual physical contact with the predator, then it makes perfect sense that a prey animal would respond adaptively to the growl by evading the predator, rather than waiting for the arrival of the predator. If a driver, in response to the sound of screeching tires from the vehicle behind, hunches her shoulders, steadies herself, and prepares for the imminent collision, she may reduce her chances of being injured should the driver behind be unable to stop. To the extent that environmental stimuli can serve as signals or predictors of additional oncoming stimuli, particularly when the latter prove especially beneficial or harmful, organisms would be expected to recognize and respond differentially to such stimulus associations. Moreover, with increased learning comes the ability to bring behavior under the control of a much larger array of stimulus events, as evidenced especially in higher order conditioning.

In a sense, Pavlovian conditioning appears to take advantage of an indelible feature of biological organisms, namely, the tendency to view events in the world as being connected. For reasons that have a largely phylogenetic basis, animals, including humans, seem to be predisposed to drawing associations or seeing functional relationships between variables in their environment. Although this tendency can be maladaptive, as when superstitious behavior develops, more often than not, identifying relationships between natural events makes good survival sense. Of course, not all events are equally connected, and this is why researchers find that certain CSs or USs lead to more rapid or stronger learning. Much of the history of Pavlovian conditioning research has been aimed at answering detailed questions about those variables that might be expected to enhance or inhibit the learning process. Keep in mind that the very discovery of the "psychic secretion" would never have occurred if dogs were not capable of recognizing cues in their environment that reliably predicted food. Thus, Pavlovian conditioning represents a powerful tool for helping organisms to sort out an otherwise confusing barrage of stimulation and to store those connections that carry significant consequences.

CHAPTER THREE

Pavlovian Conditioning
Applications

As a college student not exactly disposed to observe the four food groups when eating, Zach couldn't possibly appreciate more the fine repast before him. His roommate, Michael, has invited Zach to his home for Thanksgiving dinner, and Michael's parents have spared no effort in making the feast a memorable one. The table is laden with roast turkey, mashed potatoes, green beans, cranberries, and fresh yeast rolls for the meal, and a gourmet custard will be served for dessert. Zach digs in unabashedly, honoring his hosts' frequent reminders to "help yourself to seconds," even trying the unusual custard and finding it to his liking. Several hours later, back at the dorm, Zach is overcome by a rapidly increasing nausea, followed by a high fever and severe abdominal cramping. Several days later, having recovered from his bout with intestinal upset, Zach joins friends at a campus cafeteria. Michael returns to the table, his tray full of various culinary delights, one of which is a custardlike chocolate dessert. Glancing at Michael's tray, Zach is suddenly overcome by an unexplainable uneasiness, his stomach turns in knots, and he abruptly excuses himself, heading urgently for the restroom.

Perhaps you can relate to the opening vignette, though certainly the details of your own experience will differ. Even in technologically and medically advanced societies, germs now and then get the best of people. Although we long ago learned about the need to refrigerate certain foods, precisely monitoring such things would require a high-powered microscope as a standard piece of equipment in the kitchen. Most of us are understandably unwilling to observe such a standard, and, as a result, on occasion an undetected microbial agent wreaks havoc on our gastrointestinal system. But none of this is relevant to the psychology of learning. What is relevant is Zach's behavior in the cafeteria after his unfortunate experience in that it isn't explained at the moment by any tangible food poisoning. In a sense, Zach's reaction to his roommate's food tray is like Pavlov's "psychic secretion" because it appears to be a response to seeing Michael's custard dessert, not actual physical contact with the dessert. That is, Zach's previous encounter with custard seems to have affected his reaction to the sight of custard, and this suggests that prior experience, or learning, has played an important role.

This chapter discusses the contributions that Pavlovian conditioning makes to behavioral adaptation. The process that Pavlov uncovered has implications for how and why people develop certain food preferences, why certain features of our environment can evoke powerful emotions, both positive and negative, and even for understanding the activity of the immune system as it goes about fighting the many foreign agents that continuously invade our bodies. It also covers how Pavlovian conditioning principles have been systematically utilized to treat human fears and anxieties. Indeed, the documented effectiveness of behavioral interventions, many based on Pavlovian conditioning, is a rare and impressive success story in the history of mental health. By the end of this chapter, you'll have a better appreciation of just why psychologists get so enthusiastic about salivating dogs!

LEARNED TASTE AVERSION

Zach's food poisoning in the example at the beginning of the chapter is psychologically interesting because of its long-term consequences. Zach recovered in a few days from his illness, but the experience affected how he responded to certain foods at a later time. When Zach saw the custard dessert on his roommate's food tray, he was overcome by nausea and had to leave the room. Assuming Zach never reacted that way before to seeing custard, why did it have the effect on him that it did in the cafeteria? Recall that on the evening of the Thanksgiving dinner, Zach ate several kinds of food, many of which, like turkey and mashed potatoes, are pretty standard fare on this occasion. But the dessert was a novel kind of custard that Zach, and probably others at the table, had never been served before. When Zach later became ill, he associated the illness with having eaten the custard, for this is the stimulus that he reacted so violently to in the cafeteria. Why would he develop this aversion to custard, and not to turkey, mashed potatoes, or rolls?

If you view the Thanksgiving dinner as something like a trial in a Pavlovian conditioning experiment, Zach's sensitivity to the custard might make more sense to you. Many of the other stimuli, including the aroma, taste, and visual appearance of the turkey, mashed potatoes, and rolls have probably been encountered many times by Zach, *and without getting sick afterward.* The custard, though, being unfamiliar to Zach, served as a novel, or neutral, stimulus that perhaps got his attention. When he subsequently became ill, the custard became a primary candidate for developing an aversion because it had a perfect correlation with the illness. Zach ate the custard once in his life and became ill shortly thereafter. Consequently, the taste and appearance of the custard may have been effective conditional stimuli (CSs) for the aversion. The other stimuli present, including the common foods, had a long history of being presented without illness, and were therefore less powerful predictors of illness.

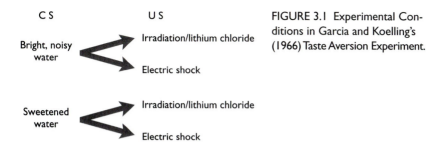

CS

Bright, noisy
water

US

Irradiation/lithium chloride

Electric shock

Sweetened
water

Irradiation/lithium chloride

Electric shock

FIGURE 3.1 Experimental Conditions in Garcia and Koelling's (1966) Taste Aversion Experiment.

The Garcia Experiment

Zach was an unwitting victim of a **learned taste aversion,** the development of a severe negative reaction to a food item due to pairing of the food with physical illness. The phenomenon was introduced in a classic article by Garcia and Koelling (1966), in which they describe the results of a study that exposed rats to different combinations of food CSs and aversive USs. The layout of the experimental conditions can be seen in Figure 3.1. Some animals were allowed to drink from water tubes containing water sweetened with saccharin. Other animals received regular water, but bright lights and loud noises occurred while they were drinking. The sweetened water and bright and noisy conditions served as the CSs. After drinking, animals received one of two kinds of USs. Some animals received an electric shock to the foot, while others were made nauseous through irradiation (X ray) or by a chemical (lithium chloride). Garcia and Koelling were interested in whether the rats would develop aversions to the CS (sweetened water, "bright, noisy" water) as a result of having been shocked or made sick.

The results of this experiment carried revolutionary implications for the psychology of learning. As you can see in Figure 3.2, those animals who received sweetened water and were then made sick through irradiation developed an aversion to the sweetened water, as evidenced in their reduced drinking rates after conditioning. Similarly, animals who received foot shock in the presence of the bright, noisy water developed an aversion to the bright, noisy water. However, neither animals who received pairings of bright, noisy water and irradiation nor those who received pairings of sweetened water and foot shock developed aversions. Garcia and Koelling had demonstrated that certain CS-US combinations produced taste aversion while others did not. Garcia's explanation of this finding would depend heavily on the concept of *preparedness,* which suggests that animals are prepared, or predisposed, to learn certain connections, especially those that "make sense" in their natural habitat. Animals in the wild often consume foods that make them sick, and it therefore makes sense that they may associate the sight, smell, texture, or taste (including sweetness) of the food with illness, thus adaptively avoiding the food in the future. Preparedness to learn certain stimulus-stimulus connections is assumed to have come about through natural selection and would be expected to vary across species and ecosystems.

Naturally, if organisms can be said to be prepared to learn certain stimulus connections with ease, it follows that other stimulus pairings might

learned taste aversion development of a severe negative reaction to a food item due to pairing the food with illness or other aversive stimulation

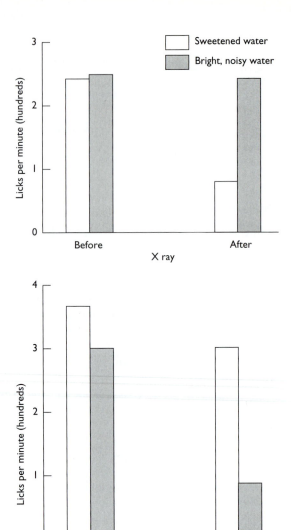

FIGURE 3.2 Response Suppression as a Result of Different CS-US Pairings. (Adapted from Garcia & Koelling, 1966.)

prove less amenable to conditioning. For example, bright lights and noises aren't typically associated with illness from ingesting food, but they might portend other aversive stimuli. Loud noises frequently signal such potentially dangerous things as crashing trees, lightning, and predators. Garcia and Koelling argued that animals in their study developed aversions to bright, noisy water when it was paired with shock because these stimuli represent a fairly natural connection between noise and painful stimulation. The Garcia and Koelling experiment garnered substantial attention among learning psychologists because the results challenged both time-honored assumptions about the learning process and previous knowledge about the role of temporal contiguity in Pavlovian conditioning. Prior to Garcia and Koelling's experiment, many scientists adhered to the notion that the stimuli used in conditioning experiments could be arbitrarily chosen by the researcher, as long as they could be detected by the animal subjects. This notion that all stimuli are created equal, or that all stimuli should support similar conditioning, is known as the *equipotentiality hypothesis*. Garcia and Koelling's results demonstrated that only certain CS-US connections (sweetened water–irradiation; bright, noisy water–shock) would support learning, as evidenced by the development of taste aversion. Moreover, the idea of preparedness suggests that the ease with which certain CS-US pairings can be learned is directly tied to the evolutionary history of the particular species being studied. Scientists who ignore the unique ecological heritage of their animal subjects do so at the risk of missing out on much of what is adaptive about learning. In the years since Garcia and Koelling's research, much has been learned about the way phylogenetic or evolutionary variables affect the learning process, and a sizable literature now exists dealing with what are called *biological constraints on learning* (Klein & Mowrer, 1989; Lolordo, 1979; Seligman & Hager, 1972).

The other aspect of the "Garcia effect" that warrants discussion is the fact that animals who were made sick through irradiation didn't develop symptoms immediately. Nor, for that matter, did Zach, in the leading vignette, become ill during or even immediately after the Thanksgiving dinner. Nevertheless, the rats in taste aversion experiments, and Zach, "connect" their illness with something consumed minutes, or even hours, earlier. The fact that conditioning occurs despite this rather long CS-US interval seems to violate much of the experimental literature on Pavlovian conditioning. Recall from the previous chapter that the optimal interval separating the CS from the US, at least in many standard laboratory preparations, is about half a second. Most researchers believe that the learning of taste aversions under conditions of long CS-US intervals further supports the idea that many animals are simply *prepared* to connect illness with ingested food, no matter how tenuous the temporal relationship between the two.

Taste Aversion and Cancer Treatment

Zach's plight shows that taste aversion isn't a phenomenon limited to the laboratory or to nonhuman animals. The business of ingesting external agents found in the environment is something of a dilemma, in that humans need to eat in order to acquire necessary nutrients, but some things we consume can be quite harmful. Thus, paying attention to what we eat and keeping track of those things that become associated with illness are clearly adaptive features of this type of learning. But sometimes the ability to learn from experience becomes a double-edged sword, and there are times when attending to food-relevant stimuli may actually prove problematic. A case in point is the use of chemotherapy as part of a treatment regimen for cancer. Although chemotherapy has become a standard form of cancer treatment, like most medical interventions, it comes at some cost. Chemotherapy often causes considerable nausea in patients, and this fact is particularly troublesome when you consider that patients are often given food along with their treatment. Because most mammals, including humans, are adept at associating illness with food intake, it follows that cancer patients receiving chemotherapy may inadvertently develop taste aversions to those foods that often accompany their treatment.

Imagine how such an aversion might develop. As a medical intervention, chemotherapy occurs in a particular context, be it a hospital room or a medical center. This context is a physical environment containing numerous forms of stimulation, including the appearance and behavior of the medical staff, the smells of disinfectants and other chemicals common to medical environments, and a nearly constant cacophony of intercom calls, patients' cries of discomfort, and the hum of high-tech automated equipment. Surrounded by this array of stimulation, patients are given treatment (usually in the form of a pill) and strongly encouraged to eat some food to go along with it. Although the effect is not immediate, the chemical properties of the medicine may produce extreme nausea, and this qualifies the medicine as an unconditional stimulus (US). In fact, in many ways chemotherapy mirrors the US properties of irradiation in Garcia and Koelling's (1966) experiment.

In most taste aversion research, separate stimuli are manipulated as conditional stimuli (CSs). Garcia and Koelling (1966) used sweetened water and flashing lights and buzzers as their CSs. Of course, in a laboratory experiment, control over such stimuli is achieved with considerable ease. In a hospital or other medical setting, it's practically impossible to control, or even be precisely aware of, all of the ambient stimuli impinging on the patient at the time of treatment. So which of these stimuli, if any, become associated with the illness produced by the chemotherapy (US)? The equipotentiality hypothesis suggests that any of the various sights, sounds, or smells encountered in the setting could become an effective CS for nausea. This is not what happens, though. In most instances, patients develop an aversion to the food that they were given along with their medication, so much so that they refuse to eat the same food in the future, even when hungry. That is, patients don't tend to associate their nausea with the various sights, sounds, or smells that permeate a medical setting. Similar to Garcia and Koelling's (1966) rats, they connect illness with something they ate, in this case the hospital food.

Bernstein (1985) has shown that such food aversions are common in cancer patients receiving chemotherapy, and strong aversions can come about even as a result of a single trial or CS-US pairing. After all, severe nausea is an aversive, and therefore memorable, experience. As a result of these learned aversions, patients may avoid those specific foods that are part of a hospital diet, and this leads naturally to poor nutrition and weight loss as well. In fact, Bernstein's work has stimulated an interesting dialogue on the possible role that taste aversion may play in many eating disorders, including anorexia nervosa (Bernstein & Borson, 1986). Fortunately, such aversions may be preventable. Introducing novel foods during chemotherapy, rather than standard fare, would take advantage of the fact that conditioning often occurs rapidly to unusual stimuli. Recall that in the chapter's opening vignette, Zach had eaten an unusual custard dessert at his friend's house. Taste aversions often develop to the novel foods, but this should not interrupt consumption of those foods making up the patient's regular diet. In addition, several authors have argued that food aversions, once developed, may be readily modified by well-documented behavior therapies (de Silva, 1990).

FIGURE 3.3 Learned taste aversion was successfully taught to coyotes in the wild.

Taste Aversion and Predator Control

You can't live in the modern world without becoming aware of the conflicts that often characterize relationships between different constituencies or groups of people, especially when their very different agendas clash. Nowhere is this more visible than in the American West, where vast areas of forests and rangeland have become the focus of volatile disputes between such varied interests as wildlife supporters, environmentalists, outdoor recreationists, loggers, and ranchers (Dagget, 1995). Increasingly, the West has become a battleground, with groups that support environmental and wildlife agendas squaring off against those who have for generations made their living off the land. When the vested interests of such disparate groups clash, the results can get pretty unpleasant. One such dispute has pitted ranchers against those who support the introduction or enhancement of populations of large predators (wolves, coyotes, mountain lions, etc.) into natural areas. The conflict arises when predators begin feeding on livestock, and the livelihood of ranchers becomes compromised.

It is at times like this that people often ask science to step in, either to provide an accurate picture of the problem or to suggest potential solutions. As it turns out, one possible remedy has come from an unlikely source—the psychology of learning. Armed with an understanding of learned taste aversion, Gustavson and colleagues attempted to bring about a change in the predatory habits of the coyote (Figure 3.3), whose fondness for sheep is legendary. The researchers contaminated chunks of lamb meat with a poison and distributed the meat throughout a sizable range of coyote habitat. The poison wasn't strong enough to kill the coyotes, but it produced rather severe gastrointestinal distress. Subsequent to experiencing the unpleasant consequences of feeding on the meat, coyotes were observed to avoid sheep that would have otherwise been easy prey (Gustavson, Garcia, Hawkins, & Rusiniak, 1974).

This study serves as an especially good example of applied science, in that the researchers implemented a real-world intervention based on well-developed and documented principles of behavior. Moreover, the results of the study were particularly desirable because the sheep remained unharmed and the coyotes simply turned their attention to other prey, including rabbits and small rodents. Such an intervention, if successful, meets the needs of both ranchers and conservationists, not to mention those of the larger four-legged creatures involved. Of course, the issue is a complicated one, and no single remedy is likely to meet with complete success. Taste aversion training has not become *the* solution to the complicated problem of livestock predation in the West, but it remains one of the more humane and inexpensive alternatives (Forthman Quick, Gustavson, & Rusiniak, 1985; Gustavson & Gustavson, 1985; Gustavson & Nicolaus, 1987).

✖ INTERIM SUMMARY

Learned taste aversion involves the avoidance of a particular food as a result of having associated the food, through Pavlovian conditioning, with illness. The phenomenon is adaptive and probably quite common in many animals, including humans. Discovery of the phenomenon forced a reconsideration of many fundamental assumptions about learning, including the historical idea that stimuli that enter into a conditioning procedure can be chosen arbitrarily. Taste aversion research has helped to shed light on food preferences and dietary habits in humans, including such maladaptive phenomena as anorexia. Finally, efforts at regulating the feeding behavior of large predators through the application of taste aversion principles has met with some limited success.

✖ THOUGHT QUESTIONS

1. In the Garcia and Koelling experiment, rats developed aversions to bright, noisy water when paired with shock. The previous chapter described a patient in a dentist's office who responded anxiously to the sound of the dentist's drill. Describe how each of these aversions makes sense from the perspective of belongingness or preparedness.

2. Imagine you are a health psychologist working on a cancer ward of a hospital. Describe in detail what you would do to help patients who were losing weight because they became nauseous whenever they were offered food.

CONDITIONING AND PHYSIOLOGY

The fact that Pavlovian conditioning results in changes in physiological activity is not surprising, since Pavlov, himself a physiologist, was particularly interested in how the process affected the central nervous system. But the nervous system is not an isolated collection of nerve pathways; rather, it is intricately connected to the body's other systems. This arrangement makes sense if you consider that in most animals, including humans, various brain centers actually regulate basic physical processes, including breathing and circulation of blood. An interesting consequence of this interconnectedness is that there isn't much going on anywhere in your body that the nervous system doesn't monitor. This does not mean, of course, that you are always aware of these physiological processes, for you usually aren't. But if the nervous system monitors all other systems, and if conditioning manifests itself in the nervous system, then could the activities of the other systems become susceptible to conditioning as well? Let's take a look at one of these systems whose job it is to protect you continuously from the countless bacterial and viral agents contained in the physical environment.

Psychoneuroimmunology

One of the body's more remarkable features is the immune system, a diverse collection of cells that respond to infection by bacterial, viral, and fungal agents (collectively known as *pathogens*). When a foreign agent invades the body, the cells of the immune system respond by creating antibodies that attack and neutralize the invading agents. We may not always appreciate the work done by the immune system because, like many other bodily systems, it operates outside of our awareness. Nevertheless, the immune system remains continuously vigilant in guarding against a nearly constant barrage of foreign agents, drawing attention to itself most often when these defenses fail and we become ill, whether with a common cold or a more life-threatening illness. That this process unfolds in response to invading foreign agents isn't itself very interesting psychologically, because it represents the body's unconditioned response to an unconditioned stimulus. What *would* be of interest is if the immune system could be shown to be responsive to external stimuli (visual, auditory, etc.) that reliably predicted the onset of the unconditioned stimuli (invading agents). This would represent a conditioning effect and would highlight an important connection between psychological events and physical functioning. Such a finding would also have implications for thinking about mind-body issues, and it would highlight the mutual interdependence of several scientific disciplines.

Conditioned Immunosuppression　　Such a connection between the immune system and external stimuli has been documented by many researchers and over the course of many years (Ader, 1985; Ader & Cohen, 1993; Alvarez-Borda, Ramirez-Amaya, Perez-Montfort, & Bermudez-Rattoni, 1995; Biondi & Zannino, 1997; Gorczynski, 1991; King & Husband, 1991). In fact, two Russian scientists were probably the first to show Pavlovian conditioning of the immune system in the early decades of the 20th century. Metalnikov and Chorine (1926, 1928) injected guinea pigs with various nonlethal foreign agents in order to boost immune system functioning. In subsequent conditions, these animals were exposed to various environmental stimuli that had previously been connected to these injections. Presentation of the environmental stimuli (lights, etc.) led also to heightened immune system activity. In a final phase of the study, these animals, as well as a control animal not previously conditioned, were infected with cholera. The conditioned animals survived their bout with cholera, but the control animal died. Apparently, the immune system enhancement produced through conditioning allowed the experimental animals to better cope with the cholera infection.

More recently, Ader and Cohen (1975, 1984, 1993) have shown that conditioning of the immune system is a reliable effect, and that different conditioning histories can bring about either increases in or suppression of immune system activity. Ader and Cohen (1984) stumbled upon this conditioned immune suppression by accident, as the purpose of their original work was to study taste aversion in rats. Animals were allowed to drink saccharin (sweetened) water and were then injected with a nausea-inducing drug, cyclophosphomide. Animals did in fact develop a taste aversion, as indicated by their subsequent avoidance of saccharin water, but an additional surprising, and somewhat disturbing, result was that many of Ader and Cohen's experimental animals became sick and died during the experiment. Upon reflection, the researchers determined that experimental animals had not only acquired a taste aversion through conditioning, but also experienced suppression of the immune system, which left them extremely vulnerable to infection. Why would immune suppression have occurred for these animals? It turns out that cyclophosphomide, the drug the researchers used to produce nausea, is also a strong immunosuppressive agent, meaning that it also has the effect of reducing immune system activity. Thus, not only were Ader and Cohen's animals behaviorally conditioned to avoid saccharin water, but their immune systems had also been conditioned to the saccharin, which had become a CS for cyclophosphomide (US).

Research that focuses on the conditioned responsivity of the immune system has recently been designated **psychoneuroimmunology,** and, like other research utilizing Pavlovian principles, much of this work has centered on identifying the kinds of conditional and unconditional stimuli and responses that can enter into the conditioning process (Ader & Cohen, 1993; Cohen & Herbert, 1996). Standard auditory and visual cues, as well as flavored water, have been the most frequently used conditional stimuli in studies of conditioned immunosuppression. Many kinds of unconditional stimuli have been shown to produce the effect, including pharmacologic agents like cyclophosphomide and morphine (Coussons, Dykstra, & Lysle, 1992); nonpharmacologic agents, such as electric shock (Zalcman, Kerr, & Anisman, 1991); and rotation on a turntable (Gorczynski, 1992).

psychoneuroimmu-
nology field that
studies the conditioned
responsivity of the im-
mune system

Allergic Reactions Although the effect of conditioning of immune reactivity is not always of a large magnitude, it has proven to be very reliable and easily reproduced, across both different laboratory preparations and species. In fact, there is mounting evidence of the effect in humans, and the phenomenon may play a role, not only in susceptibility to disease, but also in common allergic and asthmatic reactions. Ader and Cohen (1993) relate the story of a 16th-century monk whose allergy to roses was so severe that the mere sight of the flower would cause him to collapse. Experimental studies have verified that reactions can be conditioned to neutral stimuli that become associated with the unconditioned allergens. In one study, Ikemi and Nakagawa (1962) painted subjects' arms with a blue solution containing a chemical that unconditionally produced eczema, an itchy, inflammatory skin reaction. After repeated pairing of the blue solution and the chemical allergen, all subjects developed a conditioned response (inflammation of skin tissue of the arm) to the blue solution when presented in isolation. If you are one of millions of Americans who suffer from allergic reactions to grass, pollens, and molds, these findings may not surprise you all that much. Perhaps you've noticed on more than one occasion that the very act of gassing up your lawn mower brings on the classic watery eyes, running nose, and sneezing fit characteristic of an allergic reaction, *long before any actual contact with the allergen has occurred.*

Research in psychoneuroimmunology is valuable for several reasons. First, it illustrates once again the widespread applicability of this basic conditioning process to phenomena considerably beyond salivation in dogs. Pavlov uncovered some of the power of this learning principle by demonstrating higher order conditioning, generalization, and such. But this more contemporary work has extended the basic principle to physical systems other than the neocortex, which was Pavlov's major concern. In addition, as stated previously, findings from psychoneuroimmunology have helped to bring scientific credibility to the long-standing observation that mind and body are connected in intricate ways. Although people have always considered this to be the case, the claim has always had something of a mystical quality to it. Indeed, for many years, the term *psychosomatic* was taken to mean "in one's head," thus not quite real or worthy of serious clinical attention. Psychoneuroimmunology, and other areas of research within the larger discipline of *behavioral medicine,* have come a long way toward indicating that such things are not only in our heads but specifically in our nervous systems and immune systems, and that the connection between the two is not only very real but very important to our long-term health and adaptation. In fact, Ader and Cohen (1984) argue that ". . . it has become clear that there is probably no major organ system or homeostatic defense mechanism that is not subject to the influence of interactions between psychological and physiological events" (p. 117).

Drug Addiction and Overdose

The discussion of Pavlovian conditioning began in the previous chapter with the unfortunate story of Nathan, the 18-year-old who died from a heroin overdose. Among the most noteworthy features of Nathan's death was that it was surprising—it would not have been expected given his history of drug use. Because he was a habitual user of heroin, Nathan would have built up a tolerance for the drug, meaning that he could have consumed larger doses than someone with no history with the drug, and to no ill effect. But the dose that Nathan took the night he died was less than his normal dose, and this made his death all the more perplexing. Two important lessons encountered so far in this book help to make sense of Nathan's unexpected demise. First, no behavior is easily understood outside of its environmental context, and this context is defined largely by the multitude of visual, auditory, tactile, and olfactory stimuli continuously impinging on the organism. Second, as explained in Chapter 2 and this chapter, these stimuli can enter into subtle and complex relationships with behavior, even to the point of triggering activity in bodily systems that are not ordinarily associated with behavior (Figure 3.4).

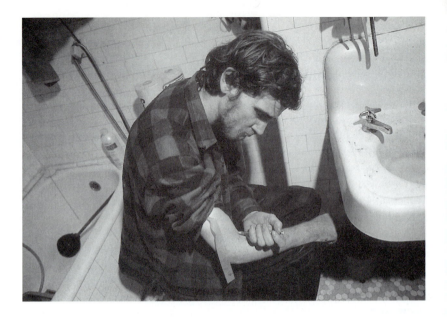

FIGURE 3.4 Role of Pavlovian Conditioning in Drug Addiction.

It will be useful to conceptualize each instance of Nathan's heroin use as something like an experimental trial. Of course, the context of this behavior is complex, and the conditions aren't identical to those of a controlled experiment in which external stimuli are specified and systematically manipulated by the researcher. But learning, as a natural phenomenon, doesn't require such systematically controlled events; indeed, it would be a poor means of adaptation if it did. When Nathan began taking heroin, he did so within a fairly common social context. Recreational drug use frequently occurs in small social groups of friends or acquaintances. Moreover, the use of illegal drugs, like heroin, often takes place in isolated or clandestine settings, in order to diminish the possibility of discovery. The secretive nature of this kind of drug use tends to engender a degree of camaraderie among the users, and a sense of community and belongingness, similar to that among any group of individuals brought together by common interests.

For many such groups, the ingestion of the drug takes on ritualistic dimensions, and the ambience surrounding drug use becomes an integral component of the experience. For any one user, the predictable presence of fellow users, characteristics of the room itself (furnishings, wall decorations, odors, etc.), music, and various drug paraphernalia (syringes, vials, etc.) are among the contextual stimuli that actually accompany drug ingestion. These stimuli, either individually or in compound, become potential conditional stimuli (CSs) for the introduction of the drug itself (US). The drug, of course, produces various physiological reactions, some of which influence psychological variables, including sensations and mood states. It is, in fact, these effects of the drug on psychological functioning that motivate use of the drug and lead to the classification of heroin as a *psychoactive* or *psychotropic* drug. In the case of heroin, psychological effects ordinarily include euphoria, relaxation, and a general sense of extreme contentment.

If the external stimuli described earlier are predictable components of drug usage, then a powerful contingent relationship between the CSs (external stimuli) and the US (heroin) has been established, and these are precisely the conditions that lead to Pavlovian conditioning. Remember that one interpretation of Pavlovian conditioning is that the conditioned response (CR) is the organism's way of preparing for the onset of the US. Salivating at the sound of a bell prepares the mouth for the presentation of food, thus aiding digestion. Withdrawal of a leg in response to a tone paired with shock may allow the organism to escape or at least diminish the aversive nature of the shock. It is certainly plausible that the external stimuli accompanying heroin use may serve to provoke bodily reactions in anticipation of drug ingestion. In fact, such a phenomenon, if repeated many times, may help explain how the body can develop a tolerance for greater and greater doses of the drug.

There is considerable evidence to support this notion. Siegel, Hinson, Krank, and McCully (1982) injected rats repeatedly with heroin, increasing the dose gradually. In the experiment's last phase, animals were injected with one large dose. Some animals received this large dose in the same environment in which previous injections had occurred, while other animals received the large dose in a novel, unfamiliar environment. Thirty-two percent of the animals injected in the familiar environment died after this large dose, but 64% of the animals injected in a novel environment died. In addition, almost all (96%) of a group of control animals who were injected only with the large dose died as well. These results reveal two things about drug addiction as a behavioral phenomenon. First, repeated injections of heroin in increasing dosages do lead to enhanced tolerance, as nearly all the control animals receiving one large injection succumbed to this dose. Second, and more important from a learning perspective, animals who were injected with the large dose in the *same* environment in which they had received previous injections better tolerated the drug, for their survival rate was highest. Animals who received the large dose in the *novel* environment, however, did not fare so well.

Additional evidence of the role played by conditioning in drug-related behavior comes from studies in which common withdrawal responses were brought under the control of conditioned stimuli. Goldberg and Schuster (1967) placed morphine-dependent rhesus monkeys in an experimental chamber in which lever pressing could periodically lead to food delivery. On occasion, a tone (CS) was sounded, followed by injection of nalorphine (US), a morphine antagonist that produces withdrawal symptoms, such as increased heart rate, excessive salivation, and vomiting. After continued exposure to these conditions, animals began exhibiting the withdrawal-like behaviors shortly after the onset of the tone and before nalorphine injection. In addition, responding on the lever for food was systematically suppressed during the tone presentation, thus representing conditioned suppression, as discussed in the previous chapter.

Research and theory on drug addiction has increasingly benefited from studies of the learning process, and professionals now recognize that addiction is not solely a biological event but a complicated behavior in which processes like Pavlovian conditioning play a central role. Shepard Siegel (1989, 1999) has been a particularly visible proponent of the idea that environmental context makes a significant contribution to many drug-related phenomena, including tolerance, withdrawal, and so-called *enigmatic overdoses,* or deaths, like Nathan's, that can't be attributed solely to the physical effects of drug dosage. In an interview conducted with several heroin addicts who were fortunate to have survived an overdose, Siegel (1984) collected information about contextual stimuli that accompanied drug ingestion. Most of Siegel's respondents reported having ingested the nearly lethal dose of heroin in unfamiliar or novel surroundings, a finding that is consistent with a growing body of research based on controlled laboratory studies (Siegel, Krank, & Hinson, 1987; Silverman & Bonate, 1997).

✖ INTERIM SUMMARY

The fact that the nervous system is intimately connected with other biological systems opens up the possibility that activity in these other systems might be susceptible to Pavlovian conditioning. The activity of the immune system, which protects the body against infection and illness, has been shown to be responsive to conditioned environmental stimuli. Numerous studies pairing neutral stimuli with chemical agents that affect immune system functioning have shown that immune activity can be brought under the control of these stimuli. In addition, recent research using both human and nonhuman subjects has demonstrated that Pavlovian conditioning likely plays a role in many drug-related phenomena, including tolerance and addiction, withdrawal, and death due to drug overdose.

✖ THOUGHT QUESTIONS

1. A friend visiting for dinner spies your plastic philodendron in the corner of your dining room. A look of disgust washes over her face and she excuses herself from the table. Heading toward the bathroom and sneezing all the way, she proclaims a strong allergy to such plants. How would you explain your friend's odd behavior, particularly in light of the fact that the plant is artificial?
2. Suppose a friend reports feeling much better after taking medicine for a headache. In actuality, you know that your friend has been given an inert pill, not a painkiller with any active substance. How would an understanding of Pavlovian conditioning help to explain this well-known *placebo effect?*

CLINICAL IMPLICATIONS

By now you probably appreciate the reverence that many psychologists feel for Pavlov and his conditioning experiments. But there's more to the story. You have only seen a small part of how Pavlovian conditioning illuminates the landscape of human behavior. This section explores some of the broader implications of the conditioning process for psychological functioning, including the regulation of emotional behavior. An additional discovery, that events in the environment effectively signal other events, holds out promise, not only for a better understanding of human behavior, but for changing it as well. The development of behavior therapy in the 1950s and 1960s represents one of the great success stories in psychology's long history, and Pavlovian conditioning helped pave the way.

Emotional Conditioning and the Legacy of Little Albert

You don't need to visit the laboratory to acknowledge that humans are emotional creatures. This part of our nature is so accepted that emotional behavior tends to draw attention to itself only when exhibited to extremes or under inappropriate circumstances. Former Indiana University basketball coach Bobby Knight, for instance, was the subject of considerable media scrutiny and a university-wide investigation when allegations surfaced concerning his legendary temper tantrums, some of which have been captured on film by national sports networks. Ultimately, Knight's outbursts cost him his job. Emotional behavior seems to have taken center stage, not just in media circles, but among experts as well. Psychologist Daniel Goleman (1995) has argued persuasively that we ignore emotional development in children at our peril and that a wise culture is one that takes seriously the emotional lives of its citizens.

Psychologists refer to *emotional intelligence* as a person's ability to be aware of her or his own and others' emotional states and to regulate emotional sensitivity in adaptive ways. Several authors have even suggested that emotional intelligence may prove more important than intellectual ability in negotiating the challenges of academic, career, and interpersonal domains (Ciarrochi, Chan, & Caputi, 2000; Goleman, 1995; Martinez-Pons, 1997).

Whether or not such claims are viable, our emotional lives do matter to us, and it is the business of psychology to ask fundamental questions that might not occur to most of us. Where do emotions come from? Why do we respond positively to one circumstance, but negatively to another? Why does a driver recovering from the injuries of a serious automobile accident cringe when approaching the intersection where the accident occurred? Why does a multimillion-dollar lottery winner feel a sense of elation when entering the local convenience store where he or she purchased the winning ticket? And why does the word *no* produce visible discomfort, and often tears, in some toddlers? None of these emotional reactions can be readily explained as inborn reflexes or fixed-action patterns that evolved because of their adaptive significance in human history. Our Pleistocene ancestors would have benefited little from a fear of cars or busy intersections, nor would the concept of a lottery or a million dollars have had any meaning. And in many of the world's thousands of human languages, the uttered sound "no" would be similarly meaningless.

It seems, then, that the significance of these stimuli must be accounted for in some other way. Personal experience must have something to do with the idiosyncratic meanings that environmental events hold for each of us, and Pavlovian conditioning seems well suited for just such a task (Bouton, Mineka, & Barlow, 2001). Although the role that conditioning might play in emotional behavior can often be readily seen in everyday settings, controlled laboratory studies have made their own contribution to understanding this complex relationship. Regrettably, the history of research on emotional conditioning is bittersweet. Important lessons have been learned and effective clinical interventions developed, but these advances have on occasion come at the expense of the long-term psychological well-being of involuntary research participants.

When you think of an emotional reaction, be it joy, sadness, or fear, you probably don't envision the response as being completely detached from its circumstances. That is, when you're afraid, you're usually afraid *of something*. Similarly, sadness doesn't usually emerge spontaneously, but in response to some relevant environmental event, such as loss of a loved one. This doesn't mean that people are always aware or cognizant of why they are reacting emotionally at any given moment, for this is most certainly not the case. Indeed, some schools of psychological thought, such as psychoanalytic theory, are essentially founded on the notion that people are *usually* unaware of the often subtle causes of their own actions and emotions. Nevertheless, a science of behavior would come to a screeching halt if psychologists were to accept the idea that any kind of behavior, emotional or otherwise, occurred spontaneously, without any connection to the world at large. In keeping with the adaptationist theme of this book, it seems unthinkable that natural selection could have designed an organism whose behavior was entirely disconnected from its surrounding environment. Fortunately for psychologists and those of us interested in studying human behavior, this is not the case. Like any other behavior, emotional responses don't occur in a vacuum, and this means that part of the psychologist's responsibility in explaining such behavior is taking account of the role that stimulus events play in emotional behavior.

If emotional responses are in part learned, it should be possible to produce such reactions intentionally and under controlled conditions. This was essentially the logic that informed one of the most notorious and unfortunate experiments in psychology's long history. John B. Watson (Figure 3.5), among the most visible and respected of American psychologists in the 1920s, was interested in the question of how human emotions, particularly fears, might be established, and what specific role learning plays in this process. Watson and his research assistant Rosalie Rayner set out to answer this question by attempting to produce an emotional response in an infant, known as Little Albert. Albert, whose mother was a nurse, had grown up in and around hospitals and was considered by the researchers to be both physically and psychologically healthy. In fact, Albert was considered especially well suited for the experiments because "He was on the whole stolid and unemotional" (Watson & Rayner, 1920, p. 1).

The experiment, which was carried out over several months (from approximately 9 months of age to a little over 1 year) began with an evaluation of Albert's normal reactions to various kinds of stimuli, including such animals as a white rat, a dog, a rabbit, and a monkey. Typical of children his age, Albert initially showed no fear or trepidation toward these animals or several other visual stimuli to which he was exposed. Such was not the case, however, when the researchers, from behind Albert, forcefully struck a metal bar with a hammer. This loud and surprising sound (US) produced a strong

FIGURE 3.5
John B. Watson.

startle reaction and crying in Albert. In the subsequent conditioning phase of the experiment, Albert was presented with the white rat:

> Just as his hand touched the animal the bar was struck immediately behind his head. The infant jumped violently and fell forward, burying his face in the mattress. He did not cry, however. . . . Just as the right hand touched the rat the bar was again struck. Again the infant jumped violently, fell forward and began to whimper. (Watson & Rayner, 1920, p. 4)

In a fairly short period of time, Watson and Rayner had produced in Albert a phobic reaction toward a white rat by way of Pavlovian conditioning. Today, the very idea of two psychologists intentionally subjecting an infant to such an emotionally trying experience is nearly inconceivable. Indeed, this same experiment could not be conducted today due to rigorous ethical standards that govern all research with both humans and nonhuman animal subjects. As misguided as the Watson and Rayner experiment was, if psychologists were able to learn something important about the origin of human fears, perhaps Albert's misfortune wasn't entirely in vain. As it turns out, the experiment *did* reveal the possibility that some fears may result from fortuitous Pavlovian conditioning. In the experiment, repeated pairing of the rat (CS) with the loud noise (US) led to eventual fear of the rat. In addition, Albert's fear reaction appeared to generalize to other animals and stimuli containing fur, such as a mask worn by Watson. It isn't difficult to imagine how this same process might account for many human emotional dispositions. The automobile accident victim overcome by anxiety when approaching the intersection where the accident occurred may have been similarly conditioned. There is in fact some evidence that accident victims, and those suffering from fears of blood and medical procedures, may have acquired their fears through conditioning procedures (Kheriaty, Kleinknecht, & Hyman, 1999; Kleinknecht, 1994; Kuch, Cox, Evans, & Shulman, 1994).

Some researchers argue that too much emphasis is placed on learning explanations of fears and phobias, and the case of Little Albert can shed only so much light on the phenomenon of human emotion (Lazarus, 1991). Of course, it is important to remember that Pavlovian conditioning has simply been identified as *one* mechanism by which fears might be acquired. No one would suggest that *all* fears or phobias are produced through this process. In fact, given the importance of attaching emotional value to objects and events in the environment, it would make sense to assume that emotional repertoires come about through processes other than Pavlovian conditioning.

The Birth of Behavior Therapy

If there was a silver lining in the Little Albert experiment, it was the realization that if a fear reaction could be produced through conditioning, then perhaps it could be eliminated as well. In fact, in their defense, Watson and Rayner had considered several avenues by which they could eliminate Albert's fear, but they were never afforded the opportunity to pursue such efforts because Albert was removed from the hospital. Although his fate remains unknown to this day, Albert's contribution to the development of treatments for phobia is incontestable. If Albert's fear was the result of Pavlovian conditioning, then our understanding of how conditioned reflexes (CRs) can be established and removed should lead to a systematic method for treating human fears.

Mary Cover Jones and the Case of Peter The idea that the principles of conditioning could be used in treatment of fear was in fact seized upon in 1924 by an American psychologist, Mary Cover Jones, believed by some to be the first behavior therapist (Gieser, 1993). Jones had been presented with the case of Peter, a 3-year-old suffering from a fear of rabbits. As is usually the case with patients who seek professional help, the fear had developed outside the laboratory, under unknown conditions. Although Jones could not be certain that Peter's phobia had emerged through a conditioning process, she was aware of both Pavlov's and Watson's research and therefore pursued a treatment based on conditioning principles.

The goal in treating a phobia is relatively straightforward, regardless of professional or theoretical orientation. The object is to reduce the client's negative emotional reaction to the feared stimulus, presumably because this reaction is preventing the client from normal, adaptive functioning. Jones knew that in a Pavlovian conditioning paradigm, conditional stimuli assume their properties through association with unconditional stimuli and that eliminating the response to the conditional stimulus requires breaking or eliminating this connection. Doing so could entail the process of extinction, which, as discussed in the previous chapter, involves presenting the CS (in Peter's case, the rabbit) repeatedly by itself or by associating the CS with an alternative US. Jones took the latter approach. She provided Peter with a snack of milk and crackers (US), stimuli ordinarily associated with positive feelings. As Peter ate the snack, Jones presented, very gradually, the feared rabbit. By presenting the rabbit first at a considerable distance and then moving the rabbit closer and closer to Peter, Jones was able to establish an association between the rabbit and the positive stimulus of the snack. Peter's emotional reaction to the rabbit changed quite rapidly, and before long he was observed playing with the rabbit in a manner typical of a child his age who was not fearful of rabbits (Jones, 1924).

The process of associating a feared CS with a positive, nonaversive US is known as **counterconditioning,** and it became a staple feature of behavior therapy. The logic of the procedure stems from the fact that an individual can't be both anxious and relaxed at the same time. These are mutually exclusive emotional reactions. By presenting the feared stimulus with emotionally positive stimuli, the client comes eventually to respond favorably to the CS. Jones's groundbreaking treatment of Peter, based on Pavlovian principles, set the stage for what could only be called a revolution in the treatment of human fears, anxieties, and other behavioral problems (Franks, 1969; Wolpe, 1958, 1969). The 1950s and 1960s would see an explosive development of **behavior therapy,** defined by Wolpe (1969) as ". . . the use of experimentally established principles of learning for the purpose of changing maladaptive behavior" (p. vii). Behavior therapy became a powerful alternative to insight-oriented therapies, such as psychoanalysis, which proclaimed that therapeutic gains could only be achieved by uncovering the complex machinery of unconscious intrapsychic conflict. Although beyond the scope of this book, the history of behavior therapy is a fascinating story about the tenuous relationship between laboratory science and clinical application and of theoretical and professional conflict. (Two recommended reviews of behavior therapy's history are Franks, 1969, and Kazdin, 1982.)

counterconditioning process of associating a feared CS with a positive US

behavior therapy interventions based on learning principles to alter maladaptive behavior

Systematic Desensitization Among the more prominent figures in the early development of behavior therapy was Joseph Wolpe (1915–1997). As was true of other significant figures in behavior therapy, Wolpe's early career was established in the laboratory, where he studied the Pavlovian conditioning of anxiety reactions in rats. In his classic book *Psychotherapy by Reciprocal Inhibition,* Wolpe (1958) described in detail the role that conditioning might play in both the development and elimination of human fears. Among his contributions was the therapeutic technique known as **systematic desensitization,** a procedure in which the anxious client is gradually exposed to the feared stimulus while practicing previously learned relaxation. The treatment usually begins with the client developing a fear hierarchy, in which the feared stimulus is represented by various forms that provoke increasing amounts of distress for the client. Table 3.1 depicts a hypothetical hierarchy of fear that might be generated by a snake phobic. Lower numbers reflect stimuli that produce (at least for this hypothetical client) only mild discomfort (for

systematic desensitization treatment for phobias entailing gradual exposure to feared stimulus under conditions of relaxation

TABLE 3.1 FEAR HIERARCHY FOR A HYPOTHETICAL SNAKE PHOBIC

8. Physical handling of the snake

7. Standing next to therapist who is handling snake

6. Standing next to cage with snake inside

5. Being in room with snake in cage (across room)

4. Watching film of person handling snake

3. Looking at still photograph of snake

2. Hearing the word *snake* spoken

1. Reading the written word *snake*

example, the written word *snake*). Higher numbers reflect stimuli that produce increasing levels of anxiety. If you or someone you know is afraid of snakes, you can probably appreciate why stimulus 8 is at the top of the list. It is probably hard for snake phobics to imagine anything more horrifying than having close physical contact with the object of their fear.

The other component of systematic desensitization is relaxation training. Although this can take many forms, the training often entails teaching the client to alternately contract and then relax various groups of muscles throughout the body. Once a relaxation response has been learned, the client is presented with the least anxiety-producing stimulus in the fear hierarchy. When the client is able to relax fully in the presence of this stimulus, the next stimulus up in the hierarchy is presented. The procedure of presenting stimuli systematically from least to most fearful is referred to as *graded exposure*. Although anxiety may not be completely eliminated, particularly in the presence of the most anxiety-provoking of the stimuli in the hierarchy, therapy is considered successful if the individual can continue to function normally in the presence of the feared object. It is, in fact, an impressive sight to see a snake phobic actually handling a live snake, and such a person is considered cured of his phobia if he can make physical contact with a snake without demonstrating obvious signs of distress. Keep in mind that prior to treatment, this person may have refused to go on walks in parks for fear of potential encounters with snakes. If, as a result of systematic desensitization, the client is able to go on such walks, perhaps even enthusiastically, then therapy has led to an adaptive change in the client's behavioral repertoire, and this is precisely the goal of behavior therapy.

Systematic desensitization may very well be the most thoroughly researched intervention in the history of therapy, as it has been the focus of hundreds of empirical studies (Emmelkamp, 1982). Although most of these studies are in agreement about the effectiveness of systematic desensitization in treating anxiety and phobias, little consensus has developed concerning the mechanism or process by which the procedure produces its therapeutic effects. For instance, relaxation training may not be a necessary condition for effective treatment (Marks, 1975). A number of studies have shown exposure to the fear hierarchy to be effective by itself, without any effort to bring about relaxation in the client (Goldfried & Goldfried, 1977; Ladouceur, 1978). But the story gets even stranger still, for neither is it necessary for clients to be exposed to the feared stimulus gradually to achieve therapeutic benefits. Exposure to those stimuli at the top of the hierarchy (most feared) is often sufficient to bring about an eventual reduction in phobic behavior (Clark, 1963; Geer & Katkin, 1966). This presents a rather interesting puzzle. On the one hand, there is little doubt that systematic desensitization is among the most effective tools in the behavior therapy arsenal. But if neither relaxation nor gradual exposure is necessary to its effectiveness, what is it about systematic desensitization that makes it work? The answer, it turns out, was right under Pavlov's nose, and the eventual development of additional techniques for treating phobias would help solve the riddle.

Flooding and Exposure Therapies   Therapeutic procedures in which clients are exposed directly to the feared stimulus and without previous relaxation training are referred to as **flooding**, or *exposure,* therapies. Flooding (also called *implosive therapy*) was first introduced by Stampfl (Stampfl & Levis,1968) and was theoretically based on Pavlovian extinction. Remember that extinction involves presentation of a CS repeatedly, but without the US. In the case of phobias, the feared stimulus (perhaps a snake) is viewed as a conditioned stimulus that has acquired the ability to provoke anxiety. By presenting this stimulus repeatedly or continuously, and preventing the occurrence of any negative US (being bitten by the snake), the anxiety reaction to the CS (snake) should diminish over time. A major distinction between flooding and desensitization is that in flooding the feared stimulus is presented at full strength, not in gradual steps (hierarchy). It is in fact the goal of flooding to produce strong anxiety at the outset and to allow this anxiety to diminish over time.

flooding phobia treatment in which a feared stimulus (CS) is presented at full strength without relaxation

A good deal of research shows flooding to be an effective treatment for phobias, in some cases even superior to systematic desensitization (Boudewyns & Wilson, 1972; Marshall, Gauthier, Christie, Currie, & Gordon, 1977). However, length of exposure is a critical feature in flooding, and numerous studies show that the effectiveness of the treatment often hinges on this variable. The client's discomfort wouldn't plummet immediately upon being presented with a stimulus that has, perhaps for many years, provoked extreme anxiety. When using exposure therapies, it is absolutely essential to continue exposure for a period sufficient to bring about reduced anxiety. Although the therapeutically effective duration of exposure will differ from client to client, and from one type of phobia to another, numerous studies attest to the fact that longer exposure durations are generally superior to shorter durations (Foa & Chambless, 1978; Stern & Marks, 1973).

To understand why both systematic desensitization and flooding- or exposure-based therapies effectively reduce phobic symptoms, let's consider what elements these strategies have in common. Since all of these procedures were inspired by work on Pavlovian conditioning, it would be prudent to ask whether all of the therapeutic procedures share some dimension of this basic conditioning paradigm. Sure enough, such a commonality exists. It turns out, all behavioral therapies aimed at reducing fear or anxiety do so through one essential strategy: exposure to the feared stimulus. Although they do this in different ways, either gradually or all at once, both systematic desensitization and flooding therapy require continued exposure to the CS. Assuming that nothing untoward happens to the client during this exposure—such as being bitten by a snake or, in the case of the automobile accident victim, having another accident in the same intersection—then exposure amounts to Pavlovian extinction—repeated or continuous presentation of the CS by itself. Thus, extinction seems to be the basic conditioning principle that unifies these procedurally disparate treatments.

Of course, there can be many variations on a basic theme, and exposure can vary along dimensions other than gradual versus maximum presentation. One of the more interesting and practical questions concerning the procedure is whether exposure to the actual object must occur in real time (referred to as *in vivo*) or if therapeutic benefits can accrue through imaginary or visualized presentations. Imagine the difficulty behavior therapists would face if they had to possess or have easy access to all of the potential stimuli—snakes, spiders, blood, farm implements (the list goes on forever)—that provoked fear in their clients. If clients could generate vivid visual images of the object and personal interactions with the object, and if such images provoked anxiety similar to that attending to the actual object, then perhaps therapy could progress without actual exposure.

A considerable amount of research has been devoted to this issue, and many studies have been conducted pitting in vivo exposure against imagined exposure. Unlike the contentious nature of studies comparing systematic desensitization and flooding, this research seems to point overwhelmingly toward the greater therapeutic effectiveness of in vivo exposure (Emmelkamp & Wessels, 1975; Johnston et al., 1976; Stern & Marks, 1973). Actual exposure may prove more effective for several reasons, not the least of which is the variation of clients' ability to visualize the feared stimulus or event. Some people are much better at creating realistic and vivid "pictures in the head." And don't forget that clinical treatment would require that the client be exposed continuously to the feared stimulus. This means that the client must be able to produce a sufficient visual image as well as maintain the strength of this image for the duration of the treatment session. This may be an unreasonable requirement for many clients. Fortunately, a recent technological innovation could prove to be an interesting solution to this problem.

Virtual Reality: The Future of Anxiety Treatment? Technological advances have a way of making themselves known in almost every human endeavor, and such developments are especially visible in health care. It may have occurred to you that one additional way to get around the logistical difficulty of maintaining an inventory of fearful objects is to be able to artificially induce perceptions of such objects in the client. Enter the new world of virtual reality (Figure 3.6). With sophisticated computer programming and specialized equipment, it is possible to create amazingly realistic, though

FIGURE 3.6 Virtual Reality Technology.

nonexistent, sensory experiences, thus making it unnecessary to rely upon the imagery abilities of any particular client. Recently, researchers and clinicians have begun using this remarkable technology to help bridge the gap between in vivo and imaginal exposure strategies. Using virtual reality exposure (VRE), Carlin, Hoffman, and Weghorst (1997) treated a 37-year-old woman suffering from a spider phobia. Twelve 1-hour sessions of VRE were conducted over 3 months, and both behavioral and self-report measures of anxiety revealed substantial reduction in symptoms over the course of therapy. Clients suffering from fear of flying have also been shown to derive as much therapeutic benefit from VRE as from traditional exposure therapy (Rothbaum, Hodges, Smith, Lee, & Price, 2000).

Similar findings have been reported for the treatment of acrophobia (fear of heights) in a 19-year-old male (Rothbaum, Hodges, & Kooper, 1997) and post-traumatic stress disorder (PTSD) in a Vietnam combat veteran (Rothbaum et al., 1999). Keep in mind that the use of virtual reality technology in no way alters the underlying principles that lead to therapeutic effectiveness, as long as the virtual stimuli produce the same kind of emotional effect as would the real thing. So far, research does seem to suggest that clients perceive the stimuli as authentic and realistic, despite an intellectual understanding that the objects are not truly present. This means that for all intents and purposes, VRE can be conceptualized as a type of exposure therapy. Only the manner in which the feared stimulus is presented is different. In the same manner, antibiotic medication works because of the chemical properties of the medicine, not according to whether it is introduced into the body orally or through injection.

When all is said and done, exposure to the feared stimulus is clearly the "active ingredient" in behavioral treatments of anxiety, though the method of exposure can vary considerably without compromising the therapeutic effect. VRE emerges as the most recent version of this general approach, and the recent success of VRE in several case studies suggests that virtual and in vivo exposure may be functionally equivalent. Moreover, the VRE technology clearly boasts an advantage both logistically and in terms of cost effectiveness (Rothbaum, Hodges, & Kooper, 1997).

✖ INTERIM SUMMARY

Research on the Pavlovian origins of emotional behavior began with the regrettable conditioning of a fear in an 11-month-old child, Little Albert. Soon after this experiment, however, researchers successfully used the same principles to eliminate phobias. Mary Cover Jones's treatment of Peter, and Joseph Wolpe's development of systematic desensitization, signaled the beginning of behavior therapy—clinical interventions based on fundamental principles of learning. All Pavlovian-based therapies for anxiety disorders have as their common element exposure of the client to the feared conditioned stimulus (CS). Several methods of exposure have been studied, including actual (in vivo) exposure to the feared stimulus, imaginal exposure, and, most recently, virtual exposure using the technology of virtual reality.

✖ THOUGHT QUESTIONS

1. How would you go about discovering whether Little Albert's fear had generalized to stimuli other than the white rat? If it had, why would this be problematic for Albert?

2. What kind of fear hierarchy would you create for someone who has a fear of elevators? Which of these stimuli would you present if using flooding to treat the fear?

Operant Conditioning and Reinforcement

Brenda, a 15-year-old high school student, experiences an ambivalent flush of terror and excitement as she works desperately to bring the mechanical monster under control. The instrument panel is a confusing array of fluorescent hieroglyphs, each telling a story Brenda can hardly comprehend. Movements of feet and hands must be made smoothly, in coordinated sequences, and often quickly in response to the constantly changing stimulation reaching her eyes and ears. Too much movement here, too little there, or any at all made out of step with the rapidly changing environment, and Brenda's future mobility, not to mention her self-esteem, will be severely compromised. Brenda, you see, is engaged in a rite of passage much anticipated by adolescents and lamented by parents: She's learning to drive.

If you have been a licensed driver for several years, you might find it difficult to empathize with Brenda. Her anxiety about driving may seem unjustified. After all, you probably give little thought to the mechanics of driving. Indeed, those of us who have been doing it for years devote little attention to the process of driving; the routine has become nearly automatic. The fact that many of us spend our time behind the wheel engaged in other pursuits, such as searching for a radio station or changing CDs, finding a suitable perch for our coffee cup, daydreaming, or holding a conversation, either with a passenger or on a cell phone, attests to the fact that driving is a behavior that, once learned, seems to unfold unconsciously. But it was not always this way. With the passing of years, we tend to forget that we were once neophytes, sitting behind the wheel, perhaps paralyzed by fear, awaiting instruction from parent or driving instructor, and convinced that we would never obtain our driver's license.

Though it may be hard to convince you, driving is actually a highly skilled behavior, requiring a good deal of vigilance to your surroundings and relatively fine coordination of movements of different muscles in your body. It is most assuredly not a fixed-action pattern, as the automobile is a relatively recent invention, and evolutionary change would not have had nearly enough time to hardwire this kind of behavior into the human nervous system. And although there may be some elements of Pavlovian conditioning involved, driving would seem to be much more than simply a collection of conditioned reflexes. In fact, the business of learning to drive requires not only attending to stimulus events in the environment that may signal other important events, but also attending to how your own behavior influences some of these events. In other words, a good deal of the stimulation that arises while you drive is directly related to your actual movements: whether you stepped on the brake or the gas, whether you turned the steering wheel to the left or to the right, or whether you shifted the transmission into drive or reverse.

Fortunately for Brenda, and the rest of us blessed with an open genetic system, each movement we make while driving, from stomping on the gas to turning the wheel sharply to the right, produces a noticeable consequence. This consequence can be very useful as feedback, in that it tells us whether we did the right thing or the wrong thing. We take advantage of such feedback, knowingly or not, and adjust our behavior accordingly. Thus, much of the learning we do is owing to the fact that we are sensitive to the consequences of our behavior, and this kind of learning is different in important ways from the learning discussed in the previous chapter. As it turns out, paying attention to the consequences of behavior has implications for everything we do, from driving a car to playing a video game, from holding a conversation to figuring a math problem. For this and other reasons, scientists have been studying this form of learning for well over a hundred years. Let's take a look at two of the more influential psychologists whose work emphasized the role that consequences play in adaptive behavior.

THE DISCOVERY OF OPERANT CONDITIONING

As mentioned in the previous chapter, Pavlov didn't really *discover* the conditioned reflex in a formal sense. Rather, he was the first to subject it to systematic laboratory study and consequently to identify many factors that determined its expression. Similarly, no single scientist can be credited with identifying the role that consequences play in learning, for people have probably always been generally aware of this relationship. It doesn't take a psychologist to predict that the family pet who is fed scraps following family meals will become an accomplished beggar, showing up faithfully during mealtimes. In addition, parents have probably always known that children will repeat behaviors that bring them positive attention from adults, hence the proverb, You catch more flies with honey than vinegar. Nevertheless, two prominent American psychologists led the way in placing this familiar phenomenon "under the microscope," and their work stimulated both large programs of basic research and applied interventions that remain influential today.

Thorndike and the Law of Effect

At the turn of the 20th century, Edward L. Thorndike (1874–1949) was among America's more celebrated psychologists. He may, in fact, be one of the discipline's most prolific writers, having authored more than 500 profes-

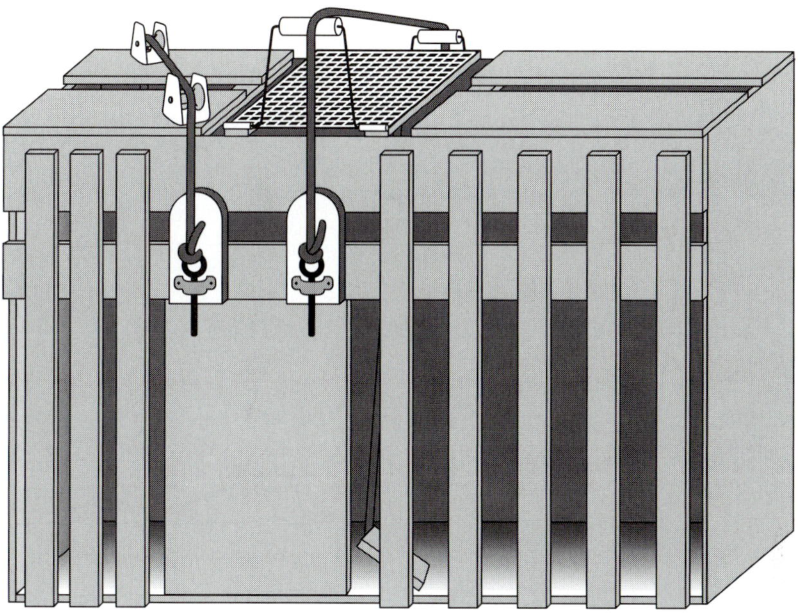

FIGURE 4.1
Thorndike's
Puzzle Box.

sional articles and books during a long and distinguished career at Columbia University. During his years as a doctoral student and throughout his professional career, Thorndike remained fascinated by the question of intelligence in both humans and nonhumans. In fact, his early experiments, carried out in William James's basement at Harvard, studied how chicks learned to negotiate simple mazes, which Thorndike constructed by placing books on end on a table. Later, Thorndike would expand his interest in problem solving and intelligent behavior in studies of cats, dogs, monkeys, and human beings.

One of Thorndike's more celebrated research programs utilized an apparatus referred to as a puzzle box, as depicted in Figure 4.1. Cats were placed inside the box, which was equipped with a rope attached at one end to the box's door and at the other to a pedal inside the box. Outside the box, and well within smelling range, Thorndike would place a tasty morsel, such as a bit of tuna. The question Thorndike had about animal intelligence and problem solving was a simple one: How long would it take the animal to discover how to get out of the box (by pressing the pedal attached to the rope), and would this amount of time change with additional attempts or trials? Thorndike began an experimental trial by placing the animal inside the box, then setting a timer to keep track of how long the animal took to escape from the box. As you might guess, animals often spent some time in the box during the first few trials. As the experiment progressed, though, Thorndike's cats spent less and less time in the box. That is, with experience, they learned to escape quite rapidly. Thorndike may have been among the first psychologists to quantify a learning curve, as represented in Figure 4.2, which plots the amount of time to escape as a function of number of trials.

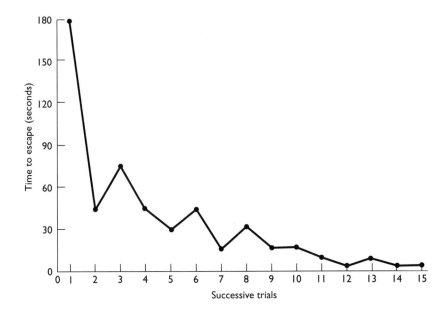

FIGURE 4.2 Typical Learning Curve in Thorndike's Puzzle-Box Experiments. (Adapted from Thorndike, 1911.)

Thorndike paid close attention to what his animals did during the experiment, and he observed some impressive regularities in their actions as they solved the puzzle-box problem. Thorndike's cats, for instance, often spent much of the first trial meandering and exploring the box, as any animal might do when placed in an unfamiliar environment. Such exploring would eventually lead, perhaps by accident, to physical contact with the pedal and an open door leading to freedom. In subsequent trials, less time would be spent engaged in aimless wandering, and more of the animal's time would be directed toward that part of the box containing the pedal. Because activity near the pedal, including actually stepping on the device, was associated with escaping the box, Thorndike observed that these behaviors increased or occurred with greater frequency over time. These observations led Thorndike to formalize a fundamental principle of behavior that achieved rather grand status in the psychology of learning while simultaneously fueling the research careers of some of the discipline's more notable scientists. Thorndike (1911) stated his principle, known as the **law of effect,** as follows:

law of effect
Thorndike's formulation that behavior that produces satisfying consequences will be repeated, and behavior that produces dissatisfying consequences will not be repeated

> Of several responses made to the same situation, those which are accompanied or closely followed by satisfaction to the animal will, other things being equal, be more firmly connected with the situation . . . those which are accompanied or closely followed by discomfort to the animal will, other things being equal, have their connections with that situation weakened. (p. 24)

Whatever else it may have accomplished, the law of effect drew attention to the fact that the consequences of a behavior are important because they affect future occurrences of the behavior. Thorndike also posited some ancillaries, or additional learning principles, that affected the strength of these behavior-consequence connections, some of which are described in Table 4.1.

TABLE 4.1 ADDITIONAL LAWS FORMULATED BY E. L. THORNDIKE AS ANCILLARIES TO LAW OF EFFECT

Ancillary	Definition
Law of readiness	This principle is similar to the notion of biological preparedness and suggests that certain behaviors may be more easily conditioned than others (such as key pecking in pigeons)
Law of exercise	The idea that simple repetition of a behavior will lead to strengthening
Law of attitude	Previous experiences, such as learning or deprivation, that may influence the ability of some event (food) to affect strength of learning
Law of response by analogy	Similar to response generalization; the idea that animals will behave in one situation as they have behaved in similar situations

Thorndike did not consider the law of effect to operate according to any mental reasoning or special cognitive ability on the part of the organism. Indeed, he viewed the learning process as one in which new connections are "stamped in" in nearly automatic fashion, without awareness on the part of the individual. Thorndike would be challenged on this and other views, and the law of effect and its supporting postulates would be modified throughout his long career (Bower & Hilgard, 1981). Nevertheless, for the young science of psychology, Thorndike's formulation was heralded as an important step toward systematically identifying behavioral laws. The law of effect would eventually be championed by a large and influential group of experimental psychologists, among them, B. F. Skinner.

Skinner and the Operant

Recall from Chapter 1, B. F. Skinner (Figure 4.3) graduated from college with a degree in English, and following a disappointing attempt at a literary career, enrolled in graduate study in psychology at Harvard. Though having no formal background in psychology, Skinner quickly established himself as an ambitious and brash young student, largely unimpressed with the psychology being taught at Harvard. He felt that much of what passed as psychology was simply armchair philosophy and idle speculation about the mysteries of the mind. Consequently, Skinner was drawn to the writings of Pavlov, whose work reflected the experimental rigor of the natural sciences, and to the philosophical pronouncements of John B. Watson, the iconoclastic American psychologist who declared psychology to be an objective science of behavior. Skinner's commitment to constructing his own brand of scientific psychology is apparent in a letter written to friends while in graduate school, in which he claimed ". . . my fundamental interests lie in the field of Psychology, and I shall probably continue therein, even, if necessary, by making over the entire field to suit myself" (1979, p. 38).

FIGURE 4.3
B. F. Skinner.

As an American psychologist interested in learning, Skinner was aware of Thorndike's research and his formulation of the law of effect. But Skinner took exception to Thorndike's methodology and the language he employed in describing the learning process. Skinner was of the opinion that by handling his cats at the beginning of each experimental trial, Thorndike might have been unintentionally affecting their behavior and, consequently, the validity of his experimental results. In an effort to resolve this problem, Skinner put his talents as an amateur engineer to work and set about building various experimental chambers, culminating with an apparatus similar to that depicted in Figure 4.4. Originally designed for rats, the chamber allowed the animal to be continuously housed throughout the duration of the experiment. By pressing a lever protruding from one of the chamber's walls, the animal could cause a food pellet to be delivered into the chamber through a tube connected to an external food supply. Thus, the animal could remain in the chamber for indefinite periods of time, and experimental conditions could be programmed by the experimenter without any disruption of the animal's behavior.

In essence, Skinner had created an environment in which Thorndike's law of effect could be studied as it continuously had an impact on the animal, rather than through the discrete trials strategy employed by Thorndike. Keep in mind that despite the differences in apparatus and subjects used, Skinner and Thorndike were both investigating the role that consequences play in the learning process.

Consistent with his aspiration to pursue an objective, natural science of behavior, Skinner declared Thorndike's language sloppy and misleading.

FIGURE 4.4 Operant Chamber.

References to such emotional states as "satisfaction" and "discomfort" were unfortunate, Skinner claimed, because they alluded to private, inaccessible feelings in nonhuman animals whose mental lives could hardly be verified by the experimenter. What was objective and proper subject matter for a science of behavior were the specific behavioral and environmental events that unfolded in the experimental space. It was these, Skinner argued, that a scientific account should emphasize. The lever press was an easily observed and quantified activity, as was the resulting delivery of food, and orderly relationships between these variables could be examined without recourse to the animal's "inner world."

Skinner reasoned that the law of effect referred to a different kind of learning than was studied by Pavlov. In fact, Skinner's doctoral dissertation at Harvard was in part devoted to teasing apart the different kinds of relationships being studied by learning psychologists. He proposed that Pavlov was interested in one type of learning, called *Type S,* in which the organism learns about the predictable relationship between two stimulus events (US and CS). In Pavlovian conditioning, the animal's behavior (the conditioned reflex) occurs only after the repeated pairing of US and CS and the occurrence of the CR marks the end of an experimental trial. On the other hand, research into the law of effect seemed to be focusing on the connection between an organism's behavior and consequential stimuli, which Skinner called *Type R* learning. That is, both Thorndike and Skinner seemed to be emphasizing stimuli that *followed* the organism's response. Indeed, escaping Thorndike's puzzle box or receiving food in Skinner's apparatus only happened if the organism engaged in a particular behavior. To further designate

operant behavior that operates on the environment to produce consequences

this specific form of learning, Skinner coined the term **operant,** because this kind of behavior *operates* on the environment to produce consequences. For this reason, Skinner termed his experimental apparatus an *operant chamber,* though it has for many years been widely referred to as a Skinner box.

✖ INTERIM SUMMARY

The initial study of operant learning can be traced to the work of two American psychologists, Edward Thorndike and B. F. Skinner. Thorndike's research utilized a wooden puzzle box, in which cats were placed at the beginning of an experimental trial. By pressing on a pedal inside the box, the animals could escape the box to obtain food outside. Thorndike observed that his subjects learned to escape through a process in which effective behaviors were "stamped in" according to the law of effect. Skinner refined Thorndike's methodology by creating the operant chamber, an experimental apparatus in which the animal could remain continuously housed during an experiment. Rats pressed levers inside the operant chamber, resulting in delivery of food pellets to the animal. Skinner referred to this kind of behavior as operant behavior and maintained that it was a different kind of learning than was studied by Pavlov.

✖ THOUGHT QUESTIONS

1. Why is Brenda's behavior in the opening vignette operant behavior? Describe some examples of specific actions she might take while driving and their potential consequences.
2. If you observed one of Thorndike's cats escaping from the puzzle box, you might be tempted to say that the cat had a "desire" to escape the box and was "trying to figure out" how to get out of the box. What reservations might Skinner have had concerning your explanation?

THE THREE-TERM CONTINGENCY

As will become increasingly apparent, much of this chapter will draw upon the work of B. F. Skinner, whose contribution to the psychology of learning, and operant behavior in particular, remains monumental. Skinner, in fact, is among the most recognizable names in the history of psychology, joining a very small list of luminaries, including Freud, Pavlov, and Piaget. A study done by Korn, Davis, and Davis (1991) found that Skinner was named by heads of psychology departments as the single most important figure in psychology's history. The range of Skinner's work was impressive, and his contributions came in many forms, as can be seen in Box 4.1. This chapter emphasizes Skinner's experimental work, but this work can't really be appreciated without an understanding of the conceptual framework used by Skinner to talk about and make sense of behavior.

At some point in the historical development of a scientific discipline, members of the discipline must decide how best to approach their subject matter. What are the fundamental units to be studied? How will they talk about these units, and what kind of criteria will be used to distinguish them?

BOX 4.1 / CONTRIBUTIONS OF B. F. SKINNER TO PSYCHOLOGY

Conceptual Contributions

• Radical behaviorism: Skinner's philosophy of science claimed that behavior is a natural phenomenon subject to discoverable cause-effect laws. Among Skinner's more controversial claims was the position that "private events," such as thoughts and images, are no different in principle from publicly observable behavior and can therefore be conceptualized within the framework of the three-term contingency.

• The operant: Skinner coined this term to refer to behavior that operates on the environment to produce consequences. Operant behavior was conceptualized as a functionally different kind of behavior than Pavlov's respondent behavior, and any particular operant is specified by its antecedent and consequent stimuli.

Methodological Contributions

• Skinner championed the study of individual organisms and was strongly opposed to the growing tendency of behavioral researchers to study large groups of subjects, producing "averaged" data that seemed irrelevant to understanding behavioral processes. Indeed, Skinner and his fellow proponents of operant behavior encountered great difficulty getting their experimental work published in standard psychology journals due to editorial practices requiring group designs. In response to this state of affairs, operant researchers established the *Journal of the Experimental Analysis of Behavior* in 1958. Devoted exclusively to publishing research data from individual subjects, *JEAB* has become one of experimental psychology's more prestigious journals.

• Skinner's engineering skills proved especially useful as he began developing various apparatuses to improve the precision of control over experimental events. For an insightful, and often humorous, article tracing the evolution of the operant chamber and cumulative record, see his article "A Case History in Scientific Method" (1956).

Empirical Contributions

• Although Skinner's philosophy of science and popular writings invited the wrath of psychologists and nonpsychologists alike (Wheeler, 1973), his reputation as an experimentalist is unassailable. The research for which he is best known is the work done with colleague Charles Ferster and published in the classic *Schedules of Reinforcement* (Ferster & Skinner, 1957).

(continued)

(continued)

- Near the end of his life, Skinner embarked on a fascinating program of research with colleagues, in which an effort was made to bring about complex behavioral repertoires in pigeons that would ordinarily be considered possible only in human beings (for example, "insight," "self-awareness," "creativity"). Skinner and Epstein were able to demonstrate that through the proper application of behavior principles (shaping, discrimination, etc.), novel behaviors could be produced that invited comparison with those of so-called higher organisms (Epstein, Lanza, & Skinner, 1980; Epstein & Skinner, 1981).

What methods of observation and analysis will prove most useful in studying the subject matter? The study of learning and behavior is no exception, and Skinner essentially began his illustrious career by bringing researchers' attention to the important differences between Pavlovian and operant learning. Just as biologists use the Linnaean classification system to differentiate between species, so too must psychologists decide how to classify behavior in ways that prove empirically or theoretically useful. For Skinner, doing so meant recognizing that behavior always takes place in an environmental context and that this context should serve not only to give behavior its meaning but also to act as the criterion for formally classifying behavior.

To appreciate how important context is to making sense of behavior, consider the following:

- A Labrador retriever stands on its hind feet, placing its front paws on the wall.
- A middle-aged woman describes the difference between meiosis and mitosis.
- A 7-year-old first grader utters the name "Abraham Lincoln."
- A young man approaches the driver of a car and, placing a gun to the window, orders the driver to get out of the car.

How would you interpret each of these behaviors? Do they make inherent sense, or is more information needed to fill in your interpretation? Consider the first example, the dog standing on its hind legs. What is the dog doing? Why would it be standing against the wall? Suppose you were told that the dog was a highly trained animal and that it was standing against the wall of an elevator, pressing the UP button in response to its disabled owner's verbal request? Now does the behavior make more sense to you? In the second instance, would your interpretation of the woman's behavior change if you knew that she was a college professor delivering a lecture to a biology class? In the third example, suppose you were to learn that the child was responding to the teacher's request to name the 16th president of the United States? Finally, in the last example, imagine that the behavior being described represents a scene from a popular television show.

In each of these cases, knowing something about the circumstances in which the behavior occurs gives the behavior some meaning or substance that it may not have had by itself. In fact, the meaning of each behavior described above can be shifted dramatically simply by changing the conditions surrounding the behavior. Suppose, for instance, that the woman discussing the difference between meiosis and mitosis was doing so at the corner of a busy downtown intersection, not in a college classroom. Would this change your interpretation of her behavior? Or imagine encountering the last scenario as you walked to school. Would you respond differently to observing a man with a gun approach a car than if you saw the same behavior on television? Notice that in these examples, the behavior remains identical to that described in the original scenarios. The only thing that has changed are the circumstances, or the context, in which behavior occurs.

Skinner was so convinced that context was crucial to understanding behavior that he developed a system for classifying behavior based exclusively on context, not on the physical properties of the behavior itself. This classification system he called the **three-term contingency**, and it referred to antecedent stimulus events, behavior, and consequent stimulus events. The three-term contingency is often called the ABCs (*Antecedents, Behaviors, Consequences*) of behavior, and this often proves a useful strategy for remembering the elements of the contingency. As conceptualized by Skinner, the three-term contingency looks something like this:

$$S: R \Rightarrow S$$

The first S in this model represents the antecedent stimuli that are present when a behavior occurs. For instance, in one of the examples above, the antecedent stimulus is a teacher asking a student to name the 16th president of the United States. In response to this antecedent stimulus, the student says, "Abraham Lincoln." The child's answer represents behavior, thus it is the R (response) in the three-term contingency. The response *produces* (hence, the directional arrow) a consequential stimulus, represented by the second S in the sequence above. In the student example, a nod of approval or verbal praise may represent the consequential stimulus. According to Skinner, all operant behavior can be conceptualized in this way, and doing so brings a certain clarity and economy to classifying an otherwise unmanageably complex and confusing subject matter. Because the three-term contingency plays such a critical role in Skinner's analysis of operant behavior, and because much of what follows in this chapter derives from this conceptualization, it might be useful to consider each component in detail.

three-term contingency conceptual system for classifying behavior in relation to antecedent and consequent stimuli

Antecedent Stimuli

To *antecede* means to precede, or come before, and in the three-term contingency an antecedent stimulus is an environmental event that precedes the behavior of interest. Of course, no behavior occurs in an environmental vacuum, and that means that numerous sources of stimulation may serve as antecedent stimuli. In the examples listed earlier, antecedents include such things as the request "Up" from the dog's owner and the question "Who was the 16th president of the United States?" If you take a close look at almost any behavior, from the very simple to the complex, you will be able to

TABLE 4.2 EVERYDAY EXAMPLES OF THE THREE-TERM CONTINGENCY

Antecedent	Behavior	Consequence
"Walk" crosswalk sign illuminated	Walk across street	Arrive safely across street
Internet server request for "Password"	Type in password	Gain access to Internet
Waiter asks, "Can I get you a drink?"	Request ice tea	Receive ice tea
Brewing cycle completes on coffeemaker	Pour coffee	Drink fresh cup of coffee
Computer Print icon illuminates	Click on OK	Paper prints
Trolley pulls up to curb and stops	Step on trolley	Ride to desired location

identify antecedent stimuli that seem pretty obviously connected to the behavior. For instance, you don't normally pick up a telephone and say, "Hello," unless it has rung first. If you're trying to type a term paper on your computer, it won't make much sense for you to begin typing while the computer is still booting up. Instead, you'll probably wait until the word processing program is loaded and visible on your monitor. And, if while driving to work you spy flashing lights in your rearview mirror, you'll likely pull off to the side of the road and slow down or stop.

There are few limitations concerning which events in the environment can function as antecedent stimuli. Obviously the stimulus must be heard, seen, smelled, touched, or tasted by the individual involved; that is, it must be of sufficient energy to excite a sensory receptor. Antecedents can be simple, such as the command "Up" uttered by the dog's owner, or more complex, such as the instruction to "turn left at the third light after the hardware store" given to a pizza delivery driver. You will recall that in Pavlovian conditioning, only some stimuli present in one's environment come to function as conditioned stimuli. Similarly, which particular stimuli in a given environment will function as antecedents for operant behavior is also determined by other components of the three-term contingency, and this will be addressed in more detail in subsequent sections. Some examples of potential antecedents and their related behavioral and consequential components can be seen in Table 4.2.

Behavior

By now, it is established that behavior is the primary subject matter of psychology, and the psychology of learning is particularly concerned with changes in behavior that result from experience. But behavior is an enormously complex subject matter that varies across an almost unlimited number of dimensions. This variability is evident even in the handful of examples provided earlier. Pressing an elevator button is a fairly discrete, simple behavior, taking little time to occur. On the other hand, describing the difference between meiosis and mitosis can be time-consuming and involve considerable subtleties of language. For Skinner (1938), "Behavior is what an organism is *doing* . . ." (p. 6), and this encompasses a class of nearly infinite events. Although for research purposes the behavior of interest is likely to be something easily observed and recorded (such as dogs salivating or rats pressing levers), observable and objective events do not exhaust the concept of behavior. In fact, although Skinner was widely misunderstood on this issue (Catania, 1991; Todd & Morris, 1992), he considered private activity, such as thinking and imagining, to be behavior as well, and therefore subject to the same kind of analysis as more publicly verifiable behavior.

Many properties of behavior have been the focus of study in the psychology of learning, and the relevance of any one of these will differ depending upon the goals of the experiment or even the theoretical position of the researcher. Pavlov measured the quantity of saliva secreted or the rapidity with which a leg was withdrawn in response to electric shock. Moreover, he was especially interested in the speed with which a conditioned reflex could be measured, as indicated by the number of CS-US trials needed to produce a CR. Thorndike monitored, among other things, how long it took his subjects to escape from the puzzle box, and this metric proved useful in describing learning curves. For Skinner, a major dimension of responding was response rate, as measured by the number of lever presses occurring in a given period of time. As discussed later, Skinner used this basic dimension to uncover some remarkable facts about the sensitivity of behavior to environmental events.

Consequent Stimuli

What set operant learning apart from Pavlovian learning most dramatically, Skinner argued, was the significance of consequent stimuli to operant learning. In Pavlovian learning, little attention is given to anything that happens after the behavior (CR) because the functional aspect of conditioning, the CS-US pairing, occurs prior to behavior. But Thorndike and Skinner both focused on stimulus events that followed behavior. Such events are called consequent stimuli because they are produced by, or occur as a consequence of, behavior. The opening of the puzzle-box door and the delivery of food to the animal inside the operant chamber are consequences that occur only because of some aspect of the subject's behavior. In fact, the essence of the law of effect is that different kinds of consequences either weaken or strengthen the behavior that produces them.

Although the law of effect drew proper attention to the role of consequences in the learning process, Skinner felt that a scientific treatment of this topic required a more precise language than offered by Thorndike. Although experimenters cannot directly tune into the degree of "satisfaction" or "annoyance" felt by a subject, be it human or nonhuman, they can observe directly the effects of particular consequences on behavior. Whatever their emotional impact, consequences tend either to strengthen or weaken behavior, and this can be determined by monitoring such aspects as the frequency or probability of the behavior over time. An important contribution of Skinner's work was a technical language for describing these effects. Consequent stimuli that increase the strength or probability of a behavior are called **reinforcers**, and the process of delivering these stimuli contingent on behavior is known as *reinforcement*. Reinforcing stimuli, however, come in many different guises, and over the years Skinner and others have suggested certain rules for classifying or distinguishing between different kinds of reinforcers. Like most taxonomies, not all reinforcers seem to fall readily into one category, but, for the most part, this method of delineation has held up among operant psychologists.

reinforcers
consequent stimuli that strengthen or increase the behavior on which they are made contingent

Primary and Conditioned Reinforcers   Both Skinner's rats and Thorndike's cats received food as the reinforcer for engaging in the appropriate behavior. Because of its obvious biological importance, food is an effective reinforcer when made contingent on behavior, and this is especially true when an animal is deprived of food before an experiment, a common practice in studies of operant behavior. Other stimuli that have significant implications for survival, including water and protection from the elements, can be used as reinforcers for the same reason. Such stimuli are often referred to as **primary reinforcers** because their ability to reinforce behavior would seem to be innately determined as a result of phylogenetic variables, as explained in the first chapter of this book. Not surprisingly, food and water have been utilized most frequently in operant learning experiments with nonhuman animals, in part because it is easy to establish deprivation of these items and they are relatively easy to deliver contingent on behavior. Although these kinds of reinforcers may be equally powerful in influencing human behavior, operant studies with humans seldom use primary reinforcers because of the larger ethical issues that surround the practice of depriving humans of such essential stimuli.

primary reinforcers
stimuli that possess reinforcing properties because of their biological significance

In studies of human operant behavior, reinforcers vary across a wide range of stimuli, including bonus points on a computer game, money, and course-related extra credit (Galizio & Buskist, 1988; Lattal & Perone, 1998; Pilgrim, 1998). The capacity of these stimuli to act as reinforcing consequences, however, seems to depend upon experience rather than on any innate biological feature. After all, money only has value within the context of an economy and, even then, only to those who understand that it can be exchanged for other things. Similarly, extra credit may be a satisfactory incentive for college students, but it would have little utility in the workplace. Because these kinds of stimuli acquire their reinforcing properties as a result of experience or because of indirect connection to primary reinforcers, they are called **secondary** or **conditioned reinforcers**. Conditioned reinforcers are pervasive in the human environment and may in fact be responsible for a good deal more behavior than are primary reinforcers. The look of approval on a parent's face, a grade of A+ on a term paper, advancing to the next level in a video game, or the sound of a favorite song can all function as conditioned reinforcers.

secondary (conditioned) reinforcers
stimuli that acquire reinforcing properties through experience or association with primary reinforcers

Whether speaking of primary or conditioned reinforcers, remember that reinforcers are defined according to their effects on behavior, not according to whether they improve one's emotional state—though they may have this effect as well. Receiving an A+ on a paper may feel good, but not all reinforcers have this effect. For instance, when you turn the ignition key in your car, the engine starts—assuming the car is in good condition. (If the engine never turned over when you turned the key, there would be little reason for you to engage in this behavior.) Although the engine turning over doesn't make any contribution to your emotional well-being, it is a reinforcing consequence to the extent that you continue turning your ignition key when you get into your car. Thus, the technical language employed by operant researchers allows for the consistent classification of consequent stimuli based on observable properties of behavior. Although his ideas regarding behavior drew more than their share of criticism, Skinner's terminological clarity was a rare accomplishment in psychology, and the study of operant behavior has long benefited from a language that lives up to its rigorous experimental methods.

Positive and Negative Reinforcement   Another dimension of reinforcing consequences has to do with precisely *how* the reinforcing event is made contingent on behavior. Because many studies of operant behavior utilize non-human animals and operant chambers, and because the logistics of doing so were long ago worked out by Skinner and others, reinforcement usually consists of the *delivery* or *presentation* to the animal of some primary reinforcer, such as food or water, contingent on a lever press or key peck. When a stimulus is presented to the organism contingent on behavior, and when this behavior-consequence contingency results in an increase or strengthening of the response, the process is called **positive reinforcement**, and the stimulus itself (in this case, food) is a *positive reinforcer*. Both primary reinforcers, such as food and water, and conditioned reinforcers, such as money or praise, may be presented contingent on behavior, in which case the procedure would be designated positive reinforcement. Positive reinforcement dominates both the basic and applied literatures in operant psychology because arranging for the presentation of stimuli dependent on behavior is usually fairly simple mechanically.

positive reinforcement process by which response-contingent presentation of a stimulus increases the probability of the behavior

Sometimes behavior results in the removal or reduction of a stimulus, and if this contingency increases the probability of the behavior, then isn't this reinforcement as well? It certainly is, at least according to the language of reinforcement. When the response-contingent removal of a stimulus leads to an increase in the behavior, **negative reinforcement** has occurred. Although this contingency may seem a bit strange when viewed in the abstract, it can be readily seen in many everyday behaviors. If you're on the phone making an important business call, and at that precise moment your sister decides to blast her stereo, a number of reactions on your part may come to mind. You may simply call out to your sister, asking her to turn down the music. Or perhaps you would shut the door separating her room from the room where you are talking on the phone. In either case, your

negative reinforcement process by which response-contingent removal of a stimulus increases the probability of the behavior

behavior will likely lead to a reduction, or perhaps even removal, of the loud music. Now, loud music may not be inherently obnoxious to you; you may in fact actually enjoy some of your sister's music. But under the circumstances, the music is undesirable and you would like to do something to diminish it. That is, the music presently is an **aversive stimulus** because you are motivated to avoid it or escape from it. Negative reinforcement occurs whenever a response or behavior is strengthened because it produces escape or avoidance from an aversive stimulus. Covering your eyes when emerging from a darkened theater following a matinee helps to reduce the aversive nature of bright sunlight. Muting your television whenever a commercial comes on is a behavior made strikingly easy by the modern remote control. Scratching an itch, taking aspirin for a headache, and stepping inside the house during summer to escape oppressive humidity are all potential examples of negative reinforcement.

aversive stimulus
object or event that an
organism is motivated
to avoid or escape

The distinction between positive and negative reinforcement has been with us for a long time, though some have argued that the difference is often meaningless. It is not always clear, even in relatively well-defined laboratory studies, whether the consequent event represents presentation or removal of a stimulus. For example, food is most definitely delivered to the animal inside the operant chamber contingent on lever pressing, so this would seem a clear-cut case of positive reinforcement, right? Suppose, however, that the consequent event in this case was interpreted as the reduction of hunger, which can be viewed as an aversive stimulus. If so, continued lever pressing for food could be conceptualized as negative, not positive, reinforcement. Similarly, is coming in out of the humid outdoors an example of removing the aversive stimulus of humid air, or is the cooler air of an air-conditioned house being presented? As you can see, it is often a toss-up as to whether a consequence should be identified as a presented stimulus or a removed stimulus, and some researchers have recommended that the distinction no longer serves any useful purpose in the language of operant behavior (Michael, 1975). However, due to its historical precedent, this distinction isn't likely to disappear from the literature anytime soon. Perhaps what is more important is to recognize the common functional properties the two processes share. Regardless of whether a stimulus is being presented or removed, both positive and negative reinforcement involve strengthening or maintaining, as opposed to weakening, behavior.

punishment process
by which response-
contingent stimulus
presentation or removal
results in reduction
or elimination of the
response

positive punishment
process by which
response-contingent
presentation of a stimu-
lus decreases the prob-
ability of the behavior

Positive and Negative Punishment It would be a simple matter if all consequences strengthened behavior, but the world doesn't work that way. Some behavior produces consequences that have the opposite effect, that of reducing or even eliminating the behavior. The term **punishment** refers to the process by which consequences produce a reduction in the frequency or strength of a behavior. But, like reinforcement, punishment can be brought about either through the response-contingent *presentation* or *removal* of a stimulus. Thus, the language of punishment mirrors that of reinforcement, although, for the same reasons described for reinforcement, not everybody agrees that this distinction is useful. For those who maintain the distinction, the phrase **positive punishment** (also called *Type I punishment*) refers to instances in which behavior is reduced or eliminated by the response-contingent presentation of an aversive stimulus. In fact, most people probably have positive punishment in mind when they think of punishing contingencies. If an experimenter delivers electric shock to an animal in an operant chamber when it presses a lever, and lever pressing reduces in frequency, then positive punishment has occurred. If a child disrupts class and is reprimanded by the teacher, positive punishment has occurred if the disruptive behavior is suppressed or eliminated. Many pets today are kept inside their yards by way of invisible fencing. If the animal approaches too close to the fence perimeter, an underground wire sends a signal to a receiver on the animal's collar, and the result is a brief electric shock. If the animal no longer approaches the fence's boundary, this particular behavior has been reduced through positive punishment. Of course, manufacturers and vendors of these pet containment systems will, quite understandably, call the aversive stimulus a "correction." It is technically a punisher if its presentation reduces the likelihood that the animal will approach the fence boundary.

The language of punishment can be a significant stumbling block, particularly for students trying to ferret out all the different response-consequence relationships that characterize operant behavior. Several scholars have pointed out that the term *punishment* is problematic in a science because it is not a pure technical term. Operant psychologists did not create the term, as it is a word that appears in ordinary language, and this means that most people use the term in everyday conversation and understand intuitively what other people mean when they use the term. The problem is that, like most words in ordinary language, *punishment* can vary in its referents as a function of context and the person using the term. A parent who has just told his child to go up to his room for yelling at the dinner table may identify this act of discipline as punishment, and people may view a prison sentence as punishment for having committed a particular crime. What is often unclear in such cases is what, precisely, makes each episode an example of punishment. Is it that the authority figure (parent, judge) intends to change the behavior of the offender? In most cases, both the parent and the judge would consider their actions punitive whether or not any substantial change occurred in the behavior of the offender.

It may be that people consider the presentation of an aversive stimulus to be punishment because of some moral or ethical stance about making the offender suffer. For instance, it could be argued that we put criminals in prison as a form of vengeance, with little concern as to whether this will alter their criminal behavior in the future. Perhaps we simply believe that one who misbehaves deserves to encounter aversive stimulation, be it a prison cell or time in one's room. Punishment, according to this view, can be seen as a form of justice doled out by relevant authority figures, but with little concern for bringing about any kind of behavior change.

The word punishment, then, plays havoc in a science of behavior, in part because its lack of precision and specificity of meaning makes it a poor candidate for a technical term. For this reason, operant researchers and behavior therapists have made a special effort to define *punishment* in a way that identifies a specific behavior-consequence operation. Doing so removes some of the idiosyncratic nature of the term as it is used in casual conversation, but it may not entirely eliminate the emotional baggage that accompanies use of the term, particularly in casual conversation. Because the term punishment is used in so many ways and often provokes emotional reactions, Harzem and Miles (1978) proposed the introduction of a new term, *disinforcement.* This term could be used, they argue, in place of *punishment,* and would refer to reductions in response rate or probability as the result of a response-contingent stimulus. As with reinforcement, disinforcement would be defined in a strictly functional manner and would not depend on the intentions of those delivering the stimulus or whether the stimulus was considered pleasant or unpleasant. This proposal has yet to be endorsed by most who work in the field. Certain terms, once introduced and adopted, take on a life of their own, and changing the linguistic repertoires of researchers and professionals often proves to be an ambitious undertaking.

Can you think of situations in which your behavior was reduced as the result of a stimulus being removed contingent on the behavior? If so, then you have probably identified an instance of **negative punishment** (*Type II punishment*). Ordinarily, this kind of punishment results from the loss or removal of a reinforcing stimulus. The inference is that to lose a reinforcing stimulus is, almost by definition, an aversive experience. For example, if I am pulled over by a state trooper and cited for speeding, this will mean a loss of a sizable amount of money. Assuming that money is a conditioned reinforcer, and that I perceive myself as working pretty hard to earn it, then it would almost assuredly be aversive for me to lose it by way of a speeding ticket. Naturally, this is precisely the idea. Fines are ordinarily levied, for speeding or for other violations of the law, in order to reduce or eliminate some undesirable behavior.

Negative punishment contingencies in which previously earned reinforcers or access to reinforcing circumstances are removed contingent on behavior are often referred to as **response cost**. Examples of response cost abound, both in the home and in the world at large. Parents often take away privileges from their children in an effort to punish inappropriate behavior. If taking a video game away from an 8-year-old, or the car keys away from an adolescent, results in the reduction of the targeted undesirable behavior (tantrums, aggression, etc.), then the response cost contingency has led to punishment of the behavior. An especially common use of response cost, particularly in schools, day care, and other institutional settings is the practice of **time-out**. The term time-out is actually an abbreviation of the phrase "time out from positive reinforcement." A surprising fact is that *time-out* actually emerged as a procedural element of stimulus control experiments with pigeons in the late 1950s. In such experiments, differential reinforcement was used to bring the pecking behavior of the birds under control of variously colored lights. If a bird responded to the wrong stimulus light, the entire experimental chamber was darkened, and no grain reinforcement was available for a predetermined period of time. This nonreinforcement interval, or time-out from positive reinforcement, proved an effective punisher for incorrect key pecks.

negative punishment process by which response-contingent removal of a stimulus decreases the probability of behavior

response cost negative punishment procedure in which previously earned reinforcers are removed contingent on behavior

time-out response cost procedure in which behavior leads to a period during which reinforcement is not available.

| | Consequent Stimulus | |
	Presented	Removed
Increased response rate	Positive reinforcement	Negative reinforcement
Decreased response rate	Positive punishment	Negative punishment

FIGURE 4.5 Response-Consequence Contingencies.

It is often difficult for students to keep all of the potential reinforcement and punishment contingencies straight in their minds. No doubt much of the confusion derives from the fact that the contingencies share certain fundamental features. For instance, both *positive* and *negative reinforcement* are contingencies that strengthen or maintain behavior. Conversely, both *positive* and *negative punishment* serve to reduce the probability of behavior. In addition, the two kinds of operations, reinforcement and punishment, are distinguished based on the presentation or removal of a stimulus. It is not surprising that students find it hard to separate one kind of contingency from another or to recognize which kind of contingency characterizes a bit of behavior in the real world. Figure 4.5 depicts the four reinforcement-punishment contingencies in a simple 2×2 matrix. The matrix takes into consideration the two major features that are the basis for classifying any behavior-consequence contingency: whether a stimulus was presented or removed contingent on the response, and whether the response subsequently increased or decreased in strength or probability.

The Premack Principle: Access to Behavior as Reinforcement

Students often view the concept of reinforcement as simplistic, perhaps in part because much of the basic research in operant behavior has involved studies of rats and pigeons responding for food reinforcement in operant chambers. But there is much more to operant behavior than this, just as there is more to Pavlovian conditioning than salivating dogs. For example, as mentioned earlier, any comprehensive list of reinforcing stimuli would be enormous because it would have to include many kinds of both primary and conditioned reinforcers. Moreover, reinforcing stimuli show tremendous variability across species and even individuals. Even if it were possible to identify all of these stimuli, there is more to the concept of reinforcement. It turns out that one of the more pervasive reinforcers is not a stimulus at all, but the opportunity to engage in a specific behavior.

An experimental psychologist named David Premack studied the complex relationships that develop between different responses in organisms placed in a *multiresponse environment*. Premack placed rats in experimental chambers that were designed to support the following behaviors: (1) drinking,

(2) eating, (3) running in an exercise wheel, and (4) paper shredding (a popular activity for rodents). His first objective was simply to observe the animals over long experimental sessions, noting how their behavior was allocated to the various freely available activities. What he observed probably won't surprise you. Animals tended to distribute their behavior unevenly. For instance, a particular animal may have spent most of its time (60%) shredding paper and relatively little time engaged in the other activities (drinking, 17%; eating, 15%; wheel running, 8%). Premack measured the animal's time allocation to each activity before manipulating any variable in order to establish that animal's baseline preferences. Just as you might choose to engage in different amounts of several activities (watching television, eating snacks, playing cards, etc.) if given freedom to do so, Premack's animals chose to distribute their behavior in certain idiosyncratic ways. Those activities that animals devoted the most time to Premack called *high probability* behaviors, and those that occupied little time he called *low probability* behaviors.

The experimental question that Premack wanted to answer was whether he could use access to one response as a reinforcer for engaging in another response. More specifically, he assumed that high probability responses, because of their greater preference, could be used to reinforce low probability behaviors. For the animal described in the previous paragraph, paper shredding would clearly be the high probability response. Premack's strategy was to restrict access to this preferred activity to below its baseline (60%) level. The animal could then gain access to paper shredding by engaging in a particular low probability response (wheel running). It also became apparent to Premack that a more precise terminology would be helpful in distinguishing these two behaviors. He chose the term *instrumental response* to refer to the behavior that the animal was required to emit (in this case, wheel running) in order to gain access to the preferred activity, or *contingent response* (in this case, paper shredding). If, as a result of this arranged contingency, instrumental responding (wheel running) was observed to increase above its baseline level (8%), Premack could conclude that access to the high probability response (paper shredding) did indeed function as a reinforcer under these conditions.

In several studies, high probability behaviors have been shown to be effective reinforcers for lower probability behaviors, and this relationship is known as the **Premack principle** (Premack, 1959, 1962, 1963). You can probably appreciate the logic of this principle in many domains of human behavior. Parents, for instance, have long recognized the merits of making preferred activities contingent on less preferred activities. Requiring children to clean their rooms before being allowed to watch television, for instance, is a fairly common application of the Premack principle. Similarly, a classroom teacher who makes recess dependent on completion of an academic assignment is arranging the same kind of behavioral contingency. Naturally, such a manipulation assumes that most children prefer watching television and playing during recess to cleaning their room or completing schoolwork. Children differ, however, just like adults, and their behavioral preferences

Premack principle
the finding that high probability behaviors can be used as contingent reinforcers for low probability behaviors

can be very individualistic. A proper application of the Premack principle would require an initial observation to assess the relative probabilities of the relevant behaviors before the arrangement of any particular contingency.

The Premack principle wasn't the final word on how various operants interact with one another. Low probability behaviors still occur under conditions in which no contingencies are in effect (*baseline*), and this would seem to suggest that they, too, have some reinforcing value. Is it possible, then, that a low probability response could be used as a contingent reinforcer in order to increase the occurrence of a high probability response? This question may seem counterintuitive. Could you imagine, for instance, a parent using room cleaning as a reinforcer for watching television? The very idea seems outlandish! Nevertheless, a number of empirical studies have shown that such a contingency is possible, *as long as the contingent response (room cleaning) is restricted to below its naturally occurring (baseline) level.* What seems to matter is that the contingent response is not as readily available as it is during the baseline condition. It may not occur with much frequency during baseline, but it still occurs at some level. Depriving an organism of a behavior below the level at which it would ordinarily occur seems to enhance that behavior's status as a potential reinforcer. This finding is consistent with classic research on operant behavior when contingent stimuli (food or water) are used as reinforcers. Deprivation of the stimulus prior to experimentation establishes the reinforcing properties of the stimulus. So too does depriving an organism of a behavior, even a low probability one, increase the potential reinforcing effects of that behavior. The idea that any behavior restricted below its baseline level can then be used as a contingent response to reinforce another (even higher probability) behavior, has been referred to as the *response deprivation hypothesis,* and it is supported by numerous studies (Timberlake, 1979, 1981, 1983, 1984; Timberlake & Allison, 1974).

✖ INTERIM SUMMARY

In an operant analysis, behavioral events are always considered within a contextual framework that includes antecedent stimulus events, the behavior itself, and consequent stimulus events. Rather than focusing on contingencies between antecedent stimuli, as is the case in Pavlovian conditioning, operant research emphasizes the contingency between behavior and consequent stimuli. Among the most important consequences are reinforcers—stimuli that strengthen the behavior on which they are made contingent. Reinforcers are also classified as either primary or conditioned and positive or negative. Punishing stimuli are consequences that reduce the future probability or strength of a behavior, and punishment contingencies are also classified according to whether the consequent stimulus is presented (positive punishment) or removed (negative punishment). Finally, David Premack's work on multiple-response classes led to the important finding that access to certain kinds of behavior can function as a reinforcer for engaging in other behavior, ultimately leading to the idea that behaviors that are restricted below their baseline level acquire reinforcing properties.

1. Suppose one person turns to another and says, "Bonjour, mon ami" (French for "Hello, my friend"). What additional information would you need in order to know whether this utterance occurred in a foreign language class or on the streets of Paris? How does the three-term contingency relate to your answer?
2. Consider a behavior you engage in daily. Describe the antecedent(s) for the behavior, the behavior itself, and the consequence(s) of the behavior.
3. Do you consider the consequence in question 2 a reinforcer? If so, is it a primary or conditioned reinforcer, and why? Is the example one of positive reinforcement or of negative reinforcement, and why?

BASIC PRINCIPLES OF OPERANT BEHAVIOR

In some respects, the cats in Thorndike's puzzle box and the rats in Skinner's operant chamber faced a similar problem, namely, how to acquire food. They solved this problem in different ways: Thorndike's subjects by escaping the puzzle box, Skinner's by pressing the lever protruding from one of the operant chamber's walls. Remember that Thorndike simply measured how long it took his subjects to escape from the box, and this was often a considerably long time, at least during the experiment's initial trials. Skinner, on the other hand, did not conduct a discrete trials procedure, because his modified apparatus allowed the animal to be housed in the operant chamber for indefinite periods of time during the experiment. This strategy is known as a *free operant procedure* because the animal is, in a sense, free to engage in any activity inside the chamber, and the experiment is not defined according to discrete occurrences or trials. Nevertheless, Skinner was interested in studying a particular kind of operant behavior, lever pressing, and it stands to reason that rats would not, when first placed in the operant chamber, immediately move toward the lever and press it. Thus, Skinner saw his task as one of teaching, or training, the animal to press the lever, in the same way that you or I would train a dog to sit or roll over.

Shaping

When first placed in the operant chamber, Skinner's rats behaved in ways similar to Thorndike's cats. They explored the chamber and, utilizing their strong olfactory sense, sniffed every nook and cranny. Although the animals showed very little initial interest in the lever, their somewhat random meanderings eventually led toward the lever or at least to a position in which they were facing the lever. When this happened, Skinner used a handheld button (similar to a television remote control) to deliver a food pellet into the chamber. Because the food delivery mechanism made an audible clicking sound, this would often result in a startle response on the part of the animal, as rats are very sensitive to sound. Having recovered from the sound, the animal approached the food trough, discovering and then consuming the food. Next, Skinner waited until the animal moved closer to the lever, then delivered a second food pellet. Subsequent food pellets were delivered only when the animal engaged in behavior that brought it successively closer to the lever, eventually making physical contact with it. Once this occurred, Skinner withheld additional pellets until the animal actually pushed down on the lever, exerting enough force to close an electrical switch, thus delivering the food pellet without the aid of the experimenter.

By requiring the animal to engage in more refined movements, acquiring the food pellets only through actions that progressively moved closer and closer to lever pressing, Skinner was able to mold the animal's behavior much as an artist molds a nondescript hunk of clay into a specific shape. Skinner referred to this process as **shaping** because it entailed reinforcing successive approximations to a desired behavior (lever pressing). Once the animal was reliably pressing the lever and acquiring food without the intervention of the experimenter, it could be said that the operant of lever pressing had been acquired. Thus, acquisition of operant behavior involves the delivery of consequent stimuli (reinforcers) contingent on some predetermined class of behavior (lever pressing in this case). Skinner observed that once the lever press had been acquired, animals in the operant chamber continued to respond for prolonged periods of time.

shaping reinforcing successive approximations to a desired behavior

Skinner used shaping to intentionally bring about a response that would not ordinarily be observed in a rat's natural repertoire, but the process would be of little interest if it only applied to rats in operant chambers. In actuality, shaping is a pervasive feature of operant behavior, easily seen not only in the training efforts of pet owners, but also in the formal activity of teachers and coaches. In teaching children to read, teachers often require small steps toward reading, such as recognizing letters of the alphabet, before requiring students to recognize and sound out words and sentences. Within this context, praise, stickers, and looks of approval usually function as the reinforcing consequences. Simply expecting a nonreading child to sit down and read a book fluently from cover to cover is comparable to expecting the naïve animal, when first placed inside the operant chamber, to go immediately to the lever and press. In addition, the world at large often does a pretty good job of shaping behavior, even without the efforts of other people. For instance, learning to play a video game is often an ongoing exercise in shaping. With each click of the mouse or movement of the joystick, visual stimuli on the screen change, providing you with immediate feedback about your progress. Because the miniscule responses you make have immediate consequences— some sending you on to more advanced levels, others leading to defeat and the end of a game—video and computer games can shape an amazingly complex repertoire in relatively short order. Indeed, the speed with which this skill can be developed is easily observed even in school-age children, many of whom negotiate the labyrinthine world of the game with the aplomb of a neurosurgeon.

Extinction

Chapter 3 explained that a previously acquired conditioned reflex could be eliminated through a process known as extinction. This chapter will show that operant behavior is subject to many of the same processes as are conditioned reflexes. If an operant is acquired as a result of reinforcing consequences being made contingent on the behavior, then it stands to reason that the behavior may cease to occur when reinforcing consequences no longer follow. In fact, **extinction** of operant behavior does occur when the reinforcer is withheld or no longer occurs contingent on behavior. As it turns out, Skinner stumbled upon extinction by accident when his apparatus broke down. Remember that one of the advantages of the operant chamber is the extent to which the researcher is removed from the moment-to-moment conduct of the experiment. This frees the researcher to pursue other things while the experiment is continuing by way of automated equipment. One day, Skinner left his lab during a conditioning experiment and, upon his return, noticed that an animal in an operant chamber had quit responding altogether. When Skinner inspected the chamber, he found the food magazine clogged, meaning that the animal had for some time not been receiving food contingent on lever pressing. Not surprisingly, the lever press had been extinguished. The same might be expected of the child playing a video game if the screen were to go black, or if points were no longer being acquired, or if new levels of the game were inaccessible.

extinction elimination of an operant by withholding the reinforcer

Extinction is not an instantaneous process. In fact, it can often take a considerable amount of time, and, along the way, behavior undergoes an interesting metamorphosis. If, for example, you were to observe an animal in an operant chamber after the lever press had been shaped, you would notice that each instance of the response looks pretty much like any other. In other words, once a response has been acquired and is being maintained by reinforcement, it becomes fairly stereotyped. You can probably recognize this pattern in much of your own behavior: Those things that you do with great frequency eventually become automatic, and little variability characterizes the behavior. Curiously, though, when behavior is placed on extinction, an amazing transformation takes place. In the case of the rat pressing a lever, extinction often leads to increased variability in the form of the behavior, including higher response rates than occurred during reinforcement (Antonitis, 1951; Eckerman & Lanson, 1969; Ferraro & Branch, 1968). This variability is also seen when animals exert more pressure on the lever during extinction (Notterman, 1959), and it isn't unusual to see signs of what could be interpreted as *emotional* behavior as well, such as biting the lever or the unfortunate experimenter who reaches inside the chamber to retrieve the animal. This change in the rate and form of behavior under extinction is referred to as *extinction-induced variability,* and it is a common occurrence observed in nonhumans and humans alike (Eckerman & Vreeland, 1973; Morgan & Lee, 1996; Morgan, Morgan, & Toth, 1992).

You can probably readily appreciate the adaptive nature of extinction-induced variability in operant behavior. Many times when a particular behavior has produced consistent consequences and then no longer does so, simply varying the behavior in some way leads to reinforcement once again. Most people, for example, have considerable experience with vending machines, and, although most of the time they acquire the desired item, sometimes the machine doesn't deliver the goods. When this happens, people often become quite creative in their interactions with the machine. They may push the buttons corresponding to all of the selections one after the other or try to get their money back by using the Change Return button. If none of this works, and there are no witnesses, some people use more violent means in an effort to get their snack or drink. Of course, if the desired item is not forthcoming, the person will eventually walk away, demonstrating the terminal effects of extinction. At times like this, it is not difficult to see a parallel between the rat biting the lever and the frustrated human assaulting the vending machine. Both are responding to a circumstance in which a particular behavior has produced reinforcement reliably in the past, and this behavior isn't simply going to disappear the first time the reinforcer is not forthcoming.

A behavior first acquired and then extinguished may also recover at some later time, indicating that operant behavior is also subject to **spontaneous recovery.** The rat whose lever pressing has been reinforced and then extinguished will, if removed from the apparatus for several days, respond once again on the lever if placed back in the chamber. Similarly, a vending machine patron who walks away disappointed following an unsuccessful effort at coaxing a drink or food item out of a stubborn machine is exhibiting operant extinction. However, this behavior is not likely to last forever. At some later time, perhaps weeks or months after the frustrating encounter, the patron may very well try his or her luck again. Operant behavior, then, exhibits some of the same features as Pavlovian conditioning, including acquisition, extinction, and spontaneous recovery.

spontaneous recovery reoccurrence of an operant that had been previously extinguished

Stimulus Control: Generalization and Discrimination

Operant behavior makes up a significant percentage of humans' entire behavioral repertoire, because much of what we do operates on or affects our environment. Fixing a meal, writing a term paper, painting a picture, driving a car, taking a test, turning on a stereo, lighting a candle are all actions that bring about consequences, some large and dramatic, others subtler and more easily unnoticed. Regardless of the differences that exist in the various forms and patterns of these behaviors, they all share certain features, including the fact that they operate on the environment. But they also share the property of occurring under somewhat specific circumstances. In other words, none of the behaviors mentioned occurs all the time or without regard to the surrounding environment. Fixing a meal is something that occurs in a kitchen, not inside a classroom. By the same token, driving a car is behavior that happens out on the roadways, not (it is hoped) in someone's kitchen.

Notice that this is simply another way of saying that behavior always happens in context, and part of this context consists of the antecedent stimuli that characterize an organism's environment at any given moment. The discussion here centers on the role that antecedent stimuli play in operant behavior and why such stimuli occupy an important position in the three-term contingency. Despite the emphasis that operant researchers place on consequent stimuli, operant behavior would have little adaptive value if it occurred randomly and without regard for context. Moreover, the ability to generalize and discriminate across various stimulus contexts is as crucial to operant behavior as it is to Pavlovian or respondent behavior. The phrase **stimulus control** refers to the processes of generalization and discrimination as they pertain to operant behavior. In fact, any instance of operant behavior can be described in terms of its stimulus control, and the consequences that follow behavior are ordinarily closely tied to this dimension of behavior.

Generalization   Imagine yourself stopped at an intersection, waiting for a green light. When the light does change, a strange hue appears, say, a pea green, instead of the darker forest green you are accustomed to seeing. Now you wouldn't expect this novel green color to incapacitate you at the intersection. Just because you have never encountered this shade of green before at a light doesn't mean you won't respond appropriately by stepping on the accelerator. In fact, if you were to hesitate too long, lost in confusion, fellow drivers behind you would probably offer a "friendly" prod to encourage you to move. Naturally, their prod would come in the form of a brief blast of their horn. Of course, this might prove problematic for you as well, for car horns don't all sound alike; they can actually have rather distinct personalities. Were you unable to generalize across relevant auditory stimuli, you might be additionally paralyzed by the unique sound of the car horn. As you can see, this scenario is an exercise in absurdity. Neither Pavlov's dogs, nor human beings in complex environments, encounter much difficulty generalizing appropriately across various stimulus dimensions. Generalization has its limits, though, and effective adaptation requires that animals recognize both the relevant and irrelevant aspects of stimulus events in their environment.

Discrimination   For you to respond successfully to the green light in the example, your behavior must show sensitivity to variations in the color of the lights. On the one hand, you need to respond to all green lights in the same manner, no matter how much they might vary along the dimension *green*. That is, pea green, forest green, bluish green, and any other vaguely green light must be treated the same. Recall that responding to all green lights by accelerating is an example of generalization. In this case, the green light functions as an antecedent stimulus for the operant of placing your foot on the accelerator.

But you also need to respond differently to green than you do to red lights. In fact, this is the very purpose of the lights; each color designates a specific, appropriate behavior. Traffic lights, and road signs as well, are there for the express purpose of regulating the driving behavior of all of us behind the wheel, and if our behavior occurred irrespective of these varying stimuli, driving would be a dangerous endeavor. What would happen if you were to approach the intersection, only to find that drivers coming through the intersection are paying absolutely no heed to the lights? That is, a driver is just as likely to drive through the intersection on a red light as on a green light. Now, granted, sometimes this kind of behavior does occur, but it usually invites the wrath of other drivers in the intersection, and for good reason. If the behavior of drivers at a busy intersection was completely unrelated to the changing lights, a simple activity like going to the store or to school would be like entering a demolition derby. Under these circumstances, it would be understandable if some of us chose never to get behind the wheel of a car again.

Fortunately, drivers at intersections usually *do* behave in accordance with traffic lights, meaning that their behavior demonstrates an appropriate balance between generalization and discrimination; that is, their behavior has come under proper stimulus control. The study of stimulus control has a long and storied history in operant psychology. In fact, many early experiments conducted by Skinner and his students and colleagues focused on how operant behavior could be produced and maintained under varying antecedent stimulus conditions. Experiments on stimulus control are often conducted with pigeons, rather than rats, mainly because birds have highly sensitive visual abilities and researchers find it easy to control visual stimuli in experimental settings. Not surprisingly, the operant chamber for pigeons is designed differently from the one for rats (shown earlier in Figure 4.4). Pigeons aren't anatomically built to press levers, but they can use their beaks to peck, and, consequently, pigeon chambers use a spring-mounted key on the wall as the response mechanism. These keys are translucent and can be illuminated with varying kinds of stimuli, from different-colored lights to geometric shapes. Pecking on the key produces reinforcement in the form of a brief presentation of grain in the food hopper at the bottom of the chamber.

In a typical stimulus control experiment, visual stimuli varying on some dimension (shape, color, size, etc.) are projected or illuminated on a response key in random order. One specific stimulus is chosen by the experimenter as the **discriminative stimulus (S^D)**, meaning that if the pigeon pecks at the key when this stimulus is illuminated, grain reinforcement will be delivered. If, however, responses occur to the key whenever other stimuli are illuminated, the experimental chamber goes dark and no reinforcer is delivered. In other words, incorrect responses lead to a time-out.

discriminative stimulus specific stimulus or stimulus dimension in whose presence a response is reinforced

Because of their visual acuity, pigeons master this task with little difficulty, and when key pecking occurs only in the presence of the S^D, and not in the presence of other stimuli (often referred to as S^Δ, or "S delta"), the pecking behavior is said to have come under discriminative control. In fact, a large literature on stimulus control demonstrates that operant behavior exhibits properties of generalization and discrimination very much like what is seen in Pavlovian conditioning. Suppose that an experimenter trains a pigeon to peck at a key illuminated with a 100-watt light. Once the bird is responding reliably to this S^D, a generalization phase is conducted during which this original light, and others of varying brightness, are randomly illuminated on the key and no grain reinforcement occurs. Do you think the bird will peck at anything other than the discriminative stimulus? If so, you're right. Responding will occur to the other stimuli, though not to the same extent that it occurs to the S^D. In fact, plotting response rate per minute for each of these stimuli will produce a response function that closely mirrors the generalization gradient for a conditioned reflex shown in Figure 2.5.

Remember that generalization and discrimination exist on a continuum, such that maximum generalization tends to correspond to minimal discrimination, and vice versa. To bring the pigeon's key pecking under strict stimulus control, the experimenter would expose the animal to many random presentations of stimuli of varying degrees of brightness, including the original S^D (100 watts). Pecking at the key illuminated with the S^D will always produce grain reinforcement, while pecks to any other stimuli (S^As) will always result in time-out. This practice of reinforcing behavior in the presence of one stimulus but not in the presence of other stimuli is referred to as **differential reinforcement.** Although the procedure may require literally hundreds of presentations of each stimulus, eventually responding will occur solely to the S^D and not to S^A, producing a steep response gradient similar to that depicted in Figure 2.5. An experimenter could make this discrimination more difficult by presenting stimuli that are increasingly similar to the S^D. If the pigeon was no longer able to respond differentially to the S^D and the various S^As, this would provide objective evidence concerning the boundary conditions of the bird's visual acuity.

differential
reinforcement
process of reinforcing
an operant in the pres-
ence of one stimulus
but not in the presence
of another

Stimulus control procedures have played a historically important role in operant psychology for many reasons, not the least of which is their strength in revealing the limits of animals' sensory capabilities (Blough, 1961, 1967; Guttman & Kalish, 1956; Terrace, 1966). Unlike human subjects, nonhuman animals cannot verbally report on their sensations. Nevertheless, through the use of differential reinforcement contingencies, these animals can, in some sense, tell us what they can hear or see. The same research strategy has paid dividends in more applied ventures as well. Verhave (1966), for instance, trained pigeons to distinguish between acceptable and defective pills on a pharmaceutical conveyer belt, thus producing a relatively inexpensive quality control inspector. Similarly, because of their superior olfactory skills, dogs have long been used to sniff out illegal drugs and explosives at international borders and airports (Johnston et al. 1998; Meyers, 1999; Wren, 1999). In perhaps the most ambitious and impressive display of stimulus control, Skinner and colleagues (1960) trained birds to guide missiles during World War II. The birds were placed inside small "cockpits" in the nose of a small missile, and pecks on a screen depicting a target at various distances and orientations provided continuous feedback to mechanisms in the missile that could redirect the missile's trajectory. The research program was amazingly successful, and, in a demonstration to top Army scientists, the birds performed flawlessly. Nevertheless, the Army never fully funded the program, perhaps because they found it difficult to accept the possibility that a million-dollar armament was being piloted by a bird brain.

Pulling It All Together: The Three-Term Contingency Revisited

A discussion of stimulus control inevitably leads back to a consideration of the three-term contingency. All of the components must be considered in order to understand how and why antecedent stimuli (both S^Ds and S^As) develop their control over behavior. Recall that in Pavlovian conditioning, a CS begins as a neutral stimulus, acquiring its ability to provoke a CR only through a process of conditioning. In operant learning, discriminative stimuli also begin as relatively meaningless or neutral stimuli. The control that they eventually exert over behavior develops gradually because of the consequences that follow when responding occurs to these stimuli. In a stimulus control experiment, if responding in the presence of a green key light reliably produces food reinforcement, then the green light will eventually provoke responding as soon as it is illuminated. Skinner suggested that the key light (S^D) "sets the occasion for responding," because it has been associated with reinforcement. Thus, the control exerted by discriminative stimuli largely depends upon what consequences have followed behavior in the presence of such stimuli.

Examples of stimulus control abound in human behavior. A student who has a question about a particular concept or fact isn't likely to ask it unless the teacher is in the room. Asking the question with the teacher present (S^D) is more likely to produce a meaningful consequence (an answer) than asking the question in the teacher's absence (S^Δ). It is also easy to see why efforts at stimulus control sometimes fail. Our human-created environment, for instance, contains many discriminative stimuli in the form of instructions and signs. Speed limit signs are a particularly good example. Speed limit signs inform drivers of the speed that they are not to exceed on a specific roadway. But people frequently drive in excess of posted speeds, in part because there are seldom any effective consequences for discouraging speeding, such as being pulled over and given a ticket. The posted speed limit sign, therefore, is a relatively weak discriminative stimulus because the consequences that would be necessary to support the stimulus are inconsistently applied, if at all.

It should be clear now why all three components of the three-term contingency are considered critical to understanding operant behavior. The range of responses any organism possesses is enormous, but these behaviors don't occur willy-nilly without regard to the surrounding environment. All behavior must be interpreted within its environmental context, and this means attending to stimulus events present prior to behavior and those that follow contingently on behavior. In an operant analysis, these stimulus events are the *controlling variables,* and any serious discussion about the causes of behavior must take them into account.

✖ INTERIM SUMMARY

Acquisition of operant behavior often occurs gradually through the process of shaping, in which approximations toward a specific response form are reinforced. Once acquired, operant behavior can be extinguished through the withholding of the reinforcing stimulus, though increased variability in the response is a common side effect of extinction. Operant behavior also exhibits generalization and discrimination, and the process by which behavior comes under the control of antecedent stimuli is referred to as stimulus control.

✖ THOUGHT QUESTIONS

1. Describe how you would use shaping to teach a first grader how to turn a forward somersault. What kind of reinforcer would you use, and what are some of the approximations that might be targeted?

2. You finish typing a manuscript and send a print command to the printer, but nothing happens. Describe how the concept of extinction-induced variability might apply to this scenario.
3. Describe an instance of your own behavior under stimulus control. What range of stimuli would your behavior have to generalize across? Across which stimuli would your behavior have to discriminate to be effective?

SCHEDULES OF REINFORCEMENT

The advent of the operant chamber ushered in an entirely new method for studying learning, but it was not without its limitations. The food pellets that Skinner used as reinforcers had to be produced in large quantities, and Skinner ordinarily took this task on himself, often arriving in his laboratory early in the morning before the day's experiments. The food pellets were made by way of a lengthy process in which a pasty food mash was laid out on a flat surface (similar to a cookie sheet), cut into small, bite-sized pellets, and then allowed to dry. Now, imagine numerous animals, all having acquired the operant of lever pressing and all remaining inside the operant chamber for prolonged periods of time. You can probably appreciate the substantial dilemma that Skinner (1956) faced:

> Eight rats eating a hundred pellets each day could easily keep up with production. One pleasant Saturday afternoon I surveyed my supply of dry pellets, and, appealing to certain elemental theorems in arithmetic, deduced that unless I spent the rest of that afternoon and evening at the pill machine, the supply would be exhausted by ten-thirty Monday morning. . . . It led me to apply our second principle of unformalized scientific method and to ask myself why *every* press of the lever had to be reinforced. (p. 226)

Once again, serendipity had pointed the way, resulting in a lengthy research program of unparalleled importance to the study of operant behavior and the most significant contribution of Skinner's career as an experimentalist. By questioning the necessity of reinforcing every response, Skinner had stumbled upon a much bigger topic than he originally recognized. The relationship between behavior and its consequences is a mercurial one, seldom described by a simple one-to-one ratio. After all, do gamblers win every time they make a bet or throw the dice? Does a golf swing always result in the ball carrying the desirable distance or trajectory? Does an angler catch a fish on every cast? Do children always comply with the requests of parents? Or parents the requests of their children? Needless to say, the answer to all of the above questions is a resounding "No." During a productive 6-year collaboration, Skinner and colleague Charles Ferster studied the effect of altering various aspects of the behavior-reinforcer relationship, or what they referred to as **schedules of reinforcement.** In the groundbreaking work *Schedules of Reinforcement* (Ferster & Skinner, 1957), they demonstrated orderly changes in response rate and response patterning as a function of

schedule of reinforcement
method of delivering reinforcement dependent on numerical and/or temporal dimensions of behavior

changing the quantitative and temporal properties of response-reinforcer contingencies.

Aside from the ingenuity of the researcher, there are very few limits on the kinds of response-reinforcer arrangements that can be created. Ferster and Skinner described the results of experiments on more than a dozen different schedules, and many others have been studied in the ensuing years (Catania, 1971; Herrnstein & Morse, 1958; Lee & Gollub, 1971; Williams & Johnston, 1992; Zeiler, 1977). Although this discussion can only scratch the surface of the schedules of reinforcement literature, the tremendous variety of this research area can at least be hinted at by considering the more basic schedules and those that have been most extensively studied. Most of these response-reinforcer arrangements can be classified based on whether the reinforcer is delivered according to a certain number of responses or according to a period of elapsed time. Let's take a look at some of the basic schedules of reinforcement.

Ratio Schedules

In the early development of his operant methodology, Skinner arranged for food pellets to be delivered contingent on each lever press or key peck. Because an experiment almost always began with a naïve animal, and shaping of the relevant operant was required before much else could be done, there was seldom any reason for Skinner to be concerned about his supply of food pellets. Once the animal had acquired the operant, responses on the lever or key no longer required the intervention of the researcher. Each response would automatically close a microswitch in the chamber, resulting in the delivery of food. This schedule in which every response produced food is often referred to as **continuous reinforcement.** However, when Skinner determined that his supply of pellets would be quickly depleted, he reasoned that it might be possible to maintain the behavior even without reinforcing every response. One possibility was to reinforce the response on every *n*th occurrence, rather than on a continuous basis. Ferster and Skinner referred to this behavior-consequence contingency as a **ratio schedule.** For example, suppose the experimenter arranged reinforcement to occur every third response. Ferster and Skinner (1957) called such a schedule a *fixed ratio schedule,* because the response-reinforcer ratio (in this case 3:1) remains constant over time. In this particular case, the schedule is a FR 3 schedule, or a fixed ratio 3 schedule, indicating that the reinforcer is delivered after every third response.

There is nothing special about a particular ratio. A schedule that requires 25 responses per reinforcer (FR 25) is also a fixed ratio schedule, so long as the response-reinforcer ratio doesn't change over time. What Ferster and Skinner (1957) discovered was that behavior could indeed be maintained by ratio reinforcement. In addition to answering a question having practical utility—remember the food pellet supply—they had uncovered an interesting fact about behavior. If behavior can be maintained by reinforcing every 3rd response, or every 25th response, then it is simply a matter of time before the following question comes up: Just how many responses will a

continuous reinforcement reinforcement schedule in which each response produces reinforcement

ratio schedule reinforcement schedule in which reinforcers are delivered according to a predetermined number of responses

single reinforcer support? That is, how far could this ratio be stretched before it would no longer maintain behavior? The answer is, pretty far, so long as the size of the ratio is increased gradually. Imagine, for instance, what an animal would do if moved immediately from a continuous reinforcement schedule to, say, a FR 200 schedule. The animal will likely never receive the reinforcer on this larger schedule because the response will extinguish before 200 responses are emitted. This breaking down of an operant due to an abrupt increase in response requirement has been referred to as *ratio strain*. On the other hand, if the animal had been exposed to gradually increasing response requirements, a single reinforcer could be shown to maintain in excess of 500 responses. This remarkable finding had obvious implications for Ferster and Skinner's food supply, but more important, it was a striking lesson in the powerful role that reinforcement could play in behavior.

Ferster and Skinner discovered some interesting aspects of behavior maintained by fixed ratio reinforcement, but, before describing this research, it's necessary to describe another of Skinner's laboratory inventions. Because he was interested in precise measurement of behavior, Skinner devoted considerable thought to the question of which dimension of behavior to monitor and how best to do this. His solution was to claim response rate as his primary objective measure, because lever presses or key pecks could occur with great frequency over extended experimental sessions. The number of responses emitted during a specific unit of time (seconds, minutes, hours) could be a sensitive metric, documenting momentary changes in response strength.

To measure this property of behavior, Skinner devised a graphing instrument he called a *cumulative recorder,* an example of which is shown in Figure 4.6. The cumulative recorder holds a large roll of graph paper, which, by way of a small motor, is pulled out of the instrument at a constant speed. An ink-filled event pen, starting at the bottom of the graph paper, takes a small, incremental vertical step on the paper with each response on the lever or key in the operant chamber. Also, whenever a reinforcer is delivered, this pen makes a downward, diagonal blip in the record. Because the graph paper is moving continuously, and because each response by the animal causes one step up of the event pen, the resulting line drawn by the pen depicts moment-to-moment changes in response rate and patterning. A rapid response rate produces a steep slope in the cumulative record, whereas slower response rates produce more level records. An absence of responding corresponds to a flat line on the record. When the event pen reaches the top of the paper, it is automatically reset to the bottom, thus tracing a straight vertical line.

In their explorations of reinforcement schedules, Ferster and Skinner programmed different values, or parameters, of a fixed ratio schedule (for example, FR 5, FR 100, FR 250). Inspection of the cumulative records produced under each schedule revealed orderly patterns unique to FR schedules. Figure 4.7 depicts typical response patterns generated by FR schedules. Even when different ratio values or parameters are programmed, the response patterning on FR schedules exhibits certain uniform features. Responding tends to occur at a fairly high and constant rate until the delivery of the reinforcer (as indi-

FIGURE 4.6 Cumulative Recorder.

cated by the small diagonal marks on the record). Immediately after reinforcer delivery, the record is flat, indicating no responding by the animal. This temporary absence of responding has been called a *postreinforcement pause* (PRP). Several studies have shown that the length of the postreinforcement pause tends to increase as a function of ratio value, with longer pauses corresponding to larger ratios (Felton & Lyon, 1966; Powell, 1968). The response pattern generated by fixed ratio schedules, represented by fairly rapid responding followed by a postreinforcement pause, has been called a *break-and-run* pattern of responding.

It occurred to Ferster and Skinner that the ratio requirement did not need to remain constant over the course of the experiment. What would happen, for instance, if the ratio of responses to reinforcers changed unpredictably over time? Such a schedule, in which reinforcers are delivered contingent on a changing ratio requirement, is called a *variable ratio schedule* (VR). A VR 10 schedule, for example, is one in which, over the course of an experimental session, reinforcers will be delivered on an average of every 10 responses. The key difference between this schedule and the fixed ratio schedule is that the actual response requirement changes from reinforcer to reinforcer in a VR schedule. An animal responding to a VR 10 schedule may receive the reinforcer after the following number of responses: 13, 8, 12, 4, 7, 1, 15, 9, 19, 12. If you add up the ratios and divide by 10, you'll discover that the *average* number of responses occurring prior to reinforcement is 10.

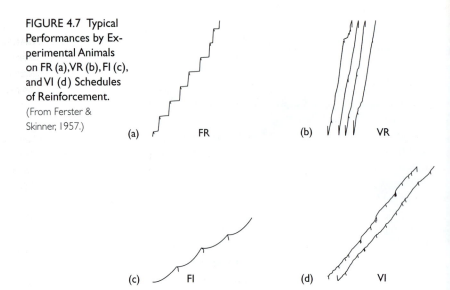

FIGURE 4.7 Typical Performances by Experimental Animals on FR (a), VR (b), FI (c), and VI (d) Schedules of Reinforcement. (From Ferster & Skinner, 1957.)

(a)   FR

(b)   VR

(c)   FI

(d)   VI

Not every new experimental manipulation proves interesting or important, and Ferster and Skinner could have discovered that a variable ratio schedule didn't produce any different kind of behavior than did FR schedules. But that is decidedly *not* what they discovered, and this is why their research on schedules of reinforcement looms large in the study of operant behavior. Animals placed on VR schedules of reinforcement produced cumulative records that look like those depicted in Figure 4.7b. If you compare these records to those produced by FR schedules (Figure 4.7a), you will notice two rather conspicuous differences. First, as indicated by the steeper slope, the overall response rate on the VR schedule is somewhat higher than on the FR schedules. Also, most dramatically, the postreinforcement pause that was so apparent in FR performance is nonexistent in the VR record. This difference may be explained, in part, by the fact that the reinforcer delivery in the VR schedule is much less predictable because it occurs contingent on a continuously changing response requirement. In a sense, the FR schedule makes the conditions of reinforcement more discriminable, either because the response-reinforcer ratio is constant or because the amount of time spent responding remains relatively constant as well and is therefore a reliable predictor of reinforcer delivery.

Interval Schedules

interval schedule
reinforcement schedule in which reinforcers are delivered according to predetermined intervals of time

Ferster and Skinner reasoned that reinforcement delivery could also be made contingent on behavior as a function of the passage of time. In **interval schedules,** reinforcement occurs contingent on the first response that follows a predetermined interval of time. As with ratio schedules, this interval of time could remain constant from reinforcer to reinforcer, or it could vary. A schedule in which the interval remains constant is referred to as a *fixed interval schedule*. A fixed interval 30-second schedule (FI 30 s), for instance, arranges reinforcement to occur every 30 seconds, but the reinforcer is only delivered when a response occurs after this 30-second interval. Responses can occur throughout the interval, but they produce no consequences. Only the first response after the interval has elapsed produces reinforcement.

As you may have guessed by now, Ferster and Skinner were interested in whether arranging reinforcers in this way would produce different behavior patterns from those seen under ratio schedules of reinforcement. Figure 4.7c depicts a typical cumulative record from an animal exposed to a FI 30 s schedule of reinforcement. The most noticeable aspect of this record is the curved nature of the response run that characterizes behavior prior to each reinforcer delivery. Remember that animals responding under fixed ratio schedules produce break-and-run patterns in which a postreinforcement pause is followed by a rapid, constant response run until the next reinforcer delivery. Performance on a fixed interval schedule differs from this break-and-run pattern in that responding following the postreinforcement pause isn't initially rapid, but very slow. As the interval elapses, and the next reinforcer draws nearer, the response rate increases, thus producing a curve, or *scallop,* in the cumulative record. This common response pattern is therefore referred to as an *FI scallop.* Once again, Ferster and Skinner had demonstrated that changing the schedule of reinforcement had brought about a different kind of behavior than either of the ratio schedules had produced.

The next logical step would be to program reinforcers to occur according to a changing temporal criterion, and this is precisely what Ferster and Skinner did. In a *variable interval schedule* reinforcers are arranged contingent on responses that follow varying intervals of time. A variable interval 30-second (VI 30 s) schedule, for example, arranges reinforcers to become available on average every 30 seconds, but this interval varies from one reinforcer to the next. In other words, as with variable ratio schedules, the availability of the reinforcer is less predictable than on a fixed interval schedule. The response pattern typical of variable interval schedules is depicted in Figure 4.7d. Notice that the VI schedule doesn't produce the scallops characteristic of FI schedules. Responding on the VI is relatively constant and exhibits little, if any, postreinforcement pausing. The absence of a postreinforcement pause is reminiscent of behavior on a variable ratio schedule, although the response rate on the VI does not match that of the VR.

One general finding, then, from reinforcement schedule research is that responding on ratio schedules almost always occurs at a higher rate than responding on interval schedules, and for good reason. On a ratio schedule, whether FR or VR, the animal can exert some control over the rate at which it receives reinforcement simply by responding rapidly. The more rapidly it responds, the more reinforcers it can acquire in a given period of time. On interval schedules, though, the reinforcer becomes available only after the predetermined interval has elapsed, and nothing the animal does can bring the reinforcer closer in time. Ferster and Skinner were often amazed at the consistently high rates of behavior that could be maintained by ratio schedules of reinforcement, and the next chapter covers the implications of such findings for human behavior.

Concurrent Schedules

The operant chamber necessarily represents a somewhat artificial environment, and scientists understand that the conditions that organisms face in their natural settings cannot be mimicked within the laboratory. In their natural habitats, for instance, most animals face circumstances that require them to choose between a variety of behavioral options. In fact, nearly any behavioral episode can be interpreted in this way—whether to turn left or right at the intersection, whether to wear the solid blue or the red and blue striped tie, whether to buy your favorite chocolate cookies or a healthier alternative, whether to major in biology or psychology. The list, quite obviously, goes on. From trivial to critical, most organisms find themselves almost continuously choosing one course of action over another, and choosing one alternative over another has consequences. Turning left at the light may bring you closer to your destination than turning right. Choosing the solid blue tie may produce looks of approval and compliments from colleagues, whereas wearing the red and blue striped tie may bring less positive attention. Choice behavior can be readily interpreted as operant behavior because the choices produce differential consequences. These consequences, in fact, often conspire to turn certain choice dilemmas into exasperating personal challenges.

If you view choice behavior as deciding among two or more possible consequences (reinforcers), then the standard operant procedure, with a few apparatus modifications, should prove capable of shedding some light on why organisms make the choices they do. One way to do this is to design an operant chamber that contains two separate response mechanisms (levers or keys), giving the animal an opportunity to distribute its responses to the keys in various proportions. In most choice experiments, reinforcement is delivered independently on each lever or key according to its own schedule; thus the

concurrent schedule condition in which two separate reinforcement schedules operate simultaneously and independently of one another

procedure is known as a **concurrent schedule** of reinforcement. The most common arrangement is two variable interval schedules. Suppose we are researchers and we conduct an experiment in which two VI 30 s schedules are in effect. Remember that what this means is that the two schedules are running at the same time, and reinforcement becomes available on average every 30 seconds on each key. Responding on one key doesn't affect the programmed schedule on the other, so reinforcers can be obtained by strategically alternating responses to the keys. The important questions in such an experiment are How will the animal distribute its responses? and What if we change the schedule so that one key delivers reinforcers more frequently than the other? The dependent variable in such an experiment is the relative amount of responding that the animal distributes to each response lever or key.

In an early attempt to quantify the relationship between responding and reinforcement rate, Richard Herrnstein (1961) presented pigeons with different concurrent variable interval schedules. In some conditions, the schedule values for the separate keys were identical (for example, VI 3 min VI 3 min), and, in others, the schedule values differed (for example, VI 1.8 min VI 9 min). If rate of reinforcement affects responding, then an animal exposed to a VI 3 min VI 3 min schedule should distribute its responses evenly to both keys, since the rate of reinforcement is equal on both keys. On the other hand, an animal exposed to a VI 1.8 min VI 9 min schedule could receive reinforcement on one key more than four times (VI 1.8 min) as often as on the other key (VI 9 min). What Herrnstein discovered was that birds distributed their key pecks in a manner that matched the rate of reinforcement. That is, if the rate of reinforcement on the two keys was equal (VI 3 min VI 3 min schedule), birds responded equally on the two keys. On the other hand, if reinforcement occurred at a greater rate on one key (VI 1.8 min) than on the other key (VI 9 min), birds responded more frequently to the key correlated with higher rates of reinforcement (VI 1.8 min). This relationship between reinforcement rate and response rate is orderly enough that Herrnstein (1970) referred to it as the *quantitative law of effect,* and it has subsequently been called the **matching law.** Expressed mathematically, the matching law originally took the following form (Herrnstein, 1970):

matching law
Herrnstein's formula relating the relative response rate to relative reinforcement rate on concurrent schedules of reinforcement

$$\frac{P_L}{P_L + P_B} = \frac{R_L}{R_L + R_B}$$

In this equation, P refers to key pecks, R refers to reinforcement, and L and B refer to the left and right keys, respectively. Thus, the equation states that the relative amount of key pecking to any key will be a function of the relative rate of reinforcement corresponding to responses on that key. This is just a mathematical way of saying that rate of response will be equivalent to rate of reinforcement for any particular response option. Herrnstein found that pigeons did distribute their key pecks in a manner that "matched" the rate of reinforcement on that particular key relative to responses to alternative keys. On a concurrent schedule in which reinforcement rate was the same on both keys (for example, VI 3 min VI 3 min), the expectation is that response rates on both keys will be similar, and in fact they were. On the other hand, if reinforcement rates were dramatically different on the two keys (VI 1.8 min VI 9 min), responses were distributed in a manner that matched the relative reinforcement rates on the respective keys.

Herrnstein's original formula proved incapable of accounting for certain results and has been revised several times in the years since it first appeared. Experiments on the matching law and choice behavior dominated operant research for nearly 20 years after Herrnstein's 1970 article, and a great deal has been learned about choice under concurrent schedules of reinforcement (deVilliers, 1977; Prelec, 1982). In addition, considerable controversy has emerged concerning the question of how matching develops as a behavioral process. After all, the matching law, as described by the formula given earlier, only indicates that the relative rate of responding to two keys will match the relative reinforcement rate to the two schedules, but the equation cannot explain the moment-to-moment process that accounts for this outcome.

Although all researchers agree that animals' performance on concurrent schedules demonstrates sensitivity to the schedules in operation and to the rate of reinforcement corresponding to those schedules, debate continues over the nature of this sensitivity. Some researchers believe that animals alter their behavior moment to moment in order to maximize the rate of reinforcement continuously, whereas others argue that matching occurs only over fairly long periods of time and that animals are not necessarily responding to momentary fluctuations in reinforcement rate (Baum, 1981; Baum & Aparicio, 1999; deVilliers, 1977; Hinson & Staddon, 1983; Rachlin, Green, Kagel, & Battalio, 1976; Shimp, 1969, 1975; Williams, 1991). To some extent, debate about matching hinges on fundamental questions about how response classes are to be defined and what specific measure of behavior serves as the unit of analysis for a particular study.

Operant researchers have found that concurrent schedules have considerable utility beyond their contribution to the study of choice behavior. Because of the mathematical uniformity of the matching law, concurrent schedule performance can become a useful benchmark, or baseline, against which to study the effects of numerous independent variables. An obvious one, the effect of reinforcement rate, characterizes a good deal of the early research on matching. But there are many other dimensions of reinforcement besides rate. For instance, reinforcer magnitude can be systematically varied as well (Catania, 1963; Grace, 1995; Meisch & Spiga, 1998). If the schedule value remains the same on both schedules, but one response produces a larger magnitude reinforcer (4 seconds access to grain) than the other (2 seconds access to grain), then preference for the larger magnitude reinforcer can be precisely assessed. Concurrent schedules have also proven valuable to research in behavioral pharmacology, in which the effects of various drugs can be readily seen against the baseline provided by concurrent schedule performance (Barrett & Sanger, 1991; McMillan & Hardwick, 2000; Thompson & Boren, 1977; Thompson & Schuster, 1968).

✖ INTERIM SUMMARY

Among the more important discoveries about operant behavior was the finding that rate and pattern of responding change when reinforcement is delivered according to various schedules. Ratio schedules deliver reinforcers contingent on a specified number of responses. This ratio remains constant on fixed ratio schedules, but varies about a mean value on variable ratio schedules, and each schedule produces idiosyncratic response patterns. Interval schedules deliver reinforcement contingent on a single response after an interval of time has elapsed. This interval remains constant in fixed interval schedules, but varies about a mean interval on variable interval schedules. Each interval schedule produces response patterns distinct both from one another and from performance generated under ratio schedules. Finally, concurrent schedules arrange reinforcement on separate mechanisms according to independently operating schedules and allow for the analysis of choice behavior. Relative response rates on the concurrent schedules tend to correspond to the reinforcement rates on the schedules, as described by Herrnstein's matching law.

✖ THOUGHT QUESTIONS

1. What practical matter led Skinner to move from studying continuous reinforcement to other schedules of reinforcement? Also, can you think of an example of human behavior reinforced on a continuous schedule?
2. Describe an example of your own behavior that produces consequences on a ratio schedule (fixed or variable). Do you think your behavior corresponds to the pattern of behavior that is typical of this schedule? Why or why not?
3. Describe how you would use a concurrent schedule of reinforcement to assess whether a rat preferred banana-flavored pellets over orange-flavored pellets.

THE ADAPTIVENESS OF OPERANT CONDITIONING

To survive, and certainly to prosper, organisms must remain sensitive to both constant and changing features of their environment. Among the sources of environmental change is behavior itself, and it is therefore difficult to imagine a biological creature that could successfully negotiate the demands of the physical environment while being oblivious to the consequences of its own actions. Of course, no such organism has been discovered, nor is such a discovery anticipated by scientists. Nearly a century of research on operant behavior, from Thorndike's original formulation of the law of effect to contemporary research and theory (Nevin & Grace, 2000), attests to the universal role that consequences play in behavioral adaptation. The adaptive nature of any learning process, though, depends upon its flexibility in accounting for a potentially large number of specific behavioral events. With regard to the research on the law of effect, this flexibility is provided by the conceptual framework of the three-term contingency. Other than obvious biological limitations, the range of events that can function as discriminative stimuli, behavior, and consequent stimuli is nearly infinite, often constrained more by apparatus and methodological limitations than by the richness of the subject matter itself.

Although the adaptive nature of operant learning is easily recognized in the experimental lever pressing or key pecking of animals whose behavior directly produces the necessities of life, the natural human environment offers more than its share of similar lessons. Failing to step on the brake pedal when approaching a red light at a busy intersection, typing in the wrong PIN number at the drive-through ATM, and inadvertently turning the power off on your computer while putting the finishing touches on a lengthy term paper all have unique and significant consequences in the human-made environment. More so than other animals, humans inhabit ever-changing environments, and different kinds of behavioral repertoires are called for in each. It is entirely appropriate to maintain a cerebral and serious demeanor in the classroom, but the same behavior will likely incur disapproval at a student picnic or party. The cardiac surgeon who asks for his nine iron rather than a scalpel in the middle of a surgical procedure may receive puzzled stares from his operating assistants—or an appointment with the hospital chief of staff. In short, we continuously attend to the world around us because doing so pays rather large dividends. Discriminative and consequential stimuli assume such a primary role in operant psychology because it is inconceivable how any organism could adapt its behavior to the demands of the environment without being attuned to these central, contextual events.

CHAPTER FIVE

Operant Conditioning
Applications

As a first-year student at a small liberal arts college, Kurt has had to make some pretty big adjustments to college life. Among his challenges has been getting used to the format for his introductory psychology class, which has proven unlike anything Kurt has encountered before in academia. To his amazement, Kurt learned the first day that there would be very few formal lectures given by the professor. In fact, most class days are devoted to testing, as Kurt and his classmates study small sections of chapters in their text and come to class prepared to take short quizzes over the material. As soon as Kurt has finished a quiz, he brings it to the front of the classroom where it is immediately graded by the instructor or an assistant. If Kurt doesn't do very well on the quiz, no big deal. He can take the quiz as many times as he needs to in order to develop complete mastery of the material. Kurt appreciates this part of the class, because even though most class time is given over to testing, the experience doesn't create the tremendous foreboding that ordinarily precedes taking a test. He is also excited about the fact that he can take the quizzes whenever he is ready, regardless of what other students are doing. The class is self-paced, meaning a student can work hard and finish the course requirements before the formal end of the semester. Kurt does so, receiving an A in the course. In addition, he finds, much to his surprise, that he can recall a good deal of what he learned in the course even a semester after having finished it. This unorthodox course format makes such an impression on Kurt that he makes every effort to sign up for other courses that are taught in the same manner.

There is nothing fictional about this description of Kurt's introductory psychology course. In fact, many courses, in psychology and other disciplines, are taught every year at U.S. colleges and universities using the format described. This self-paced, nonlecture format of instruction, referred to as *personalized system of instruction* (PSI), was introduced in the late 1960s by psychologist Fred Keller. Keller was a close friend and colleague of B. F. Skinner at Harvard, and the PSI format was developed with the goal of producing more effective instructional outcomes through the application of well-known behavioral principles, particularly operant learning. Through careful arrangement of antecedent stimuli and immediate consequences for behavior (test taking), the PSI format has proven to be an extremely efficient and effective method of instruction, and a sizable empirical literature attests to its superiority over traditional lecture format instruction (Kulik, Kulik, & Carmichael, 1974). Personalized instruction and other educational applications of operant principles will be explored in more depth later in the chapter.

Virtually all behavior produces consequences, and operant behavior can be changed by altering its consequences. This is why operant principles have been implemented across such a huge domain of human activity. In fact, it would be a challenge to identify any meaningful human behavior to which such principles have not been applied. In this book, the term **behavior modification** refers to any application of such principles to human behavior having social or clinical importance. The scope of behavior modification is immense, and operant principles have been used to modify behavior across such varied settings as the school, home, workplace, and public places. Moreover, the range of behaviors to which operant contingencies have been applied is enormous. Psychiatric patients exhibiting bizarre behaviors, and autistic and retarded children who bite and hit themselves, have been among the beneficiaries of behavioral programs. Patients suffering from chronic pain and those wishing to stop smoking or to develop better eating and exercise habits have acquired more adaptive repertoires of behavior. As a common example, teachers at every level, from preschool to college, have used operant techniques, not only to construct an environment that can better support educational objectives, but also to bring about those changes in student behavior referred to as *knowledge* and *skill*. In short, operant methodology has more than proven its mettle in varied social and clinical settings, and only a portion of this impressive success story can be covered here. Let's begin by taking a necessarily abridged look at some of the people and events that shaped the early development of behavior modification.

behavior modification application of operant principles to human behavior having social or clinical importance

BEHAVIOR MODIFICATION: A BRIEF HISTORY

As is true of most intellectual and scientific developments, the emergence of behavior modification within psychology was the result of an interesting collection of factors, including changes in the theoretical fabric of psychology as a discipline, growing frustration with existing approaches to treating maladaptive behavior, and a small cadre of laboratory scientists who believed that clinical interventions could and should be informed by basic research in learning. Let's consider the role that each of these factors played in the formative years of behavior modification.

The Rise of Behaviorism

Part of the machinery of any science are the often unspoken assumptions that researchers hold about their subject matter—its fundamental characteristics and dimensions—and how best to measure, make sense of, and even

BOX 5.1 / PSYCHOLOGICAL SCHOOLS OF THOUGHT

Despite their emphasis on objectivity and precise measurement, scientists within any particular discipline do not always agree about the nature and scope of their subject matter. Even physicists for years debated the very essence of light as a form of energy. Some theorized that light was best conceptualized as collections of individual rapidly moving particles, while others contended that light should be seen more holistically, as a wavelike phenomenon. Psychologists, too, see their subject matter in different ways. The major schools of thought, or epistemologies, characterizing the discipline of psychology are summarized here. Keep in mind that each school of thought actually boasts several variations on the general theme described, as contributed by many scientists and scholars over time.

Psychoanalytic   The psychoanalytic movement, begun in the late 1880s, was the brainchild of Sigmund Freud. Though many of Freud's close associates and colleagues would eventually split with him on several theoretical matters, all psychoanalytic theorists emphasize the significance of unconscious conflicts in determining human personality and behavior. This conflict, viewed as an inevitable product of the tension between the needs of the individual and those of the larger collectivity (society), may manifest itself in various shades of pathological (what Freud called neurotic) behavior.

Humanistic   Humanistic epistemology, partly emerging in response to psychoanalytic theory's focus on pathology, emphasizes the unique capacity that each individual has for positive growth, personal health, and what Abraham Maslow called "self-actualization." Compared with the other psychological perspectives, humanism places relatively little importance on science as a method of inquiry, valuing instead the phenomenology of first-person experience.

(continued)

talk about these dimensions. This collection of ideas about how to go about studying a particular phenomenon is referred to as **scientific epistemology**. Although such notions are not always explicitly articulated by scientists, they significantly inform every part of the scientific enterprise, from laboratory experimentation, to theory building, to discussions of the relevance of the science to everyday affairs. Psychology has its share of epistemologies, often referred to as schools of thought, and you can get some appreciation for the diversity of these schools from Box 5.1. Like the classic fable of six blind men who, when approaching an elephant from different directions, drew very different conclusions about what they had encountered, psychologists vary tremendously in defining their subject matter and in their recommendations about how best to go about understanding this subject matter.

scientific epistemology   collection of ideas scientists hold about how to go about studying a particular phenomenon scientifically

(continued)

Cognitive   The cognitive revolution began during the 1960s, largely in response to the long-standing domination of behaviorist philosophy. Many psychologists felt (often incorrectly—see Box 5.2) that behaviorism denied such private experiences as thoughts, feelings, and perceptions and that an understanding of human behavior required attention to such phenomena. Today, cognitive theory, and its focus on information processing, remains the predominant school of thought in psychology, particularly in its recent convergence with neuroscience.

Neuroscience (biological basis)   No serious student of behavior has ever denied the role that biology *must* play in behavior, and contemporary neuroscientists are well situated to shed unprecedented light on brain-behavior relationships. Modern technology allows for detailed and intimate analyses of the specific anatomical and physiological events that make possible the sensations, perceptions, thoughts, feelings, and actions that have been the historical subject matter of psychology. Neuroscientific epistemology argues that any understanding of behavior necessarily begins with an analysis of these underlying physical occurrences.

Behaviorism   There are at least as many versions of behaviorist theory as there are of psychoanalytic theory. Nevertheless, all forms of behaviorism share a common allegiance to the scientific method, particularly with respect to objective and precise behavioral measurement. Also, behaviorist philosophy tends to highlight learning as a primary vehicle for behavioral development and to place relatively less emphasis on the concept of personal agency (personality dispositions, etc.).

In the initial decades of the 20th century, psychology would undergo a significant philosophical shift, presided over by an ambitious and charismatic American, John B. Watson. Recall from Chapter 3 that Watson was the behavioral psychologist who, along with Rosalie Rayner, conditioned fear in an 11-month-old child (Little Albert) through experimental means. That Watson was pursuing explanations of human behavior based on fundamental learning principles was no accident. Several years before the famous Little Albert experiment, Watson had called for a revolutionary change in the science of psychology. He had been disappointed by the predominant psychological methodology of his day—introspection—which usually took the form of scientists isolating themselves in sound-proofed experimental cubicles and detailing their every sensation, thought, and private experience. According to many psychologists, introspection was the proper way to achieve the goals of this young science, namely, describing the basic elements or structures of the human mind.

Watson could not disagree more. He argued that the "mind" was a fanciful notion born of philosophical speculation, not experimental science, and that no sufficient instrumentation existed to "introspect" this mythical structure anyway. For this reason, Watson (1913) claimed psychology to be "a natural science of behavior," and its subject matter was to include only overt, readily observable activity, not the private, inaccessible world of mental life. Watson's proclamations came at a time in psychology's history when many psychologists were adamant about establishing the scientific status of this young discipline, and the focus on observation and measurement seemed to preclude attention to the elusive elements of mind. It is important to point out that Watson never claimed that such private events were unreal or that the activity of the brain was irrelevant to understanding behavior. His argument was largely a methodological one. There was simply no way in Watson's day to directly observe the physiological activity of the nervous system, and this made focusing on this activity less than scientific. Today's scientists benefit from a number of high-tech instruments that offer remarkable access to the nervous system, but this could not have been foreseen by Watson.

Watson's focus on overt behavior represents a scientific epistemology known as *behaviorism,* and this perspective or school of thought dominated American psychology for most of the first half of the 20th century. As a philosophy, behaviorism has always placed a premium on empirical research and on the pervasive role that learning plays in the development of a behavioral repertoire. Although behavioristic thinking has informed the work of many pioneers, such as Pavlov and Thorndike, the philosophy achieved its greatest influence within psychology in the research and writing of operant psychologists, headed up most visibly by Skinner. As discussed in the previous chapter, Skinner's contributions to psychology came in many forms, from important empirical investigations, to applications of learning principles to behavior in natural settings (Skinner, 1958, 1968), to discussions of behaviorism's underlying assumptions (Skinner, 1953, 1974) and ideas. Unfortunately, many of Skinner's contributions haven't been well appreciated by nonbehavioral psychologists, and his ideas have been systematically misrepresented even within the psychological literature and unduly criticized over the years (Catania, 1991; Todd & Morris, 1983, 1992). For a glimpse at the many misconceptions that continue to surface regarding Skinner's writings, see Box 5.2. Despite these misunderstandings and many claims about the death of behaviorism, behavioral psychology remains a viable and influential perspective within psychology, as manifested in both the laboratory and the field.

Treating Maladaptive Behavior: Leaving the Medical Model Behind

When you visit your family physician because of an illness, you have certain expectations about your appointment. You expect to be questioned about your symptoms, to be examined by the physician, and you expect this process to result in a diagnosis and a recommendation for treatment. Physicians are trained in identifying symptoms that are consistent with a particular disease or pathology, as well in how to treat the pathology by way of internal medicine, surgery, or other alternatives. As a biological system, the body is susceptible to numerous kinds of illness, so this business of diagnosing and treating pathology can be quite complicated. The entire enterprise is predicated on the notion of pathology or illness. People are believed to become

BOX 5.2 / MISCONSTRUING THE LEGACY OF B. F. SKINNER

The magnitude of Skinner's empirical and theoretical contributions to operant psychology has been amply noted so far. What has not been discussed is the considerable extent to which these contributions have been distorted or misunderstood, even by his fellow psychologists. In fact, Skinner may enjoy the rather dubious distinction of being the most thoroughly maligned and misrepresented figure in psychology's history. Todd and Morris (1983, 1992) have documented the many aspects of Skinner's thought that have been misrepresented in the psychological literature, particularly by authors of psychology textbooks. Though not exhaustive, the following represent some of the more common errors:

1. *Behaviorism is a form of stimulus-response (S-R) psychology.* Although this claim was somewhat true of earlier brands of behaviorism, Skinner's radical behaviorism envisioned a probabilistic relationship between behavior and antecedent stimuli, rather than a mechanical, one-to-one relationship usually attributed to S-R theorists.

2. *Because of its focus on environmental variables, behaviorism has often been accused of downplaying, or even ignoring, the role played by genetic endowment in behavior.* In actuality, both Watson and Skinner conducted research that would today be classified as "behavioral genetics," and Skinner (1966, 1981, 1987) wrote extensively on the complex relationship between genetic and environmental determinants of behavior.

3. *Skinner's operant principles are often perceived as being applicable only to nonhuman organisms behaving under highly controlled laboratory settings.* As described in this chapter, Skinner and his students were among the first to extend the basic findings of operant research to human environments, including medical institutions and classrooms. The development of behavior modification as a major force in clinical psychology, in fact, owes a substantial debt to Skinner's empirical laboratory work as well as his conceptual and theoretical writings.

4. *Skinner, and all behaviorists, are only interested in overt, objective behavior.* This may be the most common misconception surrounding Skinner's behaviorism. In fact, on more than one occasion, Skinner (1969) claimed that "The skin is not that important as a boundary" (p. 228), and both public and private activity were equally amenable to an analysis by way of contingencies of reinforcement. How this analysis might unfold, and its importance to behavioral science, is especially well articulated in Skinner's 1953 book *Science and Human Behavior,* in a chapter aptly titled "Private Events in a Natural Science."

sick when various external pathogens infect their body or when particular bodily systems fail or function in a less than optimal manner. The basic idea of pathology, and the logic that leads to examination, diagnosis, and treatment, is often referred to as the *medical model.*

Most people don't have any difficulty conceiving of the body as a physical system that can malfunction as the result of a disease process, so the medical model and its focus on pathology makes intuitive sense. But what about malfunctions or pathology in behavior? Is it logical to talk about behavior or psychological functioning being pathological or diseased? If so, could the medical model be extended to the assessment, diagnosis, and treatment of behavioral or psychological illness? After all, the term *mental illness,* which has been around for many years, seems to suggest that the idea of pathology can be applied to mental functioning as readily as it can be applied to physical functioning. There is in fact ample precedent for viewing psychological functioning as a phenomenon susceptible to pathology. A focus on pathology is explicit in the psychoanalytic theory of Sigmund Freud and also in the modern discipline of psychiatry. Indeed, the very bible of diagnosis, utilized by both psychiatrists and many clinical psychologists, is tellingly titled the *Diagnostic and Statistical Manual of Mental Disorders* (American Psychiatric Association, 2000) and is currently in its fourth, revised, edition. Like their counterparts in hospitals, people in psychiatric or mental institutions are referred to as patients. Moreover, the medical model and its focus on pathology is pervasive in the colloquialisms of everyday language. It is not uncommon to hear someone refer to those exhibiting strange or bizarre behavior as being "sick in the head," "touched," or "mentally ill."

Among the conceptual contributions made by behavioristic psychologists was the claim that strange, bizarre, or maladaptive behavior might have more to do with environmental experiences, such as learning, than with pathology of the mind. Rather than searching for evidence of pathology in the form of classic Freudian defense mechanisms or disordered personality structures, early behavioral psychologists chose to focus on the learning process and how basic principles might produce both adaptive and maladaptive repertoires of behavior. The position taken by these pioneering behavior therapists is well articulated by Kazdin (1982a):

> A second characteristic of the behavioral approach is the view that normal and abnormal behavior are not qualitatively different. Some behaviors are not "sick" and others "healthy" based on characteristics inherent in the behaviors. There is a continuity of behavior, and psychological principles apply to all behaviors whether or not they are identified as normal. Thus, maladaptive behavior can be unlearned and replaced by adaptive behavior. (p. 25)

A major impetus for the development of behavior therapy came out of the research on psychotherapy outcome. In a groundbreaking study in 1952, Hans Eysenck examined the clinical effects of various types of "talking" therapies, including conventional psychoanalysis. The controversial results of

Eysenck's study included the observation that those patients who received therapy, regardless of type, showed no more improvement than a control group that received no treatment. Eysenck's study ignited a firestorm of debate and subsequent research on therapy outcome, and today a good deal more is known about how the effectiveness of therapy depends upon such critical features as the therapy procedure itself, the training and competence of the clinician, and numerous client characteristics as well (Hubble, Duncan, & Miller, 1999; Seligman, 1995, 1996). Nevertheless, Eysenck's conclusions left little doubt that there was substantial room for improvement in the development of therapeutic interventions for psychological and behavioral problems.

Eysenck's research, and the discovery that fear responses could be produced and eliminated through basic conditioning processes, set the stage for a revolution in the conceptualization and treatment of psychopathology. Psychology was increasingly turning away from medical model explanations, and, by the 1940s and 1950s, Watson's epistemological revolution was in full swing. Behaviorism as a philosophy informed much of what transpired under the banner of psychology, and an emphasis on rigorous empirical practice characterized the work of both basic research and application of psychological principles. Indeed, as is typical of the development of technology, many of the original clinical applications of behavior therapy were conducted by scientists who had cut their teeth on basic laboratory research.

From the Laboratory to the Field

In 1958 a seminal event in the history of operant psychology occurred. Frustrated by the reluctance of psychology journal editors to publish studies on basic operant behavior, Charles Ferster, B. F. Skinner, and several other colleagues founded their own publication outlet, *Journal of the Experimental Analysis of Behavior (JEAB)*. The journal would eventually become one of experimental psychology's more prestigious forums, and it remains committed today to the study of behavior in individual organisms. In fact, this focus on the individual is what makes *JEAB* unique. Most of psychology had, by the 1940s, adopted the experimental logic proposed by Ronald Fisher, in which large groups of subjects, having been exposed to different experimental conditions, are compared at experiment's end on some relevant behavioral measure. This comparison ordinarily requires that the behavioral measures from the many subjects composing a group be added together, or *aggregated,* to produce a group mean or average score. Skinner (1938, 1953) and others in the operant movement argued that group averages obscured important features of individual behavior and were consequently inappropriate measurement dimensions in a science of behavior (Johnston & Pennypacker, 1993; Sidman, 1960). *JEAB*'s founding was significant, not only because its contributors had demonstrated the powerful advantages of single-subject research, but also because many of the data published in the journal proved both reliable and replicable, a relatively unprecedented occurrence in the behavioral sciences.

Skinner's methodology proved to be an extraordinarily powerful tool for studying the variables that influence behavior, and the emphasis on individual behavior that he and his many followers championed led inexorably toward questions of application. Operant researchers had demonstrated potent control over behavior by systematically altering antecedent and consequent events, and it was a small logical step to infer that similar manipulations could be conducted in natural settings to alter maladaptive behavior. By the early 1950s, the stage was set for operant psychology to move beyond the somewhat artificial confines of the laboratory and flex its muscles in the real world.

The first formal attempt to apply operant principles to maladaptive human behavior was made by Skinner and his student, Ogden Lindsley, at the Massachusetts Metropolitan State Hospital in 1954 (Lindsley & Skinner, 1954). Their original efforts were directed toward patients diagnosed as psychotic, an exceedingly debilitating condition characterized by severe disturbances in all aspects of cognitive, emotional, and behavioral functioning. Clearly, the researchers had their work cut out for them, as this particular form of pathology had long since been considered unresponsive to treatment. Using a modified operant chamber, Lindsley and Skinner programmed various reinforcers (such as cigarettes and candy) to be made available contingent on pulling a lever attached to the apparatus. Supported by the observation and measurement strategies of the operant laboratory, the researchers were able to monitor response rates with a precision seldom demonstrated in applied settings. To the surprise of many, Lindsley and Skinner showed considerable sensitivity of the patient's behavior to programmed contingencies of both reinforcement and extinction. Here was a group of patients, afflicted by the most severe of psychological disorders, whose behavior could nonetheless be shown to be responsive to antecedent and consequent events, rather than being entirely disconnected from reality, as was the conventional wisdom of the times.

By the late 1950s, the floodgates had been thrown open, and several researchers and clinicians began to enthusiastically import operant principles to psychiatric hospitals. King, Armitage, and Tilton (1960) utilized a modified version of Lindsley and Skinner's apparatus to modify the behavior of withdrawn, mute, schizophrenic patients. Operant principles were used to shape problem-solving skills and cooperative behavior in the hospital ward environment. Compared to patients receiving other kinds of therapy, the operant group experienced increased success at solving everyday problems on the ward and also demonstrated greater interpersonal competence. Moreover, these treatment benefits were observed even in nontraining circumstances, particularly in the form of spontaneous verbalizations, a rather remarkable achievement given the patients' previous verbal deficits.

The Token Economy   By the 1960s, clinical interventions based on operant learning principles were flourishing in applied settings. By far the most impressive large-scale application was conducted at Anna State Hospital in Illinois. Teodoro Ayllon and Nathan Azrin (1965, 1968) implemented a program in which all the residents in one ward of the hospital were continuously exposed to various operant contingencies. The program focused on behaviors having practical or real-world consequences, such as personal hygiene and work-related activities. An essential component of the program was the systematic training of hospital staff (nurses, aides, etc.) in how to arrange and implement appropriate reinforcement contingencies. Through appropriate behavior, residents could earn tokens, which could later be exchanged for "backup" reinforcers, including such things as grounds privileges, attending religious services, and various preferred items, such as cigarettes. (Of course, it should go without saying that the use of cigarettes as reinforcers would be considered inappropriate by today's standards.) Consistent with basic operant research, each subject served as his or her own control, and response rates for each relevant behavior were monitored throughout the program, both before and during implementation of operant contingencies.

token economy
behavior modification program delivered systematically to a large community or institution

Ayllon and Azrin (1968) had established the first **token economy,** a behavior modification program delivered systematically to a large community of individuals (hospital residents). The results, described in detail in their classic book, *The Token Economy: A Motivational System for Therapy and Rehabilitation,* were nothing short of phenomenal. Most residents were observed engaging in much higher frequencies of appropriate behaviors, while demonstrating much less of the bizarre, maladaptive behavior for which they were originally hospitalized. In fact, in a later token economy, residents were allowed to actually earn their way out of the token program by demonstrating substantial improvement in behavior (Paul & Lentz, 1977). In such a program, gradual changes in both self-help and social behavior can lead to additional levels in the token economy, in which requirements for behavior are more stringent, but privileges (backup reinforcers) are more desirable. Given sufficient improvement, residents can not only earn their way out of the token economy but out of the institution as well. Since its inception in the 1960s, the token economy has become a fairly standard treatment modality in many institutional settings, including psychiatric hospitals; drug abuse clinics (Budney, Higgins, Delaney, Kent, & Bickel, 1991); correctional facilities (Bassett & Blanchard, 1977); the workplace (Fox, Hopkins, & Anger, 1987); schools (Knapczyk & Livingston, 1973); and the home (Lowe & Lutzker, 1979).

Token economies are not without their limitations, however (Kazdin, 1982b). In fact, their widespread use in many settings has allowed for rather thorough outcome research, resulting in an impressive inventory of the token economy's strengths and weaknesses. Clearly, token programs have more than proven their mettle regarding behavior change, even in clinical populations long considered impervious to therapeutic efforts. The benefits of token economies, though, come at a considerable cost, not the least of which is substantial amounts of training and organization. Since most programs are actually administered by institutional staff (nurses, aides, guards, etc.), considerable preparation is often necessary to teach staff members how to properly respond to the behavior of residents. A token economy, after all, is not simply a large operant chamber, and consequences cannot be delivered automatically with mechanical precision. Instead, the success of the program depends upon the ability of the staff to arrange consequences properly and in a timely manner. This requirement is much more difficult to meet than it may seem. As any parent or teacher can tell you, it is pretty easy, or "natural," to pay attention to someone whose behavior is problematic or disruptive and similarly easy to leave the well-behaved person alone. But this natural reaction is often the opposite of what is needed, and considerable time and effort are often necessary to teach the staff, or behavior change agents, how to deliver consequences in an effective manner. In the end, a token economy is only as good as the training of its staff.

By far the greatest shortcoming of the token economy is the frequent failure of behavior change to generalize, or occur outside the specific environment of the institution. This is, in some sense, an understandable and perhaps expected outcome. After all, a detention center for juvenile delinquents run on the token principle, for example, is going to be designed to reinforce socially and ethically appropriate behavior and either punish or place on extinction inappropriate behavior. But should a resident eventually earn his or her way out of the facility, the most likely result will be a return to an original environment whose reinforcement contingencies are almost certain to produce a deterioration in behavior. During the 1960s and 1970s, this unfortunate drawback was simply accepted as a weak link in the token economy, but this is no longer the case. Fortunately, the past 15 years have seen a significant increase in research on treatment generalization, or transfer of training. Much is understood now about the variables that contribute to or impede treatment generalization, and today's behavior therapists consider the issue to be a crucial component of the overall therapy program, rather than an uncontrollable event left to happenstance (Horner, Dunlap, & Koegel, 1988).

Founding of AABT and *JABA*

Behavior therapy, and its supporting philosophy of behaviorism, had by the late 1950s and early 1960s become the dominant force in applied and clinical psychology. Increasingly, psychologists were being trained to both conceptualize and treat maladaptive behavior from a learning perspective, rather than from the medical model. Not surprisingly, the growing numbers of behaviorally educated psychologists eventually necessitated the establishment of a professional organization, and in 1966 the Association for the Advancement of Behavior Therapy (AABT) was formed. Consisting primarily of clinical psychologists operating from a behavioral orientation, AABT today boasts more than 4,500 members. In addition, the society publishes *Behavior Therapy* and the *Behavior Therapist*, journals dedicated to empirical research and to professional issues regarding the application of behavior therapy.

An emphasis on empirical rigor and the scientific method has always been a hallmark of behavior therapy. Indeed, behavior therapists often conceptualize a treatment regimen as not only a clinical intervention but also a single-subject experiment in which the outcome data serve useful scientific purposes. Early behavior therapists were limited in their ability to disseminate therapeutic findings, for few professional journals existed that were devoted to clinical studies of behavioral interventions. Although established

TABLE 5.1 PSYCHOLOGY JOURNALS REPRESENTING A BEHAVIORAL ORIENTATION

Advances in Behaviour Research and Therapy

Behavior Analysis Letters

The Behavior Analyst

Behavior Modification

Behavior Therapy

Behavioral Assessment

Behaviorism

Behaviour Research and Therapy

Child and Family Behavior Therapy

Journal of Applied Behavior Analysis

Journal of Autism and Developmental Disorders

Journal of Behavior Therapy and Experimental Psychiatry

Journal of Behavioral Medicine

Journal of the Experimental Analysis of Behavior

in 1958, *JEAB* was of little help, for it was a basic research journal, dedicated more to laboratory studies of operant conditioning than to applications of operant principles in natural settings. Perceiving a need for an applied journal, the Society for the Analysis of Behavior established, in 1968, the *Journal of Applied Behavior Analysis (JABA)*. For more than 30 years, *JABA* has remained the primary outlet for empirical articles concerning applications of operant principles to behavior in various settings, including institutions, homes, schools, and the workplace. *JEAB* and *JABA*, however, were simply the tip of the iceberg. By the mid-1980s, more than two dozen professional psychology journals had been established that operated primarily from a behavioral perspective (Wyatt, Hawkins, & Davis, 1986).

✖ INTERIM SUMMARY

Philosophical rumblings at the turn of the 20th century, particularly in the form of John B. Watson's influential writings, paved the way for an American psychology dominated by a behavioral orientation. By the 1940s and 1950s, the laboratory-based study of learning had taken on a decidedly operant emphasis, and the success enjoyed by these laboratory scientists would eventually lead to efforts at application. Early studies by Skinner and several of his students demonstrated that operant principles could be generalized beyond the laboratory and that such principles were equally relevant to both normal behavior and behavior traditionally viewed as maladaptive or disordered. The application of operant principles to behavior in natural settings, referred to as behavior modification, would become an influential branch of clinical psychology, leading to numerous professional organizations and scientific journals devoted to a behavioral orientation (Table 5.1).

❌ THOUGHT QUESTIONS
1. A behavioral orientation argues that maladaptive behavior may often be the result of the same learning processes that produce normal, or adaptive, behavior. What implications do you think this perspective has for the legal system, particularly the popular "insanity" defense?
2. A token is a conditioned reinforcer that can then be exchanged for backup reinforcers. Other than money, can you identify some common tokens encountered in your natural environment?

OPERANT PRINCIPLES AND BEHAVIORAL MEDICINE

Let's return to the example of a visit to the family physician. This time, you have been examined—perhaps even subjected to lengthy testing at the office or in a hospital—a diagnosis has been rendered, and a treatment will be prescribed by the physician. The nature of the treatment will naturally depend upon the diagnosis given but will almost necessarily require some follow-through on your part. For instance, you may be prescribed an antibiotic medication for an infection, and, if so, your physician, and the label on the medicine bottle, will instruct you to take all of the pills in the bottle. If you were diagnosed with either essential hypertension (high blood pressure) or diabetes, a very strict routine of medication and self-regulation of diet, and possibly exercise, would be instituted. Similar kinds of recommendations may occur if your physical symptoms are the result of smoking or being substantially overweight.

Regardless of the diagnosis and recommended treatment, a common theme tends to run through virtually any encounter with a physician: As the patient, you will be expected to follow through on or adhere to the recommended treatment. This means that the effectiveness of the treatment may depend in no small part on your willingness to comply with your physician's recommendations. That is, your behavior becomes an essential part of the treatment equation. Yet, the physician's expertise ends at the point that the diagnosis is made and treatment recommended. Despite his or her medical authority, the physician has no special credentials or knowledge for ensuring that you will adhere to the treatment program. In fact, any physician will tell you that this often becomes a serious problem, for many patients fail, for whatever reason, to adhere to treatment, be it medication, self-monitoring of blood pressure or blood sugar levels, dietary recommendations, or exercise regimens. In the end, the expertise of the physician is of little value if patients do not assume responsibility for following through on the prescribed medical treatment.

Fortunately, that point at which the physician's expertise ends is also where the expertise of another professional comes into play. Although the medical professional is not necessarily expected to know how to help patients adhere to a prescribed treatment regimen, the problem lies very much within the domain of the psychologist. After all, behavior is *the* subject matter of psychology, and taking medication, eating, exercising, and self-monitoring are all simply different types of behavior. The potential benefits of a professional collaboration between medical and behavioral scientists was officially recognized at a conference held at Yale University in 1977. The result of this interdisciplinary meeting was the field of **behavioral medicine,** defined by Blanchard (1977) as "the systematic application of the principles and technology of behavioral psychology to the field of medicine, health and illness" (p. 2). There has always been some controversy about the definition of behavioral medicine (Gentry, 1984), but this disagreement is beyond the scope of the present chapter. For purposes of this discussion, the phrase *health psychology* can just as readily be substituted for behavioral medicine with little loss of meaning.

behavioral medicine
application of basic behavior principles to behavior having significant repercussions for health and illness

Whatever the label, at the heart of behavioral medicine is the explicit acknowledgment that there exists an abiding relationship between people's actions and their physical well-being. In some sense, the field represents the most recent reincarnation of an age-old preoccupation with the connection between mind and body. But rather than being characterized primarily by philosophical speculation, behavioral medicine is a decidedly research-oriented discipline, represented by several professional organizations and scientific journals. Moreover, the field is an extremely broad one, encompassing psychologists from many theoretical orientations, not solely those endorsing a behavioristic philosophy. Research in behavioral medicine runs the gamut, from studies of how personality factors correlate with susceptibility to various illnesses, to the variables that affect compliance with medical regimens, to the especially difficult topic of modifying long-standing behavior patterns, such as diet and exercise, that influence health. Because of its immensity—indeed, behavioral medicine and health psychology are among the fastest growing subfields within psychology—the review of the field presented here will be necessarily selective. The first topic is relevant, not only to millions of individuals, but increasingly to the legal profession as well.

Smoking Cessation

The negative health consequences of smoking cigarettes are rarely contested today. Both the addictive nature of nicotine and the connection between smoking and emphysema and lung cancer are so thoroughly documented that the very future of the tobacco industry seems tenuous. Nevertheless, supporters of cigarette manufacturers are often quick to point out that people "decide" to smoke and therefore should assume some responsibility for the consequences of doing so. Regardless of how you feel about this particular argument, it does point to an inescapable fact: Cigarette smoking is behavior. A physician, having diagnosed a medical condition related to smoking, can recommend that the patient stop smoking—even plead with the patient to stop—but any physician will tell you such words typically fall on deaf ears. The problem is ultimately a behavioral one; thus it falls within the domain of the behavior therapist. Arguments about legal or moral responsibility aside, it makes sense that behavioral psychologists would be interested in understanding the dynamics of smoking, particularly the role

FIGURE 5.1 Behavioral interventions can be effective in reducing cigarette smoking.

played by antecedent and consequent stimuli in the development, maintenance, and, ultimately, elimination of the habit.

A sizable literature in behavior modification is devoted to the issue of smoking cessation, and this literature, spanning nearly four decades, represents an interesting microcosm of the developments and trends that have characterized behavior modification as a discipline (Figure 5.1). Early efforts to reduce cigarette smoking tended to rely on aversive measures. Azrin and Powell (1968), for instance, designed a cigarette case that delivered a painful electric shock when it was opened. Use of shock as an aversive proved to be short-lived, both for ethical reasons and because of limited long-term effectiveness. An alternative aversive procedure, rapid smoking, required the client to inhale continuously until a personal tolerance level was reached. Initial studies conducted on rapid smoking showed promising results, including abstinence rates of nearly 50% at follow-up 6 months later (Danaher, 1977). Later studies have reported less sterling results (Gordon, 1978) and have questioned the ethics of rapid smoking, citing possible physiological disadvantages (Russell, Raw, Taylor, Feyerabend, & Saloojee, 1978). In sum, aversive procedures have, in recent years, given way to programs based either on stimulus control principles or use of less questionable consequences.

Foxx and Brown (1979) exposed different groups of smokers to varying conditions of self-monitoring and reduced nicotine intake. The group that was required both to keep track of their own smoking behavior (self-monitoring) and to smoke cigarettes containing a progressively smaller amount of nicotine were more likely to be abstinent at the 18-month follow-up than other experimental groups. In addition, subjects in this group who were still smoking were able to maintain lower nicotine levels because of their use of the low-nicotine cigarettes. Stitzer and Bigelow (1984) offered monetary reinforcement to smokers for reducing smoking frequency. The researchers measured carbon monoxide (CO) levels in the smokers' breath each afternoon. Subjects could receive payment contingent on reducing their CO levels to below baseline, to a maximum of $12 a day. The program was successful in reducing CO levels, with greater reduction being associated with larger monetary reinforcement. Similar results were obtained by Stitzer, Rand, Bigelow, and Mead (1986) when monetary reinforcement was combined with a self-monitoring schedule.

The final chapter on behavioral interventions for smoking clearly has yet to be written. Researchers can attest to the fact that habitual behavior patterns, particularly those characterizing addictions, are extremely resistant to change, and it is unreasonable to expect easy solutions. For this reason, treatment today tends to be multimodal—that is, made up of various components, some of which might be conventional operant strategies, others borrowing more from social learning or cognitive theory. As Lichtenstein and Brown (1982) note, these multicomponent packages, though often effective, are difficult to assess scientifically, for it becomes nearly impossible to determine which of the components provided the primary clinical effect or if the effect was produced by some idiosyncratic interaction of variables.

Weight Loss and Dietary Habits

American culture seems to be in the midst of a fitness or health craze, which is well supported by a multibillion-dollar diet and physical fitness industry. Visit your local bookstore and browse the dozens of titles that promise to help you lose those excess pounds or to build muscle mass in just "minutes a day!" Turn on your television and be mesmerized by half-hour infomercials celebrating the latest home gym equipment, scientifically engineered and guaranteed to burn off fat and refine previously unused muscles. Many of these new machines come complete with instructional videos describing not only how to use the equipment but also how to tailor a workout to fit your specific needs. And it's not as if the current obsession with physical fitness is unjustified. In fact, it is ironic that in the most affluent country in the world, with access to the most advanced medical care in human history, many Americans seem to be losing the battle to stay fit. Government statistics demonstrate that obesity is nearly epidemic, and the medical complications associated with being overweight are multifarious (National Institutes of Health [NIH], 1998). Moreover, obesity is especially troubling when seen in young children, an apparently increasing percentage of the overweight population. Estimates suggest that by the mid-1990s, 13% of American children were considered overweight according to government standards, nearly double the rate observed during the 1960s (Cowley, 2000).

One culprit in the increase of obesity is the modern high-tech lifestyle. Many people work at sedentary jobs and eat foods high in saturated fats and unneeded calories but low in nutritious content. Americans also work more hours than do the people of any other industrialized nation, leaving little time to circumvent this unhealthy lifestyle with needed exercise. And most parents don't need government statistics (though such statistics are readily available) to tell them that today's crop of youngsters spends inordinate hours in equally sedentary pursuits, such as watching television and playing computer and video games. The current fitness industry is predicated on the fact that this current state of affairs bothers us, and we quite naturally find appealing all those promises of a more desirable, healthy lifestyle.

There is one very big catch in the fitness craze equation, one that is conveniently minimized by the fitness gurus on television. It isn't that the programs and equipment they advertise are useless—far from it, in fact. But substantial weight loss or increases in cardiovascular fitness or muscle mass require (you guessed it) a lot of behavior on your part; and this proves, time and time again, to be the sticking point. In fact, the reasons that so many diet and exercise programs fail are transparent to the behavioral psychologist, and you will likely recognize them from the discussion of reinforcement and punishment in the previous chapter. Basic research has clearly shown that, in general, consequences that immediately follow behavior tend to have strong effects on the behavior, and the more delayed the consequence, the less the effect. Unfortunately, the positive consequences of dieting or exercise are anything but immediate. Almost without exception, benefits from a diet or exercise program do not materialize until several weeks, maybe even months, after initiating the program. That doesn't mean there aren't relatively immediate consequences, for there are; and, unfortunately, they often work against the program's success. Suppose, for example, that you begin an exercise program after having been sedentary for many years. You begin with a bang—jogging a 2-mile course in your neighborhood. The next morning, you awaken to extraordinarily sore muscles and spend the rest of the day moving gingerly from your desk to the watercooler, vowing to decline any future temptation to exert yourself.

When trying to change your diet or level of physical activity, you face a common dilemma in which various consequences (positive and negative) are pitted against one another. The relatively immediate consequence of jogging/walking is sore muscles. Any benefits, such as better cardiovascular fitness, will not occur overnight but, instead, over a much longer period of time. It isn't hard to see, then, why so many exercise programs are terminated within the first few days of their initiation (Leith & Taylor, 1992). Similarly, weight loss tends to occur gradually, whereas increased hunger is a relatively short-term result of restricting food intake. The deprived dieter who opens the refrigerator door only to encounter a tantalizing piece of chocolate cake is simply facing nearly insurmountable odds. When pitted against a "possible" weight loss, perhaps not visible for several weeks, the immediate availability of the tasty cake becomes overwhelming. At moments like this, comments from friends or family about will power are often of little help. What is needed instead is an appreciation of the complex dynamics of diet and exercise, particularly the role played by antecedent and consequent stimuli as relevant controlling variables. Behavioral research has borne some impressive fruit in this regard.

Many behavioral interventions for weight loss and exercise focus on elements of stimulus control, which, you will recall, concern the discriminative stimuli that set the occasion for behavior. Although hunger, defined as the sensation of an empty stomach, would seem to be the primary discriminative stimulus for eating, this is decidedly not the case. In fact, the range of effective S^Ds for food consumption in the industrialized world is overwhelming. Many people, for instance, have grown accustomed to eating in front of the television. And who among us would decline an appetizer at a social gathering, even if we had come directly from eating a large meal? In fact, the tendency of party-goers to congregate in the kitchen, or wherever food is being served, is well documented, and this suggests that being hungry or food deprived is neither a necessary nor sufficient cause of eating. For this reason, behavioral programs devoted to weight loss often target antecedent stimuli (Adachi, 1989; Jeffery, 1987).

The range of visual, auditory, and olfactory stimuli that can serve as cues to eating is probably unlimited. The reading on a clock tells us how close we are to the next mealtime. For some people, simply turning the television on sets the occasion for heading to the kitchen for a snack. Of course, all of those commercials for food and drink make their own contribution. And the prominent images and the odors emanating from fast-food restaurants can be pretty hard to pass up on your way to or from work. The fact is, most of us have a low threshold for food-related stimuli and consequently give in readily to such temptations. Thus, a beginning point of many behavioral interventions for weight loss is teaching the client to recognize possible antecedents or cues for eating, with the ultimate aim being some degree of control over these cues.

Many programs teach clients to avoid turning on the television until after they have eaten a meal. It is often desirable to bring eating under the strict stimulus control of a properly set table and prescribed mealtimes. And what of the allure of the fast-food restaurant? Sometimes, stimulus control comes down to common sense. It may be possible for you to drive home from work using a route that doesn't take you by the tempting restaurant. And at home, why not make nutritious snacks, such as fruits and vegetables, readily available by placing them on the table or kitchen counter. If you simply must have sugar- and fat-loaded goodies around, keep them out of sight, not in a prominently displayed cookie jar.

As you know, antecedent stimuli aren't the whole picture. The effectiveness of a discriminative stimulus depends upon the consequences that follow behavior in its presence. Altering food-related environmental stimuli by itself is not likely to bring about clinically significant changes in eating habits. Behavioral approaches to weight loss, therefore, usually entail the use of important reinforcers as well. Stuart (1967) reported the results of the first formal attempt to apply behavior modification procedures to weight loss. All 8 subjects who remained in treatment experienced significant weight loss, a finding that generated great interest and fueled tremendous research activity during the subsequent decade. In such behavioral programs, reinforcement often comes in the form of money or points that can later be exchanged for various privileges. In addition, reinforcers can be made contingent on either weight loss itself or on behaviors that lead to weight loss, including self-monitoring and eating habits.

In a study by Aragona, Cassady, and Drabman (1975), parents of obese children deposited substantial amounts of money into a fund at the beginning of the treatment program. The money could be earned back by meeting various program goals, such as self-monitoring, attendance at group meetings, and documented weight loss. Parent/child groups were also placed on a response cost contingency, in which money could be lost permanently if treatment goals were not met. Compared to a no-treatment control group, children in groups placed on the response cost treatment lost significantly more weight. Although some of the weight was regained at an 8-week follow-up, children in the response cost group maintained weight loss more than did children in the control group.

By the late 1970s, a good deal of optimism surrounded research on behavioral treatment of obesity. Sadly, this optimism has been tempered by setbacks in recent years. Although behavioral interventions for weight loss have been well documented, long-term maintenance of these reductions has proved elusive (Kramer, Jeffery, Forster, & Snell, 1989; Stunkard & Penick, 1979). The problem of maintaining weight loss is complicated by many factors, some of which are nonbehavioral. It is well known, for example, that the body's metabolic rate slows down in response to food restriction, resulting in fewer calories burned and, ultimately, slower weight loss. Wooley, Wooley, and Dyrenforth (1979) have suggested that therapists implementing weight loss programs for obese clients keep in mind such physiological variables, as well as idiosyncrasies in the clients' sensitivity to food cues and food restriction. This means that behavioral interventions must be designed specifically for each client, based on the client's personal history, physiological status, and responsiveness to particular program contingencies.

Pain Management

For humans and nonhumans alike, painful stimulation is among the most powerful of motivators. In sufficient magnitude, pain will send the most stoic among us in search of medicinal relief, even to the emergency room in the dead of night. Those who otherwise avoid their physician's or dentist's office with zeal can be coaxed into an office visit by the right amount of discomfort. Although pain may be a fact of life, much of the activity of the multibillion-dollar health care and pharmaceutical industries is devoted to its alleviation: Pain is big business in the United States.

From a behavioral standpoint, pain is an intriguing phenomenon. On the one hand, pain is aversive stimulation. Clearly, like other health specialists, psychologists wish to help patients reduce their sensations of pain. But an equally important aspect of pain is the role it plays in the patient's behavioral repertoire. That is, pain may serve as an antecedent for many kinds of behavior. When in pain, people grimace, change their body posture, verbalize (perhaps quite loudly), sometimes act aggressively against others, and attempt to discover ways to reduce the pain. Health psychologists refer to this collection of activity as *pain behavior,* and among the purposes of behavioral medicine is understanding both the antecedents and consequences of such behavior. Before considering how such behavior is modified, let's take a look at the contribution that behavioral medicine makes to the actual reduction of pain as an aversive stimulus.

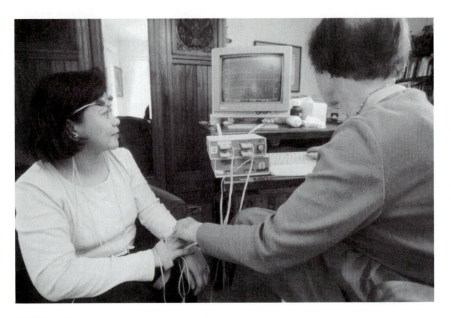

FIGURE 5.2 Biofeedback.

biofeedback

technology-based process of providing an individual with visual or auditory feedback regarding some bodily or physiological activity

One of the primary developments to come out of behavioral psychology in the late 1960s was a technological intervention known as **biofeedback,** in which instrumentation is used to provide the patient with visual or auditory information about some bodily or physiological activity (Figure 5.2). The technology of biofeedback emerged from the classic laboratory research of Neal Miller (1969; Miller & Banuazizi, 1968), who demonstrated that, when provided with reinforcement, rats were capable of controlling various physiological processes, such as heart rate and blood circulation, long believed to be automatic or involuntary. Despite the fact that this research proved difficult to replicate, the idea that such things as blood pressure and heart rate could be voluntarily controlled presented tremendous implications for health care. By the 1970s, numerous instruments had been developed for use in health clinics.

One of the more common applications of biofeedback has been to chronic headache, in which electrodes are placed on the patient's forehead to monitor the degree of tension in the muscles in the front of the head. The electrodes can then be connected to a device that provides ongoing feedback about the state of relaxation of the muscles. This feedback can be in auditory form (different musical tones) or visual form (changing colors on a computer monitor). With continuous feedback as reinforcement, many patients eventually learn to relax the forehead muscles, thus alleviating or reducing the headache discomfort (Allen & Shriver, 1998).

Since its inception, biofeedback has been applied to an increasing array of health concerns, including essential hypertension (Dubbert, 1995; Mukhopadhyay & Turner, 1997); asthma (Lehrer, 1998); generalized anxiety disorder

(Sarkar, Rathee, & Neera, 1999); cardiac arrhythmia (Engel & Bleecker, 1974); muscular rehabilitation following injury and illness (Dohrmann & Laskin, 1978); and attention deficit hyperactivity disorder (ADHD) (Boyd & Campbell, 1998). Despite its popularity, biofeedback's limitations as a clinical intervention have been amply recognized. In an early review of the literature, Ray, Raczynski, Rogers, and Kimball (1979) warned against undue optimism regarding biofeedback's effectiveness. Because of its reliance on technological gadgetry, biofeedback often proves impractical outside the clinic. In addition, the generalization and maintenance of clinically useful results beyond the clinic have been a major stumbling block. Finally, biofeedback may produce a general state of relaxation that can just as readily be achieved through meditation and relaxation training, neither of which requires technical equipment.

More recent reviews tend to cast biofeedback and its future in more positive light. Laibow (1999), for instance, argues that recent advances in technology have begun to increase the mobility of biofeedback instrumentation, meaning that patients in the future may be less constrained to the clinic for treatment. Others have suggested that, despite having been historically misunderstood and unappreciated by many medical professionals, biofeedback is increasingly being considered as a treatment of choice, particularly in the field of neurology (Carmagnani & Carmagnani, 1999). In sum, although biofeedback has yet to live up to its status as a medical panacea, as portended in the 1970s, it has nonetheless earned its place in the arsenal of health psychology and behavioral medicine.

As indicated at the beginning of this section, pain is a complex form of stimulation that gives rise to similarly complex behavior. Health psychologists have come to recognize that many of these pain behaviors are maintained by predictable environmental stimuli, and pain management interventions often strive to alter patterns of pain behavior through systematic manipulation of these variables. The general dynamics of pain behavior are all too familiar to any parent. Most parents are aware of the fact that children's reactions to minor falls and accidents often depend upon the presence of an audience. A toddler who descends a slide only to land abruptly on her behind may let out a considerable wail if Mommy or Daddy is watching. In the absence of any adult onlookers, however, precisely the same physical incident may produce nary a grimace as the child climbs nonchalantly to the top of the slide to do it again. These different scenarios illustrate that the child's behavior in response to the same occurrence (a rough landing from the slide) differs dramatically as a function of the surrounding environment (presence vs. absence of parent), not because of any difference in the sensation produced by the fall.

Though minor, the child's encounter with the slide is representative of the kinds of consequences (parental attention and nurturing) that may often result from pain behavior. Indeed, most people, when hurt or ill, appreciate the attention of loved ones; thus, such attention may function as powerful reinforcement for pain- or illness-related behavior. The downside of such a contingency is the possibility that the injured or ill person will continue to display pain behavior, not because of continued discomfort, but because such behavior has been unwittingly reinforced by others. This possibility may or may not prove problematic for the parent in the example of the slide, but it is most assuredly of concern in medical settings such as hospitals and nursing homes.

Like all forms of therapy, medical treatment is intended to be of finite duration. The ultimate goal of treatment is patient improvement, to the point of being able to leave the facility or, in the case of a nursing home, functioning more autonomously. From the patient's point of view, though, better functioning or improved health leads to a loss of attention and nurturing—reinforcers that may not be available otherwise. It isn't difficult to understand the dynamics that may lead some people to continue to manifest pain behavior under such circumstances. Nor should such patients be accused of purposely maintaining their illness or infirmities, for such contingencies can easily go unrecognized by both patient and caregiver.

Nevertheless, the continued manifestation of pain behavior is, in the long run, disadvantageous to both the patient and the health care system. By remaining dependent on caregivers, patients slow their own recovery, often compounding the problem. For instance, a patient undergoing rehabilitation following an industrial accident could benefit from physical therapy or a specific exercise regimen. If, however, the patient remains reluctant to attempt any exercise, choosing instead to focus on his or her discomfort, then therapeutic gains are unlikely. Thus, pain management intervention often focuses on teaching the patient how to manage the discomfort, possibly through biofeedback and/or relaxation, as well as on developing therapeutically helpful behaviors, perhaps including those specifically recommended by the physical therapist. Such interventions almost necessarily require the cooperation of the medical staff (doctors, nurses, aides, etc.) who interact daily with the patient.

In many respects, establishing an effective pain management program is like establishing a token economy, in that those professionals who come in contact with the patient must be trained how to objectively observe and record various pain behavior in the patients. In addition, medical personnel must be taught how to respond differentially, not reinforcing inappropriate pain behavior but reinforcing physical activity, including exercise. Naturally, interventions must be individualized, for each patient confronts different physical problems and therefore possesses different outcome goals. Well-displayed charts depicting the patient's progress have been shown to increase both the compliance of staff members with the pain management program and the compliance of the patient with the medical regimen (Steger, Shelton, Beukelman, & Fowler, 1981). As in a token economy, reinforcers are often idiosyncratic but may consist of such things as special privileges or free time— a period during which the patient is excused from the normal treatment regimen. In general, pain management programs can serve an important role in fostering behaviors that speed recovery and contribute to independent functioning and reduction of patient reliance on pain medication.

Compliance with Medical Treatment

This discussion of behavioral medicine began with the observation that a treatment program that is not adhered to is doomed to failure from the beginning, yet this "behavioral" variable is one over which the medical professional has little control. On the other hand, the behavior of complying with or adhering to a treatment plan is of special concern to the health psychologist. As the discussion has shown, the contingencies that lead to noncompliance are pervasive and readily understood. Few medical treatments produce instantaneous results, and this means that improved health, or simply absence of disease, as a predictably delayed consequence, will be a poor reinforcer for treatment compliance.

The problem faced by the health psychologist, then, is arranging other, perhaps artificial, consequences that will effectively maintain treatment compliance until the more natural consequences of improved health eventuate. In fact, the challenge is very similar to that faced by teachers charged with teaching school-age children to read. Being able to read is a behavior that produces natural and important consequences, at least at some point. Being able to read instructions or road signs helps people to negotiate a complex world, and reading for pleasure is a favored form of recreation for many. But these are consequences that await the proficient reader, not the young child still struggling with the sounds made by various letters. Thus, the reading teacher must find a way to shape this complex repertoire by encouraging recognition of letters, words, then sentences; and this encouragement usually comes in the form of praise, academic rewards, and other artificial reinforcers.

Similarly, considerable ingenuity is often required to bring about compliance with a medical regimen whose ultimate reinforcer, improved health, is a temporally remote event. Consistent with other behavioral interventions, programs that focus on compliance do so by identifying potential antecedent or consequent stimuli that influence behavior related to the medical regimen. A common case in point is failure to take prescribed medication, an offense to which most people will probably plead guilty, at least on occasion. It may simply be a case of forgetting to take the medicine, but this, and other problems, can often be remedied merely by enhancing the discriminative properties of the medicine. One way to do so is to embed the medicine within an environmental context that is predictably associated with some behavioral routine. For instance, for the inveterate coffee drinker, placing the medicine bottle on top of the coffeemaker each evening will serve as an easily identified reminder to take the medicine first thing in the morning. Other stimuli, such as self-written notes or alarm clocks, can similarly function as effective antecedents.

Of course, consequent stimuli play an equally important role, and formal programs implemented to enhance compliance seldom fail to include specific reinforcement strategies. Epstein and Masek (1978) describe a program designed to encourage college students to take vitamin C tablets. Students were required to deposit a sum of money with the researchers at the beginning of the study. Subjects were required to self-monitor their intake of the tablets, which included identifying which of several differently flavored tablets had been taken. The various flavors were used to increase the distinctiveness of the tablets as well as to enhance the likelihood of self-monitoring. In addition, one group of subjects experienced a response cost contingency, in which failure to comply with the vitamin C regimen resulted in permanent loss of a percentage of the deposited money. These contingencies resulted in increased compliance relative to baseline levels, with greatest compliance being associated with the combined self-monitoring and response cost condition.

Lundervold and Enterman (1989) report similar success in increasing medical compliance in a 32-year-old developmentally disabled woman. The subject was taught both to organize her medication (stimulus control) and to self-administer medication at appropriate times. Amari, Grace, and Fisher (1995) used the Premack principle to establish food preferences for a 15-year-old female with severe epilepsy. The foods represented choices within the ketogenic diet, a treatment seldom used because of its extreme dietary restrictions. The researchers established compliance with the diet by arranging for more highly preferred foods to be delivered contingent on consumption of less preferred foods. In addition to successful compliance with the diet, seizure activity was reduced substantially during treatment.

Contemporary research on compliance has been characterized by an encouraging interface between basic behavioral research and application. Out of the laboratory has come the concept of **behavioral momentum,** the brainchild of John Nevin. Nevin argues that operants that have a long and rich history of reinforcement may be especially resistant to change, either by way of extinction or punishment. That is, they have acquired a momentum that nearly ensures their continuance. The details of the empirical research and theory surrounding behavioral momentum are of less concern in the present chapter than are the implications of the concept for applied practice. In fact, Nevin himself has discussed the relevance of behavioral momentum to natural settings in some detail (Nevin, 1996; Nevin & Grace, 2000; Nevin, Mandell, & Atak, 1983). One of the more intriguing observations to come out of the research on behavioral momentum is that environments that have become associated with high rates of reinforcement seem to contribute to greater behavioral persistence. Surprisingly, this is true even when reinforcers are delivered randomly, not contingent on a specific response (Tota-Faucette, 1991).

The relevance of behavioral momentum to medical regimens is easily appreciated if you consider how this kind of behavior ordinarily unfolds. The patient taking medication or beginning an exercise program seldom has much difficulty *beginning* the regimen. In fact, many people tackle the initial steps of a self-improvement program with enthusiasm, as alluded to by Mark Twain, who boasted about the ease with which he could quit smoking; indeed, he had done it dozens of times! As examples have shown, maintaining behavior change is another matter, and the long-term prospects of many such programs often prove anything but impressive. The focus of research on behavioral momentum is on how to bring behavior to the point of remaining persistent, even in the presence of potentially disruptive variables or in the absence of a rich schedule of reinforcement.

The concept of behavioral momentum has been fruitfully explored in applied settings, often with an emphasis on a behavior of nearly universal significance—compliance with verbal instructions. For example, in an institution for mentally retarded adults, Mace and colleagues (1988) first reinforced patient compliance with requests that had, historically, produced high levels of compliance, such as simple salutations or greetings. That is, most people respond consistently to simple greetings, such as "Hi, how are you?"

behavioral momentum the idea that operants having a long and rich history of reinforcement may be especially resistant to change

These *high-p*, or high-probability, requests were made repeatedly, and compliance produced immediate social reinforcement. Subsequent to a sequence of reinforced high-p requests, researchers made requests that were less likely to produce compliance (*low-p* requests).

Low-p requests that immediately followed a history of compliance to high-p requests were more likely to produce compliance than were low-p requests presented without such a history. This effect was substantially diminished, however, when the low-p request was delayed and therefore not temporally contiguous with the high-p requests. Similarly, Houlihan, Jacobson, and Brandon (1994) obtained increased compliance in a 5-year-old preschooler when high-p requests were separated by a short *interprompt* interval, relative to longer intervals. Thus, behavior that is prompted frequently and produces a rich history of reinforcement does in fact acquire momentum, and this is a particularly useful finding when applied to clinical populations suffering from severe behavioral deficits. The high-p compliance tactic has also been successful in increasing the interpersonal repertoires of autistic children, a population ordinarily distinguished by severe social deficits (Davis, Brady, Hamilton, McEvoy, & Williams, 1994).

✖ INTERIM SUMMARY

Behavioral medicine, representing an interface between medical science and psychology, entails the application of basic behavioral principles to everyday activity having implications for health. Behavioral interventions in which both antecedent and consequent stimuli are systematically arranged have demonstrated moderate success in programs aimed at smoking cessation, pain management, and changes in dietary or exercise habits. A common obstacle to producing long-term changes in many such programs comes in the form of the multiple, and often competing, consequences of such behavior. A recent addition to the behavioral medicine literature is the concept of behavioral momentum, which suggests that behavior is more likely to persist in environments associated with high rates of reinforcement.

✖ THOUGHT QUESTIONS

1. Think of a time in your life when you made an effort, successful or not, to change some aspect of your lifestyle or behavior (diet, exercise, study habits, etc.). Can you identify the competing consequences that may have made this behavior change difficult for you to achieve? How would you do things differently if trying once again to modify this behavior?
2. Describe some examples of discriminative stimuli that you may have arranged in order to influence some aspect of your behavior. What consequence or consequences of this behavior influenced the effectiveness of these S^Ds?

OPERANT PRINCIPLES IN EDUCATION

If ever there was a worldly arena in which you would expect to find operant principles conspicuously applied, it would be education. After all, operant behavior is all about learning by way of consequences, and educational institutions are essentially formalized learning environments. Yet the history of operant psychology's contribution to education is a bittersweet one, perhaps as a result of the uneasy relationship that often exists between science, technology, and cultural practice. There is evidence that when appropriately arranged, operant contingencies can produce substantial, documented increases in pedagogical efficiency. Nevertheless, despite overwhelming empirical evidence supporting the promise of behavioral education, this promise remains largely unfulfilled.

Teaching Machines and Programmed Instruction

In addition to reverence for observation and measurement, a quality often attributed to behaviorism is a pragmatic or practical philosophy of science. In studying the controlling variables—namely, environmental contingencies—that influence behavior, psychologists not only learn about the whys of behavior, but they put themselves in a position to do something about behavior, that is, effect desirable changes in behavior. For this reason, behavioral psychologists have always looked at the real world as the ultimate testing ground for behavioral principles, and this helps to explain why so many of the pioneers in behavior therapy have also been leading laboratory scientists.

In 1953, Skinner visited his daughter's fifth-grade classroom to see what sorts of things transpired in a typical primary schoolroom. What he saw disappointed him but also served to inspire a lifelong desire to bring behavioral science to the U.S. educational system. Among other things, Skinner observed a disturbingly inefficient class in which the teacher, moving unsystematically through the room, stopped here and there to assist or provide feedback to students. The very structure of the classroom, both then and today, seems to prevent the teacher from attending at any length to the needs of any particular student. Yet, if the goal is to build an academic repertoire, be it reading or writing, what is needed, Skinner argued, is a nearly continuous arrangement of contingencies in which relevant behavior could be prompted and then immediately reinforced. Short of some kind of automation, he considered this possibility highly unlikely.

Armed with expertise in both the field of learning and amateur engineering skills, Skinner set about designing a series of "teaching machines" that could arrange the necessary academic contingencies needed for effective instruction. Figure 5.3 depicts one of Skinner's earlier devices. Academic material is presented, in small amounts or "frames," in a viewing window by turning the knob on the left side of the machine. An excerpt from a program designed to teach high school physics is shown in Table 5.2. The material, be it in mathematical or written form, prompts a response, such as an answer to a science question, from the student. The student writes his or her answer on a small piece of paper exposed through the window on the right. Then the student uncovers the correct response by sliding a transparent cover on the right side of the machine. In this way, the student is provided with immediate feedback concerning the accuracy of his or her answer. In this way, the student could move through a program of material, say a

FIGURE 5.3 Early Teaching Machine. (*Source:* From B. F. Skinner, *The Technology of Teaching,* Appleton-Century-Crofts, 1968. Copyright © 1968 by Meredith Corporation. Reprinted with permission of The McGraw-Hill Companies.)

lesson in physics, at his or her own pace, being continuously prompted to emit appropriate behavior and then receiving immediate feedback concerning this behavior, all without the necessity of human intervention. As is true of any piece of technology, teaching machines went through several stages of evolution, varying primarily in the details of their mechanical operation. What remained constant was their functional adherence to the fundamentals of operant learning principles.

Among the shortcomings of conventional education, Skinner said, was that students too often played a passive role, sitting silently during a lecture or while reading an assignment. But when assessed on what they had learned, students were expected to behave in such a way as to demonstrate their newly acquired knowledge or skill. Unlike the standard class format, the teaching machine required not only constant vigilance, but continual activity on the part of the student, as he or she worked through a typical program. Thus, during any one study session, a student might experience dozens, if not hundreds, of three-term contingencies (discriminative stimuli-behavior-consequence). Contemporary research has for the most part vindicated Skinner's emphasis on enhancing the activity level of the student, particularly the continuous overt responding necessitated by the program as it unfolds (Kritch & Bostow, 1998; Miller & Malott, 1997; Tudor, 1995).

By the late 1950s, Skinner and his colleagues had written many programs to teach various academic subjects, including spelling, physics, chemistry, and algebra. What was needed was a real-world application. Skinner got his chance in 1960, when he was allowed to conduct an experiment using the teaching machines in an eighth-grade classroom in Roanoke, Virginia. Rather

TABLE 5.2 EXCERPT FROM PROGRAM FOR TEACHING PHYSICS

Part of a program in high-school physics. The machine presents one item at a time. The student completes the item and then uncovers the corresponding word or phrase shown at the right.

Sentence to be completed	Word to be supplied
1. The important parts of a flashlight are the battery and the bulb. When we "turn on" a flashlight, we close a switch which connects the battery with the ____.	bulb
2. When we turn on a flashlight, an electric current flows through the fine wire in the ____ and causes it to grow hot.	bulb
3. When the hot wire glows brightly, we say that it gives off or sends out heat and ____.	light
4. The fine wire in the bulb is called a filament. The bulb "lights up" when the filament is heated by the passage of a(n) ____ current.	electric
5. When the weak battery produces little current, the fine wire, or ____, does not get very hot.	filament
6. A filament which is *less* hot sends out or gives off ____ light.	less
7. "Emit" means "send out." The amount of light sent out, or "emitted," by a filament depends on how ____ the filament is.	hot
8. The higher the temperature of the filament the ____ the light emitted by it.	brighter, stronger
9. If a flashlight battery is weak, the ____ in the bulb may still glow, but with only a dull red color.	filament
10. The light from a very hot filament is colored yellow or white. The light from a filament which is not very hot is colored ____.	red
11. A blacksmith or other metal worker sometimes makes sure that a bar of iron is heated to a "cherry red" before hammering it into shape. He uses the ____ of the light emitted by the bar to tell how hot it is.	color
12. Both the color and the amount of light depend on the ____ of the emitting filament or bar.	temperature
13. An object which emits light because it is hot is called incandescent. A flashlight bulb is an incandescent source of ____.	light

Source: From B. F. Skinner, *The Technology of Teaching,* Appleton-Century-Crofts, 1968. Copyright © 1968 by Meredith Corporation. Reprinted with permission of The McGraw-Hill Companies.

than receiving a conventional math lesson, students worked through a ninth-grade algebra curriculum using Skinner's teaching machines. The experiment was an overwhelming success, as students completed the entire ninth-grade algebra course work in only half a year. Moreover, in follow-up tests, students exposed to the teaching machines had retained more of the material to which they had been exposed than did those who were not exposed to the machines. To Skinner, though, the more impressive result was how the teaching machines had transformed complacent, easily distracted students into highly active, enthusiastic participants in a dynamic educational experience. Skinner (1987) described a particular instance in which he visited a classroom to observe:

> The director, Allen Calvin, and I entered a room in which thirty or forty eighth-grade students were at their desks using rather crude teaching machines. When I said I was surprised that they paid no attention to us, Calvin proposed a better demonstration. He asked me to keep my eye on the students. He went up to the teacher's platform, jumped in the air, and came down with a loud bang. Not a single student looked up. (p. 126)

The teaching machines were a success, Skinner argued, because they arranged effective contingencies for academic behavior in a manner that no teacher could hope to simulate. Skinner would call the process itself **programmed instruction,** for the students' academic repertoires were being shaped programmatically through continuous antecedent-consequent arrangements. In fact, the actual arrangement of such contingencies didn't even require automation, only properly written and presented stimulus materials. It occurred to Skinner that similar results could be achieved with a textbook written in such a way as to take advantage of the same principles. With colleague James Holland, Skinner wrote an introductory programmed text on behavior analysis, an excerpt of which can be seen in Figure 5.4. As you can see, the text adheres to the fundamentals of programmed instruction in that small amounts of material are presented, and then the reader is prompted to respond to a question or fill in the blank. By turning the page, the reader could then uncover the answer to the question, thus receiving immediate feedback.

programmed instruction instructional method involving systematic arrangement of academically oriented antecedent-consequence contingencies

Skinner hoped that the efficient and powerful nature of his instructional program would transform U.S. education, particularly with advances in electronic technology. In fact, though he was initially skeptical of computers, Skinner would eventually view them as playing a vital role in programmed instruction, especially given the sophisticated interactive capacities possessed by today's microcomputers. Although programmed instruction, and the behavior principles behind it, would inform the development of what is now called computer assisted instruction (CAI), Skinner remained disappointed by such developments, observing that many so-called educational programs were written by computer experts, not informed behavioral scientists.

Despite considerable empirical evidence attesting to the efficiency and power of Skinner's instructional technology, there would be no widespread adoption by educators. The fate of programmed instruction rested on many

	PART I Reflex Behavior — Page I
Set I	**Simple Reflexes**
	Estimated time: 23 minutes Turn to next page and begin
stimulus (tap on the knee) 1-7	Technically speaking, a reflex involves an eliciting stimulus in a process called elicitation. A stimulus ____ a response. 1-8
threshold 1-15	The fraction of a second which elapses between "brushing the eye" and "blink" is the ____ of the reflex. 1-16
threshold 1-23	The greater the concentration of onion juice (stimulus), the ____ the magnitude of the response. 1-24
elicit 1-31	In the pupillary reflex, a very bright flash of light elicits a response of greater ____ than a weak flash of light. 1-32
latency 1-39	A solution of lemon juice will not elicit salivation if the stimulus is ____ the threshold. 1-40
(1) magnitude (2) latency 1-47	Presentation of a stimulus is the "cause" of a response. The two form a(n) ____. 1-48

	Page 2
	A doctor taps your knee (patellar tendon) with a rubber hammer to test your ____. 1-1
elicits 1-8	To avoid unwanted nuances of meaning in popular words, we do not say that a stimulus "triggers," "stimulates," or "causes" a response, but that it ____ a response. 1-9
latency 1-16	In the patellar-tendon reflex, a forceful tap elicits a strong kick; a tap barely above the threshold elicits a weak kick. Magnitude of response thus depends on the intensity of the ____. 1-17
greater (higher, larger) 1-24	Onion juice elicits the secretion of tears by the lachrymal gland. This causal sequence of events is a(n) ____. 1-25
magnitude (intensity) 1-32	A response and its eliciting stimulus comprise a(n) ____. 1-33
below (less than, sub-) 1-40	The latency of a reflex is the (1) ____ between onset of (2) ____ and ____. 1-41
reflex 1-48	The layman frequently explains behavior as the operation of "mind" or "free will." He seldom does this for reflex behavior, however, because the ____ is an adequate explanation of the response. 1-49

FIGURE 5.4 Excerpt from Programmed Text. (*Source:* From James G. Holland and B. F. Skinner, *The Analysis of Behavior,* McGraw-Hill, 1961. Copyright © 1961 by the McGraw-Hill Book Company, Inc. Reprinted with permission of The McGraw-Hill Companies.)

variables over which Skinner had no control. Skinner had encountered difficulty in getting the machines mass-produced. Over the course of several years, his views about the scientific integrity of the teaching machines clashed with the bottom-line mentality of several manufacturing companies, ultimately leading to broken business relationships. In addition, Skinner (1968, 1987) and colleagues met with even more resistance from the educational establishment. Skepticism about the ability to teach more advanced topics using programmed instruction, coupled with the inaccurate perception that teaching machines might someday replace teachers, contributed to an overall climate of distrust among educators. Although research on programmed instruction continues to this day, the revolution fizzled. In the end, his failure to transform U.S. education would rank among Skinner's greatest professional disappointments.

Fred Keller and PSI

Although Skinner may have felt alone at times in his pursuit of a behaviorally designed education system, he in fact was surrounded by a loyal and gifted group of colleagues who shared his vision. Among these, Fred Keller,

BOX 5.3 / ELEMENTS OF KELLER'S PERSONALIZED SYSTEM OF INSTRUCTION (PSI)

Self-pacing Students acquire knowledge and skills at different rates, and ideal instructional practices should be programmed to accommodate this individual variability. PSI courses do this by allowing students to work at their own pace, not according to a time schedule imposed by the instructor.

Unit mastery An assumption of the PSI format is that students should *master*, or demonstrate proficiency on, material; only under such conditions can learning be said to have occurred. PSI courses require students to master *units*—small amounts of material—before moving on to further study.

Keeping units manageable (*chunking*) A typical textbook contains chapters that are 20 to 30 pages long, and students often take tests over several chapters at once. From a learning perspective, this mastery requirement is unreasonable, and considerable research evidence points to the superiority of presenting material in smaller units, or chunks. The PSI format does this by requiring more quizzes over much smaller amounts of material than are customary in traditional lecture courses.

Immediate performance feedback PSI courses use frequent testing for both assessment and teaching purposes. By providing immediate feedback to students on tests or quizzes covering smaller amounts of material, the PSI format takes advantage of two empirically supported learning principles: superiority of small-unit mastery and the power of immediate reinforcement (score feedback on quizzes and tests).

a friend and confidant of Skinner's from their graduate school days at Harvard, would come closest to making the dream a reality. During a long and distinguished career at Columbia University, Keller was a visible champion of the behavioral movement, convincing generations of students of both the scientific integrity and applied promise of an operant approach. Keller retired from Columbia in 1964, but his contribution to instructional design was only beginning to emerge.

Following his retirement from Columbia, Keller traveled to Brazil, where he assisted in establishing a psychology department at the University of Brasilia. There Keller taught his first course utilizing the same learning principles that he had taught for so many years and that were at the heart of Skinner's programmed instruction. Keller would call his method the **personalized system of instruction (PSI)**, though it often is referred to simply as the Keller Plan. Kurt, the student introduced in this chapter's opening vignette, is enrolled in a PSI class. The major components of a PSI class, as developed by Keller, are described in Box 5.3. It's important to note that many derivations of personalized instruction have been used over the years, not all of which conform to the system established by Keller. This has implications for

personalized system of instruction (PSI) Keller's operant-based instructional format utilizing self-pacing and unit mastery

research done to evaluate the effectiveness of the instructional format, a point addressed in more detail later.

The essence of Keller's PSI is found in the program's name—*personalized*. In agreement with his friend Skinner, Keller recognized that teachers simply could not address the needs of individual students in a typical classroom configuration. One factor working against such individualized treatment is that students master information, or acquire new skills, in different ways and at different rates. Consequently, it would seem unreasonable to assume that all the students in a classroom would benefit in the same way from an assignment or lecture. Thus, the first component defining a PSI class is individual pacing, meaning that students work through the various course assignments according to their own timetable. This means, for example, that one student may be working on material from Chapter 4 of a text at the same time that another student is just finishing the requirements for Chapter 2.

Also consistent with programmed instruction, PSI courses usually involve the presentation of small amounts of material. Whereas a conventional course may require students to read and master three or four chapters before taking a unit exam, students in a PSI course encounter information in much smaller chunks, maybe no more than a major section (say, 10 pages) of a chapter. Once a student has read and feels comfortable with this small amount of material (referred to as a *unit* or *module*), he or she would come to class prepared to take a brief quiz (multiple choice or essay) over the material. In fact, on any given day in a PSI class, students might be taking quizzes over different material, due to the self-paced nature of the class.

When the student is finished with the quiz (ordinarily only a few minutes are required to take the short quizzes), he or she takes the quiz to the front of the class where it is graded by the instructor or a student proctor. This means that the student receives nearly immediate feedback regarding performance on the quiz. Recall that immediate feedback is a critical feature of operant learning and a major procedural element in programmed instruction. Of course, the practice of receiving immediate feedback on tests and quizzes is almost unheard of in the traditional classroom. Even the most conscientious of teachers would be hard pressed to grade, record, and hand back lengthy exams so promptly, especially in a large section containing hundreds of students.

What if a student fares poorly on a quiz? Here, too, the PSI format is distinctive compared to conventional classrooms. In a standard class, a student who does poorly on an exam simply accepts the fact and prepares for the next exam, hoping that a better score will compensate in the long run. Because the instructor has a timeline to follow, and cannot afford to ensure that all students understand previously covered material, the course marches ahead, with or without those who failed to master previous material. Not so in a PSI course. If a student does poorly on a quiz, he or she has the opportunity to retake the quiz, usually in the form of an alternate quiz covering the same material, as many times as needed in order to demonstrate mastery. In most PSI courses, a mastery criterion is instituted, such that the student is not allowed to take quizzes over new material until the criterion is met. Although the criterion is clearly an idiosyncratic decision, most PSI instructors require close to 90% correct responses on quizzes. This may seem a rather high standard, but remember that students in a PSI course are allowed to retake the quiz, and the quizzes tend to cover much less material than exams in traditional classes. Under these conditions, a 90% mastery criterion is not so outlandish; in fact, it is usually met by students without much difficulty. And, as you might have guessed, students in PSI courses tend not to experience the kind of anxiety before taking quizzes as do their counterparts in traditional classrooms. In essence, quiz taking within the Keller system is not as much a pure assessment strategy as a learning mechanism for the student.

You may have noticed that this description of Keller's PSI format has had little to say about lectures. There's a good reason for this conspicuous omission—lectures play a relatively small role in such classes. The primary study material in PSI classes is written content in textbooks and study guides. Lectures are often given on an irregular schedule and serve as opportunities for discussion or integration of material, not as primary sources of course content. In fact, in most PSI courses, attendance at lectures is not mandatory. Instead, students meet on a regular basis in small discussion groups, usually overseen by the class proctors (advanced undergraduate majors or graduate students).

Class time in PSI courses is devoted primarily to taking quizzes, not to lectures. You're not alone if this strikes you as the most unorthodox aspect of the PSI system, as most people view the lecture as the quintessential academic event in higher education. But is it? Is there any reason to believe that students can't learn effectively in the absence of regularly scheduled lectures? Does true enlightenment come only to that student seated passively at the feet of the master, or can learning occur under much less conventional conditions? Rather unambiguous answers to these questions have emerged from research studies conducted over the course of more than 30 years. As with the teaching machine and programmed instruction, the story of PSI is punctuated by a regrettable fact: Adoption of new cultural practices is often influenced more by the whims and biases of specialized social groups than by the scientific evidence supporting such practices.

Keller's experience with PSI in Brazil had been uniformly positive, and, when he returned to the United States, he continued to promote both application and evaluation of PSI as an instructional tool. His dedication to college teaching, and education in general, was unfaltering. Keller was formally recognized for his scholarship and contribution to education in 1970, with the receipt of the American Psychological Foundation's Distinguished Teaching Award, and again in 1976, with the American Psychological Association's Distinguished Scientific Award for Applications of Psychology. By the late 1970s, more than 250 studies had been published attesting to the merits of PSI as a system of instruction (Kulik, Kulik, & Carmichael, 1974).

Research on PSI is something of a mixed bag, in large part because of the inherent difficulty of conducting well-controlled studies in applied settings, like college classrooms. Comparisons across studies are often treacherous because of the variability characterizing such studies. For instance, due to institutional restrictions, it isn't always possible to randomly assign students to different kinds of classes, though this is a standard control procedure in psychological research. In addition, distinguishing between the details of a PSI course and a standard lecture course can sometimes prove difficult, especially since PSI courses do include some lectures. Also, many instructors choose to adopt certain aspects of PSI (perhaps unit mastery and smaller quizzes) but not others. When this is done, the result is something of an instructional hybrid not easily compared to Keller's original system. How best to assess what students have learned remains a controversial issue for all teachers, let alone those wishing to compare PSI with other course formats. Consequently, the large literature evaluating PSI is in many ways like the research on psychotherapy outcome in that researchers understand that they are frequently reduced to comparing apples and oranges.

Fortunately, a literature this size is bound to contain some methodologically sound studies, and the PSI literature is no exception. Several studies did entail random assignment and careful designation of course format, and these more empirically rigorous studies led to some rather incontestable conclusions. Almost without exception, students taking PSI courses prefer this format to traditional lecture format and/or would recommend the PSI format to other students. Of course, student satisfaction is hardly a useful measure of teaching effectiveness, or how much learning has taken place. Thus, much of the research on PSI has examined learning outcomes by way of final exam scores and follow-up measures some time after finishing the course. In many such cases, comparisons were made between students in a PSI course and other students enrolled in a traditional course. Once again, the evidence argues for the superiority of the PSI format (Kulik, Cohen, & Ebeling, 1980; Kulik, Kulik, & Cohen, 1979), whether comparisons were for multiple choice exams or essay items (Sheppard & MacDermot, 1970). Thus, a review of the sizable literature on PSI would seem to lead even the less sophisticated reader to anticipate the demise of the traditional lecture format. As you know, this is not the case.

To a large extent, the reception that PSI received within the educational community mirrored that encountered by Skinner. After all, Keller and Skinner were not only longtime friends and colleagues but also behaviorist soul mates. It may have simply followed logically that anyone who found Skinner's operant-based approach to instructional design reprehensible would find similar fault with Keller's system. And it didn't help much that Keller's landmark article describing PSI, published in 1968 in *JABA*, was titled "Good-Bye Teacher." Though intended as tongue-in-cheek humor (Keller was a charming, self-effacing man, with a wry sense of humor), the title was undoubtedly perceived as threatening to teachers. Here was a behavioral scientist arguing that as long as schools had well-designed instructional materials and a system for testing and providing immediate test results, the teacher, as lecturer, was expendable, or at least not vital to the learning process. But the point that Keller tried to make was that a well-run PSI course actually freed the teacher to do more important things, such as presiding over discussions of content and challenging students to apply acquired knowledge. Skinner (1968), too, had often argued that automation could alleviate the need for teachers to introduce basic content to students, while providing the opportunity for more fruitful, intellectual collaboration between student and teacher.

Keller's personalized instructional method was adopted with much more enthusiasm in Brazil than it was in the United States, though it remains alive and well in various college classrooms scattered about the United States. As Buskist, Cush, and DeGrandpre (1991) have suggested, PSI probably failed to become an academic standard, not so much for scientific reasons, but for reasons having to do with the social and historical makeup of the academy. Adoption of a PSI format, and its implications for the learning process, would clearly entail sweeping changes in the structure and function of the educational institution and perhaps in professors themselves. As highly educated professionals and experts in their fields, professors may be prone to view themselves as repositories of knowledge and wisdom and the lecture as the only proper vehicle for the transmission of this wisdom. But a PSI course shines the light on the student more than on the teacher:

> In a PSI-based course, the student is the star of the show, not the teacher. For many teachers this is not a desirable state of affairs. Many teachers like to lecture, they enjoy the stardom, and are reluctant to give it up . . . to be a manager of learning just doesn't have the same ring to it. It seems, somehow, less noble than being a teacher. (Buskist, Cush, & DeGrandpre, 1991)

Placing any practice under the microscope will eventually reveal its flaws or limitations, and PSI is no exception. In addition to suggesting that PSI courses usurp the authority of the instructor, critics of personalized instruction pointed to difficulties that may be unique to this format. Some students, for instance, may not be able to meet the mastery criterion set by the instructor (Sussman, 1981), even with repeated testing. This would require that the instructor either consider optional criteria or have an explicit policy for dealing with those students who fail to meet the mastery criteria (Reiser, Driscoll, & Vergara, 1987). In addition, because personalized instruction is self-paced, much of the responsibility of the course falls on the shoulders of students. This is not problematic for mature, self-guided students, but for those who are more dependent on others, or who tend to procrastinate, self-pacing may prove disastrous.

Thus, personalized instruction failed to usher in the kind of educational revolution Keller had intended, in part because of opposition to the format's behaviorist roots and in part because of logistic complexities that must be negotiated to properly administer a PSI class. Nevertheless, Keller's system must be evaluated within the context of an ever-growing warehouse of "educational revolutions," many of which lack anything like the empirical endorsement that PSI has received. Whatever its eventual fate may be, PSI stands as a resounding testimony both to the need for research-based instructional practice and to the application of basic operant principles to human behavior in the world at large.

✖ INTERIM SUMMARY

Operant psychologists were well aware of the apparent usefulness of operant principles to the educational enterprise, and the inefficiency of the traditional classroom environment inspired Skinner, in the late 1950s, to design his first teaching machines. Through programmed instruction, including presentation of small amounts of material, prompting of student responses, and immediate presentation of relevant feedback, teaching machines could deliver instruction in various academic subjects more efficiently while also producing greater long-term retention. Using many of the same principles, Fred Keller designed his personalized system of instruction (PSI), which involved self-pacing, unit mastery requirements, and frequent testing. Though widely adopted in Brazil, PSI, like programmed instruction, was unable to replace the standard lecture format in U.S. colleges and universities, despite substantial empirical data supporting its effectiveness as an instructional format.

✖ THOUGHT QUESTIONS

1. Computer programs today are often written to be user friendly, meaning they can be easily learned by a novice. How does the phrase *user friendly* translate into the language of programmed instruction? Can you think of a computer program you have learned recently that possesses this quality? Also, can you identify some specific antecedent and consequent stimuli that help to make this program user friendly?

2. Research overwhelmingly indicates that students prefer PSI courses over traditional lecture courses. How do you think you'd like such a course? What advantages and disadvantages do you think attend to a PSI course?

CHAPTER SIX

Social Learning

In virtually every social group, there emerge leaders whose every action seems to take on unparalleled significance for others. Imo was just such a leader among her troop of macaque monkeys on the Japanese island of Koshima (Figure 6.1). Imo had somehow stumbled upon an ingenious method for solving one of nature's most common dilemmas: how to clean food before consuming it. Imo's solution was rather simple. She would take her selected food item to the shore of the island, drop it into the water, and voilà! The dirt and sand that had collected on the food was gone. This tactic proved especially useful for preparing sweet potatoes and wheat grain. In fact, Imo discovered that the wheat would float to the top, where it could easily be scooped up—free of sand, of course. But Imo's ingenuity isn't the end of the story. What amazed researchers observing this particular troop of monkeys was that this food-washing routine, originally observed only in Imo, soon spread to other monkeys, ultimately becoming something of a cultural standard among the troop. That is, Imo had not only discovered an important and adaptive form of food preparation, but she had also modeled this activity successfully for her fellow primates (Itani, 1958; Kawai, 1965).

Precisely how Imo first learned to wash her food is not known to this day, but that is hardly the point. Her story is intriguing because it portrays a powerful method of learning that may very well be universal to all highly social animal species, humans included. There is little reason to doubt that the individuals within Imo's troop could have, eventually, figured out on their own how to clean food using Imo's strategy. But why bother? Here was a *conspecific* (member of one's own species) demonstrating, whether purposefully or not, an effective way of separating one's food from dirt, sand, and other unpalatable things; so why reinvent the wheel? By simply paying attention to one of their own kind, members of the troop could almost instantaneously discover how to solve a problem that had undoubtedly perplexed generations of macaques. The lesson is simple: Watch what others do, for their actions may prove useful at some later time. The usefulness of Imo's food

FIGURE 6.1 Japanese Macaques.

washing was quite apparent, for the strategy spread rapidly among other members of the troop.

The theme of this chapter is that some of life's most important lessons are learned by simply observing others, and the propensity to do so is characteristic of all social animals, even human infants. The adaptive value of this kind of learning lies in its economy, for learning through observation often saves time, and it may also prove less dangerous than learning through more direct experience. Although observational learning has been historically portrayed as a distinct form of learning, the discussion raises the possibility that such behavior may fall easily within the purview of the traditional learning principles discussed thus far.

IMITATION: THE ROOTS OF SOCIALITY

Throughout this book you have seen that psychologists frequently find the most mundane behavior interesting and worthy of scientific study. Much of this chapter addresses one of the more common, and presumably unremarkable, aspects of human behavior: imitation. Fortunately, it doesn't take science to document the pervasiveness of this kind of behavior. Anyone visiting a preschool or elementary classroom can see how readily children imitate the actions and verbalizations of their classmates. Moreover, their tendency to repeat the behavior of adults or television actors (even when parents may prefer they don't) is well known. Yet imitative behavior is hardly limited to children. Think of the last time you attended some social gathering or function in which an unfamiliar activity was required of you. For instance, you might have attended a friend's wedding, only to discover that the ceremony, based on a religious faith unknown to you, involved a complicated series of movements and vocalizations in which all guests were to engage. To avoid embarrassment, you probably observed with keen interest the actions of other guests, taking your cue from them. Imitation probably plays a central role in the acquisition of many behavioral skills, including such things as building a model airplane, riding a horse, playing basketball, baking a cake, changing a flat tire, or playing a computer or video game. This is not to say that imitation *alone* suffices to produce these sometimes sophisticated skills, but it would be a challenge to find a behavior whose initial development was completely unaffected by imitation.

You can get a sense of the complexity of imitation by considering both the varying definitions offered by researchers over the years and the research strategies that these scientists have employed to study imitation. Gordon Allport (1954), for instance, defined imitation as ". . . any occasion where a stimulus gives rise to motor activity of a sort that resembles the stimulus situation" (p. 24). Although appearing rather technical and objective, there are several dimensions of imitative behavior this definition fails to address (Nagell, Olguin, & Tomasello, 1993; Visalberghi & Fragaszy, 1990). For instance, should the imitated behavior be physically identical to or match the actual muscle movements of the modeled behavior? Additionally, perhaps the behavior should be completely new to the imitator, not an action already present in his or her behavioral repertoire. As you can see, the attempt to subject imitation to the methods of science allows considerable quibbling and room for disagreement among those who try.

Variability also characterizes the research procedures used by scientists studying imitation, although some fairly standard techniques have emerged. One common strategy is known as a *two-action* task, in which subjects are allowed to choose between two responses, either of which will result in a reinforcing consequence, such as food delivery. For example, Zentall (1996) trained demonstrator pigeons to either peck at or step on a treadle in an operant chamber to produce grain reinforcement. Then observer birds were allowed to watch trained birds acquiring food through their previously acquired actions (pecking or stepping). A similar design was used by Bugnyar and Huber (1997), in which marmosets (monkeys) could either push in or pull out a swinging door in order to access food inside a box. Observer monkeys were exposed to previously trained demonstrator monkeys who had learned a specific response form. In both experiments, observer animals demonstrated a varied pattern of behavior, sometimes using the specific modeled behavior, and sometimes relying on the alternative response.

The dilemma faced by the researcher in such a study is how to interpret the actions of imitators who engage in the nondisplayed response alternative. For instance, suppose a pigeon that had observed a lever-*pressing* demonstrator began *pecking* at the treadle when introduced to the chamber? Or, what if a marmoset that observed a demonstrator *pulling* the pendulum door commenced *pushing* at the door when placed in the chamber? Wouldn't the observers' behavior be called imitation? Certainly the researcher would not conclude that they had failed to learn how to acquire food in the experimental chamber. In other words, does the definition of imitation require that precisely the same movements or physical topography describe the behavior of both the model (demonstrator) and the observer? Or is it sufficient that the observers learned a functionally similar behavior—acquiring the food—regardless of response topography? In other words, what specific criteria should be used to distinguish between imitation and other socially derived behaviors, or is such a distinction even necessary? These and similar questions have confronted scientists studying imitation for many years, and they suggest that the phenomenon is anything but simplistic. Indeed, in a review of the literature and its surrounding controversy, Galef (1988) identified more than a dozen terms that converge on imitation or imitation-like behavior, some of which clearly have strong phylogenetic origins.

Fortunately, the controversy over defining imitation has not stifled experimentation. At some point, scientists simply head to their laboratories, arrange experimental conditions, and record what their subjects do, perhaps leaving the question of interpretation to others. The issue of what is and what is not imitation aside, there is considerable evidence demonstrating what various animals, both human and nonhuman, do in response to observing a conspecific engaged in an experimental task. Let's consider first the growing literature from comparative psychology, which adamantly demonstrates that many nonhuman species are well equipped for observational learning.

Imitation in Nonhuman Animals

Given the importance of imitation in human behavior, it seems sensible to expect researchers to find it in many other social species as well. Indeed, imitative repertoires (some of which may surprise you) have been demonstrated in a host of both mammalian and nonmammalian species. For instance, Fiorito and Scotto (1992) allowed untrained octopuses to observe demonstrator octopuses that had been taught a simple color discrimination. When subsequently confronted with the same choice, observer octopuses were more likely to choose the same colored object that they had observed being chosen by the trained octopus. In addition, the observer octopuses acquired the discriminative response more rapidly than did the demonstrator octopuses during the original discrimination training. This finding is all the more impressive for having been observed in an invertebrate species, for scientists had long considered such complex behavior beyond the capacity of any nonmammalian species.

Further evidence for animal imitation comes from a study by Templeton (1998), in which observer starlings watched demonstrators master a discrimination task. The experiment was designed in such a way that demonstrator birds chose the correct stimulus (S+) on either 0%, 50%, or 100% of the trials. Surprisingly, observer starlings that had seen a demonstrator pick the wrong stimulus on every trial performed more successfully when exposed to the discrimination task than did observers that saw demonstrator birds respond to both the correct and incorrect stimuli. Once again, this is a rather remarkable finding given the species involved, and it suggests that observers in a social situation may be learning, not only what to do, but also what not to do in the setting. Fritz and Kotrschal (1999) showed that ravens could also benefit from observing conspecifics solve a food acquisition task. Demonstrator birds were trained to engage in a specific behavior sequence to open a box containing food. When given their chance, observer ravens utilized the same method as demonstrator birds but also exhibited response forms typical of control birds not exposed to a model. These results seem to portray imitation as a possible mechanism for behavior acquisition but not one that necessarily preempts other, nonimitative behaviors.

Not surprisingly, a preponderance of studies on social learning in nonhuman animals have focused on various primate species. Comparative psychologists favor research on monkeys, apes, and chimpanzees because of the highly social nature of these animals and because humans share with them a considerable proportion of genetic material. In general, research on nonhuman primates indicates that these species possess capabilities for social learning that rival those of humans. For instance, Whiten, Custance, Gomez, Teixidor, and Bard (1996) exposed both preschool-age children and chimpanzees to an artificial foraging task. All subjects were first exposed to models using either a "poking" or "twisting" motion to remove bolts from a test box, then additional turning or pulling responses on the handle to open the box. Both children and chimpanzees engaged in imitative responses, though the responses of the chimpanzees were less consistent. In addition, the researchers reported that the specific response topography differed somewhat among the subjects, and that several different actions were equally successful in opening the box. Whiten and colleagues (1996) recommend use of the term *emulation* to refer to imitative behaviors that produce the same consequence as the modeled behavior, despite differences in form or topography. What is important about social learning, they argue, is that observers see generally how to solve a problem, not that they match faithfully the specific motor movements observed.

In addition to laboratory research, efforts have been made to study imitative behavior in the natural habitats of several primate species. For nearly three decades, Galdikas and colleagues have studied social behavior, including imitation, in free-ranging orangutans in Borneo (Galdikas, 1985, 1988; Galdikas & Vasey, 1992; Russon & Galdikas, 1993, 1995). One of the more interesting findings reported by these researchers is that imitation among such animals does not occur haphazardly but in a way that is highly sensitive to the group hierarchy that characterizes such animals. That is, animals are more likely to imitate others with whom they have established some previous relationship or those that are relatively high in the group's dominance hierarchy. In many cases of animals that have lived and socialized with humans, this means human models become primary sources of social learning, and responses learned through imitation of human behavior often persist even after the animals have been returned to their natural habitat. Indeed, Tomasello, Savage-Rumbaugh, and Kruger (1993) suggest that whether a primate has been raised by or around humans or, instead, by its natural mother and in contact only with other members of its own species may help explain some of the conflicting findings concerning primate imitation (Byrne

& Tomasello, 1995; Tomasello, 1990). In particular, *enculturated* chimpanzees (those raised in close contact with humans) often perform much better on tasks requiring deferred imitation (imitating an action as long as 48 hours after observing) than do either mother-raised chimpanzees or human children (Tomasello et al., 1993).

In sum, the capacity for nonhuman animals to benefit from imitation seems well established, despite continuing debate over the specific criteria for imitation. Many researchers believe that science has made important inroads in recent years toward uncovering the impressive range of social learning capacities in nonhuman animals (Boysen & Himes, 1999; Galef, 1988; McGrew, 1998). Galef (1988) notes that advances in the field are largely due to increased interdisciplinary research by both biologists and psychologists. Imitative repertoires have been observed across a range of both vertebrate and invertebrate species and under controlled laboratory and natural field settings. As a final note, evolutionary models have recently been developed that promise to describe the selective pressures that would have made imitation an important adaptation in social species.

Imitation in Humans

The study of imitation in humans raises a slightly different question that is not encountered with nonhuman animals. After all, the existence of imitation in humans is simply a given. What researchers do want to know is where imitation comes from. Does everybody do it, and when do humans start imitating the behavior of others? Do humans have to be taught to imitate, or does it come as a fairly prepared behavior? Are there certain kinds of behaviors that are more likely to be imitated or specific environmental conditions that tend to favor or discourage imitation? These are all important questions because imitation is a pervasive and efficient means of acquiring new behaviors. So, let's begin by asking a seemingly innocent question: Can babies imitate?

When trying to understand the origins of a behavior, it is natural to look toward the earliest age group in which the behavior is known to occur. When it comes to imitation, preschoolers are known to already possess a pretty impressive capacity, so that means the search will have to be taken up in younger tykes, and that means infants. Now, any developmental psychologist will tell you that studying infant behavior poses unique challenges. In fact, curiously enough, those who study human infants often encounter the same problems as do those studying nonhuman animals. For one, neither nonhumans nor infants can tell the researcher much about their experiences. Researchers can't simply ask infants what they can see or hear, or give them complicated verbal instructions, the way that they can with older children and adults. What this means is that researchers studying infants must come up with experimental procedures that prompt certain kinds of behavior in the infant that can then be unambiguously interpreted. This is no small task, as perhaps you can appreciate if you ponder for a moment how you would go about setting up an experiment to discover whether a very young infant, say 3 months, could imitate. What kind of behavior would you model for the infant? It couldn't be a complicated physical movement, like a somersault, because of infants' limited motor skills. Nor could you model sophisticated verbal behavior, for this, too, would be beyond the infant's capacity.

Fortunately, babies do have a repertoire of actions from which to draw, among them various facial expressions. As any baby watcher can attest, even newborns express such universal emotions as fear, surprise, and happiness through strategic positioning of facial features, particularly the eyes and mouth. Thus, researchers frequently utilize such expressions and movements as their window for observing imitation in infants. Figure 6.2 depicts some of the facial expressions that infants have been shown to imitate, even as early as 2 or 3 weeks after birth (Field, Woodson, Greenberg, & Cohen, 1982; Meltzoff & Moore, 1977). Study of imitation in infants has advanced remarkably in the past 20 years, and the primary lesson coming out of this research is that newborns may very well come into the world much more equipped for social interaction than psychologists used to think (Heyes & Galef, 1996). In fact, many researchers argue that research on imitation, in both humans and other animals, sheds light on the evolution of sociality (Lefebvre & Giraldeau, 1996; Whiten & Custance, 1996; Zentall, 1996) as well as development of what psychologists call "theory of mind"—the understanding that people acquire of the thoughts and behavior of other people (Meltzoff, 1996). It has even been suggested that a specific brain mechanism that specializes in matching observed gestures to motor patterns in the observer may also have played a role in the evolution of language in humans (Rizzolatti & Arbib, 1998).

Not only do infants demonstrate imitative abilities within the first few weeks of life, but there also appears to be little restriction on who can serve as a model for imitation. Although many studies have utilized adults as the primary models, researchers have on occasion used other children, even infants, as models. Hanna and Meltzoff (1993) used 14- to 18-month-old infants as both demonstrators and observers. The demonstrator infants, or trained "expert peers," had been taught to engage in specific movements with a number of different objects. Observer infants were able to imitate the specific actions of demonstrators both immediately and after a 5-minute delay. Perhaps even more remarkable, observers imitated the same actions at home, 2 days after the original demonstration that had occurred in a laboratory setting. Similarly, Collie and Hayne (1999) found that 6- and 9-month-old infants imitated behavior from a single demonstration session 24 hours after exposure. These findings show not only that infants are capable of **deferred imitation**—imitation of an action after a temporal delay—but also that imitation is not confined to the environment in which the demonstrated behavior occurs. Clearly, these represent adaptive features of imitation, for they suggest that infants can draw upon their imitative repertoires when needed and in novel contexts.

Imitation, then, is a well-documented phenomenon in various nonhuman animals and in human infants. That it is similarly common in older children and adults should hardly be a surprising observation. Much of the research on imitation in older age groups has focused not so much on the occurrence of the phenomenon but on the range of behaviors that might be

deferred imitation
repeating an observed action after some temporal delay

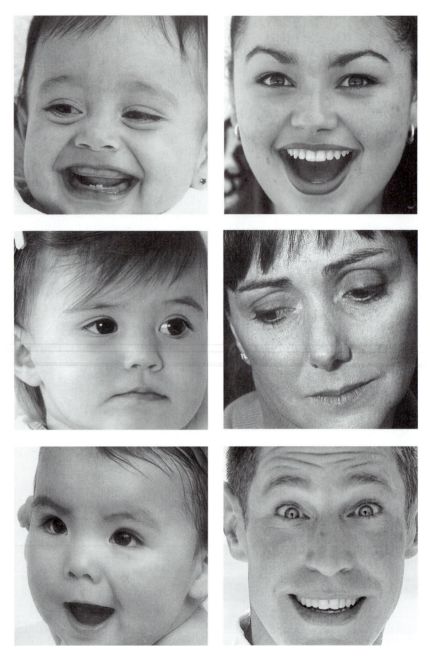

FIGURE 6.2 Facial Imitation in Neonates.

open to imitation. In addition, imitation has often been seen as a specific instance of a larger class of socially acquired behaviors, some of which may not involve direct matching or mimicking of behavior. Remember that definitions of imitation usually require either close approximations of motor movements or at least actions producing identical consequences. Yet, you and I learn more than specific muscular movements from observing the behavior of other people. We usually pay attention to the equally important antecedent conditions in which the modeled behavior occurs and the kinds of consequences produced. That is, when we observe the behavior of others, we are really attending to all elements of the three-term contingency, not just specific behavioral topography.

Sometimes, the critical question isn't whether to do as others do, but precisely *when* or *where* to do it. If you were attending a seminar on assertiveness training, the speaker might demonstrate various ways to behave assertively. It would not necessarily be effective for you to mimic these behaviors while attending the seminar. The real test of the seminar's usefulness is whether you can emit these behaviors at different times and in appropriate circumstances, say at work or in the midst of negotiations with a car salesperson. In other words, much of the behavior that we acquire socially may be beneficial to us, but not necessarily at the moment of acquisition.

Continuing Issues in the Study of Imitation

Even a seemingly trivial behavior like imitation becomes complex once it is investigated scientifically. When forced to define the behavior technically, researchers must be very specific in identifying the criteria, and some actions that appear imitative may not fit these rigorous criteria. For example, non-human animals can learn by observing members of their own species (conspecifics), but they don't necessarily duplicate the motoric actions of models. Michael Tomasello (1996, 1999, 2000) has suggested that emulation, producing the same consequences as the modeled action but without repeating the specific actions, represents a form of social learning common to nonhuman animals. Humans, on the other hand, are more likely to mimic the detailed movements of the model, and Tomasello believes that this subtle difference may explain how human culture differs from that of other species. Once an observer imitates a model, and this behavior transfers to others, it becomes something of a cultural standard. But inevitably, someone will come along who tries a variant on this standard, deviating from the original behavior and perhaps discovering a better way to accomplish the same goal. As an example, the assembly line represented a revolutionary advance in the speed and efficiency with which a product could be manufactured. This progressive development of increasingly more effective techniques, a process Tomasello calls a "ratchet effect," catches on because the larger community benefits from such methodological advances.

The ratchet effect, and the rapidity with which advances could be shared within human communities, particularly through language, set the stage, Tomasello argues, for an explosion in human culture that forever distinguished humans from nonhumans. Although this position is somewhat speculative, most social and behavioral scientists agree that there are important differences between human and nonhuman cultures, especially with respect to language and the emergence of such uniquely human institutions as the arts, science, and religion. Something must account for this difference, and perhaps the answer lies in the subtle distinctions that modern research has uncovered between human and nonhuman social learning dynamics.

✖ INTERIM SUMMARY

Though a seemingly simple behavior, imitation plays a crucial role in the development of social creatures. The study of imitation has been complicated by the difficulty of distinguishing imitative behavior from other kinds of socially influenced behavior, and by the inherent problems associated with studying very young research participants, including human infants. Both humans and nonhumans appear to benefit significantly from observing conspecifics, and imitation, as a fundamental instance of social learning, may be among the important building blocks of culture. There are subtle differences in how humans and nonhumans imitate, and some scientists believe that these differences have implications for many kinds of social behavior, including the remarkable cultural achievements of human beings.

✖ THOUGHT QUESTIONS

1. Why is deferred imitation so important to the development of new behaviors? Also, describe an instance of your own behavior that could be categorized as deferred imitation.
2. Imitation makes its most profound contribution to culture through what Tomasello calls the ratchet effect. Describe an example of the ratchet effect and how it has influenced some aspect of contemporary American culture.

SOCIAL LEARNING: THE COGNITIVE PERSPECTIVE

social learning a process by which organisms acquire behavior by observing others

Psychologists use the phrase **social learning** to refer to the process by which humans acquire behavior by observing others, and this includes but is not limited to pure instances of imitation. In fact, some scientists, including Albert Bandura, believe that social learning accounts for a much greater amount of learned behavior in humans than do basic learning principles like Pavlovian and operant conditioning. For many years Bandura has been the most visible proponent of social learning theory, the essential tenets of which were articulated in his groundbreaking book *Social Learning Theory* (1977). The book outlines the fundamental principles of observational (vicarious) learning, discusses the role of expectations in human learning, and describes research, much of it conducted by Bandura himself, on observational learning.

Like most theories, social learning theory has evolved over the years, benefiting from a diverse collection of both applied and basic research programs. Today, social learning theory commands a central position in psychology, with a scope of influence over the entire field. Clinical psychologists, in particular, have found social learning theory to be relevant to understanding the dynamics of behavior change, and its basic principles have been fruitfully extended to a range of applied phenomena, including anxiety (Williams, 1995); depression (Maddux & Meier, 1995); marital violence (Mihalic &

Elliott, 1997); human sexuality (Adih & Alexander, 1999; Hogben & Byrne, 1998); adolescent cigarette smoking (Epstein, Botvin, & Diaz, 1999); and career choice (Hackett & Betz, 1995). This list is merely representative, not exhaustive. The ubiquity of social learning theory in psychological science is testimony to its influence within the field. Let's begin the discussion of the theory by considering the essential concept of observational learning.

Observational Learning

The idea of observational learning may seem somewhat familiar because the previous discussion of imitation addressed a fairly specific instance of this kind of learning. But remember that you may just as easily learn how *not* to behave from watching a model. If a student in your psychology class answers, "Freud," in response to the question of who invented the operant chamber, and the instructor informs the student of his or her error, you would be unlikely to repeat the same response. Now, you may not know the answer is Skinner, but you almost certainly won't offer Freud as your answer, and this means that you learned something from the other student's behavior. Bandura would claim that your experience was one of observational (sometimes referred to as *vicarious*) learning because you benefited from the behavior and consequences of another person. Among the most important aspects of Bandura's presentation of social learning theory is his argument that observational learning accounts for much more learning, particularly in humans, than do the processes of Pavlovian and operant conditioning.

Bandura began pursuing the phenomena of observational learning during the early 1960s in a series of studies in which both adults and children were exposed to models engaged in various kinds of behavior. In one particularly famous study, boys and girls in a nursery school observed either a male or female adult model aggressing against a life-size inflated Bobo doll (Bandura, Ross, & Ross, 1961). After exposure to the model, children were observed playing with various objects, including the Bobo doll, but in a separate room from the one in which observation took place. Children who had observed the adult model behave aggressively toward the Bobo doll engaged in similar aggressive responses, whereas children who were not exposed to an aggressive model engaged in few instances of aggression toward the doll (Figure 6.3).

In order to ensure that the children's aggressive behavior was a result of observational learning, the adult models engaged in specific acts of aggression, including sitting on the doll and punching its nose repeatedly, hitting it in the head with a mallet, tossing the doll into the air and kicking it, and saying such things as "sock him in the nose" and "hit him down." Children who observed this aggression were much more likely to repeat these specific forms of aggression than were those who observed no aggressive behavior in the model. Thus, it wasn't simply the case that children were influenced to generally aggress against the doll; they had, instead, acquired particular forms of aggressive behavior as a result of observing the model's behavior. An additional and interesting finding from this study was that male models who demonstrated aggressive behavior produced higher frequencies of

FIGURE 6.3 Adult Modeling Aggression and Children Imitating Aggressive Behavior.

imitated aggression than did female models. In fact, many of the children seemed taken aback by the aggression of the female model, offering such observations as "Who is that lady? That's not the way for a lady to behave. Ladies are supposed to act like ladies . . ." (Bandura et al., 1961, p. 581). Keep in mind that this study was conducted 40 years ago, and the children's responses to the female model, though perhaps comical by today's standards, were not unrepresentative of American culture at that time.

In the years since Bandura's experiment, literally hundreds of studies have been done to further illustrate the conditions under which observational learning occurs. Remember that, when you observe someone else's behavior, it isn't just the motor movements you see, but important features of the immediate environment as well. In other words, you observe behavior in context, and it stands to reason that you pay attention to both the behavior and its surrounding context. One critical feature of the environment, as identified in the three-term contingency, is the consequence that any particular behavior produces. As discussed in the previous two chapters, these consequences can generally be categorized as reinforcers or punishers. This leads to two questions: Do observers pay attention to the consequences of the model's behavior? and Does this influence the observer's tendency to repeat the behavior? The answer to these questions is a resounding yes! Numerous studies indicate that observers are much more inclined to repeat behaviors for which models have been reinforced and are less likely to repeat actions that have been punished in models (Levy, McClinton, Rabinowitz, & Wolkin, 1974; Rosekrans & Hartup, 1967).

FIGURE 6.4 Children's television-watching habits have received a large share of research attention.

Nor is observational learning limited to instances in which an observer views the behavior of a live model. In fact, a good deal of research on observational learning over the years has focused on the role that various media may play in the development of both prosocial and negative behaviors. Because it has become such a fixture in American culture, and commands a sometimes disturbing amount of the attention of children, television has received a disproportionate share of research attention from social scientists (Figure 6.4). In one of many such studies, Liebert and Baron (1972) divided young children into two groups. The experimental group watched an extremely violent televised police program while members of the control group saw an exciting, but nonviolent, sports program. After viewing the programs, children were placed in a condition in which they were allowed to press a red button that would cause a painful stimulus to be delivered to another child. Children who had viewed the violent program were more likely to push the button than those who had seen the sports program.

Although not all studies of televised violence reach the same conclusion, the overall consensus is that children, and adults as well, do learn from images portrayed in the media (Eron, Huesmann, Lefkowitz, & Walder, 1996; Geen, 1994). Whether, when, and how this learning manifests itself in the observer's behavior is a complex issue. For instance, in much of this research, exposure to violent media occurs only once and for a brief period of time. In the real world, children may encounter thousands of violent images over a period of many years. The brief presentations characteristic of experimental research may not tell everything there is to know about saturation exposure over the course of childhood. In sum, the effect of modeled behavior in the media clearly depends on a mosaic of variables, many of which may interact in unpredictable ways and over long periods of time. Fortunately, some of these variables have been studied fairly comprehensively. Let's consider one such variable—model characteristics.

Various characteristics of the model, including behavior and status in the social situation, play a role in the observational learning process. As it turns out, not everyone is an equally good candidate as a behavioral model. Not surprisingly, the authority or social standing of the model makes a difference. In one study, college student subjects who thought they were observing an assistant to the experimenter demonstrated more behavior change than those who believed they were observing another student (Berger, 1971). This tendency to give a disproportionate amount of attention to authority provides the logic behind testimonials in advertisements. There is something especially convincing about Christie Brinkley singing the praises of the latest cosmetic product or Charlton Heston leading a rally for the NRA and espousing gun rights. It's not surprising that companies will pay such celebrities a handsome sum to endorse their product or service.

There is also evidence that people are more likely to pay attention to models viewed as similar to themselves in personality, religious and cultural background, or political values (Bandura & Walters, 1963). In one study, leaders in the Liberal and Socialist parties in the Dutch Parliament gave identical television interviews (Wiegman, 1985). Despite the fact that the presentations were the same, the effect they had on their audience was not. Liberal speakers were viewed as more convincing by members of their own party than by members of the Socialist party, and the reverse was true for the Socialist speaker. Thus, not everyone is equally effective as a behavioral model; people pick and choose their models, sometimes based on rather specific criteria.

The Role of Cognition in Social Learning

The development of social learning theory must be understood within the historical context that characterized psychology during the 1960s. Many theorists at this time were reacting to what they considered to be the rigid theoretical shackles of behaviorism and stimulus-response psychology. Remember that for methodological purposes, Watson had argued that psychology should concern itself only with observable behavior-environment interactions. By the late 1950s, and into the 1960s, psychologists began to consider once again the role that private experience might play in determining behavior. For some, this meant viewing the organism as an information processing system that organized and structured sensory input, coordinating this information with motor output, or behavior. Critics of behavioristic psychology claimed that stimulus-response conceptualizations viewed the organism as a helpless automaton, responding blindly to environmental stimulation. The resurgence of "mind," consciousness, and the information processing metaphor borrowed from computer science ushered in the cognitive revolution in psychology in conspicuous fashion. Social learning theory remains among the most influential products of this revolution.

Although Bandura acknowledged the role played by basic conditioning principles (Pavlovian and operant learning), he believed that a full account of human learning required something more. In fact, even these simple processes, he argued, should be seen as something other than automatic, mechanical stamping-in of behavior. People don't merely respond to stimuli, they process them, make sense of them, and relate them in meaningful ways to their behavior. For Bandura, the way in which conditioned (Pavlovian) and discriminative and reinforcing (operant) stimuli influence behavior depends on the details of how and why they are processed by the individual, and much of his theory is a description of how this processing takes place.

Attentional, Encoding, and Retention Processes You can't very well learn from a model to whom you are not attending, so the initial activity on the part of an observer is to pay attention to relevant aspects of the model and his or her behavior. Naturally, not everything about the model is pertinent. If you are observing someone operating a drill press, noticing the type of pants worn or the color of the model's hair will serve little purpose. What you do attend to are the specific behaviors that the model uses in operating the machine. Thus, observers must pick up on or distinguish meaningful from meaningless information when viewing a model, at least if they are to learn something from what the model does. Bandura suggests, then, that basic attentional and discriminative activity on the part of the observer is a beginning point in any instance of observational learning.

It is similarly necessary that the relevant dimensions of the model's behavior be successfully placed in memory, a process known as **encoding.** As the next chapter will explain, encoding is a fundamental aspect of any information processing system. An information processing system that can't accommodate new information is pretty useless, whether it is a computer or a human brain. Consequently, Bandura's theory borrows heavily from the discipline of cognitive psychology, which addresses the details of information processing, including how people retain information over time. For present purposes, it is sufficient to understand that encoding of relevant features of a model's behavior is an integral part of observational learning. This is particularly true when what is observed is not immediately used to guide or inform behavior, and, as discussed earlier, this is commonplace in imitation, even among very young children.

> **encoding** the process of placing information into a memory system

Because information that is placed in memory doesn't do much good if it doesn't remain there or is not available when needed, a method for retaining encoded information is necessary. Cognitive psychologists call this process **storage.** Much of the research on memory, in both nonhumans and humans, focuses on storage of information over time and the variables that influence both successful retention and memory loss. Observational learning is incomplete if what people observe at one time is not available to help guide their behavior at another time, so Bandura views retention, or storage, as an essential element of observational learning. Again, the question of what sorts of factors influence retention has been thoroughly addressed by researchers in cognitive psychology, and some of the details of this research will be examined in the following chapter.

> **storage** the process of retaining information in memory over time

Transforming Observations Into Overt Action   Once an observer has attended to a model's behavior, encoded relevant aspects, and retained this information over the necessary time period, he or she must translate this information into actions. That is, there must be a process by which to coordinate sensory and cognitive activity with motor output in the form of behavior. This is actually a very complicated process, and researchers are still scratching their heads over how, precisely, this transformation is accomplished. Unraveling this process entails understanding the complex communication that must occur between the different regions of the brain responsible for integration of sensory information and coordination of this information with the brain's motor centers. Much of the answer probably lies in the area of **cognitive neuroscience**, that interface between biology and psychology that attempts to discover the specific neural machinery and activity that underlies all behavior. The development of high-tech imaging techniques, such as PET scans and MRIs, has revolutionized research in the neurosciences, allowing researchers to better identify the labyrinthine nature of neural networks—aggregates of nerve cells that collectively contribute to some psychological or behavioral process.

Regardless of what research on the nervous system reveals about how sensory information is encoded and integrated, then transferred to neural networks that elicit overt behavior, the ability of the observer to actually produce the behavior becomes a major constraining factor. Recall that researchers pursuing imitation in newborns had to recognize that certain kinds of behavior were simply out of the question because of infants' limited muscular control. Having a concert pianist demonstrate piano playing to a 3-year-old child by playing a sophisticated piece of classical music would be absurd. Even if the child could successfully attend to the model's key strokes, the limited manual dexterity of a child this age would preclude any meaningful repetition of the behavior. (Of course, you and I might be similarly inept at repeating the agile movements of an Olympic gymnast, so infants have no monopoly on imitative constraint.) It stands to reason, then, that modeled actions that are fairly simple and involve few movements are both more easily attended to and repeated, especially by younger observers.

Self-Efficacy and Contemporary Social Learning Theory

First proposed in the late 1970s, social learning theory has evolved into a mature theory of behavior acquisition within social contexts. Sometimes, in the development of theories, and the research programs that support them, a central concept virtually forces itself to the front, commanding special attention. For Bandura (1977), what eventually emerged as central was the notion that through both direct experience and observational learning, people piece together a perception of themselves as being behaviorally competent or incompetent:

> An outcome expectancy is defined as a person's estimate that a given behavior will lead to certain outcomes. An efficacy expectation is the conviction that one can successfully execute the behavior required to produce the outcome. (p. 193)

cognitive neuroscience   a scientific discipline concerned with the relationship between brain function and cognition

Thus, **self-efficacy** refers to the individual's degree of belief that he or she can accomplish some behavioral task in order to produce some desirable consequence. As a part of one's overall sense of self, self-efficacy becomes a powerful internal determinant of behavior, according to Bandura (1982). In recent years, self-efficacy has matured into one of the most prodigiously researched constructs in psychology. In fact, in an electronic search of the psychological literature, typing in the term *self-efficacy* will turn up more than 5,000 research articles, and that's just since 1984 (Bandura, 1997; Maddux, 1995).

Because of the attention that self-efficacy has received, it's reasonable to inquire into the variables that contribute to efficacy expectations. That is, where does self-efficacy come from, what kinds of factors may increase or decrease self-efficacy, and why do people differ in the degree of self-efficacy they demonstrate? Bandura (1977) has suggested that there are four primary sources of self-efficacy: performance accomplishments, vicarious experiences, verbal persuasion, and physiological cues.

Previous *performance accomplishments* are an especially important factor in determining self-efficacy. A person who has run numerous marathons is more likely to view him- or herself as capable of finishing, perhaps even winning, an upcoming race than someone who has never entered a footrace before. Research has shown that performance history is often among the strongest predictors of self-efficacy (Burke & Putai, 1996; Luzzo, Hasper, Albert, Bibby, & Martinelli, 1999), and this finding has an intuitive appeal. There is nothing like past success to engender perceptions of competence and confidence when undertaking new endeavors.

Yet previous experiences of success are not always necessary for efficacy expectations to develop. Through *vicarious experiences,* people may also develop a sense of competence, even though they may not have previously encountered the task at hand (Delorenzo, 1999; Sterrett, 1998). Upon observing a neighborhood adolescent rollerblading down the street, you may decide that you are up to the challenge yourself and strap on a pair of blades. The behavior of others, then, may serve both modeling and motivational functions. Sterrett (1998) had welfare recipients participate in a job club that met twice weekly for several weeks. Formal agendas were followed during each meeting, and participants were required to complete homework assignments. Both prior to participation and just before the last group meeting, self-efficacy measures were taken from each participant. At follow-up, all measures of efficacy, including vicarious learning, showed increases relative to the baseline measure.

A sense of efficacy can also be modified through *verbal persuasion.* Perhaps you have had friends or colleagues cajole and convince you of your ability to tackle a difficult task. Luzzo and Taylor (1993–1994) exposed college freshmen to a counseling intervention related to career choice. For some students, verbal persuasion was utilized within the counseling session, and for other students, persuasion was not used. Career decision-making self-efficacy (CDMSE), as measured after the counseling session, was greater for those students who had been exposed to the verbal persuasion condition. Hagen, Gutkin, Wilson, and Oats (1998) obtained similar results with a group

self-efficacy an individual's degree of belief that he or she can accomplish some behavioral task in order to produce desirable consequences

of preservice teachers. Teachers viewed a videotape depicting various strategies for teaching difficult-to-teach children, including persuasive appeals and teacher testimonials. Measured self-efficacy after exposure was greater for this group than for a control group who watched a videotape having no relevance to teaching strategies. It appears that the right words from the right source can go a long way toward convincing people of their ability to accomplish a difficult task. It may in fact be that the singular genius of highly successful coaches is their ability to deliver inspiring and motivational speeches to their athletes, modifying efficacy expectations and engendering higher caliber performance.

Finally, the feedback from your body is potent information in the development of efficacy expectations (Arch, 1987; O'Leary & Brown, 1995). The fear and anxiety that often precede uncomfortable or threatening tasks can serve as a powerful reminder of a sense of competency (or lack of it). For many people, speaking in front of a large group is a daunting and anxiety-provoking challenge. Butterflies in the stomach, rapid breathing, and sweaty hands are not-too-subtle cues that may be interpreted as further evidence of ineptitude.

Bandura's (1977) theory, and the sizable research literature that supports it, paints a picture of self-efficacy as a complicated cognitive structure, influenced by numerous sources of both personal (performance history, physiological cues) and social (vicarious learning, verbal persuasion) information. The significance of the construct, however, according to Bandura, is its ability to predict future behavior, such as a person's willingness to engage in and persist in a challenging task. Much of the literature on self-efficacy is devoted to studies of how efficacy expectations are related to such varied behavior as career choice, marital dynamics, and cigarette smoking. In Bandura's conception, self-efficacy is an internal determinant, or causal mechanism, that regulates overt behavior. Naturally, not all psychologists agree with this claim. The next section considers some of the criticisms that have been raised concerning self-efficacy's causal status and explains how psychologists of a more behavioral persuasion make sense of the many behavioral phenomena encompassed by the term *social learning,* including imitation and observational learning.

✖ INTERIM SUMMARY

Most animals, including humans, learn a good deal by observing members of their own species behave. Social learning makes an especially large contribution to human behavior, and Bandura's influential theory describes the cognitive processes that account for social learning. To benefit from observational learning, people must encode, store, and retain social information. As a result of both personal and vicarious experience, people develop a sense of competency, or self-efficacy, that affects their willingness to engage in and persevere at certain behavioral tasks.

✖ THOUGHT QUESTIONS

1. Describe an instance of your own behavior in which observational learning took place. Who was the model? Did the model's behavior lead to

reinforcement or punishment? What specific behavior do you think you learned in this situation?

2. Suppose a friend invites you on a white-water kayaking trip for the weekend. Would you consider yourself to have high or low self-efficacy for this trip? What kinds of personal or vicarious experiences have led to this self-efficacy?

SOCIAL LEARNING: THE BEHAVIORAL PERSPECTIVE

There isn't much reason to deny or ignore the facts of social learning. The fact that both humans and nonhumans imitate and acquire behavioral repertoires through observation is so well established as to invite little debate. Considerable disagreement does emerge, though, when the question of explanation arises. Psychologists operating from different theoretical orientations don't necessarily see eye to eye on the hows and whys of social learning. Bandura's theory of social learning is a decidedly cognitive one, in that the theory details the processes by which the individual attends to, encodes, stores, and retrieves observed information and then transforms this cognitive input into overt action. In addition, the construct of self-efficacy is, by definition, an internal, cognitive mechanism that regulates outward behavior.

It is possible, of course, to acknowledge the empirical facts of imitation and observational learning without necessarily agreeing on the process that Bandura invokes to explain these facts. Behavioral psychologists argue that social learning phenomena are well accounted for by basic learning principles and that recourse to internal mechanisms is superfluous (Deguchi, 1984; Masia & Chase, 1997). The status of self-efficacy as a causal mechanism has come under particular scrutiny, in part because it has been wielded and defined in an inconsistent manner (Kirsch, 1985). In addition, Lee (1998) claims that the self-efficacy construct possesses no explanatory power; the term simply describes a particular behavior-environment relation, not an internal mechanism that governs behavior. Further, Biglan (1987) suggests that subjects' verbal reports of self-efficacy are themselves behavior and that they may or may not correspond to other behavioral classes to which they refer. Rather than being envisioned as the causes of efficacious behavior, though, reports of self-efficacy are conceptualized as resulting from the same environmental contingencies that produced the efficacious behavior itself.

Because cognitive and behavioral psychologists envision the subject matter of their science differently, and locate the causes of behavior in different domains, their theoretical positions are difficult to reconcile. In fact, Hineline (1984) has argued that these differences are so crucial as to render any future rapprochement between the two unlikely. The issue, after all, hinges not simply on semantics but rather on fundamental aspects of philosophy of science, including how to conceptualize, measure, and draw causal inferences about the subject matter. Let's explore how this difference plays itself out in the behavioral treatment of social learning.

Social Learning and the Three-Term Contingency

For behavioral psychologists, all behavioral episodes can be meaningfully conceptualized within the context of the three-term contingency. This perspective identifies antecedent and consequent stimuli as the causes of behavior. In the social world, people serve as antecedent stimuli and provide potent behavioral consequences to one another, frequently in the form of approval and disapproval. The fact that people, and their actions, can serve discriminative stimulus functions may be difficult to appreciate, because most of the basic research on stimulus control has used simple visual and auditory stimuli (lights, tones, etc.) in laboratory settings. This is done, of course, because such stimuli are objective and easy to present and monitor in a controlled environment. But the physical or structural dimensions of a stimulus have little to do with its controlling function, and naturally occurring stimuli often possess multiple structural properties. For example, members of a prey species must be able to respond to many features of a potential predator—including sounds, movements, perhaps even olfactory cues—in order to successfully evade capture. And the human driver at an intersection must adjust his or her behavior both to the traffic lights and to the actions of other drivers.

It becomes clear, then, that behavior in natural settings is ordinarily under the control of complex stimulus conditions. In social contexts, the actions of other people play a prominent role as antecedent stimuli. Let's consider why this is the case. An animal in an operant chamber pays vigilant attention to the stimulus lights illuminated in the chamber, because these lights have become correlated with specific important events, such as reinforcers and punishers. In most highly social species, particularly humans and other primates, attending closely to the behavior of others pays similar dividends. The discussion has already shown that imitation is pervasive in such animals, even human newborns. To the evolutionary biologist, a behavior pattern this universal tells a revealing story. Behaviors that develop in a predictable manner, at an early age, and in nearly all members of a species strongly call out for an adaptationist interpretation. The pervasiveness of imitation suggests that the tendency to attend to the actions of conspecifics has contributed to the adaptive behavior of many animals, humans included, over countless generations. Thus, humans are perhaps phylogenetically prepared to imitate and simultaneously capable of differentiating between who, when, and where to imitate. That is, our native penchant for imitating is supported in kind by a flexible capacity for attending to the antecedent and consequent stimuli that help us fine-tune our imitative repertoires.

Imitation, and other forms of social learning, may very well be universal behavior patterns among many animals, but such behavior does not occur constantly, or stereotypically, like the modal-action patterns discussed in Chapter 1. Instead, the way humans benefit from the behavior of others is highly variable; recall that people often end up behaving in a manner precisely opposite to that of the model. Any complete attempt to explain social learning, then, must account for this variability in expression, and the behavioral psychologist would argue that doing so requires focusing on the environmental factors associated with a particular behavioral episode and the observer's history with respect to observational learning. Part of this story has in fact been told already, and in considerable detail, by Bandura and others who have explored the specific conditions under which modeling does or does not occur.

Among the most salient predictors of imitation is whether the model's behavior is or is not reinforced. Take a moment to consider how this difference may affect the probability of imitation in an observer. That the observer even attends to the model may be partly explained by evolutionary history, as most social animals have probably acquired this tendency as a result of long-standing selective pressures. But just as important to the current episode are environmental factors that the observer would be expected to notice. If the model engages in a specific response, and this response produces reinforcing consequences, then the observer has actually seen a rather complex discriminative stimulus (S^D)—the model's behavior *and its consequences*. It can also be assumed that most people have a history of imitating the behavior of others under this condition and have experienced similar consequences. If I observe you at a grocery store picking up several food items that have been drastically discounted, it would certainly make sense for me to do the same. In essence, your behavior has functioned as an S^D for me because it sets the occasion for similar behavior on my part.

On the other hand, when a model's behavior does not result in reinforcing consequences, or leads to punishment, the actions and consequences function as an S^Δ, meaning the observer is not as likely to engage in behavior similar to that of the model. This kind of analysis suggests that other people's behavior serves as a complex antecedent for the behavior of individuals. As it turns out, similar complexity can be demonstrated in the laboratory setting. Figure 6.5 depicts a study in which pigeons learned to respond discriminatively on the basis not of a single stimulus but of a combination of stimulus properties. Operant chambers can be illuminated generally with a house light, much like you illuminate your room or office with an overhead light. When the overhead house light is turned on, pecks to a triangle projected on one of the chamber's response keys produce grain reinforcement, whereas pecks to the circle produce a time-out. When the house light is turned off, however, the reinforcement contingencies are reversed. That is, pecks to the triangle now produce time-out and pecks to the circle produce reinforcement. This contingency is referred to as a **conditional discrimination,** because the consequences of pecking a particular geometric figure (triangle or circle) are conditional upon, or depend upon, whether the house light is on or off.

conditional discrimination a contingency in which the consequences of responding to one antecedent stimulus depend upon the presence or absence of a second antecedent stimulus

In order for the bird's behavior to come under effective stimulus control, the bird must simultaneously attend to two features of the immediate environment (geometric shapes and house light illumination). As it turns out, this is not an overwhelmingly difficult task, and pigeons master it uneventfully. Conditional discriminations confront organisms in the real world all the time. The driver at a traffic light must attend to both the color of the lights and the actions of other drivers in order to safely negotiate the intersection. That is, the light alone can't be relied upon, because other stimuli in

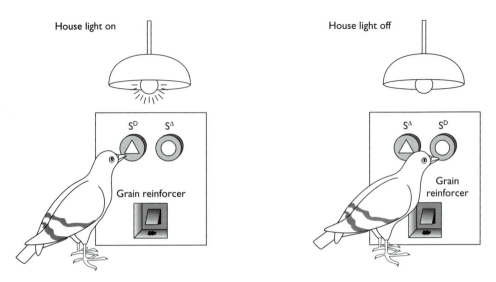

FIGURE 6.5 Conditional Discrimination. Differential reinforcement of key pecks to S^D (circle or triangle) is conditional upon illumination of the house light.

the environment may be predictive of aversive consequences for driving through the intersection. Likewise, a physician diagnosing a patient's illness may have to attend to more than one symptom, as many diseases have several symptoms in common. This kind of complex stimulus control is probably the rule rather than the exception in natural environments. In social contexts, both the model's behavior and the consequences of the behavior serve as potential discriminative stimuli, and the effects of one stimulus property may often depend upon other properties.

Perhaps just as important to a behavioral explanation of social learning is the fact that each person accumulates, throughout his or her life, a wealth of experience in observing other people's behavior and the associated consequences. As a result, the tendency to imitate the behavior of others may emerge not simply in isolated circumstances, but as a generalized response class. Several researchers have delivered reinforcement to children contingent on imitation of modeled behavior (Baer, Peterson, & Sherman, 1967; Kymiss & Poulson, 1994; Young, Krantz, McClannahan, & Poulson, 1994). As expected, children imitate the specific behaviors for which reinforcement is received. However, the children also demonstrate an increase in imitation of behaviors even when reinforcement is not made contingent on such imitation. This phenomenon, **generalized imitation**, suggests that a few instances of reinforced imitation may "spread" considerably beyond the specific location and time of reinforcement. A child observing a parent writing a check at the grocery store isn't merely learning some things about writing checks. He or she is learning that the parent's behavior is effective in the environment in ways that matter, and this is as important a lesson as anything specific that the child learns about check writing. But such a realization comes with a cost. The phenomenon of generalized imitation makes no useful dis-

generalized imitation the tendency to imitate behavior seen in others that has not been reinforced tinction between appropriate and inappropriate behavior, and it is possible, therefore, that children will readily imitate both. This likelihood may account for the favored, though ineffective, proclamation of parents to "Do as I say, not as I do." Thus, as a behavioral phenomenon, generalized imitation would seem to generate little fanfare, since generalization as a dimension of learned behavior is well documented. The concept of generalized imitation is important, though, because it illustrates how a relatively basic learning principle can account for a substantially diverse collection of social behaviors.

From Acquisition to Maintenance:
Explaining Behavior Over Time

One of the great challenges for a science of behavior is to explain a phenomenon that is, by its very nature, relatively continuous and extended in time. Most meaningful human behavior is not a one-time occurrence, having a discrete beginning and ending. There are, of course, exceptions to this rule. There are those rare accomplishments in life that we anticipate experiencing but one time: Marriage (it is hoped), graduating college, and paying off the mortgage on a home come to mind as such milestones. Much more of our behavioral repertoire, however, manifests itself, sometimes in an agonizingly repetitive manner, over days, weeks, months, even years. Everyday routines, such as washing the clothes and dishes, putting out the trash, mowing the lawn, grocery shopping, paying the bills, balancing a checkbook, and, yes, reading assignments for college course work, happen with predictable frequency. The apparent mundane quality of such behavior can be deceiving, because the temptation is to see the behavior as always occurring for the same reason. But it is important to distinguish between a learned behavior's acquisition and its maintenance over time, because different controlling variables may be in effect at different times. In fact, the distinction between behavioral acquisition and maintenance has particularly critical implications for social learning.

In actuality, it is always difficult to establish with any certainty the very first occasion of any behavior, and for several reasons. On the one hand, some behavioral firsts may simply be hard to categorize as such. First-time parents often relish documenting their infant's first word, or first step in the world, but identifying the exact occurrence is more often an exercise in wishful thinking than objective observation. Are fathers more likely than mothers to interpret the 4-month-old's vocalization "daga" as an attempt at saying "Daddy"? And consider the infant who takes that initial, bold step away from the supportive couch, only to tumble to the ground before completing the second step. Should the parents chalk this episode up as the child's first independent stroll? In addition, some behavioral firsts occur in private and can't therefore be verified by an objective observer.

What all of this means is that, whether parents or researchers, we probably seldom have the luxury of observing the very first instance of a behavior, and once the behavior occurs, it makes contact with environmental contingencies that weren't in effect on its initial occurrence. Skinner

(1968) recognized the ethereal nature of original behaviors, suggesting that ". . . there is always an element of mystery in the emission of any operant response" (p.137). Thus, we don't always know why a behavior occurs on its first occasion. But once a response occurs, regardless of its initial causes, it produces consequences that alter its future probability. These consequences (reinforcers and punishers) help to explain how the behavior is maintained over long periods of time, even though they may have had nothing to do with its initial acquisition.

Imitation and other forms of social learning are unquestionably pervasive forms of human learning, but their predominant effect is on the acquisition process, not necessarily on maintenance. That is, social learning may be conveniently viewed as a way to jump-start behavior. Consider the preschooler who, having just listened to a teenage sibling's conversation with a friend, walks up to her parents and repeats several choice words overheard in the older sibling's conversation. After recovering from their shock at hearing such language from a toddler, Mom and Dad offer a brief lecture on the inappropriateness of "bad words" and then institute a suitable disciplinary tactic. Now, a complete understanding of the preschooler's "learning" experience in this episode would have to account for two separate phases—the initial acquisition of the verbal behavior and its eventual contact with subsequent contingencies. Any parent will testify to young children's propensity to repeat actions and verbalizations that they observe in the behavior of others. Indeed, a major contention of social learning theory is that a sizable percentage of human behavior is acquired in this way. But recall that all behavior operates on the environment to produce consequences, and this means that the toddler's colorful language, initially an instance of imitation, becomes an immediate candidate for reinforcement or punishment, and its future occurrence will likely be strongly determined by such consequences. In the present example, those consequences are most likely to be delivered by the toddler's perplexed parents.

The distinction between behavioral acquisition and maintenance has repercussions for the national conversation regarding the influence of mass media on children's behavior. Social scientists have for several decades studied the relationship between content of televised programs and behavior in children, particularly with an emphasis on aggression (Danish & Donohue, 1996; Heath, Bresolin, & Rinaldi, 1989; Huesmann & Malamuth, 1986). The finding that children will readily imitate the actions of characters seen on television surprises no one, squares well with the casual observations of parents, and converges with the large literature on modeling, including Bandura's famous Bobo doll studies. Indeed, this chapter argues that humans, like many social animals, may be phylogenetically prepared to attend to and repeat the actions of conspecifics.

A larger question emerges from both the research and casual observation, and that is Should television and other forms of mass media be held specifically responsible for aggression and other antisocial behavior, especially in children? In other words, just because children (and adults, too) may pick up novel behaviors from models, does it necessarily mean that repeated occurrences of the behavior can be attributed to the initial modeling? Such a claim seems questionable when you consider the well-documented role that consequences play in maintaining behavior. In fact, many such behaviors would probably merit little attention if they occurred once, never to be repeated. When these behaviors become firmly ingrained in an individual's repertoire, the larger culture begins to take notice, and explaining habitual behavior requires consideration of factors that come into play after the initial modeling experience. While it may be more convenient to identify a single, conspicuous instance of modeling as the "cause" of the behavior and ignore the effect that long-term contingencies might play, doing so may end up neglecting the very factors that, when manipulated as part of a systematic intervention, can help to change or modify the behavior in more desirable directions.

In the end, getting a handle on the causes of behavior is a difficult business, in part because of the temporal characteristics of the subject matter. The independent variables of which behavior acquisition are a function may be quite separate from the variables responsible for maintenance. People do indeed learn new behaviors by observing others, but the result is seldom a fixed, rigidly stereotypic response emitted without regard to other environmental factors. Like most other species, humans are sensitive to the way their behavior operates on the environment, and this fact better accounts for the long-term persistence of many behaviors.

Rule-Governed Behavior Versus Contingency-Shaped Behavior

The power and flexibility of social learning is owing to much more than imitation or observational learning. Episodes of human social behavior are distinguished by the existence of a particular habit that many psychologists believe is unique to humans—language. Whether or not other animals share our penchant for linguistic behavior is an interesting point of debate, and this issue will be addressed in more detail in Chapter 9. For purposes of the present chapter, language takes on specific importance because it provides a certain economy to interpersonal behavior that is often missing in private encounters with the world. According to linguists and anthropologists, a chief advantage of language is its contribution to culture, through such devices as storytelling, mentoring, and simply providing information. Recall Imo, the macaque whose food-washing propensity was observed by and eventually transmitted to other members of her troop. Clearly, the other troop members benefited from observing Imo's cleansing routine, in that they didn't have to discover this functional behavior on their own.

Imagine how much more efficient this social transmission of information would have been if Imo could have called a troop meeting in which she verbally instructed the members of the troop in the fine art of potato washing. Parents and teachers instruct children, sometimes continuously it seems, on a nearly unlimited array of behavioral routines, from how to put bread in the toaster, to how to move the cursor on a computer screen (OK, maybe the kids do more of the instructing on this one!), to how to simultaneously let out the clutch and step on the gas pedal when learning to drive a vehicle with a manual transmission. Such verbal instructions, if provided carefully, can speed up the process of acquiring a new skill, strongly reducing the time and effort that would be required in the absence of such instruction. It may in fact be difficult to appreciate just how much behavior is acquired, not by observing others engaged in the same behavior, but from written or verbal instructions. Parents and teachers may seem to do a disproportionate amount of instructing, but they, like everyone else, also benefit from instruction. From learning a new computer program to how to put together that new Christmas toy for an excited 8-year-old, people follow instructions of some sort nearly every day of their lives.

When people adjust their behavior in response to written or verbal instructions, they are engaging in what Skinner (1969, 1974) referred to as **rule-governed behavior.** A rule, of course, is a stimulus, be it a brief injunction to "Put on Hard Hat When Entering Work Area" or a lengthy, step-by-step description of how to construct a new gas grill (Figure 6.6). But remember that stimuli in natural environments, particularly those inhabited by humans, are often complex and multidimensional. Researchers' interest lies in the function that such a stimulus plays in the adaptive behavior of the person responding, not in the structural features of the stimulus. Many rules describe both the behavior to be accomplished and the results (consequences) that will follow from doing so. In other words, a rule is often a description of a behavior-consequence contingency. For example, my backpacking stove comes with instructions that describe a sequence of behaviors (opening a valve, operating a pump, then placing a lit match to the burner) that must be completed in order to successfully light the stove. If these steps are not taken, or are not executed correctly, the stove does not light—an altogether unpleasant experience when cold evening air settles upon me and I'm hungry from a long day on the trail. This entire sequence of events just described—a written description of how to light the stove, completion of the behaviors required by the rule, and, finally, a lit stove—should strike you as familiar. It is an example of a three-term contingency, in which the antecedent stimulus is the set of instructions for lighting the stove.

A behavioral approach to rule-governed, or instructed, behavior brings a very large category of human activity under the common conceptual framework of operant psychology—the three-term contingency. Written and spoken rules function as antecedent (discriminative) stimuli because they ordinarily specify what actions to undertake and often identify as well what results will follow from these actions. Naturally, the control that a rule will exert over behavior is largely a function of the consequences that actually follow rule-following. A researcher can, for example, ensure that a pigeon's key pecking is always reinforced in the presence of a lighted key (S^D) in an operant chamber but not in its absence (S^Δ). As a result of this differential reinforcement contingency, the bird's key-pecking behavior will come under strict stimulus control; it will, in effect, be possible to turn the response on or off almost like a water faucet.

Unfortunately, the real world is somewhat messier than the operant chamber, and the connection between the components of the three-term con-

rule-governed behavior acquiring or emitting a behavior in response to written or verbal instructions

FIGURE 6.6 Rule-Governed Behavior.

tingency often turns out to be a hit-or-miss proposition, particularly in the social environment of human beings. There are many antecedent stimuli, in the form of rules, that have little effect on human behavior because of a breakdown in the three-term contingency. A particularly good example is the speed limit sign. A speed limit sign contains a rule that specifies the legal speed at which drivers on a particular road can travel. Drivers, of course, are notorious for violating such rules. Why does this happen? Remember that a discriminative stimulus is only as powerful as the consequent stimuli with which it is associated. As long as drivers benefit by driving faster (reinforcement), and tend not to suffer negative consequences (accidents or being pulled over by a police officer), the rule (speed limit sign) would not be expected to exert much effect on driving behavior. Of course, this effect can be substantially altered by the presence of a state trooper on the side of the road. Under such conditions, drivers come under the control of a conditional discrimination because the consequences of obeying the speed limit are conditional, or depend, on the presence of an additional stimulus (state trooper).

Scientists are still unsure of exactly how and when humans developed language, but there can be no doubt that this occurrence marked a substantial milestone in our species' history. The ability to codify, in either spoken or written form, the thousands of behavior-consequence contingencies that affected humans must have had an enormous adaptive advantage for our ancestors. Whether manifested in stories, songs, prayers, or official legal documents, rules describing human activity and its consequences became a mainstay, and you and I benefit from such arrangements in our contemporary world in countless ways. But rule-following, like imitation, achieves its greatest potential when it attains the level of a generalized response class.

That is, the act of responding to any specific rule is not, by itself, very monumental; it is the tendency, or readiness, to respond to rules that affords so much flexibility to this kind of learning. The questions to answer, then, are How does rule following come about initially? and Why is it that humans sometimes follow rules and sometimes don't?

Rule-following, like imitation, occurs in a robust social context. Human beings pay attention to other human beings, and rule-following probably has its origins in simple interactions between adults and infants. Parents and other adults frequently provoke responses from babies simply by doing what comes naturally: smiling at the child, making various faces, vocalizing, and making dramatic gestures. When infants respond in turn, either by laughing, smiling, or repeating the adults' actions, consequences follow, usually in the form of enthusiastic and animated adult behavior. It is difficult to overestimate the potency of such adult reactions. After all, babies simply don't get what they need in life without the intervention of big people; consequently, anything an infant can do to solicit the attention of an adult will likely be remembered.

Later, as children become more mobile, able to move about their environment, they will be variously enjoined to accomplish certain tasks: "Bring Daddy the bottle," "Come to Mommy," "Give sister a hug," and so on. Such requests, as antecedent stimuli, describe specific behaviors and, as such, function as rules of conduct. Responding to such simple injunctions likely results in positive attention (smiles, hugs, words of praise), and these consequences serve to strengthen further instances of both the reinforced behavior and general rule-following. Thus, it is hardly an exaggeration to suggest that the seeds for rule-following can be found in the normal, day-to-day interactions that characterize most families.

As a child matures, the instructions or rules that he or she can respond to become both quantitatively and qualitatively more complex. But this increased complexity doesn't alter the fundamental properties of rules as antecedent stimuli nor how they function in the three-term contingency. Children, like adults, respond effectively to some rules and not to others, and understanding why requires identifying the consequences for rule-following. Recall the earlier example of drivers who refuse to comply with speed limit signs. Such failure to follow instructions is not uncommon. People litter, park illegally in handicapped parking spaces, fail to report taxable income, enter a grocery store's express line with many more items than they should, ignore memos sent by colleagues at work, and so on. In most of these instances, reinforcing and/or punishing consequences occur with considerable inconsistency or with such delay as to make them relatively ineffective. In other words, instructions, as antecedent stimuli, are effective prompts for behavior only when reliable consequences follow such behavior. This simple realization probably accounts for the nearly universal complaint by parents that their children don't mind them. Child behavior therapists often admonish parents for a lack of consistency, suggesting that compliance with verbal prompts (such as "Pick up your toys," "Wipe your shoes,") be backed up immediately with reinforcement. Similarly, if a negative or aversive consequence is threatened (loss of a privilege or time-out) for misbehavior, the consequence should reliably follow noncompliance. Like the boy who cried wolf, parents' instructions (rules) can lose effectiveness, just like speed limit signs, if no effective consequences follow for rule-following.

To acknowledge that much human behavior is acquired through rule-following is not to suggest that all learning falls into this category. It is probably impossible to anticipate every novel circumstance that a person may encounter, and it is consequently unlikely that a rule or instructional prompt will always be available to guide behavior. In addition to watching others and responding to their various instructions, people are also pretty good at simply acting and paying attention to how their actions affect the world at large. Skinner coined the phrase **contingency-shaped behavior** to refer to learning that occurs only in response to the contingencies themselves and not to antecedent rules or instructions. Many new skills can in fact be acquired this way, although the road is often longer and bumpier. Suppose you have just purchased a new video game, the goal of which is to move a medieval magician through a forest filled with dangerous creatures to the safety of a distant castle. You could simply turn the game on and, using the computer's joystick, try to figure out how to move the magician while simultaneously evading the creatures. Each movement of the joystick or button press will produce some outcome on the screen, and this procedure will eventually teach you what you need to know about the game. Of course, your first few efforts may meet with limited success, and it will probably be some time before you can successfully get the magician to the castle.

> **contingency-shaped behavior** behavior that is acquired as a result of direct exposure to behavior-consequence contingencies

There are any number of behaviors that you and I master in this way, without any special instruction or formal guide to help us. More often, though, learning involves a mix of both contingency-shaped and rule-governed behavior. Learning to drive a car is an especially good example of this interaction. Many teenagers are required to take a driving instruction course during their high school careers. This course involves reading materials (often the state driving booklet) and perhaps verbal instruction from the teacher. That is, the class entails both instruction on how to operate a motor vehicle and exposure to the rules of the road. Now, any parent who has taught a child to drive knows that instruction only goes so far, and at some point the real world comes into play. No matter how much, and in what detail, new drivers are told about how to press down on the brake or how much to turn the steering wheel, nothing can specifically prepare them for how the automobile will react when they comply with the instructions. Too little pressure on the brake will fail to stop the vehicle, and too much will . . . well, you get the point. The student's initial efforts at operating the vehicle are the result of instruction, but once the behavior actually makes contact with the contingencies (in this case, the vehicle not slowing down or coming to a jolting halt), instructional control tends to fade into the background. Driving is a complex skill, and that means that a good deal of time must be spent learning the "feel" of the car, that is, learning specific relationships between the driver's movements and the resulting movement of the car. The car "shapes" our driving behavior in much the same way that an operant chamber shapes the key pecking of the pigeon.

The distinction between rule-governed and contingency-shaped behaviors is important in part because of its widespread application to human learning. But equally important is the emerging finding that behavior that is shaped by direct exposure to contingencies may be more malleable, or responsive to changes in contingencies, than behavior that is rule governed. Several researchers have exposed human subjects to laboratory tasks in which verbal instructions (rules) are pitted against experimental contingencies in order to examine the relative power that each exerts over behavior. In many such studies, participants are exposed to written or verbal instructions that describe how to earn points on a computer screen by responding on the keyboard. Points are delivered according to standard reinforcement schedules (FR, FI, VR, etc.). The use of reinforcement schedules affords researchers several advantages, not the least of which is the fact that, once responding on a particular schedule stabilizes, the corresponding response rate and pattern becomes a useful benchmark or baseline against which to evaluate the effects of schedule changes. In general, the degree to which response rate and/or patterning change in response to changes in reinforcement contingencies is usually seen as a metric of sensitivity—that is, whether behavior is coming under effective control of the experimental variables.

A number of these studies have shown that people respond differently in such experiments depending upon whether they are instructed on how to respond (rule-governed condition) or simply exposed to the programmed reinforcement contingencies (contingency-shaped condition). Subjects who are instructed on how to respond to obtain points do in fact acquire points when exposed to the contingencies, but when the contingencies change (for instance, from a FI to a FR schedule), the subjects don't always change their response rate or pattern to reflect the new schedule (Joyce & Chase, 1990; Shimoff, Catania, & Matthews, 1981). Instead, they tend to respond in a manner consistent with the instructions and the original schedule. In such studies, it is often possible for subjects to continue to receive reinforcement (points) by responding as they were initially instructed, even though the reinforcement contingencies change. However, when following instructions leads to loss of points because the instructions improperly describe experimental contingencies, subjects will alter their responding to be consistent with the contingencies (Galizio, 1979).

It is apparent, then, that rules can exert strong control at the beginning of the experiment, but long-term compliance with the rule does not occur if such compliance results in a reduction in reinforcement. In other words, consistent rule-following requires reliability in the consequences that follow compliance. In many ways, this finding squares well with how people respond to instructions in the real world. Because they have a lengthy personal history of rule-following, they initially try to comply with instructions, especially if tackling a novel task. The parent who tries to follow the instructions for putting together a toy on Christmas morning may become frustrated if the various pieces fail to fit together. As a result, he or she may simply discard the instructions and rely on past experience and the contemporary contingencies that are in operation when trying to put together the toy. Thus, behavior in the world at large is often a subtle mix of rule-governed and contingency-shaped activities, and it is frequently difficult to identify with any certainty where one ends and the other begins. Because of the historical importance of instructions as antecedent stimuli, written and verbal rules probably exert their greatest impact during the acquisition phase of novel behavior. Once behavior produces consequences, instructional control may diminish, and this is particularly true when consequences do not correspond to those implied by or explicitly stated in the instructions.

✖ INTERIM SUMMARY

Behavioral psychologists view the phenomena of social learning within the causal framework of the three-term contingency. The behavior of other people functions as antecedent stimulation, and the consequences of attending to such behavior serve to maintain such observational repertoires. Verbal and written instructions also serve antecedent stimulus functions and play a substantial role in the acquisition of many new behaviors. Behavior that emerges initially in response to such stimuli is referred to as rule-governed behavior, in contrast to contingency-shaped behavior, which occurs in the absence of explicit rules or instructions. Ultimately, rule-governed behavior, once emitted, produces consequences, and the long-term maintenance of behavior often comes under the control of such consequences. Many behavioral repertoires represent complex response classes that have come about as the result of an interaction of rules and exposure to contingencies.

✖ THOUGHT QUESTIONS

1. Driving the speed limit in the presence of both a speed limit sign and a state trooper is an example of a conditional discrimination. Think of an example of your own behavior that demonstrates a conditional discrimination. Why is your behavior in the presence of the combined stimulus conditions different from your behavior in the presence of either stimulus by itself?

2. Suppose you were teaching a parenting class to young mothers of preschool-age children. How would you go about explaining to these young parents how to increase their children's compliance with verbal instructions? What specific points would you want to make in such a presentation?

THE ADAPTIVE NATURE OF SOCIAL LEARNING

Humans have evolved as a social species, and this simple, undeniable fact has many repercussions for understanding behavior. Because each human being comes into the world relatively helpless, unable to tend to its own need for food, shelter, and safety, dependence on others is an inescapable feature of the human condition. It is no mystery, therefore, that we show nearly immediate interest in the activity of others, particularly those large, competent creatures who respond to our cries, provide sustenance, and generally oversee our survival. There is good reason to believe that most social animals are prepared to observe what other members of their species do—how they interact with their world to get what they need. That human babies come into the world ready to do so is becoming increasingly obvious. Discovering the imitative capacity of human newborns took considerable research ingenuity on the part of developmental psychologists, but the eventual payoff has been impressive. The research has revealed that newborns come fully equipped to interact with others, appreciate the delicate turn taking that characterizes social interaction, and benefit enormously from watching what other humans do.

The tendency to observe others and learn from their behavior is no doubt jump-started by biology, but once we enter into social interactions, our behavior makes contact with explicit contingencies that further refine and extend our social repertoires. We learn to attend, not only to others' behavior, but to how their behavior operates on the environment. In doing so, we learn to differentiate conditions in which imitative responding will prove beneficial from those in which imitation may be costly. Moreover, in observing the consequences of others' behavior, or responding to instructional stimuli, we can acquire sometimes sophisticated repertoires without direct exposure to contingencies. In this way, social learning provides a shortcut method of behavior acquisition that probably enhances, exponentially, the speed with which new repertoires can be developed. Of course, such repertoires, once manifested, will necessarily produce consequences, so that behavior initially acquired through observation will soon be subject to the acid test of real-world contingencies. Over the course of a lifetime, response classes develop that are complicated combinations of rule-governed, or observational, and contingency-shaped repertoires. It is probably not an exaggeration to suggest that the sheer speed with which humans can acquire new behaviors, especially through social learning, may explain the unique cultural accomplishments, such as the arts, science, and religion, that have accrued to our species.

CHAPTER SEVEN

Remembering and Forgetting

Imagine yourself 10 years from now—your college education behind you, a career in full swing, a loving spouse and several small mouths to feed. There is little to remind you of your life as a college student. Suppose, however, that your old psychology professor contacted you to ask if you would participate in an experiment on long-term memory. Your task in the experiment is to confine yourself to a quiet room, gather your thoughts, and in 1 hour's time write down as many concepts, names, and research findings as you can recall from your psychology of learning course taken all those years ago.

How accurate and complete do you think your recall would be of the material covered in this class 10 years from now? Would you remember 10 basic concepts, or perhaps 100? Would the name Ivan Pavlov ring a bell? B. F. Skinner? How about the distinction between positive and negative reinforcement? Would you recall the phenomenon of taste aversion and the experimental methodology utilized by Garcia in his research? Would you remember the basic results of this research and the significant implications of taste aversion for the study of learning?

Naturally, no one would expect your recall of material to be either comprehensive or extremely accurate, at least not over such a long time span. A considerable amount of water has passed under the bridge in the form of other classes taken since your psychology of learning class, the rigors of job training, time and energy expended in forming intimate relationships, and other events and passages that define a life. Instead, your memory of the material in this class would be fragmentary, incomplete, and, yes, sometimes inaccurate. Such is the nature of human memory. Humans are not infallible processors of information, but given to bias and distortion. Memory proves to be something of a paradox, for it is a generally adaptive feature of our cognitive makeup that nevertheless sports a nasty penchant for omitting or manufacturing detail.

You probably do not view as extraordinary your remembering how to tie your shoes this morning when getting dressed. After all, you have been doing it since you were 5 or 6 years old. To psychologists, however, even such trivial capacities loom as fascinating evidence of the necessity—indeed, the very survival value—of memory. Why psychologists place so much importance on our ability to remember and, conversely, on our similarly inconvenient tendency to forget is the theme of this chapter. Research on memory has been developing over more than a century, and advances in procedures and technology have allowed researchers to explore the cognitive capacities of nonhuman animals, resulting in some unexpected but impressive findings. Such research holds implications for scholars and nonscholars alike.

HISTORICAL APPROACHES AND THEORIES OF MEMORY

What if you had to learn and then relearn how to tie your shoes, fix breakfast, or drive a car each morning after awakening. Suppose you were unable to remember the names of friends, fellow workers, professors, or even your fiancee, spouse, or other family members. And did you finish that term paper for English literature, or was that last semester? Last year? As you can see, the ability to remember facts, names, places, and events is so much a part of our daily experience that we seldom give it any thought at all. Unless, of course, this ability fails us or becomes impaired in some very noticeable way. This is precisely the plight of individuals suffering from Alzheimer's disease and other degenerative neurological conditions. For such people, the wonders of everyday memory are seldom taken for granted. Of course, none of us is immune to at least occasional memory lapses. Who among us can claim never to have forgotten where we parked our car when the time comes to leave the shopping mall? Or whether we turned off the stove before leaving the house? Such common occurrences serve as frequent, even sobering, reminders that humans are imperfect information processors. The silver lining in this cloud is that the various causes of remembering and forgetting have increasingly surrendered themselves to scientific scrutiny.

Ebbinghaus and the Nonsense Syllable

Hermann Ebbinghaus (1850–1909), a German scientist, was the first person to bring the logic of experimental control to the study of memory (Ebbinghaus, 1885/1964). Before he could submit human memory to systematic study, Ebbinghaus had to attend to certain methodological concerns. For example, if you wanted to find out how people learn the concept of meiosis in biology, you wouldn't want to study biologists already familiar with the concept, would you? In order to observe how learning takes place, you would choose people who had never encountered the concept. From this starting point, you would be able to follow the process in detail, observing how long it takes a person to learn the concept and how quickly, if at all, the concept is forgotten, and so forth. This is precisely what Ebbinghaus did. His first task was to develop the stimulus material to be learned. Ebbinghaus first considered words, but this proved inherently problematic, because the words of one's native language have already been learned; therefore they already have meaning. His solution to the problem was to create collections of letters having no meaning within his language. These meaningless three-letter combinations, or *trigrams,* were called **nonsense syllables** and usually consisted of a vowel surrounded by two consonants. Such combinations as TIL, VOX, or JIV, for instance, would be nonsense syllables, for they represent no known words or phrases in English. Thus, their usefulness in memory research is obvious. Because nonsense syllables have no prior meaning to participants, whatever learning or memory of the stimuli occurs can be attributed solely to the experimental conditions, not to any previous experience.

Ebbinghaus served as his own subject in a series of experiments conducted over the course of 5 years. Because the British empiricists had claimed repetition was an important mechanism for forming associations, Ebbinghaus's first experiments involved measuring the number of times that lists of nonsense syllables had to be rehearsed in order to be mastered, which for Ebbinghaus meant the ability to recall the items without error. Not surprisingly, he found that longer lists required more rehearsals than shorter lists to master completely. In fact, he was able to specify quantitative relationships between list length and required rehearsal time. It is important to understand that this kind of systematic control of variables (list length, etc.), and accurate observation and measurement are distinguishing features of the scientific method. Although Ebbinghaus's results may not be particularly surprising, keep in mind that common sense is often misleading, and a function of rigorous experimentation is to check the validity of intuition and casual observation.

Ebbinghaus also found that even when people forget information that at one time was well learned, all is not lost. When reexposed to the material, they relearn it much faster than it was originally learned, a phenomenon that Ebbinghaus called **savings.** As a college student, you are a beneficiary of this aspect of memory, though perhaps unknowingly. For example, if you took a psychology course in high school, no one would expect you to be able to remember all of the facts and concepts that you encountered in that class. On the other hand, you will probably find much of what you read or hear about in many of your college psychology classes quite familiar. The savings phenomenon simply means that it will take you less time to master this material the second time around.

Ebbinghaus's contribution to the study of learning and cognition can hardly be overstated. Contemporary research on memory, conducted in laboratories containing technological gadgetry that would have awed Ebbinghaus, has understandably added to knowledge of how memory works, but his original findings remain valid today. Perhaps most important, Ebbinghaus helped to establish learning and cognition as legitimate and important subject matters for the then-emerging science of experimental psychology.

Bartlett and Memory in the Real World

Ebbinghaus's use of the nonsense syllable was a stroke of genius as a control procedure because it eliminated the problem of confounding by previously established associations. Sometimes, however, the practices used by

nonsense syllables three-letter combinations (usually consonant-vowel-consonant) used in memory experiments by Ebbinghaus

savings rapid mastery of material that has been previously learned

researchers to establish strong experimental control also have the negative consequence of making research findings difficult to interpret when applied to life outside the laboratory. In other words, although Ebbinghaus removed the possibility that prior knowledge of the material would contaminate his procedure, of what relevance is the recall of such a meaningless item (the nonsense syllable TIL, for example) in the context of tying shoes, cooking meals, and driving cars in the real world?

In 1932 the Englishman Sir Frederic C. Bartlett published *Remembering: A Study in Experimental and Social Psychology,* which describes his research program on human perception and memory. In reviewing Ebbinghaus's work, Bartlett claimed that use of nonsense syllables was problematic, for in everyday circumstances people are more likely to be asked to recall familiar, as opposed to unfamiliar, material. Bartlett considered this to be an especially critical point, for although a researcher might expect a subject to rehearse a nonsense syllable repetitiously in order to recall it later, people seldom use mere repetition or rote memorization when attempting to commit more familiar information to memory. Instead, they are more likely to rehearse material by comparing or associating it with other similar, highly familiar information already stored in memory.

Because he felt that studies of memory should utilize more familiar materials, Bartlett presented research subjects not with nonsense syllables, but with folk stories, short essays, or descriptions of various human activities. One item used by Bartlett, for example, was a description of a cricket match between Middlesex and Kent in England. It is interesting to note that in doing so, Bartlett was essentially making the same argument that has resurfaced in cognitive psychology, namely, that research on memory ought to focus on the conventional functions and capacities of memory in the everyday environment, not memory for meaningless material presented in the artificial setting of the laboratory (Conway, 1991; Loftus, 1991).

After allowing subjects to read a story or essay, Bartlett would ask them to reproduce it for him. How accurate was their recall? It turns out that much of what Bartlett discovered stands up quite well to modern-day scrutiny. One general conclusion was that, although subjects remember the overall gist or theme of a story, including main characters, types of interactions, and so on, their reports often omit specific details. It is pretty easy to empathize with Bartlett's subjects. How well, for example, do you recall the previous paragraph? If asked to reproduce it, could you do so precisely? Bartlett's research suggests that although you would be able to say something about the importance of using material of everyday significance in memory research, you would not likely be able to provide a verbatim account of the paragraph. And, of course, in most situations complete accuracy of recall is not necessary. More often than not, what is important is that you recall in general what claim or statement was made, not specifically how it was made.

Bartlett's (1932) research also foreshadowed much of the contemporary psychological literature that claims human memory to be rather more inventive than people would sometimes like to think. In his own words:

The first notion to get rid of is that memory is primarily or literally reduplicative, or reproductive. . . . In fact, if we consider evidence rather than presupposition, remembering appears to be far more decisively an affair of construction rather than one of mere reproduction. (pp. 204–205)

For example, in remembering what you have done today, you will probably fail to remember certain details. However, rather than leaving these details out, you will use your knowledge of a typical day, or memory from yesterday or the day before, to fill in where details seem fuzzy. In other words, recall of any particular event is composed of actual memory of that event and reconstructions of various memories of other similar events.

As several previous chapters have shown, psychologists are model builders. In order to explain a phenomenon, they often develop a structural facsimile, be it mathematical, pictorial, or verbal, to depict or simulate the phenomenon in which they are interested. Theories of memory are no exception to this rule, and many influential models have been developed to explain how and why memory works the way it does.

The Stage Model

Models in cognitive psychology often take the general form of a flowchart, perhaps because the human being is considered to be an information processor, and the concept *processing* implies a sequence of events or stages. An influential model of the stages through which information passes in human memory was provided by Atkinson and Shiffrin (1968). As you can see in Figure 7.1, the stage model suggests that information from the environment, usually in the form of visual or auditory stimulation, can be viewed as moving through three separate modes or processing stages: the sensory store, the short-term store, and the long-term store. Let's examine in more detail how, according to the model, information makes its way through the processing system, and what characteristics or attributes distinguish the separate processing stages from one another.

The Sensory Store   When you first come into contact with information of any kind, you do so through your senses. You cannot process or remember anything until you have read it, heard it, felt it, or in some other way made contact with it through a sensory modality. For this reason, the **sensory store** is considered the first stage through which all information must pass before it can be processed further. The sensory store has certain characteristic features that separate it from both the short-term and the long-term stores. For instance, just how much information is available to the sensory store is limited only by the physical nature of the sensory receptors. As you gaze across the room in which you are now sitting, you actually perceive a rather large (180 degree) panorama. You don't see the entirety of this panorama clearly; you see much of it indistinctly through peripheral vision. If you were to close your eyes rapidly, the image that was focused on your retina just milliseconds before remains for a fleeting moment. In other words, the information

sensory store the first stage of information processing in which some sensory receptor is stimulated by external energy

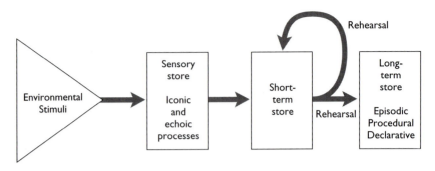

FIGURE 7.1 Stage Model of Memory. (Adapted from Atkinson & Shiffrin, 1968.)

that was available to your eyes persists, however briefly, after the stimulus no longer impinges upon the receptors.

The capacity of the sensory store was first demonstrated in a series of clever experiments by Sperling (1960). In order to ascertain the capacity for the visual sensory store, Sperling created a matrix (three rows by four columns) of letters that was presented to participants for 50 milliseconds ($\frac{1}{20}$ of a second). Immediately after the matrix was terminated, a brief tone sounded. Tones differing in pitch signaled that participants were to report as many letters as possible from one of the three rows of the matrix. If a brief visual image persisted after termination of the matrix, participants should have been able to report most, if not all, of the matrix when signaled to do so.

Participants were in fact able to recall an average of 3 out of 4 letters from whichever row was signaled by the tone. This indicates that almost the entire array (9 out of 12 letters) is available in the sensory store immediately upon termination of the visual stimulus. However, when the tone was delayed for even brief periods, the number of items recalled dropped substantially. Thus, Sperling had demonstrated that a good deal of information is available in the form of a visual image, but that this image fades rapidly and information is lost if not further acted upon. Sperling called this brief persisting image an **iconic image**, and it is often referred to as a *memory trace*.

Such memory traces are not limited strictly to visual information. There is also evidence for **echoic images**, which are briefly persisting traces of sound stimulation after the presentation of an auditory stimulus. The fact that the memory trace fades so rapidly testifies to the fleeting nature of information in sensory memory. In order for the information to be retained for later use, it must be acted upon by the subject. In other words, simple stimulation of a sense modality, be it vision, audition, or any other sense, does not guarantee later availability of the information for recall. This is where the second stage in Atkinson and Shiffrin's (1968) model becomes operative. People must attend to or rehearse information actively if it is to make its way from the sensory store to the next processing stage, the **short-term store.** Let's have a look at what researchers have found out about the capacity and retention characteristics of the short-term store.

iconic image the brief persisting image of a visual stimulus after removal of the stimulus

echoic image the brief persistence of an auditory stimulus after presentation of the stimulus

short-term store the second stage of memory, often called working memory, characterized by limited capacity and retention time

The Short-Term Store   Suppose you are driving to a friend's house, and she has just given you her street address over your cell phone. You hang up the phone without writing down the address, so you need to retain it while you drive. How will you accomplish this? You would probably rehearse the address, either out loud or silently, as you drive. Psychologists would say that, as you rehearse the address, it is being *processed* in your working memory, or short-term store. Thus, the short-term store contains the words, images, numbers, or any other information to which you are attending at a given moment. The short-term store, however, is quite different from the sensory store, both in terms of how much information it can handle and how long this information can be retained.

In a now-classic paper, cognitive psychologist George Miller (1956) presented evidence that the short-term store can hold approximately 5 to 9 items of information for brief periods of time. For example, if you were read a list of 25 words, approximately 1 word presented every other second, and were then asked after the last word was presented to recall as many words from the list as you could, how well would you do? According to Miller, most people can recall somewhere between 5 and 9 words, with of course some people recalling fewer than 5 and some recalling more than 9. This finding would seem to explain why most people could recall an item such as a street address or a phone number, since they typically don't contain more than nine items. An important point made by Miller, however, is that how much information can be placed in the short-term store really depends upon how an *item* of information is defined. Suppose that, in the example just used, each word in the list contains an average of six letters, and as a subject in the experiment, you were able to recall 7 words. If each *word* is an item, then you recalled 7 items. On the other hand, if each *letter* is an item, you have recalled approximately 42 items.

Miller's point in discussing how to define an item of information has considerable implications for memory. Although most individuals' short-term store has a limited capacity of about seven items, it is possible for each of these items to contain a considerable amount of information (Baddeley, 1994). In fact, in the everyday world, people frequently reduce larger amounts of information into smaller, more readily managed pieces of information through a process called **chunking**. An example of chunking is the *acronym*, a verbal device used with increasing frequency these days. Here is a short list of commonly encountered acronyms and their expanded meanings:

chunking any strategy that reduces larger amounts of material into smaller, more readily encoded information

NOW (National Organization of Women)

PGA (Professional Golfers' Association)

SCUBA (Self-Contained Underwater Breathing Apparatus)

NRC (Nuclear Regulatory Committee)

ACLU (American Civil Liberties Union)

PTA (Parent-Teachers Association)

CPU (Central Processing Unit)

TRL (Total Request Live)

Notice that each of these acronyms contains much more information than the 3 to 5 letters of which they consist. In its longhanded form, for example, SCUBA actually contains 41 letters. The purpose of the acronym, of course, is to provide a shortcut for processing and utilizing information. The use of such cognitive effort-saving devices is quite common. In fact, you could probably generate a long list of acronyms from newscasts, newspapers, magazines, and other sources of mass communication. The hyphen used to separate the seven digits of a phone number serves a similar purpose, in that a longer sequence of numbers is reduced to a more manageable pair of information chunks.

Remember that, in addition to being limited to approximately seven chunks of information, the short-term store can also retain information for only a brief period of time. What happens, for instance, to the street address once you have arrived at your friend's house? Chances are it's forgotten quite rapidly. In fact, research has shown that once information is no longer attended to in the short-term store, it is likely to be lost within approximately 20 to 30 seconds. Given this limitation, how do humans ever establish more lasting, or even permanent, memories? Obviously, we must be able to do so, or every new day would involve such overwhelming challenges as relearning how to drive, cook, and even tie our own shoes.

The Long-Term Store Atkinson and Shiffrin's (1968) theory of memory holds that the repeated rehearsal of information in the short-term store can lead to transference of the information into the long-term store. The **long-term store** is considered to be a permanent and limitless reservoir for information. You can generally assume that if information makes its way to the long-term store, it will remain there permanently. This does not mean, of course, that information held in the long-term store is accessed easily—only that it is in fact available, given appropriate retrieval strategies.

Researchers make a distinction among three types of long-term memory: episodic, procedural, and declarative (Cohen, 1984; Tulving, 1972). **Episodic memory** is memory for particular events in one's life. Remembering a dinner party you attended a week ago or recalling your 16th birthday party are examples of long-term episodic memories. Especially critical to everyday functioning are **procedural memories,** such as remembering how to cook, tie your shoes, drive, dress yourself, and balance a checkbook. And **declarative memory** refers to knowledge of facts about the world or word meanings: for example, remembering at what temperature water boils, who discovered gravity, and what an isotope is. As a college student, you rely daily upon semantic memory. The distinction among types of long-term memory is significant because there is evidence that certain types of memory loss, such as that common among Alzheimer's patients, occur for one type of memory but not for another (Eslinger & Damasio, 1986; Schacter, 1983). This may mean that episodic, procedural, and declarative memories represent qualitatively different memory processes or even involve separate regions of the brain (Eichenbaum, 1997; McKoon, Ratcliff, & Dell, 1986; Schacter & Tulving, 1994).

long-term store the final stage of memory, characterized by unlimited capacity and permanence of the memory trace

episodic memory long-term retention of specific events in one's life

procedural memory long-term retention of a specific skill, procedure, or practice

declarative memory long-term retention of a specific fact or concept

Levels of Processing Theory

Despite its intuitive appeal, the stage theory of memory has had its share of critics. Craik and Lockhart (1972), for instance, argue that the distinction between the short-term store and the long-term store may be unimportant. At what point, for example, has information made it into the long-term store—35 seconds, 2 weeks, 1 year? Another source of criticism of stage theory is its proponents' claim that the major variable responsible for transferring information from short-term to long-term memory is rehearsal, usually in the form of mere repetition. According to Craik and Lockhart (1972), however, it isn't the quantity (number of repetitions) but the quality (type of processing) of rehearsal that determines how well people recall information later.

On the basis of this criticism of stage theory, Craik and Lockhart (1972) proposed the **levels of processing theory** of memory, suggesting that information is recalled better if it is processed deeply than if it is processed superficially. Just how do these two levels of processing differ? Imagine yourself as a participant in the following experiment. You are asked to view words as they are projected on a screen in front of you. Sometimes you are asked to make a judgment about whether the word was printed in upper- or lowercase letters. On other occasions you are asked to judge whether the word rhymes with another word, and on still other presentations you are asked whether the word fits into a particular category or if the word could be put into a specific sentence. You are never told that the study is a memory experiment, and only after having viewed all the words are you asked to recall as many as possible.

levels of processing theory a theory of memory that claims depth of processing and likelihood of recall are determined by quality, not quantity, of rehearsal

The levels of processing theory predicts that you will recall best those words that you were asked to place into categories or sentences because deciding the meaning or semantic quality of a word is believed to require deep processing. Judging either the physical features (upper- vs. lowercase lettering) or the sound (rhyming) of a word is a shallower form of processing, and would be expected to lead to poorer recall. In fact, as you can see in Figure 7.2, this is exactly what happens in such experiments (Craik & Tulving, 1975; Moeser, 1983). Participants had much better recall of those words that were processed semantically than those that were processed either structurally or acoustically. It is crucial to understand that in this experiment *amount* of rehearsal is held constant for all words; only *type* of rehearsal differs. The levels of processing approach suggests that it is not how often or for how long you rehearse information, but the level (shallow vs. deep) at which you process information that determines likelihood of recall.

The implications of the levels of processing approach for memory should be apparent to you. For example, in studying the concept of *reinforcement,* would you be wise simply to repeat the definition of the term over and over until you could produce it verbatim? Not according to Craik and Lockhart (1972). They argue that sheer repetition, what they call **maintenance rehearsal,** is a poor strategy for getting information into long-term memory. You can repeat a phone number to yourself many times before dialing, but you aren't likely to remember the phone number an hour later.

maintenance rehearsal use of sheer repetition for the purpose of transferring information to long-term memory

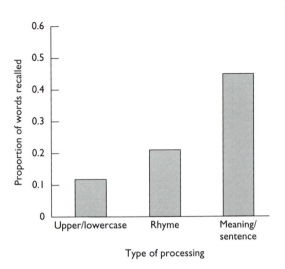

FIGURE 7.2 Recall as a Function of Depth of Processing. (Adapted from Craik & Tulving, 1975.)

elaborative rehearsal semantic or meaning-oriented rehearsal believed to lead to deep processing of information

On the other hand, rehearsing information by attending to its meaning or semantic properties, called **elaborative rehearsal,** is more likely to ensure recall of the material at a later time. The effect does not appear to depend upon verbal material, however. Adler, Gerhardstein, and Rovee-Collier (1998) demonstrated that a levels of processing effect could be obtained with 3-month-old infants using visual stimuli.

There is some evidence that elaborative rehearsal may involve different regions of the brain than does simple maintenance rehearsal (Chwilla, Brown, & Hagoort, 1995; Ferlazzo, Conte, & Gentilomo, 1993). Recent advances in medical technology have allowed contemporary researchers to monitor nervous system activity during various kinds of cognitive tasks. One method involves measurement of *event-related potentials.* Individual nerve cells, called neurons, ordinarily carry a negative electrical charge when not active, or when in their resting state. When activated by stimulation, however, the cells undergo a change in electrical potential. This change is known as an *action potential,* and can be measured by electrodes placed near a collection of cells. These action potentials can then be measured in response to various kinds of stimulation or tasks given to the participant.

Research using event-related potentials can help researchers to differentiate types of information processing. For example, participants might be asked either to discriminate between words and nonwords (semantic task) or to identify whether words are in uppercase or lowercase (structural task). An event-related potential, known as the *P400 priming effect,* occurs in response to the semantic task, but not the structural task (Chwilla et al., 1995). This kind of finding helps researchers to determine how the nervous system processes different kinds of information.

✖ INTERIM SUMMARY

The study of memory has been advanced both by controlled experiments of memory for artificial information (Ebbinghaus's nonsense syllables) and more realistic, daily fare (Bartlett's stories). The storage model of memory suggests that information passes through three separate processing stores and that the amount of rehearsal largely determines whether information becomes encoded in long-term memory. Levels of processing theory, alternatively, argues that permanence of memory depends upon the type of processing involved, as opposed to the amount of processing.

✖ THOUGHT QUESTIONS

1. This chapter presented a quote from Bartlett about memory. Take a few minutes to try to reproduce this quote as precisely as you can without going back and looking it up. After you have written it down, read the actual quote. How close is your rendition? Is it consistent with the general theme of the quote?

2. What is the chief advantage of a levels of processing model of memory over a stage model? What kind of evidence supports the levels of processing model?

FORGETTING: CAUSES AND CORRECTIONS

Psychologists often use the computer metaphor to describe memory because both computers and humans can be viewed as types of information processors. In fact, most contemporary research and theory in human memory is infused with computer language. Whether an electronic device or a biological organism, all information processors are assumed to operate according to three central functions: encoding, storage, and retrieval. You may remember from the previous chapter that *encoding* refers to the process by which information is placed into the information processor. A keyboard, for example, is one device through which information can be encoded into a computer. In human beings, encoding occurs through the senses. *Storage* refers to the retention of information over time, and **retrieval** is the process of accessing or using previously stored information. Unfortunately, problems may occur at any one of these processing stages, resulting in information loss (Schacter, 1999). In the human case, such information loss is called **forgetting,** an all-too-familiar phenomenon.

Forgetting may not be the best term to describe information loss, since it implies that something becomes lost only after having first been learned. As students of memory, however, we are just as interested in knowing what can go wrong during the initial process of encoding that makes recall unlikely later. By the same token, problems in retrieval may be evidence of poor encoding or of insufficient retrieval cues, but this does not necessarily mean information has been forgotten in the conventional sense of that word. Keep in mind that ultimately we would like to explain what sorts of errors can occur when humans attempt to encode, store, and retrieve information and how these errors can disrupt the ability to function in the natural environment.

retrieval the process of accessing or withdrawing information from a memory system

forgetting loss of information due to ineffective encoding or retrieval failure

Decay Theory

At some point during your early academic career, you probably had to learn many standard facts about the world. For example, perhaps you learned the sequence of geological time periods, such as the Precambrian, Ordovician, Silurian, Devonian, Paleolithic, Jurassic, and so on. Can you now remember the names of all these time periods and their correct order? If not, and assuming that at one time you did know such things, what could account for this apparent forgetfulness? Could it be that you learned this information so long ago that it has simply faded away? This very reasonable explanation is sometimes referred to as **decay theory**, the idea that information processed at one time decays or fades merely as a function of time. The longer it has been since you learned the names of the geological epochs, the less likely you would be to recall such information.

decay theory an early theory of forgetting claiming that information simply fades or decays over time

Because of its intuitive appeal, the idea that information fades or decays with time has been a favorite explanation for memory loss. Decay theory, however, has one fatal flaw. In order to test decay theory, a researcher would have to present some material to a participant, and after some predetermined retention interval, ask the subject to recall that information. It would be critical that the participant do absolutely nothing during the retention interval in order to avoid any additional processing of that information. Remember, decay theory states that the information will decay or fade away *only* as a result of time, not as the result of additional learning or information processing during the retention interval. Is such a study possible? It's hard to imagine how. If you were the subject in such a study, could you literally turn off your mind, becoming entirely inactive and inattentive to your environment, during the retention interval? Obviously, the answer is no. During even relatively short retention intervals, humans still see, hear, smell, think, imagine; in short, they process information. For this reason, there is no empirical test for whether information simply fades from memory or whether it instead gets jostled or bumped aside by things that happen during the retention interval.

Interference Theory

Because it cannot easily be verified through experiment, decay theory is not considered a suitable candidate to explain memory loss. Instead, forgetting would seem to be better accounted for by **interference theory**, the notion that information is lost due to competition from other information. As a student, you will appreciate the central theme of interference theory. Is it possible that, in the process of reading your text or notes for one course, other material learned for another course becomes misplaced or overridden in your memory by the more recent study session? If so, memory researchers would say that memory loss in this case is due, not to decay, but to direct interference.

interference theory a theory of forgetting claiming that information is lost from a system as additional information is added or attended to

Research has identified two fundamental ways in which recall of information may suffer from interference. Suppose you are studying today for a psychology exam coming up next week. Tomorrow you will be studying sociology, because your sociology exam comes up at the end of this week. When you sit down to take your sociology exam, you find that the material that you learned while studying psychology comes to mind and interferes with your recall of the sociology material. In this particular case, you have experienced what researchers call **proactive interference**. Information that you learned first (psychology) interfered with your ability to recall the information you learned later (sociology). As you might imagine, proactive interference becomes more likely as you study and acquire more and more information. When asked to recall a particular type of information, many other previously learned items may come to mind. The difficulty is in deciding which of these is most relevant to the immediate task at hand.

Now, let's deal with the problems that might arise when taking your psychology exam next week. Recall that this week you studied psychology first, followed by sociology. Your task now is to recall the information that you studied first, that is, psychology. If, during your psychology exam, you recall information from sociology, you are experiencing **retroactive interference**. In this case, what you learned most recently (sociology) is interfering with your recall of previously learned material (psychology). Interference is retroactive in this case because more recently learned material seems to be interfering with recall of the previously learned material (Howe, 1995).

Interference effects are probably quite common, but obviously they do not render you completely helpless, or most of what you do in life simply would be impossible. This is especially true for college students. What sorts of factors make interference effects more or less likely? Probably the most important variable relevant to this issue is the similarity of material to be recalled. In the example of the conflicting exams, sociology and psychology may interfere with one another because of their general similarity. Both disciplines deal with human behavior, and their respective vocabularies are often quite similar. Fortunately, it is much less likely that significant interference would occur for disparate materials. For example, while taking a chemistry exam, you are not likely to be faced with the decision of whether the concept of an iconic image is relevant to answering questions on the test, despite the fact that you had recently studied psychology. Research has shown consistently that interference effects can be reduced drastically when learned material consists of unrelated information (Bower, Thompson, & Tulving, 1994; Russ-Eft, 1979).

Amnesia

There are of course some occasions when memory loss may not be due to interference. In the case of **amnesia**, forgetting results either from emotional or physical trauma. Might there be times when it would actually be an advantage to forget a particular fact or incident? Sigmund Freud, the father of psychoanalysis, certainly believed so. He argued that people often are motivated to forget emotionally threatening or disturbing events. In fact, his brand of therapy had as a major objective the identification of such repressed memories, raising them to a conscious level where they could be adequately confronted. Repression was not, however, exclusively a product of psychological disturbance. In fact, Freud (1910) considered repression to be a common mechanism by which all people defend themselves against potentially uncomfortable memories. Thus repression is sometimes referred to as *psychogenic* amnesia because it is brought on by emotional factors.

proactive interference memory loss for recently learned information due to interference by previously learned information

retroactive interference memory loss for previously learned information due to interference by recently learned information

amnesia memory loss due to either emotional arousal or damage to the nervous system

Amnesia can also be brought on by physical trauma, such as head injuries or disturbances in nervous system functioning. Accident victims, for instance, frequently fail to recall what they were doing just before the accident (Brown & Chobor, 1995). Similarly, patients who receive electroconvulsive therapy, in which controlled amounts of electric current are passed through the brain, often are at a loss to remember anything that happened just before treatment (Summers, Robins, & Reich, 1979). Both of these examples illustrate the phenomenon of **retrograde amnesia**, the loss of memory for events occurring *before* the traumatic event (such as accident, electroconvulsive therapy).

retrograde amnesia memory loss for information presented before damage to the nervous system

This amnesic effect is believed to occur because the trauma occurring to the brain disrupts the encoding of the information, also known as *consolidation* (Hebb, 1949). Consolidation is a physiological event that requires some time, and if the nervous system is being compromised by trauma, the process of incorporating information into a memory trace cannot unfold normally. Imagine picking up a model airplane that you have just glued together and shaking it violently. You wouldn't expect it to hold together, would you? Pick the airplane up several hours after gluing it, however, and it would probably be little damaged by such treatment. The nervous system also needs time to form solid memories. In a classic experiment, Duncan (1949) presented shock to rats at intervals ranging from 20 seconds to 4 hours *after* trials in a T-maze. Consistent with the notion of consolidation, animals receiving shock shortly after running the maze performed much more poorly than those receiving delayed shock.

In still other cases, memory loss occurs for events that follow the physical trauma. Perhaps the most celebrated case of such memory loss was the medical patient, known only as H. M., whose severe seizures had proven resistant to antiepileptic medications. H. M. then underwent a radical surgical technique involving the removal of several brain structures, including the hippocampus and amygdala. Although successful in reducing seizure activity, the operation had the unfortunate consequence of reducing H. M.'s ability to remember recent events. Although he was able to recall events that had occurred even years prior to surgery, following surgery H. M. had tremendous difficulty committing new information to memory, usually forgetting the information within 30 to 40 seconds (Corkin, 1984; Milner, 1966, 1970). This inability to recall events that occurred after the injury, called **anterograde amnesia**, is also common among elderly people suffering from organic brain syndromes and patients diagnosed as having Korsakoff's syndrome, a disease associated with alcohol abuse (Meudell, 1992). As you can imagine, amnesia of this type can have extremely debilitating consequences. A person who turns on the stove to cook, becomes distracted by a knock at the door, and subsequently forgets about turning the stove on, may become a danger to him- or herself and lose the capacity for independent functioning.

anterograde amnesia memory loss for information presented after damage to the nervous system

Taken together, interference effects and amnesia would seem to paint a rather sobering picture of human memory. You might wonder how it is that humans can ever adapt successfully to the environment given an extraordinary penchant for misplacing, distorting, or otherwise mishandling information on a day-to-day basis. Fortunately, the picture is not so bleak after all. Ordinarily, human memory is more than up to the task. In addition, when pressed into hard duty, there is considerable evidence that the capacity to remember can be significantly enhanced through a few selective strategies. In fact, for college students, the proper use of such strategies may spell the difference between academic failure and success. Let's consider some of the ways in which human memory can be put to better use in negotiating the challenges of modern life.

Improving Memory

Scholars and scientists have long wondered whether the ability to remember can be improved or enhanced. If so, such a possibility could have tremendous implications for most of us, particularly as we confront the challenges of living in the so-called information age. The question is whether there exists a "magic memory pill," available for those whose responsibilities entail encoding large amounts of information. The question is not an outlandish one given recent advances in the neurosciences. If there is a chemical basis for memory, and if scientists can determine the complex brain activity that corresponds to specific kinds of memories, then it would seem logical to suggest that enhancing memory becomes merely a matter of chemical intervention. Naturally, this is a rather big *if*, and, although understanding of the physiological underpinnings of memory is increasing rapidly, no such magical pill has yet emerged. Considerable effort has been directed toward the synthesis and examination of several types of drugs believed to have some potential for enhancing memory. Though some experiments on laboratory animals have been promising (Meck, Smith, & Williams, 1989), there is as yet little evidence that such drugs have any practical benefit to humans (Thal, 1989). For the time being, then, you might want to exercise a bit of skepticism when encountering those ads for memory-boosting drugs so often found in the pages of popular self-help and health-oriented magazines.

Mnemonics   A chemical panacea for memory problems may not be on the immediate horizon, but a variety of time-honored behavioral strategies are available for improving memory—and they are absolutely free to the taker. These memory improvement strategies, called **mnemonics**, usually rely on visual imagery and can be mastered with little effort by most people. One such device, the *method of loci,* involves placing items or information to be recalled within various nooks and crannies of a familiar environment. For example, if you wished to memorize a list of grocery items before going shopping, you would first select an environment that you know quite well, perhaps your bedroom. Next you would *vividly* imagine each item placed somewhere within this specialized environment, preferably in a manner that creates a very distinct image. As you walk through the store, you simply bring up the image of your room, walk yourself gradually through the room, and, if the images you created were distinct enough, the items to be recalled will come readily to mind. The method of loci was a favorite of Greek orators, who often used this device to commit long and impressive speeches to

mnemonics strategies used to enhance memory (often visually based)

memory. If for no other reason than to break the monotony of a tiresome task, the next time you head for the store, try using the method of loci rather than your standard grocery list. In addition to saving on paper, you may discover that your ability to remember, like many other habits, improves with practice.

Although the method of loci and other imagery-guided mnemonics may be useful in memorizing grocery lists, you may wonder just how well they apply to scholastic pursuits. Can they really help you to understand and remember key concepts in psychology, chemistry, or political science? Will application of such techniques lead to higher test scores? These are legitimate questions, and learning psychologists are in a position to provide some tentative answers. Medical students and others required to commit to memory large lists of anatomical parts or other items may find some use for mnemonic strategies (Reeves & Bullen, 1995; Swartz, 1998). In addition, mnemonics might be especially helpful to learning disabled students or students for whom other methods of instruction have proven ineffective (Manalo, 1997). Education, however, entails more than simple memorization. The conceptual mastery of information consists of a different kind of information processing, and for this purpose mnemonics probably have limited applicability. Fortunately, mastery of just about any kind of content can be enhanced through the use of some rather simple and well-researched principles.

Distributed Practice As is true of any other specialized group of people, students often have their own terminology for describing their lifestyle. Is the phrase *all-nighter* a part of your vocabulary? You would be the exceptional student if it were not. Despite their professors' recommendations not to do so, college students frequently find themselves cramming for exams—staying up all night before a test, conducting marathon study sessions. This practice is unfortunate, for a good deal of research indicates that such cramming is a poor strategy for encoding information into long term-memory. Several studies have shown that if research participants are allowed to rehearse information for, say, 1 hour, how they divide their rehearsal time influences later recall. In such a study, one group of participants might be asked to distribute their 1 hour into four 15-minute study periods, evenly spaced throughout the day. A second group would use only one study session, taking up the full hour. Which group do you think would fare better later when asked to recall the information? If you are a student who studies some every day, rather than waiting until the night before an exam to study, give yourself a pat on the back. In experiments like this, the group that distributes its study time recalls more later (Fanselow & Tighe, 1988). Here, then, is the scientific support behind your professor's suggestion that you space your study sessions out rather than try to study everything at once. This is a fairly straightforward principle, yet large numbers of college students fail to take advantage of the benefits of distributed practice. If you are among them, you might in the future take steps to alter your study schedule, relying less on cramming for tests.

Encoding Specificity   No behavior takes place in a vacuum, and everything we learn, from solving geometry problems to programming a computer, occurs in a particular context. Since parts of our environment can become associated in some way with the learning experience, does it not make sense to take advantage of this fact for the purpose of enhancing memory? The concept of **encoding specificity** suggests that certain stimuli that are present in our environment when we learn can become powerful retrieval cues at a later time. Research supports the notion that we remember things better when presented with cues that were present during original encoding. For example, subjects in one experiment first learned the word combination *strawberry jam*. During a later recognition phase, subjects were likelier to remember seeing *jam* in the original phase if *strawberry* rather than *traffic* was presented in the recognition phase (Light & Carter-Sobell, 1970). Research on encoding specificity reveals that we don't merely represent solitary items in memory; rather individual items are embedded in a larger context, or *stimulus array,* and this array becomes important later when attempting to access the specific item (Buschke, Sliwinski, Kuslansky, & Lipton, 1997).

encoding specificity the principle that stimuli present during encoding become potential recall cues at a later time

Keeping context in mind should emerge as a priority for anyone attempting to commit material to memory, especially college students. For this reason, it makes sense to try to ensure that the environment in which you learn is as similar as possible to the environment in which you will be asked to recall what you've learned. Should you study while relaxing in a recliner, listening to the stereo, and holding a conversation with your roommate? Of course not, unless you will be allowed to re-create this environment while taking your test. Practical circumstances may prevent you from duplicating the testing environment while studying, but a bit of ingenuity may go a long way. Can you actually study in the classroom in which you will be taking the test? At the very same desk? If not, how similar to this environment is the library? Can your dorm room or apartment be made similar to the classroom?

State-Dependent Learning   While studying, you are not only processing the various sights and sounds coming to you from the external environment. There is additional stimulation arising from your own body, some of which may be encoded as recall cues just like those more external happenings. **State-dependent learning** refers to the fact that physiological states in effect during encoding may serve as retrieval cues if also present at the time of recall. Perhaps you are hungry during a study session. Or maybe you have consumed large quantities of coffee. Coffee contains caffeine, a central nervous system stimulant, and the physiological arousal it produces may serve as an important recall cue during the test (Overton, 1985). Similarly, Bower (1981) has shown that an emotional state can serve as a recall cue. Subjects who are made happy during a learning experience are more likely to recall what they learned later if in a happy mood than if depressed. Keep in mind that these effects are often small or moderate and are not likely to be the deciding factor in whether you remember some piece of information. In fact,

state-dependent learning a phenomenon in which physiological states that are in effect during encoding serve as retrieval cues during recall

Blaney (1986) has argued that the effect of mood on state-dependent learning is not well documented.

Elaborative Rehearsal   Remember that research has shown that simple repetition of material is generally a less effective memory strategy than is semantic, or meaning-based, encoding (Craik & Tulving, 1975). When studying for a test in any class, do you find yourself relying on sheer repetition, reading your chapters or class notes over and over, somehow assuming that your test performance will be directly related to the number of times your eyes wandered over material? Ask your instructor how many times he or she has heard the following: "I don't know why I did so poorly on the test; I read the chapter three times." It is regrettable that so many students continue to use study skills more relevant to short-term encoding than to long-term encoding to study for exams.

What can you do to increase both the efficiency and proficiency of your study time? For one thing, you might try reading your textbooks in a different manner than you read a magazine or a newspaper. It doesn't really matter whether you remember what you read in the newspaper at the breakfast table, does it? You are not likely to be questioned on it at a later time. You will, however, be expected to remember what you read in your textbook. For this reason, reading a textbook should be a much more active and engaging process than reading a newspaper. As you read your text, try to develop the habit of stopping after a few paragraphs or sections and asking yourself what you have just read. If you find yourself drawing a blank, you may have just wasted your time. You will find that with some practice you will be better able to recall major concepts and research findings as a result of this self-quizzing method.

In addition, try as much as possible to go back to major concepts and paraphrase them: that is, redefine them using your own words. It really isn't all that helpful simply to reread the textbook's definition over and over, especially if the words don't make sense to you. By paraphrasing the definition, you are processing the concept at a semantic rather than structural level, and this should improve your recall of the concept later. To most instructors, defining a concept in different words while retaining the meaning will serve as better evidence of learning than a verbatim recitation of the term.

A final tip: You can make otherwise difficult abstract material more meaningful if you find a way to relate it to yourself or to other people in your life. Fortunately, psychology is a discipline ready made for this practice, and students often find it not only instructive, but also enjoyable, to figure out how such concepts as *reinforcement, proactive interference,* and *state-dependent learning* help them to make sense of their own behavior. If you can personalize the information you are studying, you will probably find it easier to recall later.

The tactics described here are not effortless, nor are they miraculous memory-enhancing charms. They are methods that follow from a certain compelling logic and are supported by a large body of research data. If you are returning to college after a considerable absence from the classroom, or if you have never developed systematic study habits, these tactics may be of some benefit to you. In fact, if you were to inquire into the study habits of friends you know to be excellent students, you might be surprised to hear that such tactics are an established part of their academic repertoire, although they may not call them by such technical names.

✖ INTERIM SUMMARY

The notion that memory traces simply fade over time is an unlikely explanation of forgetting. Interference effects, however, are well documented and probably are responsible for most information loss. In addition, memory loss in the form of amnesia can occur in response both to emotional factors and to head injury. Although forgetting may often take center stage in the study of memory, methods to enhance memory have been well documented as well. In particular, the use of memory-enhancing strategies—such as visually based mnemonics, distributed practice, elaborative rehearsal, and techniques that take advantage of environmental cues present during encoding—can go a long way toward improving memory in the real world.

✖ THOUGHT QUESTIONS

1. As a student, you are enrolled in several classes during any given semester. This means that you must distribute your study time across several different subject matters. This kind of course arrangement presents numerous opportunities for interference effects. Can you think of a different way to arrange courses that might reduce the probability of interference effects?

2. The concept of adaptation is a central theme of this text. How can this be reconciled with the phenomenon of forgetting? Under what circumstances could forgetting be considered to be adaptive?

3. Lying in his bed in his dorm room, Matthew cracks open his chemistry book at 11:30 p.m. the night before his big chemistry exam, scheduled for 8:00 a.m. the next morning. He reads the necessary chapters swiftly, then reads them a second time, all the while sipping hot coffee. Matthew flunks the exam the next day. What advice would you give him about altering his study habits?

INCIDENTAL MEMORY

The college student and the participant in a memory experiment have one important thing in common: They are both usually making an intentional, effortful attempt to commit material to memory. There are many times, however, when people are not so obviously attentive to what is happening around them. It seems logical to assume that, at times like this, information present in the environment is simply not encoded into memory. This assumption couldn't be farther from the truth. Recall that basic conditioning principles, like Pavlovian and operant conditioning, often occur outside of your awareness and in many settings outside the psychology laboratory. The same is true of memory. Many of the sights and sounds making up the everyday environment actually make their way into memory, but the process by which this happens is subtle and clandestine. It turns out that people are often especially poor witnesses of their own memory processes.

The idea that information becomes encoded in memory without effort or awareness may seem like an incredible claim to you as a college student, particularly when you consider the amount of intentional effort you expend studying course information and preparing for exams. The idea isn't so silly when you consider some fundamental facts about humans as a biological species. First, throughout most of our history as a species, formal schools or places of instruction were nonexistent. Our early ancestors spent little time musing over the distinction between positive and negative reinforcement, the formal properties of the Rescorla-Wagner model, or how flashbulb memories are represented in the nervous system. None of this means that memory didn't serve these early hominids. In fact, were it not for their ability to quickly and adequately process and retain information about their environment including how to obtain food and how to recognize dangerous elements in their environment, you would not be reading this passage. In short, the human nervous system evolved as an information processing system. Its primary function is to be responsive to stimulus conditions in the environment, and coordinate this information with the ongoing behavior of the organism. A valuable part of this process is the retention of important information over time, thus ensuring availability of the information when needed.

Memory, then, is an absolutely essential and fundamental aspect of human adaptation, so much so that it would be remarkable if it only functioned under the highly artificial conditions of an academic institution. This realization eventually led cognitive psychologists to the study of **incidental memory,** the recollection of information that is processed unintentionally. The result has been a fascinating chapter in the history of memory research. It turns out that a significant amount of the information processing that people do in a given day goes on beneath the veil of consciousness. In addition, despite its pervasiveness, incidental memory is far from perfect. In fact, it can lead people astray in ways that may have serious consequences, both for themselves and others.

incidental memory
recall of information without remembering its original source

Eyewitness Testimony and False Memories

Suppose you are walking home late at night from the movie theater. You hear some harsh but muffled words being spoken, and turning in the direction of the sound, you spot a man, holding a brown paper bag and a handgun, making a hasty exit from a nearby convenience store. The man runs directly toward you, but, at a distance of just a few feet, he turns sharply and disappears down an alley. Although it seems that time has momentarily stood still, the whole incident has transpired in seconds. After taking a few minutes to regain your composure, you decide to fulfill your civic duty by reporting what you have seen to the police. Several weeks later, the police ask you to come to the police station to identify a recently apprehended robbery suspect. Could you do so? How likely is it that you will remember the details of this rather frightening event that unfolded so quickly and in the dead of night, especially weeks later?

You can probably appreciate the importance of answering this question. On a daily basis, in courtrooms throughout the country, witnesses to crimes, accidents, and other significant happenings are asked to describe what they remember of these events. The question of whether they can accurately recall such events has enormous implications, not just for psychologists, but for the judicial system and society as well. Juries, for instance, are asked to make critical decisions about a person's guilt or innocence based on such evidence (Figure 7.3). Such decisions are hardly trivial academic exercises, for they can permanently affect the lives of those involved, sometimes in a devastating way. Imagine, for example, the consequences of falsely convicting someone of a crime as the result of eyewitness testimony. First, the convicted person loses his or her freedom, perhaps for a period of time measured in years. And it is difficult, if not impossible, to measure the effects of the conviction on the person's family, friends, and coworkers. Finally, society pays a heavy price in two ways: by losing the productivity and contributions of a valuable member of society and by remaining threatened by the person actually responsible for the crime, who is presumably still at large.

Thus, the consequences of wrongful conviction due to inaccurate eyewitness testimony are both numerous and severe. Regardless of how rare such wrongful convictions may be, they are nevertheless sobering reminders that the judicial system is disturbingly susceptible to error, and the problem is of interest to the psychologist precisely because it is due to the nature of human information processing. Judicial decisions, after all, are based on evidence and information, all of it supplied by human beings. For this reason, the courtroom becomes a fascinating and dramatic environment for the study of human behavior. Several dimensions of information processing have significant bearing on both the trial process and the eventual outcome. For instance, just how accurate is eyewitness testimony, and under what conditions is it rendered inaccurate? In addition, how much weight do juries place on eyewitness testimony, and is their confidence in such testimony justified? Fortunately, answers to some of these questions are now available.

For the most part, research has not painted an optimistic picture of the accuracy of eyewitness testimony. Instead, the evidence points rather disturbingly to the conclusion that an eyewitness's recall of an incident may very well be influenced both by the initial processing of the event and by how questions about the event are asked during the trial. In an intriguing experiment by Loftus and Palmer (1974), five groups of participants viewed the same film of two cars involved in an accident. Later, all subjects were asked to fill out questionnaires about what they had seen. One question asked, "About how fast were the two cars going when they _____ each other?" For each group, one of the following verbs completed the sentence: contacted, hit, collided, or smashed. Since all subjects saw the same film, researchers would expect their estimates of speed to be pretty much the same.

Participants' speed estimates, however, differed depending on which verb was used in the question. Those who heard the verb *contacted* gave an average estimate of 32 miles per hour. Participants who heard the verb *smashed* averaged estimates of 41 miles per hour. Even more startling was the

FIGURE 7.3 The courtroom is a dramatic environment for the study of human behavior.

finding that those who heard the verb *smashed* were much more likely to report having seen broken glass in the film than other groups. Amazingly, there was no broken glass depicted at any time during the film. Subjects' memory of the broken glass was not a memory at all, but a fabrication created by the questions themselves. This experiment not only questions the validity of eyewitness testimony but also serves as an additional reminder of Bartlett's (1932) contention that memory for an event is often a process of active reconstruction, not faithful copying of the event.

The bad news doesn't stop here, though. For instance, it is a fact that jurors are likely to be persuaded by testimony delivered by an eyewitness who is quite confident in what he or she has seen. Does this mean that testimony should be interpreted according to how sure eyewitnesses seem to be of themselves? Unfortunately, research does not square well with this bit of common sense. In several studies, eyewitness confidence or degree of certainty was found to be uncorrelated with accuracy of testimony (Brigham, 1990; Luus & Wells, 1994). Yet, an eyewitness account that is delivered with enthusiasm and certainty has a surface validity to it, and as such it may carry significant weight in the decision making of the jury. In some respects, this is not surprising. After all, people pay considerable attention to the nuances of a person's demeanor, because these subtleties often have important implications in interpersonal episodes. However, empirical research suggests, somewhat counterintuitively, that juries should pay little heed to the confidence of an eyewitness.

There is perhaps no more sobering example of the malleable nature of memory than the recent controversy over the construction of false memories (Conway, 1997; Kihlstrom, 1997; Spiegel, 1997). The issue has become particularly visible because of its implications for childhood memory of sexual abuse, a matter having enormous legal, professional, and personal ramifications. Obviously, the abuse of a child is a serious matter, and accusations of abuse must necessarily be treated seriously. At the heart of the matter, however, is the sticky question of how well people remember childhood experiences, particularly years, even decades, after their occurrence. Can such memories be relied on, and should they serve as relevant testimony in a court of law?

Sadly, there is no clear-cut answer to this question at the moment. The ethereal nature of memory, first demonstrated by Bartlett (1932), and the susceptibility of memory to alteration within the context of questioning or the therapeutic process, are potentially alarming when you consider that memory may be used to convict people of crimes (Intons-Peterson & Best, 1998). A growing literature attests to the ease with which false memories can actually be created at will (Loftus, 1997a, 1997b; Loftus, Nucci, & Hoffman, 1998). Subjects have, for example, been instructed to create vivid childhood fantasies as part of an experimental task. When these fantasies are consistent with generic expectations or beliefs about childhood, they become strongly established and are reported later as having actually been experienced (Dubreuil, Garry, & Loftus, 1998).

In addition, such false memories are enhanced when family members are recruited to assist in their creation. Subjects were more likely to believe that, as a child, they had been lost in a shopping mall or had spilled punch at a family wedding, if relatives had been instructed to report having witnessed the event as well (Loftus, 1997a). As with eyewitness testimony, false memories are often reported with great confidence, so degree of certainty cannot be used as an index of whether an event actually happened (Loftus, 1997b). Thus, the research on false memories is particularly troubling in light of the fact that many legal proceedings, and the decisions they engender, are based to a large extent on events that may have transpired in the distant past and for which there is no independent confirmation.

The problem of false memory is not restricted to adults attempting to recall childhood incidents. Increasingly, children are taking the stand in legal proceedings and being asked to describe relatively recent incidents involving parents, day care instructors, and other caretakers. Given the ease with which false memories can be created in adults, researchers wonder whether children may be similarly easy targets for such distortions. Research on this topic does seem to point toward a greater suggestibility for young children. In fact, there is a rather predictable relationship between age and susceptibility to false memory, with preschoolers being more prone to such distortions than school-age children, who are, in turn, more prone to suggestion than are adults (Ceci & Bruck, 1993; Ceci, Bruck, & Battin, 2000). However, a somewhat optimistic note emerges from this research. Young children are not necessarily subject to suggestive questioning or interviewing. The effect is much likelier to occur as the result of a decidedly biased questioner asking leading questions repetitively over time. Under the right conditions, even preschoolers may offer useful testimony in the forensic setting. In general, so long as the conditions under which the child first reported an incident are well known, the interview is conducted by a well-trained, nonbiased adult (presumably neither prosecuting or defending attorney), and the child's report doesn't change substantially over time, the testimony of a young child may possess as much credibility as any other witness.

Although consistent with historical accounts of memory as a constructive, malleable phenomenon, much of the research on eyewitness testimony and false memory flies in the face of common sense and intuition. There is something almost unexplainably compelling about a verbal report of an incident given by a witness, and most people find it hard to imagine that the witness's recall of the event could be inaccurate. For this reason, today's social and behavioral scientists have a responsibility to convince the judicial system of the perils associated with memory for real events. In this case, understanding the conditions under which people may be led astray by memory has significance well beyond the confines of the psychology laboratory.

Implicit Memory

implicit memory
the tendency to forget the source or origin of familiar information

Suppose you had witnessed the robbery described in the previous section. At the police station you are first asked to view mug shots of potential suspects. Later you are brought to a special viewing room to see a lineup of potential suspects. You are struck by an overwhelming sense of familiarity for one of the suspects in the lineup. You tell the police that this person looks familiar and that you're pretty sure he's the one you saw running out of the convenience store. The suspect is charged and ultimately convicted of the robbery. Is it safe to claim that justice has been served in this case? Perhaps not, according to psychologists who study **implicit memory,** the tendency to forget the source of familiar information (Engelkamp & Wippich, 1995; Stadler & Frensch, 1998). Let's examine an experiment on implicit memory to discover why researchers believe the police procedure described here may result in improper suspect identification.

As a participant in this experiment, you are shown a list of people's names and asked to pronounce the names as quickly and correctly as possible. Approximately 24 hours later you are given a new list of names, some of which are repeated from the first list. Using the new list of people, you are asked to tell how famous they are. This second list contains some names of famous people in addition to a few less well known people and a few made-up names. An interesting thing happens during your attempt to identify the famous people on this list. Some of the names seem familiar to you, but you don't necessarily attribute this familiarity to the first list. Instead, you assume that if they sound familiar to you, it must be because they are famous. In other words, you have remembered having seen these names before, but you don't remember where you saw them. What this means is that sometimes people recall having seen or heard something before, but they mistakenly attribute it to the wrong source. This is the phenomenon of implicit memory, and it has been demonstrated across a range of both visual (Bradley, Greenwald, Petry, & Lang, 1992) and auditory stimuli (Jacoby, Allan, Collins, & Larwill, 1988). There is, in addition, physiological evidence that implicit memory is a distinct form of information processing: The neural activity occurring during implicit memory differs from that associated with explicit memory tasks, suggesting that the distinction between these two kinds of memory is not simply procedural (Rugg et al., 1998). To see how implicit memory might be problematic in a nonlaboratory setting, let's return to the suspect identification scenario.

Remember that in the example, one of the potential suspects in the lineup looks familiar. But are you remembering the suspect from the night of the robbery, or is there another source of this familiarity? Could it be that this person looks familiar to you from the mug shots seen earlier? If so, then it would most certainly be a miscarriage of justice to identify this "suspect" as the man you saw running out of the convenience store. And yet, this is a very real possibility, according to research on implicit memory. In fact, it is such a likely source of misidentification that the Supreme Court in 1968 declared that this was an unacceptable means of obtaining suspect identification (Simmons et al. *v.* United States, 1968).

Flashbulb Memories

While driving down a familiar road, you happen on the site of an automobile accident. You slow down as you pass the accident, noticing large numbers of police vehicles, ambulances, firefighters, and paramedics on the scene. As you move past the wreckage, it becomes clear that this has been a terrible accident, almost certainly involving fatalities. Understandably, this is an emotional event, and you find yourself thinking back to it, recalling the images, and contemplating the tragedy of the incident throughout the rest of the day.

Now let's leap ahead to a year after the accident. What kind of recall do you have of the incident and the circumstances surrounding it? Of course, the fact that you recall the accident is not surprising by itself. What is a bit unusual, however, is that you may be able to remember, in considerable detail and vividness, particulars of the incident that have nothing to do with the accident itself. For instance, you may remember what day it was, or that you were just beginning your summer vacation. Perhaps you remember who was in the car with you, where they were sitting, or what they were saying to you as you came on the accident. You might even remember something as unremarkable as the clothes you were wearing that day, or that you had forgotten your watch when dressing that morning. Psychologists call these vivid memories for the circumstances surrounding a highly emotional event **flashbulb memories** (Brown & Kulik, 1977). They are an especially dramatic example of everyday memory, in that they demonstrate that even the presumably unimportant details of an event may become permanently encoded when that event is of a highly emotional nature.

flashbulb memory
particularly vivid recall of one's surroundings produced by exposure to a dramatic event

Flashbulb memories have often been studied in response to such widely publicized tragedies as the assassination of President Kennedy in 1963, John Lennon's murder in 1980, the space shuttle *Challenger*'s explosion in 1986, and the untimely death of Princess Diana in an automobile accident in 1997 (Figure 7.4). Can you recall where you were, what you were doing, or who was with you when you heard the news of the Princess Diana tragedy? If so, how vividly or clearly do you recall this information?

FIGURE 7.4 Princess Diana. Flashbulb memories are often connected with highly publicized tragedies.

There appears to be some controversy among researchers as to just how accurate flashbulb memories might be. In one study (McCloskey, Wible, & Cohen, 1988), subjects were asked to report on their recall of events surrounding the *Challenger* explosion, once 3 days after the accident and then again 9 months later. Despite subjects' reports that their memories surrounding the event remained vivid months later, details of their reports differed substantially over time. Thus, like other kinds of memories, flashbulb memories seem to be susceptible to the effects of distortion and interference. In addition, there remains some disagreement as to whether flashbulb memories occupy a unique structure or involve any special mechanism in the nervous system (Cohen, McCloskey, & Wible, 1988).

There is some evidence that flashbulb memories can be formed, not only for negative or tragic events, but for emotionally positive events as well. Scott and Ponsoda (1996) asked Scottish university students to fill out questionnaires concerning a large number of both positive and negative events that had occurred over a 10-year period. Memories for both types of events were similar, indicating that flashbulb memories are not distinctly dependent on tragedy. Similarly, Weaver (1993) had participants fill out questionnaires about an "ordinary event," in order to determine whether flashbulb memories might be formed in the absence of any spectacular or distinguishable feature of the event. As it happened, the bombing of Iraq to begin the Persian Gulf War occurred on the same day. Participants were asked to fill out questionnaires both several months and 1 year after these two events. No differences in recall accuracy occurred for the separate events, although participants believed their recall of the bombing to be superior. Weaver argued that flashbulb memories can be formed for relatively indistinct events and that such memories are probably not unique, other than in the extreme confidence with which they seem to be held.

✖ INTERIM SUMMARY

Humans process a good deal of information to which we do not consciously attend. Eyewitness recall, false memories, implicit memory, and flashbulb memories all represent effortless types of information processing. Although such memories develop outside of conscious awareness, they are prone to the same kinds of distortions that afflict intentional memories. Contemporary research on incidental memory has been directed toward identifying both the causes of memory distortion and the real-world consequences of such distortions.

✖ THOUGHT QUESTIONS

1. In the "trial of the century," O. J. Simpson was found not guilty of murdering Nicole Brown Simpson and Ronald Goldman. Although the prosecuting attorneys claimed to have a "mountain" of physical evidence, including DNA samples, that incriminated Simpson, there were no eyewitnesses to the actual crime. Should the absence of an eyewitness be considered a major liability in the case against Simpson? Why or why not?
2. Try to recall a significant (positive or negative) event from your childhood. Take a few moments to write down in as much detail as you can how the event unfolded. If possible, have someone else who witnessed the event (a family member or friend) do the same. Do your two descriptions match? If not, what kinds of differences did you uncover? How would you explain the discrepancy in the two reports?

MEMORY IN NONHUMANS

A consistent theme throughout this book has been that much of the knowledge acquired about learning is the result of experiments on nonhuman animals. Animal experiments are conducted for many reasons, including some convenience and ethical considerations. In addition to these reasons, researchers study animals because they assume that what they learn about animals may hold true for humans as well. This concept of continuity, attributed largely to Darwin, suggests that certain fundamental similarities characterize all species in their struggle to survive. Learning would seem to be one of these fundamental processes. And what of memory? Can nonhuman animals remember objects, events, or episodes in their lives? If so, do they show the same types of memory functions as do humans? Do they forget as humans do? Are they as susceptible to interference effects? Answers to such questions contribute to better understanding of the cognitive abilities of nonhuman animals, and help to clarify the many differences and similarities between humans and nonhumans.

Recent years have seen a prolific increase in research on the cognitive capacities of nonhuman animals. Studies of short-term and long-term memory, spatial and serial memory, visual imagery, and foraging in both laboratory and nonlaboratory settings have become so popular as to have been identified as a separate discipline, referred to as either *animal cognition* (Boysen & Himes, 1999; Wasserman, 1997) or *comparative cognition* (Roitblat, 1987; Roitblat & von Fersen, 1992). As Roitblat (1987) has aptly pointed out, research in comparative cognition no longer asks whether animals have minds. Rather, the focus is on describing how the minds of different species function and what their capacities are as information processing systems.

Research with animals and, for that matter, human infants, differs in significant ways from research with adult humans. Both human infants and animals are nonverbal organisms, meaning that they can't tell researchers whether they remember something or how they feel. Such private events must be inferred on the basis of overt behavior. For this reason, the study of animal cognition, including memory processes, relies on the kinds of equipment and research methodology made popular by early learning psychologists. Apparatuses like the radial-arm maze and the operant chamber are used frequently by researchers interested in animal cognition. You may want to review some of the basic processes of conditioning from early chapters before reading the rest of the chapter. In particular, the concepts of stimulus control, discrimination, and differential reinforcement are all important to understanding the methods used by researchers studying animal memory. In some sense, animals can "tell" researchers what they remember by responding in particular ways to stimulus conditions controlled by the experimenter.

Memory for Visual Stimuli

Because of its superior vision, the pigeon has been a popular research subject in studies of animal memory. In a standard operant chamber, visual stimuli differing on any number of dimensions can be presented on response keys, removed for varying periods, and then presented again to test for recall. The procedure most frequently used to test for memory in pigeons is the delayed-matching-to-sample (DMTS) task (Figure 7.5). At the beginning of a trial, the middle of three horizontally aligned response keys is illuminated to capture the pigeon's attention. When the pigeon pecks this middle key, it changes into the *sample* stimulus, such as a series of lines, a geometric figure, or a particular color. After some predetermined period of illumination, the sample turns off, followed by a retention interval during which all keys remain dark. During the last, or *comparison*, phase of the trial, both side keys are lit, one with the previously displayed sample stimulus, the other with a stimulus different from the sample.

During this final phase of the trial, the pigeon is to peck the key that matches the sample presented previously. If it pecks the correct key, all lights are extinguished and grain reinforcement is delivered through a food tray. An incorrect response results in darkening of the experimental chamber and no food. In other words, the bird's behavior of responding to the previously presented sample stimulus is differentially reinforced. A typical experiment

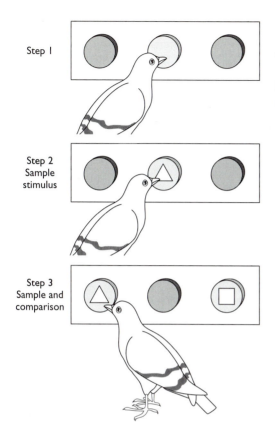

FIGURE 7.5
Delayed-Matching-to-Sample (DMTS) Procedure Used to Study Memory in Animals.

Step 1

Step 2
Sample stimulus

Step 3
Sample and comparison

will involve perhaps hundreds of trials, and the number of correct responses by the pigeon is believed to indicate memory ability.

There are actually many variations on the DMTS task. In *identity matching,* for example, the subject is required to select the comparison stimulus that directly matches the sample stimulus. This is precisely the procedure just described. In *symbolic matching,* comparison and sample stimuli are usually from different stimulus dimensions, and the correct comparison stimulus bears no physical relationship to the sample stimulus (Roberts, Macuda, & Brodbeck, 1995). For example, geometric (triangle and square) shapes may appear first as sample stimuli, but red and green lights appear during the comparison phase of the trial. The bird may be required to peck the green key when the triangle has been presented as the sample, and the red key when the square has been presented as the sample. Many researchers believe symbolic matching is a critical procedure because it requires the animal to form a rule relating the sample to the comparison stimulus rather than simply responding to the same stimulus when presented a second time.

The same is true of *oddity matching,* in which the animal is required to respond to whichever comparison stimulus does *not* match the sample. If a triangle is presented as the sample, for instance, and the triangle and a square appear as comparison stimuli, the subject's behavior will be reinforced only for responding to the square, not the triangle. Some researchers suggest that the subject must develop a formal rule, such as "respond to anything that isn't a triangle," in order to solve this particular problem (Zentall, Hogan, & Edwards, 1984). Attributing rule-governed behavior to nonhuman animals would have been nearly unthinkable during the early decades of the 1900s, but it is an increasingly seductive inference for today's researchers. It is clear that researchers have gotten better at devising instruments and techniques for posing complex questions to other animals under well-controlled conditions allowing for more sophisticated conclusions. In many cases, nonhuman animal subjects have provided impressive answers.

So, how often do pigeons respond correctly in such experiments? As you might suspect, that depends on many factors, such as how long the sample stimulus remains illuminated and how long the retention interval is between the sample and the comparison stimuli. Consistent with common sense, correct responses increase with longer sample times and shorter retention intervals. In fact, with sample durations of 14 seconds, correct responding remains quite high even after retention intervals of 60 seconds (Grant, 1976). In other words, like humans, pigeons recall events much better after having been exposed to them for longer periods of time and when little time has passed since the events occurred. It may in fact be safe to assume that this kind of limitation would be expected of any kind of biological information processing system, be it mammalian, avian, or otherwise.

Much forgetting in humans seems due to interference effects; can the same be said of pigeons? Several studies seem to suggest that pigeons do indeed experience both proactive and retroactive interference. For example, shortening the time between trials, called the *intertrial interval* (ITI), reduces pigeons' accuracy in delayed-matching-to-sample tasks. This would be equivalent to your being required to learn several short lists of words, one after the other. Apparently, as trials become more closely spaced in time, differentiating between correct sample stimuli becomes difficult, thus producing the classic proactive interference effect (Roberts, 1980). Also, if pigeons are required to respond to comparison stimuli from trials much earlier in an experiment, the expectation would be that the intervening trials may interfere with recall of earlier sample stimuli. This retroactive interference effect has indeed been demonstrated in pigeons working DMTS tasks (Roberts & Grant, 1978) and also rats negotiating T-mazes (Terry, 1996).

Don't be misled into thinking all DMTS research is conducted with pigeons. Pigeons are frequently used because of their acute vision, but the DMTS procedure has been used to examine short-term memory in several other species, including rats (Wallace, Steinert, Scobie, & Spear, 1980), monkeys (Colombo & Graziano, 1994), and dolphins (Herman & Thompson, 1982)—with essentially the same results. Thus, many nonhuman species appear to be susceptible to interference effects.

Spatial Memory

Perhaps the delayed-matching-to-sample task appears too artificial to you. You may ask, "What has this to do with how an animal uses its memory in adapting to its natural habitat?" This is a good question, and you can be certain that it has occurred to researchers as well. Other procedures and apparatus have been utilized for the purpose of exploring just how well animals remember events having important biological consequences. For example, in their natural environment, many animals must constantly search, or forage, for food. In so doing, they must remember such things as where they last found food, whether they have depleted the food from that particular location, and so on. To discover how well animals accomplish this task, researchers use such instruments as the radial-arm maze, or they construct laboratory environments that simulate the natural habitats of different animal species. Recall that rats perform quite impressively in foraging for food in a radial-arm maze. Keep in mind that this ability makes perfect sense given the rat's evolutionary history and its status as a natural forager. Other species demonstrate similarly remarkable spatial memories that assist them in adapting to their peculiar habitats.

In order to bring a sense of ecological realism to their experiments, some researchers have designed laboratory settings that simulate the environment in which animals forage naturally. Such settings decrease the artificiality of the laboratory while allowing for relatively precise measurement and control of variables. Many bird species, including Clark's nutcracker, acquire large amounts of seeds and then place them in specific locations, called *caches,* which they can later access when needed. Of course, in order to take advantage of this form of food storing, the birds must be able to remember, sometimes weeks or months later, exactly where they placed the seeds. Balda and Turek (1984) designed an indoor aviary and allowed birds to distribute a tray of seeds in several caches beneath the aviary's sandy floor. The birds were then removed from the aviary for 31 days. Before the birds were returned to the aviary, half of the seed caches established by the birds were removed by the experimenters. Upon their return, birds revisited most of the cache locations they had previously constructed and seldom searched in locations where they had not hidden seeds.

Also, when visiting a cache location from which the experimenter had removed seeds, birds increased the intensity of their digging and searching behavior and extended their search to areas immediately adjacent to the previously established cache. This increase in response variability and intensity at pilfered cache locations bears a remarkable similarity to the response burst that often follows from extinction conditions (Stokes, 1995). In other words, the birds were acting as if a reinforcer in this particular location was expected, a finding consistent with the notion that the birds recalled where they had previously hidden seeds.

Shettleworth and Krebs (1982) demonstrated a similar ability to recover caches in another bird species, the marsh tit. Birds were allowed to store seeds in the holes of numerous tree limbs hanging from the ceiling of an experimental cubicle (Figure 7.6). There were 97 possible locations for establishing caches. After depositing all the seeds into caches, the birds were removed from the cubicle for an interval ranging from 2 to 3 hours. Upon returning to the cubicle, birds recovered 65% percent of the cached seeds, seldom visiting possible cache sites that were not used to store seeds (Shettleworth, 1983).

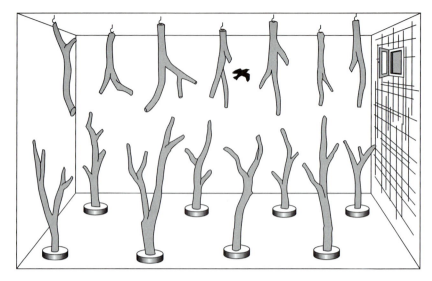

FIGURE 7.6 Experimental Aviary Used to Study Spatial Memory in Birds.
(From Shettleworth, 1983).

In summary, the results of cache location studies with birds are consistent with the foraging studies with rats, in that both types of animals demonstrate an impressive capacity for recalling food locations, whether naturally occurring or self-established. In fact, the ability to remember food locations remained intact even when experimenters explicitly created conditions that should have produced interference effects (Bednekoff, Kamil, & Balda, 1997). Findings like this are consistent with a phylogenetic interpretation of behavior. It follows that foraging species are highly prepared to encode and retain information relevant to food location, for this ability is an essential survival skill.

Metacognition

As more studies of nonhuman animals are conducted from a perspective that takes their unique evolutionary history into account, people may come to appreciate their considerable cognitive capacities. But when pressed, most people would still maintain that, memory for important food locations aside, animals differ from humans cognitively in important ways. It is often said, for example, that only humans possess consciousness, defined as the ability to reflect on our own behavior, thoughts, and state of being. In other words, although animals can remember important biological events in their lives, they aren't likely to be conscious of such memories. They remember locations quite well, but do they remember having been responsible for establishing those locations?

The question at hand inevitably invites some discussion of *consciousness,* a concept with a considerably troubling history in psychology. Psychologists have long debated what, precisely, it means to be conscious or have consciousness, and definitions of the term abound (Rychlak, 1997).

Despite the conceptual disagreement surrounding use of the term, most definitions of consciousness include some reference to self-awareness. This self-awareness or capacity to attend to one's own behavior or cognitive states is called **metacognition.** From a research perspective, then, the question becomes Just how can we tell whether a nonhuman animal pays attention to itself? Answering this question has required experimenters to develop innovative, often ingenious, experimental methods.

metacognition the process of thinking about or attending to one's own thoughts and/or behavior

Although they can't literally tell researchers about their own behavior, other animals can reveal something of their awareness of self when they respond to the conditions established in operant experiments. For example, Shimp (1982) had pigeons peck the right and left keys of a three-key matrix in an alternating fashion. After either two or five alternating key pecks, the center key was lit and the two side keys extinguished. Pecking the middle key caused the two side keys to light up red and green. If the pigeon had just completed a two-response alternation, pecking the red key produced reinforcement. If a five-run alternation had just been completed, pecking the green key was reinforced. Incorrect responses produced a temporary blackout of the experimental chamber and no reinforcement. The essence of this experiment was that birds could have responded correctly only if they could remember what they had just done in the previous part of the experiment. Demonstrating memory for their own previous behavior, birds did in fact respond correctly on most trials. According to Shimp (1982), the birds responded in a manner similar to humans when we are demonstrating *metaknowledge*— awareness or memory of our own behavior.

In a similar experiment, Kramer (1982) used an interesting variation of the symbolic DMTS task to study pigeons' memory for their own behavior. During the first component of a trial, a center key was lit. In a random order, birds were required either to peck the center key once or not to peck it at all. If birds responded correctly to the center key, it was extinguished and a short retention interval was begun. At the end of the retention interval, the two side keys were illuminated white. If the bird had pecked the center key during the first phase of the trial, a response to one of the side keys was reinforced. If the bird had not pecked the center key, responding to the other side key produced reinforcement. Incorrect responses during this phase produced a blackout and no reinforcement. Remember, during the first phase the center key was turned on, regardless of whether birds pecked the key. Therefore, they could not have been responding to the key itself as a discriminative stimulus. Nor could the birds be responding according to the duration of the sample phase, because this was held constant regardless of whether birds were required to peck or not peck the center key. They could only respond discriminatively on the basis of their own previous behavior.

Consistent with Shimp's (1982) results, birds responded above chance levels, even during trials in which the retention interval approached 1 minute. These findings support the idea that under properly arranged circumstances, animals may be capable of "reporting" on their own behavior. Of course, you'll have to decide for yourself whether these results demonstrate that animals other than humans have consciousness and, if so, whether it can be compared to human self-awareness. Findings like this are important if only because they challenge people to rethink the distinctions they draw between humans and nonhuman animals. Keep in mind too, that as much as people make of human consciousness, this chapter has shown that unconscious or unintentional information processing may be the rule for humans, not the exception. In other words, consciousness may make up a rather small percentage of human behavior, and it clearly isn't absolutely necessary to much of our functioning (Bargh & Chartrand, 1999).

✖ INTERIM SUMMARY

This section explored the provocative questions being entertained about the memory and cognitive capacities of nonhuman animals. Research in animal cognition suggests that the cognitive prowess of humans is perhaps not unique but that other creatures possess sometimes remarkable memories. From long-term memory of feeding locations to reporting on aspects of their own behavior, other animals may call upon skills as highly adapted to their distinct niches as are our human memory skills.

✖ THOUGHT QUESTIONS

1. Why do some researchers believe that animals must be able to develop a rule in order to respond to a symbolic matching task? Do you think household pets, such as cats and dogs, possess such symbolic abilities? Why or why not?
2. Some psychologists believe that metacognition, the ability to reflect on one's own behavior, is a unique feature of human consciousness. Do you agree? What kind of evidence might suggest that other animals can attend to aspects of their own behavior as well?

THE ADAPTIVE NATURE OF MEMORY

You don't have to look far to see how much everyday functioning depends upon memory. Being a college student, you are probably overly sensitized to the importance of memory, as your capacity to recall names, dates, events, and procedures is tested systematically and, perhaps to your way of thinking, unrelentingly. But your reliance on recall and recognition served you long before your admission to college, and its relevance to further success in life will not terminate when you receive your degree. Indeed, memory may be the cognitive equivalent of breathing, in that much of the time, you are hardly aware of the fact that negotiating your environment without memory would be impossible. So, too, people seldom think much about the constant work being done by their lungs to bring fresh oxygen into their bodies; only when breathing becomes difficult, such as during an asthma attack or in an extremely dusty or polluted environment, do they deliberate on the wonders of something so simple as drawing a breath.

The ability to remember places, events, objects, and procedural routines is so much a part of any behavioral episode that it's a challenge to envision any animal, human or otherwise, adapting to a complex world in its absence. Indeed, the adaptive necessity of memory is often most dramatically seen in those unfortunate enough to have suffered memory loss through injury or disease. The case of H. M., or the growing population of elderly (including former President Ronald Reagan) who weather the daily inconveniences and indignities of Alzheimer's disease, serve as reminders that the capacity to act on previous information or experience is no luxury at all, but an evolved device of unrivaled significance.

Perhaps one of the most adaptive features of memory is the extent of information processing that goes on behind the scenes, without any awareness on our part. As suggested by the various instances of incidental memory, we automatically process a good deal of information about our environment, despite not always being able to recall the information's source. Psychologists are only now learning that considerable amounts of information processing, from memory to social judgment making, actually occur automatically and outside of awareness. That such automatic processing of information is adaptive can be seen readily in the many procedural memories we use to negotiate the world. Imagine having to spend inordinate amounts of mental effort on ordinary, well-mastered tasks like driving a car or getting dressed. By not having to commit much information processing effort to these tasks, we're able to more selectively decide which kinds of activities require conscious, effortful processing, such as studying for an exam or filling out a job application. What must be remembered, though, is that these more intentional and observable examples of memory in action are but the tip of the iceberg of a much busier, often unnoticed information processing system.

CHAPTER EIGHT

Conceptual Behavior

It has been one of those days when you are convinced that the stars and planets must be aligned against you in some nefarious astronomical conspiracy. A 15-page term paper is due in 2 days in your Ancient History class, and your roommate, unbeknownst to you, just loaded a new word processing program on the computer the two of you share in your dorm room. Your task? To master this new program and use it to write your paper, all in the next 48 hours! At first, the task seems overwhelming, for the new program, though impressive in its power and flexibility, also boasts several unfamiliar features and unusual key functions. You struggle at first, making several unintentional formatting changes and accidentally deleting a section of your paper. But with time, the newness of the program wears off, and your confidence increases. Although this new program is different from the one you are used to, the two programs have enough in common that progress is made quickly. As it turns out, your knowledge of the previous program serves you well, and the few nuances of the new program prove manageable after all. In the end, the 2-day marathon typing session yields a most satisfactory paper, turned in on time, and you emerge with greater confidence in your ability to master new computer programs.

As is true of any other group of professionals, biologists don't always see eye to eye on many of the issues pertaining to their science. But on one central issue, there is consensus: The planet we call home is literally teeming with life. So much so, in fact, that biologists are reluctant to put a number on how many species of trees, plants, mammals, fish, and other life-forms occupy the globe. The difficulty of properly cataloging life on earth is embodied in the work of an entomologist (Erwin, 1983) who embarked on a remarkable study of insect life within the forest canopy (upper levels of trees) in South America. Erwin's strategy was to spread a large tarp beneath a target tree, then shoot a cloud of insecticide into the tree. Several minutes later, the canopy would literally rain dead insects onto the tarp, where they would be collected and returned to the laboratory for precise identification. The result? Nearly 80% of the insects that fell from the canopy turned out to be unknown to scientists. Even when Erwin moved a short distance to a new tree, the procedure yielded large numbers of insects as yet unclassified by entomologists. So much for the old expression, There is nothing new under the sun! This astounding finding is testimony not only to the earth's nearly unimaginable biodiversity, but also to the amount of work yet to be done by contemporary biologists.

CONCEPTS AS ABSTRACTIONS

Of course, the natural world has no monopoly on diversity. We humans also have a considerable reputation for tinkering, and our ingenuity and resourcefulness has led to a similarly dizzying array of artifacts. Our human-constructed environments contain such standard items as lawn mowers, edge trimmers, automobiles, stereos, chairs, tables, computers, cell phones, electronic toys, sports equipment, and other inanimate objects with which most of us are familiar. In short, we live in a very busy world, populated by an inconceivable number of *things,* both natural and artificial. To a large extent, successful adaptation requires that we deal effectively with these objects. We need to learn to avoid those that may prove harmful, but approach, and perhaps collect, those that may be beneficial. This is especially true with respect to the many gadgets and devices that define life in the industrialized world. Many of the high-tech instruments that we use every day are tools whose usefulness depends upon knowledge and our ability to operate them properly. In many work environments, the ability to use such tools with skill is a defining aspect of the job description.

Thus, our ability to meet the demands of our environment requires that we respond appropriately to the things that populate our world. But doing so entails an even more fundamental task: identification and classification. We cannot very well avoid an animal that poses a threat if we haven't first identified it as a dangerous animal. And we must distinguish between edible and inedible items if we are to acquire proper sustenance—a point perhaps obvious to an adult, but not to the 7-month-old whose list of consumables may include such delicacies as cigarette butts and dead insects. And for many taxpayers, distinguishing between those services or commodities that are tax deductible and those that are not may have important implications when filing a tax return each April. In these scenarios and countless others, acting effectively means, among other things, recognizing that objects in the world belong to certain meaningful classes.

This chapter explores the process by which we come to identify objects according to category membership and how this simple ability helps us to negotiate a complex world. In addition, it describes how researchers discovered that the ability to identify classes of objects develops early in life, for human infants as well as other animals.

Making a Complex World Simple

In the opening vignette, you are faced with a challenge that is becoming common in this increasingly computer-dominated world. Each year, new computer programs, or revised versions of programs, devoted to word processing and data management appear. Although the process of relearning a program can be frustrating, most people resign themselves to the task, seldom finding the experience quite as exasperating as they may have feared. When you load a new word processing program and begin working with it, you will no doubt be greeted by some unfamiliar features—perhaps a new way to select text, a toolbar with menu items that differ from your previous program, or maybe even some formatting selections that you have never seen before. On the other hand, many features will remain the same, such as the general functions of the letter keys, the Spacebar, and the Delete key. In other words, once you begin using the program, you will recognize it as a word processing program as opposed to a spreadsheet program because the program does most of the same things that other word processing programs do but doesn't do the sorts of things that a spreadsheet program does. Even though you have never encountered this specific word processing program before, you find learning this one to be fairly uneventful because of your considerable previous experience with word processing programs.

conceptual behavior behavior under the control of generalized or abstract stimulus properties rather than specific attributes

In learning a new word processing program, you exhibit what psychologists refer to as **conceptual behavior,** because you respond to a particular object (specific word processing program) that shares certain features with a larger category of such objects (all word processing programs). This one program may be only one of a dozen; it is a member of a larger class of programs used for word processing. The new program represents an abstraction, or representative example, of all word processing programs. In this complicated world, we encounter new objects or situations all the time, and there would be little adaptive benefit to studying each new situation intensively before acting. Many circumstances simply don't allow for deliberation and contemplation. Fortunately, most organisms, both humans and nonhumans, have a penchant for sizing up novel circumstances quickly, usually by comparing the unfamiliar with other more familiar objects or events. We make a "quick-and-dirty" assessment of the novel item, compare it to other items that already exist in well-known categories or classifications, and then act toward this new item in a manner that is consistent with our classification. In this way, we expend minimal effort and time in recognizing the object before responding.

This kind of conceptual undertaking is a way of economizing on cognitive effort while meeting the behavioral demands of encountering something new. Conceptual behavior often comes down to recognizing whether some new object or situation has enough in common with some category of objects or events to justify treating it as a member of this category. So why categorize at all? Why not just keep a list of all things in the world handy, then simply consult the list when necessary? Take a look at the items in Table 8.1. Imagine that you were given 2 minutes to rehearse the items in the list for purposes of recalling as many as possible. How would you rehearse this list? You might simply go through the list, in rote manner, as many times as possible in the allotted 2 minutes. But recall from the previous chapter that this is a decidedly ineffective way to remember the list. The list contains 30 words, and it would be pretty difficult for most people to remember this

TABLE 8.1 ITEMS TO BE MEMORIZED FOR RECALL TEST

Crescent wrench	stapler
coffee cup	Phillips screwdriver
donuts	keyboard
sledgehammer	pencil
floppy disk	granola bar
router	saltine crackers
printer cartridge	trail mix
paperweight	drill bits
Post-it notes	wintergreen mints
Twinkies	Rolodex
pipe wrench	telephone book
jelly beans	carpenter's level
soldering gun	butterscotch candies
paper clips	galvanized nails
pretzels	potato chips

many words on the basis of only 2 minutes of rehearsal time, especially if the time is devoted to simple repetition, or rote memorization.

There is a much more effective and efficient way to handle this list. You may have noticed that the list contains several kinds, or categories, of items. Ten of the items fit into the category of *tool* (sledgehammer, Crescent wrench, carpenter's level, etc.), 10 items fit into the category of *work desk* (stapler, Rolodex, keyboard, etc.), and 10 items fit into the category of *snack foods* (trail mix, jelly beans, Twinkies, etc.). Perhaps it occurred to you that you could memorize the list by thinking of these different categories and then placing each item into the appropriate category. As it turns out, this would be an efficient means of organizing this rather long list of words. Then, when asked to recall as many as possible, you would want to call up the name of a category label, such as *tool*. The word *tool* then becomes a recall cue for all members of that category. Not surprisingly, this tactic is more effective than simply rehearsing the words over and over, and this makes perfect sense given what is known about humans' ability to process information. All organisms possess limited capacities of working memory, and this means that it is unlikely that we store information randomly or in some haphazard way. Instead, we tend to organize things in memory in meaningful ways, such as in categories or classification systems. The benefits of doing so become apparent not only during a memory task such as this, but also when the world confronts us with novel objects or circumstances.

Conceptual behavior, then, occurs whenever we respond to a specific object or situation because of its perceived similarity to a larger class of objects or situations. The difficult question to be answered by researchers is

What makes for category membership in the first place? Why do we respond to a particular item as if it belongs to one category of things and not another? Sometimes category membership is not so obvious after all. For instance, in Table 8.1, *pencil* is perhaps more "at home" in the category *work desk,* but it could just as well be a member of the category *tool,* couldn't it? In fact, in the real world of objects and events, the rules for classifying are sometimes quite complex. Many objects can belong to multiple categories at the same time. For instance, *stapler* may be conceptualized as belonging to such varied categories as *office supply, tool, fastening devices,* and perhaps even *weapon.*

To make matters even more complicated, some categories are created on the spot when the need arises. Imagine a professor walking into a classroom and requesting that students separate into two groups, those who like statistics and those who don't. Now, as difficult as it may be for you to believe, the professor would expect the classroom to divide into two groups (OK, the group that likes statistics may be somewhat smaller), and this division is based on the arbitrary criteria of liking or not liking statistics. The same could be done on the basis of any number of other similarly arbitrary criteria, such as class rank, gender, major, height, weight, political affiliation, and so on. What this means is that conceptual categories are sometimes fluid, temporary means of organizing information. One of the impressive things about conceptual behavior is the ease with which it occurs, regardless of the parameters for defining a category. As psychologists, we wish to know how people manage, so effortlessly it seems, to categorize what they encounter and then respond appropriately, most of the time, to these defined parameters.

Emergence of Concepts

Conceptual behavior is sometimes best seen in people who are in the process of acquiring a new concept, such as infants learning labels for things in their environment. Even at the age of 2 years, a child has already formed a large number of concepts. For example, a 2-year-old who has played with balls for any length of time can recognize new instances or members of the class of *balls* with considerable ease. Let's assume a child has only played with a few types of balls, say a green tennis ball, a red Nerf football, and an orange spongy basketball. If the child's father brings home a new, large, multicolored beach ball and rolls it on the floor in front of the child, what kind of reaction would you expect from the child? Most likely, the child would point to or in some other way show acknowledgment of the ball, perhaps even saying the word *ball.*

If you stop to consider what is going on, you will appreciate what a remarkable behavioral feat has just occurred. The child has never seen this particular object before but responds appropriately by classifying it as a ball. This capacity for recognizing new examples of a conceptual category is important, especially when the concept is so large that the individual is not likely to have previously encountered every possible member. Of course, *ball* is just one example of a concept acquired quite early by most children. Their repertoire of concepts is, however, much broader and includes such significant members as *food, clothes, toy, dog, cat, game,* and a host of others. In each case, the child understands that the label itself refers not to any particular object, but potentially to all members of the class. Perhaps even more impressive is that category learning can be seen in infants as young as 3 to 4 months (Behl, 1996; Colombo, O'Brien, Mitchell, & Roberts, 1987; Quinn, Eimas, & Rosenkrantz, 1993), and these early concepts appear to set the stage for more sophisticated concept learning in adulthood (Eimas, 1994).

An additional and puzzling aspect of concepts is that people are often hard pressed to explain even the simplest of concepts. For example, take a moment to come up with a formal definition of the concept *dog*. Or, more challenging yet, suppose you had the job of explaining to a 2-year-old how to identify a dog. Could you verbalize what characteristics distinguish *dog* from other concepts, such as *cat*? If you try this exercise, you will discover that visually identifying members of the concepts is easy, but formal definitions can be tricky. For instance, you wouldn't define a dog as *a furry, four-legged creature with a tail* because this definition includes cats as well. Perhaps you would suggest that dogs are big animals compared to cats. But there are, of course, exceptions to this rule: A tiger, for instance, is much larger than even the grandest German shepherd. You might suggest that dogs bark, while cats meow. But even a toddler can distinguish dogs from other animals on the basis of visual information alone, and there are species of dogs that do not bark at all. Yet, despite being unable to define *dog* easily, neither you nor the 2-year-old has any difficulty recognizing many different types of dogs and cats. Conceptual behavior would seem to be a complex skill; yet, paradoxically, it develops quite rapidly and without great difficulty even in young children.

✖ INTERIM SUMMARY

Conceptual behavior occurs when humans respond to objects or events not because of their specific attributes but because of their membership in larger classes or categories. Our ability to respond to stimuli on the basis of category membership is most likely advantageous, as it allows for more economical processing of our surrounding world. Despite its apparent complexity, conceptual behavior may be well accounted for by standard processes of stimulus control.

✖ THOUGHT QUESTIONS

1. What does it mean to say that concept formation is an economical way to process information? What evidence suggests that humans acquire concepts nearly effortlessly?

2. How would you go about trying to teach a 2- or 3-year-old the difference between cows and horses? Can you identify distinguishing features that will always lead to proper categorization of these animals?

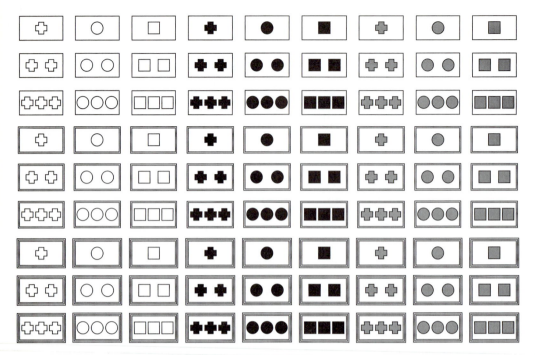

FIGURE 8.1 Stimuli Used by Bruner et al. (1956) to Study Concept Learning.

HUMAN CONCEPTUAL BEHAVIOR

Psychologists have been studying concept learning in humans for more than four decades, and the methods used have often rivaled in complexity the phenomenon itself. In perhaps the best-known study of concept formation, Bruner, Goodnow, and Austin (1956) presented participants with a series of 81 visual stimuli (Figure 8.1). Each stimulus contains four dimensions, with each dimension consisting of three attributes. The dimensions and accompanying shapes were as follows:

Shape: circle, square, cross

Color: red, green, black

Number of borders: one, two, three

Number of objects: one, two, three

In one version of the experiment, participants were asked whether a particular stimulus represented the concept that the experimenter had in mind. In other words, they had to guess which of 12 possible features (4 dimensions × 3 attributes) was correct or representative of the concept, while disregarding all other attributes. When participants responded to a stimulus that matched the correct attribute, the experimenter replied by saying yes. Incorrect responses led to a reply of no.

Bruner and his colleagues found that participants differed in the strategies they used to discover the correct concept. Some participants developed

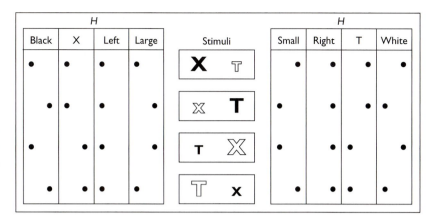

FIGURE 8.2 Concept Learning Stimuli and Corresponding Subject Hypotheses (*H*).
(From Levine, 1969.)

what the researchers called a **wholist strategy,** in which all attributes of the stimulus associated with a yes response were remembered. For example, let's assume I say that a stimulus containing three red squares encircled by one border is an instance of the concept, and the experimenter confirms this guess. If on the next stimulus, one of these attributes is missing but the stimulus is identified as an instance of the concept, my new concept will include only those features that were common to both stimuli. That is, I retain what worked from my first guess and what has been added to it on the second trial. The researchers suggest that this is an effective strategy, especially when the participant is placed under a time restriction to identify the concept. It is effective probably because all of the attributes from the first response can be considered simultaneously on each trial.

> **wholist strategy**
> responding to all attributes of a conceptual class or category

In contrast, the **partist strategy** involves focusing on only one attribute when a guess is confirmed by the experimenter. In the previous example, after being told yes on my first response, I may guess that red is the relevant attribute. If so, I will state that the next stimulus is an instance of the concept only if it contains red figures, regardless of whether all of the other attributes differ from the first stimulus. According to Bruner and colleagues (1956), this strategy will work, but it is more challenging because it requires that I keep in mind each previous hypothesis, so as not to repeat those that have been ineffective.

> **partist strategy**
> focusing on a single attribute of a conceptual class or category

Note that in the experiment just described, participants are said to make guesses, or form hypotheses, about the relevant dimension. The notion that concept learning involves hypothesis testing is a central assumption for some researchers (Levine, 1969, 1975; Livingston & Andrews, 1995). In a series of experiments, Levine demonstrated that human participants do indeed test hypotheses during simple discrimination tasks. In a typical experiment, participants were presented with a set of stimulus cards like those shown in Figure 8.2. As you can see, each card contains both a letter *X* and a letter *T*. The two letters also differ on three other dimensions, including size (large-small), shading (black-white), and position on the card (left-right). Participants were told to say the name of the letter they believed was correct over a series of trials. The correct dimension—either letter, size, color, or position—was chosen arbitrarily by the experimenter before the experiment began.

Suppose the correct dimension is *black*. As a participant, your task is to identify this correct dimension and then respond to this dimension on each card, disregarding the letter, size, or position of the black stimulus. If you respond to a letter that is not black, the experimenter reports that the response is incorrect. If, on the other hand, you respond to the letter that is black, regardless of all other dimensions, the experimenter reports that the response is correct.

You might ask, "How did Levine know which hypothesis the participant was using when responding to the cards?" If you look at Figure 8.2, you will notice that if the cards are presented in the order depicted, certain patterns of responding are peculiar to each possible hypothesis. Let's say that you chose *black* as the hypothesis. If presented with the cards in sequence from top to bottom in Figure 8.2, you should respond to the letters *X, T, T, X*, in that order. In order to ascertain a participant's hypothesis, Levine ran several series of what he called "blank trials," during which the participant received no feedback about the hypothesis. It was nevertheless easy to tell which hypothesis a participant had used during these blank trials, as each hypothesis produced a distinct response pattern. In the figure, the columns containing black dots represent the sequences of responses that participants would have emitted given the several possible hypotheses. Levine found that participants maintained a specific hypothesis until they had received negative or disconfirming feedback from the experimenter. When they were told their response was correct, participants again tended to keep the same hypothesis until such time that the hypothesis was disconfirmed by the experimenter. Similar results have been obtained from groups engaged in cooperative problem-solving tasks (Laughlin, Shupe, & Magley, 1998).

The idea that participants develop hypotheses that are then tested through feedback is a popular theory of conceptual behavior, but it is not without problems. Analyses of hypothesis testing have revealed a complex interaction between the subjects' stated hypotheses and feedback from the experimenter. There is still some disagreement, for instance, about whether confirmatory and disconfirmatory feedback play equivalent roles in shaping further hypotheses. In addition, participants are likely to forget hypotheses that they have tested as the experiment progresses, and this is especially true when the stimuli used consist of several dimensions (Kellogg, Robbins, & Bourne, 1978; Schroth, 1984). In Levine's experiments, participants tested hypotheses concerning only one dimension of the stimulus figures, such as size, shape, letter, or card position. Correct feedback in these experiments was based on whether this single dimension had been correctly identified. The experimental task could be made more difficult, though, if the participant had to identify a more complex concept. For example, on any particular series of trials, the experimenter might consider correct figures to be those that are both *large* and *black* meaning that responses to any figures not containing both features would be incorrect. This would be an example of a

conjunctive concept, because positive instances of the concept require the presence of both attributes.

On the other hand, the experimenter might require the participant to identify a **disjunctive concept,** defined by the presence of either one or the other of two dimensions. Using the same example, any figure that is either *large* or *black* would be considered a positive instance. Of course, ingenious experimenters can think up increasingly complex concepts. They could require participants to identify concepts that consist of a number of intricately related attributes, similar to the conditional discriminations discussed in previous chapters. Under these conditions, subjects must attend to two or more separate dimensions in order to successfully identify the concept. Several studies have shown that such conditional concepts can take many more trials to master than do simpler concepts (Bourne, 1970; Choi, McDaniel, & Busemeyer, 1993).

Natural Concepts and Hierarchical Organization

The discussion thus far has been limited to experiments in which human participants have been presented with relatively arbitrary geometric or pictorial stimuli and asked to make judgments about category membership. The responses of subjects are themselves easily classified as correct or incorrect because the parameters of the concept are predetermined by the researcher. Although there are procedural advantages to using arbitrary stimuli and unambiguous classification rules in such studies, the controlled laboratory environment limits the conclusions that can be drawn about how humans and other animals classify objects and events in their natural habitats. Identifying and responding effectively to an object as a *tool* or a *ball* is perhaps more representative of the kind of conceptual behavior psychologists wish to understand. Such natural categories, far from being predetermined and discrete, often have ambiguous boundaries, with members identified only on the basis of what the philosopher Wittgenstein (1953) called "family resemblances."

How do people make category judgments about the everyday objects encountered in their daily lives? Rosch and her colleagues have discovered that most people develop very similar categories for objects in the world and that these categories are arranged in a hierarchical fashion (Rosch, Mervis, Gray, Johnson, & Boyes-Braem, 1976; Rosch, Simpson, & Miller, 1976). Let's take a look at how this works, according to Rosch.

Superordinate Level   The **superordinate level** of any concept is the most generic or inclusive level of the concept. An example of a concept at this level is that of *tool*. People recognize that this category label refers to all implements that help to achieve some task, such as writing a paper, digging a hole, building a bridge, or cooking dinner. People use all sorts of tools, including pens and pencils, hammers, drills, screwdrivers, scissors, and others to achieve these objectives. It would take a long time to name all of the objects that belong to the category *tool*. Thus, were a friend to ask you to bring him or her a tool, how would you respond to such a request? Is a request at this level helpful? Is the friend asking for a hammer? A wrench? An electric beater? A stapler?

Basic Level   In reality, your friend would probably not simply request a tool, but would specify the kind of tool. If he or she asks for a hammer, wrench, electric beater, or stapler, the request seems more informative, not to mention more helpful. You are in a much better position to assist your friend if you have this information. Rosch claims that this enhanced and more specific information represents the **basic level** of the concept *tool*. All of these individual objects belong to the larger concept *tool*, but they are particular types of tools, useful for different types of tasks.

basic level   the most useful level of a concept, characterized by neither too much nor too little information

Subordinate Level   It is possible that your friend might ask for a sledgehammer, a pipe wrench, a five-speed hand mixer, or a pocket-size stapler. These requests would be almost as unlikely as the request for a tool, but for different reasons. For many circumstances, it isn't necessary to provide this kind of detailed information. At the **subordinate level**, concepts are highly specific and often add little information to what has already been communicated by the basic level.

subordinate level the most restrictive, specific level of a conceptual category

Notice that this hierarchical arrangement can be used to characterize many natural concepts, not just that of *tool*. Table 8.2 depicts other examples of everyday concepts and some exemplars at the superordinate, basic, and subordinate levels, respectively. According to Rosch, what is interesting about this hierarchical arrangement is that some levels provide more information than others and consequently ought to be more useful. Indeed, a number of studies suggest that people often operate at the basic level of concepts. As noted in the preceding example, your friend is not likely to ask either for something as vague as a tool (superordinate) or something as specific as a 16-lb. sledgehammer (subordinate). Rather, the request is more likely to be made at the basic level, where there is considerably more information than at the superordinate level, but not as much information as at the subordinate level. The request for a hammer occurs at this basic level. Perhaps some additional examples will clarify why Rosch believes that people operate more efficiently and frequently at this basic level.

If you were asked right now to name the object in which you are seated, how would you reply? Would you say that you are seated in a piece of furniture? This would be a rather odd reply, wouldn't it? Although correct, it would probably seem puzzling to those who heard it. On the other hand, you would probably not say that you were seated in a Lazy-Boy recliner, though this too may be entirely true. Most likely, you would say that you are sitting in a chair. This reply, representing the basic level of the concept *furniture*, conveys just enough specific information without providing unneeded detail.

Rosch and her associates have demonstrated that basic level concepts have more in common than do superordinate level concepts and that not much additional information is gained at the subordinate level (Rosch et al., 1976). For example, do hammers, wrenches, screwdrivers, electric mixers, and staplers share many common features? Not really, other than member-

TABLE 8.2 HIERARCHICAL ARRANGEMENT OF NATURAL CONCEPTS

Superordinate Level	Basic Level	Subordinate Level
Food	Meat	Hamburger, fish, chicken
	Fruit	Apple, orange, banana
	Grain	Bread, cracker, oatmeal
Tool	Wrench	Socket, pipe, Crescent
	Hammer	Sledge, ball-peen
	Screwdriver	Phillips, slotted
Clothing	Hat	Derby, fedora, cowboy
	Shirt	Polo, dress, flannel
	Pants	Jeans, dress, bell bottoms

ship in the larger category of *tool*. Notice, however, that within any one of these basic level categories, say *hammer*, commonalities do emerge. All hammers are used for striking other objects. Moreover, this commonality doesn't disappear on the subordinate level, though there are differences in shape and some other uses between, say, sledgehammers and ball-peen hammers.

Also interesting is the fact that physical movements in relation to certain objects are more similar at the basic level than at the superordinate level. For example, the movements necessary to put on a shirt differ from those used to put on a pair of pants. Of course, both shirts and pants represent basic level members of the superordinate concept *clothing*, but here the similarity ends. Putting on a shirt is a fairly uniform act, regardless of whether it's a dress shirt or a casual shirt. Thus, most shirts are put on in a similar way—but in a different way from that used to put on a pair of pants. Similarly, using a hammer involves essentially the same movements, regardless of the type of hammer, but these movements are not the same as those entailed in the proper use of a wrench. Thus, there seems to be ample evidence that under many circumstances, people operate most comfortably at the basic level of a concept, rather than at higher or lower levels of the concept.

Concepts as Prototypes

If you were asked to say the name of a type of bird as quickly as you can, which of the many thousands of species would you name? Do you think you would be more likely to say robin than penguin? Suppose you were read a list of the following words: car, truck, plane, unicycle, elevator. After each word is read, you are asked to decide as quickly as possible whether or not the object is a vehicle. Would you find some of these judgments easier than others? Research demonstrates that some members of a category seem to be better examples of the concept than others, perhaps because they are more typical. In other words, you would be more likely to come up with robin or canary as an example of a bird than either penguin or ostrich (Barsalou, 1985; Barsalou & Sewell, 1985). You would also classify car, truck, and plane more readily than unicycle and elevator as examples of vehicles (McCloskey & Glucksberg, 1979; Rosch, Simpson, & Miller, 1976). These kinds of findings support the idea that concepts are arranged hierarchically and that certain members of each category are more readily accessible to working memory.

prototype a member of a conceptual category exhibiting a collection of typical features or attributes

These findings are often taken as evidence that many concepts consist of a **prototype**, or a member of the larger class that seems most typical or representative of the concept. For most people, a robin is a prototypical bird, in that they are more likely to think of it as being birdlike than either a penguin or an ostrich. According to prototype theory, when people encounter unfamiliar objects, the task of classifying the object first involves consulting the prototype. Whether they ultimately classify the object as a member of the particular concept depends upon how well the object matches their prototype for that object. Naturally, some objects match a prototype better than others. In the previous example of vehicles, the term *elevator* is to be considered as a possible type of vehicle. However, your concept of *vehicle* probably utilizes a more common example as a prototype, perhaps a car. In deciding whether an elevator is a vehicle, then, you compare the elevator to your car prototype. Notice that, in this case, the structural or physical similarities between car and elevator are pretty minimal. Yet both are devices used to get from one place to another. Thus, you might conclude that an elevator is indeed an example of a vehicle, though not as good an example as a car. According to proponents of prototype theory, members of a concept share many "family resemblances," despite their sometimes superficial differences.

The major limitation of prototype theory is its inability to explain how members differing substantially from the prototype come to be included in the larger category or concept. Continuing the same example, your prototype for *vehicle* is car, yet you understand that an elevator may also belong to this category. Indeed, sometimes objects that clearly belong in a category show little or no resemblance to the prototype, yet they are properly classified. Perhaps you have an old shoe that, having seen better days, now serves as a chew toy for the family dog. The appearance of the shoe will quite obviously change as the dog begins to chew and tear away bits and pieces. But at what point is it no longer recognizable as your shoe? Chances are, even when there is not much more left than the sole and part of the heel, most people would still see it as a shoe. This is a remarkable perceptual feat when you consider that the object no longer comes close to matching the prototype of *shoe*. On the other hand, there are times when objects bear a remarkable resemblance to a prototype, but do not belong in the conceptual category. A counterfeit bill is a good example. A good counterfeit bill is one that so strongly resembles a real bill that it is treated as legal tender. Yet it is not real nor does it belong, technically, to the concept of *money*.

Despite the inherent difficulty of classifying atypical objects, there appear to be advantages to appealing to prototypes. One advantage is the cognitive economy that they afford—prototypes may be efficient means of classifying otherwise unmanageable amounts of information. In any particular situation, drawing upon the prototype may be useful, because it shares

FIGURE 8.3 Examples of Members of the Conceptual Category *dog*.

certain critical features with the object of concern. Although people can change their response to an object if the prototype proves to be wrong, use of the prototype is an economical way of classifying an object when it is first encountered. Human stereotypes, such as ethnic and gender stereotypes, may reflect this tendency to classify information. You might, for instance, possess a stereotype of *college professor* that includes such descriptors as *intellectual, authoritative, rigid,* and *conservative.* Although this description is certainly untrue of many professors, it may serve as a prototype against which to evaluate individual members of this category. Despite the fact that such stereotypes often prove wrong and lead to unfortunate prejudice and discrimination, they may function to reduce and make manageable large amounts of social information (Andersen & Klatzky, 1987; Fiske & Neuberg, 1990; Krebs & Denton, 1997).

The Exemplar Approach to Concepts

Some researchers believe that when people attempt to classify novel objects, they don't always use prototypes as comparison stimuli (Fodor & Lepore, 1996). Instead, they rely on actual, specific objects with which they are familiar. These well-known objects are called **exemplars** because they represent particular examples, not averaged combinations, of category members. All of the items in Figure 8.3 belong to the larger category *dog.* If you were asked to imagine the concept of *dog,* do you think you would come up with

exemplar a specific example or member of a larger category or conceptual class

any of these particular members? Notice that prototype theory would predict that your image would not be of any one of these specific dogs, but it would probably possess features common to many of them. Exemplar theory, on the other hand, predicts that you might come up with one of the specific members depicted in the figure, be it a German shepherd, a Chihuahua, or some other breed. What does research have to say about the validity of exemplar theory?

Dopkins and Gleason (1997) conducted a study in which participants classified visual stimuli into one of two categories and received feedback from the researcher regarding correct and incorrect classification. In a generalization phase of the study, participants classified novel stimuli. Participants were more likely to assign novel stimuli to categories resembling an exemplar than a prototype of the original stimuli. Other researchers have also demonstrated that there are occasions when people use specific exemplars as comparison stimuli (Brooks, 1987; Hintzman, 1986; Medin, Altom, Edelson, & Freko, 1982; Myers, Lohmeier, & Well, 1994; Vandierendonck, 1995). What isn't yet clear from research is why people would utilize, in any particular case, an exemplar approach rather than a prototype, or vice versa. Let's speculate on how you might have responded to the example in Figure 8.3. Perhaps whether you conjured up an average prototype of *dog* or a clear image of a German shepherd may be due to whether you are a dog owner. If so, it would hardly be surprising if you immediately visualized your own dog, rather than a generalized prototype. Keep in mind that prototype theory and exemplar theory do make one similar assumption, namely, that people make a direct comparison between the new, unfamiliar object and a familiar model, be it an average prototype or a specific exemplar.

The final word on concept formation by prototype or exemplar is certainly not in. In fact, classification of novel stimuli may occur based not so much on similarity of the object to a prototype or exemplar, but on the basis of a verbal rule for classification. Smith, Patalano, and Jonides (1998) present evidence from neuroimaging experiments suggesting that rule-based classification and classification based on visual similarity involve different neural circuits. Indeed, the neurological underpinnings of concept learning have become a major focus of contemporary research, and this is the topic of the next section.

Concepts as Neural Networks

Recall that cognitive psychologists frequently use machines, especially computers, as models for explaining human learning and behavior. However, using the computer as a metaphor for the human mind has its shortcomings. In addition to the fact that the computer is an electronic machine and the brain an organic structure, the way that each processes information may differ in important ways. Computers, for example, are designed to process information sequentially. Information in the computer must be taken in steps through successive processing stages before a solution emerges. Of course, today's powerful computers can process information, including complicated mathematical equations, at nearly inconceivable speed. For example, try solving the following problem without the aid of a calculator:

$$3{,}875 \times 401{,}899 \times 64.5567 = x$$

In the few milliseconds it would take a computer to solve this problem, you and I might have just begun to reach for the paper and pencil we would need to carry out this calculation.

The human brain consists of billions of individual nerve cells, called neurons, connected in intricate, labyrinthine networks. At any given moment, many of these networks are active, processing information simultaneously. For this reason, scientists often call the brain a *parallel processor*, because humans don't process information sequentially like computers. It is this parallel processing that allows us to engage in simple activities, such as driving a car and holding a conversation, at the same time. As it turns out, even the most sophisticated and powerful computers fail at some of the more mundane tasks that you and I carry out with little conscious effort every day.

Increasingly, cognitive psychologists have begun to explain human cognition and behavior by appealing to the physical properties of the "machine" known as the human nervous system. An example of this practice is the **neural network model,** which attempts to account for some cognitive or behavioral phenomena by describing possible connections between various groups of neurons in the brain. Although neural networks have been proposed to explain a wide array of learning and cognitive abilities (Tryon, 1993), this discussion will focus on their application to the complex task of concept formation.

neural network model cognitive theory suggesting that concepts consist of various excitatory connections between neurons or groups of neurons

Because a neural network model is a physiological explanation, the level at which it attempts to explain a behavioral phenomenon is necessarily that of the individual neuron or groups of neurons. Remember, though, that an explanation at a physiological level does not automatically discount explanations at other levels. Neural network models can be viewed as attempts to describe the fundamental physiological happenings that must always accompany the learning process, not necessarily as alternative explanations of these phenomena. For example, suppose in the middle of a lively conversation with your professor, you unwittingly let slip a particularly juicy obscenity that you would not ordinarily air in such company. Upon realizing your indiscretion, you respond with understandable embarrassment, your face blushing a deep crimson. What causes the sudden flush of color in your cheeks? One cause is the social context. In a different setting, such as your dorm room, the same verbalization would probably lead to no embarrassment at all. In fact, it might produce some backslapping and looks of approval from your roommates. At a strictly physiological level, however, the red tinge in your face is the result of increased blood flow to small facial capillaries. Clearly, neither one of these explanations is incorrect. They do, however, utilize different facts and describe different aspects of the same happening. As long as you understand that they are descriptions of events at different levels of observation, you are not likely to be confused by their apparent differences.

The essence of neural network explanations is that connections between neurons or groups of neurons are either strengthened or weakened during the learning process (Goldstone, 1996; Nosofsky, Kruschke, & McKinley, 1992). Perhaps a specific example will illustrate how this might happen. Suppose that, in a standard learning experiment, an animal learns to respond to a red stimulus light. For purposes of this example, it doesn't matter whether the experiment is a Pavlovian or an operant learning situation. In fact, part of the appeal of neural network models is their apparent ability to account for diverse kinds of learning phenomena.

During the conditioning process, the light becomes predictive of something important in the experiment. In the case of a Pavlovian conditioning experiment, the red light may be followed by food directly, and, in the operant experiment, pressing a lever in the presence of the light may produce food. In either case, the red light eventually comes to stimulate activity in a particular neuron or group of neurons. These neurons, in turn, become associated with a specific response (either salivation or lever pressing). Over time, the association between the red light and the neural activity responsible for the response reaches a maximum strength. Thus, whenever the animal is presented with the light, it engages in the correct response. The major tenet of neural network models is that the connection that develops can be seen as a physiological event, not just a correlation between a stimulus and a response.

According to several researchers, neural network models can account quite well for human conceptual behavior. Much of the research conducted to test this belief has involved computer programs designed to simulate neural network models presented with concept formation tasks. The basic idea behind these models is that neurons or groups of neurons in the network respond differentially to aspects of a given concept or stimulus (Jones, Wills, & McLaren, 1998). Recognition of a concept such as *dog*, for example, depends upon a particular pattern of activity within the neural network. An important claim made by neural network theorists is that only certain features of a given concept are necessary to stimulate the proper collection of neurons. In other words, although the concept of *dog* may include many details, such as fur, tail, four legs, and barking, not all of these features are required for the network to recognize an instance of the class *dog*. However, the pattern of neural activity produced by a dog stimulus must necessarily be different from the neural activity produced by a cat stimulus. Clearly, these two stimuli will produce some overlap in the neural activity they elicit, as the two concepts share several attributes.

Neural network models, as simulated by computer programs, do a reasonably good job of differentiating between such concepts as *dog, cat,* and, of all things, *bagel* (McClelland & Rummelhart, 1985). In fact, in some instances, neural network models appear to account for learning phenomena at least as well as the highly influential Rescorla-Wagner model discussed in Chapter 3 (Gluck & Bower, 1988; Gluck & Thompson, 1987; Kehoe, 1988). In addition, contemporary models attempt to predict concept learning regardless of whether such learning is driven by prototypes, exemplars, or verbal rules (Erickson & Kruschke, 1998; Milliken, 1998). Regardless of which theoretical model researchers endorse, a primary function of concepts seems to be their usefulness in reducing large amounts of information into manageable packages.

✖ INTERIM SUMMARY

Rosch has demonstrated that people organize natural concepts in a hierarchical arrangement based upon the amount of specific information contained in each category member. People tend to use concepts that impart a moderate amount of information, being neither too vague nor too specific. They also classify novel or unfamiliar objects according to their similarity either to average prototypes or to specific examples of already existing category members. Recent cognitive theory has proposed that conceptual behavior can best be accounted for through the understanding of excitatory connections between neurons.

✖ THOUGHT QUESTIONS

1. For each of the following category labels, what would you consider to be the most prototypical member of each category? Least prototypical?

   Tool   Clothing   Fruit   Game   Vehicle   Machine

2. Can you identify superordinate, basic, and subordinate levels for the concept *vehicle*? In what way are basic members of this category alike while being different from superordinate and subordinate members?

CONCEPTUAL BEHAVIOR IN NONHUMAN ANIMALS

At this point in the book, you won't be surprised to learn that many psychologists consider nonhuman animals capable of conceptual behavior. In fact, many chapters have already shown that advances in technology and experimental procedures have put researchers in a position to ask some provocative and important questions about learning and cognition in nonhuman organisms. The study of concept formation in nonhuman species occupies a central position in the modern animal cognition literature (Commons, Herrnstein, Kosslyn, & Mumford, 1990; Wasserman, 1993). This current development can be traced to somewhat distant events in the history of learning. This part of the chapter describes the historical literature and evaluates what the prospects for understanding animal conceptual behavior appear to be from the current perspective.

Harlow's Research on Learning Sets

During the 1940s and 1950s, comparative psychologist Harry Harlow conducted a series of classic experiments on learning. Although Harlow is perhaps best known for his developmental research on isolation and maternal deprivation in rhesus monkeys, he also provided some crucial data on learning curves and the nature of generalization, discrimination, and problem solving. Although his work is not generally identified with the literature on concept formation, the tasks he presented to his participants are remarkably like those used by concept formation researchers today.

The layout of Harlow's experiments resembles the delayed-matching-to-sample (DMTS) procedure used by animal researchers today (described in Chapter 7). Essentially, in Harlow's experiments, a monkey was presented with two stimulus objects. Responding to one object produced a food reinforcer, while responding to the other object resulted in no food and an intertrial interval. On the next trial, reinforcement was delivered only if the animal responded to the same or a matching stimulus. Harlow also conducted experiments on oddity matching, in which reinforcement was delivered only when a response was made to the object that did not match the previous stimulus. Consistent with much of the literature on animal and human learning, Harlow (1949) discovered that these relatively simple discriminations (identity and oddity matching) developed only after numerous trials. These findings are not particularly noteworthy by themselves, nor do they bear much relevance to conceptual behavior. But Harlow went further than this, and the importance of what he found will become apparent if you remember that concept learning involves abstraction or generalization.

Once an animal has learned a discrimination, how rapidly will it acquire a new discrimination involving novel stimuli? For example, if a monkey has first learned to respond to whatever object does not match a triangle, what happens if it is asked to respond to any object that is not a circle? Would you expect this discrimination to take as long to form as the first one? If so, you would be wrong. Harlow showed that when exposed to several discrimination tasks, the amount of time needed to master each new task decreased substantially. In fact, a well-trained animal will make a minimum of errors, perhaps only one, when confronted with a new discrimination task (Bailey & Thomas, 1998).

learning set application of previously learned rules or responses to novel circumstances

Psychologists refer to this ability to apply what has been learned earlier to novel circumstances as a **learning set.** Perhaps most important, at least in regard to concept formation, is that learning sets seem to represent an abstraction, or a rule that can be applied to any setting, regardless of the details of that setting (Rumbaugh, 1997). In a very real sense, students may be the master of the learning set, sometimes also referred to as "learning to learn." This is true because the academic success of a student depends upon being able to adapt quickly to changing requirements, from semester to semester. This is not as true of many people in the workforce, for example, whose duties, once mastered, become rather mundane and predictable routines.

Think for a moment how much your success as a student depends on this ability to adapt quickly to new academic challenges. Each semester you are introduced to new instructors, new course content, and new grading requirements. Your job, as a student, is to find out as much as you can, and as quickly as possible, about what you need to do to succeed in each course. This is a tall order for a number of reasons. First, instructors are often very different: Some encourage a great deal of class participation and assign grades accordingly; some instructors use multiple-choice exams, and others use essay exams; some offer extra credit, and others don't; some expect students to memorize and recite information verbatim, and others require students to think creatively and apply information; some give final exams, and some don't; some differ dramatically in their lecture and class presentation styles.

Students must also adapt to differing course contents, particularly at liberal arts colleges and universities where they may be taking history, English, physics, psychology, art, and math, all in one semester. In addition, the presentation of information, in texts and other sources, may vary considerably as well. In short, the adaptive success of the student is largely dependent on an ability to rapidly identify studying and preparation strategies that will prove effective across several "course environments."

Whether you are aware of it or not, you figured out, probably during high school or early in your college years, how to make these adjustments in order to succeed academically. Indeed, colleges and universities are increasingly recognizing the importance of assisting students in developing such skills, sometimes even offering minimal course credit for a class that deals specifically with such strategies. The university where I work, for instance, requires all first-year students to take a course titled Successful Student Strategies, which focuses on such skills as note taking, textbook reading and highlighting, active studying, test taking, and other habits considered necessary to the college student's success. Though not advertised explicitly as such, the course is really an exercise in enhancing the capacity for learning to learn, which is, after all, the lifeblood of the college student.

The Transposition Effect

In 1939, Wolfgang Kohler presented chickens with an interesting discrimination task. The animals were shown two visual stimuli, one a relatively light shade of gray, the other a darker gray. Pecks to the lighter stimulus were reinforced, while pecks to the darker stimulus were not reinforced. After this discrimination had been learned, Kohler presented the animals with a new choice. In the new task, the positive, or reinforced, stimulus from the first task was presented alongside a new, even lighter stimulus. To which stimulus did the birds respond? Surprisingly, the chickens responded not to the positive stimulus from the earlier discrimination, but to the brand-new, lighter gray stimulus. This finding puzzled researchers, for it was assumed that in discrimination tasks the organism is learning to identify the specific stimulus associated with reinforcement and, alternatively, the stimulus not associated with reinforcement.

Kohler's study, however, seemed to suggest that it is not the absolute characteristic of either stimulus that controls responding in a discrimination task, but the relative difference between the two stimuli. In other words, discriminations might be formed on the basis of the relationship between the stimuli. On any particular trial, the *larger* or *smaller*, or *lighter* or *darker*, stimulus may control responding. In Kohler's (1939) study, the *lighter* stimulus changes from one trial to another, so responding does not always occur to the same stimulus, even if responses to that stimulus had previously produced reinforcement. This phenomenon has been called the **transposition effect**, because the organism is said to *transpose* the relationship between the first two stimuli to later stimulus pairs. The transposition effect has been demonstrated

transposition effect responding to a relationship between two stimuli rather than to discrete characteristics of either stimulus

for many species, including humans, and across a large array of visual stimuli (Alberts & Ehrenfreund, 1951; Ehrenfreund, 1952; Kuenne, 1946; Pasnak & Kurtz, 1987; Schusterman & Krieger, 1986; Sugimura, 1985).

Transposition, like the phenomenon of learning sets, represents an application of a general rule to novel circumstances, thus it strongly invites comparison with the process of concept formation. You may recall that many animal researchers believe that in traditional learning and discrimination tasks, animals are acquiring not situationally specific responses, but problem-solving strategies appropriate under numerous conditions. If the participant learns the rule "Choose the larger stimulus," this rule can then be applied to any collection of stimuli, regardless of other stimulus dimensions, such as color, shape, and so on. In this case, responding is controlled not by the *correct* stimulus itself, but by the relationship between this stimulus and the alternatives. In addition, learning a generalizable rule is more economical and thus more adaptive than having to memorize details across varied circumstances.

Conceptual Behavior as Abstract Stimulus Control

Throughout this book you have seen a number of instances in which the same behavioral phenomenon has received different empirical and theoretical treatment from psychologists of varying conceptual orientations. The study of conceptual behavior has historically been viewed as part of the subject matter of cognitive psychology; thus most of the research methodology and language that have characterized the study of concept learning have been informed by cognitive epistemology. Indeed, the very idea that organisms acquire concepts suggests that an explanation of concept learning must ultimately turn inward to an assessment of the information processing features of the organism, and this has long been the primary research goal of cognitive psychology.

Yet, complex behavior does not necessarily require similarly complex machinery. In fact, many kinds of physical systems and processes, including biological evolution, draw upon a few relatively simple operating principles to bring about tremendous complexity. As mentioned early in this chapter, the magnitude of biological diversity characterizing life on earth is as yet unmeasured by scientists. Nevertheless, this tremendous morphological variability has come about chiefly as a result of two fundamental processes— genetic variation and natural selection—interacting dynamically over millions of years. Even neural network theories of information processing systems suggest that the complexity of the operating system is actually invoked by parallel, interactive communication of relatively simple connectionist units. Thus, there is ample precedent in science for utilizing simple, well-understood principles to explain what appears to be more sophisticated phenomena. Conceptual behavior would seem to be a good candidate for such an analysis, given its complicated dimensions—remember the idea of teaching a 2-year-old how cats and dogs differ? The question arises, then, as to whether concept learning requires a new set of processes or if it can instead be explained in terms of well-known principles of behavior.

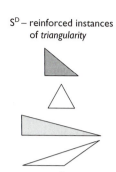

S^D – reinforced instances
of *triangularity*

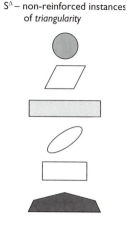

S^Δ – non-reinforced instances
of *triangularity*

FIGURE 8.4 Stimuli Used to Condition the Concept of *triangularity* in Pigeons. (From Ferster & Culbertson, 1982.)

As it turns out, behavioral psychologists have argued that concept learning needn't be viewed as a special class of behavior, requiring additional explanatory schemes. Rather, it may very well be that conceptual behavior emerges from the same fundamental principles that have proven effective in accounting for other aspects of humans' behavioral repertoire. This argument is somewhat compelling in light of the comparisons that can be made between concept learning experiments and the traditional stimulus control literature (Fields, Reeve, Adams, & Verhave, 1991). Howard (2000) has argued that concept learning does represent a form of stimulus generalization and is therefore understandable from a basic learning perspective.

To appreciate how concept learning may be regarded as an instance of stimulus control, consider the effort by Ferster and Culbertson (1982) to bring a pigeon's key-pecking behavior under control of the abstract concept of *triangularity*. In less precise but functional ordinary language, it can be said that a participant, be it human or nonhuman animal, has developed the concept of *triangularity* if it can respond effectively to all instances of triangles, regardless of size, orientation, color, or any other irrelevant dimension. Figure 8.4 shows some of the geometric stimuli that might be used to test whether a participant can acquire the concept of *triangularity*. Notice that the stimuli on the left include many figures that meet the technical definition of a triangle—a closed, three-sided figure whose angles sum to 180 degrees. However, in every other respect, these triangles differ from one another: They represent varying sizes, shades, and orientations. On the right side of the figure are examples of nontriangular geometric shapes, including squares, circles, and rectangles. Notice that these shapes resemble the triangles in size, shading, and orientation but not on the formal requirements for *triangularity*.

The procedures used to bring the participant's behavior under the control of *triangularity* are those discussed in previous chapters on stimulus control. The geometric stimuli, triangles and nontriangles alike, are presented on a translucent key in random order, so that the sequence of stimulus presentations cannot be the discriminative stimulus controlling responding.

Whenever a triangle is projected on the key, pecks to the key produce reinforcement. Pecks to any other geometric figure, regardless of size, shading, or orientation, produce a temporary blackout of the experimental chamber and no reinforcement. Because this procedure involves many stimuli, both similar and different from one another on several dimensions, the experimenter would expect discriminative control to take considerable time to develop. Nevertheless, with sufficient exposure to these conditions, a pigeon will eventually come to respond only to those figures meeting the formal requirements for *triangularity* and will not respond to other figures.

Of course, this might merely be a case of discriminative behavior, in that the participant might have memorized which stimuli are triangles and which are not. The test for a concept of *triangularity*, however, comes when the animal is presented with a new series of stimuli, both triangular and nontriangular, that it has never encountered. If the animal has acquired the concept of *triangularity*, it should respond to novel instances of triangles and not to novel nontriangular stimuli. This is, in fact, what happens. By responding to novel instances of triangles, the animal is demonstrating that it isn't a particular triangle or stimulus that controls responding, but a broader abstraction that could be called *triangularity*.

Ferster and Culbertson (1982) argue that this behavior is best described as an example of control by an "abstract property of a stimulus" (p. 201). They believe that this is a more useful description of conceptual behavior because it draws attention to an objective feature of the environment rather than to purportedly internal processes in the participant. To many researchers, especially behavior analysts, this type of explanation is more parsimonious, in that it uses a minimum number of well-defined concepts (for example, differential reinforcement, generalization, and discrimination) to explain a fairly complex behavior. Let's now examine whether this account of stimulus control can be extended to explain nonhuman conceptual behavior in more natural settings.

In an experiment on natural concept learning, Lubow (1974) presented pigeons with 80 different slides made from aerial photographs. Forty of the slides were photographs of man-made objects, such as skylines and city streets, and 40 slides contained no man-made objects, depicting instead natural stimuli such as forests and lakes. Figure 8.5 shows some of the slides representing each category (man-made vs. not man-made). Responding to the slides depicting man-made objects (S^D) was reinforced by access to grain, and responses to the slides not containing man-made objects (S^Δ) resulted in an auditory tone but no food reinforcement. By the end of training, animals were responding reliably to the positive slides (man-made objects) but not to the negative slides (no man-made objects). In a follow-up generalization test, 10 novel slides (5 positive and 5 negative) were presented to the birds. Differential responding to the positive slides occurred above chance levels, indicating that the animals had generalized the concept of *man-made* to novel instances of this class.

Natural concept learning in pigeons has also been reported by Herrnstein and his associates (Herrnstein & deVilliers, 1980; Herrnstein, Loveland, & Cable, 1976), who demonstrated that key pecking in pigeons can come under the control of such "abstract" stimuli as trees, water, people, and fish. In their experiments, pigeons were presented with slides of photographs, some of which contained positive instances of a concept and others which did not. For example, in one such experiment, between 500 and 700 slides, some depicting trees and others not depicting trees, were projected on a response key. The tree photographs differed from one another markedly: There were pictures of whole trees and pictures of parts of trees, pictures of trees with leaves and others without leaves, pictures of large trees and small trees, and so on. The negative, or nontree, slides also differed from one another in a variety of ways, but differed from the tree slides only in that they contained no pictures of trees.

Using a standard discrimination procedure, the researchers showed that over time pigeons came to respond predominantly to the "correct" tree slides and little to slides not containing trees. In addition, they argue that the birds must have been developing a concept of *tree*, for it would have been highly unlikely that the birds could have memorized so many slides. Moreover, when a new series of both positive (tree) and negative (nontree) slides was presented, discriminative responding showed virtually no reduction. Similar results were obtained when slides of water or of a particular human being were used as positive instances.

Of course, one explanation of Herrnstein, Loveland, and Cable's (1976) findings might be that trees, water, and to some extent, people, represent innate concepts to the pigeon. In other words, it might be that trees, water, and people have been familiar aspects of the pigeon's environment for many generations. Thus, perhaps pigeons are highly prepared for phylogenetic reasons to recognize specific instances of these conceptual classes. This interpretation, however, shortchanges the pigeon, whose conceptual abilities appear somewhat more sophisticated.

Herrnstein and deVilliers (1980) showed that pigeons can develop the unlikely concept of *fish under water*. This is a remarkable finding because of the lack of any evolutionary pressures to facilitate the pigeon's familiarity with fish, especially those under water. It is probable that no pigeon has ever had the opportunity to view a fish from this perspective; in fact, for laboratory bred pigeons, it is impossible. Nevertheless, pigeons learned to respond discriminatively to this concept, including novel instances during a testing phase. The researchers also report that the *fish under water* concept required no more time to learn than did the presumably more natural concepts of *tree, water,* and *people*.

In support of both Lubow's (1974) and Herrnstein and deVillier's (1980) work, additional research has shown that pigeons are also capable of learning complex sample-comparison relationships in matching-to-sample tasks (Wright, 1997) and such artificial concepts as the letter *A* (Morgan, Fitch, Holman, & Lea, 1976). Similarly impressive findings have been reported by Pepperberg (1990, 1992) who argues that a gray parrot, Alex, acquired more than 70 same-different concepts and responded to novel instances of this concept across various stimulus dimensions, including color, shape, and action. Some researchers believe that such complex conceptual behavior must be due to the acquisition of a simple same-different rule that

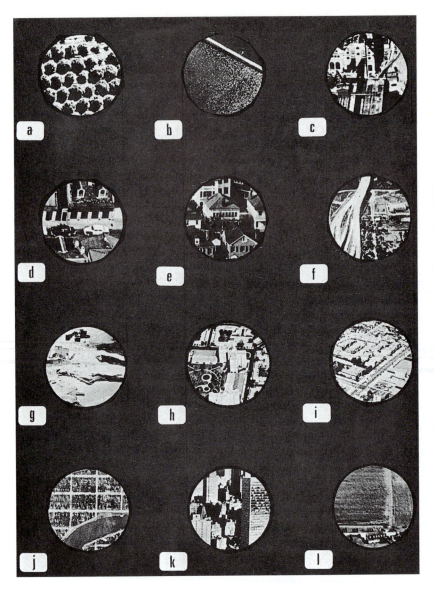

FIGURE 8.5 Positive Slides (S^D, *a–l*) and Negative Slides (S$^\Delta$, *m–x*).

can be successfully applied to large classes of novel stimuli differing along several dimensions (Cook, Katz, & Cavoto, 1997).

The ease with which even nonhuman subjects acquire fairly complex concepts seems to invite the observation that concept learning may be highly prepared behavior, perhaps for all species. Clearly, human infants must be ready to assimilate the many concepts that they will acquire, since most adults would be hard pressed to explain how to actively teach such concepts to children. In fact, primates, in general, appear especially gifted in this regard. Schrier and Brady (1987) found that rhesus monkeys mastered the

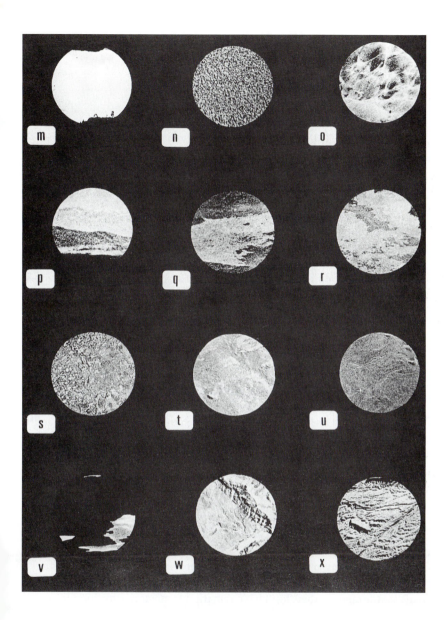

same human-nonhuman concept learning task demonstrated in pigeons but did it with many fewer trials than avian species. Oden, Thompson, and Premack (1990) report that infant chimpanzees (9–21 months of age) needed training on only one pair of same-different stimulus objects to be able to generalize this relationship to novel stimuli. These authors suggest that many natural concepts may be innately perceived and that training merely increases the animal's ability to utilize the concept for future benefit. The distinction may be similar to the human infant's ability to comprehend speech long before actively producing speech.

In sum, considerable work with various nonhuman species indicates that conceptual behavior is probably not a distinguishing feature of human cognition. In fact, the more sophisticated research methods become, the more astonishing the conceptual abilities of nonhuman animals appear. It may be that the ability to quickly parse objects in the environment into workable categories is so fundamentally necessary for adaptation that such an ability may be nearly universal in the animal kingdom. To date, researchers looking for conceptual abilities in nonhuman animals have seldom been disappointed.

✖ INTERIM SUMMARY

There is ample evidence that nonhuman animals can behave in ways easily interpreted as conceptual in nature. That many animal species respond to relationships between stimuli and to abstract characteristics of stimuli is apparent both in Harlow's and Kohler's demonstrations of learning sets and the transposition effect, respectively, as well as in the more contemporary literature on natural concepts. Thus, the evolution of conceptual behavior in many species may have afforded important advantages in the struggle to survive.

✖ THOUGHT QUESTIONS

1. Why do behavioral psychologists believe the processes of generalization and discrimination are relevant to the issue of concept formation? In what way is generalization like abstraction?

2. Do you believe that the process by which the pigeon in Herrnstein and deVillier's (1980) experiment learned the concept of *fish under water* is the same as the process by which the human infant learns the concept of *ball*? Why or why not?

THE ADAPTIVE NATURE OF CONCEPTUAL BEHAVIOR

In discussing many types of learning, this book emphasizes how important a particular behavior might be to the organism involved. For example, animals that forage for their food have remarkable memories for food locations that they have recently visited. This ability is understandable given their particular evolutionary history and environmental niche. Failing to remember such locations would seriously compromise this kind of animal's survival. Humans, too, have a particular evolutionary history, and it might be helpful to ask, "What do abstract categories, or concepts, do for us?" Do concepts help us deal more effectively with our environment? You may not be able to recognize or name every type of dog that you encounter, but you understand that each is an example of a dog—and not a cat, mouse, or other type of animal. Why would this ability to group all members of a particular class of animals, tools, toys, or any other number of objects be useful to you?

Remember that humans are far from perfect as information processors. Our limitations include the fact that we can process or act upon only a limited amount of information at any given time. When faced with a situation in which some course of action or decision is required, we may not have access to all of the information that might be desirable. Nevertheless, it might be important to act promptly, even in the absence of comprehensive information. It is at times like this that concepts prove extremely useful, if not necessary, to adaptive functioning. If you encountered a snake in the forest, you could act appropriately by avoiding it even if you couldn't identify the particular species. It is important, though, that you recognize it as a snake, and not a dog or cat, for your reaction to either of these latter animals would be quite different. If you were a herpatologist, you might be able to identify the snake as an Eastern timber rattler, and although that would certainly enhance your knowledge of what you encountered, it might not lead to any different behavior.

In the same way, the 2-year-old described early in the chapter will presumably respond appropriately by rolling, throwing, or kicking the beach ball, despite never before having seen this type of ball. In other words, concepts help us to reduce large, burdensome amounts of information into smaller, more manageable chunks. This ability may be an especially adaptive trait in the information-rich environment of the modern technological world. Although our general tendency to group similar objects is probably an innate property of our mammalian nervous system, the specific categories we form and the members that constitute those categories probably arise from learning experiences, motivation, and personal convictions and beliefs.

Remember, too, that the tendency to categorize information is not limited to inanimate objects or things, despite a long history of laboratory research utilizing only these kinds of stimuli. Indeed, as a strongly social species, humans would be expected to classify information about the social world into meaningful categories as well. Sedikides, Olsen, and Reis (1993) have in fact shown that people readily classify individuals into such groupings as *married couple,* indicating that different kinds of social relationships may fall into natural categories. And social psychologists have long documented the ease with which we distinguish between the in-group, to which we belong, and the out-group, toward which we may direct all manner of ill will (Sherif, Harvey, White, Hood, & Sherif, 1961; Tajfel, 1982). In fact, even when individual subjects are assigned randomly to groups, feelings of group allegiance emerge almost immediately. It is almost as if humans, and perhaps other social species, inherently understand and value the concept of *group belongingness.* It appears, then, that the economy of arranging information categorically helps us to negotiate, not only the inanimate physical environment, but also the vast social networks that define us as a species.

CHAPTER NINE

Acquiring and Using Language

Sarah is 6 years old and, lacking the ability to speak, has never uttered a word. She is learning, however, to identify hundreds of plastic symbols that stand for everyday objects and actions. She communicates with others by placing the plastic symbols on a magnetized board in specific, vertically arranged orders. In the presence of several types of fruit, Sarah arranges her plastic "words" in such a way as to say, "Give Sarah apple." When offered the apple, Sarah sits contentedly and consumes her prize.

You may not find such behavior noteworthy, particularly if exhibited by a 6-year-old child. In fact, you would probably be most interested in learning what kind of disability rendered Sarah incapable of speech in the first place. But Sarah is not a child. She is a chimpanzee—one of several trained by psychologist David Premack—and her exploits are intriguing because they force researchers to entertain some potentially disturbing questions about human beings and the other animals with whom we share this planet. In particular, Sarah's behavior, as well as that of dozens of other chimpanzees, has implications for how psychologists think about language and the role it plays in the lives of humans and nonhuman animals.

One of the more interesting facts about humans is our apparent desire to distinguish ourselves from other animals. It would seem that recognizing the continuities that bind all animal life together is to admit something almost scandalous about ourselves. Consequently, much intellectual energy has been expended in defining the essential characteristics that make us *human,* and, alternatively, those that relegate other life-forms to the category of *animal.* It has been observed, for example, that at various times throughout history humans have been identified as hunter-gatherers, toolmakers, and language users—each one of these behaviors presumably setting us apart from our animal cousins (Strum, 1987).

Unfortunately, such a tidy classification system has proved inadequate, as all of these distinguishing characteristics have been seriously questioned as criteria for identifying what is uniquely human. The designation of humans as hunter-gatherers and toolmakers, for instance, has not stood up to the thorough field observations of Jane Goodall (1971), who for more than three decades has studied the chimpanzees native to the Gombe Stream Reserve in Africa. Goodall has amply documented not only instances of hunting and gathering among chimpanzees, but also an equally marvelous talent for fishing: Chimpanzees have been observed pulling small branches from trees, stripping them of their leaves, poking them into termite mounds, and fishing out what is apparently a delicacy to the chimpanzee.

In fact, tool use is widely practiced, even in animal species much less related to us than the chimpanzee. Some examples include sea otters using rocks to break open clams and other hard-shelled mollusks, Egyptian vultures dropping rocks from above to crack open the shells of ostrich eggs, and archer fish spitting water in concentrated streams to stun insect prey (Alcock, 1972; van Lawick-Goodall, 1970). It seems, then, that as research on nonhuman animal behavior progresses, drawing a clear line of demarcation between ourselves and the rest of the animal kingdom becomes more and more difficult.

All of this is not to say that humans do not differ in important ways from other animals. Most assuredly we do. This chapter examines what many scientists believe to be the best candidate for distinguishing humans from nonhumans—our capacity for language. Unraveling the mystery of language may be among the greatest of all challenges to behavioral science. Language is an immensely complex, yet subtle, and important form of human behavior. Researchers approach the study of language from a diverse range of theoretical and methodological persuasions. Despite this diversity, scientists have uncovered some fascinating regularities in the nature of language development and usage throughout the human community. The chapter examines these universal features as well as the process of language development in the individual human child. Also considered is the provocative hypothesis, embraced by some psychologists and primatologists, that language may not be unique to humans after all.

LANGUAGE FUNDAMENTALS

The Definitional Problem

The challenge of coming up with an acceptable definition of language is not merely an intellectual exercise; it has important implications for research and the kinds of conclusions researchers will ultimately draw about language and behavior. Indeed, as will become apparent in later sections of this chapter, much of the current debate about language in nonhuman species boils down to how language is defined. At a general level, however, there exists a surprising degree of consensus as to what defines a language. For most researchers, **language** represents a highly structured symbol system that allows for creative and meaningful communication between organisms. In addition, most linguists suggest that all human languages contain specific rules that speakers use to construct an unlimited number of utterances out of the finite set of sounds that characterize any natural language.

language a highly structured symbol system that allows for creative and meaningful communication between organisms

There are, of course, forms of communication throughout the animal kingdom that would not be considered linguistic. For example, vervet monkeys in the wild often emit vocal alarm calls in response to the presence of predators, and these calls differ in sound quality depending upon whether the predator is airborne or on the ground. Monkeys who have not seen the predator, but have heard the alarm calls, respond appropriately by escaping to the nearest cover (Figure 9.1; Seyfarth & Cheney, 1992). What makes this communication symbolic is that the alarm calls function to designate or refer to the approaching predator. In other words, a symbol is a stimulus (usually appearing visually or auditorally) that stands for or refers to some other stimulus. Thus, much animal communication in the wild is clearly symbolic, though many scientists do not consider it to have all the properties of human language. Such communicative efforts tend to be highly specific, showing little variability from one occurrence to the next. Also, such behaviors tend to occur under limited and predictable stimulus conditions in the environment, and, this doesn't seem to characterize human language. Distinguishing language from other forms of communication is a complex issue, and, as discussed later in the chapter, some experts believe that non-human animals are capable of linguistic feats that approach the level of sophistication seen in human language.

Language Development and Universals

Scientific attempts to understand any natural phenomenon usually include the development of a technical vocabulary and formal postulates or theories. However, researchers often disagree about the nature of theory and vocabulary as applied to the phenomenon of interest, and the study of language is no exception. Given the considerable disharmony characterizing research and theory in language acquisition, it would be tempting to claim that next to nothing is known about this presumably most important of human behaviors. But such pessimism would be unjustified. Remember that science begins with observation, and one can collect volumes of empirical information about a subject matter regardless of whether or not a theoretical system exists for explaining these data. Fortunately, both past and present students of human behavior have taken seriously the task of documenting the nature of language acquisition in humans. The following discussion will put aside the problem of theory building and explore some facts about language of which scientists are quite certain.

Among the most interesting characteristics of human language are what scientists call *universals*. Universals are those features of language that appear to be true of all language users, regardless of the language one speaks or the culture in which one lives. Even though the many human languages differ, often dramatically, in terms of vocabulary and grammatical structure, they nevertheless share certain fundamental properties. For these particular features to have become so prominent among human beings, they would have had to bestow certain adaptive benefits on countless generations of humans. For this reason, scientists interpret the existence of universal language features as evidence of natural selection at work.

FIGURE 9.1 Vervet Monkey Alarm Calls.

Auditory Discrimination   One universal feature of language acquisition is that all human newborns appear to be prepared, at birth, to distinguish among different kinds of speech sounds. You may wonder how scientists know this, because newborns cannot talk about their sensory experiences. Consequently, developmental psychologists, and others who study newborns, have marshaled a considerable amount of ingenuity to develop instruments and procedures that allow them to reliably observe and record activity in nonverbal subjects. One such strategy is known as the *habituation-dishabituation* technique, which relies on the well-known fact that most organisms respond with less intensity to a stimulus that is presented repeatedly or continuously. One way to evaluate what a newborn can see or hear is to present a novel visual or auditory stimulus and closely monitor the newborn's reaction to this stimulus. With continued presentation of the stimulus, the child will eventually turn away or demonstrate disinterest (habituate). Then, if a new stimulus is presented in place of the one that has been repeatedly presented, the newborn will once again orient to, or show an interest in, the stimulus (dishabituate). Since the newborn can only behave discriminatively to stimuli that it can detect, alternating habituation and dishabituation responses can inform the experimenter about the newborn's ability to distinguish between various sights and sounds.

Using a habituation-dishabituation procedure, researchers have demonstrated that newborns' capacity for recognizing human speech is quite well developed, particularly when the speaker's voice is familiar. Ockleford, Vince, Layton, and Reader (1988) exposed newborns (from birth to 5 days old) to brief recordings of both their mother's and strangers' voices and measured heart rate as the index of attention or arousal. Infants' heart rates increased when presented with the mother's voice and decreased in response to the stranger's voice. However, when the mother's voice was presented for longer periods of time, heart rate eventually decreased—a finding the researchers attributed to habituation. The mother's voice, after all, is a familiar sound to newborns due to prenatal exposure and is not therefore a completely novel stimulus when presented in the context of such experiments.

Ramus, Hauser, Miller, Morris, and Mehler (2000) used a habituation-dishabituation procedure to assess discrimination of different languages among both human newborns and cotton-top tamarin monkeys. Recordings of both Dutch and Japanese sentences were played forward and backward to subjects. Both human newborns and monkeys demonstrated patterns of habituation and dishabituation, indicating an ability to discriminate between the two languages, but only when the sentences were played forward. Discrimination did not occur to recordings of either language played backward. The researchers suggest that the relevant cues to identifying any human language are only present in forward spoken, or naturally occurring, sentences. Moreover, they argue that the equivalent performances of the human newborns and the tamarin monkeys suggest that speech recognition may be a universal feature of the primate auditory system, not an ability peculiar to humans. This hypothesis has obvious implications for the study of language in nonhumans, a matter that will be taken up at the end of this chapter.

Researchers have also utilized operant contingencies to study speech recognition and preference in newborns. In one particularly clever strategy, referred to as *contingent sucking,* newborns are allowed to suck on nipples attached to audio equipment. The newborn can activate a tape recording of human speech by sucking on the nipple. In a typical experiment, infants are presented with two nipples. Sucking on one produces a tape recording of the mother's voice, and sucking on the other produces a stranger's voice. The duration of the taped speech is directly related to how long the infant sucks on the nipple. This research has led to some interesting conclusions about the auditory abilities and preferences of babies. Not surprisingly, newborns spend more time sucking on the nipple associated with their mother's voice than on the nipple associated with the voice of a stranger, and this preference emerged at only 3 days of age (DeCasper & Fifer, 1980). Newborns also show a preference for tape recordings of their native language compared to a foreign language (Moon, Cooper, & Fifer, 1993). Finally, the fact that newborns come into the world prepared to accommodate human speech is evident in the finding that newborns show a preference for passages of prose that were read to them prenatally (DeCasper & Spence, 1986).

The research on auditory preferences is interesting because it allows newborns to communicate their likes and dislikes, but an even more fundamental lesson can be learned from this research. Babies possess at birth sophisticated skill in recognizing and distinguishing between some remarkably subtle properties of human speech. For example, 2- and 3-month-old children can differentiate between such vowels as *a* and *i,* even when pitch and speaker vary (Marean, Werner, & Kuhl, 1992). In fact, cross-cultural studies have shown that newborns can distinguish all of the basic sounds that constitute the more than 4,000 human languages that have been documented to date (Comrie, 1987; Ruhlen, 1994). This amazing feat is not long lived, though. By the end of their first year, infants perceive only the specific sounds, words, and expressions of their native culture (Eimas, 1985; Kemler-Nelson, Jusczyk, & Cassidy, 1989). It's almost as if the human nervous system equips us initially with the ability to handle all of the variability that human languages entail, but that exposure to a verbal community whittles away at this flexibility as we acquire our native tongue. This finding is consistent with the well-documented observation that second language learning becomes more difficult as a function of maturation (Johnson & Newport, 1989).

The Social Nature of Language   However else researchers may wish to characterize language, it's pretty hard to ignore its social dimensions. In fact, most theories of language evolution argue that language was selected for as an adaptation because of the tremendous advantages it afforded our ancestors in coordinating and organizing such social activities as hunting, gathering, and caring for children (Bickerton, 1990). Indeed, the social aspects of language are evident in newborns long before they utter their first words. Conversations, after all, are social episodes, and their smooth unfolding requires a certain kind of interpersonal choreography that most of us take for granted. Though not yet conversationalists, newborns demonstrate many precursors of language in their daily interactions with adults. Caregivers, for instance, will speak in an interactive way to their cooing and babbling newborns, as if holding a conversation with them. More interesting, however, is that the newborn will remain silent and attentive during the caregiver's discourse (Snow, 1984), indicating an almost immediate responsiveness to the social turn taking that marks interpersonal speech. Though not yet capable of putting that first sentence together, the newborn seems to have an inherent understanding of the give-and-take that characterizes conversations.

An interesting discovery, however, is that it may not be the mother's voice per se that captures the attention of the newborn. Instead, researchers believe what matters is the special quality of speech that most people employ when talking to newborns and infants. When talking to an infant, most people speak more slowly than usual, increase the pitch of their voice, and exaggerate intonation. These distinct changes in speech patterning make up what is referred to as **motherese**, though mothers obviously have no monopoly on its usage. Research has shown that it is this special speech quality that infants prefer (Cooper & Aslin, 1990), regardless of whether it comes from a male or a female (Werker & McLeod, 1989). Moreover, infants apparently attend even to nonspeech sounds as long as they show the same cadence and intonational features as motherese (Cooper & Piston, 1991).

motherese speech patterns consisting of slow pronunciation, increased pitch, and exaggerated intonation, ordinarily used by adults when speaking to infants and young children

Development of Sentences   Usually, by the end of the first year, infants have begun to acquire a vocabulary of single-word utterances, or **holophrases.** Not surprisingly, these one-word utterances typically refer to physical objects in the infant's immediate environment (Bloom, 1990; Bloom & Lahey, 1978; Nelson, 1981). The infant's prowess in naming objects is in fact prolific at this time, to which any parent can attest. While holophrases might at first glance seem rather limited in function, the infant is actually able to wield these single-word phrases as meaningful propositions. For example, an infant who vocalizes "ball" in a high-pitched voice rather than in a lower register has probably already picked up on the role that voice intonation plays in distinguishing questions or requests from simple declarative statements (Gallagan, 1987). Eventually, these single-word utterances become two- and three-word phrases. Because the language of the 1½- to 2-year-old tends to include only truly necessary words, such as nouns and verbs, this rather Spartan language is sometimes referred to as **telegraphic speech.** A child who requests, "Baby up?" in the presence of an adult may be omitting the articles, prepositions, and pronouns that sprinkle the adult's more sophisticated speech, but the essential meaning of the utterance is hardly in question.

holophrase a single-word utterance ordinarily referring to important objects or events in an infant's environment

telegraphic speech short (2–3 word) utterances, usually consisting only of nouns and verbs, used by children from 1½ to 2 years of age

Telegraphic speech soon gives way to longer and more complex sentences. In a pioneering study of language development, Brown (1973) measured the mean length of utterance (MLU) in three children throughout early childhood. This measure (MLU) represents the average number of *morphemes,* or basic units of speech meaning, occurring in a given utterance. As can be seen in Figure 9.2, the three children observed by Brown exhibited a rapid increase in MLU over the observational period. Both length and complexity of sentences show remarkable gains in these young language

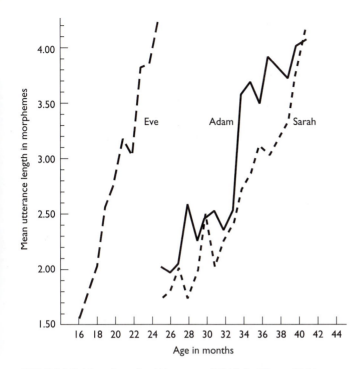

FIGURE 9.2 Mean Length of Utterance (MLU) for Three Children.

learners. In general, most children are competent in wielding their native language long before they begin formal schooling. Although their vocabularies do not match that of the average adult, most preschoolers' utterances are relatively complete, syntactic, and, perhaps most important, meaningful efforts at communication.

The Preparedness of Language   To many researchers, the single most impressive characteristic of language development is that it unfolds in the absence of any formal training. When you think about many of the ordinary skills that you possess, such as driving a car, balancing a checkbook, or cooking a three-course meal, can you recall the circumstances under which you acquired these skills? Although you may not remember the details, you cannot deny that at some time you received some degree of intentional instruction (parental or academic) along these lines. Amazingly enough, such is not the case with language. Humans become competent language users despite never having been schooled in the finer art of conversation. This is not to say that language does not develop in a social context or that this context plays no role in language acquisition, for clearly it does. But we are not formally taught how to talk in the same way that we formally learn algebra or how to play the piano.

Most of us, in fact, resist any attempt to understand the rules and regulations that govern our speech. Can you describe the difference between a preposition and an article? If you are like most people, you may be hard pressed to offer a definition of these components of language, despite the fact that you use them properly in everyday speech. All of this would seem to point toward another language universal, namely, that humans acquire language readily and with only minimal environmental input. This observation suggests that humans are highly prepared to acquire language.

Language and the Sensitive Period   It is tempting to view development as a process highly dependent upon experience, as if all major human milestones must await proper stimulation or support from the environment. This assumption, however, often proves false. In fact, many important developmental events unfold irrespective of environmental input and according to a time scale that is similarly uniform and subject to little modification. Psychologists often refer to the time period during which some developmental milestone will be reached as a **sensitive period.** If the milestone is not reached during this period, the likelihood that it will ever emerge is substantially reduced.

The concept of a sensitive period is easily seen in the precocial birds, including ducks and geese. Upon hatching, the young birds almost immediately establish close contact with the mother, following her every move and even following her if she moves away from the nest. This tendency to attach promptly to a mother figure shortly after coming into the world is called **imprinting.** But imprinting is not entirely automatic: It is a highly time-dependent phenomenon. For example, the likelihood of imprinting is strongest during a temporal window somewhere between 12 and 15 hours after hatching. Although imprinting can still occur beyond the sensitive period, its formation may require more experience or exposure to the imprinted object (Brown, 1975).

Also, imprinting can sometimes go strangely awry. Mother birds, it seems, have little monopoly as attachment figures. Several studies have shown that newly hatched birds will imprint upon whatever moving object appears most salient in their early environment, including such unlikely maternal candidates as trains (Fabricus & Boyd, 1954), footballs (Ramsay, 1951), and ultralight airplanes (Jensen, 1994). Of course, in its natural habitat, the duckling or gosling is unlikely to confront such unusual stimuli. Clearly, the adaptive nature of imprinting depends on the highly probable presence of the bird's mother in the posthatching environment.

Certain milestones in human development may be characterized by a sensitive period similar to that seen in imprinting. There is some evidence that language acquisition may be a time-constrained developmental phenomenon. Children in all cultures, regardless of which language they speak, move through a sequence of linguistic stages—from babbling, to holophrases, to telegraphic speech, to complete sentences—and the age at which each milestone is achieved is remarkably consistent from one child to the next and from one culture to the next. Although their sentences will be somewhat shorter and evidence a more limited vocabulary than adult speakers, most children are, by age 3 or 4, extremely competent users of their native language. They construct rich and flexible utterances, complete with verbs, nouns, articles, and prepositions, in order to make requests, join conversations, convey the

sensitive period limited time period during which a developmental milestone can be most readily achieved

imprinting   tendency of infants to develop rapid and strong attachments to a parental figure; most frequently seen in precocial birds

varied terrain of their emotional lives, and, as more than one parent has observed, simply to hear themselves talk!

But early childhood may be a privileged time when it comes to language acquisition (Lenneberg, 1967). Numerous studies converge on the conclusion that if language is not acquired during the first few years of life, later acquisition is often more difficult and progresses more slowly (Johnson & Newport, 1989; Long, 1990; Schacter, 1996). In further support of a sensitive period for language learning is the finding that deaf children learning American Sign Language (ASL) demonstrate the same developmental pattern as children acquiring spoken language. Children who use sign language progress through the same syntactic and grammatical stages of language use as speaking children (Poizner, Klima, & Bellugi, 1987), and their ability to acquire language is much greater during early than late childhood (Newport, 1990). Researchers are careful to recognize, however, that learning language can occur at any point in the life span. That is, if you are trying to learn a foreign language, you needn't despair altogether. But you should expect the process to require more conscientiousness and effort than was necessary when learning your native language.

✖ INTERIM SUMMARY

Language is a complex symbolic behavior allowing for creative communication between organisms. Scientists agree that language exhibits certain universal features in its development, and that these are probably the result of selective pressures occurring throughout human evolution. Despite cultural differences, all human children acquire language through uniform developmental stages and demonstrate a greater capacity for language development during early childhood than during any other portion of the life span. Unlike many other learned skills, language acquisition occurs in the absence of any formal instruction.

✖ THOUGHT QUESTIONS

1. Would you consider Sarah's use of plastic "words," as described in the opening vignette, an instance of language use? Why or why not? How does her behavior differ from the alarm calls of vervet monkeys in the wild?
2. The identification of language universals is often interpreted as evidence of language as an evolved adaptation in human history. What kind of advantages might language have afforded early humans?

THE PSYCHOLINGUISTIC APPROACH TO LANGUAGE

This book has pointed out several times that psychologists approach their subject matter from many different perspectives. These perspectives often reflect the diverse backgrounds, training experiences, and theoretical interests of the researchers. Although these differences can be categorized in many ways, one especially important distinction helps to describe how researchers differ with respect to the study of language. In particular, some researchers begin their study of language from a *functional* position, asserting that language should be viewed as behavior that contributes to the adaptive functioning of the organism. Such an approach emphasizes how language helps the user negotiate daily routines, solve problems, and, in general, get about effectively in the world. On the other hand, researchers may be interested in the *structural* properties of language, conducting an analysis of its component parts and the rules for combining these building blocks.

Building Blocks of Language

The study of virtually any natural phenomenon usually begins with an analysis of its essential components. For example, a botanist who has discovered a new species of plant will likely begin by describing its various parts (pistil, stamen, etc.). This exercise might be followed by an attempt to compare the new species to others in order to discover the correct taxonomic class in which to place the new species. The botanist, at least initially, is engaged in an analysis of the new plant's structural properties. Does the study of language have a parallel?

psycholinguistics branch of science historically devoted to understanding the properties of human language and the mechanisms responsible for language acquisition

The discipline of **psycholinguistics** has traditionally been concerned with identifying the building blocks of language and the various grammatical rules used to put these basic components together. For instance, the smallest unit of speech sound in all human languages is called the **phoneme.** Phonemes can be sounds made by single letters, such as *t, b,* or *i,* or sounds produced by simple letter combinations, such as *sh* or *th.* Natural languages differ with respect to the number of phonemes they contain; English has approximately 40 phonemes.

phoneme smallest unit of speech sound

By themselves, however, phonemes are meaningless. They acquire meaning only when combined in strategic ways with other phonemes. The **morpheme** is the smallest *meaningful* unit of speech sound and is made up of two or more phonemes. Morphemes can be single words, such as *cat, word,* or *pencil,* or meaningful prefixes and suffixes, such as *-s* at the end of a noun or *-ed* at the end of a verb to indicate past tense. The word *talked,* for example, actually consists of two morphemes, *talk* and *-ed.*

morpheme smallest meaningful unit of speech sound

But human speech is more complex than the simple phonemes and morphemes of which it consists. Perhaps the most noteworthy aspect of language is the way we put these elements together to form complicated sentences and to convey information to others. There are, of course, rules that dictate how we can combine these building blocks. For example, while the phrase "We went to the park" is meaningful to any English speaker, the phrase "Park to we the went" is uninterpretable. Notice that the two phrases contain precisely the same phonemes and morphemes; yet the second phrase is nonsense. What differs between the two phrases is the order or sequence of the words. Every human language contains a **syntax**—a set of rules for describing how words are combined to create meaningful sentences. Among the goals of psycholinguistics is discovering what these rules are and how they are acquired by the individual language user. An interesting question is

syntax rules of a language that determine the ordering of words to make sentences

whether these rules are learned or whether they represent an innate property of the human mind. Indeed, much of the controversy surrounding the study of language revolves around this central issue.

Studying language also entails understanding **semantics**—the meaning or interpretation given to the spoken or written word. You may have had the experience of arguing or debating an issue with a friend, only to be told that the conflict is largely a semantic one. Suppose, for example, that in a conversation with a friend you refer to an episode in which you confronted a store manager about an allegedly unfair policy. Although you feel justified in describing your behavior in the incident as assertive, your friend counters that you were being aggressive. The disagreement in this case is about the meaning or interpretation of such terms as *assertive* and *aggressive*. Needless to say, rather heated conflicts can arise in communications when two or more persons attribute entirely different meanings to the same word.

semantics meaning or interpretation given to the spoken or written word

Although much of their attention has been directed to structural aspects of language, psycholinguists have not ignored the performance or functional aspects of language. When researchers explore the ways in which language is used in social contexts to communicate or to bring about desired consequences for the speaker, they are studying the **pragmatics** of language. For example, the practice of speaking loudly when trying to be heard over annoying background noise is a pragmatic or functional aspect of language use, as is the use of stuffy, parliamentarian language in the midst of a professional committee meeting or casual idiom in the locker room. Notice that these features of language have little to do with syntax, the rules used to put sentences together. Rather, they are properties of language use that are sensitive to aspects of the surrounding environment. A full understanding of language entails not only a description of its formal structural properties but also the many ways in which it must conform to the vagaries of a changing environment.

pragmatics use of language in social contexts to bring about desired consequences

Chomsky's Revolution

Many behavioral scientists would agree that the most important contribution to psycholinguistics has been the work of Noam Chomsky. Beginning in the late 1950s, Chomsky began to present a theory of language that characterized the subject matter in an entirely unprecedented way (Chomsky, 1957, 1965, 1975). A brief look at some fundamental concepts may demonstrate why many believe that Chomsky has almost single-handedly ushered in a new era in the study of language.

The Language Acquisition Device (LAD)   Remember from an earlier section on language universals that despite the tremendous differences in spoken language, dialects, and so on, children throughout the world progress through stages of language development in an orderly and highly uniform way. Chomsky (1965) has argued that the existence of such universals strongly suggests that language is hardwired into the human nervous system. In other words, for reasons that are not yet understood, humans have evolved language as a *species-specific* behavior.

Thus, it may well be that the general features of language structure reflect, not so much the course of one's experience, but rather the general character of one's capacity to acquire knowledge—in the traditional sense, one's innate ideas and innate principles. (Chomsky, 1965, p. 59)

Chomsky's claim is not necessarily outlandish. After all, biologists and ethologists who study nonhuman animal behavior frequently refer to behaviors that are observed in all members of a species as "instinctive" or "innate." There would seem to be no better way of accounting for a behavior pattern seen in every member of a species than to claim that the behavior has been selected for at some time in the species' evolutionary history. Just as the rat appears to be highly prepared to learn associations between food characteristics and physical illness, humans might similarly be prepared to acquire language as a means of communicating.

language acquisition device (LAD) an evolved mechanism believed responsible for language acquisition in humans

Chomsky refers to this innate mechanism as the **language acquisition device (LAD)**. Although he has not attempted to specify precisely what structure or which brain region may have evolved this function, that is not a major shortcoming of his idea. Internal mechanisms are often given theoretical status in an explanatory system, despite researchers' inability to identify or locate them. Freud, for instance, believed that ultimately the science of neurology would shed light on the physical representations of the id, ego, and superego in his theory of human personality. Regardless of whether this ambition is ever realized, one can talk meaningfully about the roles played by these separate components of personality in the development of the person. Similarly, the assumption that there exists a property of the human nervous system that makes language acquisition a highly prepared behavior is not predicated on whether or not this structure can be identified.

Recently, some debate has emerged regarding the nature of the physical representation of the LAD. Some researchers have argued, for example, that our capacity for language may be partitioned into several separate neurological regions or structures (Fodor, 1987). In fact, this argument is consistent with much recent theory about the "modularity of mind," which states that different parts of the nervous system are considered to have evolved at different times and to have developed different types of cognitive operations (Bickerton, 1990; Fodor, 1983; Piatelli-Palmarini, 1994).

Transformational Grammar Recall that all languages consist of a limited or finite number of elements, the phonemes and morphemes. Out of this limited array of components an unlimited and diverse collection of utterances can be constructed. This is the generative property of a language. According to Chomsky, the language acquisition device must be especially proficient at combining these elements into coherent and effective sentences. This process of generating novel sentences is carried out by what Chomsky calls the **transformational grammar**. The idea of a transformational grammar is based upon an important distinction made by linguists. In using language to communicate, one person is trying to convey some meaning or idea to another person. The meaning or intent of what people are saying is referred to as the

transformational grammar process by which deep structures become expressed in novel and unlimited surface structures or sentences

deep structure of the sentence. However, there are an unlimited number of ways in which people could communicate a single meaning.

Suppose, for example, that you and I are sitting at opposite ends of a table at dinnertime. I would like the salt, but it is presently at your end of the table. Consequently, it would make sense for me to ask you to pass me the salt. Notice, though, that I can make this request in an unlimited number of ways. Here are just a few possibilities:

"Could you pass the salt, please?"

"I'd like the salt, if you don't mind."

"Would you please pass the salt?"

"Salt, please!"

"Mind passing the salt this way?"

"Pass the damn salt, will you?"

Although the underlying meaning remains the same—namely, a request for the salt—all of these utterances differ from one another in terms of the words used and their syntactical arrangement. Linguists would say that this single deep structure has been represented by several distinct **surface structures,** the actual ordering or arranging of words into a sentence. This capacity of the transformational grammar to translate a single deep structure into an unlimited number of surface structures is what allows people to produce entirely novel sentences. Similarly, it is possible that the same surface structure could have different deep structures. For example, the sentence "They are flying planes" is potentially confusing. Upon reading the sentence, you cannot be sure whether the *they* in the sentence refers to the planes or to the persons piloting the planes. The ambiguity of the sentence can probably be resolved only by considering the circumstances under which the sentence is uttered. Of course, this information is usually available when you are listening to a speaker. Most important, however, is that the language acquisition device, representing an evolutionary adaptation in humans, allows us to discover these transformation rules with little effort, according to Chomsky, and this is what makes language such a rich and complex subject matter.

deep structure
intended meaning underlying an utterance or sentence

surface structure
syntactic arrangement of words in an utterance or sentence

Contemporary Psycholinguistics

There is little question that Chomsky's work ushered in a new era in linguistics and psychology, and the study of language today continues to draw heavily from his ideas concerning the transformational grammar and the language acquisition device. But, in recent years, the landscape of language research and theory has become a diverse mosaic of experimental procedures and conceptual approaches, contributed to by scientists from many disciplines, including psychology, linguistics, anthropology, and evolutionary biology. Although Chomsky's influence remains significant, contemporary researchers have increasingly directed their attention to the details of language development, both phylogenetically in human history and ontogenetically in the life of the individual.

The Origins of Human Language As discussed early in the book, the details of human evolution remain shrouded in mystery, in part because these details are relegated to the remote past. Although evolutionary biologists disagree about details concerning when and why humans diverged from other hominids, on other matters consensus is high. In particular, most scientists view the development of language as a particularly seminal event in human history, perhaps making possible the many achievements, like science and religion, that seem to be unique to our species (Leakey, 1994; Bickerton, 1990).

Just as there are unanswered questions about human evolution in general, the nuts and bolts of the evolution of language remain a source of contention. Part of this difficulty stems from the fact that language doesn't "fossilize." That is, unlike skeletons, which not only provide relatively permanent records for scientists to study but also offer significant insight into the physical stature and behavioral capabilities of early humans, our facility for language is not similarly preserved in the evidence collected by paleontologists (Botha, 1998, 1999). This means that the understanding of language evolution is necessarily speculative, as scientists have had to be content with suggesting the possible ecological conditions in the early human environment that may have selected for linguistic behavior.

Naturally, there is no shortage of such speculation. Numerous ideas have been put forth by linguists, anthropologists, and psychologists concerning the likely scenarios for language development in human evolution. These ideas share certain fundamental features—to be expected of evolutionary accounts of any physical or behavioral characteristic. Clearly, an evolutionary interpretation of language must claim that linguistic behavior would have bestowed certain adaptive benefits on its users. Indeed, it isn't hard to envision any number of advantages that early humans may have accrued from the ability to speak, including

- Simple communication about important matters, such as the location of food and water or the presence of predators
- Freeing up of the hands for other kinds of activities, such as tool use and self-defense
- Coordination of group behavior for purposes of hunting, foraging, warfare
- Communicating to others one's emotional states and/or the intent to behave in beneficial or harmful ways toward others

Theories of language evolution differ, however, on the matter of when and how language came about in human history. For instance, some theorists believe that language shares particular features with, and perhaps even evolved from, other related cognitive abilities, such as problem solving and concept formation. These scientists are often referred to as *continuity theorists,* because they view language as existing on a continuum of cognitive processes, not as a separate or distinct mental module (Cartmill, 1990;

Hockett, 1960; Lieberman, 1991). One consequence of this approach to language is that any animal that can be shown to possess problem-solving and conceptual learning skills may, in principle, be expected to show some linguistic capacity as well. This is, in fact, the position taken by some continuity theorists, particularly those who endorse the existence of rudimentary language ability in nonhuman primates. In addition, continuity theory suggests that gestural communication skills, observed in both humans and nonhuman primates, may be viewed as precursors to language.

On the other hand, many linguists claim that language is a unique type of communication that should not be lumped together with other cognitive or behavioral capabilities. These *discontinuity theorists* claim that human language emerged, through natural selection, as a unique ability qualitatively different from the many communicative skills seen throughout the animal kingdom (Bickerton, 1990; Davidson & Noble, 1993; Pinker, 1994). These theorists tend to view language as not only distinctly human but also as a particularly noteworthy example of the modularity of mind (Fodor, 1983). You may recall that such a position states that the nervous system, as an evolved structure, is viewed as a collection of relatively specialized modules, each having been selected for because of its contribution to adaptation. Many contemporary students of language consider Chomsky's language acquisition device to be equivalent to a mental module that, once evolved, became the catalyst for further human evolution, increased intelligence, and, ultimately, the tremendous cultural, scientific, and technological achievements of our species (Bickerton, 1990). The question of whether language should be viewed as a unique module or simply as part of a broader cognitive system has been the focus of considerable contemporary debate among linguists (Goodluck, 2000; MacWhinney, 1999; Sabbagh & Gelman, 2000) and is unlikely to be resolved in the near future.

Evolutionary psychologist Steven Pinker (1994, 1995) has been an enthusiastic and articulate proponent of the modular approach to language. In his influential book *The Language Instinct*, he argues that language must be viewed as an evolved adaptation and that a major agenda for modern linguistic study is piecing together the pressures in the early human environment that would have selected for this most important of abilities. By posing the question "What kinds of skills and behaviors would our early ancestors need to possess in order to solve the adaptive problems that they faced?" researchers can begin to hypothesize the sorts of information processing tasks that the nervous system would have to accomplish. In other words, viewing language as an evolved adaptation leads to the same kinds of questions that scientists might ask about our upright stance or our opposable thumb. This practice of determining the kinds of problems that the human mind would have to solve, referred to as *reverse engineering*, helps to determine the operating parameters of the information processing system—in this case, a language module.

An additional aspect of Pinker's treatment of language, quite conspicuous in his book's title, is his reference to the concept of an *instinct*. Pinker claims that the *instinct* concept, long viewed as conceptually weak and irrelevant to much human behavior, actually deserves center stage in the study of language:

> Language is not a cultural artifact that we learn the way we learn to tell time or how the federal government works. Instead, it is a distinct piece of the biological makeup of our brains. . . . I prefer the admittedly quaint term 'instinct.' It conveys the idea that people know how to talk in more or less the sense that spiders know how to spin webs. Web-spinning was not invented by some unsung spider genius and does not depend on having the right education or on having an aptitude for architecture or the construction trades. Rather, spiders spin spider webs because they have spider brains, which give them the urge to spin and the competence to succeed. (1994, p. 18)

Cognitive-Functional Linguistics   One current trend in modern language research is **cognitive-functional linguistics,** which focuses on longitudinal studies of language acquisition in children and a greater appreciation for the practical and functional issues that characterize this process. This focus is at odds with the approach, championed by Chomsky, of creating and analyzing artificial statements for the purpose of identifying universal features of grammar and syntax. Much of the work of traditional linguistics has been done by way of this kind of formal analysis of sentence structure, not necessarily by observing and recording the actual linguistic behavior of everyday people, particularly infants and children acquiring their first language.

cognitive-functional linguistics approach to language study that emphasizes longitudinal studies of language acquisition in children and the practical and functional issues that characterize this process

A major proponent of the cognitive-functional linguistic movement is Tomasello (1995, 1998, 1999, 2000), whose experimental work has focused on the spontaneous utterances of infants acquiring language. Such utterances, Tomasello argues, do not support the traditional claims of linguists that language is instinctual or that newborns possess an innate understanding of syntactic rules for generating sentences. In fact, certain syntactic properties, such as verb-object order or subject location, show tremendous variability across languages. This is a sizable problem for theories of universal grammar, because such claims are founded on the idea that there are invariant, or universal, syntactic features in all languages. Linguistic theory in the Chomskian tradition suggests that children extract these syntactic universals and then generate novel, creative utterances from them in the course of language development. Natural languages differ, however, not only in vocabulary, but in terms of specific syntactic features (Dryer, 1997; Slobin, 1997), and this variability poses serious problems for the concept of an *instinct,* which, by any definition, involves rather rigid stimulus control.

An increasing number of detailed analyses of language acquisition in children cast doubt on the idea of a universal grammar. When children's spontaneous utterances are evaluated for syntactic properties, they are often found to exhibit much less creativity and generativity than would be predicted from traditional linguistic theory. Early language learners, particularly from 1 to 3 years of age, tend to construct sentences in a consistent and restrictive manner, based both on their previous utterances (Lieven, Pine, & Baldwin, 1997; Pizuto & Caselli, 1994) and on sentences uttered by parents (Rubino & Pine, 1998). Tomasello (2000) argues that language acquisition should be viewed as simply another example of the human adaptation for culture, so much of which depends on social behavior. Young children are, he suggests, "'imitation machines,' as they attempt to understand and reproduce virtually all of the activities they see in the cultural activities around them" (p. 240). Thus, children are socialized into language as they are socialized into other kinds of activities, including tool use and general problem solving (Carpenter, Nagell, & Tomasello, 1998). Because so much of their early experience is social in nature, children have unlimited opportunities to try out new behaviors, both linguistic and nonlinguistic, and receive nearly continuous feedback from the adults in their world.

Tomasello's theory of language acquisition is referred to as a "usage-based" theory because it embeds language in a larger social context, and it suggests that fundamental learning and cognitive processes play an essential role in language learning. Simply invoking the idea of preparedness does little to explain the moment-to-moment details of how language is acquired, and traditional linguistics has paid little attention to this process.

> There is no question that human children are biologically prepared to acquire a natural language in any number of ways involving basic processes of cognition, social interaction, symbolization, and vocal-auditory processing. But this does not mean that they have to possess from the beginning the final adult syntactic structures in all of their complexity and abstractness. (Tomasello, 2000, p. 247)

✖ INTERIM SUMMARY

The psycholinguistic approach to language attempts to classify the elements of language as well as explain language acquisition in the human child. This approach gained much of its influence through the work of Noam Chomsky, who claimed that humans possess an innate mechanism, the language acquisition device (LAD), that allows the developing child both to understand and produce language. In addition, the transformational grammar serves to translate any given deep structure into an unlimited number of surface structures, leading to the generative property of language. More recent work in linguistics has focused both on explaining when and how language evolved in human beings and on the social details of language acquisition in young children.

✖ THOUGHT QUESTIONS

1. Consider the sentence "After reading the paper, Jack went for a long walk in the country." How many morphemes would you say this sentence contains? Also, how would you go about changing the surface structure of the sentence while retaining the deep structure?
2. With respect to the evolution of language, do you agree more with the continuity theorists or the discontinuity theorists, and why?
3. Do you agree with Pinker's claim that language is an instinct? Why or why not?

THE BEHAVIORAL APPROACH TO LANGUAGE

The psycholinguistic approach has provided a useful way to classify the different components of language as well as a reasonable account of language universals. In addition, modern linguists are beginning to turn their attention to the details of language acquisition in young children. In doing so, these researchers inevitably move toward a more functional or pragmatic account of language. Indeed, Tomasello's (2000) usage-based approach to language clearly identifies language as a functional, adaptive form of social behavior. As it turns out, this focus on language as functional behavior corresponds well to the perspective that has been taken for many decades by behavioral psychologists. This section describes how human beings *use* language to operate more effectively on their environment, and some of the specific ways in which learning plays a role in the acquisition and use of language. Also addressed is the possibility that a functional approach to language study is complementary, not contradictory, to structural investigations as has often been suggested.

Skinner's Functional Analysis of Verbal Behavior

In 1957, B. F. Skinner published what he considered to be his most important contribution to behavioral science, the book *Verbal Behavior*. In it, Skinner outlined a potential interpretation of language founded on basic learning principles, particularly operant conditioning. Skinner believed that language, though unquestionably complex and of unequaled significance in human beings, is nevertheless a part of our behavioral repertoire. Thus, the same learning principles that have helped to shed light on other kinds of behavior ought to be helpful in explaining how language is actually used in the course of individual adaptation. This is a crucial point in understanding Skinner's analysis, because, unlike much of psycholinguistics, a behavioral analysis focuses on the individual language user, not the process by which language evolved in humans as a species-specific capability. The fact that language evolved at some point in our species' history is not ignored by behavioral psychologists. In fact, Skinner (1986) himself speculated at length about how language became such an integral part of our behavior.

Nor does a behavioral approach to language claim verbal and nonverbal behavior to be identical, for this is not the case. In addition to the rather obvious differences in their mode of expression, verbal and nonverbal behavior produce consequences in disparate ways. Most nonverbal behavior operates on the physical or mechanical environment. For example, when I turn a doorknob far enough in one direction, the beveled latch clears the strike plate and the door pulls open, allowing me to pass through. In this case, my behavior has had an effect directly upon the physical world (the door), producing the desirable outcome of an open door. Verbal behavior, however, ordinarily produces consequences indirectly through a listener. In the earlier example of the table salt, what effect could my verbal request have had if there had been no other persons sitting at the table? In this case, the desired consequence (receipt of the salt) could occur only through the action of another person, the listener. Thus, verbal behavior is different from nonverbal behavior, not because it isn't affected by antecedent and consequent events, but because of the method according to which these events operate.

> Indeed, it is characteristic of such behavior that it is impotent against the physical world. Rarely do we shout down the walls of a Jericho or successfully command the sun to stop or the waves to be still. Names do not break bones. The consequences of such behavior are mediated by a train of events no less physical or inevitable than direct mechanical action, but clearly more difficult to describe. (Skinner, 1957, pp. 1–2)

Remember that an understanding of operant behavior requires asking what function a particular behavior serves for the organism. In particular, researchers are interested in how behavior is acquired and maintained by antecedent and consequent events in the speaker's past and present environments. Skinner's analysis of verbal behavior is an attempt to classify the kinds of relationships that may exist between these elements of the three-term contingency. The antecedents (discriminative stimuli) and the consequences (reinforcers and punishers) are often called the *controlling variables* in behavior analysis, because it is their operation that determines the many dimensions (frequency, intensity, duration, etc.) of behavior. Skinner's analysis in *Verbal Behavior* is an effort at interpretation, perhaps even theory building, and no experimental data are reported in the book. However, experimental analyses of language from a behavioral perspective have blossomed in the past two decades, and a journal founded in 1982, *Analysis of Verbal Behavior,* has become the primary outlet for such research (Normand, Fossa, & Poling, 2000).

One attribute that makes language seem so complex and foreboding as a research subject is its generative nature. You may remember that this refers to the fact that people can create an infinite number of utterances out of a limited number of basic units, the phonemes and morphemes. The incredible array of responses that any scientific explanation of language must accommodate ranges from such simple statements as "Here" in response to your name being called during class roll to the complete recitation of a lengthy poem.

To add to the confusion, these verbal responses may occur under a similarly diverse number of circumstances, such as reading a book, responding to a professor's question in class, talking to yourself while driving, holding a conversation on the phone, greeting a neighbor across the fence in the morning, and a host of others. Given the sheer number of response and stimulus dimensions that characterize verbal behavior, the pessimism shared by many psychologists concerning a behavioral explanation of language becomes somewhat understandable. However, much of the complexity of language is structural, not functional, and behavior principles may in fact be essential to accounting for certain aspects of this most perplexing human endowment.

Verbal Behavior and the Three-Term Contingency

As functional behavior, language can be conceptualized using the same explanatory model that psychologists apply to other kinds of behavior—the three-term contingency. The antecedent stimuli that occasion verbal utterances are often quite conspicuous. In perhaps the simplest case, the antecedent is some object or property of an object in the immediate environment. Just as discriminative stimuli control many nonverbal behaviors (such as stepping on the brakes in response to a red light), much verbal behavior occurs in response to stimuli in a functionally identical manner. The utterance itself, whether a holophrasic request from an infant or a long-winded discourse by a professor, constitutes the response class. And verbal behavior, like nonverbal behavior, has consequences for the speaker. In other words, verbal behavior can be readily interpreted within the standard operant framework. The process by which verbal repertoires become established is easily observed in the toddler, whose successful adaptation depends heavily upon the ability to produce effective verbal behavior under appropriate stimulus control. Let's look at an example to see why this might be so.

When I was a graduate student, I had the good fortune to become a father for the first time. My daughter proved herself to be a consummate behavioral expert even at 10 months of age. During one particular episode in the family kitchen, she pointed emphatically toward the higher cabinets (to which, strategically, she had no access) and asked, in true holophrasic splendor, for a "cacka." Believing myself to be particularly gifted in deciphering toddlerspeak, I reached up confidently and pulled down a box of generic crackers. Clearly offended by this inconceivable transgression, my daughter shook her head and delivered a most resounding, "No!" followed by an even more adamant request, once again, for "Cacka!"

Turning around to glance once more at the cabinet, I realized that a box of cookies, sitting immediately beside the crackers, was the true object of my daughter's desire. Having seen the error of my ways, I dutifully fetched the cookies for her. Before handing her the prize, however, I held up the box, pointed to its contents, and slowly enunciated "cookie;" then, with equal aplomb, I pointed to the cracker box on the upper shelf and uttered "cracker." The lesson having ended, she retired to her room to enjoy the sugary treat and, no doubt, to deliberate on the questionable intelligence of fathers.

For the time being let's ignore my blunder in not requiring my daughter to articulate "cookie" before providing her with the prized snack. Instead, let's look at how this scenario might be captured by a behavioral analysis. You can assume that the child was in a state of deprivation such that any behavior successful in acquiring food would have a high momentary probability. By 10 months most children have long since figured out where in the house food is located, so her presence in the kitchen is hardly surprising. The dilemma faced by a child this age, however, is that many important commodities in the environment are beyond reach, for obvious safety reasons. Consequently, children must use an intermediary, usually a parent, to acquire these desirable items. In the example, my daughter's request for a "cacka" occurs in response to several antecedent stimulus conditions: (1) hunger (state of deprivation), (2) kitchen cabinets containing known foods, and (3) the father. Although the first two antecedents may not be considered absolutely necessary for the verbal behavior to occur, the same cannot be said of the father. Such a request would be almost unthinkable in the absence of another person whose presence makes reinforcement of the request possible.

In this particular case, Skinner (1957) would say that the child's request was a *mand,* which is a somewhat altered version of *command.* **Mands,** according to Skinner, are verbal operants that occur under conditions of deprivation or aversive stimulation. An important part of the definition of the mand is that it can only be reinforced by reduction in either the state of deprivation or aversive stimulation. In other words, mands occur under rather specific circumstances because the type of consequent event that will reinforce such verbal behavior is very limited. The request for salt described earlier also belongs in this category. Such a request is unlikely under circumstances where food is not being consumed and where there are no other people present. Moreover, the only meaningful consequence of a request for salt is receipt of the salt itself. If such a request never led to receipt of salt (or any other requested item), such verbal requests would most likely not continue to be a part of the speaker's repertoire.

mands verbal operants occurring under specific states of deprivation or aversive stimulation

Thus, the mand, as a verbal operant, is defined according to the same criteria used to classify other operant behavior—the antecedent and consequent stimuli that control its occurrence. This means that it is not the words themselves or their syntactic arrangement that make this request a mand. In fact, a similar verbal utterance may be classified differently if it occurs under different stimulus conditions. If, for example, the toddler had uttered "salt" in response to an adult having pointed to and enunciated "salt," the response would not be categorized as a mand by Skinner, but as an *echoic* response. **Echoic** operants are verbalizations that bear an acoustic relationship to, or mimic, the antecedent stimulus ("salt" in response to "salt"), and their emission is not reinforced by receipt of the commodity itself. In fact, adults trying to assist toddlers in vocabulary development will often offer verbal praise and other interpersonal consequences when children correctly imitate the adult's pronunciation. The important point to remember is that in a behavioral analysis, the response itself is not *the* defining aspect of a verbal unit. Making sense of behavior requires viewing it in its environmental context, and this is why the three-term contingency plays such a key role in a behavioral account of language.

echoic verbal operant whose structural properties match those of the antecedent stimulus

The mand and echoic do not exhaust the functional categories of verbal behavior. Table 9.1 presents the major categories of verbal operants in Skinner's analysis. You can probably see that an emphasis on contextual variables makes identifying such structural elements as phonemes, morphemes, words, sentences, and so on, less critical because all of these properties can vary across many functional properties. In short, a functional system like that in Table 9.1 allows utterances to be parceled into practical categories without having to distinguish specific surface structures. Thus, the statements "Pass the salt, please" and "Can I have the salt?" though structurally different, would both be considered members of a single operant class, in this case a mand.

TABLE 9.1 FUNCTIONAL CATEGORIES OF VERBAL BEHAVIOR

	Antecedent	Behavior	Consequence
Mand	State of deprivation	Verbal utterance	Reinforcer that reduces state of deprivation

Example: You have just come in from mowing the yard and you are thirsty (antecedent). You request a drink (behavior) from your friend. Your friend grants your request by bringing you a glass of water (consequence).

	Antecedent	Behavior	Consequence
Echoic	Verbal utterance from another person	Repetition of what the speaker says	Conditioned reinforcement (praise, etc.) from other person

Example: The parent of an infant (1½ years old) points to a pitcher of milk and says "milk" (antecedent). The infant repeats the utterance "milk" (behavior). The parent responds with social reinforcement, such as praise or a smile (consequence).

	Antecedent	Behavior	Consequence
Tact	Stimulus (usually object) in the environment	Verbal utterance naming or referring to object	Conditioned reinforcement from other person

Example: Dog walks into room (antecedent) in presence of infant and parent (see above example). Infant points to dog and says "doggie" (behavior). Parent provides social reinforcement (such as, "That's right, that's a dog") to infant (consequence).

	Antecedent	Behavior	Consequence
Intraverbal	Verbal utterance (often as question) from another person	Verbal response (often answer to question)	Verbal feedback or reinforcement

Example: Biology teacher asks a student in the class which kind of cell division occurs for the gametes, or sex cells (antecedent). The student replies, "mitosis" (behavior). The teacher tells the student. "Yes, that's correct" (consequence).

Source: Adapted from Skinner, 1957.

Chomsky-Skinner: The History of a Nondebate

Skinner's analysis of language could probably not have been more ill timed, for it appeared on the scene just as the theoretical pendulum in psychology was to swing strongly in a cognitive direction. Indeed, it is ironic that in the same year that *Verbal Behavior* was published, Chomsky would publish *Syntactic Structures,* a book that contributed significantly to psychology's shift toward a cognitive orientation. In addition, in 1959, Chomsky published a scathing, no-holds-barred critique of Skinner's book in the journal *Language.* This review, in addition to making Chomsky's name a fixture within psychology, would resonate throughout every corner of the discipline and, in the opinion of many, forever condemn behavioral analyses of complex behavior to a theoretical graveyard.

The crux of Chomsky's criticism of a behavioral account of language is that conditioning principles cannot possibly explain either the universal features of language development seen throughout the human species or the tremendous generativity observed in language expression. Chomsky (1959) suggested that a stimulus-response psychology treated a sentence as a simple behavioral chain in which each word serves as a stimulus for the next word, and so on. The problem with such an analysis, according to Chomsky, is that there is no way to predict the utterance of any one word given its predecessor in a sentence.

For example, take the word *the* as it appears in this sentence. Can you predict *the* from the word that precedes it, in this case, *take*? Of course not, because any number of words may precede *the* in a given sentence. In fact, in this chapter alone, the word *the* is preceded by such various words as *of, from, and, be, entertain, about,* and *include.* It becomes even more challenging to predict what words would follow *the* in any given sentence. A short list of words following *the* in this chapter would include *problem, study, human, mystery, provocative, challenge, wild,* and *chapter.* Because it is nearly impossible to know ahead of time which words will follow one another in any utterance, critics of the behavioral position have argued that any and all behavioristic analyses of language will prove similarly impoverished (Brown & Hanlon, 1970; Chomsky, 1957, 1970; Lashley, 1951).

Much of the criticism leveled at Skinner's analysis of language, however, has been shown to be misdirected. Unlike previous forms of behaviorism, Skinner's analysis of behavior was not a stimulus-response (S-R) theory (Catania, 1988), nor did he contend that a sentence is merely a behavioral chain in which each word functions as a stimulus for the next word in the sentence (MacCorquodale, 1969, 1970). Most important, Skinner's critics, especially Chomsky, appear to have misunderstood the most fundamental element of a Skinnerian account, the operant. Remember that an operant is defined functionally, not structurally. This means that the basic unit of analysis in any given utterance is determined not by the utterance itself, but by the antecedents and consequences surrounding the utterance. This means that "Salt, please," "Please pass the salt," and "Can I have the salt?" could all be considered members of the same operant, despite the fact that they differ syntactically from one another. That is, a behavioral approach to language makes a distinction between the structural (surface) elements of an utterance and its functional (deep) dimensions just as does a psycholinguistic account, though it does so in a different way.

Neither a behavioral nor a psycholinguistic theory of language finds it necessary to be able to predict the precise syntax or word order that a given statement will take. Under most circumstances, the deep structure of an utterance can be conveyed through many different surface structures. But there may, on occasion, be quite rigid contingencies that require even the form of the response to be rather precise. For example, if asked to name the first president of the United States, a student would probably get credit for the response "George Washington" but not for the response "The guy who cut down the cherry tree." In other words, sometimes individuals must emit responses that fall within a fairly narrow range of topography, or form.

Indeed, teachers often spend considerable time agonizing over the level of generality or specificity to accept in students' answers to test questions.

The notion of requiring verbal utterances to have a particular topography has parallels in the animal conditioning laboratory. For instance, in many operant experiments, researchers don't really care whether an animal presses a lever with its left paw or its right paw. They could, however, impose some requirement on this dimension of the response by differentially reinforcing responses with one paw or the other. In fact, they could choose to reinforce responses according to any number of specific response characteristics, such as the amount of downward pressure exerted on the lever or response key (Chung, 1965) or the volume of a subject's voice (Miller, 1968). Research has shown, in fact, that nearly any dimension of behavior may become an operant class if that dimension is differentially reinforced. Neuringer and colleagues (Denney & Neuringer, 1998; Neuringer, 1991, 1993; Neuringer, Deiss, & Olson, 2000), for example, have studied variability by requiring subjects to emit different sequences of left-right lever presses in order to obtain reinforcement. When reinforcement was made contingent on variable topography, as defined by no repetitions of left-right sequences for a predetermined period of time, sequence variability increased. This exciting research program demonstrates that variability itself can be identified as an operant class and that the kind of behavior referred to as *creativity* in the vernacular may be open not only to experimental analysis, but also to systematic efforts at modification.

An additional aspect of Chomsky's critique focused on the apparent lack of formal training that characterizes human language development. Because parents and other adults don't purposefully or formally teach language to young children, psycholinguists have long assumed that environmental contingencies, at least in the form of parental feedback, have little to do with language acquisition in children. In an early examination of child-parent interactions, Brown and Hanlon (1970) discovered that parents neither consistently correct their children's ungrammatical utterances nor reinforce grammatical statements. Parental feedback seems to be based on the meaning or the validity of the child's statement, not its formal syntactic properties. This observation has been interpreted as evidence against a behavioral account, since such an explanation would seem to require that adults differentially reinforce grammatically correct sentences in order for effective language learning to occur (Marcus, 1993).

More recent research has cast a different light on the role of parental feedback in language learning. Moerk (1983) reanalyzed Brown's (1973) claim and discovered that parental feedback was differentially contingent on children's grammatical and ungrammatical sentences. Grammatical sentences led to qualitatively different kinds of verbal reinforcement than did ungrammatical sentences, and parents frequently corrected children's ungrammatical sentences. Yet, the idea that every sentence uttered by a child must meet with swift and powerful consequences (reinforcing or punishing) in order for learning to occur is as silly as the claim that every key peck or lever press emitted by an animal in an operant chamber must produce consequences. Parents cannot be expected to respond to every utterance a child emits with either positive or negative feedback, nor is this kind of consistency demanded by a learning approach to language. As discussed in Chapter 4, behavior can be maintained at considerable strength through intermittent reinforcement. Moreover, unless the contingencies demand specificity in form, individual lever presses or key pecks may vary considerably across a session. The effect of a reinforcer is to strengthen the *operant class,* not specific responses. Similarly, a behavioral explanation of language suggests that parental feedback may influence the future probability of certain kinds of utterances, not a specific surface structure.

In order for operant learning to affect language learning, ongoing experience or exposure to a functional language is necessary, and this is pretty much a given for most children. In a normal social environment, infants and children encounter hundreds of thousands of verbal episodes, sometimes merely as listeners, sometimes as speakers, and often as both. In essence, it might be fruitful to view childhood as a developmental period marked by an enormous number of, for lack of a better phrase, experimental trials, in which the child has the opportunity to experience the advantages of behaving verbally. The power of these episodes to enhance language acquisition can be further appreciated by recalling that many kinds of learning, such as conditioned taste aversion, require very few trials or exposure to contingencies. Because most psychologists view language as a highly prepared behavior in humans, they don't expect to find language learning to be an extremely effortful process or one requiring numerous encounters with specific lessons. Instead, they would predict that children pick up on the nuances of syntax and grammar rather quickly and from a limited number of modeled sentences and/or personal exposure to verbal contingencies. In short, a learning account of language suggests the ontogenetic processes responsible for language development, but in doing so it hardly negates the phylogenetic history and the resulting preparedness of language acquisition in humans.

It is unfortunate that history has often pitted Chomsky and Skinner against one another, as if their accounts of language were inevitably contradictory and one or the other had to hold sway as *the* theory of language. In reality, both scientists have made lasting and substantial contributions to behavioral science, and it is unlikely that either one would have presented an unsophisticated or poorly reasoned account of language. In actuality, contemporary behavioral psychologists recognize the universal features that characterize language development and also agree with the argument that language is a highly prepared human propensity that must have proven adaptive to humans many generations ago. But language use also exhibits tremendous variability, across both individuals and circumstances. How do psychologists account for one child learning English and another learning Japanese? Even standard English finds expression in diverse dialects, as heard in different regions of the United States. Why do people speak in motherese only to infants and not adults? And what accounts for the disparity between the church whisper and the football stadium cheer?

The answer is that the environment cannot be disregarded in any explanation of language use. The contingencies that characterize what Skinner referred to as the "verbal community" must be taken into account when attempting to explain the ontogenetic development and use of language by the individual. That is, the universal aspects of language development as well as the more momentary adaptations that language use exhibits in everyday life must be considered. This kind of analysis does not substitute for, nor does it compete with, a psycholinguistic account of language. In fact, contemporary research in cognitive-functional linguistics has adopted the strategy of formally analyzing language development within its natural, social context (Tomasello, 2000). Acknowledging that structural and functional approaches to language are in fact complementary (Andresen, 1991) may prove to be an important advance, especially in the context of the multidisciplinary endeavor that the study of language has become.

✖ INTERIM SUMMARY

Behavioral psychologists view language as functional behavior that, like all behavior, contributes to individual adaptation. Unlike a traditional psycholinguistic approach, a behavioral perspective is less concerned with describing the building blocks of language and more interested in describing verbal episodes within the context of the three-term contingency. The focus is on how language helps the individual solve pragmatic problems in his or her immediate environment. Such an emphasis on functional, rather than structural, properties is not antagonistic to a psycholinguistic account; indeed, both kinds of analyses are necessary to fully explain language as a natural behavior.

✖ THOUGHT QUESTIONS

1. How does the behavioral psychologist conceptualize language as operant behavior, and what role does the three-term contingency play in this conceptualization?
2. Consider the phrase "Gentlemen, start your engines." How is it possible that this utterance could be either a mand or an echoic in Skinner's system? What kind of antecedent and consequent events would lead you to classify the utterance as a mand?
3. Describe at least five different stimuli that may act as reinforcers for verbal behavior. Is verbal behavior reinforced on a continuous or intermittent schedule?

LANGUAGE IN NONHUMANS

This book has stressed the importance of nonhuman animal research in understanding learning and cognition. The practice of conducting research on other animals is validated, in part, by the simple recognition that all biological creatures must solve functionally similar problems in order to survive. For countless centuries, both human and nonhuman animals have faced the challenges of finding food, shelter, and mates and remaining safe from predators or aggressors. Part of the rationale, then, for conducting research on nonhuman animals is the desire to identify the similar ways in which different species learn about and solve problems in their natural habitat. This is important, remember, because science often seeks general rules or principles that apply across several domains. Such principles can be remarkably powerful if they prove generalizable across different settings, tasks, or species. As an example, the law of effect, formalized by Thorndike and later studied by Skinner and many others, has proven to be an impressively generic fact about behavior. Despite the fact that different animals may engage in responses that differ physically (key pecking, lever pressing, typing) and receive different kinds of reinforcers (access to grain, food pellets, letters on a computer screen), the law of effect serves to unify these observations because they share the common attribute of behavior being influenced by its consequences.

Of course, research on nonhuman animals has its drawbacks as well. Scientists wish to avoid, for example, the trap of **anthropomorphism**, the tendency to attribute human thoughts and feelings to nonhumans. In short, it is sometimes difficult to maintain an appropriate balance between scientific skepticism and open-mindedness when the question of nonhuman cognitive ability arises. Nowhere has this issue stirred up more heated debate than the question of whether other animals possess language or can acquire language through training.

anthropomorphism tendency to attribute humanlike characteristics to nonhuman animals

Historical Precedents

The story of nonhuman animal language as a subject of psychological research began with a husband-and-wife team, the Kelloggs (1933), who undertook the ambitious task of teaching a baby chimpanzee, Gua, to speak English. Unfortunately, the project met with little success. Although Gua was able to follow some verbalized instructions (*receptive language*), speaking (*expressive language*) was simply not in the cards for this diminutive pupil. Another husband-and-wife team, the Hayeses (1951), met with slightly more success in teaching Vicki, another chimpanzee, to speak, but her verbal repertoire, acquired only through painstakingly slow and intensive training, was very limited and never even approached that of a human toddler.

Initial attempts to teach chimps to speak were probably doomed from the start. Many primates, chimpanzees included, do not have vocal musculature like that of humans, and it was probably unreasonable to expect spoken language from them. Recognizing this crucial limitation, yet another couple, the Gardners (1969), set about trying to teach their young pupil, Washoe, to communicate using American Sign Language, a much more logical endeavor given the chimp's superior manual dexterity. Washoe proved to be a very capable student and acquired more than 200 signs in a few years. Perhaps most impressive about Washoe's development was her facility for putting words together into what appeared, to the Gardners at least, to be true sentences. She became especially adept at making her momentary desires known to the Gardners, including such pragmatic requests as "Give me sweet drink."

The Gardners' success opened the floodgates to an era of ape-language research, as several scientists sought new ways to demonstrate the linguistic potential of humankind's closest primate relative. In some cases, chimps were trained using plastic symbols on magnetic boards, with each symbol standing for an object or action in the real world (Premack, 1983; Premack & Premack, 1972). In other laboratories, chimps learned symbols that were illuminated on a console. Figure 9.3 shows the computerized keyboard used by Savage-Rumbaugh and her colleagues at the Yerkes Primate Center in Georgia (Savage-Rumbaugh, 1984; Savage-Rumbaugh, Pate, Lawson, Smith, & Rosenbaum, 1983). In most of these studies, chimps were intensively trained in the meaning of the symbols themselves, how to respond to requests (receptive language) made by experimenters using the symbols, and, finally, how to put strings of symbols together to communicate (expressive language) in "sentences" to the experimenters. By the late 1970s the language acquisition literature, not to mention the nightly news, was sprinkled with the names of Washoe, Lana, Koko, and Sherman, all afforded celebrity status by virtue of their mastery of a skill previously considered unique to humans. Whether pressing keys corresponding to words on a computer keyboard or strategically manipulating plastic tokens to create sentences, these language-wielding chimps altered forever the way that scientists would look at language and its role in human behavior.

Current Controversies

It is the nature of scientists to be skeptical, so the claim that chimpanzees can learn language could not remain unchallenged for long. And it most certainly hasn't. Among the most ardent critics of the chimp language research is Herbert Terrace, who, ironically, was responsible for teaching sign language to Nim Chimpsky. (Can you guess the noted linguist for whom this chimp was named?) Nevertheless, Terrace (1979) would eventually become convinced that neither Nim nor the other heralded chimpanzees had really acquired anything like human language. Instead, he argued, they had acquired admittedly impressive repertoires of nonlinguistic behavior through the processes of stimulus control and operant conditioning, in much the same way that laboratory animals acquired key-pecking and lever-pressing behaviors.

Terrace's conclusions are based on several important considerations as well as detailed observation of videotaped material of both Nim and Washoe. Terrace makes the case that the animals seldom sign spontaneously and that most of their signing activity consists either of immediate imitations of trainers' behavior or requests for visible objects in the animal's environment. In other words, the chimps may be learning what they need to do to get desirable goodies, just as the rat or pigeon in an operant chamber learns what behavior produces reinforcement. This kind of behavior may be interpreted rather parsimoniously as instances of discriminated operants and, as such, bear little resemblance to linguistic behavior. Although you and I clearly use language to ask for things, we also speak to ourselves when others are not present and talk about things and ideas that are not part of our immediate environment.

Perhaps more important, Terrace refutes the claim that signing chimps understand syntax (the rules for combining words into sentences). For

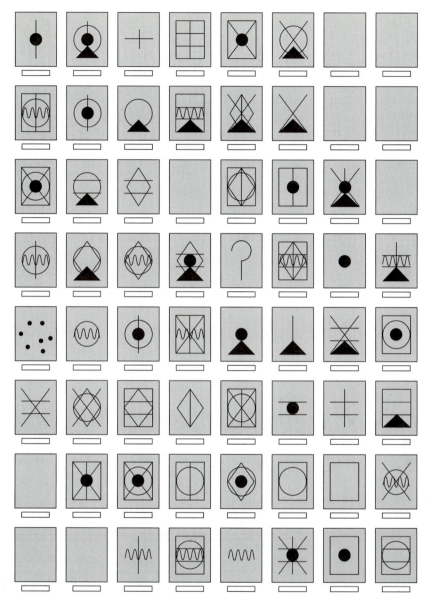

FIGURE 9.3 Keyboard Used to Teach Language to Nonhuman Primates.
(From Savage-Rumbaugh et al., 1983.)

example, the sign "give orange me give eat orange me eat orange give me eat orange give me you" was produced by Nim. This 16-word statement looks impressive on the surface, but it is highly redundant and does not conform to the rules of English grammar. In fact, the order of words appears nearly random, unlike the sentences of even very young children, for whom word order is usually predictable and consistent with the syntax of their native language. Nim's sentence doesn't begin to compare to the simple utterance "Mother, may I please have an orange?" which, despite containing less than half as many words, represents a syntactically correct sentence that would not be difficult for a 5- or 6-year-old child. Most of Nim's "sentences," according to Terrace, were less than 2 MLUs (mean length of utterance), considerably below that of most 3- and 4-year-old children. In essence, the argument being made here is not that the trained chimpanzees are not acquiring something like a vocabulary, but that there is more to language production than the possession of a few building blocks. Chimpanzees, according to Terrace, do not yet exhibit the subtle properties of language production that even very young children master before beginning their formal schooling.

Also, remember that language is remarkably generative. That is, out of a limited number of letters in their native alphabet, people construct an unlimited number of utterances throughout their lives, many of which have never been uttered before, either by themselves or others. It is this feature of language that renders this particular kind of communication so flexible and powerful. Terrace argues that trained chimpanzees, no matter how many words they may have learned, evidence little, if any, generativity in the expressions they construct. Instead, they produce stereotypic "sentences" that are highly dependent on the immediate environment and the animal's history of training.

Terrace's arguments notwithstanding, the final chapter in the ape-language controversy has yet to be written. Researchers in the field continue to endorse the chimpanzee's linguistic skills (Hixon, 1998; Langs, Badalamenti, & Savage-Rumbaugh, 1996), suggesting that language development in chimps exhibits the same social features, including turn taking, that mark language acquisition in humans (Greenfield & Savage-Rumbaugh, 1993). Along similar lines, Bickerton (1990) suggests that chimpanzees, and other nonhuman primates, may possess the rudiments of linguistic capacity in the form of what he refers to as "protolanguage." Unlike formal language, protolanguage does not place restrictions on word order, lacks many of the grammatical features of language, and lacks the capacity for combining phrases and clauses into complex sentence structures. Protolanguage is evident both in the unusual word orders of language-trained chimps and in the 2-year-old human's telegraphic speech, and Bickerton believes that the concept of protolanguage may prove to be a useful window through which to view the evolution of language. Also, some researchers have reported that linguistic skills have actually been handed down from one generation of signing chimps to the next (Brakke & Savage-Rumbaugh, 1995; Savage-Rumbaugh, 1990; Savage-Rumbaugh, McDonald, Sevcik, Hopkins, & Rupert, 1986). This claim, if true, would be remarkable, for it would seem to contradict the idea that nonhuman animals acquire language, if at all, through a concrete, purposeful, and time-intensive training regimen, not through the informal, unintentional experience that seems to mark human language acquisition.

Critics maintain that a healthy skepticism is in order until the evidence concerning language use in nonhumans becomes unequivocal (Ristau & Robbins, 1982). At this point, it is hard to say that the data argue strongly for the possession of linguistic skills in nonhuman primates. Keep in mind, however, that most of the research discussed here has involved efforts to teach an artificial language to nonhumans, and in many ways this may be similar to teaching a second language to a human being—a process that is also notoriously difficult, at least in older children and adults. The question of whether nonhumans can acquire a "human" language is logically separate from the issue of whether animals already possess a natural language of their own. It may very well be the case that more detailed and sophisticated observations of animals communicating in their natural environments will change the way people think about language and other forms of communication. This brings the discussion full circle to a consideration of what counts and what does not count as language, and this is a conceptual issue on which experts are likely to disagree for some time to come.

✖ INTERIM SUMMARY

Early attempts to teach language to nonhuman primates (usually chimpanzees) were unsuccessful because of the animals' limited vocal abilities. Several animals have been trained to communicate using sign language and computerized or magnetized symbol manipulation. Though several researchers argue that this symbol usage is comparable to human language, others suggest that this animal communication lacks the kind of spontaneity, generativity, and general grammatical properties that characterize human language.

✖ THOUGHT QUESTIONS

1. Do you agree or disagree with Terrace's interpretation of Nim's 16-word "sentence"? Would you call this utterance language? Why or why not?
2. Have you ever taught a pet, such as a family dog, to sit, stay, speak, or follow any other command? If so, do you think the animal is demonstrating what linguists refer to as receptive language? Does this count as linguistic behavior? Why or why not?

THE ADAPTIVE NATURE OF LANGUAGE

The study of language is characterized by very different theoretical persuasions, and these differences have at times led to rather bitter disagreements. Linguists have tended toward a more formal analysis of language's building blocks and, more recently, of the ecological conditions under which language may have evolved in human ancestors. Behavioral psychologists, on the other hand, have chosen to emphasize the functional or pragmatic aspects of language in the individual and the many ways in which language use contributes to adaptive behavior throughout one's life. Despite these differences in perspective, there is a noticeable common ground in the study of language, and that is the recognition of language as an enormously important means of adaptation. This is true whether psychologists take a phylogenetic or an ontogenetic view.

Language presumably evolved in humans because it afforded unprecedented advantages in solving the problems of survival. The ability to use the vocal tract to communicate to others about the availability of food or the presence of a dangerous animal in the environment would have proven immensely useful to our ancestors. Moreover, the capacity for planning and organizing group behavior would have saved an enormous amount of effort and time and may have led, eventually, to storytelling, oral traditions, and the benefits of rule-governed behavior. The tendency to share descriptions of behavior-environment contingencies with members of one's group would have afforded early humans tremendous advantages by making actual contact with certain aversive contingencies (that fire hurts, for instance) unnecessary. In short, the evolution of language in human history may have served essential survival functions, but it also may have ultimately become a catalyst for other significant developments in human history, such as advanced civilization, religion, and science.

The adaptive nature of language in the lifetime of an individual is similarly compelling. Infants grow up in a highly verbal environment and learn early on that words can do wonders, especially in the presence of those big people who have access to important objects in the world. Throughout our lives, language remains important as a means of interpersonal communication, from resolving problems and conflicts with loved ones or coworkers, to establishing and maintaining intimate relationships, to meeting the demands of a formal education. Language, in fact, is very much on center stage for the college student. Listening to and understanding a lecture, asking questions in class, and reading and writing are all essentially linguistic activities. Much of your success as a student depends upon mastering the nuances of language. A substantial part of understanding any particular science, from physics to psychology, involves a mastery of that discipline's technical language, and the study of great literature is, among other things, a celebration of language. Thus, whether language is unique to humans or shared by other creatures, there is little question that the acquisition and use of language is of unparalleled significance to human beings as we go about meeting the demands of our busy world.

CHAPTER TEN

Biology, Learning, and Cognition

By the time the firefighters arrived, Miriam's modest two-bedroom suburban home was engulfed in flames, with little hope of anything worthwhile being re- covered. Miriam was by herself and had called the fire department and left the house just moments after she saw smoke coming from the kitchen. At 72 years of age, Miriam had lived by herself, independently, since becoming a widow 10 years ago. She had always prided herself on being autonomous and being able to "take care of myself." For the past several months, however, Miriam's for- getfulness had become noticeable, not only to herself, but also to friends and her children and grandchildren. First there was the incident at the grocery store, where Miriam searched for half an hour for her parked car, even though she had only run into the store for a loaf of bread. Then there was the day she called her daughter twice in the same hour, having completely forgotten the initial phone conversation. Today she had put some oil in a pan and turned the stove burner on high. When the telephone rang, Miriam went into the hallway to answer it and soon found herself immersed in a lengthy talk with an old friend. It wasn't until she saw smoke pouring out of the kitchen that Miriam recalled having turned the burner on under the oil.

Miriam's tragedy is a hypothetical one; but similar stories, some of them with equally devastating consequences, play out each day in the lives of thousands of people affected by Alzheimer's disease, a cruel form of demen- tia that produces serious memory impairment as well as other debilitating symptoms. Alzheimer's has received more and more attention in recent years, in part because of former President Ronald Reagan's ongoing battle with the disease. But perhaps the most sobering reason is the increasing number of people affected by this disease. Although Alzheimer's can strike younger adults, it is a condition predominantly affecting the elderly, and seniors are among the fastest growing segment of the population. Approximately 5% of individuals age 65 to 74 suffer from the disorder, and this number climbs to nearly 50% of the population in those 85 years and older (Evans et al., 1989).

All forms of dementia, including Alzheimer's disease, involve progressive loss of intellectual ability leading to problems in everyday functioning. There is currently a flurry of research activity surrounding Alzheimer's, including several journals devoted exclusively to its possible causes, treatment, and potential prevention. Although there is much to learn, overwhelming evidence attributes the cognitive impairment characteristic of Alzheimer's to well-documented pathology in the brain. Autopsies reveal that Alzheimer's patients have experienced widespread atrophy and death of nerve cells in several regions of the brain, including those that play an important role in learning and memory. Thus, this devastating disease serves as a distressing reminder that the day-to-day adaptive behaviors that people take for granted depend continuously on a fully functioning nervous system. When pathology strikes the brain, the repercussions are felt well beyond the nervous system. Indeed, family members who provide care for a relative with Alzheimer's are often taken aback by the dramatic impact of the disease on their loved one's emotional life and personality as well as memory.

This book looks at learning as a remarkably powerful mode of adaptation that most animals use daily to negotiate the contingencies of a sometimes exacting world. But doing so requires some essential anatomical and physiological machinery, much of which is contained in the nervous systems of even primitive animals. This chapter explores this machinery with an aim toward giving you an appreciation for how the nervous system manages the formidable task of organizing experience so as to help human and non-human animals meet the ever-changing demands of the physical world. Modern research in neuroscience is generating, at an explosive pace, new knowledge about the underlying physiology of learning and cognition. Insight into the connections between the brain, learning, and cognition comes from the basic laboratory as well as the applied world of the clinic. The organizing theme of this book—adaptation—is revisited in this context. The ability to benefit from experience is itself an immensely critical adaptation, enjoyed by both humans and nonhuman animals. The chapter, and the book, close by considering the advantages of viewing learning and cognition through an evolutionary lens.

LEARNING AND THE NERVOUS SYSTEM

The nervous system can be thought of as the control center of the body, particularly where behavior is concerned. It is the billions of cells making up the nervous system that keep humans in contact with the outside world through various bodily senses. It is also the nervous system that renders this information meaningful through often unconscious organizational feats that scientists are still trying to understand. Ultimately, it is the nervous system that generates the muscular activity that gives rise to adaptive behavior. Although psychologists may not care to know all that much about human anatomy and physiology (say, where the liver is located and what it does), the nervous system is one significant exception. Psychologists wish to understand how the nervous system does its job, and what happens when it doesn't,

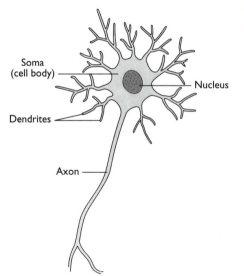

Soma
(cell body)

Nucleus

Dendrites

Axon

because what goes on at this physiological level has overriding implications for all behavior, including learning and cognition.

The Neuron: Building Block of the Nervous System

Any system, whether organic or mechanical, is made up of various interrelated parts, and these parts are the system's building blocks. The building blocks of the nervous system are individual nerve cells, or **neurons.** The typical human nervous system contains billions of neurons, many of which make up specific pathways or organized collections that carry out some particular function. As you can see in Figure 10.1, neurons have certain structural characteristics in common with other cells, including a cell body, or *soma,* and a *nucleus.* For purposes of this discussion, though, the important parts of a neuron are those that assist the cell in carrying out its primary function— that is, to communicate with other neurons or with sensory or motor systems. The **dendrites** of a neuron are short, branchlike extensions that receive input from neighboring cells. The longer protruding part of the neuron is the **axon,** and it acts as the transmitting end of the cell. Although there are exceptions, axons of many nerve cells carry the cell's message to the dendrites of neighboring cells. Neurons are not physically connected to one another in the nervous system. Rather, they are separated by a microscopically small gulf, known as the **synaptic gap.** The chemical events that unfold within this gap are of monumental importance to adaptive behavior, including learning and memory.

Neural Transmission as an Electrochemical Process   The cells that make up a nervous system carry a small electric charge and transmit chemical messages to one another. For this reason, it is accurate to say that neural transmission, the process by which neurons communicate with one another, is an

neurons   individual nerve cells that make up the nervous system

dendrite   structure of neuron that receives input or message from neighboring cells

axon   structure of neuron that transmits action potential to neighboring nerve cells

synaptic gap   area separating two neurons

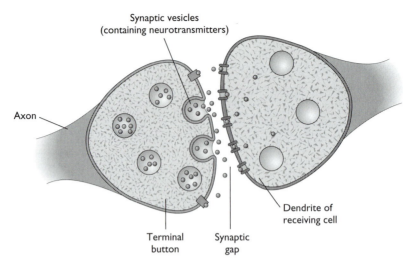

Synaptic vesicles
(containing neurotransmitters)

Axon

Terminal
button

Synaptic
gap

Dendrite of
receiving cell

FIGURE 10.2 Synaptic Activity During Action Potential (Nerve Impulse).

resting state nega-
tive charge within a
cell when the action
potential is not being
produced

action potential
change in electrical
charge of cell from
negative to positive

synaptic vesicles
spherical sacs in termi-
nal button containing
neurotransmitters

neurotransmitters
chemical messengers
released by axon into
synaptic gap

electrochemical one. That is, all of the cells that make up a nervous system
speak a common physical language. Ordinarily the fluid that surrounds a
neuron (extracellular fluid) contains a large number of positively charged
molecules—primarily sodium (Na^+) and chloride (Cl^-). The inside of the
cell contains other molecules, most notably potassium (K^+), and there is a
negative charge inside the cell relative to the outside. When in this state (negative charge inside relative to outside), the cell is inactive, or in its **resting
state.** But neurons are almost continuously receiving messages from other
cells, and, depending upon the nature of these messages, a cell's electrical
charge can change. This happens because the membrane of the cell's wall is
semipermeable, meaning that it can actually allow ions to flow in and out of
the cell.

Given certain kinds of stimulation from surrounding cells, a neuron's
semipermeable membrane may allow a large influx of positively charged
ions to rush into the cell, while at the same time pumping many of the negatively charged ions outside the cell. This exchange of ions results in a change
in the electrical potential of the neuron, from negative to positive, and is
referred to as an **action potential.** Thus, the neuron has now become active,
having produced, in ordinary language, a nerve impulse. This change in electrical potential then moves like a wave down the length of the neuron's axon.
When the action potential reaches the end of the axon (sometimes called the
terminal button), small, spherical **synaptic vesicles** become activated (Figure
10.2). These vesicles contain the chemicals, called **neurotransmitters,** that
will carry the cell's message to the next neuron. When the action potential
reaches the terminal button, the vesicles migrate to the end of the button,
rupture, and release the neurotransmitters into the synaptic gap. The neurotransmitters then make their way across the gap and make contact with
receptor sites on the adjacent cell's dendrites in a lock-and-key fashion.
Depending on its location in the nervous system and its specific chemical

makeup, the neurotransmitter tends to either facilitate (excite) or impede (inhibit) an action potential in this adjacent neuron.

It has taken you much longer to read this section than it takes the actual process of neural transmission to occur. In fact, if this were not the case, you would have perished long ago, the victim of an inept nervous system. Fortunately, taking into consideration the number of neurons that make up a nervous system, the large numbers of connections that form between neurons, and the speed at which neurons can conduct an action potential, the working system is both powerful and efficient. After all, the human nervous system must be able to produce such varied accomplishments as a baby's first steps, a basketball player's slam dunk, a chess master's comprehensive knowledge of moves, an actor's perfect recall of a script, and the deft movements of a surgeon's knife. As it turns out, many of the cells in the nervous system can conduct hundreds of action potentials per second, making possible all of these behaviors and many more. Of course, the complex repertoires that humans are capable of aren't due simply to the random firing of large numbers of neurons.

Needless to say, some order must reign in the nervous system if the actions of any organism are going to be appropriately responsive to contingencies in its immediate environment. It follows, then, that neurons must be arranged in some kind of meaningful relationship to one another, for organization and integration are among the chief responsibilities of a nervous system. Many advances being made in modern neuroscience revolve around identifying organized collections of neurons that carry out or contribute in important ways to specific behavioral functions. In addition, functional connections between neurons can be strengthened through various kinds of experiences, including those that have been formally studied by psychologists interested in learning and memory.

Neural Networks and Integration of Information   Chapter 8 alluded to the concept of a *neural network*—a collection of individual nerve cells that function as a unit to solve some perceptual or behavioral problem. Scientists who propose neural networks to explain behavioral phenomena are sometimes referred to as *connectionists*, because their models emphasize the fundamental fact that neurons working together in concert are capable of amazingly powerful functions that could not be carried out by individual cells. Connectionists build theoretical models of neural networks to explain domain-specific tasks, such as discriminating a triangle from a square, identifying a specific animal as a dog rather than a cat, or applying a grammatical rule, such as when to place the suffix *-ed* at the end of a verb to indicate past tense. Although such models are hypothetical, connectionists argue that they are based on the fundamental excitatory and inhibitory properties of neurons and are therefore consistent with the empirical findings of neuroscience.

The individual components that make up a neural network are referred to as **neurodes,** and they are the conceptual equivalent of neurons in an actual nervous system. Figure 10.3 depicts a simple neural network composed of neurodes A, B, and C. As you can see, neurodes A and B both provide input to neurode C. In this case, neuorde A provides positive, or

neurode hypothetical nerve cell meant to symbolize a neuron within a neural network

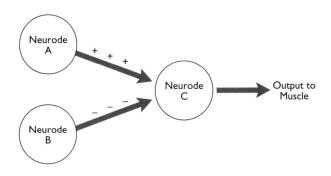

FIGURE 10.3 Simple Neural Network.

excitatory, input, whereas neurode B provides negative, or inhibitory, input to C. Whether or not neurode C "fires" in the neural network will depend on the summary of excitatory and inhibitory information it receives from neurodes A and B. Activation of neurode C may represent the response to a discrimination or conceptual task or the decision of whether or not to apply a grammatical rule. Or neurode C may be directly linked to some muscle system such that its output determines whether or not a specific movement occurs. The neural networks proposed by researchers are much more complicated than the one depicted in Figure 10.3 because they are intended to illustrate the activity of a real nervous system in which individual neurons may form thousands of connections with other neurons. Consequently, even hypothesized neural networks can contain numerous neurodes and complex connections.

In order for a neural network to be flexible and powerful in explaining behavior, it must be amenable to modification. This means that the strength and direction of connections between neurodes must be sensitive to experience, or, in the language of connectionism, the neurode must be "trainable." A neural network that has the job of classifying objects as either *dog* or *not dog* must be able to adjust its criteria based on feedback, and most neural network models make explicit how the system can alter its functions as a result of experience (Rosenblatt, 1958; Rummelhart & McClelland, 1986). Providing additional power to the neural network is the fact that information in the system is distributed throughout various neurode collections, not housed centrally in one unit. That is, several collections of neurodes may be contributing unique information to the entire network's output, and these separate functions may be carried out simultaneously. Researchers use the phrase **parallel processing** to refer to an information processing system that can distribute processing demands across different subsystems, each working at the same time. This contrasts with sequential processors, like those found in computers, that must deal with the demands of information processing in a serial manner, one piece of information at a time. Neural networks, and the actual nervous system on which such models are based, operate as parallel processors and are consequently capable of the kinds of information processing feats that a biological organism must accomplish to adapt to a constantly changing world.

parallel processing distribution of information processing demands across different subsystems, each working at the same time

Building Connections Through Learning

If the nervous system were unmodifiable—incapable of benefiting from experience—you would not be reading this book. Nor would you be engaged in any number of activities that you have long since mastered, from balancing a checkbook to surfing the Internet. The nervous systems of most animals, however, are ever changing, particularly in response to important encounters with the environment. Especially in childhood, new connections form between neurons at an amazing rate, and new neural connections or networks may be formed whenever people are confronted with new tasks or problems to be solved. The ability of the nervous system to undergo structural and functional change as a result of experience is sometimes referred to as *plasticity,* and the book you hold in your hands right now would be inconceivable in the absence of this simple feature.

To a large extent, the manner in which your body parts have come together during your development was scripted by your genetic blueprint. Certain cells were going to become bone, others skin, still others were destined to be blood cells, and so on. Even the development of your brain and spinal cord was largely predetermined at the moment of your conception. But the real clue to a nervous system's functioning is not so much the presence of several billion cells, but the specific number and complexity of connections that form between these cells. Scientists now know that experience plays a crucial role in the manner in which the brain gets "wired up" throughout people's lives.

Several experiments, for instance, have shown how critical early sensory input is to the development of a visual system that will later have to deal with a complex visual world. When kittens are deprived of vision in one eye (usually by stitching the eyelids closed), they become functionally blind in that eye, though vision in the unaffected eye remains normal (Rittenhouse, Shouval, Paradiso, & Bear, 1999). In addition, animals exposed early on to a visual field made up exclusively of horizontal lines are later unable to respond to lines of a vertical orientation (Stryker & Sherk, 1975; Stryker, Sherk, Leventhal, & Hirsch, 1978). Early deprivation affects the development of cells in the animal's visual cortex, though the magnitude of the effect depends on the length of deprivation and on the nature of later visual experiences (Kirkwood, Lee, & Bear, 1995).

The enrichment provided by a stimulating environment clearly has implications for brain development. Rosenzweig and Bennett (1996) raised two groups of rats in different kinds of environments, one fairly impoverished, the other providing rich stimulation and opportunities for various kinds of learning. Comparison of the two groups revealed numerous differences in brain structure and organization. The animals exposed to an enriched environment possessed a thicker neocortex and had larger accumulations of acetylcholine, a neurotransmitter known to play a substantial role in learning and memory. In addition, these animals' brains contained more glial cells, which are cells that surround neurons and provide various support and protective functions for neurons. Thus, the kinds of experiences that organisms encounter, especially early in life, have much to do with how the brain becomes wired, and these experiences set the stage for later experience as well.

Pavlovian Conditioning and the Brain   If simple sensory input can be shown to influence the types of connections formed between neurons, it follows that similar effects would take place during learning experiments. In fact, you may recall that Pavlov, being a physiologist, was specifically interested in viewing classical conditioning as a phenomenon occurring at the level of the nervous system. Remember, the subtitle of his classic work was *An Investigation of the Physiological Activity of the Cerebral Cortex* (1927). Pavlov believed that the behavioral facts of conditioning—dogs learning to salivate in the presence of bells and lights—were directly tied to connections being formed within the brain. Modern scientists might suggest that Pavlov was studying the formation of specialized neural networks. Pavlov, however, was at a considerable disadvantage because it was simply not possible, in his time, to directly observe the activity of the cerebral cortex during conditioning.

Figure 10.4 depicts a potential assembly of cells whose connections might be altered as the result of a conditioning procedure. Assume that cell A is a neuron in the animal's sensory cortex that responds to the tactile sensation of food (US) being placed in the mouth. Ordinarily this cell would, by way of an action potential, communicate a strong message to cell C, a motor neuron connected to the salivary glands. Thus, a message from cell A to cell C would produce the unconditional reflex of salivation when food is placed in the mouth of the animal. Cell B is a neuron in the sensory cortex that is responsive to auditory (sound) stimulation. During conditioning trials, this neuron is stimulated by presentation of an initially neutral stimulus, a ringing bell. At the beginning of conditioning, stimulation of cell B provokes no response in cell C; that is, there is no link between the sound of a ringing bell and the activity of the salivary glands. There is, however, a strong relationship between cells A and C, a connection largely due to phylogenetic history; all mammals naturally salivate to food being placed in the mouth.

During conditioning, the already strong connection between cells A and C is repeatedly paired with the neutral stimulus (bell) that activates cell B. Eventually, activation of cell C spreads or transfers to cell B, which previously responded only to the neutral stimulus (bell). At some point the presentation of the bell by itself will produce salivation, indicating the acquisition of a conditioned reflex. At the neural level, cell B has formed a strong connection to cell C as a result of repeated activation simultaneously with activation of cell A. The three cells now form a neural circuit, and stimulation of cell B by itself is sufficient to produce salivation. Keep in mind that this is a rather simplistic depiction of what actually goes on in an intact nervous system. The example isolates a small number of cells to portray a neural network that might be responsible for a specific conditioned reflex. In actuality, such a network would be more complicated, involving many more individual neurons, many of which would have connections to other sensory and motor neurons throughout the nervous system. In fact, this would have to

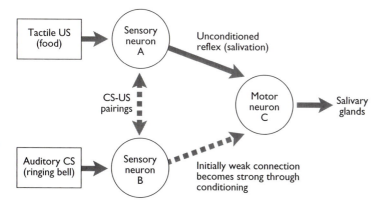

FIGURE 10.4 Strengthening of Neural Connections Through Pavlovian Conditioning.

be the case to explain such phenomena as generalization, higher order classical conditioning, and other Pavlovian phenomena.

It is also important to acknowledge that the generic neural network described here could in fact be created in many places in the nervous system, depending upon the nature of the sensory and motor systems involved. For instance, several researchers have attempted to identify those regions of the nervous system in which particular kinds of conditioning might occur. A case in point is the conditioned emotional reaction. Chapter 3 stated that the adaptive value of Pavlovian conditioning is primarily owing to an organism's ability to identify stimuli in the environment that signal or predict other events having important biological consequences. Being able to recognize stimuli that portend dangerous events, such as a falling tree or a nearby predator, would be of significant survival value. Psychologists might expect, then, that sights, sounds, or smells that evoke strong emotions, including fear, may be easily conditioned and that particular regions in the brain may have evolved specialized circuits for this kind of learning.

LeDoux and his colleagues (LeDoux, 1992, 1995, 1998, 2000; LeDoux, Sakaguchi, & Reis, 1984; Rogan, Staeubli, & LeDoux, 1997) carried out a series of experiments in which rats were classically conditioned to an auditory stimulus. Foot shock was used as the US, a stimulus to which rats ordinarily respond by jumping or running in an effort to get away from the stimulus. In addition, there are standard physiological responses to such a stimulus, including increased respiration and secretion of adrenaline and stress hormones. Once the animals had experienced several paired presentations of the shock with the auditory stimulus (CS), the CS, when presented by itself, came to provoke these same reactions. In addition, animals often became completely immobile during presentation of the CS. This *freezing response* is a species-typical defense reaction that many smaller mammals exhibit in the wild under conditions of threat. Of course, the researchers were interested in more than the overt physical reactions of the animals to the conditioning procedure. After all, even Pavlov had shown that animals could be conditioned to many neutral stimuli that portended aversive events, such as shock. LeDoux was trying to identify which structures or regions in the brain were altered as a result of the conditioning procedure.

The answer turned out not to be surprising. In fact, it converged rather nicely with what brain researchers had long observed about the neural regulation of emotional behavior. In mammals, an assortment of relatively primitive structures, collectively known as the **limbic system** (Figure 10.5), is known to have numerous effects on both emotional responding and motivated behavior, such as mating and eating and drinking. One of these structures, the **amygdala,** has been specifically implicated in strong emotional arousal. LeDoux and colleagues found that several nuclei, or collections of cells, in the amygdala showed increased activity during conditioned emotion experiments. One particular nucleus, the *central nucleus,* seems to be especially important in regulating emotional reactions in animals. When the central nucleus of the amygdala is electrically stimulated, animals display behaviors that are typically provoked by dangerous or threatening stimuli. If stimulation of the nucleus continues, animals not only exhibit a prolonged stress reaction, but also become susceptible to developing ulcers (Henke, 1982). Alternatively, if the central nucleus is destroyed, animals become unusually docile and do not respond in a typical way to threatening stimuli (LeDoux, 1992).

The amygdala takes on special importance in the case of aversive stimuli, but conditioning can occur to nonaversive stimuli as well, and the amygdala does not necessarily play a role in all instances of Pavlovian conditioning. Another species that has contributed much to understanding the neural basis of conditioning is the rabbit, whose somewhat unusual eyelid construction lends itself well to Pavlovian procedures. Rabbits possess what is often thought of as a third eyelid, called a nictitating membrane, that serves to protect the eye from potentially damaging objects. The *nictitating membrane* closes automatically, covering the sensitive cornea, under potentially damaging conditions, such as an abrupt sandstorm. Closure of the membrane clearly represents an unconditional response to an unconditional stimulus, and researchers correctly surmised that this response could be brought under Pavlovian control. Using a tone as a conditioned stimulus (CS), and a brief puff of air to the eye as the unconditioned stimulus (US), experimenters have been able to demonstrate Pavlovian conditioning of the nictitating membrane in a manner consistent with Pavlov's original research (Gormezano, Kehoe, & Marshall, 1983; Gormezano, Schneiderman, Deaux, & Fuentes, 1962).

In addition to the behavioral evidence, contemporary research has successfully identified brain regions that appear to be activated during the conditioning process. In particular, nuclei contained in the cerebellum show no response prior to conditioning, but become increasingly active throughout the conditioning process. Of course, the cells in this particular nucleus in the cerebellum have connections with many other structures in the brain, so you might be wondering if the conditioned response was actually "learned" in the cerebellum or in one of the other structures. Through a series of ingenious experiments, Thompson (1986) was able to rule out these alternative explanations. For instance, when activity in the cerebellar nucleus was chem-

limbic system collection of primitive brain structures influencing motivation and emotion

amygdala structure in limbic system associated with strong negative emotions, such as rage

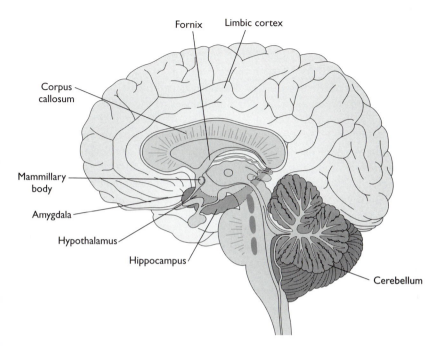

Fornix   Limbic cortex

Corpus
callosum

Mammillary
body

Amygdala

Hypothalamus

Hippocampus

Cerebellum

FIGURE 10.5 Major Structures of the Limbic System.

ically suppressed, standard Pavlovian conditioning had no effect. When the nucleus was allowed to recover from this suppressed state, however, standard CS-US pairing led to successful conditioning. Further experiments demonstrated that although additional brain structures may play a role in outward expression of the conditioned response, the original learning, or acquisition, was specifically attributable to the cerebellar nucleus. Although humans don't have a nictitating membrane, our eyelids serve essentially the same protective function, and eye-blink conditioning has been demonstrated in humans. Moreover, the cerebellum appears to play as important a role in eye-blink conditioning in humans as it does in other mammals (Logan & Grafton, 1995; Woodruff-Pak, Papka, & Ivry, 1996).

Operant Conditioning and the Brain   Pavlovian conditioning involves a contingency between two environmental stimuli (CS-US), and contemporary research has done much to vindicate Pavlov's position that the conditioning process leads to the strengthening of neural connections. Might the same be true of operant conditioning, in which contingencies develop between behavior and consequent stimuli? In some ways, the question is a more involved one, because operant learning actually involves connections between three separate components—discriminative stimuli, behavior, and consequences (the three-term contingency). It follows, then, that the neurological activity that underlies operant learning may entail a similarly complex collection of neural networks operating in an integrative fashion. Research seems to bear this notion out.

To get a sense of what researchers must account for physiologically, let's consider what kinds of behavioral facts make up even a relatively simple operant. Recall that in a *discriminated operant,* an organism must learn to engage in a specific response in the presence of one stimulus, but not in its absence. This particular kind of behavior is ordinarily produced through differential reinforcement, in which responses to the correct stimulus produce reinforcement and responses to the incorrect stimulus produce either no consequence or aversive consequences. Thus, for behavior to come under discriminative control, the organism must first attend to relevant features of the environment, and that means that pertinent sensory receptors (visual, auditory, olfactory, etc.) must receive stimulation and convey this information to higher centers of the nervous system. This relevant sensory information must then be transmitted to several regions of the motor-cortex in order to give rise to the appropriate response on the part of the organism. There is more to the story, of course, because operant behavior *operates on the environment to produce consequences.* These consequences are stimuli, sometimes boasting several dimensions (food, for instance, has visual, olfactory, and gustatory characteristics) that further impinge on sensory receptors. This information must not only be relayed to appropriate regions of the brain, but also connected in meaningful ways to the stimulation produced by the discriminative stimulus and the neural activity responsible for the actual behavior. That is, the operant must become a behavioral whole and be represented in the nervous system as an integrated unit.

basal ganglia structures lying beneath the cortex that serve to integrate sensory input and motor functioning

Although many regions of the brain are undoubtedly implicated in operant learning, a collection of structures beneath the cortex, the **basal ganglia,** serve the indispensable function of integrating sensory information and motor activity. Structures of the basal ganglia form an immense labyrinth of connections with both the sensory cortex and the several motor cortices, and they constantly monitor activity in these regions (Houk, Davis, & Beiser, 1995). It is interesting to note that the basal ganglia do not appear to be critical to the initial development of operant behavior, but seem largely responsible for "taking over" the automatic execution of an operant once it has been acquired. Many operant repertoires, even complex ones like driving a car or operating a computer, become fairly automatic once mastered, and activity in the basal ganglia corresponds more to this automatic behavior than to the operant during acquisition. In addition, increased activity in the basal ganglia occurs when behavior is under the control of instructional stimuli, that is, when behavior is rule governed. Further evidence for the basal ganglia's role in operant learning comes from studies in which these structures have been damaged. McDonald and White (1993) found that lesions to the basal ganglia of rats impaired their ability to learn a simple operant task.

Structures of the basal ganglia have been shown to have similar repercussions for human learning. Several studies have demonstrated learning deficits in patients with Parkinson's disease, a degenerative neurological disease whose symptoms include muscle rigidity, tremors, and impairment in initiating movement. Parkinson's is believed to result from degeneration of cells in the *nigrostriatal system,* which includes structures of the basal gan-

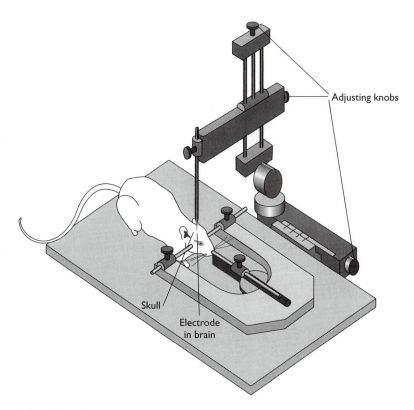

FIGURE 10.6 Stereotaxic Apparatus Used in Small-Animal Research.

glia. Parkinson's patients have exhibited deficits in visual discrimination tasks (Owen et al., 1992) and appear not to benefit from feedback when learning to predict probabilistic outcomes, such as weather forecasting (Knowlton, Mangels, & Squire, 1996).

In many ways, the defining event in operant learning is the consequence itself. Reinforcing stimuli, by definition, strengthen the behavior that produces them, and this must mean that some critical event occurs in the nervous system when a reinforcing stimulus is made contingent on a specific behavior. Physiological psychologists have pursued the neurological basis of reinforcement for many years, and, like other such stories in science, the enterprise has been colored by its fair share of laboratory drama and serendipity. In 1954, Olds and Milner were exploring the effects of electrical stimulation of the brain in rats. Now, the brain of a rat is relatively small, and delivering electrical stimulation to a highly specific region is difficult, requiring stealth and precision. Such procedures therefore require both an immobilized animal and equipment that allows for such precision. Using stereotaxic apparatus, scientists conduct a surgical procedure to achieve accurate placement of electrodes (Figure 10.6).

Once the electrodes are implanted, the animal can be allowed some freedom of movement within an experimental apparatus, such as a maze or an operant chamber. Now, no two brains are exactly alike, and, although the details of brain anatomy were relatively well known in the 1950s, there is always a margin of error when attempting to place the electrode. Fortunately for the science of psychology, Olds and Milner erred in the placement of their electrode. Rather than stimulating the animal's *reticular system,* the electrode is thought to have ended up in a portion of the animal's **hypothalamus,** a structure that is known to assist in the regulation of motivated behavior (eating, drinking, mating, etc.) in many mammals, including humans.

hypothalamus brain structure known to be associated with motivated behavior, particularly appetitive and sexual behavior

The results of stimulating this region of the brain were both dramatic and surprising. Olds and Milner were assuming that the stimulation would have aversive properties, but what they observed convinced them otherwise. The researchers discovered that the animals would return immediately to that location in the experimental chamber in which they received the stimulation. Soon, the animals were spending all of their time in this specific location. Olds and Milner surmised that the electrode must be stimulating a "pleasure center" in the brain, not producing aversive stimulation as they had originally intended. In further experiments, the researchers connected the electrode to the lever in an operant chamber, allowing animals to deliver their own stimulation, or to *self-stimulate.* The strength of this stimulation as a reinforcer is well attested to by Olds and Milner's observation that animals would self-stimulate at rates approaching 1,000 responses per hour.

Olds and Milner's groundbreaking study opened up an entire field of neuroscience, as researchers enthusiastically began mining the nervous system, searching for different locations that might function as reinforcement centers (Milner, 1991). Although many such candidates exist, considerable research has emphasized the *medial forebrain bundle (MFB),* whose axons pass through the lateral hypothalamus on their way to connecting regions of the midbrain and forebrain. The lateral hypothalamus was probably the region accidentally stimulated by Olds and Milner, and modern researchers often target this area intentionally, with much the same result. In fact, stimulation of several regions in the MFB functions as a reinforcer (Olds & Fobes, 1981; Routtenberg & Malsbury, 1969), and blocking receptors in the same area reduces this effect (Stellar, Kelley, & Corbett, 1983).

Electricity is but one means of stimulating brain tissue. Recall from the beginning of this chapter that the brain actually speaks an *electrochemical* language, and the release and subsequent fate of neurotransmitters in the synapse contribute enormously to behavior. Increasingly, contemporary research on the brain's reinforcement centers has focused on the role of chemistry, including both the neurotransmitters that occur naturally in the brain and the many legal and illegal substances long known by humans to produce pleasurable feelings. The primary neurotransmitter activated within the MFB is dopamine, and increased dopamine activity corresponds to the delivery of many natural or primary reinforcers, including food, water, and access to sexual stimulation. In addition, Ljungberg, Apicella, and Schultz (1992) have demonstrated increased dopamine activity in monkeys when the sight and sound of a door opening was paired with a small piece of apple. The increased dopamine activity in response to the door opening suggests that dopamine plays a role not only in primary reinforcement, but also in the development of conditioned reinforcers. Finally, many addictive drugs, including alcohol, cocaine, and nicotine, stimulate release of dopamine in the MFB, a fact that many researchers believe will help shed light on the dynamics of drug tolerance and addiction (Di Chiara, 1995; Hyman, 1996; Milner, 1991; Robinson & Berridge, 1993).

✖ INTERIM SUMMARY

Advances in neuroscience have made it possible for researchers to get a close look at the nervous system activity that corresponds to Pavlovian and operant conditioning. Consistent with Pavlov's original speculation, modern neuroscientists view learning as a process by which neural networks, as specific functional units, become strengthened over time. In the case of Pavlovian conditioning, these networks have been located chiefly in the limbic system and the cerebellum. Regulation of operant behavior, particularly complex operants that become well established, has been linked to activity in the basal ganglia, and several reinforcement centers have been identified, especially in networks that project through the medial forebrain bundle (MFB).

✖ THOUGHT QUESTIONS

1. The chapter discusses how much more power and flexibility accrues to a parallel processing system than to a serial processing system. Think of a relatively complex behavioral activity you engage in (one that is not mentioned in this chapter). In as much detail as possible, describe the parallel processing that your nervous system would have to achieve in order for you to accomplish the behavior.

2. Olds and Milner's rats were engaged in self-stimulation. Other than through drugs and/or sexual contact, describe some ways in which people (yourself included) might self-stimulate. How would you classify the reinforcers in your example: primary or conditioned?

MEMORY AND THE NERVOUS SYSTEM

This chapter's opening vignette is a reminder of how much people take certain behavioral abilities for granted—until, of course, they lose them. Miriam's personal tragedy resulted from what might have been a rather trivial memory lapse: She simply forgot that she had put a pan on the stove and turned the burner on. But unlike perhaps dozens of other such lapses, this one cost Miriam her home—and almost her life. Sadly, the scenario is not an unusual one. Today, many elderly Americans are confined to nursing homes and other supervised living arrangements, sometimes because of a degree of forgetfulness that could prove dangerous, either to themselves or to loved ones. Modern medicine is a long way from an effective cure for such memory deficits, but rapidly accumulating research is providing a welcome look at the underlying machinery (Gabrieli, 1998; Tulving, 1998). You won't be surprised to read that this "machinery" is none other than the human nervous system.

How Memory Is Localized in the Nervous System

In response to an exam item asking you to identify the founder of behaviorism, you come up with the name John B. Watson. Or when asked for your phone number, you rattle off the seven-digit number with little effort or hesitation. And when a friend lets you borrow his car, you get behind the wheel and refamiliarize yourself quickly with the mechanics of driving a stick shift, even though it has been years since you drove anything other than an automatic. When you remember John B. Watson, or your phone number, or how to drive a stick shift, where exactly in your nervous system was this memory located? How did it get there in the first place, and how was it activated when you needed it? These questions may seem relatively simple to answer. After all, if everything you think and do is in some way represented in your brain, it should be a relatively straightforward task to "find" the location of specific memories and to come to an understanding of how they are formed and then retrieved when needed. But of course this is no simpler than locating Pavlovian or operant conditioning in the nervous system, both of which rely upon several, sometimes intricately connected, neural networks. The story on memory is much the same, perhaps even more convoluted. As Chapter 7 explained, memory comes in many forms and serves many different functions. Contemporary research has shown that these different types of memory are not all created equal, even at the level of the nervous system.

Lashley and the Equipotentiality Hypothesis   Among the founders of modern physiological psychology was Karl Lashley (1890–1958), a student of John B. Watson's at the University of Chicago. Lashley devoted much of his career to studying the effects of damage to the brain on learning, particularly maze running, in rats. The results of such experiments, often involving cutting various regions of the subjects' neocortex, puzzled Lashley. Frequently, the cuts had no negative impact on maze learning, leading Lashley to refute Pavlov's speculation that conditioning resulted in new connections being formed in the cortex. Lashley was eventually able to produce impairment, usually by making numerous cuts in the neocortex, but his results did not seem to point to any specific location as being critical for learning. Consequently, Lashley reasoned that all brain matter is roughly the same, making the same contribution to learning and behavior—a position that became known as the **equipotentiality hypothesis.** His experimental results also led him to believe that although location of damage didn't matter, overall amount of damage did. Thus Lashley also contributed the hypothesis of *mass action*, meaning that the quantity or amount of cortex involved, not location, is what affects learning and behavior.

equipotentiality hypothesis Lashley's notion that all brain matter is functionally equivalent, capable of producing equal amounts and types of learning

Contemporary research has not been especially kind to Lashley's ideas about nervous system functioning. As already discussed, neuroscientists have discovered that even simple learning involves multiple regions of the brain, including those that lie beneath the neocortex. In addition, modern precision instruments have allowed for much more specific monitoring; thus it is now easier to isolate specific pathways or regions for purpose of analysis. Perhaps most important, though, is the finding that different functional categories of memory (declarative, episodic, procedural, etc.) are represented in different ways and often in different regions of the brain. This fact should not be too surprising, considering the way various systems and organs of the body "specialize" at different functions. For that matter, the different components of man-made machines do the same. The carburetor, pistons, spark plugs, and alternator all serve different functions in starting and running a car engine, and your lungs, heart, and kidneys carry on important, though distinct, biological activities. Memory, too, is a diverse collection of cognitive processes, and the way these processes are distributed in the nervous system is similarly diverse. Nevertheless, neuroscientists have discovered some specific operating principles that appear necessary to most forms of memory, regardless of nervous system location. Let's take a look at one such principle.

The Hebb Rule and Long-Term Potentiation (LTP)   All episodes of learning and memory involve long-term changes in behavioral potential, and this temporal dimension must somehow be represented in the nervous system. In other words, neural activity produced during learning experiences must endure in some form, or else there would not be anything very adaptive about the ability to learn. What good would it do you to know how to calculate a standard deviation on Monday but forget it before Friday's test? Can you imagine having to be reminded of your best friend's name every day? Or having to relearn how to use a telephone every time you made a phone call? Happily, these are problems that most people with intact learning and memory skills don't encounter because, when they learn something, changes occur in the nervous system that help to maintain the original learning. As covered earlier, Pavlov speculated about the physiological underpinnings of conditioning, and Lashley further pursued, with limited success, the physical representation of memory. Although all the details have not been worked out, contemporary neuroscientists are more convinced than ever that the physical process responsible for the relative permanence of learning and memory has been identified.

In 1949, psychologist Donald Hebb suggested that the enduring nature of learning and memory must be due to some permanent alteration in a neuron's sensitivity to stimulation. The first section of this chapter discussed a hypothetical neural network, or collection of functionally connected nerve cells. Cells A and B each sent axons to cell C, which was in turn connected to a particular muscle. Hebb reasoned that if cell A produces an action potential, and this impulse reaches cell C, activity in cell C may increase at the same time that an impulse is being transmitted from cell B. Because the impulse from cell B reaches cell C during a period of increased activity, the connection between cells B and C actually strengthens. Hebb believed that certain chemical and structural properties in cell C become altered by this simultaneous activity, such that cell C becomes increasingly responsive to activity in cell B in the future, a position known as the *Hebb rule*.

Hebb's speculations about what was happening in the synapse have been largely confirmed by recent findings from neuroscience. When the dendrites of a particular neuron have been activated, and the cell receives additional input from other neurons, changes in the properties of the receiving dendrites do in fact occur (Bliss & Lomo, 1973). Several studies have shown that dendritic synapses become more receptive to glutamate, a major excitatory neurotransmitter in the nervous system (Liao, Hessler, & Malinow, 1995; Meberg, Barnes, McNaughton, & Routtenberg, 1993; Sanes & Lichtman, 1999; Tocco, Maren, Shors, Baudry, & Thompson, 1992). In essence, the dendrites have become sensitized, or *potentiated,* and this makes them even more receptive to further stimulation. In addition, changes in the actual structure of the synapse have been documented. Using sophisticated microscopy, Hosokawa, Rusakov, Bliss, and Fine (1995) showed that the dendritic branches of the receiving cell actually elongated as a result of continued activity, thus allowing a larger area of stimulation. There is also evidence that the dendrites may send out additional spines or fingers, a process known as dendritic branching, which also allows for more synapses with the presynaptic neuron (Engert & Bonhoeffer, 1999; Toni, Buchs, Nikonenko, Bron, & Muller, 1999).

When the receiving cell experiences input in the form of multiple, rapid impulses from several axons, the dendrites become much more sensitive or responsive to the same kind of stimulation. This increased responsiveness can last for days or weeks and has therefore been called **long-term potentiation (LTP).** Long-term potentiation has been confirmed in several regions of the brain (Rogan et al., 1997), especially the hippocampal region, and may represent the physiological representation of memory so long sought by the likes of Pavlov, Lashley, and Hebb. Let's not forget how, on more than one occasion, the detective work involved in tracking down the precise physiological correlates of a specific learning or memory episode has gone awry. Stevens (1998) has cautioned researchers against viewing long-term potentiation as an all-encompassing explanation for the large number of behavioral phenomena that fall under the heading of learning and cognition. History has often shown the soundness of such advice.

long-term potentiation (LTP) increased and long-lasting responsiveness of dendrites due to repeated stimulation

Evidence for Different Memory Systems

Today's imaging devices have revolutionized the neurosciences, but much was known about the information processing capacity of the nervous system before such technology came on the scene—a good deal of it provided by clinical case studies. A particularly noteworthy example is patient H. M., first discussed in Chapter 7, who underwent radical surgery in 1953 to treat severe epileptic seizures (Milner, 1968, 1972). The surgery involved removal of several structures in the medial temporal region, including the amygdala and hippocampus, both of which have been shown to play a role in various kinds of learning. Though successful in reducing seizure activity, the surgery resulted in several side effects that soon made themselves known in H. M.'s daily attempts to process information about his world. One deficit that became apparent was his inability to remember experiences that had preceded the surgery by several years, a form of memory loss called retrograde amnesia. Retrograde amnesia is a fairly common occurrence in cases of brain trauma, such as that associated with serious vehicular accidents. In recovering from such an incident, people often have little or no memory of the events that immediately preceded the accident.

In addition, H. M. suffered from anterograde amnesia, an inability to form new memories subsequent to the surgery. The latter amnesia proved especially exasperating, for H. M., like Miriam in the chapter's opening vignette, was prone to forgetting such things as activities he had just taken part in or people he had just met. These specific memory deficits were all the more surprising given H. M.'s normal functioning in so many other cognitive domains. He had little difficulty remembering events or episodes in his life that preceded the surgery by many years (childhood and early adulthood experiences), and neither his language nor intellectual abilities exhibited any decline after the surgery.

The fact that H. M.'s amnesia was selective suggested to researchers the possibility of various memory systems, perhaps each represented uniquely in the nervous system. The distinction between long-term and short-term memory is one example, and the case of H. M. is often taken as support for this classification system. But there is more to memory than this simple distinction, and in-depth assessment of H. M. revealed some remarkable nuances in how people commit different types of information to memory. For instance, a common measure of short-term memory is the digit-span test, in which subjects are presented, usually verbally, with a sequence of digits, then immediately asked to recall the digits in their proper sequence. Consistent with Miller's (1956) famous "seven, plus or minus two" depiction of short-term memory (see Chapter 7), most people can accomplish this task with relative ease when the number of digits is between 5 and 9. With practice, most people can handle considerably more digits (up to 20), though mastering a longer list requires more rehearsal. H. M., on the other hand, was unable to extend his digit-span recall beyond six digits, even with continued practice, and this has been shown to be true of other amnesic patients as well (Drachman & Arbit, 1966; Talland, 1965). What this finding seems to indicate is that H. M.'s short-term memory is functional, but it has a much more limited capacity than that of most people.

The short-term/long-term distinction refers to the temporal quality of memory, but there are other important dimensions along which memories differ. For example, researchers distinguish between declarative memory (the recall of facts and concepts that one has learned) and procedural memory (recall of particular skills or habits previously acquired). Considerable research has demonstrated that amnesics suffer significant deficits in declarative memory, both for information acquired prior to the disease or injury onset, and for novel information encountered afterward (Cohen & Squire, 1981; Shimamura & Squire, 1987). Procedural memory, however, shows little disruption in many amnesic patients. Most patients, H. M. included, retain basic skills that they possessed prior to their illness or injury, such as how to drive a car, play an instrument, cook a meal, and so on. In addition, new skills can often be learned and exhibit improvement with practice. In a mirror-tracing task, for instance, subjects must use a pencil to trace a line inside a geometric figure whose image they are looking at through a mirror. H. M. demonstrated increased performance at this as a function of practice, and demonstrated similar improvement in several other manual tasks (Brooks & Baddeley, 1976; Corkin, 1965). Subjects often do not remember when or how they learned or acquired the skill, but their measured improvement clearly indicates their having done so (Squire, 1987).

The functional distinction between declarative and procedural memory may even have an evolutionary basis. Rozin (1976) has suggested that procedural memory may be an antiquated component of the nervous system of many animals, having been selected because of its contribution to many adaptive problems. An organism's ability to solve problems posed by the environment, and to readily recall what it did to solve the problem, may be among the most critical information processing tasks assigned to the nervous system. This information need not be available to consciousness, as long as it can be tapped under relevant environmental conditions. That is, an organism doesn't have to have intentional awareness of how or why it learned to respond in a specific way to an environmental challenge; it simply needs to respond in an effective manner. Thus, procedural memory may be a primitive, but highly adaptive, information processing ability, while declarative memory may have emerged as an adaptation much more recently in our phylogenetic history. Consistent with this argument is the observation that procedural memory develops earlier in childhood than does declarative memory (Mandler, 1984; Nadel & Zola-Morgan, 1984).

Anterograde amnesia is easily the most striking feature of H. M.'s and other amnesic patients' memory deficits. Moreover, contemporary neuroscience has increasingly honed in on the brain structure that appears to bear a good deal of responsibility. The **hippocampus,** one of several structures within the limbic system, may make one of the most critical singular contributions to the formation of memories (Eichenbaum, 1994; Henke, 1999), and recall that forming new memories is precisely the difficulty in anterograde amnesia. Damage to the hippocampus has now been clearly identified as a common cause of anterograde amnesia. Bechara and colleagues (1995) presented three patients with a conditioned emotion task in which an aversive noise was paired with one of several randomly presented colored lights. One subject had experienced hippocampal damage, another had experienced damage to the amygdala, and the third subject had damage to both areas. Neither of the two subjects who had experienced damage to the amygdala developed an emotional reaction to the light paired with the aversive noise, whereas the subject with only hippocampal damage did. Conversely, the subjects with hippocampal damage were unable to articulate after the experiment the conditions to which they were exposed, regardless of whether they had in fact been emotionally conditioned. Thus, there appeared to have been a dissociation between the emotional conditioning and memory for the task itself, with hippocampal damage primarily being implicated in the latter.

Additional evidence for the role of the hippocampus in declarative memory comes from autopsies of amnesic patients. Zola-Morgan, Squire, and Amaral (1986) documented anterograde amnesia in a male patient who suffered a heart attack at age 52. Though surviving the heart attack, the patient experienced substantial anoxia, or loss of oxygen, which produced brain damage. When the patient died several years later, an autopsy revealed dam-

hippocampus structure in the limbic system having significant implications for formation of long-term memory

age to a specific region of the hippocampus, the CA1 field. Subsequent research identified damage to cells in the CA1 in other patients suffering from anterograde amnesia (Victor & Agamanolis, 1990). Also, nonhuman animals exposed to periods of anoxia have shown damage to this region of the hippocampus, along with corresponding anterograde amnesia (Auer, Jensen, & Whishaw, 1989). The CA1 field is a major hippocampal locus for the occurrence of long-term potentiation and is believed to play a prominent role in the formation of declarative memories. Imaging studies have revealed increased activity in this field during both encoding and retrieval of declarative information (Gabrieli, Brewer, Desmond, & Glover, 1997; Squire et al., 1992).

✖ INTERIM SUMMARY

The search for the neural representation of memory is a long and noble tradition in psychology, instigated by Pavlov's early speculations about conditioning and the nervous system. The experimental work and theories of Lashley and Hebb set the stage for modern neuroscience and the discovery of long-term potentiation, the enduring physical change in the synapse that allows the kind of permanence required of many learning and memory phenomena. Continued advances in neuroscience technology, combined with information from clinical cases of memory deficit, have led scientists to identify separate structures and regions of the nervous system responsible for memories that differ along several dimensions. The hippocampus, a structural component of the limbic system, has emerged as the most heralded and thoroughly researched "seat" of learning and memory, both because of its many connections to other brain regions and because of its well-documented capacity for long-term potentiation.

✖ THOUGHT QUESTIONS

1. Lashley was not very successful in localizing specific memories. How does the contemporary view that the nervous system is a parallel processor help to explain Lashley's failure?
2. From what you have learned about evolutionary adaptations in this book, how would you explain the fact that procedural memories appear to be more fundamental and enduring than declarative memories?

THE PHYLOGENY OF LEARNING AND COGNITION

This book's final section will come full circle, revisiting how learning and cognition are viewed as adaptive processes. Doing so will require a major change in perspective, for the chapter thus far has dealt with the details of nervous system functioning—the physical minutia, if you will, underlying learning and cognition. But a nervous system is an evolved organic structure, shaped over millions of years by the forces of natural selection. Consequently, it is important to remember that all of the information processing that humans do, including the many forms of learning and cognition discussed so far, is possible only because generations of hominids who came before us used these skills to successfully solve the riddles of survival and reproduction. We are, therefore, the beneficiaries of a long line of predecessors who learned the dangers of lightning and predators, fashioned tools to help bring down prey, found their way home from remote hunting grounds, found or constructed effective shelter from the elements, and negotiated dozens of additional obstacles in adapting to the world. The complex combinations of genes that afforded such abilities survive in us and, to a large extent, define us still.

The notion that modern humans learn, think, feel, and solve problems in essentially the same way that our early ancestors did is hard for some to swallow. The idea may even seem insulting to those of us who live in industrialized, technologically sophisticated cultures. Surely, modern humans, surrounded as we are by the triumphs of science and technology, cannot be compared to primitive hunter-gatherers eking out an existence on the African savanna. But much of the "progress" of the modern world has been developed only in the past century and can't be accounted for by any meaningful change in the human nervous system. Biological evolution occurs on a time scale measured in geological epochs, meaning that the remarkable advances enjoyed by those of us living in the 21st century are the product of the same human brain that discovered fire and built primitive stone tools. Psychologists, though historically reluctant to acknowledge this fact, have increasingly come to appreciate the role that evolution has played in fashioning our cognitive and behavioral dispositions, and this realization is beginning to bear impressive fruit.

Modern Evolutionary Psychology

In their provocative and insightful book, *New World New Mind,* Robert Ornstein and Paul Ehrlich (1989) describe the unique problems that modern humans encounter due to the striking mismatch between our primitive nervous system and the challenges of a technological, rapidly changing world. The lesson to be found in their book is a simple, though not necessarily appeasing, one. Our opposable thumbs and bipedal posture aren't the only products of our evolutionary heritage. Our psychological makeup, including the way we think and react to our world, is similarly shaped by natural selection, and this means that a serious assessment of learning and cognition cannot proceed without addressing a fundamental question: What essential adaptive problems did our ancestors need to solve in order to survive and reproduce, and what specific cognitive and behavioral skills contributed to their success? This question lies at the heart of **evolutionary psychology,** a conceptual approach that seeks the evolutionary, or adaptive, roots of all behavioral phenomena of interest to psychology—not only learning and cognition, but also human development, motivation and emotion, intelligence, social psychology, even behavioral pathology. Evolutionary psychology is a growing and increasingly visible force in contemporary psychology, as reflected in the publication of several recent textbooks (Buss, 1999; Crawford & Krebs, 1998; Gaulin & McBurney, 2001; Simpson & Kenrick, 1997). Although evolutionary psychologists have addressed the implications of our evolutionary past for all aspects of our behavior, the discussion here will

evolutionary psychology contemporary school of thought devoted to discovering the evolutionary roots of psychological processes, including learning and cognition

attend primarily to those that concern learning and cognition, beginning with a consideration of the kinds of problems that our ancestors faced in that original human environment of so long ago.

The Environment of Evolutionary Adaptedness (EEA)   Among the major goals of evolutionary psychology is identifying specific cognitive systems, or modules, that help organisms to adapt to and solve real-world problems. An evolutionary perspective necessarily holds that in any evolved species, many of these modules would have evolved long ago, having served our ancestors in meeting the unique demands of their environment. This original environment, consisting of selection pressures that operated on particular physical traits (both anatomical and behavioral), is referred to by evolutionary psychologists as the **environment of evolutionary adaptedness (EEA)** (Bowlby, 1969). In the case of human beings, the EEA is generally agreed to have been the ecology of the African savanna during the Pleistocene period, from 1.8 million years ago until about 11,000 years ago. Like all biological organisms, early humans had to solve numerous problems encountered in this environment in order to survive and pass on genes to further generations, ultimately leading to the present one. Although any number of problems might have existed, most evolutionary theorists assume certain adaptive problems to be universal. Humans, like many other animals, had to survive long enough to achieve reproductive maturity, be successful in finding a mate, provide adequate parenting for offspring, and in general aid both offspring and other biological relatives so as to ensure further replication of shared genetic material (Buss, 1999).

> **environment of evolutionary adaptedness (EEA)** primary ecological features and selection pressures that have operated on the physical traits of a species over time

These are fairly disparate problems, and each one of them might require any number of specific sensory/perceptual and information processing abilities. Cosmides and Tooby (1989, 1992, 1994) have argued that early humans would have had to develop numerous cognitive mechanisms to solve particular adaptive problems. These **evolved psychological mechanisms** would be domain specific; that is, they would be relevant to a particular adaptive problem, not applied generically to any kind of challenge. For instance, early hunter-gatherer humans would have benefited from an ability to distinguish perceptually between landscapes that provided useful and important resources (those containing access to water, vegetation, and cover) and those offering few such resources (barren plains). In fact, this tendency to differentially perceive natural environments is readily observed in modern humans. Several studies have shown that subjects asked to rate pictures of differing kinds of landscape overwhelmingly prefer those that appear to offer access to biologically important resources and protection from both predators and the elements (Balling & Falk, 1982; Kaplan, 1987; Orians & Heerwagen, 1992; Ulrich, 1983). In short, evolutionary thinking leads to a different kind of understanding of why so many people adorn their walls with photographs and paintings of beautiful natural settings.

> **evolved psychological mechanism** domain-specific cognitive modules selected for because of their contribution to solving adaptive problems in the environment

In addition, it would have been adaptive for our ancestors to be able to perceive and react appropriately to things in the environment that may have posed immediate danger, such as poisonous snakes or other dangerous animals. Evolving as highly social creatures, it would have been important for early humans to master numerous social nuances, such as identifying potential mates, protecting and providing for offspring, and entering into the tenuous but critical domain of social exchange of resources. Evolutionary psychologists believe that humans possess specific cognitive modules that represent adaptations resulting from the early exploits of hominids during the Pleistocene period.

Don't forget, though, that adaptations are the result of historical selection pressures, and, given the slow rate of biological evolution, it doesn't necessarily follow that these cognitive mechanisms serve us well in all of the environmental domains occupied by modern humans. In fact, the idea that our high-tech modern world has somewhat outstripped our more primitive cognitive architecture is a major theme in evolutionary psychology, known as *environmental mismatch theory* (Bailey, 1995). Our unprecedented ability to master new skills means that many of us today use tools and machines that even our grandparents couldn't have dreamed of, much less our paleolithic forebears. We inhabit varied human-made environments, including grocery and department stores, schools, tanning salons, movie theaters, football stadiums, and scores of others, none of which existed in the EEA of early humans. Successfully negotiating these different milieus often requires behavioral variations that simply could not have been anticipated by early humans. Environmental mismatch theory suggests that our efforts to adjust to such novel environments may entail anxiety and a general sense of not fitting in or belonging. Perhaps these kinds of feelings are part of the reason that so many people, wishing to escape the rat race, seek natural environments and wilderness areas for rest, relaxation, and rejuvenation.

In addition, our lifestyles diverge in substantial ways from that of a hunting-gathering group, particularly with respect to physical exertion. After all, technological advances are usually heralded because they free us from some difficult or distasteful task, relieving some of the physical challenges of hard work. It is no secret that people in industrialized nations live remarkably sedentary lives. This combination of a sedentary lifestyle with the overconsumption of high-caloric and high-fat foods, produced with ease and in great quantity by modern industry, becomes a recipe for cardiovascular disaster, as recognized by contemporary medical and behavioral scientists (Howson, 1998; Orth-Gomer & Schneiderman, 1996). The human EEA was a challenging world in which long periods of hard work and exertion were the rule, not the exception, and the ratio of calories taken in to those burned through activity was a relatively equitable one. Not so for the typical citizen of today's industrialized world. Most people take in many more calories than they will burn in a given day, and many of these calories are empty or of questionable nutritious value.

The human body, shaped as it was in our EEA, was predisposed to prize foods high in energy value (high levels of sugar and fat), though such natural foods were in small supply. In *The Paleolithic Prescription*, Eaton, Shostak, and Konner (1988) argue that people would do well to return to a diet low in fats, but high in proteins and carbohydrates, and to refamiliarize themselves with the kind of physical exercise and exertion that marked most of human evolutionary history. The goal of such recommendations is to help reduce the mismatch that exists between contemporary lifestyles and those that were characteristic of our ancestors some 40,000 years ago.

Beyond Nature Versus Nurture   There is probably no more timeless debate known to scholars and scientists than the question of whether human behavior is a product of genetic endowment (nature) or personal experiences (nurture). Far from being immune to this contentious issue, psychologists have historically embraced it, and, as you might guess, opinions have been vehemently and eloquently articulated on both sides of the issue. In fact, psychology's early history as a discipline was in part defined by how various scholars viewed this issue. At the turn of the 20th century, nature reigned supreme, as manifested in the thinking of such nativists as William James and William McDougall, who argued that the behavior, personality, and intelligence of individuals were largely the product of genetic makeup and that environmental variables played a minor role in the expression of behavioral traits. McDougall (1908) was famous for having suggested an essential list of human instincts, including curiosity, parenting, and self-assertion. Thus, the tendency of parents to worry about and protect their young could be easily attributed to a parenting instinct. Similarly, our propensity for opening up strange cans or boxes, or touching novel objects, may be generic manifestations of a curiosity instinct.

By the 1920s, instinct theory had fallen on hard times, for several reasons. First, critics were quick to point out that labeling a behavior as instinctive is at best description but does little to explain the behavior. In other words, to say that a mother cuddles and feeds her offspring because of a "maternal instinct" is not an explanation but simply a name given to a collection of behaviors. In addition, John Watson's behaviorism, a strong form of environmentalist (nurture) theory, was gaining ground. Watson was a charismatic and articulate proponent of the idea that human behavior is nearly infinitely malleable and that upbringing and experience make tremendous contributions to personal development. Behaviorist theory, coupled with empirical and theoretical advances in the study of learning, dominated the discipline of psychology until the cognitive revolution that began to take hold in the 1950s and 1960s.

The nature-nurture issue has not receded completely into the background today; it still raises its head from time to time, most often in the form of some outlandish magazine article applauding the discovery of an "intelligence" gene. Fortunately, modern researchers have a more sophisticated understanding of gene-environment interactions, and it is now clear that the early notion that behavior could be solely attributed to one or the other was overly simplistic and almost assuredly wrong. Imagine being asked to describe whether it is the length or width of a rectangle that contributes most to the rectangle's area. You would rightly consider the question nonsensical, as the only way to figure the rectangle's area is to multiply its length times its width. And so it is with nature and nurture. Genes code for a range of possibilities, but how they actually express themselves phenotypically

facultative trait

phenotypic expression (physical feature or behavior) that is highly sensitive to changing characteristics of the environment

depends very much on environmental stimulation. Evolutionary biologists use the term **facultative trait** to refer to a phenotype (morphological characteristics or behavior) whose expression is highly dependent on environmental input. This chapter gives several examples of how the connections formed in a developing nervous system are shaped by experience. Genes provide a basic blueprint for constructing a body, but the details of how and when various systems become configured are responsive to a host of environmental variables, including nutrition and sensory experience.

For evolutionary psychologists, the nature-nurture distinction is especially confusing because it suggests a false dichotomy. Nature and nurture do not occupy distant poles of a causal continuum, and they are not separate forces acting on the organism at different times or under separate circumstances. Contemporary researchers claim that the instinct concept can remain useful, if understood to refer to behavioral routines that are relatively universal within a species, but occur under well-specified environmental conditions, and are somewhat responsive or modifiable under changing environmental contingencies (Kenrick, Sadalla, & Keefe, 1998; Pinker, 1994). That is, as species-specific adaptations, instinctive behaviors might be best conceptualized, not as rigid, overly determined reflexes, but as organized patterns of perceiving and reacting to a range of environmental events that would have been consistent with the particular species' EEA. This is an important part of evolutionary psychology's theoretical stance, and it has particular repercussions for those instances of behavior that fall under the general headings of learning and cognition.

The Limits of Learning and Cognition

You may recall from this book's first chapter the concept of *preparedness*, the notion that for all animals, some kinds of behaviors and environmental stimuli are more easily learned than others. The idea of preparedness was introduced by Seligman (1970) in a classic article that served to remind psychologists that learning and cognition are not arbitrary mechanisms of adaptation but species-specific strategies for adapting to specific environmental conditions. Seligman took exception to the historical research on learning, much of which was founded on the assumption that animals, including humans, could form associations between any two stimuli (CS-US) in a Pavlovian procedure or that any movement could be reinforced through operant conditioning. Seligman suggested that learning was instead a relatively specialized ability to draw connections between ecologically relevant stimuli or to recognize the consequences of one's behavior on the natural environment. Consistent with modern evolutionary psychology, Seligman argued that not all connections are created equal, and organisms master those learning tasks that bear relevance in their natural environment, but they have difficulty learning those that don't. Thus, Seligman was anticipating evolutionary psychology's focus on conceptualizing all behavior as a type of adaptation to a given species' EEA.

The idea of preparedness shed a welcome light on the psychology of learning and cognition, especially certain experimental findings that proved somewhat puzzling to the learning theories that dominated psychology before the 1960s. The phenomenon of taste aversion, as discussed in Chapter 3, is a case in point. You may recall that taste aversion occurs when an organism avoids a particular food stuff after experiencing an association between the sight or smell of the food and physical illness. At first blush, taste aversion appeared to be a perfect example of Pavlovian conditioning, with odors or sights serving as conditioned stimuli and illness serving as the unconditioned stimulus. But, in several respects, taste aversion showed itself to be something of an anomaly, for it violated several well-known "facts" about Pavlovian conditioning. First, the aversion was seen to occur as a result of a single pairing of the food with illness, whereas most laboratory studies of Pavlovian conditioning had revealed the need for several such pairings. In addition, taste aversion proved to be a robust phenomenon despite a considerable time delay between presentation of the food and illness, and most studies of Pavlovian conditioning had shown that conditioning dropped off significantly with delays beyond a second or two. In taste aversion, the delay is often measured in hours, and this fact was difficult to reconcile with most of the empirical research.

Garcia's (Garcia & Koelling, 1966) famous research on taste aversion was a powerful demonstration that only CS-US connections that make sense ecologically support learning. Animals made nauseous when exposed to saccharin water associated their illness with the taste of the water but not with meaningless lights and sounds. Conversely, when animals were presented lights and sounds along with saccharin water, then shocked, an aversion to the "bright, noisy" water developed. Garcia had shown that CS-US associations that reflected contingencies likely to be encountered in natural settings—illness following food consumption, for instance—would be readily learned, whereas unnatural, arbitrary pairings would be learned with great difficulty, if at all.

Similar attention to species-specific adaptations appeared in the work of Breland and Breland (1961). Students of B. F. Skinner and consummate operant conditioners, the Brelands were employed as successful commercial animal trainers. But, in the process of attempting to shape novel behavior through operant means, the Brelands frequently encountered unforeseen problems. In one instance, pigs were taught to pick up wooden tokens, or "coins," and to carry the coins and deposit them in a "piggy bank." On several occasions, however, the animals were observed dropping the coins and rooting, or pushing them with their nose, around in the dirt. In their natural habitat, pigs often engage in such rooting behavior as a part of their normal appetitive repertoire. Such behavior proved maladaptive for the Brelands, for the pigs' training was often disrupted by these natural behaviors, referred to by the Brelands as **instinctive drift.**

The Brelands documented several other examples of instinctive drift in an influential paper titled "The Misbehavior of Organisms" (1961; a not-too-subtle parody of Skinner's 1938 *The Behavior of Organisms*). Taken together, the research by Garcia and the Brelands stimulated an increasing interest in how basic learning principles might be influenced, even restrained, by species-specific, evolved adaptations. By the 1970s, viewing learned

instinctive drift disruption of conditioned behavior by natural, or innate, behavioral repertoires

behavior through this kind of evolutionary lens became a major focus of an area of research known as *biological constraints on learning.*

Today, such empirical findings, once considered anomalous, seem altogether consistent with a worldview that conceptualizes learning as an evolved adaptation. In fact, once psychologists acknowledge the falsity of the nature-nurture dichotomy, a great deal of the adaptive behavior observed in all species can be seen as facultative expressions of domain-specific learning modules. Ethologist Niko Tinbergen (1951) was among the first scientists to systematically identify complex behavioral repertoires in insects, many of which rely heavily on specialized learning abilities. In a series of landmark studies, Tinbergen examined how a particular species of wasp manage to find their burrows following lengthy hunting expeditions. Tinbergen observed that these *wolf bees*—so called because mothers of this wasp species prey on bees to feed their young—flew in an ever-widening circular pattern when leaving their burrows. Tinbergen inferred that the wasps were encoding relevant landmarks in the environment in order to enhance wayfinding on the return trip to the burrow. When the experimenter disrupted these cues by moving certain critical landmarks shortly after the mother wasp left her burrow, wayfinding was in fact disrupted and the wasp was unable to locate the burrow upon her return.

The wayfinding ability of the wolf bees is but one example of how animals use varying environmental cues to modify adaptive behavior. As discussed in Chapter 7, animals that forage for food must encode information about when and where food is found and also when food has been depleted from a particular location. Even species historically assumed to have limited learning capacity may possess domain-specific learning strategies that allow them to solve important adaptive problems. One species of foraging ant acquires its sustenance by locating small portions of dead insects distributed widely in the hot Tunisian desert. Researchers have found that these ants use feedback about direction of travel and distance traveled to find their way back from circuitous foraging trips that often take them hundreds of meters from their underground colonies. If the ants are displaced by experimenters during their foraging trips, their wayfinding behavior is based on the directional and distance information their original movement would have provided, not their objective location after displacement (Wehner & Srinivaisan, 1981; Wohlgemuth, Ronacher & Wehner, 2001).

Similarly, animals that store food in caches that can be accessed later must rely on specific cues in the environment. Such species as the Clark's nutcracker (Balda & Turek, 1984) recover previously cached food with remarkable success. When food is removed from caches during a retention interval, birds behave as if the food is still available, flying to the site and searching in vain for the anticipated food. There is also considerable evidence that animals who exhibit seasonal migration, such as salmon and many bird species, utilize naturally occurring location cues to guide their long treks. Indigo buntings, for example, navigate by the stars, learning specific star clusters and orienting to the earth's seasonal center of rotation. Young birds not yet exposed to the relevant astronomical cues exhibit no migratory behavior, nor do adults whose visual field is obscured by clouds (Emlen, 1969a, 1969b).

Thus, this complex behavior is species specific, but depends substantially on the incorporation of changing environmental stimulation, implicating learning as an essential ingredient in this sophisticated repertoire.

It is clear, then, that many animal species solve the pervasive problems of survival by way of evolved, domain-specific learning modules. Might the same be said of humans? To the evolutionary psychologist, the answer is an unequivocal yes. As an evolved species, humans would be expected to have acquired, through natural selection, a collection of specialized, highly modifiable behavior patterns that contributed to the survival of our early ancestors. Evolutionary psychologists argue that the human mind consists of many such modules, each evolved to help solve a specific adaptive problem encountered during the early human EEA. Although a comprehensive discussion of all such evolved psychological mechanisms is beyond the purview of this book, the next few sections will consider a few of those most pertinent to the study of learning and cognition.

Language   You don't need to look very far to appreciate the tremendous variability of human language. Linguists have identified thousands of distinct languages, many of which take on even more variability in the form of slang and regional dialects. Even people speaking the same language do not necessarily possess identical vocabularies. The words used by the typical American teenager, for instance, will not be the same as those used by the average 4-year-old. Nor does a physics lecture have much in common with a sociology lecture, in part because of the different technical languages developed by these disparate disciplines. And you and I, in the course of any given day, modify our linguistic output in countless ways. Sometimes we whisper, sometimes we yell. We converse in the high-pitched, stilted language of motherese when addressing an infant but not when talking to a fellow adult. Thus, language use has a chameleon-like quality, in that both the things we say and the way we say them vary, sometimes drastically, from moment to moment, in response to different environmental conditions.

To view language as an evolved adaptation, evolutionary psychologists look not for the momentary changes or modifications that describe verbal activity in any particular person, but for the universal features of language—those aspects of language and its development that remain constant across the human family. After all, any organismic feature (anatomical or behavioral) that has become an adaptation, must have been represented in many generations of humans, and many of its features would need to exhibit constancy over long periods of time. Language, by almost any accounting, appears to meet such criteria. In fact, as discussed in Chapter 9, modern linguists consider the existence of *language universals* to be among the strongest evidence for language's status as an adaptation. Psychologist Steven Pinker (1994) makes the same point in his book, *The Language Instinct,* arguing that language development in humans follows a circumscribed path—as would be expected given an evolved mechanism—responding in specific ways to specialized input from the environment.

Human babies the world over develop language through a sequence of steps, from recognition of basic phonemes, to babbling and cooing, to the construction of initial, telegraphic sentences. This developmental sequence occurs predictably during the first 2½ to 3 years of life, as long as the child has had normal exposure to a verbal community. In addition, language development occurs in the absence of any formal, planned instruction. Unlike so many other skills that human children will have to be explicitly taught (reading, writing, riding a bicycle, etc.), healthy children naturally acquire language simply by being exposed to other language users. Language, then, may be among the best examples of a highly prepared human behavior, a specialized adaptation whose parameters are genotypically established, but whose ongoing expression depends heavily upon the environmental features that characterize the learning process.

Concept Learning   Chapter 8 discussed experiments in which animals who were exposed to large numbers of stimuli, differing on many dimensions, managed to extract some kind of essential, common information from the stimuli. In doing so, an organism is behaving conceptually, responding in a similar manner to stimuli perceived as belonging to a meaningful category due to shared properties. Human children master a nearly unimaginable number of concepts: some verbal, some nonverbal, some referring to animate objects, others to the many inanimate articles that populate the human environment. Although the process of acquiring concepts is most certainly an instance of learning, like language development, concept learning occurs with a tremendous rapidity and with little intentional support from the environment. It is tempting, then, to view concept learning as another case of preparedness, in humans and nonhumans alike. The ability to classify, or place numerous specific items into a coherent category, is an exercise in cognitive economizing that would appear to afford any organism considerable advantages when sizing up a complex physical environment.

Like other highly social species, humans employ categorical, or conceptual, thinking to virtually everything, including other people. After all, what else is a stereotype if not a label that we apply, relatively indiscriminately, to an entire group of people, despite obvious differences between the group's members? The history of social psychology is replete with accounts of stereotype-wielding humans and the unfortunate prejudice and discrimination that can follow from stereotypical thought (Horowitz & Bordens, 1995). But social psychologists have tended to focus more attention on the negative consequences of stereotyping than on the question of why stereotypic thinking is so pervasive. To evolutionary psychologists, this latter question is of more significance, particularly if stereotyping is but another manifestation of an evolved tendency to categorize environmental stimuli. If you view college professors as verbose, absent-minded nerds, this perception serves as a useful anchoring point for initial encounters with unfamiliar professors. You may adjust your thinking if you come into contact with a professor whose personal characteristics violate your concept, but until this kind of individuating experience occurs, the stereotype may remain the least effortful and therefore most economical way of categorizing this large group of individuals.

Our propensity for classifying people into meaningful, though not necessarily accurate, stereotypes is well supported by social psychological research. One of the more telling examples is what social psychologists refer to as the *minimal group phenomenon*. In an experiment, members of a large group, perhaps a class of college students, are randomly assigned to two separate groups. Random assignment is important because it pretty much ensures that the groups won't differ systematically on some important characteristic such as gender, ethnicity, or academic major. The groups are then given some trivial task to accomplish, such as rating the quality of a group of paintings or estimating the number of dots in a visual stimulus (Tajfel, 1981, 1982). It is important to note that the groups are not squared off against one another in a competitive, or even interactive, exercise. After completing their task, members of each group are asked to evaluate their liking for members of their own group as well as members of the other group. The result is nearly always the same. Members of each group tend to evaluate their fellow in-group members more positively than they evaluate members of the out-group. Social psychologists were surprised by this outcome because the groups were not competing and random assignment should have ensured equivalent groups. Thus, there is no overwhelming reason to expect that members of the groups would so readily develop an allegiance.

To the evolutionary psychologist, the nearly immediate "in-group versus out-group" phenomenon makes sense. Early humans belonged to small groups of closely knit, often biologically related individuals. These groups worked together, in continual face-to-face fashion, solving the adaptive problems faced by all animals. A tendency to readily favor those with whom you have close and ongoing contact may have evolved as a useful adaptation in early human groups, and this may well survive in modern humans in the minimal group phenomenon. Just as we are quick to classify other objects into meaningful groups, we easily develop loyalty to groups, even those to which we have been randomly assigned. There seems to be something about being a member of a group that bolsters and validates us as individuals, and this sense of belongingness manifests itself in positive feelings about our in-group and less positive perceptions of the out-group. As social psychologists have long known, the intensity of this loyalty to the in-group and the corresponding ill will for the out-group can be easily enhanced. Numerous studies show that when such groups are pitted against one another in competition for scarce resources, the end result is often heightened intergroup conflict, hostility, and even aggression (Sherif, Harvey, White, Hood, & Sherif, 1961; Sherif & Sherif, 1973).

Acquired Fears and Anxieties   A final example of prepared learning comes from clinical psychopathology. Because the human environment consists of so many things, both animate and inanimate, the range of items to which fears and phobias might be attached is nearly limitless. It is theoretically conceivable, that is, for people to develop phobias (debilitating and irrational fears) of computers, coffee cups, wastebaskets, streetlights, staplers, sports magazines, or virtually anything else. Although on occasion a client shows up in a therapist's office boasting a fear of some unusual object, most human fears turn out to be rather predictable and, in the eyes of an evolutionary psychologist, consistent with human evolution as a species. Far from being naturally maladaptive, fear offers numerous advantages to biological organisms (DeBecker, 1997; Marks, 1987). In many animals fear induces a freezing response, and an animal that remains completely still is hard to detect by a potential predator whose visual system is only sensitive to movement. Fear also causes animals to escape and avoid feared stimuli, many of which may prove dangerous. Also, fear often motivates aggressive behavior, which can prove effective in driving a potential predator or aggressor away.

Thus, it is important to realize that fear is an adaptive emotion, and the kinds of fears that any particular species possesses will normally be dictated by the sorts of stimuli that proved dangerous during that species' EEA. Buss (1999) confirms that this seems to be the case with humans:

> A large body of evidence suggests that humans are far more likely to develop fears of dangers that were present in the ancestral environment, but far less to dangers in the current environment. Snakes, for example, are hardly a problem in large urban cities, but automobiles are. Fears of cars, guns, electrical outlets, and cigarettes are virtually unheard of, since these are evolutionarily novel hazards—too recent for selection to have fashioned specific fears. The fact that more city dwellers go to psychiatrists with fears of snakes and strangers than fears of cars and electrical outlets provides a window into the hazards of our ancestral environment. (p. 87)

Needless to say, the acquisition of any particular fear is an idiosyncratic event, one in which learning can play a key role. After all, Little Albert did not naturally fear white rats, but a phobic reaction to this stimulus was not difficult to engender through conditioning, as demonstrated by Watson and Rayner (1920). Although such an experiment would not be justified, one wonders whether such conditioned fears could just as easily be produced for novel, but evolutionarily meaningless, stimuli such as cigarettes, cars, electrical outlets, and the like. An evolutionary perspective would predict that such fears, if subject to conditioning at all, would require more pairings than was required with rats and other animal stimuli and perhaps also that elimination of such fears through extinction might progress more rapidly. An evolutionary account does not negate the role that learning plays in fear acquisition but suggests that the range of stimuli that would be expected to provoke a fear reaction would be limited to those that made up the human EEA.

✖ INTERIM SUMMARY

Human's ability to benefit from experience, as manifested in various learning and cognitive phenomena, is as much a product of our evolutionary history as is our bipedal stance or our opposable thumb. We process information and adapt to Pavlovian and operant contingencies in our environment because similar abilities in our Pleistocene ancestors helped solve real-world problems in the environment of evolutionary adaptedness. A focus on the evolutionary development of learning and cognition has led modern psychologists to rethink the traditional nature versus nurture issue and to reconceptualize such varied behavioral phenomena as language, concept learning, and acquired fears as species-specific facultative traits.

✕ THOUGHT QUESTIONS

1. Come up with a list of skills that you have learned during your lifetime, not including language, reading, writing, and others discussed in this chapter. Rank these skills on a continuum of preparedness, from low to high. Use an evolutionary analysis to explain why the highly prepared skills were so easy for you to learn or acquire.
2. Using the tenets of environmental mismatch theory, suggest some possible remedies to some of the social ills (crime, environmental problems, geopolitical conflict) that affect modern humans. Also, can you describe any type of activity you engage in personally that may represent an attempt to recapture or return to the human EEA?

THE ADAPTIVE NATURE OF LEARNING AND COGNITION: SUMMING UP

This book began with the claim that learning and cognition represent means by which biological organisms adapt to a changing environment. In fact, the general theme of adaptation proves essential to understanding everything about organisms, both their physical makeup and their behavioral repertoires. At times it is easy to lose sight of this principle, however, when steeped in the details and language of specific experiments and scientific concepts. The learning and cognitive phenomena discussed throughout this book are pervasive; that is, they characterize the behavioral activity of all biological species, from invertebrates to primates, despite differences in expression. Thus, learning and cognition are universal adaptive mechanisms whose specific features have been shaped over phylogenetic time by the forces of natural selection. The processes by which particular learning and cognitive episodes unfold ontogenetically are remarkably constant, but the content of and rapidity with which such adaptations occur are variable in a manner predicted by an evolutionary consideration. Organisms solve the moment-to-moment riddles of a changing world by invoking both species- and domain-specific modules that proved adaptive in that species' particular EEA. Far from being inflexible and unresponsive, such modules are sensitive to a range of environmental input, and this allows for an often impressive degree of behavioral modifiability.

In the end, an organism's ability to survive and pass its genes on to further generations is a product of a complex equation. Part of this equation consists of the unique physical features the organism shares with other members of its species, such as the human's upright posture, the turtle's protective shell, or the giraffe's long neck. But these physical or anatomical features are the result of an evolutionary process occurring over immense time periods and the adaptive successes enjoyed by previous generations. Individual organisms, though, must contend with an immediate environment that may change in unpredictable ways and over relatively short time periods. The ability to benefit from past experience (learn) and to effectively process relevant information about one's environment (cognition) emerged as adaptive mechanisms well suited to handling the ongoing, moment-to-moment demands of a complex world.

References

ADACHI, Y. (1989). The effect of behavioral treatment of obesity and correlates of weight loss in treatment and at a 2-year follow-up. *Japanese Journal of Behavior Therapy, 15,* 36–55.

ADER, R. (1985). Conditioned taste aversions and immunopharmacology. *Annals of the New York Academy of Sciences, 443,* 293–307.

ADER, R., & COHEN, N. (1975). Behaviorally conditioned immunosuppression. *Psychosomatic Medicine, 37,* 333–340.

ADER, R., & COHEN, N. (1984). Behavior and the immune system. In W. D. Gentry (Ed.), *Handbook of behavioral medicine.* New York: Guilford Press.

ADER, R., & COHEN, N. (1993). Psychoneuroimmunology: Conditioning and stress. *Annual Review of Psychology, 44,* 53–85.

ADIH, W. K., & ALEXANDER, C. S. (1999). Determinants of condom use to prevent HIV infection among youth in Ghana. *Journal of Adolescent Health, 24,* 63–72.

ADLER, S. A., GERHARDSTEIN, P., & ROVEE-COLLIER, C. (1998). Levels-of-processing effects in infant memory? *Child Development, 69,* 280–294.

ALBERTS, E., & EHRENFREUND, D. (1951). Transposition in children as a function of age. *Journal of Experimental Psychology, 41,* 30–38.

ALCOCK, J. (1972). The evolution of the use of tools by feeding animals. *Evolution, 26,* 464–473.

ALLEN, K. D., & SHRIVER, M. D. (1998). Role of parent-mediated pain management strategies in biofeedback treatment of childhood migraines. *Behavior Therapy, 29,* 477–490.

ALLPORT, G. W. (1954). The historical background of modern social psychology. In G. Lindsey (Ed.), *Handbook of social psychology: Vol. I. theory and method* (pp. 3–56). Reading, MA: Addison-Wesley.

ALTMANN, G. T. M. (2001). The language machine: Psycholinguistics in review. *British Journal of Psychology, 92*(1), 129–170.

ALVAREZ-BORDA, B., RAMIREZ-AMAYA, V., PEREZ-MONTFORT, R., & BERMUDEZ-RATTONI, F. (1995). Enhancement of antibody production by a learning paradigm. *Neurobiology of Learning & Memory, 64,* 103–105.

AMARI, A., GRACE, N. C., & FISHER, W. W. (1995). Achieving and maintaining compliance with the ketogenic diet. *Journal of Applied Behavior Analysis, 28,* 341–342.

AMERICAN PSYCHIATRIC ASSOCIATION. (1994). *Diagnostic and statistical manual of mental disorders* (4th ed.). Washington, DC: Author.

ANDERSEN, S. M., & KLATZKY, R. L. (1987). Traits and social stereotypes: Levels of categorization in person perception. *Journal of Personality and Social Psychology, 53,* 235–246.

ANDRESEN, J. (1991). Skinner and Chomsky 30 years later or: The return of the repressed. *Behavior Analyst, 14,* 49–60.

ANTONITIS, J. J. (1951). Response variability in the white rat during conditioning, extinction, and re-conditioning. *Journal of Experimental Psychology, 42,* 273–281.

ARAGONA, J., CASSADY, J., & DRABMAN, R. S. (1975). Treating overweight children through parental training and contingency contracting. *Journal of Applied Behavior Analysis, 8,* 269–278.

ARCEDIANO, F., MATUTE, H., & MILLER, R. R. (1997). Blocking of Pavlovian conditioning in humans. *Learning & Motivation, 28(2),* 188–199.

ARCH, E. C. (1987). Differential responses of females and males to evaluative stress: Anxiety, self-esteem, self-efficacy and willingness to participate. In R. Schwarzer & H. M. Van der Ploeg (Eds.), *Advances in test anxiety research* (Vol. 5, pp. 97–106). Berwyn, PA: Swets North America.

ARCHER, J. (1992). *Ethology and human development.* Savage, MD: Barnes & Noble.

ATKINSON, R. C., & SHIFFRIN, R. M. (1968). Human memory: A proposed system and its control processes. In K. W. Spence & J. T. Spence (Eds.), *The psychology of learning and motivation* (Vol. 2, pp. 89–105). New York: Academic Press.

AUER, R. N., JENSEN, M. L., & WHISHAW, I. Q. (1989). Neurobehavioral deficit due to ischemic brain damage limited to half of the CA1 section of the hippocampus. *Journal of Neuroscience, 9,* 1641–1647.

AYLLON, T., & AZRIN, N. H. (1965). The measurement and reinforcement of behavior of psychotics. *Journal of the Experimental Analysis of Behavior, 8,* 357–383.

AYLLON, T., & AZRIN, N. H. (1968). *The token economy: A motivational system for therapy and rehabilitation.* New York: Appleton-Century-Crofts.

AYRES, J. J. B., HADDAD, C., & ALBERT, M. (1987). One-trial excitatory backward conditioning as assessed by suppression of licking in rats: Concurrent observations of lick suppression and defensive behaviors. *Animal Learning & Behavior, 15,* 212–217.

AZRIN, N. H., & POWELL, J. (1968). Behavioral engineering: The reduction of smoking behavior by a conditioning apparatus and procedure. *Journal of Applied Behavior Analysis, 1,* 193–200.

BAARS, B. J. (1986). *The cognitive revolution in psychology.* New York: Guilford Press.

BADDELEY, A. (1994). The magic number seven: Still magic after all these years? *Psychological Review, 101,* 353–356.

BAER, D. M., PETERSON, R. F., & SHERMAN, J. A. (1967). The development of imitation by reinforcing behavioral similarity to a model. *Journal of the Experimental Analysis of Behavior, 10,* 405–416.

BAILEY, A. M., & THOMAS, R. K. (1998). An investigation of oddity concept learning by rats. *Psychological Record, 48,* 333–344.

BAILEY, K. (1995). Mismatch theory and paleopsychopathology. In C. B. Crawford (Chair), *Human behavior and evolution society conference.* Symposium conducted at the meeting of Human Behavior and Evolution Society, Los Angeles, California.

BALDA, R. P., & TUREK, F. J. (1984). Memory in birds. In H. L. Roitblat, T. G. Bever, & H. S. Terrace (Eds.), *Animal cognition.* Hillsdale, NJ: Erlbaum.

BALLING, J. D., & FALK, J. H. (1982). Development of visual preference for natural environments. *Environment and Behavior, 14,* 5–28.

BANDURA, A. (1977). *Social learning theory.* Englewood Cliffs, NJ: Prentice-Hall.

BANDURA, A. (1982). Self-efficacy mechanism in human agency. *American Psychologist, 37,* 122–147.

BANDURA, A. (1997). *Self-efficacy: The exercise of control.* New York: W. H. Freeman.

BANDURA, A., ROSS, D., & ROSS, S. A. (1961). Transmission of aggression through imitation of aggressive models. *Journal of Abnormal and Social Psychology, 63,* 575–582.

BANDURA, A., & WALTERS, R. W. (1963). *Social learning and personality development.* New York: Holt, Rinehart, & Winston.

BARGH, J. A., & CHARTRAND, T. L. (1999). The unbearable automaticity of being. *American Psychologist, 54,* 462–479.

BARLOW, G. W. (1977). Modal action patterns, in T. A. Sebeok (Ed.), *How animals communicate* (pp. 98–134). Bloomington: Indiana University Press.

BARRETT, J. E., & SANGER, D. J. (1991). Behavioral pharmacology in the era of neuroscience. *Journal of the Experimental Analysis of Behavior, 56,* 167–169.

BARSALOU, L. W. (1985). Ideals, central tendency, and frequency of instantiation. *Journal of Experimental Psychology: Learning, Memory, and Cognition, 11*, 629–654.

BARSALOU, L. W., & SEWELL, D. R. (1985). Contrasting the representation of scripts and categories. *Journal of Memory and Language, 24*, 646–665.

BARTLETT, F. C. (1932). *Remembering: A study in experimental and social psychology.* Cambridge, MA: Cambridge University Press.

BARUCH, I., HEMSLEY, D. R., & GRAY, J. A. (1988). Differential performance of acute and chronic schizophrenics in a latent inhibition task. *Journal of Nervous and Mental Disease, 176*, 598–606.

BASSETT, J. E., & BLANCHARD, E. B. (1977). The effect of the absence of close supervision on the use of response cost in a prison token economy. *Journal of Applied Behavior Analysis, 10*, 375–379.

BAUM, W. M. (1981). Optimization and the matching law as accounts of instrumental behavior. *Journal of the Experimental Analysis of Behavior, 36*, 387–403.

BAUM, W. M. (1994). *Understanding behaviorism: Science, behavior, and culture.* New York: HarperCollins College Publishers.

BAUM, W. M., & APARICIO, C. F. (1999). Optimality and concurrent variable-interval variable-ratio schedules. *Journal of the Experimental Analysis of Behavior, 71*, 75–89.

BECHARA, A., TRANEL, D., DAMASIO, H., ADOLPHS, R., ROCKLAND, C., & DAMASIO, A. R. (1995). Double dissociation of conditioning and declarative knowledge relative to the amygdala and hippocampus in humans. *Science, 269*, 1115–1118.

BEDNEKOFF, P. A., KAMIL, A. C., & BALDA, R. P. (1997). Clark's nutcracker (*Aves: Corvidae*) spatial memory: Interference effects on cache recovery performance? *Ethology, 103*, 554–565.

BEHL, C. G. (1996). Basic-level and superordinate-like categorical representations in early infancy. *Cognition, 60*, 105–141.

BERGER, S. M. (1971). Observer perseverance as related to a model's success: A social comparison analysis. *Journal of Personality and Social Psychology, 19*, 341–350.

BERNSTEIN, I. L. (1985). Learning food aversions in the progression of cancer and its treatment. *Annals of the New York Academy of Sciences, 443*, 365–380.

BERNSTEIN, I. L., & BORSON, S. (1986). Learned food aversion: A component of anorexia syndromes. *Psychological Review, 93*, 462–472.

BICKERTON, D. (1990). *Language and species.* Chicago: University of Chicago Press.

BIGLAN, A. (1987). A behavior-analytic critique of Bandura's self-efficacy theory. *Behavior Analyst, 10*, 1–15.

BIONDI, M., & ZANNINO, L.-G. (1997). Psychological stress, neuroimmunomodulation, and susceptibility to infectious diseases in animals and man: A review. *Psychotherapy & Psychosomatics, 66*, 3–26.

BLANCHARD, E. B. (1977). Behavioral medicine: A perspective. In R. B. Williams & W. D. Gentry (Eds.), *Behavioral approaches to medical treatment.* Cambridge, MA: Ballinger.

BLANEY, P. H. (1986). Affect and memory: A review. *Psychological Bulletin, 99*, 229–246.

BLISS, T. V. P., & LOMO, T. (1973). Long-lasting potentiation of synaptic transmission in the dentate area of the anaesthetized rabbit following stimulation of the perforant path. *Journal of Physiology (London), 232*, 331–356.

BLOOM, L. M., & LAHEY, M. (1978). *Language development and language disorders.* New York: Wiley.

BLOOM, P. (1990). Syntactic distinctions in child language. *Journal of Child Language, 17*, 343–356.

BLOUGH, D. S. (1961). Animal psychophysics. *Scientific American, 205*, 113–122.

BLOUGH, D. S. (1967). Stimulus generalization as signal detection in pigeons. *Science, 158*, 940–941.

BOTHA, R. P. (1998). Neo-Darwinian accounts of the evolution of language: 3. Questions about their evidential bases, logic and rhetoric. *Language and Communication, 18*, 17–46.

BOTHA, R. P. (1999). On the testability of theories of language evolution. *Stellenbosch Papers in Linguistics, 32*, 1–52.

BOUCHARD, T. J., JR. (1994). Genes, environment, and personality. *Science, 264,* 1700–1701.

BOUDEWYNS, P. A., & WILSON, A. E. (1972). Implosive therapy and desensitization therapy using free association in treatment of inpatients. *Journal of Abnormal Psychology, 79,* 252–268.

BOURNE, L.E., JR. (1970). Knowing and using concepts. *Psychological Review, 77,* 546–556.

BOUTON, M. E., MINEKA, S., & BARLOW, D. H. (2001). A modern learning theory perspective on the etiology of panic disorder. *Psychological Review, 108*(1), 4–32.

BOWER, G.H. (1981). Mood and memory. *American Psychologist, 36,* 129–148.

BOWER, G. H., & HILGARD, E. R. (1981). *Theories of learning* (5th ed.). Englewood Cliffs, NJ: Prentice-Hall.

BOWER, G. H., THOMPSON, S. S., & TULVING, E. (1994). Reducing retroactive interference: An interference analysis. *Journal of Experimental Psychology: Learning, Memory, and Cognition, 20,* 51–66.

BOWLBY, J. (1969). *Attachment and loss* (Vol. 1.) New York: Basic Books.

BOYD, W. D., & CAMPBELL, S. E. (1998). EEG biofeedback in the schools: The use of EEG biofeedback to treat ADHD in a school setting. *Journal of Neurotherapy, 2,* 65–71.

BOYSEN, S. T., & HIMES, G. T. (1999). Current issues and emerging theories in animal cognition. *Annual Review of Psychology, 50,* 683–705.

BRADLEY, M. M., GREENWALD, M. K., PETRY, M. C., & LANG, P. J. (1992). Remembering pictures: Pleasure and arousal in memory. *Journal of Experimental Psychology: Learning, Memory, and Cognition, 18,* 379–390.

BRAKKE, K. E., & SAVAGE-RUMBAUGH, E. S. (1995). The development of language skills in bonobo and chimpanzee: I. Comprehension. *Language and Communication, 15,* 121–148.

BRAUNSTEIN-BERCOVITZ, H., & LUBOW, R. E. (1998). Latent inhibition as a function of modulation of attention to the preexposed irrelevant stimulus. *Learning and Motivation, 29*(3), 261–279.

BREBION, G., SMITH, M. J., GORMAN, J. M., & AMADOR, X. (1996). Reality monitoring failure in schizophrenia: The role of selective attention. *Schizophrenia Research, 22,* 173–180.

BRELAND, K., & BRELAND, M. (1961). The misbehavior of organisms. *American Psychologist, 16,* 681–684.

BRENNAN, J. F. (1998). *History and systems of psychology* (5th ed.). Upper Saddle River, NJ: Prentice-Hall.

BRIGHAM, J. C. (1990). Target person distinctiveness and attractiveness as moderator variables in the confidence-accuracy relationship in eyewitness identification. *Basic and Applied Social Psychology, 11,* 101–115.

BROOKS, D. N., & BADDELEY, A. (1976). What can amnesic patients learn? *Neuropsychologia, 14,* 111–122.

BROOKS, L. R. (1987). Decentralized control of categorization: The role of prior processing episodes. In U. Neisser (Ed.), *Concepts and conceptual development.* Cambridge, MA: Cambridge University Press.

BROWN, J. L. (1975). *The evolution of behavior.* New York: Norton.

BROWN, R. (1973). *A first language: The early stages.* Cambridge, MA: Harvard University Press.

BROWN, R., & HANLON, C. (1970). Deviational complexity and order of acquisition in child speech. In J. R. Hayes (Ed.), *Cognition and the development of language* (pp. 11–53). New York: Wiley.

BROWN, R., & KULIK, J. (1977). Flashbulb memories. *Cognition, 5,* 73–99.

BROWN, W., & CHOBOR, K. L. (1995). Severe retrograde amnesia. *Aphasiology, 9,* 163–170.

BRUNER, J. S., GOODNOW, J. J., & AUSTIN, G. A. (1956). *A study of thinking.* New York: Wiley.

BUDNEY, A. J., HIGGINS, S. T., DELANEY, D. D., KENT, L., & BICKEL, W. K. (1991). Contingent reinforcement of abstinence with individuals abusing cocaine and marijuana. *Journal of Applied Behavior Analysis, 24,* 657–665.

BUGNYAR, T., & HUBER, L. (1997). Push or pull: An experimental study on imitation in marmosets. *Animal Behavior, 54,* 817–831.

BURKE, S. T., & PUTAI, J. (1996). Predicting performance from a triathlon event. *Journal of Sport Behavior, 19,* 272–287.

BUSCHKE, H., SLIWINSKI, M. J., KUSLANSKY, G., & LIPTON, R. B. (1997). Diagnosis of early dementia by the double memory test: Encoding specificity improves diagnostic sensitivity and specificity. *Neurology, 48*, 989–997.

BUSKIST, W., CUSH, D. T., & DEGRANDPRE, R. J. (1991). The life and times of PSI. *Journal of Behavioral Education, 1*, 215–234.

BUSS, D. M. (1999). *Evolutionary psychology: The new science of mind.* Boston: Allyn & Bacon.

BYRNE, R. W., & TOMASELLO, M. (1995). Do rats ape? *Animal Behaviour, 50*, 1417–1420.

CAMUTO, C. (1990). *A flyfisherman's blue ridge.* New York: Henry Holt.

CARLIN, A. S., HOFFMAN, H. G., & WEGHORST, S. (1997). Virtual reality and tactile augmentation in the treatment of spider phobia: A case report. *Behaviour Research and Therapy, 35*, 153–158.

CARLSON, N. R. (1998). *Physiology of behavior* (6th ed.). Boston: Allyn & Bacon.

CARMAGNANI, A., & CARMAGNANI, E. F. (1999). Biofeedback: Present state and future possibilities. *International Journal of Mental Health, 28*, 83–86.

CARPENTER, M., NAGELL, K., & TOMASELLO, M. (1998). Social cognition, joint attention, and communicative competence from 9 to 15 months of age. *Monographs of the Society for Research in Child Development*, Vol. 63.

CARTMILL, M. (1990). Human uniqueness and theoretical content in paleoanthropology. *International Journal of Primatology, 11*, 173–192.

CASSADAY, H. J. (1997). Latent inhibition: Relevance to the neural substrates of schizophrenia and schizotypy? In G. Claridge (Ed.), *Schizotypy: Implications for illness and health* (pp. 124–144). Oxford: Oxford University Press.

CATANIA, A. C. (1963). Concurrent performances: A baseline for the study of reinforcement magnitude. *Journal of the Experimental Analysis of Behavior, 6*, 299–300.

CATANIA, A. C. (1971). Reinforcement schedules and psychophysical judgments: A study of some temporal properties of behavior. In W. N. Schoenfeld (Ed.), *The theory of reinforcement schedules.* Englewood Cliffs, NJ: Prentice-Hall.

CATANIA, A. C. (1988). The operant behaviorism of B. F. Skinner. In A. C. Catania & S. Harnard (Eds.), *The selection of behavior: The operant behaviorism of B. F. Skinner: Comments and consequences.* Cambridge, MA: Cambridge University Press.

CATANIA, A. C. (1991). The gifts of culture and of eloquence: An open letter to Michael J. Mahoney in reply to his article "Scientific psychology and radical behaviorism." *Behavior Analyst, 14*, 61–72.

CECI, S. J., & BRUCK, M. (1993). Suggestibility of the child witness: A historical review and synthesis. *Psychological Bulletin, 113*(3), 403–439.

CECI, S. J., BRUCK, M., & BATTIN, D. B. (2000). The suggestibility of children's testimony. In D. F. Bjorklund (Ed.), *False-memory creation in children and adults: Theory, research, and implications* (pp. 169–201). Mahwah, NJ: Erlbaum.

CHOI, S., MCDANIEL, M. A., & BUSEMEYER, J. R. (1993). Incorporating prior biases in network models of conceptual rule learning. *Memory and Cognition, 21*, 413–423.

CHOMSKY, N. (1957). *Syntactic structures.* The Hague: Mouton.

CHOMSKY, N. (1959). Review of Skinner's *Verbal Behavior. Language, 35*, 26–58.

CHOMSKY, N. (1965). *Aspects of the theory of syntax.* Cambridge, MA: MIT Press.

CHOMSKY, N. (1970). The case against B. F. Skinner. *New York Review of Books*, 18–24.

CHOMSKY, N. (1975). *Reflections on language.* New York: Pantheon.

CHUNG, S. (1965). Effects of effort on response rate. *Journal of the Experimental Analysis of Behavior, 8*, 1–7.

CHWILLA, D. J., BROWN, C. M., & HAGOORT, P. (1995). The N400 as a function of the level of processing. *Psychophysiology, 32*, 274–285.

CIALDINI, R. B. (1988). *Influence: Science and practice.* Glenview, IL: Scott, Foresman/Little, Brown.

CIARROCHI, J. V., CHAN, A. Y. C., & CAPUTI, P. (2000). A critical evaluation of the emotional intelligence construct. *Personality and Individual Differences, 28*, 539–561.

CLARK, D. F. (1963). The treatment of hysterical spasm and agoraphobia by behaviour therapy. *Behaviour Research and Therapy, 1*, 245–250.

COHEN, N. J. (1984). Preserved learning capacity in amnesia: Evidence for multiple memory systems. In L. R. Squire & N. Butters (Eds.), *Neuropsychology of memory*. New York: Guilford.

COHEN, N. J., MCCLOSKEY, M., & WIBLE, C. G. (1988). There is still no case for a flashbulb-memory mechanism: Reply to Schmidt and Bohannon. *Journal of Experimental Psychology: General, 117,* 336–338.

COHEN, N. J., & SQUIRE, L. R. (1981). Retrograde amnesia and remote memory impairment. *Neuropsychologia, 19,* 337–356.

COHEN, S., & HERBERT, T. B. (1996). Health psychology: Psychological factors and physical disease from the perspective of human psychoneuroimmunology. *Annual Review of Psychology, 47,* 113–142.

COLE, R. P., & MILLER, R. R. (1999). Conditioned excitation and conditioned inhibition acquired through backward conditioning. *Learning and Motivation, 30,* 129–156.

COLLIE, R., & HAYNE, H. (1999). Deferred imitation by 6- and 9-month old infants: More evidence for declarative memory. *Developmental Psychobiology, 35,* 83–90.

COLOMBO, J., O'BRIEN, M., MITCHELL, D. W., & ROBERTS, K. (1987). A lower boundary for category formation in preverbal infants. *Journal of Child Language, 14,* 383–385.

COLOMBO, M., & GRAZIANO, M. (1994). Effects of auditory and visual interference on auditory-visual delayed matching-to-sample in monkeys (*Macaca fascicularis*). *Behavioral Neuroscience, 108,* 636–639.

COMMONS, M. L., HERRNSTEIN, R. J., KOSSLYN, S. M., & MUMFORD, D. B. (Eds.). (1990). *Quantitative analyses of behavior: Vol. 8. Behavioral approaches to pattern recognition and concept formation.* Hillsdale, NJ: Erlbaum.

COMRIE, B. (1987). Introduction. In B. Comrie (Ed.), *The world's major languages.* New York: Oxford University Press.

CONWAY, M. A. (1991). In defense of everyday memory. *American Psychologist, 46,* 19–26.

CONWAY, M. A. (Ed.). (1997). *Recovered memories and false memories.* Oxford: Oxford University Press.

COOK, R. G., KATZ, J. S., & CAVOTO, B. R. (1997). Pigeon same-different concept learning with multiple stimulus classes. *Journal of*

Experimental Psychology: Animal Behavior Processes, 23, 417–433.

COOPER, R. P., & ASLIN, R. N. (1990). Preference for infant-directed speech in the first month after birth. *Child Development, 61,* 1584–1595.

COOPER, R. P., & PISTON, J. (1991). Young infants' processing of prosodic contours in infant-directed speech. Paper presented at the meeting of the Society for Research in Child Development, Seattle, WA.

CORKIN, S. (1965). Tactually guided maze-learning in man: Effects of unilateral cortical excisions and bilateral hippocampal lesions. *Neuropsychologia, 3,* 339–351.

CORKIN, S. (1984). Lasting consequences of bilateral medial temporal lobectomy: Clinical course and experimental findings in H. M. *Seminars in Neurology, 4,* 249–259.

COSMIDES, L., & TOOBY, J. (1989). Evolutionary psychology and the generation of culture: Part II. Case study: A computational theory of social exchange. *Ethology and Sociobiology, 10,* 51–97.

COSMIDES, L., & TOOBY, J. (1992). Cognitive adaptations for social exchange. In J. Barkow, L. Cosmides, & J. Tooby (Eds.), *The adapted mind.* New York: Oxford University Press.

COSMIDES, L., & TOOBY, J. (1994). Origins of domain specificity: The evolution of functional organization. In S. Gelman & L. Hirshfield (Eds.), *Mapping the mind: Domain specificity in cognition and culture.* New York: Cambridge University Press.

COUSSONS, M. E., DYKSTRA, L. A., & LYSLE, D. T. (1992). Pavlovian conditioning of morphine-induced alterations of immune status. *Journal of Neuroimmunology, 39,* 219–230.

COWLEY, J. (2000, July 3). Generation XXL. *Newsweek,* 40–44.

CRAIK, F. I. M., & LOCKHART, R. S. (1972). Levels of processing: A framework for memory research. *Journal of Verbal Learning and Verbal Behavior, 11,* 671–684.

CRAIK, F. I. M., & TULVING, E. (1975). Depth of processing and the retention of words in episodic memory. *Journal of Experimental Psychology: General, 104,* 268–294.

CRAMER, R. E., WEISS, R. F., STEIGLEDER, M. K., & BALLING, S. S. (1985). Attraction in context: Acquisition and blocking of person-directed action. *Journal of Personality and Social Psychology, 49*(5), 1221–1230.

CRAWFORD, C., & KREBS, D. L. (Eds.). (1998). *Handbook of evolutionary psychology: Ideas, issues, and applications.* Mahwah, NJ: Erlbaum.

DAGGETT, D. (1995). *Beyond the rangeland conflict: Toward a West that works.* Layton, UT: Gibbs Smith in cooperation with the Grand Canyon Trust.

DALY, M., & WILSON, M. (1983). *Sex, evolution and behavior* (2nd ed.). Boston: Willard Grant.

DANAHER, B. G. (1977). Research on rapid smoking: Interim summary and recommendations. *Addictive Behaviors, 2,* 151–166.

DANISH, S. J., & DONOHUE, T. R. (1996). Understanding the media's influence on the development of antisocial and prosocial behavior. In R. L. Hampton, P. Jenkins, et al. (Eds.), *Preventing violence in America. Issues in children's and families' lives* (Vol. 4, pp. 133–155). Thousand Oaks, CA: Sage.

DARWIN, C. (1859). *On the origin of species.* London: J. Murray.

DAVIDSON, I., & NOBLE, W. (1993). On the evolution of language. *Current Anthropology, 34,* 165–166.

DAVIS, C. A., BRADY, M. P., HAMILTON, R., MCEVOY, M. A., & WILLIAMS, R. E. (1994). Effects of high-probability requests on the social interactions of young children with severe disabilities. *Journal of Applied Behavior Analysis, 27,* 619–637.

DAY, W. (1980). The historical antecedents of contemporary behaviorism. In R. W. Rieber & K. Salzinger (Eds.), *Psychology: Theoretical-historical perspectives* (pp. 203–262). New York: Academic Press.

DEBECKER, G. (1997). *The gift of fear: Survival signals that protect us from violence.* Boston: Little, Brown.

DECASPER, A., & FIFER, W. (1980). Newborns prefer their mothers' voices. *Science, 208,* 1174–1176.

DECASPER, A., & SPENCE, M. J. (1986). Prenatal maternal speech influences newborns' perception of speech sounds. *Infant Behavior and Development, 9,* 133–150.

DEGUCHI, H. (1984). Observational learning from a radical-behavioristic viewpoint. *Behavior Analyst, 7,* 83–95.

DELORENZO, D. R. (1999). The relationship of cooperative education exposure to career decision-making self-efficacy and career locus of control. *Dissertation Abstracts International Section A: Humanities & Social Sciences, 59,* 4066.

DENNEY, J., & NEURINGER, A. (1998). Behavioral variability is controlled by discriminative stimuli. *Animal Learning & Behavior, 26*(2), 154–162.

DE SILVA, P. (1990). The modification of human food aversions: New applications of behaviour therapy. In H. Zapotoczky, W. Thomas, et al. (Eds.), *The scientific dialogue: From basic research to clinical intervention. Annual series of European research in behavior therapy* (Vol. 5, pp. 177–180). Amsterdam: Swets & Zeitlinger.

DE VILLIERS, P. (1977). Choice in concurrent schedules and a quantitative formulation of the law of effect. In W. K. Honig & J. E. R. Staddon (Eds.), *Handbook of operant behavior.* Englewood Cliffs, NJ: Prentice-Hall.

DEWSBURY, D. A. (1978). What is (was?) the fixed action pattern? *Animal Behaviour, 26*(1), 310–311.

DICHIARA, G. (1995). The role of dopamine in drug abuse viewed from the perspective of its role in motivation. *Drug and Alcohol Dependency, 38,* 95–137.

DODSON, C. S., JOHNSON, M. K., & SCHOOLER, J. W. (1997). The verbal overshadowing effect: Why descriptions impair face recognition. *Memory and Cognition, 25*(2), 129–139.

DOHRMANN, R. J., & LASKIN, D. M. (1978). An evaluation of electromyographic feedback in the treatment of myofascial pain-dysfunction syndrome. *Journal of the American Dental Association, 96,* 656–662.

DOPKINS, S., & GLEASON, T. (1997). Comparing exemplar and prototype models of categorization. *Canadian Journal of Experimental Psychology, 51,* 212–230.

DRACHMAN, D. A., & ARBIT, J. (1966). Memory and the hippocampal complex. II. Is memory a multiple process? *Archives of Neurology, 15,* 52–61.

DRYER, M. (1997). Are grammatical relations universal? In J. Bybee, J. Haiman, & S. Thompson (Eds.), *Essays on language function and language type.* Amsterdam: John Benjamins.

DUBBERT, P. M. (1995). Behavioral (life-style) modification in the prevention and treatment of hypertension. *Clinical Psychology Review, 15,* 187–216.

DUBREUIL, S. C., GARRY, M., & LOFTUS, E. F. (1998). Tales from the crib: Age regression and the creation of unlikely memories. In S. J. Lynn & K. M. McConkey (Eds.), *Truth in memory* (pp. 137–160). New York: Guilford.

DUNCAN, C. P. (1949). The retroactive effect of electroshock on learning. *Journal of Comparative and Physiological Psychology, 42,* 32–44.

DURKIN, M., PRESCOTT, L., FURCHTGOTT, E., CANTOR, J., & POWELL, D. A. (1993). Concomitant eyeblink and heart rate classical conditioning in young, middle-aged, and elderly human subjects. *Psychology and Aging, 8,* 571–581.

EARLY, J. C. (1968). Attitude learning in children. *Journal of Educational Psychology, 59,* 176–180.

EATON, S. B., SHOSTAK, M., & KONNER, M. (1988). *The paleolithic prescription: A program of diet and exercise and a design for living.* New York: Harper & Row.

EBBINGHAUS, H. (1885/1964). *Memory.* New York: Dover.

ECKERMAN, D. A., & LANSON, R. N. (1969). Variability of response location for pigeons responding under continuous reinforcement, intermittent reinforcement, and extinction. *Journal of the Experimental Analysis of Behavior, 12,* 73–80.

ECKERMAN, D. A., & VREELAND, R. (1973). Response variability for humans receiving continuous, intermittent or no positive experiment feedback. *Bulletin of the Psychonomic Society, 2,* 297–299.

EHRENFREUND, D. (1952). A study of the transposition gradient. *Journal of Experimental Psychology, 43,* 81–87.

EIBL-EIBESFELDT, I. (1970). *Ethology: The biology of behavior.* New York: Holt, Rinehart & Winston.

EICHENBAUM, H. (1994). The hippocampal system and declarative memory in humans and animals: Experimental analysis and historical origins. In D. L. Schacter & E. Tulving (Eds.), *Memory systems.* Cambridge, MA: MIT Press.

EICHENBAUM, H. (1997). Declarative memory: Insights from cognitive neurobiology. *Annual Review of Psychology, 48,* 547–572.

EIFERT, G. H. (1984). The effects of language conditioning on various aspects of anxiety. *Behavior Research and Therapy, 22,* 13–21.

EIMAS, P. D. (1985). The perception of speech in early infancy. *Scientific American, 252,* 46–52.

EIMAS, P. D. (1994). Categorization in early infancy and the continuity of development. *Cognition, 50,* 83–93.

ELDREDGE, N., & GOULD, S. J. (1972). Punctuated equilibria: An alternative to phyletic gradualism. In T. J. M. Schopf (Ed.), *Models in paleobiology* (pp. 82–115). San Francisco: Freeman, Cooper.

EMLEN, S. (1969a). The development of migratory orientation in young indigo buntings. *Living Bird, 8,* 113–126.

EMLEN, S. (1969b). Bird migration: Influence of physiological state upon celestial orientation. *Science, 165,* 716–718.

EMMELKAMP, P. M. G. (1982). Anxiety and fear. In A. S. Bellack, M. Hersen, & A. E. Kazdin (Eds.), *International handbook of behavior modification and therapy.* New York: Plenum.

EMMELKAMP, P. M. G., & WESSELS, H. (1975). Flooding in imagination vs. flooding *in vivo:* A comparison with agoraphobics. *Behaviour Research and Therapy, 13,* 7–16.

ENGEL, B. T., & BLEECKER, E. R. (1974). Application of operant conditioning techniques to the control of cardiac arrhythmias. In P. A. Obrist, A. H. Black, J. Berner, & L. V. DiCara (Eds.), *Cardiovascular psychophysiology.* Chicago: Aldine.

ENGELKAMP, J., & WIPPICH, W. (1995). Current issues in implicit and explicit memory. *Psychological Research, 57,* 143–155.

ENGERT, F., & BONHOEFFER, T. (1999). Dendritic spine changes associated with hippocampal long-term synaptic plasticity. *Nature, 399,* 66–70.

EPSTEIN, J. A., BOTVIN, G. J., & DIAZ, T. (1999). Social influence and psychological determinants of smoking among inner-city adolescents. *Journal of Child and Adolescent Substance Abuse, 8,* 1–19.

EPSTEIN, L. H., & MASEK, B. J. (1978). Behavioral control of medicine compliance. *Journal of Applied Behavior Analysis, 11,* 1–9.

EPSTEIN, R., LANZA, R. P., & SKINNER, B. F. (1980). "Self-awareness" in the pigeon. *Science, 212,* 695–696.

EPSTEIN, R., & SKINNER, B. F. (1981). The spontaneous use of memoranda by pigeons. *Behavior Analysis Letters, 1,* 241–246.

EPSTEIN, S., & BURSTEIN, K. R. (1966). A replication of Hovland's study of stimulus generalization to frequencies of tones. *Journal of Experimental Psychology, 72,* 782–784.

ERICKSON, M. A., & KRUSCHKE, J. K. (1998). Rules and exemplars in category learning. *Journal of Experimental Psychology: General, 127,* 107–140.

ERON, L. D., HUESMANN, L. R., LEFKOWITZ, M. M., & WALDER, L. O. (1996). Does television violence cause aggression? In D. F. Greenberg (Ed.), *Criminal careers* (Vol. 2, pp. 311–321). The International Library of Criminology, Criminal Justice, and Penology. Aldershot, England: Dartmouth Publishing.

ERWIN, T. L. (1983). Beetles and other insects of tropical rain forest canopies at Manaus, Brazil, sampled by insecticidal fogging. In S. L. Sutton, T. C. Whitmore, & A. C. Chadwick (Eds.), *Tropical rain forest: Ecology and management* (pp. 59–75). London: Blackwell.

ESLINGER, P. J., & DAMASIO, A. R. (1986). Preserved motor learning in Alzheimer's disease: Implications for anatomy and behavior. *Journal of Neuroscience, 6,* 3006–3009.

ESTES, W. K., & SKINNER, B. F. (1941). Some quantitative properties of anxiety. *Journal of Experimental Psychology, 29,* 390–400.

EVANS, D. A., FUNKENSTEIN, H. H., ALBERT, M. S., SCHERR, P. A., COOK, N. R., CHOWN, M. J., HEBERT, L. E., HENNEKENS, C. H., & TAYLOR, J. O. (1989). Prevalence of Alzheimer's disease in a community population of older persons. *Journal of the American Medical Association, 262,* 2551–2556.

EYSENCK, H. J. (1952). The effects of psychotherapy: An evaluation. *Journal of Consulting Psychology, 16,* 319–324.

FABRICUS, E., & BOYD, H. (1954). Experiments on the following reactions of ducklings. *Wildfowl Trust Annual Report, 6,* 84–89.

FANSELOW, M. S., & TIGHE, T. J. (1988). Contextual conditioning with massed versus distributed unconditional stimuli in the absence of explicit conditional stimuli. *Journal of Experimental Psychology: Animal Behavior Processes, 14,* 187–199.

FELTON, M., & LYON, D. O. (1966). The postreinforcement pause. *Journal of the Experimental Analysis of Behavior, 9,* 131–134.

FERLAZZO, F., CONTE, S., & GENTILOMO, A. (1993). Event-related potentials and recognition memory within the "levels of processing" framework. *Neuroreport: An International Journal for the Rapid Communication of Research in Neuroscience, 4,* 667–670.

FERRARO, D. P., & BRANCH, K. H. (1968). Variability of response location during regular and partial reinforcement. *Psychological Reports, 23,* 1023–1031.

FERSTER, C. B. & CULBERTSON, S. A. (1982). *Behavior principles* (3rd ed.). Englewood Cliffs, NJ: Prentice-Hall.

FERSTER, C. B., & SKINNER, B. F. (1957). *Schedules of reinforcement.* Englewood Cliffs, NJ: Prentice-Hall.

FIELD, T. M., WOODSON, R., GREENBERG, R., & COHEN, D. (1982). Discrimination and imitation of facial expressions by neonates. *Science, 218,* 179–181.

FIELDS, L., REEVE, K. F., ADAMS, B. J., & VERHAVE, T. (1991). Stimulus generalization and equivalence classes: A model for natural categories. *Journal of the Experimental Analysis of Behavior, 55,* 305–312.

FIORITO, G., & SCOTTO, P. (1992). Observational learning in *Octopus vulgaris. Science, 256,* 545–547.

FISCHER, H., ANDERSSON, J. L. R., FURMARK, T., & FREDRICKSON, M. (2000). Fear conditioning and brain activity: A positron emission tomography study in humans. *Behavioral Neuroscience, 114,* 671–680.

FISKE, S. T., & NEUBERG, S. L. (1990). A continuum of impression formation from category-based to individuating processes: Influences of information and motivation of attention and interpretation. In M. P. Zanna (Ed.), *Advances in experimental social psychology* (Vol. 23, pp. 1–73). New York: Academic Press.

FOA, E. B., & CHAMBLESS, D. L. (1978). Habituation of subjective anxiety during flooding in imagery. *Behaviour Research & Therapy, 16,* 391–399.

FODOR, J., & LEPORE, E. (1996). The red herring and the pet fish: Why concepts still can't be prototypes. *Cognition, 58*, 253–270.

FODOR, J. A. (1983). *The modularity of mind: An essay on faculty psychology*. Cambridge, MA: MIT Press.

FODOR, J. A. (1987). *Psychosemantics*. Cambridge, MA: MIT Press.

FORTHMAN QUICK, D. L., GUSTAVSON, C. R., & RUSINIAK, K. W. (1985). Coyote control and taste aversion. *Appetite, 6*, 253–264.

FOX, D. K., HOPKINS, B. L., & ANGER, W. K. (1987). The long-term effects of a token economy on safety performance in open-pit mining. *Journal of Applied Behavior Analysis, 20*, 215–224.

FOXX, R. M., & BROWN, R. A. (1979). Nicotine fading and self-monitoring for cigarette abstinence or controlled smoking. *Journal of Applied Behavior Analysis, 12*, 111–125.

FRANKS, C. M. (1969). Introduction: Behavior therapy and its Pavlovian origins: Review and perspectives. In C. M. Franks (Ed.), *Behavior therapy: Appraisal and status*. New York: McGraw-Hill.

FREUD, S. (1910). The origin and development of psychoanalysis. In R. M. Hutchins (Ed.), *Great Books of the Western World* (Vol. 54, pp.1–20). Chicago: Encyclopaedia Britannica.

FRITZ, J., & KOTRSCHAL, K. (1999). Social learning in common ravens, *Corvus corax. Animal Behaviour, 57*(4), 785–793.

GABRIELI, J. D. E. (1998). Cognitive neuroscience of human memory. *Annual Review of Psychology, 49*, 87–115.

GABRIELI, J. D. E., BREWER, J. B., DESMOND, J. E., & GLOVER, G. H. (1997). Separate neural bases of two fundamental memory processes in the human medial temporal lobe. *Science, 276*, 264–266.

GALDIKAS, B. M. F. (1985). Orangutan sociality at Tanjung Puting. *American Journal of Primatology, 9*, 101–119.

GALDIKAS, B. M. F. (1988). Orangutan diet, range, and activity at Tanjung Puting, Central Borneo. *International Journal of Primatology, 9*, 1–35.

GALDIKAS, B. M. F., & VASEY, P. (1992). Why are orangutans so smart? Ecological and social hypotheses. In F. D. Burton (Ed.), *Social processes and mental abilities in non-human primates*. Lewiston, New York: Edward Mellon.

GALEF, B. (1988). Imitation in animals: History, definition, and interpretation of data from the psychological laboratory. In T. R. Zentall & B. G. Galef, Jr. (Eds.), *Social learning: Psychological and biological perspectives*. Hillsdale, NJ: Erlbaum.

GALIZIO, M. (1979). Contingency-shaped and rule-governed behavior: Instructional control of human loss avoidance. *Journal of the Experimental Analysis of Behavior, 31*, 53–70.

GALIZIO, M., & BUSKIST, W. F. (1988). Laboratory lore and research practices in the experimental analysis of human behavior: Selecting reinforcers and arranging contingencies. *Behavior Analyst, 11*, 65–69.

GALLAGAN, R. (1987). Intonation with single words: purposive and grammatical use. *Journal of Child Language, 14*, 1–22.

GARCIA, J., KOELLING, R. A. (1966). Relation of cue to consequence in avoidance learning. *Psychonomic Science, 4*, 123–124.

GARDNER, H. (1985). *The mind's new science*. New York: Basic Books.

GARDNER, R. A., & GARDNER, B. T. (1969). Teaching sign language to a chimpanzee. *Science, 165*, 664–672.

GAULIN, S. J. C., & MCBURNEY, D. H. (2001). *Psychology: An evolutionary approach*. Upper Saddle River, NJ: Prentice-Hall.

GAZZANIGA, M. S. (Ed.). (2000). *Cognitive neuroscience: A reader*. Malden, MA: Blackwell.

GEEN, R. (1994). Television and aggression: Recent developments in research and theory. In D. Zillmann, J. Bryant, & A. C. Huston (Eds.), *Media, children, and the family: Social scientific, psychodynamic, and clinical perspectives*. Hillsdale, NJ: Erlbaum.

GEER, J. H., & KATKIN, E. S. (1966). Treatment of insomnia using a variant of systematic desensitization: A case report. *Journal of Abnormal Psychology, 71*, 161–164.

GENTRY, W. D. (Ed.). (1984). *Handbook of behavioral medicine*. New York: Guilford.

GIESER, M. T. (1993). The first behavior therapist as I knew her. *Journal of Behavior Therapy & Experimental Psychiatry, 24*, 321–324.

GLUCK, M.A., & BOWER, G.H. (1988). From conditioning to category learning: An adaptive network model. *Journal of Experimental Psychology: General, 117,* 227–247.

GLUCK, M. A., & THOMPSON, R. F. (1987). Modeling the neural substrates of learning: A computational approach. *Psychological Review, 94,* 176–191.

GOLDBERG, S. R., & SCHUSTER, C. R. (1967). Conditioned suppression by a stimulus associated with nalorphine in morphine-dependent monkeys. *Journal of the Experimental Analysis of Behavior, 10,* 235–242.

GOLDFRIED, M. R., & GOLDFRIED, A. P. (1977). Importance of hierarchy content in the self-control of anxiety. *Journal of Consulting and Clinical Psychology, 45,* 124–134.

GOLDSTONE, R. L. (1996). Isolated and interrelated concepts. *Memory and Cognition, 24,* 608–628.

GOLEMAN, D. (1995). *Emotional intelligence.* New York: Bantam Books.

GOODALL, J. (1971). *In the shadow of man.* Boston: Houghton Mifflin.

GOODLUCK, H. (2000). Buzzsaws and blueprints: Commentary. *Journal of Child Language, 27*(3), 734–736.

GORCZYNSKI, R. M. (1991). Conditioned immunosuppression: Analysis of lymphocytes and host environment of young and aged mice. In R. Ader, D. L. Felton, et al. (Eds.), *Psychoneuroimmunology* (2nd ed). San Diego: Academic Press.

GORCZYNSKI, R. M. (1992). Conditioned stress responses by pregnant and/or lactating mice reduce immune responses of their offspring after weaning. *Brain, Behavior, and Immunity, 6,* 87–95.

GORDON, J. R. (1978). The use of rapid smoking and group support to induce and maintain abstinence from cigarette smoking. *Dissertation Abstracts International, 39* (5-A), 2831. (University Microfilms No. 7820725.)

GORMEZANO, I., KEHOE, E. J., & MARSHALL, B. S. (1983). Twenty years of classical conditioning research with the rabbit. In J. M. Sprague & A. N. Epstein (Eds.), *Progress in psychobiology and physiological psychology* (Vol. 10, pp. 198–264). New York: Academic Press.

GORMEZANO, I., SCHNEIDERMAN, N., DEAUX, E. B., & FUENTES, I. (1962). Nictitating membrane: Classical conditioning and extinction in the albino rabbit. *Science, 138,* 33–34.

GOULD, J. L. (1982). *Ethology: The mechanisms and evolution of behavior.* New York: W. W. Norton.

GOULD, S. J. (1995). *Dinosaur in a haystack: Reflections in natural history.* New York: Harmony Books.

GRACE, R. C. (1995). Independence of reinforcement delay and magnitude in concurrent chains. *Journal of the Experimental Analysis of Behavior, 63,* 255–276.

GRANT, D. S. (1976). Effect of sample presentation time on long-delay matching in the pigeon. *Learning and Motivation, 7,* 580–590.

GREENFIELD, P. M., & SAVAGE-RUMBAUGH, E. S. (1993). Comparing communicative competence in child and chimp: The pragmatics of repetition. *Journal of Child Language, 20,* 1–26.

GUHA, D., DUTTA, S. N., & PRADHAN, S. N. (1974). Conditioning of gastric secretion by epinephrine in rats. *Proceedings of the Society for Experimental Biology and Medicine, 147,* 817–819.

GUSTAVSON, C. R., GARCIA, J., HAWKINS, W. G., & RUSINIAK, K. W. (1974). Coyote predation control by aversive conditioning. *Science, 184,* 581–583.

GUSTAVSON, C. R., & GUSTAVSON, J. C. (1985). Predation control using conditioned aversion methodology: Theory, practice, and implications. *Annals of New York Academy of Sciences, 443,* 348–356.

GUSTAVSON, C. R., & NICOLAUS, L. K. (1987). Taste aversion conditioning in wolves, coyotes, and other canids: Retrospect and prospect. In H. Frank et al. (Eds.), *Man and wolf: Advances, issues, and problems in captive wolf research. Perspectives in vertebrate science* (Vol. 4, pp. 169–203). Dordrecht, Netherlands: Dr. W. Junk.

GUTTMAN, N., & KALISH, H. I. (1956). Discriminability and stimulus generalization. *Journal of Experimental Psychology, 51,* 79–88.

HACKETT, G., & BETZ, N. (1995). Self-efficacy and career choice and development. In J. E. Maddux (Ed.), *Self-efficacy, adaptation, and adjustment: Theory, research, and application.* New York: Plenum.

HAGEN, K. M., GUTKIN, T. B., WILSON, C. P., & OATS, R. G. (1998). Using vicarious experience and verbal persuasion to enhance self-efficacy in pre-service teachers: "Priming the pump" for consultation. *School Psychology Quarterly, 13,* 169–178.

HANNA, E., & MELTZOFF, A. N. (1993). Peer imitation by toddlers in laboratory, home, and day-care contexts: Implications for social learning and memory. *Developmental Psychology, 29,* 701–710.

HARLOW, H. F. (1949). The formation of learning sets. *Psychological Review, 56,* 51–65.

HARZEM, P., & MILES, T. R. (1978). *Conceptual issues in operant psychology.* Chichester, England: John Wiley & Sons.

HAYES, K. J., & HAYES, C. (1951). The intellectual development of a home-raised chimpanzee. *Proceedings of the American Philosophical Society, 95,* 105–109.

HEATH, L., BRESOLIN, L. B., & RINALDI, R. C. (1989). Effects of media violence on children: A review of the literature. *Archives of General Psychiatry, 46,* 376–379.

HEBB, D. O. (1949). *The organization of behaviour.* New York: Wiley-Interscience.

HEIT, E. (1997). Knowledge and concept learning. In K. Lamberts, D. R. Shanks, et al. (Eds.), *Knowledge, concepts and categories.* Cambridge, MA: MIT Press.

HENKE, K. (1999). The roles of the hippocampus in memory. In L.-G. Nilsson & H. J. Markowitsch (Eds.), *Cognitive neuroscience of memory.* Seattle: Hogrefe & Huber.

HENKE, P. G. (1982). The telencephalic limbic system and experimental gastric pathology: A review. *Neuroscience and Biobehavioral Reviews, 6,* 381–390.

HERMAN, L. M., & THOMPSON, R. K. R. (1982). Symbolic, identity, and probe delayed matching to sounds by the bottle-nosed dolphin. *Animal Learning and Behavior, 10,* 22–34.

HERRNSTEIN, R. J. (1961). Relative and absolute strength of response as a function of frequency of reinforcement. *Journal of the Experimental Analysis of Behavior, 4,* 267–272.

HERRNSTEIN, R. J. (1970). On the law of effect. *Journal of the Experimental Analysis of Behavior, 13,* 243–266.

HERRNSTEIN, R. J., & DEVILLIERS, P. A. (1980). Fish as a natural category for people and pigeons. In G. H. Bower (Ed.), *Psychology of learning and motivation* (Vol. 14). New York: Academic Press.

HERRNSTEIN, R. J., LOVELAND, D. H., & CABLE, C. (1976). Natural concepts in pigeons. *Journal of Experimental Psychology: Animal Behavior Processes, 2,* 285–302.

HERRNSTEIN, R. J., & MORSE, W. H. (1958). A conjunctive schedule of reinforcement. *Journal of the Experimental Analysis of Behavior, 1,* 15–24.

HEYES, C., & GALEF, B. (Eds.). (1996). *Social learning in animals: The roots of culture.* New York: Academic Press.

HINELINE, P. N. (1984). Can a statement in cognitive terms be a behavior-analytic interpretation? *Behavior Analyst, 7,* 97–100.

HINSON, J. M., & STADDON, J. E. R. (1983). Matching, maximizing, and hill-climbing. *Journal of the Experimental Analysis of Behavior, 40,* 321–331.

HINTZMAN, D. L. (1986). "Schema abstraction" in a multiple-trace memory model. *Psychological Review, 93,* 411–428.

HIXON, M. D. (1998). Ape language research: A review and behavioral perspective. *Analysis of Verbal Behavior, 15,* 17–39.

HOCKETT, C. F. (1960). The origin of speech. *Scientific American, 203,* 89–96.

HOGBEN, M., & BYRNE, D. (1998). Using social learning theory to explain individual differences in human sexuality. *Journal of Sex Research, 35,* 58–71.

HORNER, R. H., DUNLAP, G., & KOEGEL, R. L. (Eds). (1988). *Generalization and maintenance: Life-style changes in applied settings.* Baltimore: Paul Brookes.

HOROWITZ, I. A., & BORDENS, K. S. (1995). *Social psychology.* Mountain View, CA: Mayfield.

HOSOKAWA, T., RUSAKOV, D. A., BLISS, T. V. P., & FINE, A. (1995). Repeated confocal imaging of individual dendritic spines in the living hippocampal slice: Evidence for changes in length and orientation associated with chemically induced LTP. *Journal of Neuroscience, 15,* 5560–5573.

HOUK, J. C., DAVIS, J. L., & BEISER, D. G. (Eds.). (1995). *Models of information processing in the basal ganglia.* Cambridge, MA: MIT Press.

HOULIHAN, D., JACOBSON, L., & BRANDON, P. K. (1994). Replication of a high-probability request sequence with varied interprompt times in a preschool setting. *Journal of Applied Behavior Analysis, 27,* 737–738.

HOVLAND, C. I. (1937). The generalization of conditioned responses: I. The sensory generalization of conditioned responses with varying frequencies of tone. *Journal of General Psychology, 17,* 125–148.

HOWARD, R. W. (2000). Generalization and transfer: An interrelation of paradigms and a taxonomy of knowledge extension processes. *Review of General Psychology, 4*(3), 211–237.

HOWE, M. L. (1995). Interference effects in young children's long-term retention. *Developmental Psychology, 31,* 579–596.

HOWSON, C. P. (Ed.). (1998). *Control of cardiovascular diseases in developing countries: Research, development, and institutional strengthening.* Washington, DC: National Academy Press.

HUBBLE, M. A., DUNCAN, B. L., & MILLER, S. D. (Eds.). (1999). *The heart and soul of change: What works in therapy.* Washington, DC: American Psychological Association.

HUESMANN, L. R., & MALAMUTH, N. M. (1986). Media violence and antisocial behavior: An overview. *Journal of Social Issues, 42,* 1–6.

HYDE, L. A., HOPLIGHT, B. J., & DENENBERG, V. H. (1998). Water version of the radial-arm maze: Learning in three inbred strains of mice. *Brain Research, 785,* 236–244.

HYMAN, S. E. (1996). Shaking out the cause of addiction. *Science, 273,* 611–612.

IKEMI, Y., & NAKAGAWA, S. (1962). A psychosomatic study of contagious dermatitis. *Kyushu Journal of Medical Science, 13,* 335–350.

INTONS-PETERSON, M. J., & BEST, D. L. (Eds.). (1998). *Memory distortions and their prevention.* Mahwah, NJ: Erlbaum.

ITANI, J. (1958). On the acquisition and propagation of a new food habit in the troop of Japanese monkeys at Takasakiyama. *Primates, 1,* 131–148.

IWATA, J., LEDOUX, J. E., MEELEY, M. P., ARNERIC, S., & REIS, D. J. (1986). Intrinsic neurons in the amygdaloid field projected to by the medial geniculate body mediate emotional responses conditioned to acoustic stimuli. *Brain Research, 383*(1–2), 195–214.

JACOB, F. (1977). Evolution and tinkering. *Science, 196,* 1161–1166.

JACOB, F. (1982). *The possible and the actual.* Seattle: University of Washington Press.

JACOBY, L. L., ALLAN, L. G., COLLINS, J. C., & LARWILL, L. K. (1988). Memory influences subjective experience: Noise judgments. *Journal of Experimental Psychology: Learning, Memory, and Cognition, 14,* 240–247.

JAMES, W. (1890/1981). *The principles of psychology* (Vol. 1). Cambridge, MA: Harvard University Press.

JEFFERY, R. W. (1987). Behavioral treatment of obesity. *Annals of Behavioral Medicine, 9,* 20–24.

JENKINS, H. M., & MOORE, B. R. (1973). The form of the autoshaped response with food or water reinforcers. *Journal of the Experimental Analysis of Behavior, 20,* 163–181.

JENSEN, K. (1994). Birds of a feather. *Air & Space, 9,* 62–66.

JESTE, D. (1990). The genetics of behavioral disorders. In J. Weiner (Ed.), *Behavioral neuroscience.* New York: John Wiley & Sons.

JOHNSON, J. S., & NEWPORT, E. L. (1989). Critical-period effects in second language learning: The influence of maturational state on the acquisition of English as a second language. *Cognitive Psychology, 21,* 60–99.

JOHNSTON, D. W., LANCASHIRE, M., MATHEWS, A. M., MUNBY, M., SHAW, P. M., & GELDER, M. G. (1976). Imaginal flooding and exposure to real phobic situations: Changes during treatment. *British Journal of Psychiatry, 129,* 372–377.

JOHNSTON, J. M., & PENNYPACKER, H. S. (1993). *Strategies and tactics of behavioral research* (2nd ed.). Mahwah, NJ: Erlbaum.

JOHNSTON, J. M., WILLIAMS, M., WAGGONER, P., EDGE, C. C., DUGAN, R. E., & HALLOWELL, S. F. (1998). Canine detection odor signatures for mine-related explosives. In A. Dubey, J. F. Harvey, & J. R. Broach (Eds.), Detection and remediation technologies for mines and mine-like targets III (pp. 490–501). *Proceedings of the International Society for Optical Engineering, 3392,* Bellingham, WA.

JONES, E. E., & HARRIS, V. A. (1967). The attribution of attitudes. *Journal of Experimental Social Psychology, 3,* 2–24.

JONES, F. W., WILLS, A. J., & MCLAREN, I. P. L. (1998). Perceptual categorization: Connectionist modeling and decision rules. *Quarterly Journal of Experimental Psychology: Comparative and Physiological Psychology, 51B,* 33–58.

JONES, M. C. (1924). A laboratory study of fear: The case of Peter. *Pedagogical Seminary, 31,* 308–315.

JONES, S. H., GRAY, J. A., & HEMSLEY, D. R. (1992). Loss of the Kamin blocking effect in acute but not chronic schizophrenics. *Biological Psychiatry, 32,* 739–755.

JOYCE, J. H., & CHASE, P. N. (1990). Effects of response variability on the sensitivity of rule-governed behavior. *Journal of the Experimental Analysis of Behavior, 54,* 251–262.

KAMIN, L. J. (1965). Temporal and intensity characteristics of the conditioned stimulus. In W. F. Prokasy (Ed.), *Classical conditioning: A symposium* (pp. 118–147). New York: Appleton-Century-Crofts.

KAMIN, L. J. (1968). "Attention-like" processes in classical conditioning. In M. R. Jones (Ed.), *Miami symposium on the prediction of behavior* (pp. 9–31). Miami: University of Miami Press.

KAMIN, L. J. (1969). Predictability, surprise, attention, and conditioning. In B. A. Campbell & R. M. Church (Eds.), *Punishment and aversive behavior* (pp. 279–296). New York: Appleton-Century-Crofts.

KAPLAN, S. (1987). Aesthetics, affect, and cognition: Environmental preference from an evolutionary perspective. *Environment and Behavior, 19,* 3–32.

KASPROW, W. J., CACHEIRO, H., BALAZ, M. A., & MILLER, R. R. (1982). Reminder-induced recovery of associations to an overshadowed stimulus. *Learning and Motivation, 13,* 155–166.

KAWAI, M. (1965). Newly acquired precultural behavior of the natural troop of Japanese monkeys on Koshima Island. *Primates, 6,* 1–30.

KAZDIN, A. E. (1982a). History of behavior modification. In A. S. Bellack, M. Hersen, & A. E. Kazdin (Eds.), *International handbook of behavior modification and therapy.* New York: Plenum.

KAZDIN, A. E. (1982b). The token economy: A decade later. *Journal of Applied Behavior Analysis, 15,* 431–445.

KEHOE, E. J. (1988). A layered network model of associative learning: Learning to learn and configuration. *Psychological Review, 95,* 411–453.

KELLOGG, R. T., ROBBINS, D. W., & BOURNE, L. E., JR. (1978). Memory for intratrial events in feature identification. *Journal of Experimental Psychology: Human Learning and Memory, 4,* 256–265.

KELLOGG, W. N., & KELLOGG, L. A. (1933). *The ape and the child: A study of environmental influence upon early behavior.* New York: Hafner.

KEMLER-NELSON, D., JUSCZYK, P., & CASSIDY, K. (1989). How the prosodic cues of motherese might assist language learning. *Journal of Child Language, 16,* 55–68.

KENRICK, D. T., SADALLA, E. K., & KEEFE, R. C. (1998). Evolutionary cognitive psychology: The missing heart of cognitive science. In C. Crawford & D. L. Krebs (Eds.), *Handbook of evolutionary psychology: Ideas, issues, and applications.* Mahwah, NJ: Erlbaum.

KHERIATY, E., KLEINKNECHT, R. A., & HYMAN, I. E., JR. (1999). Recall and validation of phobia origins as a function of a structured interview versus the Phobia Origins Questionnaire. *Behavior Modification, 23,* 61–78.

KIHLSTROM, J. F. (1997). Memory, abuse, and science. *American Psychologist, 52,* 994–995.

KIMMEL, H. D., & LACHNIT, H. (1988). The Rescorla-Wagner theory does not predict contextual control of phasic responses in transswitching. *Biological Psychology, 27(2),* 95–112.

KING, G. F., ARMITAGE, S. G., & TILTON, J. R. (1960). A therapeutic approach to schizophrenics of extreme pathology: An operant-interpersonal method. *Journal of Abnormal and Social Psychology, 61,* 276–286.

KING, M. G., & HUSBAND, A. J. (1991). Altered immunity through behavioral conditioning. In J. G. Carlson, R. A. Seifert, et al. (Eds.), *International perspectives on self-regulation and health. Plenum series in behavioral psychophysiology and medicine* (pp. 197–204). New York: Plenum.

KIRKWOOD, A., LEE, H.-K., & BEAR, M. F. (1995). Co-regulation of long-term potentiation and experience-dependent synaptic plasticity in visual cortex by age and experience. *Nature, 375,* 328–331.

KIRSCH, I. (1985). Self-efficacy and expectancy: Old wine with new labels. *Journal of Personality and Social Psychology, 49,* 824–830.

KLEIN, S. B., & MOWRER, R. R. (1989). *Contemporary learning theories: Instrumental conditioning and biological constraints on learning.* Hillsdale, NJ: Erlbaum.

KLEINKNECHT, R. A. (1994). Acquisition of blood, injury, and needle fears and phobias. *Behaviour Research & Therapy, 32,* 817–823.

KNAPCZYK, D. R., & LIVINGSTON, G. (1973). Self-recording and student teacher supervision: Variables within a token economy structure. *Journal of Applied Behavior Analysis, 6,* 481–486.

KNOWLTON, B. J., MANGELS, J. A., & SQUIRE, L. R. (1996). A neostriatal habit learning system in humans. *Science, 273,* 1399–1402.

KOHLER, W. (1939). Simple structural functions in the chimpanzee and the chicken. In W. D. Ellis (Ed.), *A sourcebook of gestalt psychology.* New York: Harcourt Brace.

KOP, P. F. M., & DE KLERK, L. F. W. (1994). Influential mathematical models in the psychology of learning. In M. A. Croon & F. J. R. Van de Vijver (Eds.), *Viability of mathematical models in the social and behavioral sciences* (pp. 143–161). Lisse, Netherlands: Swets & Zeitlinger.

KORN, J. H., DAVIS, R., & DAVIS, S. F. (1991). Historians' and chairpersons' judgments of eminence among psychologists. *American Psychologist, 46,* 789–792.

KRAMER, F. M., JEFFERY, R. W., FORSTER, J. L., & SNELL, M. K. (1989). Long-term follow-up of behavioral treatment for obesity: Patterns of weight regain among men and women. *International Journal of Obesity, 13,* 123–136.

KRAMER, S. P. (1982). Memory for recent behavior in the pigeon. *Journal of the Experimental Analysis of Behavior, 38,* 71–85.

KREBS, D. L., & DENTON, K. (1997). Social illusions and self-deception: The evolution of biases in person perception. In J. A. Simpson & D. T. Kenrick (Eds.), *Evolutionary social psychology* (pp. 21–47). Mahwah, NJ: Erlbaum.

KRITCH, K. M., & BOSTOW, D. E. (1998). Degree of constructed-response interaction in computer-based programmed instruction. *Journal of Applied Behavior Analysis, 31,* 387–398.

KUCH, K., COX, B. J., EVANS, R., & SHULMAN, I. (1994). Phobias, panic, and pain in 55 survivors of road vehicle accidents. *Journal of Anxiety Disorders, 8,* 181–187.

KUENNE, M. R. (1946). Experimental investigation of the relation of language to transposition behavior in young children. *Journal of Experimental Psychology, 36,* 471–490.

KUHN, T. S. (1970). *The structure of scientific revolutions* (2nd ed.). Chicago: University of Chicago Press.

KULIK, J. A., COHEN, P. A., & EBELING, B. J. (1980). Effectiveness of programmed instruction in higher education: A meta-analysis of findings. *Educational Evaluation and Policy Analysis, 2,* 51–64.

KULIK, J. A., KULIK, C., & CARMICHAEL, K. (1974). The Keller Plan in science teaching. *Science, 183,* 379–383.

KULIK, J. A., KULIK, C. C., & COHEN, P. A. (1979). A meta-analysis of outcome studies of Keller's personalized system of instruction. *Journal of Personalized Instruction, 3,* 2–14.

KYMISS, E., & POULSON, C. L. (1994). Generalized imitation in preschool boys. *Journal of Experimental Child Psychology, 58,* 389–404.

LADOUCEUR, R. (1978). Rationale of systematic desensitization and covert positive reinforcement. *Behaviour Research and Therapy, 16,* 411–420.

LAIBOW, R. (1999). Medical applications of neurobiofeedback. In J. R. Evans & A. Abarbanel (Eds.), *Introduction to quantitative EEG and neurofeedback.* San Diego: Academic Press.

LANGS, R., BADALAMENTI, A. F., & SAVAGE-RUMBAUGH, S. (1996). Two mathematically defined expressive language structures in humans and chimpanzees. *Behavioral Science, 41,* 124–135.

LASHLEY, K. S. (1951). The problem of serial order in behavior. In L. A. Jeffries (Ed.), *Cerebral mechanisms in behavior: The Hixon symposium.* New York: Wiley.

LATTAL, K. A., & PERONE, M. (Eds.). (1998). *Handbook of research methods in human operant behavior*. New York: Plenum.

LAUGHLIN, P. R., SHUPE, E. I., & MAGLEY, V. J. (1998). Effectiveness of positive hypothesis testing for cooperative groups. *Organizational Behavior and Human Decision Processes, 73*, 27–38.

LAZARUS, A. A. (1991). A plague on Little Hans and Little Albert. *Psychotherapy, 28*, 444–447.

LEAKEY, R. (1994). *The origin of humankind*. New York: Basic Books.

LEDOUX, J. (1992). Brain mechanisms of emotion and emotional learning. *Current Opinion in Neurobiology, 2*, 191–197.

LEDOUX, J. (1995). Emotion: Clues from the brain. *Annual Review of Psychology, 46*, 209–235.

LEDOUX, J. (1998). Fear and the brain: Where have we been, and where are we going? *Biological Psychiatry, 44*, 1229–1238.

LEDOUX, J. (2000). Cognitive-emotional interactions: Listen to the brain. In R. D. Lane, L. Nadel, et al. (Eds.), *Cognitive neuroscience of emotion. Series in affective science* (pp. 129–155). New York: Oxford University Press.

LEDOUX, J., SAKAGUCHI, A., & REIS, D. J. (1984). Subcortical efferent projections of the medial geniculate nucleus mediate emotional responses conditioned to acoustic stimuli. *Journal of Neuroscience, 4*, 683–698.

LEE, C. (1998). *Alternatives to cognition: A new look at explaining human social behavior*. Mahwah, NJ: Erlbaum.

LEE, J. K., & GOLLUB, L. R. (1971). Second-order schedules with fixed-ratio components: Variation of component size. *Journal of the Experimental Analysis of Behavior, 15*, 303–310.

LEFEBVRE, L., & GIRALDEAU, L. (1996). Is social learning an adaptive specialization? In C. M. Heyes & B. G. Galef, Jr. (Eds.), *Social learning in animals: The roots of culture*. San Diego: Academic Press.

LEHRER, P. M. (1998). Emotionally triggered asthma: A review of research literature and some hypotheses for self-regulation. *Applied Psychophysiology and Biofeedback, 23*, 13–41.

LEITH, L. M., & TAYLOR, A. H. (1992). Behavior modification and exercise adherence: A literature review. *Journal of Sport Behavior, 15*, 60–74.

LENNEBERG, E. (1967). *Biological foundations of language*. New York: Wiley.

LEVINE, M. A. (1969). Neo-continuity theory. In G. H. Bower & J. T. Spence (Eds.), *The psychology of learning and motivation* (Vol. 3, pp. 101–133). New York: Academic Press.

LEVINE, M. A. (1975). *A cognitive theory of learning*. Hillsdale, NJ: Erlbaum.

LEVY, E. A., MCCLINTON, B. S., RABINOWITZ, F. M., & WOLKIN, J. R. (1974). Effects of vicarious consequences on imitation and recall: Some developmental findings. *Journal of Experimental Child Psychology, 17*, 115–132.

LIAO, D., HESSLER, N. A., & MALINOW, R. (1995). Activation of postsynaptically silent synapses during pairing-induced LTP in CA1 region of hippocampal slice. *Nature, 375*, 400–404.

LICHTENSTEIN, E., & BROWN, R. A. (1982). Current trends in the modification of cigarette dependence. In A. S. Bellack, M. Hersen, & A. E. Kazdin (Eds.), *International handbook of behavior modification and therapy* (pp. 575–611). New York: Plenum.

LIEBERMAN, P. (1991). *Uniquely human: The evolution of speech, thought, and selfless behavior*. Cambridge, MA: Harvard University Press.

LIEBERT, R. M., & BARON, R. A. (1972). Some immediate effects of televised violence on children's behavior. *Developmental Psychology, 6*, 469–475.

LIEVEN, E., PINE, J., & BALDWIN, G. (1997). Lexically-based learning and early grammatical development. *Journal of Child Language, 24*, 187–220.

LIGHT, L. L., & CARTER-SOBELL, L. (1970). Effects of changed semantic context on recognition memory. *Journal of Verbal Learning and Verbal Behavior, 9*, 1–11.

LINDSLEY, O. R., & SKINNER, B. F. (1954). A method for the experimental analysis of the behavior of psychotic patients. *American Psychologist, 9*, 419–420.

LIVINGSTON, K. R., & ANDREWS, J. K. (1995). On the interaction of prior knowledge and stimulus structure in category learning. *Quarterly Journal of Experimental Psychol-*

ogy: *Human Experimental Psychology, 48A,* 208–236.

LJUNGBERG, T., APICELLA, P., & SCHULTZ, W. (1992). Responses of monkey dopamine neurons during learning of behavioral reactions. *Journal of Neurophysiology, 67,* 145–163.

LOCKE, J. (1690/1959). *An essay concerning human understanding.* New York: Dover.

LOFTUS, E. F. (1991). The glitter of everyday memory . . . and the gold. *American Psychologist, 46,* 16–18.

LOFTUS, E. F. (1997a). Creating childhood memories. *Applied Cognitive Psychology, 11,* S75–S86.

LOFTUS, E. F. (1997b). Memories for a past that never was. *Current Directions in Psychological Science, 6,* 60–65.

LOFTUS, E. F., NUCCI, M., & HOFFMAN, H. (1998). Manufacturing memory. *American Journal of Forensic Psychology, 16,* 63–75.

LOFTUS, E. F., & PALMER, J. C. (1974). Reconstruction of automobile destruction: An example of the interaction between language and memory. *Journal of Verbal Learning and Verbal Behavior, 13,* 585–589.

LOGAN, C. G., & GRAFTON, S. T. (1995). Functional anatomy of human eyeblink conditioning determined with regional cerebral glucose metabolism and positron-emission tomography. *Proceedings of the National Academy of Sciences, 92,* 7500–7504.

LOLORDO, V. M. (1979). Selective associations. In A. Dickenson & R. A. Boakes (Eds.), *Mechanisms of learning and motivation.* Hillsdale, NJ: Erlbaum.

LONG, M. (1990). Maturational constraints on language development. *Studies in Second Language Acquisition, 12,* 251–286.

LOWE, K., & LUTZKER, J. R. (1979). Increasing compliance to a medical regimen with a juvenile diabetic. *Behavior Therapy, 10,* 57–64.

LUBOW, R. E. (1974). High-order concept formation in the pigeon. *Journal of the Experimental Analysis of Behavior, 21,* 475–483.

LUBOW, R. E. (1989). *Latent inhibition and conditioned attention theory.* Cambridge, England: Cambridge University Press.

LUBOW, R. E. (1998). Latent inhibition and behavior pathology: Prophylactic and other possible effects of stimulus preexposure. In W. T. O'Donohue (Ed.), *Learning and behavior therapy* (pp. 107–121). Boston: Allyn & Bacon.

LUBOW, R. E., & GEWIRTZ, J. C. (1995). Latent inhibition in humans: Data, theory, and implications for schizophrenia. *Psychological Bulletin, 117,* 87–103.

LUNDERVOLD, D., & ENTERMAN, M. (1989). Antecedent and consequent control of medical regimen adherence skills of an adult with developmental disabilities. *Education and Training in Mental Retardation, 24,* 126–132.

LUUS, C. A. E., & WELLS, G. L. (1994). Eyewitness identification confidence. In D. F. Ross, J. D. Read, & M. P. Toglia (Eds.), *Adult eyewitness testimony: Current trends and developments.* Cambridge, England: Cambridge University Press.

LUZZO, D. A., HASPER, P., ALBERT, K. A., BIBBY, M. A., & MARTINELLI, E. A., JR. (1999). Effects of self-efficacy-enhancing interventions on the math/science self-efficacy and career interests, goals, and actions of career undecided college students. *Journal of Counseling Psychology, 46,* 233–243.

LUZZO, D. A., & TAYLOR, M. (1993/1994). Effects of verbal persuasion on the career self-efficacy of college freshmen. *California Association for Counseling & Development (CACD) Journal, 14,* 31–34.

MACCORQUODALE, K. (1969). B. F. Skinner's *Verbal Behavior:* A retrospective appreciation. *Journal of the Experimental Analysis of Behavior, 12,* 831–841.

MACCORQUODALE, K. (1970). On Chomsky's review of Skinner's *Verbal Behavior. Journal of the Experimental Analysis of Behavior, 13,* 83–99.

MACE, F. C., HOCK, M. L., LALLI, J. S., WEST, B. J., BELIFORE, P., PINTER, E., & BROWN, D. K. (1988). Behavioral momentum in the treatment of noncompliance. *Journal of Applied Behavior Analysis, 21,* 123–141.

MACWHINNEY, B. (Ed.). (1999). *The emergence of language.* Mahwah, NJ: Erlbaum.

MADDUX, J. E. (Ed.). (1995). *Self-efficacy, adaptation, and adjustment: Theory, research, and application.* New York: Plenum.

MADDUX, J. E., & MEIER, L. J. (1995). Self-efficacy and depression. In J. E. Maddux (Ed.), *Self-efficacy, adaptation, and adjustment: Theory, research, and application.* New York: Plenum.

MANALO, E. (1997). Applications of mnemonics in education: A brief review. In G. M. Haberman, et al. (Eds.), *Looking back and moving forward: 50 years of New Zealand psychology*. Wellington: New Zealand Psychological Society.

MANDLER, J. (1984). Representation and recall in infancy. In M. Moscovitch (Ed.), *Infant memory*. New York: Plenum.

MARCUS, G. F. (1993). Negative evidence in language acquisition. *Cognition, 46*, 53–85.

MAREAN, G. C., WERNER, L. A., & KUHL, P. K. (1992). Vowel categorization by very young infants. *Developmental Psychology, 28*, 396–405.

MARKS, I. (1987). *Fears, phobias, and rituals: Panic, anxiety, and their disorders*. New York: Oxford University Press.

MARKS, I. M. (1975). Behavioural treatments of phobic and obsessive-compulsive disorders: A critical appraisal. In M. Hersen, R. M. Eisler, & P. M. Miller (Eds.), *Progress in behavior modification* (Vol. 1). New York: Academic Press.

MARSHALL, W. L., GAUTHIER, J., CHRISTIE, M. M., CURRIE, D. W., & GORDON, A. (1977). Flooding therapy: Effectiveness, stimulus characteristics, and the value of brief in vivo exposure. *Behaviour Research and Therapy, 15*, 79–87.

MARTINEZ-PONS, M. (1997). The relation of emotional intelligence with selected areas of personal functioning. *Imagination, Cognition, & Personality, 17*, 3–13.

MASIA, C. L., & CHASE, P. N. (1997). Vicarious learning revisited: A contemporary behavior analytic interpretation. *Journal of Behavior Therapy & Experimental Psychiatry, 28*(1), 41–51.

MAYR, E. (1970). *Populations, species, and evolution*. Cambridge, MA: Harvard University Press.

MAYR, E. (1976). *Evolution and the diversity of life: Selected essays*. Cambridge, MA: Belknap Press.

MCCLELLAND, J. L., & RUMMELHART, D. E. (1985). Distributed memory and the representation of general and specific information. *Journal of Experimental Psychology: General, 114*, 159–188.

MCCLOSKEY, M., & GLUCKSBERG, S. (1979). Decision processes in verifying category membership statements: Implications for models of semantic memory. *Cognitive Psychology, 11*, 1–37.

MCCLOSKEY, M., WIBLE, C. G., & COHEN, N. J. (1988). Is there a special flashbulb-memory mechanism? *Journal of Experimental Psychology: General, 117*, 171–181.

MCDONALD, R. J., & WHITE, N. M. (1993). A triple dissociation of memory systems: Hippocampus, amygdala, and dorsal striatum. *Behavioral Neuroscience, 107*, 3–22.

MCDOUGALL, W. (1908). *Introduction to social psychology*. London: Methuen.

MCGREW, W. C. (1998). Culture in nonhuman primates? *Annual Review of Anthropology, 27*, 301–328.

MCKOON, G., RATCLIFF, R., & DELL, G. (1986). A critical evaluation of the semantic/episodic distinction. *Journal of Experimental Psychology: Memory and Cognition, 12*, 295–306.

MCMILLAN, D. E., & HARDWICK, W. C. (2000). Drug discrimination in rats under concurrent variable-interval variable-interval schedules. *Journal of the Experimental Analysis of Behavior, 73*, 103–120.

MEBERG, P. J., BARNES, C. A., MCNAUGHTON, B. L., & ROUTTENBERG, A. (1993). Protein kinase C and F1/GAP-43 gene expression in hippocampus inversely related to synaptic enhancement lasting 3 days. *Proceedings of the National Academy of Sciences, 90*, 12050–12054.

MECK, W. H., SMITH, R. A., & WILLIAMS, C. L. (1989). Organizational changes in cholinergic activity and enhanced visuospatial memory as a function of choline administered prenatally or postnatally or both. *Behavioral Neuroscience, 103*, 1234–1241.

MEDIN, D. L., ALTOM, M. W., EDELSON, S. M., & FREKO, D. (1982). Correlated symptoms and simulated medical classification. *Journal of Experimental Psychology: Learning, Memory, & Cognition, 8*, 37–50.

MEISCH, R. A., & SPIGA, R. (1998). Matching under nonindependent variable-ratio schedules of drug reinforcement. *Journal of the Experimental Analysis of Behavior, 70*, 23–34.

MELTZOFF, A. N. (1996). The human infant as imitative generalist: A 20-year progress report on infant imitation with implications for comparative psychology. In C. M. Heyes & B. G. Galef, Jr. (Eds.), *Social learning in animals: The roots of culture.* San Diego: Academic Press.

MELTZOFF, A. N., & MOORE, M. K. (1977). Imitation of facial and manual gestures by human neonates. *Science, 198,* 75–78.

METALNIKOV, S., & CHORINE, V. (1926). Role des reflexes conditionnele dans limmunite. *Annales de l'Institut Pasteur, 40,* 893–900.

METALNIKOV, S., & CHORINE, V. (1928). Role des reflexes conditionnels dans la formation des anticorps. *Comptes Rendes de la Societe de Biologie, 99,* 142–145.

MEUDELL, P. R. (1992). Irrelevant, incidental and core features in the retrograde amnesia associated with Korsakoff's psychosis: A review. *Behavioral Neurology, 5,* 67–74.

MEYERS, H. (1999). Search and rescue—exciting, challenging, life-saving teamwork. *Veterinary Technician, 20*(3), 159.

MICHAEL, J. (1975). Positive and negative reinforcement, a distinction that is no longer necessary: Or, a better way to talk about bad things. *Behaviorism, 3,* 33–44.

MIHALIC, S. W., & ELLIOTT, D. (1997). A social learning theory model of marital violence. *Journal of Family Violence, 12,* 21–47.

MILLER, G. A. (1956). The magical number seven, plus or minus two: Some limits on our capacity for processing information. *Psychological Review, 63,* 81–97.

MILLER, G. A., GALANTER, E., & PRIBRAM, K. H. (1960). *Plans and the structure of behavior.* New York: Holt, Rinehart & Winston.

MILLER, L. K. (1968). The effect of response force on avoidance rate. *Journal of the Experimental Analysis of Behavior, 11,* 809–812.

MILLER, M. L., & MALOTT, R. W. (1997). The importance of overt responding in programmed instruction even with added incentives for learning. *Journal of Behavioral Education, 7,* 497–503.

MILLER, N. E. (1969). Learning of visceral and glandular responses. *Science, 163,* 434–445.

MILLER, N. E., & BANUAZIZI, A. (1968). Instrumental learning by curarized rats of a specific visceral response, intestinal or cardiac. *Journal of Comparative and Physiological Psychology, 65,* 1–7.

MILLER, R. R., BARNET, R. C., & GRAHAME, N. J. (1995). Assessment of the Rescorla-Wagner model. *Psychological Bulletin, 117,* 363–386.

MILLIKEN, R. G. (1998). A common structure for concepts of individuals, stuffs, and real kinds: More Mama, more milk, and more mouse. *Behavioral and Brain Sciences, 21*(1), 55–100.

MILNER, B. (1966). Amnesia following operation on the temporal lobes. In C. W. M. Whitty & O. L. Zangqill (Eds.), *Amnesia.* London: Butterworth.

MILNER, B. (1968). Visual recognition and recall after right temporal-lobe excision in man. *Neuropsychologia, 6,* 191–209.

MILNER, B. (1970). Memory and the medial temporal regions of the brain. In K. H. Pribram & D. E. Broadbent (Eds.), *Biology and memory.* New York: Academic Press.

MILNER, B. (1972). Disorders of learning and memory after temporal lobe lesions in man. *Clinical Neurosurgery, 19,* 421–446.

MILNER, P. M. (1991). Brain-stimulation reward: A review. *Canadian Journal of Psychology, 45,* 1–36.

MOERK, E. L. (1983). *The mother of Eve—As a first language teacher.* Norwood, NJ: Ablex.

MOESER, S. D. (1983). Levels of processing: Qualitative differences or task-demand differences? *Memory and Cognition, 11,* 316–323.

MOON, C., COOPER, R. P., & FIFER, W. P. (1993). Two-day-olds prefer their native language. *Infant Behavior & Development, 16*(4), 495–500.

MORGAN, D. L., & LEE, K. (1996). Extinction-induced response variability in humans. *Psychological Record, 46,* 145–159.

MORGAN, D. L., MORGAN, R. K., & TOTH, J. M. (1992). Variation and selection: The evolutionary analogy and the convergence of cognitive and behavioral psychology. *Behavior Analyst, 15,* 129–138.

MORGAN, M. J., FITCH, M. D., HOLMAN, J., & LEA, S. E. G. (1976). Pigeons learn the concept of an "A." *Perception, 5,* 57–66.

MUKHOPADHYAY, P., & TURNER, R. M. (1997). Biofeedback treatment of essential hypertension: Review and enhancements. *Social Science International, 13,* 1–9.

MYERS, J. L., LOHMEIER, J. H., & WELL, A. D. (1994). Modeling probabilistic categorization data: Exemplar memory and connectionist nets. *Psychological Science, 5,* 83–89.

NADEL, L., & ZOLA-MORGAN, S. (1984). Toward the understanding of infant memory: Contributions from animal neuropsychology. In M. Moscovitch (Ed.), *Infant memory*. New York: Plenum.

NAGELL, K., OLGUIN, R. S., & TOMASELLO, M. (1993). Processes of social learning in the tool use of chimpanzees (*Pan troglodytes*) and human children (*Homo sapiens*). *Journal of Comparative Psychology, 107,* 174–186.

NATIONAL INSTITUTES OF HEALTH. (1998). *Clinical guidelines on the identification, evaluation, and treatment of overweight and obesity: The evidence report.* (NIH Publication No. 98–4083). Bethesda, MD: NIH.

NEISSER, U. (1967). *Cognitive psychology.* New York: Appleton-Century-Crofts.

NELSON, K. (1981). Individual differences in language development: Implications for development and language. *Developmental Psychology, 17,* 170–187.

NEURINGER, A. (1991). Operant variability and repetition as a function of interresponse time. *Journal of Experimental Psychology: Animal Behavior Processes, 17*(1), 3–12.

NEURINGER, A. (1993). Reinforced variation and selection. *Animal Learning & Behavior, 21*(2), 83–91.

NEURINGER, A., DEISS, C., & OLSON, G. (2000). Reinforced variability and operant learning. *Journal of Experimental Psychology: Animal Behavior Processes, 26*(1), 98–111.

NEVIN, J. A. (1996). The momentum of compliance. *Journal of Applied Behavior Analysis, 29,* 535–547.

NEVIN, J. A., & GRACE, R. C. (2000). Behavioral momentum and the law of effect. *Behavioral and Brain Sciences, 23,* 73–90.

NEVIN, J. A., MANDELL, C., & ATAK, J. R. (1983). The analysis of behavioral momentum. *Journal of the Experimental Analysis of Behavior, 39,* 49–59.

NEWELL, A. (1990). *Unified theories of cognition.* Cambridge, MA: Harvard University Press.

NEWPORT, E. L. (1990). Maturational constraints on language learning. *Cognitive Science, 14,* 11–28.

NILSSON, L.-G, & MARKOWITSCH, H. J. (Eds.). (1999). *Cognitive neuroscience of memory.* Kirkland, WA: Hogrefe & Huber.

NORMAND, M. P., FOSSA, J. F., & POLING, A. (2000). Publication trends in the Analysis of Verbal Behavior: 1982–1998. *Analysis of Verbal Behavior, 17,* 167–173.

NOSOFSKY, R. M., KRUSCHKE, J. K., & MCKINLEY, S. C. (1992). Combining exemplar-based category representations and connectionist learning rules. *Journal of Experimental Psychology: Learning, Memory, and Cognition, 18,* 211–233.

NOTTERMAN, J. M. (1959). Force emission during bar pressing. *Journal of Experimental Psychology, 58,* 341–347.

OCKLEFORD, E. M., VINCE, M. A., LAYTON, C., & READER, M. R. (1988). Responses of neonates to parents' and others' voices. *Early Human Development, 18*(1), 27–36.

OLDS, J., & MILNER, P. (1954). Positive reinforcement produced by electrical stimulation of septal area and other regions of rat brain. *Journal of Comparative and Physiological Psychology, 47,* 419–427.

OLDS, M. E., & FOBES, J. L. (1981). The central basis of motivation: Intra-cranial self-stimulation studies. *Annual Review of Psychology, 32,* 523–574.

O'LEARY, A., & BROWN, S. (1995). Self-efficacy and the physiological stress response. In J. E. Maddux (Ed.), *Self-efficacy, adaptation, and adjustment: Theory, research, and application.* New York: Plenum.

OLTON, D. S. (1978). Characteristics of spatial memory. In S. H. Hulse, H. Fowler, & W. K. Honig (Eds.), *Cognitive processes in animal behavior.* Hillsdale, NJ: Erlbaum.

OLTON, D. S. (1992). Tolman's cognitive analyses: Predecessors of current approaches in psychology. *Journal of Experimental Psychology: General, 121,* 427–428.

OLTON, D. S., COLLISON, C., & WERZ, M. A. (1977). Spatial memory and radial arm maze performance of rats. *Learning and Motivation, 8,* 289–314.

OLTON, D. S., & SAMUELSON, R. J. (1978). Remembrance of places passed: Spatial memory in rats. *Journal of Experimental Psychology: Animal Behavior Processes, 2,* 97–116.

ORIANS, G. H., & HEERWAGEN, J. H. (1992). Evolved responses to landscapes. In J. Barkow, L. Cosmides, & J. Tooby (Eds.), *The adapted mind.* New York: Oxford University Press.

ORNSTEIN, R., & EHRLICH, P. (1989). *New world new mind*. New York: Simon & Schuster.

ORTH-GOMER, K., & SCHNEIDERMAN, N. (Eds.). (1996). *Behavioral medicine approaches to cardiovascular disease prevention*. Mahwah, NJ: Erlbaum.

OVERTON, D. A. (1985). Contextual stimulus effects of drugs and internal states. In P. D. Balsam & A. Tomie (Eds.), *Context and Learning*. Hillsdale, NJ: Erlbaum.

OWEN, A. M., JAMES, M., LEIGH, P. N., SUMMERS, B. A., MARSDEN, C. D., QUINN, N. P., LANGE, K. W., & ROBBINS, T. W. (1992). Fronto-striatal cognitive deficits at different stages of Parkinson's disease. *Brain, 115,* 1727–1751.

PAGE, M. M. (1969). Social psychology of a classical conditioning of attitudes experiment. *Journal of Personality and Social Psychology, 11,* 177–186.

PALEY, W. (1802). *Natural theology*. London: Charles Knight.

PAPINI, M. R., & BITTERMAN, M. E. (1990). The role of contingency in classical conditioning. *Psychological Review, 97,* 396–403.

PASNAK, R., & KURTZ, S. (1987). Brightness and size transposition by rhesus monkeys. *Bulletin of the Psychonomic Society, 25,* 109–112.

PAUL, G. L., & LENTZ, R. J. (1977). *Psychosocial treatment of chronic mental patients: Milieu versus social learning program*. Cambridge: Harvard University Press.

PAVLOV, I. P. (1927/1960). *Conditioned reflexes: An investigation of the physiological activity of the cerebral cortex*. New York: Dover.

PAVLOV, I. P. (1957). *Experimental psychology and other essays*. New York: Philosophical Library.

PELLON, R., GARCIA, J. M., & SANCHEZ, P. (1995). Blocking and electrodermal conditioning in humans. *Psicologica, 16,* 321–329.

PEPPERBERG, I. M. (1990). Cognition in an African gray parrot (*Psittacus erithacus*): Further evidence for comprehension of categories and labels. *Journal of Comparative Psychology, 105,* 318–325.

PEPPERBERG, I. M. (1992). Proficient performance of a conjunctive, recursive task by an African gray parrot (*Psittacus erithacus*). *Journal of Comparative Psychology, 106*(3), 295–305.

PIATELLI-PALMARINI, M. (1994). Ever since language and learning: Afterthoughts on the Piaget-Chomsky debate. *Cognition, 50,* 315–346.

PILGRIM, C. (1998). The human subject. In K. A. Lattal & M. Perone (Eds.), *Handbook of research methods in human operant behavior*. New York: Plenum.

PINKER, S. (1994). *The language instinct: How the mind creates language*. New York: William Morrow.

PINKER, S. (1995). Language acquisition. In L. R. Gleitman & M. Liberman (Eds.), *Language: An invitation to cognitive science* (2nd ed., Vol. 1, pp. 135–182). Cambridge, MA: MIT Press.

PINKER, S. (1997). *How the mind works*. New York: Norton.

PIZUTTO, E., & CASELLI, C. (1994). The acquisition of Italian verb morphology in a cross-linguistic perspective. In Y. Levy (Ed.), *Other children, other languages*. Hillsdale, NJ: Erlbaum.

PLOMIN, R., DEFRIES, J. C., MCCLEARN, G. E., & RUTTER, M. (1997). *Behavioral genetics*. New York: W. H. Freeman.

POIZNER, H., KLIMA, E. S., & BELLUGI, U. (1987). *What the hands reveal about the brain*. Cambridge, MA: MIT Press/Bradford Books.

POWELL, R. W. (1968). The effect of small sequential changes in fixed-ratio size upon the post-reinforcement pause. *Journal of the Experimental Analysis of Behavior, 11,* 589–593.

PRELEC, D. (1982). Matching, maximizing, and the hyperbolic reinforcement feedback function. *Psychological Review, 89,* 189–230.

PREMACK, A. J., & PREMACK, D. (1972). Teaching language to an ape. *Scientific American, 227,* 92–99.

PREMACK, D. (1959). Toward empirical behavior laws: I. Positive reinforcement. *Psychological Review, 66,* 219–233.

PREMACK, D. (1962). Reversibility of the reinforcement relation. *Science, 136,* 255–257.

PREMACK, D. (1963). Rate-differential reinforcement in monkey manipulation. *Journal of the Experimental Analysis of Behavior, 6,* 81–89.

PREMACK, D. (1983). The codes of men and beast. *Behavioral and Brain Sciences, 6,* 125–168.

QUINN, P. C., EIMAS, P. D., & ROSENKRANTZ, S. L. (1993). Evidence for representations of perceptually similar natural categories by 3-month-old and 4-month-old infants. *Perception, 22,* 463–475.

RACHLIN, H., GREEN, L., KAGEL, J. H., & BATTALIO, R. C. (1976). Economic demand theory and psychological studies of choice. In G. H. Bower (Ed.), *The psychology of learning and motivation* (Vol. 10). New York: Academic Press.

RACHMAN, S. (1990). The determinants and treatment of simple phobias. *Advances in Behavioral Research and Therapy, 12,* 1–30.

RAMSAY, A. O. (1951). Familial recognition in domestic birds. *Auk, 68,* 1–16.

RAMUS, F., HAUSER, M. D., MILLER, C., MORRIS, D., & MEHLER, J. (2000). Language discrimination by human newborns and by cotton-top tamarin monkeys. *Science, 288* (5464), 349–351.

RASKIN, D. C. (1969). Semantic conditioning and generalization of autonomic responses. *Journal of Experimental Psychology, 79,* 69–76.

RAY, W. J., RACZYNSKI, J. M., ROGERS, T., & KIMBALL, W. H. (1979). *Evaluation of clinical biofeedback.* New York: Plenum.

RAZRAN, G. H. S. (1961). The observable unconscious and the inferable conscious in current Soviet psychophysiology: Interoceptive conditioning, semantic conditioning, and the orienting reflex. *Psychological Review, 68,* 81–147.

REEVES, R. R., & BULLEN, J. A. (1995). Mnemonics for ten DSM-IV disorders. *Journal of Nervous and Mental Disease, 183,* 550–551.

REISER, R. A., DRISCOLL, M. P., & VERGARA, A. (1987). The effects of ascending, descending, and fixed criteria on student performance and attitude in a mastery-oriented course. *Educational Communications and Technology Journal, 35,* 195–202.

RESCORLA, R. A. (1967). Pavlovian conditioning and its proper control procedures. *Psychological Review, 74,* 71–80.

RESCORLA, R. A. (1988). Pavlovian conditioning: It's not what you think it is. *American Psychologist, 43,* 151–160.

RESCORLA, R. A., & WAGNER, R. A. (1972). A theory of Pavlovian conditioning: Variations in the effectiveness of reinforcement and nonreinforcement. In A. H. Black & W. F. Prokasy (Eds.), *Classical conditioning II: Current research and theory* (pp. 64–99). New York: Appleton-Century-Crofts.

RISTAU, C. A., & ROBBINS, D. (1982). Language in the great apes: A critical review. In J. S. Rosenblatt, R. A. Hinde, C. Beer, & M. C. Busnel (Eds.), *Advances in the study of behavior* (Vol. 12). New York: Academic Press.

RITTENHOUSE, C. D., SHOUVAL, H. Z., PARADISO, M. A., & BEAR, M. F. (1999). Monocular deprivation induces homosynaptic long-term depression in visual cortex. *Nature, 397,* 347–350.

RIZZOLATTI, G., & ARBIB, M. A. (1998). Language within our grasp. *Trends in Neurosciences, 21,* 188–194.

ROBERTS, W. A. (1980). Distribution of trials and intertrial retention in delayed matching to sample with pigeons. *Journal of Experimental Psychology: Animal Behavior Processes, 6,* 217–237.

ROBERTS, W. A. (1998). *Principles of animal cognition.* New York: McGraw-Hill.

ROBERTS, W. A., & GRANT, D. S. (1978). An analysis of light-induced retroactive inhibition in pigeon short-term memory. *Journal of Experimental Psychology: Animal Behavior Processes, 4,* 219–236.

ROBERTS, W. A., MACUDA, T., & BRODBECK, D. R. (1995). Memory for number of light flashes in the pigeon. *Animal Learning and Behavior, 23,* 182–188.

ROBINSON, T. E., & BERRIDGE, K. C. (1993). The neural basis of drug craving: An incentive-sensitization theory of addiction. *Brain Research Reviews, 18,* 247–291.

ROGAN, M. T., STAEUBLI, U. V., & LEDOUX, J. E. (1997). Fear conditioning induces associative long-term potentiation in the amygdala. *Nature, 390,* 604–607.

ROITBLAT, H. L. (1987). *Introduction to comparative cognition.* New York: W. H. Freeman.

ROITBLAT, H. L., & VON FERSEN, L. (1992). Comparative cognition: Representations and processes in learning and memory. *Annual Review of Psychology, 43,* 671–710.

ROSCH, E. H. (1975). Cognitive representations of semantic categories. *Journal of Experimental Psychology: General, 104,* 192–233.

ROSCH, E. H., MERVIS, C. B., GRAY, W. D., JOHNSON, D. M., & BOYES-BRAEM, P. (1976). Basic objects in natural categories. *Cognitive Psychology, 8,* 382–439.

ROSCH, E. H., SIMPSON, C., & MILLER, R. S. (1976). Structural bases of typicality effects. *Journal of Experimental Psychology: Human Perception and Performance, 2,* 491–502.

ROSEKRANS, M. A., & HARTUP, W. W. (1967). Imitative influences of consistent and inconsistent response consequences to a model on aggressive behavior in children. *Journal of Personality and Social Psychology, 7,* 429–434.

ROSENBLATT, F. (1958). The perceptron: A probabilistic model for information storage and organization in the brain. *Psychological Review, 65,* 386–408.

ROSENZWEIG, M. R., & BENNETT, E. L. (1996). Psychobiology of plasticity: Effects of training and experience on brain and behavior. *Behavioural Brain Research, 78,* 57–65.

ROSS, L. (1977). The intuitive psychologist and his shortcomings: Distortions in the attribution process. In L. Berkowitz (Ed.), *Advances in experimental social psychology* (Vol. 10). New York: Academic Press.

ROTHBAUM, B. O., HODGES, L., ALARCON, R., READY, D., SHAHAR, F., GRAAP, K., PAIR, J., HEVERT, P., GOTZ, D., WILLS, B., & BALTZELL, D. (1999). Virtual reality exposure therapy for PTSD Vietnam veterans: A case study. *Journal of Traumatic Stress, 12,* 263–271.

ROTHBAUM, B. O., HODGES, L., & KOOPER, R. (1997). Virtual reality exposure therapy. *Journal of Psychotherapy Practice and Research, 6,* 219–226.

ROTHBAUM, B. O., HODGES, L., SMITH, S., LEE, J. H., & PRICE, P. (2000). A controlled study of virtual reality exposure therapy for the fear of flying. *Journal of Consulting and Clinical Psychology, 68(6),* 1020–1026.

ROUTTENBERG, A., & MALSBURY, C. (1969). Brainstem pathways of reward. *Journal of Comparative and Physiological Psychology, 68,* 22–30.

ROZIN, P. (1976). The psychobiological approach to human memory. In M. R. Rosenzweig & E. L. Bennett (Eds.), *Neural mechanisms of learning and memory.* Cambridge, MA: MIT Press.

RUBINO, R., & PINE, J. (1998). Subject-verb agreement in Brazilian Portuguese: What low error rates hide. *Journal of Child Language, 25,* 35–60.

RUGG, M. D., MARK, R. E., WALLA, P., SCHLOERSCHEIDT, A. M., BIRCH, C. S., & ALLAN, K. (1998). Dissociation of the neural correlates of implicit and explicit memory. *Nature, 392,* 595–598.

RUHLEN, M. (1994). *The origin of language: Tracing the evolution of the mother tongue.* New York: John Wiley & Sons.

RUMBAUGH, D. M. (1997). The psychology of Harry F. Harlow: A bridge from radical to rational behaviorism. *Philosophical Psychology, 10,* 197–210.

RUMMELHART, D. E., & MCCLELLAND, J. L. (1986). *Parallel distributed processing: Explorations in the microstructure of cognition* (Vol. 1). Cambridge, MA: MIT Press.

RUSS-EFT, D. (1979). Proactive interference: Buildup and release for individual words. *Journal of Experimental Psychology, 5,* 422–434.

RUSSELL, M. A. H., RAW, M., TAYLOR, C. , FEYERABEND, C., & SALOOJEE, Y. (1978). Blood nicotine and carboxyhemoglobin levels after rapid-smoking aversion therapy. *Journal of Consulting and Clinical Psychology, 46,* 1423–1431.

RUSSON, A. E., & GALDIKAS, B. M. F. (1993). Imitation in free-ranging rehabilitant orangutans (*Pongo pygmaeus*). *Journal of Comparative Psychology, 107,* 147–161.

RUSSON, A. E., & GALDIKAS, B. M. F. (1995). Constraints on great apes' imitation: model and action selectivity in rehabilitant orangutan (*Pongo pygmaeus*). *Journal of Comparative Psychology, 109,* 5–17.

RYAN, R. S., & SCHOOLER, J. W. (1998). Whom do words hurt? Individual differences in susceptibility to verbal overshadowing. *Applied Cognitive Psychology, 12,* S105–S125.

RYCHLAK, J. F. (1997). *In defense of human consciousness.* Washington, DC: American Psychological Association.

SABBAGH, M. A., & GELMAN, S. A. (2000). Buzz-saws and blueprints: What children need (or don't need) to learn language. *Journal of Child Language, 27*(3), 715–726.

SAGAN, C. (1995). *Science as a candle in the dark: The demon-haunted world.* New York: Random House.

SANANES, C. B., & DAVIS, N. (1992). N-methyl-D-aspartate lesions of the lateral and baso-lateral nuclei of the amygdala block fear-potentiated startle and shock sensitization of startle. *Behavioral Neuroscience, 106,* 72–80.

SANES, J. R., & LICHTMAN, J. W. (1999). Can molecules explain long-term potentiation? *Nature Neuroscience, 2,* 597–604.

SARKAR, P., RATHEE, S. P., & NEERA, N. (1999). Comparative efficacy of pharmacotherapy and bio-feedback among cases of generalised anxiety disorder. *Journal of Projective Psychology and Mental Health, 6,* 69–77.

SAVAGE-RUMBAUGH, E. S. (1984). Acquisition of functional symbol usage in apes and children. In H. L. Roitbalt, T. G. Bever, & H. S. Terrace (Eds.), *Animal cognition.* Hillsdale, NJ: Erlbaum.

SAVAGE-RUMBAUGH, E. S. (1990). Language acquisition in a nonhuman species: Implications for the innateness debate. *Developmental Psychobiology, 23,* 599–620.

SAVAGE-RUMBAUGH, E. S., MCDONALD, K., SEVCIK, R., HOPKINS, W., & RUPERT, E. (1986). Spontaneous symbol acquisition and communicative use by pygmy chimpanzees. *Journal of Experimental Psychology: General, 115,* 211–235.

SAVAGE-RUMBAUGH, E. S., PATE, J. L., LAWSON, J., SMITH, S. T., & ROSENBAUM, S. (1983). Can a chimpanzee make a statement? *Journal of Experimental Psychology: General, 112,* 457–492.

SCHACTER, D. L. (1983). Amnesia observed: Remembering and forgetting in a natural environment. *Journal of Abnormal Psychology, 92,* 236–242.

SCHACTER, D. L. (1999). The seven sins of memory: Insights from psychology and cognitive neuroscience. *American Psychologist, 54,* 182–203.

SCHACTER, D. L., & TULVING, E. (1994). *Memory systems 1994.* Cambridge, MA: MIT Press.

SCHACTER, J. (1996). Maturation and the issue of universal grammar in second language acquisition. In W. C. Ritchie & T. K. Bahtia (Eds.), *Handbook of second language acquisition* (pp. 159–193). San Diego: Academic Press.

SCHNEIDERMAN, N., & GORMEZANO, I. (1964). Conditioning of the nictitating membrane of the rabbit as a function of CS-US interval. *Journal of Comparative and Physiological Psychology, 57,* 188–195.

SCHRIER, A. M., & BRADY, P. M. (1987). Categorization of natural stimuli by monkeys (*Macaca mulatta*): Effects of stimulus set size and modification of exemplars. *Journal of Experimental Psychology: Animal Behavior Processes, 13,* 136–143.

SCHROTH, M. L. (1984). Memory for intratrial events in concept formation. *Perceptual and Motor Skills, 59*(1), 23–29.

SCHULTZ, D. P., & SCHULTZ, S. E. (2000). *A history of modern psychology* (7th ed.). Fort Worth, TX: Harcourt Brace.

SCHUSTERMAN, R. J., & KRIEGER, K. (1986). Artificial language comprehension and size transposition by a California sea lion (*Zalophus californicanas*). *Journal of Comparative Psychology, 100,* 348–355.

SCOTT, D., & PONSODA, V. (1996). The role of positive and negative affect in flashbulb memory. *Psychological Reports, 79,* 467–473.

SEDIKIDES, C., OLSEN, N., & REIS, H. T. (1993). Relationships as natural categories. *Journal of Personality and Social Psychology, 64,* 71–82.

SELIGMAN, M. E. P. (1970). On the generality of laws of learning. *Psychological Review, 77,* 406–418.

SELIGMAN, M. E. P. (1995). The effectiveness of psychotherapy: The Consumer Reports study. *American Psychologist, 50,* 965–974.

SELIGMAN, M. E. P. (1996). Science as an ally of practice. *American Psychologist, 51,* 1072–1079.

SELIGMAN, M. E. P., & HAGER, J. L. (Eds.). (1972). *Biological boundaries of learning.* New York: Appleton-Century-Crofts.

SEYFARTH, R. M., & CHENEY, D. L. (1992). Meaning and mind in monkeys. *Scientific American, 267,* 122–128.

SHATZ, C. J. (1992). The developing brain. *Scientific American, 267*(9), 60–67.

SHEPPARD, W. C., & MACDERMOT, H. G. (1970). Design and evaluation of a programmed course in introductory psychology. *Journal of Applied Behavior Analysis, 3,* 5–11.

SHERIF, M., HARVEY, O. J., WHITE, J., HOOD, W., & SHERIF, C. (1961). *Intergroup conflict and cooperation: The robber's cave experiment.* Norman: University of Oklahoma, Institute of Intergroup Relations.

SHERIF, M., & SHERIF, C. W. (1973). *Groups in harmony and tension.* New York: Octagon Books.

SHETTLEWORTH, S. J. (1983). Memory in food hoarding birds. *Scientific American, 248*(3), 102–111.

SHETTLEWORTH, S. J., & KREBS, J. R. (1982). How march tits find their hoards: The roles of site preference and spatial memory. *Journal of Experimental Psychology, 8,* 354–375.

SHIMAMURA, A. P., & SQUIRE, L. R. (1987). A neuropsychological study of fact memory and source amnesia. *Journal of Experimental Psychology: Learning, Memory, & Cognition, 13*(3), 464–473.

SHIMOFF, E., CATANIA, A. C., & MATTHEWS, B. A. (1981). Uninstructed human responding: Sensitivity of low-rate performance to schedule contingencies. *Journal of the Experimental Analysis of Behavior, 36,* 207–220.

SHIMP, C. P. (1969). Optimal behavior in free-operant experiments. *Psychological Review, 76,* 97–112.

SHIMP, C. P. (1975). Perspectives on the behavioral unit: Choice behavior in animals. In W. K. Estes (Ed.), *Handbook of learning and cognitive processes* (Vol. 2). Hillsdale, NJ: Erlbaum.

SHIMP, C. P. (1982). Metaknowledge in the pigeon: An organism's knowledge about its own adaptive behavior. *Animal Learning and Behavior, 10,* 358–364.

SIDMAN, M. (1960). *Tactics of scientific research: Evaluating experimental data in psychology.* New York: Basic Books.

SIEGEL, S. (1983). Classical conditioning, drug tolerance, and drug dependence. In Y. Israel, et al. (Eds.), *Research advances in alcohol and drug problems* (Vol. 7). New York: Plenum.

SIEGEL, S. (1984). Pavlovian conditioning and heroin overdose: Reports by overdose victims. *Bulletin of the Psychonomic Society, 22,* 428–430.

SIEGEL, S. (1989). Pharmacological conditioning and drug effects. In A. J. Goudie & M. W. Emmett-Oglesby (Eds.), *Psychoactive drugs: Tolerance and sensitization* (pp. 115–180). Clifton, NJ: Humana Press.

SIEGEL, S. (1999). Drug anticipation and drug addiction: the 1998 H. David Archibald lecture. *Addiction, 94,* 1113–1124.

SIEGEL, S., & ALLEN, L. G. (1996). The widespread influence of the Rescorla-Wagner model. *Psychonomic Bulletin & Review, 3,* 314–321.

SIEGEL, S., HINSON, R. E., KRANK, M. D., & MCCULLY, J. (1982). Heroin "overdose" death: Contribution of drug-associated environmental cues. *Science, 216,* 436–437.

SIEGEL, S., KRANK, M. D., & HINSON, R. E. (1987). Anticipation of pharmacological and nonpharmacological events: Classical conditioning and addictive behavior. *Journal of Drug Issues, 17,* 83–110.

SIEMANN, M., & DELIUS, J. D. (1992). Variability of forage pecking in pigeons. *Ethology, 92,* 29–50.

SILVERMAN, P. B., & BONATE, P. L. (1997). Role of conditioned stimuli in addiction. In B. A. Johnson, J. D. Roache, et al. (Eds.), *Drug addiction and its treatment: Nexus of neuroscience and behavior* (pp. 115–133). Philadelphia: Lippincott-Raven.

SIMMONS ET AL. V. UNITED STATES, 390 U.S. 377 (1968).

SIMPSON, J. A., & KENRICK, D. T. (1997). *Evolutionary social psychology.* Mahwah, NJ: Erlbaum.

SKINNER, B. F. (1938). *The behavior of organisms: An experimental analysis.* Englewood Cliffs, NJ: Prentice-Hall.

SKINNER, B. F. (1950). Are theories of learning necessary? *Psychological Review, 57,* 193–216.

SKINNER, B. F. (1953). *Science and human behavior.* New York: Macmillan. (There is also a 1965 edition published by Free Press in New York.)

SKINNER, B. F. (1956). A case history in scientific method. *American Psychologist, 11,* 221–233.

SKINNER, B. F. (1957). *Verbal behavior.* Englewood Cliffs, NJ: Prentice-Hall.

SKINNER, B. F. (1958). Teaching machines. *Science, 128,* 969–977.

SKINNER, B. F. (1960). Pigeons in a pelican. *American Psychologist, 15,* 28–37.

SKINNER, B. F. (1966). The phylogeny and ontogeny of behavior. *Science, 153,* 1205–1213.

SKINNER, B. F. (1968). *The technology of teaching.* New York: Appleton-Century-Crofts.

SKINNER, B. F. (1969). *Contingencies of reinforcement: A theoretical analysis.* Englewood Cliffs, NJ: Prentice-Hall.

SKINNER, B. F. (1974). *About behaviorism.* New York: Knopf.

SKINNER, B. F. (1979). *The shaping of a behaviorist: Part two of an autobiography.* New York: Knopf.

SKINNER, B. F. (1981). Selection by consequences. *Science, 213,* 501–504.

SKINNER, B. F. (1986). The evolution of verbal behavior. *Journal of the Experimental Analysis of Behavior, 45,* 115–122.

SKINNER, B. F. (1987). *Upon further reflection.* Englewood Cliffs, NJ: Prentice-Hall.

SLOBIN, D. (1997). On the origin of grammaticalizable notions: Beyond the individual mind. In D. I. Slobin (Ed.), *The cross-linguistic study of language acquisition* (Vol. 5). Hillsdale, NJ: Erlbaum.

SMITH, E. E., PATALANO, A. L., & JONIDES, J. (1998). Alternative strategies of categorization. *Cognition, 65,* 167–196.

SNOW, C. E. (1984). Parent-child interaction and the development of communicative ability. In R. L. Schiefelbusch and J. Pickar (Eds.), *The acquisition of communicative competence.* Baltimore: University Park Press.

SPERLING, G. (1960). The information available in brief visual presentations. *Psychological Monograph, 74,* Whole No. 498.

SPIEGEL, D. (1997). Memories: True and false. *American Psychologist, 52,* 995–996.

SQUIRE, L. R. (1987). *Memory and brain.* New York: Oxford University Press.

SQUIRE, L. R., & KANDEL, E. R. (1999). *Memory: From mind and molecules.* New York: Scientific American Library/Scientific American Books.

SQUIRE, L. R., OJEMANN, J. G., MIEZIN, F. M., PETERSEN, S. E., VIDEEN, T. O., & RAICHLE, M. E. (1992). Activation of the hippocampus in normal humans: a functional anatomical study of memory. *Proceedings of the National Academy of Science, 89,* 1837–1841.

STAATS, A. W. (1975). *Social behaviorism.* Homewood, IL: Dorsey Press.

STAATS, A. W., STAATS, C. K., & CRAWFORD, H. L. (1962). First-order conditioning of a GSR. *Journal of General Psychology, 67,* 159–167.

STAATS, A. W., STAATS, C. K., & HEARD, W. G. (1959). Language conditioning of meaning using a semantic generalization paradigm. *Journal of Experimental Psychology, 57*(3), 187–192.

STADLER, M. A., & FRENSCH, P. A. (Eds.). (1998). *Handbook of implicit learning.* Thousand Oaks, CA: Sage.

STAMPFL, T. G., & LEVIS, D. J. (1968). Implosive therapy: A behavioral therapy? *Behaviour Research and Therapy, 6,* 31–36.

STEGER, J., SHELTON, J., BEUKELMAN, D., & FOWLER, R. (1981). Pinpointing: One method of improving staff compliance with rehabilitation regimens. *Journal of Behavioral Medicine, 4*(1), 53–64.

STELLAR, J. R., KELLEY, A. E., & CORBETT, D. (1983). Effects of peripheral and central dopamine blockade on lateral hypothalamic self-stimulation: Evidence for both reward and motor deficits. *Pharmacology, Biochemistry, and Behavior, 18,* 433–442.

STERN, R., & MARKS, I. M. (1973). Brief and prolonged flooding: A comparison in agoraphobic patients. *Archives of General Psychiatry, 28,* 270–276.

STERRETT, E. A. (1998). Use of a job club to increase self-efficacy: A case study of return to work. *Journal of Employment Counseling, 35,* 69–78.

STEVENS, C. F. (1998). A million dollar question: does LTP = memory? *Neuron, 20,* 1–2.

STITZER, M. L., & BIGELOW, G. E. (1984). Contingent reinforcement for carbon monoxide reduction: Within-subject effects of pay amount. *Journal of Applied Behavior Analysis, 17,* 477–483.

STITZER, M. L., RAND, C. S., BIGELOW, G. E., & MEAD, A. M. (1986). Contingent payment procedures for smoking reduction and cessation. *Journal of Applied Behavior Analysis, 19,* 197–202.

STOKES, P. D. (1995). Learned variability. *Animal Learning and Behavior, 23,* 164–176.

STORMS, M. D. (1973). Videotape and the attribution process: Reversing actors' and observers' points of view. *Journal of Personality and Social Psychology, 27,* 165–175.

STRUM, S. C. (1987). *Almost human: A journey into the world of baboons.* New York: W. W. Norton.

STRYKER, M. P., & SHERK, H. (1975). Modification of cortical orientation selectivity in the cat by restricted visual experience: A reexamination. *Science, 190,* 904–906.

STRYKER, M. P., SHERK, H., LEVENTHAL, A. G., & HIRSCH, H. V. B. (1978). Physiological consequences for the cat's visual cortex of effectively restricting early visual experience with oriented contours. *Journal of Neurophysiology, 41,* 896–909.

STUART, R. B. (1967). Behavioral control of overeating. *Behaviour Research and Therapy, 5,* 357–365.

STUNKARD, A. J., & PENICK, S. B. (1979). Behavior modification in the treatment of obesity: The problem of maintaining weight loss. *Archives of General Psychiatry, 36,* 801–806.

SUGIMURA, T. (1985). A comparison of what is learned in transposition and oddity tasks. *Japanese Psychological Research, 27,* 21–28.

SUMMERS, W. K., ROBINS, E., & REICH, T. (1979). The natural history of acute organic mental syndrome after bilateral electroconvulsive therapy. *Biological Psychiatry, 14,* 905–912.

SUSSMAN, D. M. (1981). PSI: Variations on a theme. In S. W. Bijou & R. Ruiz (Eds.), *Behavior modification: Contributions to education.* Hillsdale, NJ: Erlbaum.

SWARTZ, C. M. (1998). Seven mnemonics for some common psychiatric applications. *Journal of Nervous and Mental Disease, 186,* 58–59.

TAIT, R. W., & SALADIN, M. E. (1986). Concurrent development of excitatory and inhibitory associations during backward conditioning. *Animal Learning and Behavior, 14,* 133–137.

TAJFEL, H. (1981). *Human groups and social categories.* Cambridge, England: Cambridge University Press.

TAJFEL, H. (1982). *Social identity and group relations.* Cambridge, England: Cambridge University Press.

TALLAND, G. A. (1965). *Deranged memory.* New York: Academic Press.

TEMPLETON, J. J. (1998). Learning from others' mistakes: A paradox revisited. *Animal Behaviour, 55,* 79–85.

TERRACE, H. S. (1966). Stimulus control. In W. K. Honig (Ed.), *Operant conditioning: Areas of research and application.* Englewood Cliffs, NJ: Prentice-Hall.

TERRACE, H. S. (1979). *Nim: A chimpanzee who learned sign language.* New York: Washington Square Press.

TERRY, W. S. (1996). Retroactive interference effects of surprising reward omission on serial spatial memory. *Journal of Experimental Psychology: Animal Behavior Processes, 22,* 472–479.

THAL, L. J. (1989). Pharmacological treatment of memory disorders. In F. Boller & J. Grafman (Eds.), *Handbook of neuropsychology* (Vol. 3, pps. 247–267). New York: Elsevier.

THOMPSON, R. F. (1986). The neurobiology of learning and memory. *Science, 233,* 941–947.

THOMPSON, T., & BOREN, J. J. (1977). Operant behavior pharmacology. In W. K. Honig & J. E. R. Staddon (Eds.), *Handbook of operant behavior.* Englewood Cliffs, NJ: Prentice-Hall.

THOMPSON, T., & SCHUSTER, C. R. (1968). *Behavioral pharmacology.* Englewood Cliffs, NJ: Prentice-Hall.

THORNDIKE, E. L. (1898). Animal intelligence: An experimental study of the associative processes in animals. *Psychological Review Monograph, 2*(4), 1–109.

THORNDIKE, E. L. (1911). *Animal intelligence.* New York: Hafner.

TIMBERLAKE, W. (1979). Licking one saccharin solution for access to another in rats: Contingent and noncontingent effects in instrumental performance. *Animal Learning & Behavior, 7,* 277–288.

TIMBERLAKE, W. (1981). Bliss points and utility functions. *Behavioral and Brain Sciences, 4,* 404–405.

TIMBERLAKE, W. (1983). The functional organization of appetitive behavior: Behavior systems and learning. In M. D. Zeiler & P. Harzem (Eds.), *Advances in analysis of behavior: Vol 3. Biological factors in learning* (pp. 177–221). Chichester: Wiley.

TIMBERLAKE, W. (1984). Behavior regulation and learned performance: Some misapprehensions and disagreements. *Journal of the Experimental Analysis of Behavior, 41,* 355–375.

TIMBERLAKE, W., & ALLISON, J. (1974). Response deprivation: An empirical approach to instrumental performance. *Psychological Review, 81,* 146–164.

TINBERGEN, N. (1951). *The study of instinct.* New York: Oxford University Press.

TOCCO, G., MAREN, S., SHORS, T. J., BAUDRY, M., & THOMPSON, R. F. (1992). Long-term potentiation is associated with increased [³H]AMPA binding in rat hippocampus. *Brain Research, 573,* 228–234.

TODD, J. T., & MORRIS, E. K. (1983). Misconception and miseducation: Presentations of radical behaviorism in psychology textbooks. *Behavior Analyst, 6,* 153–160.

TODD, J. T., & MORRIS, E. K. (1992). Case histories in the great power of steady misrepresentation. *American Psychologist, 47,* 1441–1453.

TOMASELLO, M. (1990). Cultural transmission in the tool use and communicatory signaling of chimpanzees? In S. T. Parker & K. R. Gibson (Eds.), *"Language" and intelligence in monkeys and apes: Comparative developmental perspectives.* Cambridge, England: Cambridge University Press.

TOMASELLO, M. (1995). Language is not an instinct. *Cognitive Development, 10,* 131–156.

TOMASELLO, M. (1996). Do apes ape? In J. Galef & C. Heyes (Eds.), *Social learning in animals: The roots of culture.* New York: Academic Press.

TOMASELLO, M. (1998). *The new psychology of language: Cognitive and functional approaches.* Mahwah, NJ: Erlbaum.

TOMASELLO, M. (1999). *The cultural origins of human cognition.* Cambridge, MA: Harvard University Press.

TOMASELLO, M. (2000a). Culture and cognitive development. *Current Directions in Psychological Science, 9*(2), 37–40.

TOMASELLO, M. (2000b). Do young children have adult syntactic competence? *Cognition 74,* 209–253.

TOMASELLO, M., SAVAGE-RUMBAUGH, S., & KRUGER, A. C. (1993). Imitative learning of actions on objects by children, chimpanzees, and enculturated chimpanzees. *Child Development, 64,* 1688–1705.

TONI, N., BUCHS, P.-A., NIKONENKO, I., BRON, C. R., & MULLER, D. (1999). LTP promotes formation of multiple spine synapses between a single axon terminal and a dendrite. *Nature, 402,* 421–425.

TOTA-FAUCETTE, M. E. (1991). *Alternative reinforcement and resistance to change.* Unpublished doctoral dissertation, University of North Carolina at Greensboro.

TOUWEN, B. C. L. (1984). Primitive reflexes—conceptual or semantic problem? In H. F. R. Prechtl (Vol. Ed.), *Continuity of neural functions from prenatal to postnatal life: Vol. 94. Clinics in Developmental Medicine.* Cambridge, MA: Cambridge University Press.

TRYON, W. W. (1993). Neural networks: II. Unified learning theory and behavioral psychotherapy. *Clinical Psychology Review, 13,* 353–371.

TUDOR, R. M. (1995). Isolating the effects of active responding in computer-based instruction. *Journal of Applied Behavior Analysis, 28,* 343–344.

TULVING, E. (1972). Episodic and semantic memory. In E. Tulving & W. Donaldson (Eds.), *Organization of memory* (pp. 381–403). New York: Academic Press.

TULVING, E. (1998). Brain/mind correlates of human memory. In M. Sabourin & F. Craik (Eds.), *Advances in psychological science: Vol. 2. Biological and cognitive aspects* (pp. 441–460). Hove, England: Psychology Press/Erlbaum (UK) Taylor & Francis.

ULRICH, R. (1983). Aesthetic and affective response to natural environment. In I. Altman & J. F. Wohlwill (Eds.), *Behavior and the natural environment.* New York: Plenum.

VAITL, D., & LIPP, O. V. (1997). Latent inhibition and autonomic responses: A psychophysiological approach. *Behavioural Brain Research, 88,* 85–93.

VANDIERENDONCK, A. (1995). A parallel rule activation and rule synthesis model for generalization in category learning. *Psychonomic Bulletin and Review, 2,* 442–459.

VAN LAWICK-GOODALL, J. (1970). Tool-using in primates and other invertebrates. *Advances in the Study of Behavior, 3,* 195–249.

VERHAVE, T. (1966). The pigeon as quality-control inspector. *American Psychologist, 21,* 109–115.

VICTOR, M., & AGAMANOLIS, J. (1990). Amnesia due to lesions confined to the hippocampus: A clinical-pathological study. *Journal of Cognitive Neuroscience, 2,* 246–257.

VISALBERGHI, E., & FRAGASZY, D. M. (1990). Do monkeys ape? In S. T. Parker & K. R. Gibson (Eds.), *"Language" and intelligence in monkeys and apes: Comparative developmental perspectives.* Cambridge, England: Cambridge University Press.

WALLACE, J., STEINERT, P. A., SCOBIE, S. R., & SPEAR, N. E. (1980). Stimulus modality and short-term memory in rats. *Animal Learning and Behavior, 8,* 10–16.

WASSERMAN, E. A. (1993). Comparative cognition: Beginning the second century of the study of animal intelligence. *Psychological Bulletin, 113,* 211–228.

WASSERMAN, E. A. (1997). The science of animal cognition: Past, present, and future. *Journal of Experimental Psychology: Animal Behavior Processes, 23,* 123–135.

WATSON, J. B. (1913). Psychology as the behaviorist views it. *Psychological Review, 20,* 158–177.

WATSON, J. B. (1961). Autobiography. In C. Murchison (Ed.), *A history of psychology in autobiography* (Vol. 3, pp. 271–281). New York: Russell & Russell.

WATSON, J. B., & RAYNER, R. (1920). Conditioned emotional reactions. *Journal of Experimental Psychology, 3,* 1–14.

WEAVER, C. A. (1993). Do you need a "flash" to form a flashbulb memory? *Journal of Experimental Psychology: General, 122,* 39–46.

WEHNER, R., & SRINIVASAN, M. V. (1981). Searching behavior of desert ants, genus *Cataglyphis* (Formicidae, Hymenoptera). *Journal of Comparative Psychology, 142,* 315–338.

WELLS, A. (1998). Evolutionary psychology and theories of cognitive architecture. In C. Crawford & D. L. Krebs (Eds.), *Handbook of evolutionary psychology: Ideas, issues, and applications* (pp. 235–264). Mahwah, NJ: Erlbaum.

WERKER, J. F., & MCLEOD, P. J. (1989). Infant preference for both male and female infant-directed talk: A developmental study of attentional and affective responsiveness. *Canadian Journal of Psychology, 43,* 230–246.

WHEELER, H. (Ed.). (1973). *Beyond the punitive society.* San Francisco: W. H. Freeman.

WHITEN, A., & CUSTANCE, D. (1996). Studies of imitation in chimpanzees and children. In C. M. Heyes & B. G. Galef, Jr. (Eds.), *Social learning in animals: The roots of culture.* San Diego: Academic Press.

WHITEN, A., CUSTANCE, D. M., GOMEZ, J. C., TEIXIDOR, P., & BARD, K. A. (1996). Imitative learning of artificial fruit processing in children (*Homo sapiens*) and chimpanzees (*Pan troglodytes*). *Journal of Comparative Psychology, 110,* 3–14.

WIEGMAN, O. (1985). Two politicians in a realistic experiment: Attraction, discrepancy, intensity of delivery, and attitude change. *Journal of Applied Social Psychology, 15,* 673–686.

WILLIAMS, B. A. (1991). Choice as a function of local versus molar reinforcment contingencies. *Journal of the Experimental Analysis of Behavior, 56,* 455–473.

WILLIAMS, D. A., & OVERMIER, J. B. (1988). Some types of conditioned inhibitors carry collateral excitatory associations. *Learning and Motivation, 19,* 345–368.

WILLIAMS, D. C., & JOHNSTON, J. M. (1992). Continuous versus discrete dimensions of reinforcement schedules: An integrative analysis. *Journal of the Experimental Analysis of Behavior, 58,* 205–228.

WILLIAMS, L. M. (1996). Cognitive inhibition and schizophrenic symptom subgroups. *Schizophrenia Bulletin, 22,* 139–151.

WILLIAMS, S. L. (1995). Self-efficacy and anxiety and phobic disorders. In J. E. Maddux (Ed.), *Self-efficacy, adaptation, and adjustment: Theory, research, and application.* New York: Plenum.

WISHAW, I. Q., & GORNY, B. P. (1994). Food wrenching and dodging: Eating time estimates influence dodge probability and amplitude. *Aggressive Behavior, 20,* 35–47.

WITTGENSTEIN, L. (1953). *Philosophical investigations.* (G. E. M. Anscombe, Trans.). Oxford: Blackwell.

WOHLGEMUTH, S., RONACHER, B., & WEH-
NER, R. (2001). Ant odometry in the third dimension. *Nature, 411*(6839), 795–798.

WOLPE, J. (1958). *Psychotherapy by reciprocal
inhibition.* Stanford, CA: Stanford University
Press.

WOLPE, J. (1969). *The practice of behavior
therapy.* New York: Pergamon.

WOODRUFF-PAK, D. S., PAPKA, M., & IVRY, R. B.
(1996). Cerebellar involvement in eyeblink
classical conditioning in humans. *Neuropsychology, 10,* 443–458.

WOOLEY, S. C., WOOLEY, O. W., & DYREN-
FORTH, S. R. (1979). Theoretical, practical
and social issues in behavioral treatments of
obesity. *Journal of Applied Behavior Analysis, 12,* 3–25.

WREN, C. S. (1999, August 17). Harnessing the
powerful secrets of a dog's nose. *New York
Times on the Web,* http://www.newyorktimes.
com

WRIGHT, A. A. (1997). Concept learning and
learning strategies. *Psychological Science,
8*(2), 119–123.

WYATT, W. J., HAWKINS, R. P., & DAVIS, P.
(1986). Behaviorism: Are reports of its death
exaggerated? *Behavior Analyst, 9,* 101–105.

YOUNG, J. M., KRANTZ, P. J., MCCLANNAHAN,
L. E., & POULSON, C. L. (1994). Generalized
imitation and response-class formation in
children with autism. *Journal of Applied
Behavior Analysis, 27,* 685–697.

ZALCMAN, S., KERR, L., & ANISMAN, H. (1991).
Immunosuppression elicited by stressors
and stressor-related odors. *Brain, Behavior,
and Immunity, 5,* 262–273.

ZEILER, M. D. (1977). Schedules of reinforcement: the controlling variables. In W. K.
Honig & J. E. R. Staddon (Eds.), *Handbook
of operant behavior.* Englewood Cliffs, NJ:
Prentice-Hall.

ZENER, K. (1937). The significance of behavior
accompanying conditioned salivary secretion
for theories of the conditioned response.
American Journal of Psychology, 50, 384–
403.

ZENTALL, T. R. (1996). An analysis of imitative
learning in animals. In C. M. Heyes & B. G.
Galef, Jr. (Eds.), *Social learning in animals:
The roots of culture.* New York: Academic.

ZENTALL, T. R. (Ed.). (1993). *Animal cognition:
A tribute to Donald A. Riley.* Hillsdale, NJ:
Erlbaum.

ZENTALL, T. R., HOGAN, D. E., & EDWARDS,
C. A. (1984). Cognitive factors in conditional
learning by pigeons. In H. L. Roitblat, T. G.
Bever, & H. S. Terrace (Eds.), *Animal cognition.* Hillsdale, NJ: Erlbaum.

ZOLA-MORGAN, S., SQUIRE, L. R., & AMARAL,
D. (1986). Human amnesia and the medial
temporal region: Enduring memory impairment following a bilateral lesion limited to
the CA1 field of the hippocampus. *Journal of
Neuroscience, 6,* 2950–2967.

Credits

Name Index

Glossary/Index

artificial intelligence, 33

Association for the Advancement of Behavior Therapy (AABT), 143

associationism, 47–48, 203

associative strength, 64, 66

asthma
biofeedback for, 152
psychoneuroimmunology of, 78

asymptote, of learning curve, 66

attention deficit hyperactivity disorder (ADHD), 153

attitude, law of, 97

auditory discrimination, 268–269

aversive stimulus: object or event that an organism is motivated to avoid or escape, **108,** 109
freezing response to, 305–306
pain as, 151
for smoking cessation, 147
verbal behavior and, 285

axon: structure of neuron that transmits action potential to neighboring nerve cells, **299**

backward conditioning, 43

Bandura, Albert, 178, 183, 189
Bobo doll studies, 179–180, 192
self-efficacy and, 184–185, 186, 187

Bartlett, Frederic C., 204–205

basal ganglia: structures lying beneath the cortex that serve to integrate sensory input and motor functioning, **308**

baseline level of behavior, 113

basic level: the most useful level of a concept, characterized by neither too much nor too little information, **246,** 247

behavior
acquisition vs. maintenance of, 191–193
maladaptive, 87, 134, 139, 141, 143
Skinner's definition of, 105
in three-term contingency, 103, 104–105

behavioral genetics, 138

behavioral medicine: application of basic behavior principles to behavior having significant repercussions for health and illness, **145–146**
compliance with treatment and, 154–157
pain management and, 151–154
psychoneuroimmunology in, 79
smoking cessation and, 146–148
weight loss and, 148–151

behavioral momentum: the idea that operants having a long and rich history of

reinforcement may be especially resistant to change, **156–157**

behavioral pharmacology, 130

behavioral psychology
behavioral medicine and, 146
vs. cognitive psychology, 34–37
concept learning and, 257–262
language and, 282–290, 295
vs. medical model, 139
pragmatism in, 158
social learning and, 187–199

behaviorism, 136, 137
clinical psychology and, 143
methodological, 30–31, 182
misunderstandings about, 138
nature-nurture issue and, 321
psychopathology and, 140
radical, 31, 35, 101, 138
See also Skinner, B. F.; Watson, John B.

behavior modification: application of operant principles to human behavior having social or clinical importance, **134**
institutional applications, 141–143
laboratory scientists and, 134, 140–141
medical model and, 137, 139–140, 143
theoretical basis of, 134–137
See also behavioral medicine; behavior therapy; education

behavior potential, 12

behavior therapy: interventions based on learning principles to alter maladaptive behavior, **87**
desensitization in, 87–89, 90
early development of, 86–87
flooding in, 89–90
generalization in, 143
journals of, 143–144
operant conditioning in (*see* behavior modification)
professional society for, 143
virtual reality in, 90–92

biases, 26. *See also* prejudice

biodiversity, 236–237, 256

biofeedback: technology-based process of providing an individual with visual or auditory feedback regarding some bodily or physiological activity, **152–153,** 154

biological constraints on learning, 73, 324

blocking: initial conditioning to a CS_1 impairs later conditioning to a separate CS_2, **46–47,** 66

evolution, 2–11
    constraints on learning and, 73, 324
    genetic variation and, 2–4, 5, 7, 8, 11
    of imitation, 174, 175, 188, 189
    of language, 175, 278–280, 282, 296
    of open genetic program, 16
    theories of, 7–11
    See also adaptation; natural selection
evolutionary psychology: contemporary
    school of thought devoted to discovering
    the evolutionary roots of psychological
    processes, including learning and cogni-
    tion, 14, 18, **318–319**
    Descartes' rationalism and, 28
    EEA in, 319–321, 322, 325, 328
    language and, 279–280
evolved psychological mechanisms: domain-
    specific cognitive modules selected for
    because of their contribution to solving
    adaptive problems in the environment,
    319
excitatory conditioning, 51, 66
exemplars: a specific example or member of a
    larger category or conceptual class,
    249–250, 252
exercise
    law of, 97
    pain and, 154
    for weight loss, 148–150
experience
    empiricism and, 28–29
    learning and, 12, 13, 19
experimentation
    in psychology, 29, 30–31, 37
    theories and, 22
exposure therapies, 89–92
expressive language, 291, 292
extinction: the process leading to the
    elimination of a response (conditioned
    reflex or operant) that has been previously
    acquired through conditioning (classical
    or operant)
    behavioral momentum and, 156
    in behavior therapy, 87, 89, 90
    of maladaptive behavior, 141, 143
    of conditional response, **50**
    of operant behavior, **115–117**
    Rescorla-Wagner model and, 66
extinction-induced variability, 116–117
eye-blink conditioning, 307
eyewitness testimony, 220–222, 224
Eysenck, Hans, 139–140

facial expressions, imitation of, 175
facultative trait: phenotypic expression (physi-
    cal feature or behavior) that is highly sen-
    sitive to changing characteristics of the
    environment, **322**, 324
false memories, 222–224
family resemblances, 245, 248
fear
    adaptiveness of, 327–328
    See also anxiety; phobias
fear hierarchy, 87–88, 89
feedback, in PSI, 163, 164
Ferster, Charles, 122–127, 140
FI scallop, 127
Fisher, Ronald, 140
fixed-action patterns: highly stereotyped, in-
    born behavior patterns involving multiple
    muscle systems, **17–18**
fixed interval (FI) schedule, 127
fixed ratio (FR) schedule, 123–125
flashbulb memories: particularly vivid recall of
    one's surroundings produced by exposure
    to a dramatic event, **225–226**
flooding: phobia treatment in which a feared
    stimulus (CS) is presented at full strength
    without relaxation, **89–90**
forgetting: loss of information due to ineffec-
    tive encoding or retrieval failure, **211**
    amnesia, 213–215, 314–317
    decay theory of, 211–212
    of information source, 224
    interference theory of, 212–213, 230, 232
free operant procedure, 114
freezing response, 305, 328
Freud, Sigmund, 135, 139, 213, 276
functional approach to language, 274, 282,
    287, 290, 295
fundamental attribution error: the tendency to
    view others' behavior as resulting from
    personal dispositions rather than from
    situational factors, **25–26**

Garcia experiment, 71–73, 323
generalization: tendency to respond to stimuli
    similar to the CS, despite no explicit train-
    ing to these stimuli, **53–55**, 56–57, 59
    in concept learning, 254, 257
    of operant behavior, 118, 119, 120
    response by analogy and, 97
    of treatment change, 143
generalization gradient, 54
generalized anxiety disorder, 152–153

generalized imitation: the tendency to imitate behavior seen in others that has not been reinforced, **190–191**

generativity of language, 276, 283, 287, 294

genetics, behavior and, 138, 321–322

genetic variation: the fact that individual genotypes, or genetic characteristics, differ within any group of organisms, **2–4**, 5, 7, 8, 11

glutamate, 314

graded exposure, 88, 89

grammar. *See* syntax

group belongingness, 263

H. M. (amnesia patient), 214, 314–316

habituation: decrease in intensity of response to a repeatedly presented stimulus, **11**, 45, 51

habituation-dishabituation technique, 268

Harlow, Harry, 253–254

headache, biofeedback for, 152

health psychology, 146. *See also* behavioral medicine

Hebb rule, 313–314

Heraclitus, 53–54

heroin use, 63–64, 79–80, 81, 82

Herrnstein, Richard, 128–129

higher order conditioning: conditioning to a neutral stimulus as the result of pairing with a previously established CS, **57–59**, 68

high-p requests, 157

high probability behaviors, 112

hippocampus: structure in the limbic system having significant implications for formation of long-term memory, 314, **316–317**

Holland, James, 161

holophrase: a single-word utterance ordinarily referring to important objects or events in an infant's environment, **270**, 272, 284

humanistic psychology, 135

hypertension, biofeedback for, 152

hypothalamus: brain structure known to be associated with motivated behavior, particularly appetitive and sexual behavior, **310**

hypothesis: an educated guess about relationships between variables that can be tested through experimentation, **21–22**

in concept learning, 243–244

testing of, 23–24

iconic image: the brief persisting image of a visual stimulus after removal of the stimulus, **206**

identification, 237

identity matching, 229, 254

imitation, 169–178

adaptiveness of, 174, 175, 188

deferred, 174, 175

definitions of, 171–172, 176, 177

emulation and, 173, 177

evolution of, 174, 175, 188, 189

generalized, 190–191

in language acquisition, 281

in nonhuman animals, 172–174

three-term contingency and, 188–191, 192

immune conditioning, 77–79

implicit memory: the tendency to forget the source or origin of familiar information, **224–225**

implosive therapy, 89–90

imprinting: tendency of infants to develop rapid and strong attachments to a parental figure; most frequently seen in precocial birds, **272**

incidental memory: recall of information without remembering its original source, **219–220**

adaptiveness of, 235

eyewitness testimony and, 220–222, 224

false, 222–224

flashbulb, 225–227

implicit, 224–225

independent variable: factor manipulated by an experimenter to evaluate its effect on other variables, **24**

information processing

chunking in, 207–208

cognitive psychology and, 14, 32–33, 34, 36, 136, 182

evolutionary psychology and, 28, 319

by language module, 279

by neural networks, 250–251, 256, 301–302

parallel, 251, 256, 302

in procedural memory, 316

in social learning, 183, 187

information theory: the ability to process information from the environment is dependent on properties of the system (human or machine), **32–33**

inhibitory conditioning, 51–53, 66

innate ideas
    Chomsky on, 276
    Descartes' doctrine of, 28
instinct concept, 321, 322
    language and, 279–280
    See also fixed-action patterns
instinctive drift: disruption of conditioned behavior by natural, or innate, behavioral repertoires, **323–324**
instrumental response, 112
interference theory: a theory of forgetting claiming that information is lost from a system as additional information is added or attended to, **212–213**, 230, 232
intertrial interval (ITI), 230
interval schedules: reinforcement schedule in which reinforcers are delivered according to predetermined intervals of time, **126–128**
intraverbal operant, 286
introspection, 136
in vivo exposure, 90, 92

James, William, 47, 95, 321
Jones, Mary Cover, 86–87
journals in behavioral psychology, 144
    Analysis of Verbal Behavior, 283
    JABA, 144
    JEAB, 101, 140, 144

Keller, Fred, 133, 162–164, 165, 166, 167
knowledge
    philosophy of, 27–29
    See also epistemology
Kohler, Wolfgang, 255
Korsakoff's syndrome, 214
Kuhn, Thomas, 33–34

language: a highly structured symbol system that allows for creative and meaningful communication between organisms, **265–266**
    acquisition of, 268–273, 275–276, 277, 280–281, 288–289, 325–326
    adaptiveness of, 269, 274, 278, 279, 282, 289, 295–296
    auditory discrimination and, 268–269
    behavioral approach to, 282–290, 295
    Chomsky's theory of, 275–277, 279, 280, 286–287, 288, 289
    evolutionary psychology and, 325–326
    evolution of, 175, 278–280, 282, 296

generativity of, 276, 283, 287, 294
human uniqueness and, 264–265
in nonhumans, 264–265, 266, 268, 279, 290–295
psycholinguistic approach to, 273–281, 282, 287, 288, 290
rule-governed behavior and, 193–194, 195, 296
semantic conditioning, 58–59
social nature of, 269–270, 282
universals of, 266, 268, 272, 275, 280, 287, 289–290, 325–326
language acquisition device (LAD): an evolved mechanism believed responsible for language acquisition in humans, **275–276,** 277
The Language Instinct (Pinker), 279, 325
Lashley, Karl, 312, 314
latent inhibition (LI): impaired conditioning due to previous presentation of the CS by itself (also referred to as CS preexposure effect), 45, **51–52**
law of attitude, 97
law of effect: Thorndike's formulation that behavior that produces satisfying consequences will be repeated, and behavior that produces dissatisfying consequences will not be repeated, **96–97**, 291
    adaptation and, 131
    quantitative, 129
    Skinner and, 98, 99, 105, 291
law of exercise, 97
law of readiness, 97
learned taste aversion: development of a severe negative reaction to a food item due to pairing the food with illness or other aversive stimulation, **69–73**
    in cancer patients, 73–74
    evolutionary psychology and, 323
    predator control and, 75–76
learning: a relatively permanent change in behavior potential brought about by experience, **12–13**
    adaptive nature of, 1–2, 12, 14–16, 18–20, 37, 329–330
    associationism and, 47–48, 203
    behaviorism and, 31–32, 136, 137
    behavior therapy and, 139, 143
    cognitive approach to, 32
    early research on, 29–30
    evolutionary limits on, 73, 322–324
    to learn, 254–255

cognitive revolution and, 182
immune function and, 77, 79
theory of, 175
See also consciousness; private events
mind-body problem, 28
minimal group phenomenon, 327
"The Misbehavior of Organisms" (Breland & Breland), 323
MLU (mean length of utterance), 270, 294
mnemonics: strategies used to enhance memory (often visually based), 27, **215–216**
modal-action pattern, 18
modeling. *See* imitation
modularity of mind, 276, 279
module, in PSI, 164
morphemes: smallest meaningful unit of speech sound, 270, **274**, 276, 283
motherese: speech patterns consisting of slow pronunciation, increased pitch, and exaggerated intonation, ordinarily used by adults when speaking to infants and young children, **270**, 289, 325
multiresponse environment, 111–112
mutations: spontaneous, generally unpredictable changes in genetic material, **4**, 8

nativists, 321
natural selection: differential reproduction of organisms within a population, 2, **4–7**, 8, 11
of learning and cognition, 19, 325
of open genetic program, 16
of preparedness, 71, 73
principle of continuity and, 36
See also adaptation; evolution
nature-nurture issue, 321–322, 324
negatively accelerated learning function, 65–66
negative punishment: process by which response-contingent removal of a stimulus decreases the probability of behavior, **110**, 111
negative reinforcement: process by which response-contingent removal of a stimulus increases the probability of the behavior, **107–108**, 111
Neisser, Ulric, 33
neonatal reflexes: collection of inborn responses to specific stimuli and common to all humans at birth, **16–17**
nervous system, 298–301
adaptiveness of, 317–318

learning and, 303–311, 313
modularity of, 276, 279
physiological regulation by, 76–77
plasticity of, 303
stimulus substitution theory and, 60–61
See also brain
neural network models: cognitive theory suggesting that concepts consist of various excitatory connections between neurons or groups of neurons, **250–253**, 256, 301–302
of Pavlovian conditioning, 304–305
neurode: hypothetical nerve cell meant to symbolize a neuron within a neural network, **301–302**
neurons, individual nerve cells that make up the nervous system, **299–301**
long-term potentiation and, 313–314
neuroscience, 136
behavioral psychology and, 35–36
cognitive, 35, 184
neurotransmitters: chemical messengers released by axon into synaptic gap, **300–301**
dopamine, 310–311
glutamate, 314
Nevin, John, 156
New World New Mind (Ornstein & Ehrlich), 318
nictitating membrane, 306–307
nigrostriatal system, 308–309
nonsense syllables: three-letter combinations (usually consonant-vowel-consonant) used in memory experiments by Ebbinghaus, **203**
normal science, 34
nurture vs. nature, 321–322, 324

observational learning, 170, 172, 178, 179–182. *See also* social learning
oddity matching, 229–230, 254
Olton, David, 22–23, 24
On the Origin of Species (Darwin), 7, 9, 10
ontogeny: development of the individual organism throughout its lifetime, **11–12**, 19, 329
language and, 290, 295
open genetic program: characteristic of organisms possessing a nervous system capable of being modified by experience (learning), **16**

operant: behavior that operates on the environment to produce consequences, **100**, 101
    verbal, 285, 287
operant behavior, 101, 102–111
    adaptiveness of, 131–132
    conditioned suppression of, 52–53
    discovery of, 94–100
    evolutionary psychology and, 322, 323
    extinction of, 115–117
    generalization in, 118, 119, 120
    initial acquisition of, 192
    language and, 282–290
    memory and, 228–230, 233
    neurological basis of, 252, 307–311
    vs. Pavlovian conditioning, 99–100, 102, 105
    Premack principle and, 111–113, 156
    schedules of reinforcement and, 122–131
    shaping of, 114–115
    vs. social learning, 178, 179, 183
    stimulus control in, 117–120, 149–150, 256–262, 284
    See also behavior modification; education; reinforcement; three-term contingency
operant chamber, 98, 100, 101, 105
    for choice experiments, 128
    extinction in, 116
    food pellets for, 122
    free operant procedure in, 114
    for pigeons, 119
    for psychiatric patients, 141, 142
operant class, 288, 289
orienting (rooting) reflex, 16
overshadowing: differential conditioning to one element of a compound stimulus when stimuli are presented simultaneously, **45–46**, 47, 66

P400 priming effect, 210
pain behavior, 151, 153–154
pain management, 151–154
The Paleolithic Prescription (Eaton, Shostak, & Konner), 320
Paley, William, 8
paradigm, 33–34
parallel processing: distribution of information processing demands across different subsystems, each working at the same time, 251, 256, **302**
Parkinson's disease, 308–309
partist strategy: focusing on a single attribute of a conceptual class or category, **243**

Pavlov, Ivan, 29, 38–41, 47
    behaviorism and, 137
    discrimination and, 56
    explanation of CR by, 59–61
    extinction and, 50
    generalization and, 54–55
    higher-order conditioning and, 57–58
    nervous system and, 304, 314
    Skinner and, 31, 97, 99
Pavlovian conditioning, 41–42
    adaptiveness of, 67–68
    behavior therapy and, 83, 86–90
    compound stimuli in, 45–47, 51, 66
    contingency in, 47–49, 50, 81
    defined, 42
    discovery of, 40–41
    discrimination in, 55–57
    drug tolerance and, 63–64, 79, 81, 82
    emotions and, 58–59, 61, 83–86, 305–306
    evolutionary psychology and, 322, 323
    explanations of, 59–67, 252
    extinction in, 50, 66, 87, 89, 90
    generalization in, 53–55, 56–57, 59
    higher order, 57–59, 68
    inhibitory, 51–53, 66
    methods of, 42–43
    neural basis of, 59–61, 252, 304–307
    vs. operant behavior, 99–100, 102, 105
    of physiologic responses, 76–82
    reconditioning in, 50–51
    semantic, 58–59
    vs. social learning, 178, 179, 183
    spontaneous recovery of, 50
    taste aversion and, 69–76, 323
    variables in, 43–45
personalized system of instruction (PSI): Keller's operant-based instructional format utilizing self-pacing and unit mastery, 133–134, **163–167**
persuasion, verbal, 185–186
phenotype, environment and, 321–322
philosophy, 27–29. *See also* epistemology
phobias
    adaptive basis of, 327–328
    latent inhibition and, 52
    Little Albert experiment, 84–85, 86, 136
    treatment of, 86–92
phonemes: smallest unit of speech sound, **274**, 276, 283, 325
phylogeny: evolution and development of a species over time, **2–11**, 329
    constraints on learning and, 73

fixed-action patterns and, 18
imitation and, 188
language and, 289, 295
Pinker, Steven, 279–280, 325
Plans and the Structure of Behavior (Miller, Galanter, & Pribram), 33
plasticity, neural, 303
pleasure center, 310
Pleistocene period, 319, 320
positive punishment: process by which response-contingent presentation of a stimulus decreases the probability of the behavior, **108–109**, 111
positive reinforcement: process by which response-contingent presentation of a stimulus increases the probability of the behavior, **107–108**, 111
time-out from, 110, 119, 120
postreinforcement pause (PRP), 125, 126, 127
post-traumatic stress disorder (PTSD), 91
pragmatics: use of language in social contexts to bring about desired consequences, **275**, 282, 295
predator control, by taste aversion, 75–76
preexposure effect, 45, 51–52
prejudice, 249, 326. *See also* biases
Premack principle: the finding that high probability behaviors can be used as contingent reinforcers for low probability behaviors, **111–113**, 156
preparedness, 71–73, 97, 322–323
primary reinforcers: stimuli that possess reinforcing properties because of their biological significance, **106**
Principles of Psychology (James), 47
private events
cognitive psychology and, 34, 136, 182
Skinner and, 31, 99, 101, 105, 138
Watson and, 136–137
See also mind
proactive interference: memory loss for recently learned information due to interference by previously learned information, **213**, 230
procedural memory: long-term retention of a specific skill, procedure, or practice, **208**, 234, 235, 313, 315–316
programmed instruction: instructional method involving systematic arrangement of academically oriented antecedent-consequence contingencies, **161–162**
protolanguage, 294

prototypes: a member of a conceptual category exhibiting a collection of typical features or attributes, **247–249**, 250, 252
PRP (postreinforcement pause), 125, 126, 127
pseudoscience, 20, 26
PSI (personalized system of instruction), **133–134**, 163–167
"psychic secretions," 40, 42, 68
psychoanalysis, 84, 135, 139, 213
vs. behavior therapy, 87
outcomes of, 139
psychogenic amnesia, 213
psycholinguistics: branch of science historically devoted to understanding the properties of human language and the mechanisms responsible for language acquisition, **274–275**
vs. behavioral approach, 287, 288, 290
Chomsky's revolution in, 275–277
contemporary, 277–281, 282
psychology, schools of thought in, 34–37, 135, 136
psychoneuroimmunology: field that studies the conditioned responsivity of the immune system, **77–79**
psychosomatic phenomena, 79
psychotherapy, outcomes of, 139–140
Psychotherapy by Reciprocal Inhibition (Wolpe), 87
PTSD (post-traumatic stress disorder), 91
punctuated equilibrium, 7
punishment: process by which response-contingent stimulus presentation or removal results in reduction or elimination of the response, **108–111**
behavioral momentum and, 156
as controlling variable, 283
social learning and, 180, 189, 192
puzzle box, 95–96, 99, 105, 114

quantitative law of effect, 129

radial arm maze, 22–23, 231
radical behaviorism: B. F. Skinner's philosophy stating that private experience is a legitimate subject matter of behavioral science, **31**, 35, 101, 138
RAND conference, 33
ratchet effect, 177
rationalism: the idea that knowledge and truth are to be sought through logical reasoning, **28**

ratio schedules: reinforcement schedule in which reinforcers are delivered according to a predetermined number of responses, **123–126**, 127–128
ratio strain, 124
Rayner, Rosalie, 84, 85, 86, 136, 328
readiness, law of, 97
receptive language, 291, 292
reflexes
    Descartes' speculations on, 28
    vs. instincts, 322
    neonatal, 16–17
    releasing stimuli for, 15
    unconditional response as, 41
    See also conditional response
rehearsal, 209–210
    distributed, 216
    elaborative, 210, 218–219
reinforcement, 106–108, 111
    behavioral momentum and, 156, 157
    biofeedback and, 152
    continuous, 123
    differential, 120, 308
    extinction and, 116
    of imitation, 180, 189, 190
    neurological basis of, 309–311
    of rule-governed behavior, 196–197
    schedules of, 122–131
reinforcers: consequent stimuli that strengthen or increase the behavior on which they are made contingent, **106–107**
    as controlling variables, 283
    magnitude of, 130
relaxation training, 88–89, 153, 154
relearning, 50–51, 203
releasing stimuli: environmental stimuli that provoke a simple reflex, **15**
Remembering (Bartlett), 204
Rescorla, Robert, 48
Rescorla-Wagner model: a mathematical model describing the accelerating course of learning in studies of Pavlovian conditioning and other forms of learning, **64–67**, 252
respondent conditioning. *See* Pavlovian conditioning
response
    in Pavlovian conditioning, 41
    in three-term contingency, 103
    See also conditional response; unconditional response
response by analogy, 97

response cost: negative punishment procedure in which previously earned reinforcers are removed contingent on behavior, **110**
    in behavior therapy, 151, 155–156
response deprivation hypothesis, 113
response rate, 105
    in human experiments, 141, 142
    schedules of reinforcement and, 122–123, 124, 129
response strength, 64, 65, 66
resting state: negative charge within a cell when the action potential is not being produced, **300**
retention. *See* storage
retrieval: the process of accessing or withdrawing information from a memory system, **211**, 317
retroactive interference: memory loss for previously learned information due to interference by recently learned information, **213**, 230
retrograde amnesia: memory loss for information presented before damage to the nervous system, **214**, 314–315
reverse engineering, 279
rooting (orienting) reflex, 16
rule-based classification, 250, 252
rule-governed behavior: acquiring or emitting a behavior in response to written or verbal instructions, **193–197**, 198–199, 200
    basal ganglia and, 308
    language and, 193–194, 195, 296
    in nonhuman animals, 230, 256

salivation, conditioned, 40–42, 43
    discrimination in, 55–56
    extinction of, 50
    generalization in, 54, 56
    higher order conditioning and, 57–58
    neural network model of, 304
savings: rapid mastery of material that has been previously learned, 50–51, **203**
schedules of reinforcement: method of delivering reinforcement dependent on numerical and/or temporal dimensions of behavior, **122–123**
    concurrent schedules, 128–130
    interval schedules, 126–128
    ratio schedules, 123–126, 127–128
    rule-governed behavior and, 198
Schedules of Reinforcement (Ferster & Skinner), 101, 122

spontaneous recovery: re-emergence of a response (conditioned reflex or operant)
that has been previously acquired through
conditioning (classical or operant)
of operant behavior, **117**
of Pavlovian conditioning, **50**
stage model of memory, 205–208, 209
state-dependent learning: a phenomenon in
which physiological states that are in effect during encoding serve as retrieval
cues during recall, **217–218**
stereotaxic apparatus, 309
stereotypes, 249, 326
stimulus (stimuli), 41
ecologically relevant, 322
equipotentiality hypothesis, 73
relationship between, 255–256
social, 188
See also antecedent stimuli; conditional
stimulus; consequent stimuli; discriminative stimulus; unconditional stimulus
stimulus array, 217
stimulus control: extent to which an operant
exhibits stimulus generalization and discrimination, **117–120**
abstract, 256–262
in verbal behavior, 284
weight loss and, 149–150
stimulus-response (S-R) psychology
vs. behaviorism, 138
language and, 287
vs. social learning theory, 182
stimulus substitution theory: Pavlov's idea that
the CS becomes a neural substitute, or
representation, for the US, **60–61**
storage: the process of retaining information in
memory over time, **183**, 187, 211
structural approach to language, 274, 287, 290
subordinate level: the most restrictive, specific
level of a conceptual category, **246**, 247
sucking, contingent, 269
sucking reflex, 16
summation test, 51
superordinate level: the most generic and encompassing level of a conceptual category,
245–246
surface structure: syntactic arrangement of
words in an utterance or sentence, **277**,
287, 289
symbolic matching, 229

synaptic gap: area separating two neurons,
299, 300
Hebb rule and, 313–314
synaptic vesicles: spherical sacs in terminal
button containing neurotransmitters, **300**
Syntactic Structures (Chomsky), 286
syntax: rules of a language that determine the
ordering of words to make sentences,
274–275, 277, 280, 281
chimp sign language and, 292–294
language acquisition and, 288–289
operant behavior and, 287
systematic desensitization: treatment for phobias entailing gradual exposure to feared
stimulus under conditions of relaxation,
87–89, 90

tabula rasa, 28
tact operant, 286
taste aversion. *See* learned taste aversion
teaching machines, 158–162
telegraphic speech: short (2-3 word) utterances,
usually consisting only of nouns and verbs,
used by children from 1 1/2 to 2 years of
age, **270**, 272, 294, 326
television, children's behavior and, 181,
192–193
terminal button, 300
Terrace, Herbert, 292–294
thalamus, in Pavlovian conditioning, 61
theory: a series of statements about relationships between variables that, taken
together, attempt to explain some natural
phenomenon, **21–22**
of evolution, 7–8
Rescorla-Wagner model as, 66–67
Skinner on, 31–32
theory of mind, 175
third-order conditioning, 58
Thorndike, Edward L., 94–97, 291
Skinner and, 97, 98, 99, 105, 106, 114,
137
thought. *See* private events
three-term contingency: conceptual system for
classifying behavior in relation to
antecedent and consequent stimuli, **103**,
120–121
adaptation and, 131
neural basis of, 307–311
private events and, 101
in programmed instruction, 159
in rule-governed behavior, 194–195, 196

in social learning, 177, 180, 188–191

in verbal behavior, 283, 284–285

time-out: response cost procedure in which behavior leads to a period during which reinforcement is not available, **110**, 119, 120

Tinbergen, Niko, 324

token economy: behavior modification program delivered systematically to a large community or institution, **141–143**, 154

Tomasello, Michael, 177, 280–281, 282

topography of behavior, 61

imitative, 173

variable, 288

verbal, 287–288

trace conditioning, 43

transformational grammar: process by which deep structures become expressed in novel and unlimited surface structures or sentences, **276–277**

transposition effect: responding to a relationship between two stimuli rather than to discrete characteristics of either stimulus, **255–256**

triangularity, 257–258

twin studies, 3

Twitmyer, Edwin, 42

two-action task, 171–172

Type I punishment, 108

Type II punishment, 110

Type R learning, 99

Type S learning, 99

unconditional response (UR): involuntary or automatic response to a US, **41**, 61

unconditional stimulus (US): event in the environment producing reflexive, involuntary reaction, **41–43**, 42, 44

compensatory response and, 62

contingency and, 47–49, 50, 81

discrimination and, 56

drug use as, 80, 81

intensity of, 44

in Rescorla-Wagner model, 64, 65, 66

stimulus substitution and, 61

types of, 44

verbal, 58–59

unit mastery, 163, 164, 166

universals of language, 266, 268, 272

behavioral psychology and, 289–290

Chomsky and, 275, 280, 287

evolutionary psychology and, 325–326

usage-based approach to language, 281, 282

variable interval (VI) schedule, 127

concurrent, 128–129

variable ratio (VR) schedule, 125–126

variables, 24

controlling, 121, 283

in Pavlovian conditioning, 43–45

verbal behavior, 282–290

Verbal Behavior (Skinner), 282, 283, 286

verbal conditioning, 58–59

verbal overshadowing effect (VOE), 46

verbal persuasion, 185–186

verbal rules. *See* rule-governed behavior

vicarious learning, 185, 186

violence. *See* aggression

virtual reality exposure (VRE), 90–92

visual stimuli

brain development and, 303

memory for, 228–230

Wallace, Alfred Russell, 10

Watson, John B., 30–31, 36, 136–137, 140

behavioral genetics and, 138

Lashley and, 312

Little Albert experiment, 84–85, 86, 136, 328

nature-nurture issue and, 321

Skinner and, 97

weight loss, 148–151

wholist strategy: responding to all attributes of a conceptual class or category, **243**

Wolpe, Joseph, 87

working memory. *See* short-term store